ScottForesman
EXPLORING
MATHEMATICS

AUTHORS

L. Carey Bolster
Coordinator of Mathematics
Baltimore County Public Schools
Towson, Maryland

Clem Boyer
Coordinator of Mathematics, K-12
District School Board of Seminole County
Sanford, Florida

Thomas Butts
Associate Professor,
Mathematics Education
University of Texas at Dallas
Richardson, Texas

Mary Cavanagh
Math/Science Coordinator
Solana Beach School District
Solana Beach, California

Marea W. Channel
Mathematics Resource Teacher
Los Angeles Unified School District
Los Angeles, California

Warren D. Crown
Associate Professor of
Mathematics Education, Rutgers,
The State University of New Jersey
New Brunswick, New Jersey

Jan Fair
Mathematics Department
Allan Hancock College
Santa Maria, California

Robert Y. Hamada
District Mathematics Specialist, K-12
Los Angeles Unified School District
Los Angeles, California

Margaret G. (Peggy) Kelly
Associate Professor
California State University, San Marcos
San Marcos, California

Miriam Leiva
Professor of Mathematics
University of North Carolina at Charlotte
Charlotte, North Carolina

Mary Montgomery Lindquist
Callaway Professor of Mathematics Education
Columbus College
Columbus, Georgia

William B. Nibbelink
Professor, Division of Early Childhood and
Elementary Education, University of Iowa
Iowa City, Iowa

Linda Proudfit
University Professor of Mathematics
and Computer Education, Governors State
University, University Park, Illinois

Cathy Rahlfs
Mathematics Coordinator
Humble Independent School District
Humble, Texas

Rosie Ramirez
Assistant Principal
Highland Elementary School
Silver Spring, Maryland

Jeanne F. Ramos
Assistant Principal
Nobel Middle School
Northridge, California

Gail Robinette
Vice-Principal
Fresno Unified School District
Fresno, California

David Robitaille
Head, Department of Mathematics
and Science Education
University of British Columbia
Vancouver, British Columbia,
Canada

James E. Schultz
Project LITMUS
University of Georgia
Athens, Georgia

Richard Shepardson
Professor, Division of Early Childhood
and Elementary Education
University of Iowa
Iowa City, Iowa

Jane Swafford
Professor of Mathematics
Illinois State University, Normal, Illinois

Benny Tucker
Dean, School of Education and Human Studies
Union University
Jackson, Tennessee

John Van de Walle
Professor of Education
Virginia Commonwealth University
Richmond, Virginia

David E. Williams
Former Director of Mathematics Education
School District of Philadelphia
Philadelphia, Pennsylvania

Robert J. Wisner
Professor of Mathematics
New Mexico State University
Las Cruces, New Mexico

Multicultural Reviewers

Cherry McGee Banks
University of Washington
Seattle, Washington

Armando Ayala
Director of Bilingual Education
Placer County, California

Diane Deckert Jost
Field Museum of Natural History, Chicago, Illinois

**Patricia Locke
(Ta Wacin Waste Win)**
Lakota, Chippewa Educator
Wakpala, South Dakota

Vicky Owyang Chan
Multicultural Educator
Fremont, California

Seree Weroha
Kansas State University, Manhattan, Kansas

Efrain Melendez
Dakota School, Los Angeles, California

Linda Skinner
Choctaw Educator, Edmond, Oklahoma

ScottForesman
A Division of HarperCollinsPublishers

Editorial Offices: Glenview, Illinois   Regional Offices: Sunnyvale, California • Tucker, Georgia • Glenview, Illinois • Oakland, New Jersey • Dallas, Texas

CONSULTANTS

Reading
Robert A. Pavlik
Professor, Reading/Language
Arts Department,
Cardinal Stritch College, Milwaukee, Wisconsin

At-Risk Students
Edgar G. Epps
Marshall Field Professor of Urban Education
Department of Education
University of Chicago
Chicago, Illinois

Limited-English-Proficient Students
Walter Secada
Department of Curriculum and Instruction
University of Wisconsin, Madison, Wisconsin

Mainstreaming
Roxie Smith
Associate Provost, Northwestern University
Evanston, Illinois

Gifted Students
Christine Kuehn Ebert
Associate Professor of Education,
University of South Carolina
Columbia, South Carolina

CRITIC READERS

Bruce C. Burt
East Bradford Elementary School
West Chester, Pennsylvania

Howard Cohn
Lone Star Elementary
Jacksonville, Florida

Tom Daly
Pitt County Schools
Greenville, North Carolina

Ruth Eliott
Hopkinsville Middle School
Hopkinsville, Kentucky

Margaret Foster
Calleyville Middle School
Evansville, Indiana

Guy Garrett
West School
Hillsborough, California

Randy Hamblin
Tierra Buena Elementary
Yuba City, California

Consuelo Dominguez Hernandes
Burleson Elementary School
El Paso, Texas

William Kasper
Our Lady of Perpetual Help School
Glenview, Illinois

Walter G. Kealey, Jr.
Benjamin Franklin Elementary School
Indiana, Pennsylvania

Barbara Lindley
Butler Elementary
Arlington, Texas

Patty McGuffey
Central Intermediate School
Brownsville, Texas

Theresa Frazier Norris
Crest Hills Middle School
Cincinnati, Ohio

Robert A. Potter
School #86
Buffalo, New York

Jean Reherman
Taft Middle School
Oklahoma City, Oklahoma

Calvin Rohrbaugh
Roanoke County School Division
Salem, Virginia

Lisa Stayton
Russell Cave School
Lexington, Kentucky

Acknowledgments appear after the index.

Contents

Chapter 1   Building Number Concepts

Chapter 2   Multiplying Whole Numbers and Decimals

Chapter 3 Dividing Whole Numbers

Chapter 4 Dividing Decimals

Chapter 5 Using Geometry

Chapter 6 Relating Number Theory and Fraction Concepts

Chapter 7 Adding and Subtracting Fractions

Chapter 8 Multiplying and Dividing Fractions

Chapter 9 Using Measurement

Chapter 10 Relating Geometry and Measurement

Chapter 11 — Understanding Ratios, Proportions, and Percents

Chapter 12 — Relating Percents, Fractions, and Decimals

Chapter **13** Applying Statistics

Chapter **14** Investigating Probability

Chapter 15 Understanding Integers

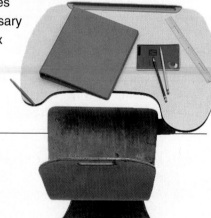

WELCOME TO
EXPLORING
MATHEMATICS

Mathematics is valuable and
interesting. The next ten pages
describe some of the ways your book
will help you explore and discover
more of the wonders of mathematics.

Your book will help you build your
Math Power

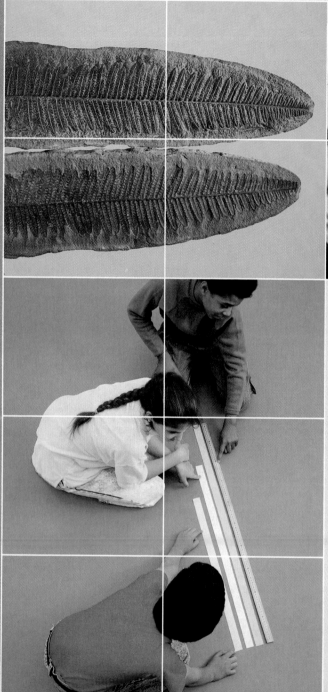

Build your math power by doing
Problem Solving and Critical Thinking

You'll need to use math to solve problems all your life. So, as you solve problems in your book, you will do more than find answers, you will also learn how to think mathematically.

In Chapter 1, tell the page numbers where these first occur.

1 "Problem-Solving Guide"
   — Understand
   — Plan and Solve
   — Look Back

2 "Tips for Problem Solvers"

3 An exercise called "Critical Thinking"

Build your math power by looking for
Connections

Your book will help you explore connections between mathematics, the real world, and other school subjects. Multicultural connections show the part mathematics plays in many cultures and societies.

4 On what page does "Multicultural Connection" first appear at the top?

5 On page 29, find a problem which involves a consumer decision.

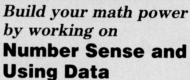

Build your math power by working on
Number Sense and Using Data

To work with numbers sensibly, you need to understand numbers, estimate, and do mental math. To read and use data, you need to be able to gather, organize, display, and analyze data.

1 Find a chapter that begins with a Number Sense Project about roller coasters. Then find where this project is continued. (Hint: Find the Problem-Solving Workshop within the chapter.) On what page is the project continued?

2 On page 92, what are the numbers called that are used for estimating?

3 On what page is the Data File that you'll use with exercise 35 on page 78?

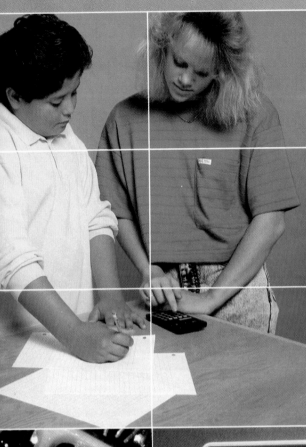

Build your math power by using
Calculators and Computers

Calculators and computers can help you solve problems and learn mathematics. It's important to know when calculators can help you and when they are not needed.

4 On page 218, what math topic does a calculator help you learn?

5 On page 247, what math topic does a computer help you learn?

6 What pages in the Independent Study Handbook explain how to use a calculator?

7 Which exercises on page 133 ask you to tell whether or not you would use a calculator?

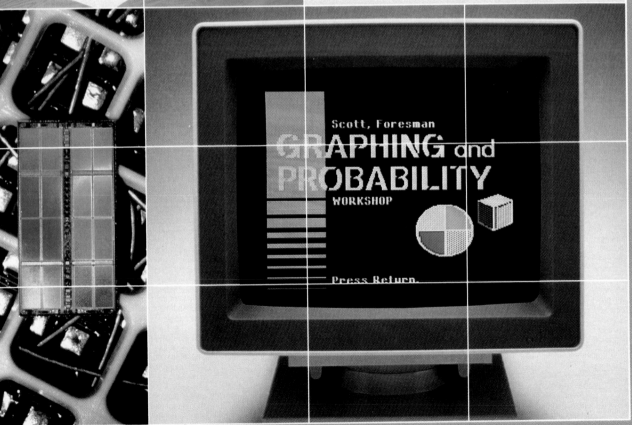

Use your book to help you

Do Your Best

To do your best,
Expect to Succeed

When you want to learn something, it helps to believe in yourself. Whether you are learning a sport, a musical instrument, or mathematics, a positive attitude can make a big difference.

To do your best,
Build Your Understanding

When you understand what you're doing, you do it better and remember it longer. So, it pays to study the "Build Understanding" part of the lessons.

1 On page 164, why is it easy to see what new math words are being taught?

To do your best, learn ways to do
Independent Study

One of the most important things you can learn from a math book is how to learn math even when a teacher is not there to help.

2 On page 4, look to the right of the words "Check Understanding." On what page can you find another example for that lesson?

3 On page 5, look to the right of the word "Practice." On what page can you find more practice for that lesson?

4 There is an Independent Study Handbook in the back of your book. On what page does the "Math Study Skills" section begin?

5 Name the first and last words defined in the glossary on page 573.

PLAN YOUR WORK

SET GOALS

WORK HARD

STUDY

THINK POSITIVELY

Your book will help you experience
Active Learning

You'll learn math by doing
Math Activities

Activities help you understand math. Some activities use materials that help you show numbers, measure objects, do experiments, explore shapes, or solve problems.

1 What materials are used in the activity on page 88?

2 Draw a circle using your "Math Sketcher" (or a compass). Shade one half of the circle.

Doing math includes
Reading, Writing, Talking, Listening

Reading, writing, talking, and listening in math class will help you think mathematically.

3 In Chapter 1, tell the page numbers where these first occur.

"Talk About Math"

"Write About Math"

"Reading Math"

A good way to learn is by Working in Groups

In real life and in math class, people can often solve problems better by working together.

4 How many should work together to do the activity on page 68?

5 In the "Explore As a Team" on page 20, what is the "Tip for Working Together"?

To have a math adventure, catch the spirit of Exploration

Be a Math Explorer and discover new ideas. Look for patterns, check out your hunches, and try different approaches to problems.

6 What lesson in Chapter 1 explores a number pattern for building stair steps made of cubes?

7 In the "Explore Math" on page 143, what are you asked to do in problems 43–46?

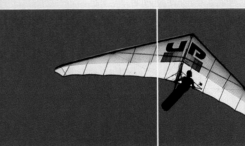

A key ingredient to learning math is
Enjoying Math

Your book will help you
Enjoy Math at School

The explorations in your book will help you discover and enjoy the wonders of mathematics.

1 In Chapter 2, what page asks you to explore the results of folding a piece of paper?

2 Fold a sheet of paper in half; continue to fold it as many times as possible. How many times could you fold it? Try different size paper.

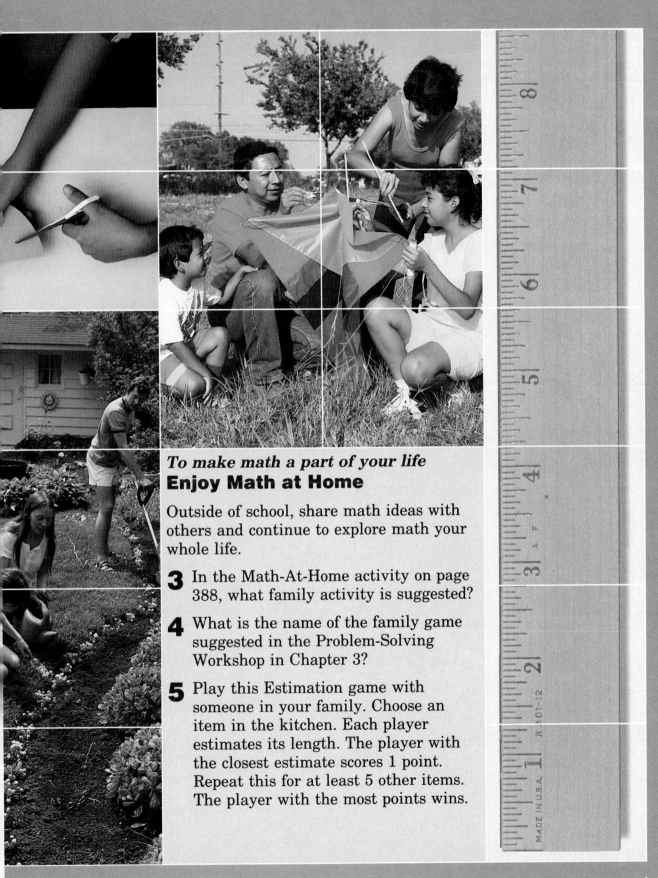

To make math a part of your life
Enjoy Math at Home

Outside of school, share math ideas with others and continue to explore math your whole life.

3 In the Math-At-Home activity on page 388, what family activity is suggested?

4 What is the name of the family game suggested in the Problem-Solving Workshop in Chapter 3?

5 Play this Estimation game with someone in your family. Choose an item in the kitchen. Each player estimates its length. The player with the closest estimate scores 1 point. Repeat this for at least 5 other items. The player with the most points wins.

Building Number Concepts

1

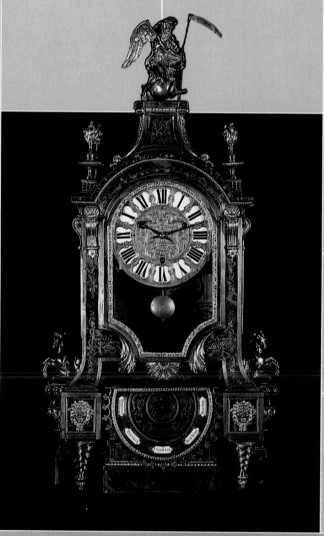

2

Number-Sense Project

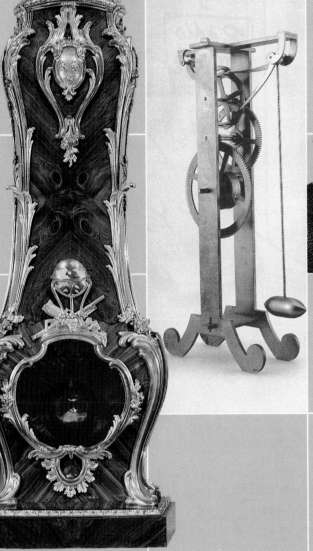

Estimate

Do you think it takes a long pendulum more time or less time to make a swing than it takes a short pendulum?

Gather Data

Make at least three pendulums of different lengths. With the second hand on a clock or a stopwatch time 20 full swings of each pendulum. Record the results.

Analyze and Report

As the pendulum length increases, does the time for 20 swings increase or decrease? Estimate the time it would take for a 50-cm and then a 100-cm pendulum to make 20 swings.

3

Numbers and Their Purposes

Build Understanding

A world without numbers would be a difficult place in which to live. How could you call a friend, buy a record, ask for shoes in your size, or send invitations to a party?

Here are some kinds of numbers and examples of situations in which they are used.

Whole numbers	24 people at a party 6 guitar strings A poster 2 feet by 4 feet
Fractions and decimals	$\frac{1}{2}$ pizza 98.5 on your radio dial $1\frac{1}{4}$ hour
Ratios	55 miles per hour (55 to 1) 3 out of 5 students (3 to 5) 6 cans for $3 (6 to 3)
Ordered pairs	At the corner of Third Street and Fourth Avenue (3, 4)

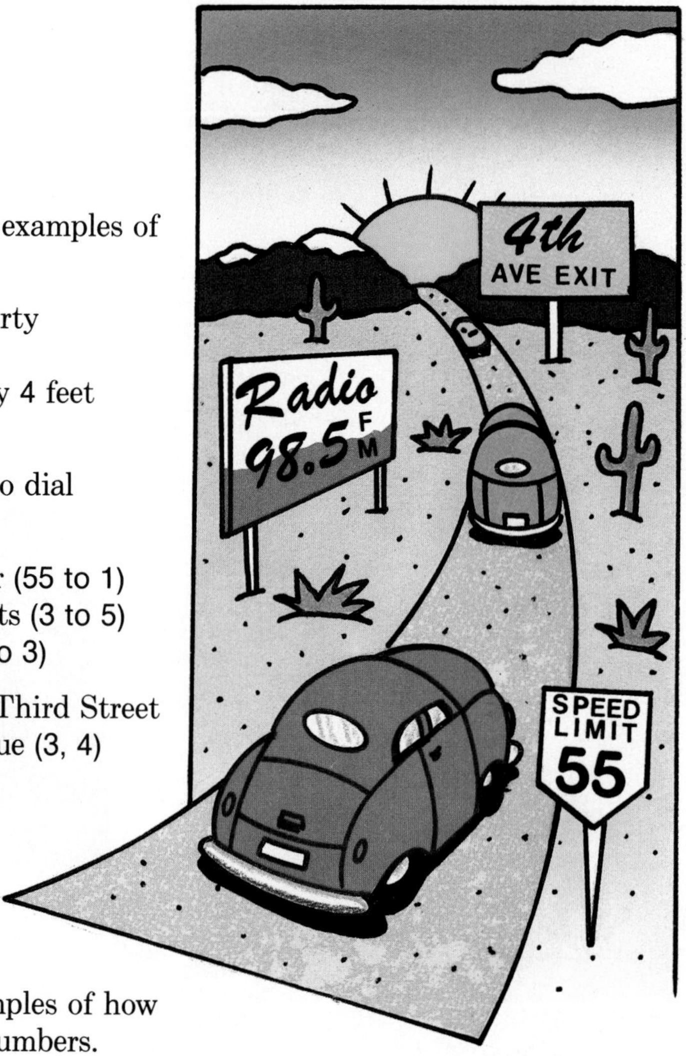

■ **Write About Math**   Give five examples of how your life would be different without numbers.

Check Understanding

For another example, see Set A, pages 38–39.

Name the kinds of numbers you might use for each activity. Then give examples.

1. Reading maps

2. Determining miles per gallon

3. Counting

4. Dividing a piece of wood into 5 equal pieces

5. Reading graphs

4

Practice

For More Practice, see Set A, pages 40–41.

Decide what kind of number to use in each situation.

6. Measuring a board that is between 10 and 11 inches long

7. Recording the finish times of runners in hundredths of seconds

8. Finding a street on a map

9. Taking a child's temperature

10. Comparing the number of girls who like country music to the number of boys who like country music

11. Counting the number of people entering the arena for a rock concert

12. Determining the number of pages in a book

13. Describing the location of a piece on a chess board according to rank (the rows across a chess board) and file (the columns up and down the board)

14. Computing miles traveled by car

Problem Solving

Number Sense   Choose the pair of numbers that fit each problem. Then solve.

$8\frac{1}{2}, 10\frac{1}{2}$ 4, 0.9   7, 5   71,000, 44,000

15. Point Reyes National Seashore in California covers about ⬚ acres. On the other coast, Cape Cod National Seashore covers about ⬚ acres. About how many acres larger is Point Reyes?

16. Find the perimeter of a picture that is ⬚ inches long and ⬚ inches wide. **Remember** that perimeter is the total length of all four sides.

17. The difference between 4.9 and ⬚ is ⬚. What is the sum?

18. What is the total cost of ⬚ frozen pizzas that cost $⬚ each?

Number Sense in Measurement

Build Understanding

Do you think Robin's travel agent found her note difficult to understand? What would have been the sensible unit for Robin to use to tell the length of time she was gone?

Days would have been the sensible unit to express the length of time she was gone.

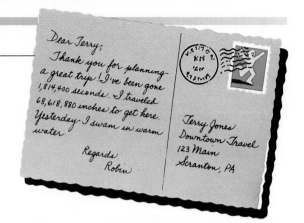

Dear Terry,
Thank you for planning a great trip! I've been gone 1,814,400 seconds. I traveled 68,618,880 inches to get here. Yesterday I swam in warm water.

Regards,
Robin

Terry Jones
Downtown Travel
123 Main
Scranton, PA

Customary Units of Length, Time, and Temperature

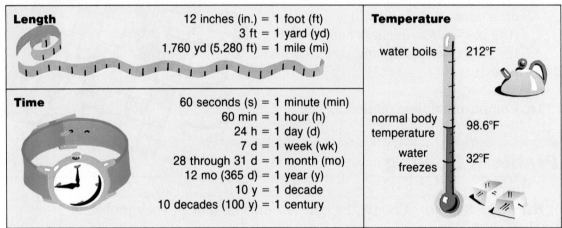

Length	
	12 inches (in.) = 1 foot (ft)
	3 ft = 1 yard (yd)
	1,760 yd (5,280 ft) = 1 mile (mi)

Time	
	60 seconds (s) = 1 minute (min)
	60 min = 1 hour (h)
	24 h = 1 day (d)
	7 d = 1 week (wk)
	28 through 31 d = 1 month (mo)
	12 mo (365 d) = 1 year (y)
	10 y = 1 decade
	10 decades (100 y) = 1 century

Temperature

water boils	212°F
normal body temperature	98.6°F
water freezes	32°F

■ **Talk About Math** Why do we use several different units to express length and time?

Check Understanding

Answer each question.

1. Which unit would be sensible for Robin to use to tell how far she traveled?

2. **Estimation** Determine the approximate temperature of the water that Robin swam in.

What unit would you use to measure the length of

3. a travel brochure?　　4. a travel office?　　5. a travel movie?

Practice

Use the table on page 6. Choose the most sensible unit
to express each measurement in Exercises 6–11.

6. The time it takes Robin to fly from the United States to Europe

7. The time it takes Robin to open her road map

8. How much taller Robin is than her twin sister

9. The length of Robin's summer vacation from school

10. The length of an airport runway

11. The dimensions of Robin's suitcase

Estimation Estimate an appropriate temperature.

12. A pleasant spring day in Texas

13. A very cold winter day in Colorado

14. A hot day in the Mojave Desert

15. Inside the freezer of a refrigerator

Replace each underlined part with sensible measures.

16. Robin is 2 decades old.

17. Robin is 60 inches tall.

18. Robin was on vacation for 0.5 month.

19. Robin walked more than 5,280 feet each morning.

Problem Solving

Complete each sentence with a sensible unit of measure.

20. It takes about 5 __?__ for Robin to fly from Denver, Colorado, to Boston, Massachusetts. This is a distance of 1,770 __?__.

21. The precipitation in Boston during January averages about 3.69 __?__. The precipitation in Denver during January averages only 0.61 __?__.

22. The average temperature in Los Angeles, California, in September is 69 __?__. Los Angeles is 414 __?__ from San Francisco.

First Quadrant Graphing

Build Understanding

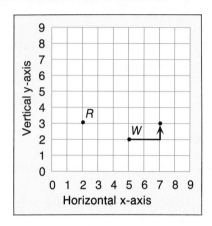

A. The grid represents the layout of Double Fun Park. The roller coaster is located at point R. The location of the entrance can be given as the ***ordered pair*** (0, 0). Use an ordered pair to describe the location of the roller coaster.

Start at the ***origin,*** the point for the entrance. Move right 2 units. Then move up 3 units. The x-coordinate is 2, and the y-coordinate is 3. The ordered pair is (2, 3).

B. The owner moved the water ride *(W)* further into the park. It was moved 2 units to the right and 1 unit up. What are the coordinates for the new location of the water ride?

Original coordinates: (5, 2)   New coordinates: (7, 3)

■ **Write About Math**   Describe how to locate points on a grid.

Check Understanding

For another example, see Set B, pages 38–39.

Draw a 10-by-10 grid. Label the x-axis and the y-axis. Use the grid as the map of a park and label the point (0, 0) as the entrance to the park.

1. Locate a refreshment stand 4 units right of the entrance and 3 units up. Label it with its ordered pair.

2. Move the refreshment stand. Label the new location with its ordered pair.

Practice

For More Practice, see Set B, pages 40–41.

On your grid from Exercises 1 and 2, graph and label these points.
Remember to move along the *x*-axis first.

3. *A* (0, 0)   **4.** *B* (1, 3)   **5.** *C* (3, 3)   **6.** *D* (6, 3)   **7.** *F* (2, 0)   **8.** *G* (0, 2)

9. *H* (4, 6)   **10.** *I* (2, 5)   **11.** *J* (3, 7)   **12.** *K* (0, 5)   **13.** *L* (6, 6)   **14.** *M* (7, 0)

Write the coordinates of each point.

15. *J*   **16.** *K*   **17.** *L*   **18.** *M*

19. *N*   **20.** *T*   **21.** *H*   **22.** *P*

23. *S*   **24.** *Q*   **25.** *V*   **26.** *R*

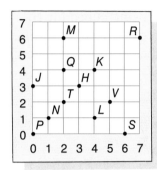

Write the new coordinates for each ordered pair.

	Move up 3 units.	Move left 1 unit.	Move left 1 unit, and down 2 units.	Move right 2 units, and up 4 units.
(2, 3)	**27.**	**28.**	**29.**	**30.**
(5, 2)	**31.**	**32.**	**33.**	**34.**
(4, 4)	**35.**	**36.**	**37.**	**38.**

Problem Solving

39. Number Sense   Ordered pairs with a *y*-coordinate of zero are always located on the *x*-axis. Write a statement about points located on the *y*-axis.

Explore ———— Math

Changing Locations

40. Graph four points *J*, *K*, *L*, and *M*. Move each point the same number of units on the *x*-axis and on the *y*-axis. Label the new points J_1, K_1, L_1, and M_1. Describe how you moved each point.

41. Give the paper with the graphed points to two classmates. Have them describe how the points were moved. Compare their descriptions with the one you wrote.

Number Patterns: Tables

Build Understanding

A. Students at Milford School are making models of buildings in the community. They are using cubes for the outside steps to each building. How many cubes are needed to build six steps?

Here is the pattern for the steps:

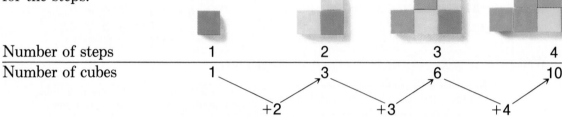

Number of steps	1	2	3	4
Number of cubes	1	3	6	10

+2   +3   +4

If you extend the table, you will find that six steps require 21 cubes.

Number of steps	1	2	3	4	5	6
Number of cubes	1	3	6	10	15	21

+2 +3 +4 +5 +6

B. Write a method for calculating y if you know x. Then complete the table.

x	y
0	2
1	3
2	4
5	7
8	
15	

To get from 0 to 2, add 2.
To get from 1 to 3, add 2.
To get from 2 to 4, add 2.
To get from 5 to 7, add 2.

The rule is: Add x and 2, or $y = x + 2$.
For $x = 8$, $y = 8 + 2 = 10$.
For $x = 15$, $y = 15 + 2 = 17$.

Talk About Math Describe the pattern in Example A.

Use the rule to complete each table.

1. Rule: $y = 2x$

x	0	1	2	4	9	20
y	0	2	4			

2. Rule: $y = x - 4$

x	4	5	6	7	17
y			2		

Practice

Find the rule for calculating x or y. Then copy and complete each table.

3.

x	y
1	5
2	
5	25
8	
10	

4.

x	y
14	20
	16
6	12
	10
0	6

5.

x	y
2	1
4	
6	
8	4
12	

6.

x	y
3	
5	
7	70
8	
9	90

7.

x	y
	2
5	5
	9
12	12
	15

8.

x	y
5	15
6	
7	17
8	18
9	

9.

x	y
2	10
	11
4	12
5	13
	14

10.

x	y
8	7
	9
12	11
	13
16	15

11.

x	y
1	1
2	
4	7
6	11
8	

12.

x	y
3	2
6	4
	6
12	8
	10

Problem Solving

The sculpture in the center of the Town Plaza is made of marble blocks. The top layer is a square 2 blocks by 2 blocks. It sits on top of a square 3 blocks by 3 blocks, and so on. There are five layers in the sculpture.

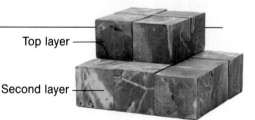

Top layer

Second layer

13. What are the dimensions of the fifth layer?

14. How many marble blocks are in the fifth layer?

15. How many marble blocks are there altogether in the first, third, and fifth layers?

16. If marble blocks cost $1,000 each, how much did all of the marble for the sculpture cost?

Using a Problem-Solving Guide

Build Understanding

Solving a problem is like taking a journey. The Problem-Solving Guide is like a map to help you find your way.

The Atlantic Coast has 2,069 miles of coastline. The Gulf Coast has 1,631 miles of coastline. The Pacific Coast has 7,623 miles of coastline. These three coasts make up the coast of the United States. How many miles of coastline does the United States have?

PROBLEM SOLVING GUIDE

Understand
QUESTION
FACTS
KEY IDEA

Plan and Solve
STRATEGY
ANSWER

Look Back
SENSIBLE ANSWER
ALTERNATE APPROACH

PROBLEM SOLVING GUIDE

Understand
QUESTION _____
What are you asked to find?

FACTS _____
What facts are given?

KEY IDEA _____
How are the facts
and question related?

Plan and Solve
STRATEGY _____
What can you do to solve
the problem?

ANSWER _____
Give the answer in a sentence.

Look Back
SENSIBLE ANSWER
Did you check your work?

ALTERNATE APPROACH _____
Is there another way to get
the same answer?

Understand

QUESTION   How many miles of coastline does the United States have?

FACTS   The Atlantic Coast has 2,069 miles, the Gulf Coast has 1,631 miles, and the Pacific Coast has 7,623 miles.

KEY IDEA   The Gulf, Pacific, and Atlantic coasts make up the coast of the United States.

Plan and Solve

STRATEGY   Add to find how many miles of coastline the United States has.
2,069 + 1,631 + 7,623 = 11,323

ANSWER   The United States has 11,323 miles of coastline.

Look Back

ALTERNATE APPROACH   Add the numbers in a different order.

7,623 + 2,069 + 1,631 = 11,323

The answer is the same.

■ **Talk About Math**   What would you do if the alternate approach gives a different answer?

Check Understanding

1. What are the three steps of the Problem-Solving Guide?

2. What facts are given?

> Alaska has 5,580 miles of coastline. This is more than any other state in the United States. California is second to Alaska with 840 miles of coastline. How much more coastline does Alaska have than California?

3. How are the facts related?

4. What can you do to solve the problem?

5. Solve the problem. Give your answer as a sentence.

6. Explain how you checked your answer.

Practice

Answer each exercise about the problem at the right.

7. What facts are not needed to solve the problem?

8. Rewrite the problem in your own words.

> The Gulf Coast includes Alabama, Florida, Louisiana, Mississippi, and Texas. Alabama has 53 miles of coastline, and Florida has 770 miles. How many miles of coastline do Alabama and Florida have together?

Solve each problem. Use the Problem-Solving Guide to help you.

9. California has 840 miles, Oregon has 296 miles, and Washington has 157 miles of coastline. What is the total length of coastline for these states?

10. The New England states have a total of 473 miles of coastline. Maine has 228 miles, and New Hampshire has 13 miles of coastline. How much more coastline does Maine have than New Hampshire?

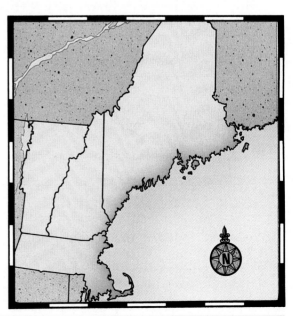

Naming Whole Numbers and Decimals

Build Understanding

A. The *standard form* for an approximation of the distance in miles that light travels in a day is 16,070,400,000. You can use a place-value chart to read this number.

trillions			billions			millions			thousands			ones		
hundred-trillions	ten-trillions	trillions	hundred-billions	ten-billions	billions	hundred-millions	ten-millions	millions	hundred-thousands	ten-thousands	thousands	hundreds	tens	ones
				1	6,	0	7	0,	4	0	0,	0	0	0

Read: Sixteen billion, seventy million, four hundred thousand

B. The human eye can see light with wavelengths between 0.000191 inch and 0.000089 inch.

hundreds	tens	ones	tenths	hundredths	thousandths	ten-thousandths	hundred-thousandths	millionths	ten-millionths	hundred-millionths
0	0	0.	0	0	0	1	9	1		

Read: One hundred ninety-one millionths

C. When there is a whole-number part in a decimal number, read the decimal point as "and."

3.49 Read: Three and forty-nine hundredths

■ **Talk About Math** Explain why it is necessary to read the decimal point as "and" in numbers such as "three hundred and twelve thousandths."

Check Understanding

For another example, see Set C, pages 38–39.

Write each number in standard form.

1. One billion, eight hundred million, five thousand, ten

2. Forty-three thousand, six and two hundred fifty-six thousandths

Practice

For another example, see Set C, pages 40–41.

Use the number 8,197,352,000,000.5469. What digit is in the

3. ones place? **4.** hundredths place? **5.** ten thousands place?

6. billions place? **7.** thousandths place? **8.** hundred millions place?

Write each number in words.

9. 500,840,092   **10.** 9,003,702,149,340   **11.** 61,000,398,000,129

12. 0.2451   **13.** 15.99703   **14.** 4.000077   **15.** 200.106   **16.** 10.08709

17. 20.987   **18.** 509.678   **19.** 1,432.06   **20.** 365,547   **21.** 908.888

Write each number in standard form.

22. Seven trillion, twelve billion, four hundred thousand

23. Seven hundred trillion, four million, fifty

24. One hundred forty-five millionths

25. One hundred and forty-five millionths

Problem Solving

Number Sense Light travels at about 186,000 miles per second.

26. About how far will light travel in 1 minute?

27. About how far will light travel in 1 hour?

28. How long do you think it takes light to travel 1 trillion miles?

Reading ———— Math

Vocabulary Complete the paragraph by using the words below.

and   decimal point   thousandths   place value   millions

1. The number 3,100,400.502 has the digit 2 in the __?__ place, and the digit 3 in the __?__ place. The __?__ of the digit 4 is hundreds.

2. The decimal point is read as __?__. The __?__ follows the whole-number part of the decimal.

Comparing and Ordering Whole Numbers and Decimals

Build Understanding

ACTIVITY

Comparing Mission
Groups: Small groups of 3–5 students

a. Your mission control team has agreed to develop a method for comparing whole numbers and decimals. For each mission, compare numbers from the charts. Be sure to select the correct type of number for your mission. Use the symbols *greater than* > and *less than* < to show comparisons. Record how you solved each mission.

Planet	Distance from Sun (in kilometers)
Earth	149,600,000
Jupiter	777,000,000
Mars	228,000,000
Mercury	57,900,000
Neptune	4,500,000,000
Pluto	5,900,000,000
Saturn	1,400,000,000
Uranus	2,900,000,000
Venus	107,800,000

Mission 1: If two whole numbers have the same number of digits, how will you know which is greater than the other?

Mission 2: If two decimals are each greater than 1 and have equal whole-number parts, which one is greater?

Planet	Size in Relation to Earth
Earth	1.0
Jupiter	11.22978
Mars	0.53086
Mercury	0.37694
Neptune	3.92650
Pluto	0.45547
Saturn	9.34506
Uranus	3.69091
Venus	0.95021

MERCURY   VENUS   EARTH   MARS   JUPITER   SATURN   URANUS   NEPTUNE   PLUTO

b. When does aligning decimal points make comparing easier? Should you start by looking at the first digit or the last digit when comparing numbers?

c. Present your method for comparing whole numbers and decimals to other mission-control teams in your class. Did every team develop the same method?

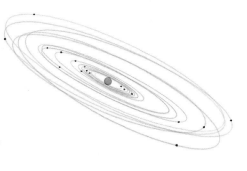

d. Challenge another team to find examples for which your method of comparison does not work. If necessary, revise your method.

■ **Talk About Math** A comet is 778,290,000 kilometers from the sun. Explain how you would decide if the comet or Jupiter is closer to the sun.

Check Understanding

For another example, see Set D, pages 38–39.

Complete each number to make the expression true.

1. 0.30▦9 < 0.3019 **2.** 16,788 < 16,7▦8 **3.** 3.416 > ▦.416

Use the charts on page 16 for Exercises 4 and 5.

4. Which is farther from the sun, Mars or Pluto?

5. Which is smaller, Mars or Mercury?

Are the numbers in Exercises 6–10 in order from least to greatest? Write *yes* or *no*. If they are not, write them in order from least to greatest.

6. 3.05; 3.50; 5.3

7. 2,342; 3,412; 2,431

8. 2; 0.002; 0.2

9. 7.081; 7.801; 7.108

10. 0.003; 0.03; 0.3

Practice

For More Practice, see Set D, pages 40–41.

Compare. Use >, <, or =. **Remember** to line up the decimal points.

11. 5,345 ⦂ 11,206   **12.** 7,437,628,107 ⦂ 7,437,826,107

13. 2.37 ⦂ 2.37   **14.** 3.994 ⦂ 3,999   **15.** 2.003 ⦂ 1.99

16. 0.345 ⦂ 0.29   **17.** 17.6 ⦂ 1.706   **18.** 0.03243 ⦂ 0.0342

19. 25.0 ⦂ 25   **20.** 1,067 ⦂ 1,067.1   **21.** 178,871 ⦂ 178,789

22. 0.99 ⦂ 0.100   **23.** 3,437 ⦂ 3,537   **24.** 10,000 ⦂ 9,999

Write the numbers in order from least to greatest.

25. 0.08; 0.8; 8.080; 0.008   **26.** 109,041; 104,091; 401,001

27. 7.7706; 7.7660; 7.76; 7.78   **28.** 2,057; 2,500; 5,499; 2,994

29. 45.928; 45.2895; 45.82; 45.2   **30.** 698; 458.3; 99.999; 9.029

31. 3.9; 0.00039; 39.0; 309.0; 0.39; 390.9; 390,000.0

Problem Solving

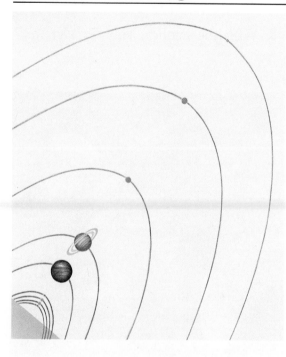

Use the information given in the tables on page 16 for Problems 32–34.

32. The table shows the distances the planets are from the sun. Make a list showing the planets in order of their distance from the sun.

33. Make a list showing the planets in order of size from least to greatest.

34. Which planet is closest to the earth in size?

35. **Use Data**   Write the diameters of Jupiter, Saturn, Neptune, and Mars from least to greatest. Use the information on page 383.

Scientists sometimes use astronomical units (AUs) to compare distances in space. One astronomical unit is equal to the average distance from the earth to the sun. Use the information given in the table on page 16 for Problems 36–37.

36. Which planet is less than $\frac{1}{2}$ AU from the sun?

37. Which planet is between 1 and 2 AUs from the sun?

Critical Thinking   Write the times in order from least to greatest.

38. 5 days; 144 hours; 3,600 minutes

39. 90 days; 5 weeks; 2 months

Midchapter ——— Checkup

Decide what kind of number to use in each situation.

1. Finding a city on a map

2. Counting railroad cars

Give the most sensible unit for each measure.

3. The time it takes you to eat dinner

4. The length of your shirt sleeve

Write the coordinates of each point.

5. *N*   **6.** *V*   **7.** *C*

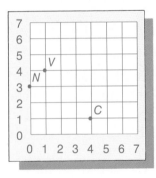

8. Move *N*, *V*, and *C* to new locations by adding 2 to each *x*-coordinate and 3 to each *y*-coordinate. What are the new coordinates?

Copy and complete the table.

9. Rule: $y = x \div 5$

x	0	10	20	30	40
y					

Write each number in words.

10. 93,000,093,000   **11.** 17.0017   **12.** 0.000038   **13.** 27.3

Write each number in standard form.

14. Three billion, six hundred fifty-eight thousand

15. Three billion and six hundred fifty-eight thousandths

Explore as a Team

Special telephone numbers are often requested by businesses so that customers can remember the number easily.

One way to remember a telephone number is to make a code word for it. A code word is made by matching each digit in the telephone number to one of the three letters on the telephone. For example, an airline might choose the phone number 247-7678.

247-7678

Ⓐ G P   Ⓟ M P Ⓣ
B Ⓗ Ⓡ   R N Ⓡ U
C Ⓘ S   S Ⓞ S V

1. Work with your team to find the numbers for the following code words: POPCORN, BIKEBAG, FRIENDS, and LIBERTY.

2. Write a code word for each business listed below.

  a. Pet Shop   264-6257

  b. Beauty Shop   742-6766

  c. Jewelry Shop   342-6663

  d. Make a phone number for a team. Base it on something special about that team.

  e. Choose a business and write a special telephone number for it.

Explore with a Computer

Use the *Graphing and Probability Workshop Project* for this activity.

At marching band practice, cones were set up to mark the corners of the field. The ordered pairs in the table show where the cones were placed.

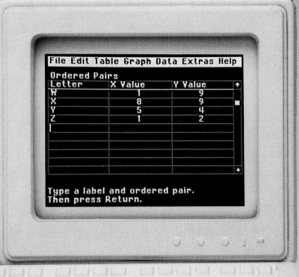

File Edit Table Graph Data Extras Help

Ordered Pairs

Letter	X Value	Y Value	
W	1	9	
X	8	9	
Y	5	4	
Z	1	2	
I			

Type a label and ordered pair.
Then press Return.

1. At the computer, display the ordered pairs in the table as a graph.

2. Which point should be changed to make a rectangle? Change the ordered pair to move the point.

3. The marching band wants to form a triangle. Plot three more points on the graph to mark the corners of a triangle. The triangle should be inside the rectangle. Type the ordered pairs in the table and display the graph.

Number-Sense Project

Look back at pages 2-3.

1. The data to the right gives the time it would take the pendulums to make 20 full swings under ideal conditions. Graph these ordered pairs.

2. On the same grid, graph the data you found when you experimented with pendulums of different lengths. How do your results compare with the ideal results?

3. A 20-meter pendulum would take about 3 minutes to make 20 swings. How long do you think it takes a 73-ft-long pendulum to make 20 full swings?

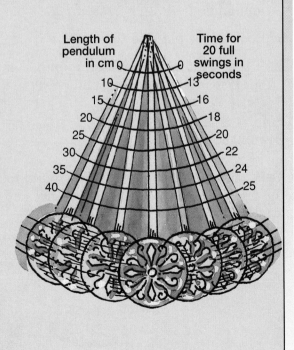

Length of pendulum in cm	Time for 20 full swings in seconds
0	0
10	13
15	16
20	18
25	20
30	22
35	24
40	25

Rounding Whole Numbers and Decimals

Build Understanding

Examine this chart. Round the value of the half dollars to the nearest hundred dollars.

Coins Minted at Denver and Philadelphia, 1987

Coin	Number Minted	Value
Half dollar	99,481	$ 49,740.50
Quarter	1,238,094,177	$309,523,544.25
Dime	1,415,912,883	$141,591,288.30

Round $49,740.50 to the nearest hundred dollars.

You could use a number line. It's hard to tell whether the answer is 49,700 or 49,800.

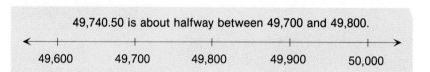

49,740.50 is about halfway between 49,700 and 49,800.

49,600   49,700   49,800   49,900   50,000

Try using a place-value chart instead.

a. Locate the place to which you are rounding.

b. Look at the place to the right.

c. If that digit is 5 or greater, round up. If it is less than 5, round down.

Since 4 is less than 5, round $49,740.50 to $49,700.

┌ ten thousands
  ┌ thousands
    ┌ hundreds
      ┌ tens
        ┌ ones
          ┌ tenths
            ┌ hundredths

4   9,   7   4   0.   5   0

■ **Talk About Math** When you round to the nearest thousand, how do you decide whether to round up or round down?

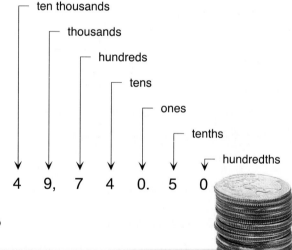

Check Understanding

For another example, see Set E, pages 38–39.

Choose the best answer.

1. 37.482 rounded to the nearest tenth is
a. 40.0.   **b.** 37.4.   **c.** 37.5.

2. 825,406.917 rounded to the nearest hundred is
a. 825,400.   **b.** 825,406.92.   **c.** 825,500.

Practice

For More Practice, see Set E, pages 40–41.

Round 2,109.7265 to the nearest

3. thousandth.   **4.** tenth.   **5.** one.   **6.** hundred.   **7.** thousand.

Round 3,476,542,099 to the nearest

8. million.   **9.** billion.   **10.** ten million.   **11.** hundred.   **12.** thousand.

Round 0.03846 to the nearest

13. hundredth.   **14.** tenth.   **15.** thousandth.   **16.** ten-thousandth.

Mixed Practice   Find each answer. Round each answer to the nearest ten.

17.
$$358.39 + 459.56$$

18.
$$352.32 - 201.65$$

19.
$$1,253 + 6,850$$

20.
$$765.08 - 123.72$$

21. $10,052 - 9,348$ **22.** $146.98 - 51.53$ **23.** $895.60 - 18.09$

Problem Solving

Critical Thinking   Write a number that has 5 in the ones place and rounds to

24. 8,000 when rounded to the nearest thousand.

25. 8,400 when rounded to the nearest hundred.

26. 8,380 when rounded to the nearest ten.

27. 8,375.0 when rounded to the nearest one.

Use the chart on page 22.

28. To the nearest million, what was the number of quarters minted in 1987?

29. To the nearest million dollars, what was the value of the quarters minted in 1987?

Estimating Sums and Differences

Build Understanding

Ingredients for
Jollof Rice

1 lb chicken $\frac{1}{2}$ cabbage
$\frac{1}{2}$ lb beef   4 onions
1 lb rice
1 eggplant   1 tomato
   1 green pepper
$\frac{1}{2}$ lb carrots   2 c peanut oil
3 cloves of $1\frac{1}{3}$ qt stock
garlic
3 T tomato   salt
paste
   pepper

Since meat is a very expensive food in West Africa, jollof rice is generally prepared for special occasions.

A. Laritha and Bill are shopping for the ingredients for jollof rice which they will serve at a dinner they are hosting. Laritha and Bill have all the ingredients with the exception of the chicken, rice, and carrots. The chicken costs $4.05; the rice is $2.59; and the carrots are $0.99. Before getting in line at the checkout counter, they decided to estimate to see if $10 would be enough to pay for the groceries.

Here is a way to estimate.

Front-end digits		Front-end digits plus 1
4 ⟵	$4.05 ⟶	5
2 ⟵	2.59 ⟶	3
0 ⟵	0.99 ⟶	1
$\overline{6}$		$\overline{9}$

Round each given amount down to the nearest whole number. The estimate is less than the exact answer.

Round each given amount up to the nearest whole number. The estimate is greater than the exact answer.

The two estimates provide a *range.* The exact answer is between $6 and $9.
$10 is enough money to pay for the groceries.

B. You can also estimate by *clustering*.

$1.89 The numbers cluster around
2.14 $2.00. Estimate:
1.93 2 + 2 + 2 + 2 = 8.
+ 2.05

The total is about $8.00.

C. Another method for estimating sums and differences is to round to the same place.

6.723 ——————→ 6.7   Choose the decimal place so
9.478 ——————→ 9.5   that each addend has at least
+ 0.81 —————→ 0.8   one digit that is not 0. In this
                17.0   case, round to tenths so that
                        0.81 rounds to a nonzero digit.

The estimated sum is 17.0, or 17.

$1,890.23 ——————→ 1,900   Choose a place so that each
−   443.18 ——————→ 400   number has at least one
                    1,500   nonzero digit. In this case
                             choose hundreds.

This African bowl, which was used for serving meat, was stained with roots and darkened with a hot iron.

The difference is about $1,500.00.

■ Talk About Math   When can you be sure that the exact answer is less than your estimate? greater than your estimate?

Check Understanding

For another example, see Set F, pages 38–39.

Use the subtraction example above to answer Exercises 1 and 2.

1. Why would you not choose to round to thousands?

2. If you rounded to ones instead of hundreds, would your estimate be closer to the exact answer? Explain.

Which estimation technique would you use to estimate each sum or difference? Will your estimate be *greater than* or *less than* the exact answer or *unknown*?

3. $1.46   **4.** $808.76   **5.** $301.94   **6.** $9,867   **7.** $85.98
       0.65   798.12   − 12.88   − 6,325   − 29.06
       6.01   780.80
     + 3.33   + 811.90

Practice

For More Practice, see Set F, pages 40–41.

Estimate each sum or difference by rounding to the nearest tenth.

8. 7.0467
      − 2.4680

9. 41.56095
      + 14.0006

10. 0.8394
       + 9.0011

11. 520.045701
       − 10.00002

12. Estimate each sum or difference for Exercises 8–11 by rounding to the nearest one.

13. Estimate each sum or difference for Exercises 8–11 by rounding to the nearest hundredth.

14. Estimate each sum or difference for Exercises 8–11 by rounding to the same place.

15. For Exercises 8–11 use front-end digits to give a range for each sum or difference.

Estimate each sum or difference. Then add or subtract.
Is your estimate greater than or less than the exact answer?

16. 6.09
       4.97
     + 5.49

17. 643.5
      − 34.7

18. 0.62
       0.0043
     + 0.023

19. 88.007
      − 60.7

20. 160.8
        71.2
     + 70.5

21. 1,596.01
      −   378.5

22. 8.006
      − 0.24

23. 4,044.3
      +   721.65

Number Sense   Give two examples of everyday situations in which you would want your estimate to be

24. greater than the exact number.

25. less than the exact number.

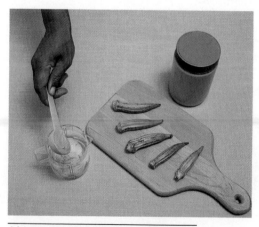

African peanut soup or stew can be found on the menus of European and American restaurants.

Suppose Laritha decides to make peanut stew instead of jollof rice. The beef needed for this recipe costs $4.59; the onions are $0.85; the okra is $1.87; and the peanut butter is $2.15.

26. Does she have enough money to make this recipe?

27. Which is more expensive to make— jollof rice or peanut stew?

Problem Solving

Adela and her friends are planning an international dinner. They are buying the foods from a catering service. Use the display to help you solve each problem. **Remember** to round prices up to help you decide if they have enough money for their purchases.

28. Dolores has $45. Can she buy Polish pierogi and Vietnamese fried rice?

29. Roy has $44.80. He wants to buy the Cuban potato omelet and either Japanese sukiyaki or Turkish pilaf. Which additional dish can he buy?

30. LaToya has $15.60. Adela has $21.19. If they combine their money, can they buy Vietnamese fried rice?

31. Kyoko bought Greek salad. Jim bought Indian curried crab. About how much more did Jim spend than Kyoko?

32. Critical Thinking Determine whether $100 is enough money to buy any five different dishes. Explain your answer.

Visualize the problem in your mind to help you understand it better.

AROUND THE WORLD CATERING
TODAY'S SPECIALS*

Polish pierogi	$14.95
Cuban potato omelet	$19.95
Vietnamese fried rice	$32.25
Japanese sukiyaki	$24.95
Turkish pilaf	$21.95
Indian curried crab	$36.75
Greek salad	$9.25

* Each dish serves 8–10 people

Skills ———— **Review**   pages 14–15

Write each number in standard form.

1. Eighty-two   **2.** Five thousand, sixty-four   **3.** Fourteen thousand

4. Two hundred ninety-four thousand, forty-eight   **5.** Four million, six

6. Eighty-five thousandths   **7.** Five hundred and four thousandths

Write in words.

8. 258   **9.** 696   **10.** 3,916   **11.** 26,062   **12.** 19,131   **13.** 504,746

A
L
G
E
B
R
A

Adding Whole Numbers and Decimals

Build Understanding

The table at the right shows the prices of baseball equipment, including sales tax.

How much will a T-shirt with the name Jesse printed on it cost?

Since you need to combine amounts, you can add. First, estimate by rounding each price to the nearest dollar: $9 + 2 + 0 = 11$. Jesse will need about $11.00.

Find $8.99 + 2.00 + 0.25$.

Item	Price
Baseball	$ 5.50
Bat	$14.00
Mitt	$15.00
T-shirt	$ 8.99
Jacket	$21.00
Cap	$ 6.67
Printing 4 or fewer	
letters	$ 2.00
additional letters	$ 0.25 each

Pencil and Paper

T-shirt	8.99
4 letters	2.00
additional letter	0.25
	11.24

Jesse will need $11.24.

Calculator

Press: 8.99 [+] 2 [+] .25 [=]

Display: *11.24*

Commutative Property of Addition It does not matter in what order you add numbers.

$8.99 + 2.00 = 2.00 + 8.99$

Associative Property of Addition It does not matter how you group numbers when you add.

$(8.99 + 2.00) + 0.25 = 8.99 + (2.00 + 0.25)$

Addition Property of Zero Adding zero to a number does not change the number.

The cost of one T-shirt and zero letters: $8.99 + $0.00 = $8.99, the cost of one T-shirt.

■ **Talk About Math** When adding decimals, how do you align the numbers to be added? Where do you place the decimal point in the answer?

Check Understanding

For another example, see Set G, pages 38–39.

Use the table on page 28. Give an example of each property of addition.

1. Commutative property   **2.** Associative property   **3.** Property of zero

Mental Math   Use mental math to find each sum.

4. 6.2 + 7.0 + 2.1   **5.** 8 + 5.0 + 2.1   **6.** 7.3 + 0.2 + 10.4

Practice

For More Practice, see Set G, pages 40–41.

For Exercises 7–27, tell whether you would use mental math, paper and pencil, or a calculator. Then add.

7. $\begin{array}{r} 1.25 \\ + 0.75 \end{array}$ **8.** $\begin{array}{r} 3.48 \\ + 5.00 \end{array}$ **9.** $\begin{array}{r} 21.50 \\ + 79.00 \end{array}$ **10.** $\begin{array}{r} 4.6 \\ + 3.2 \end{array}$ **11.** $\begin{array}{r} \$7.56 \\ + 9.87 \end{array}$

12. $\begin{array}{r} 9.99 \\ + 11.00 \end{array}$ **13.** $\begin{array}{r} 14.18 \\ + 28.79 \end{array}$ **14.** $\begin{array}{r} 98 \\ + 93 \end{array}$ **15.** $\begin{array}{r} 13.25 \\ + 48.59 \end{array}$ **16.** $\begin{array}{r} \$98.57 \\ + 63.89 \end{array}$

17. $\begin{array}{r} 9.9 \\ + 10.0 \end{array}$ **18.** $\begin{array}{r} \$6.05 \\ + 0.15 \end{array}$ **19.** $\begin{array}{r} 2.3 \\ + 0.59 \end{array}$ **20.** $\begin{array}{r} 0.83 \\ + 1.22 \end{array}$ **21.** $\begin{array}{r} 6,869.5 \\ + 1,504.2 \end{array}$

22. 4.8 + 3.0 + 6.9   **23.** 53 + 86 + 99   **24.** 28.0 + 2.6 + 6.5

25. 102 + 68 + 45   **26.** 9.1 + 12.3 + 32.8   **27.** 75 + 23 + 12

Mental Math   Use mental math to find each sum.

28. 2.5 + (2.5 + 5.0)   **29.** (2.5 + 2.5) + 5.0   **30.** (3 + 7) + (2.2 + 7.8)

31. (1.6 + 4.4) + 9.3   **32.** 5.5 + (0.7 + 3.3)   **33.** 10.9 + 2.1 + (1.9)

Problem Solving

Use the table on page 28 to solve each problem.

34. Juana wants to buy a cap with her name printed on it and a bat. How much will they cost?

35. Estimation   Which costs more, a baseball, bat, and mitt, or a jacket and a T-shirt?

36. Raul has $20.00. Name two items he could buy. Could he have his name printed on both items?

37. List five ways 3 sisters could spend $100 on baseball uniforms and equipment.

Subtracting Whole Numbers and Decimals

Build Understanding

On July 28, 1976, a jet-powered plane reached a record speed of 2,193.167 miles per hour. On July 30, 1983, a plane powered by a piston engine reached a record speed of 517.055 miles per hour. How much greater was the speed of the jet?

Vehicle	Record Speed (mph)
Jet-powered plane	2,193.167
2 race car	633.6
962C bike	124.087
Piston-engine plane	517.055
TGV train, France	135.4
Metroliner, U.S.A.	97.8

To find how much greater (or less) one quantity is than another, you can subtract.

First, estimate. Round both numbers to the nearest hundred: 2,200 − 500 = 1,700. The jet's speed was about 1,700 miles per hour greater. Then solve.

Paper and Pencil
Line up decimal points before you subtract.

```
  1 11 8 13
  2,1 9 3.1 6 7
−   5 1 7.0 5 5
  1,6 7 6.1 1 2
```

Calculator
Press: 2193.167 $\boxed{-}$ 517.055 $\boxed{=}$

Display: *1676.112*

The answer is close to the estimate. The speed of the jet was 1,676.112 miles per hour greater than the speed of the plane.

■ **Talk About Math** If you start with a number, subtract 6, and then add 6, what is the result? How can you use addition to check the subtraction above?

These vehicles are part of the rapid transit system used in Durham, North Carolina.

Check Understanding

For another example, see Set H, pages 38–39.

Complete each exercise.

Estimate. Then subtract.

1. 727
    − 412
    ▦▦▦

2. 727
    − ▦▦▦
    412

3. ▦▦▦
    − 25.3
    17.09

4. 42.3
    − 17.0

5. 58.9
    − 4.6

6. 9.06
    − 3.25

Practice

For More Practice, see Set H, pages 40–41.

Estimate. Then subtract. **Remember** to align the decimal points before you subtract.

7. 245,307
    − 89,281

8. 37,096
    − 6,329

9. 437.9
    − 182.68

10. 12.07
     − 11.03

11. 690.78
     − 305.99

12. 845.31
     − 52.06

13. 48.69
     − 15.66

14. 68.05
     − 30.77

15. 70.12
     − 54.70

16. 834.1
     − 62.5

17. 513,805 − 48,006

18. 6.21 − 3.6

19. 0.04467 − 0.00922

Mixed Practice For Exercises 20–28, tell whether you would use mental math, paper and pencil, or a calculator. Then find each answer.

20. 5.69 + 3.007 + 8.9

21. 99.37 − 19.37

22. 447.83 + 29.703

23. 447.83 − 27.03

24. 29.703 + 418.127

25. 25 + 5 + 40

26. 8.593 + 0.9 − 5

27. 208.7 + 1,366.8 − 934.5

28. 85 + 15 + 0.15

Problem Solving

Critical Thinking Decide whether these properties apply to subtraction.

29. Commutative property
    Does 16 − 8 = 8 − 16?

30. Associative property
    Does 12 − (6 − 4) = (12 − 6) − 4?

Use the table on page 30 to solve each problem.

31. How much less was the record speed of the TGV train than the record speed of the piston-engine plane?

32. How much farther can the piston-engine plane travel in two hours than the Metroliner?

Solving Equations

Build Understanding

A 25-pound radish was grown in Florida in 1977. The same year, a 513-pound squash was grown in Indiana. If the radish were on one side of a huge balance scale and if the squash were on the other, how many pounds in weights would you need to balance the scale?

To solve the problem, use a ***variable*** to stand for the number of pounds needed to balance the scale. A variable is a letter or symbol that represents an unknown quantity.

Then you can solve an equation.

$$25 + w = 513$$

In this case, w represents the unknown weight.

Will w be greater than or less than 513?

Remember that the left and right sides of the equation must stay balanced. Find a way to have w on one side of the equation by itself.

$$25 + w = 513$$
$$25 - 25 + w = 513 - 25$$
$$0 + w = 488$$
$$w = 488$$

Subtract 25 from both sides of the equation.

You would need 488 pounds in weights to balance the scale.

■ **Talk About Math** Why can you use subtraction to solve an equation like the one above?

Check Understanding

For another example, see Set I, pages 38–39.

Refer to the example. Answer each question.

1. What does the w stand for in the equation?

2. Why was 25 subtracted from both sides of the equation?

Tell what to subtract from both sides to solve each equation. Then solve.

3. $100 + p = 370$ **4.** $76 = d + 39$ **5.** $19 + k = 49$ **6.** $57 = x + 39$

Practice

For More Practice, see Set I, pages 40–41.

Solve each equation.

7. $8 + a = 32$ **8.** $17 + b = 21$ **9.** $6 + c = 19$ **10.** $d + 3 = 8$

11. $e + 17 = 43$ **12.** $f + 23 = 56$ **13.** $g + 5 = 8$ **14.** $36 + h = 52$

15. $193 = 146 + m$ **16.** $157 + n = 377$ **17.** $p + 451 = 713$

18. $357 = 79 + q$ **19.** $r + 150 = 377$ **20.** $431 + 200 + x = 700$

21. $s + 897 = 915$ **22.** $f + 250 = 625$ **23.** $109 + t + 122 = 415$

 **Calculator**   Solve for n.

24. $7,058 = 2,999 + n$ **25.** $3,564 + n = 8,440$ **26.** $2,500 = n + 856$

27. $5,798 + n = 19,843$ **28.** $3,792 = 431 + n$ **29.** $n + 925 = 57,098$

Problem Solving

Solve each problem.

30. A 55-pound cantaloupe was grown in North Carolina in 1982. In 1984 a 255-pound watermelon was grown in Oklahoma. How much heavier was the watermelon than the cantaloupe?

31. At the 1988 World Pumpkin Confederation contest the first-place pumpkin weighed 627 pounds. The second-place pumpkin weighed 616 pounds. How much did the two pumpkins weigh together?

32. In 1988 the record weight for the world's biggest squash was 653 pounds. In 1986 the record weight for a squash was 595 pounds. By how many pounds was the record broken in 1988?

33. What is the difference in weight between the 1988 first-place pumpkin in Problem 31 and the 1988 world record squash in Problem 32?

Write an Equation

Build Understanding

During the nineteenth century, the first transcontinental railroad in the Americas was completed across the Isthmus of Panama. It was 14 years later, in 1869, that the driving of the "golden spike" in Utah signified the joining of the east and west coasts of the United States by rail. When was the Panamanian railroad completed?

Understand   QUESTION   In what year was the Panamanian railroad completed?

FACTS   The United States transcontinental railroad was completed in 1869, 14 years after the Panamanian railroad was completed.

KEY IDEA   The words "years later" suggest using addition to solve this problem.

$$\xleftarrow{\hspace{1em}} 14 \text{ years} \xrightarrow{\hspace{1em}}$$

Panamanian   1869

Plan and Solve   STRATEGY   You can use an equation to solve this problem:
$$y + 14 = 1869$$
$$y + 14 - 14 = 1869 - 14 \quad \text{Subtract 14 from both sides.}$$
$$y = 1855$$

ANSWER   The Panamanian railroad was completed in 1855.

Look Back   SENSIBLE ANSWER   Check by replacing y with 1855 in the equation $y + 14 = 1869$. $1855 + 14$ does equal 1869, so the answer is correct.

PROBLEM SOLVING
GUIDE

Understand
QUESTION
FACTS
KEY IDEA

Plan and Solve
STRATEGY
ANSWER

Look Back
SENSIBLE ANSWER
ALTERNATE APPROACH

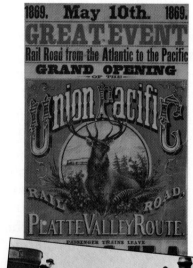

The world's first transcontinental rail line was completed at Promontory, Utah, on May 10, 1869.

■ **Talk About Math** Suppose the Panamanian railroad had been completed 14 years after the completion of the United States transcontinental railroad. What equation would you use to find the completion date?

Check Understanding

In Exercises 1 and 2, use the equation $y + 14 = 1869$.

1. What does the y stand for?

2. Why is 14 subtracted from both sides of the equation?

Write an equation for each. Then solve.

3. What number plus 5 is 12?

4. 8 plus what number is 17?

Practice

Write and solve an equation for each problem.

5. Work began on the Panama Canal in 1881. The Canal was first opened in 1917. How long did it take to build the canal?

6. The Panama Canal is about 51 miles long. The Gaillard Cut, the narrowest part, is about 8 miles long. About how long is the rest of the Canal?

7. French teams excavated about 80 million cubic yards of earth for the Canal. The total amount excavated by the French and United States teams was about 290 million cubic yards. About how much earth was excavated by the United States team?

8. Before the Panama Canal was built, a ship traveling from San Francisco to Cuba had to sail about 13,000 miles. The trip is about 4,600 miles via the Canal. About how much longer was the trip before the Canal was built?

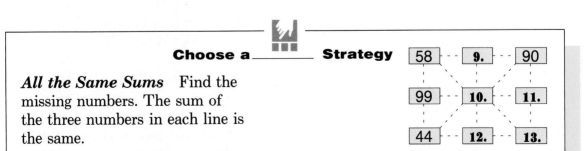

Choose a _____ Strategy

All the Same Sums Find the missing numbers. The sum of the three numbers in each line is the same.

58	9.	90
99	10.	11.
44	12.	13.

Skills Review

1. Name the kind of number you might use to find an intersection on a map.

2. Give the most sensible unit for measuring the length of time it takes you to brush your teeth.

Write the coordinates of each point.

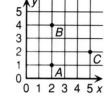

3. A **4.** B **5.** C

6. Write the rule for calculating y.

x	0	1	2	3	4
y	0	2	4	6	8

Write each number in standard form.

7. Fourteen million, three hundred twenty-six thousand, forty-one

8. Seven hundred five and nine thousandths

Compare. Use >, <, or =.

9. 135.234 ▦ 135.24

10. 0.036 ▦ 0.0346

Round 4,195.082 to the nearest

11. hundredth. **12.** tenth. **13.** one.

Estimate. Then compute.

14.   4.5   **15.**   45.003   **16.**   67.84
      + 2.3   − 28.449   + 29.46

Solve each equation.

17. $5 + a = 21$ **18.** $100 = b + 35$

Problem-Solving Review

Solve each problem.

19. Pluto's distance from the sun ranges from 2,756,000,000 miles to 4,551,000,000 miles. Write Pluto's nearest distance to the sun in words.

20. Ruth made a stair-step design of stars to decorate her T-shirt. The bottom step has 6 stars. The top step has 1 star. How many stars are in the design in all?

21. In 1984 the number of $2 bills in circulation was 707,773,472. Round the number of bills to the nearest million.

22. Oscar had $10.00. He bought a notebook for $5.48 and paper for $1.59. Does he have enough money left to buy pens for $1.95?

23. Mary harvested a total of 92 pounds of squash and beans from her garden. She harvested 33 pounds of beans. Write and solve an equation to find how many pounds of squash she harvested.

24. **Data File** Use the data on pages 124–125. Suppose you have $50 to spend on rocket models, accessories, pamphlets, or books. What would you order? How much money would be left?

25. **Make a Data File** Use an almanac or an encyclopedia to make a table of the populations of six cities in your state. List the cities in order of population from greatest to least.

Name the kind of number you might use in each situation.

1. Counting the people in line

2. Cutting a pizza into equal pieces

Choose the most sensible unit to express each measurement.

3. The time it takes to run 1 mile

4. The height of a flagpole

Write the coordinates of each point.

5. *A*   **6.** *B*   **7.** *C*   **8.** *D*

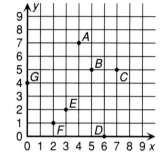

Give the letter that names the point located by each ordered pair.

9. (2, 1)   **10.** (0, 4)   **11.** (3, 2)

Copy and complete each table.

12.

x	1	2	3	4	5	6
y	3	4	5			

13.

x	2	3	4	5	6	7
y	1	2	3			

Write each number in words.

14. 301.25   **15.** 4,125.6   **16.** 15.098   **17.** 700,400,149

Write the numbers in order from least to greatest.

18. 0.23; 0.023; 2.03; 2.30   **19.** 37.142; 37.421; 37.241; 37.214

Round 44,502.174 to the nearest

20. hundredth.   **21.** tenth.   **22.** one.   **23.** hundred.   **24.** thousand.

Estimate. Then add or subtract.

25. $\begin{array}{r} 1{,}654 \\ +\ 2{,}428 \end{array}$ **26.** $\begin{array}{r} 48{,}250 \\ -\ 6{,}925 \end{array}$ **27.** $\begin{array}{r} 65.9 \\ +\ 2.6 \end{array}$ **28.** $\begin{array}{r} 15.03 \\ -\ 11.42 \end{array}$ **29.** $\begin{array}{r} 5.0095 \\ +\ 0.9811 \end{array}$

30. 5.3 + 6.2 + 2.9   **31.** 99.4 − 86.3   **32.** 0.32 + 1.25 + 4.98

33. 264.3 − 98.2   **34.** 125 + 95 + 8   **35.** 9.26 − 3.2

Solve each equation.

36. 10 + a = 63   **37.** b + 38 = 52   **38.** c + 125 = 490

Reteaching

Set A   pages 4–5

Each of these situations uses a certain kind of number.

Timing a 100-yard dash: decimals
Length of relay race: whole numbers
Length of a bolt: fractions

Remember that numbers are necessary for many activities and situations in daily life.

Decide what kind of number to use.

1. Setting an alarm clock

2. Measuring a page in this book

Set B   pages 8–9

On the grid, the coordinates of point *D* are 3 and 4. As an ordered pair, this is written as (3, 4).

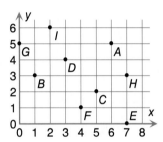

Remember that the first number of an ordered pair tells you the number of units on the *x*-axis.

Write the coordinates of each point.

1. *A*   **2.** *B*   **3.** *C*   **4.** *E*

5. *F*   **6.** *G*   **7.** *H*   **8.** *I*

Set C   pages 14–15

A place-value chart will help you to read or write numbers, such as 53.000486.

hundreds	tens	ones	tenths	hundredths	thousandths	ten-thousandths	hundred-thousandths	millionths	ten-millionths	hundred-millionths
	5	3.	0	0	0	4	8	6		

Read: Fifty three and four hundred eighty-six millionths

Remember to read the decimal point as "and."

Write each number in standard form.

1. One hundred twelve and five hundred sixteen millionths

2. Two and three hundred twenty-one millionths

Set D   pages 16–19

Compare 2.527 and 2.448.

Line up the decimal points.
2.527
2.448
The whole number parts are equal.
Compare the tenths.
5 > 4
Therefore, 2.527 > 2.448.

Remember to line up the decimal points when comparing numbers.

Compare. Use >, <, or =.

1. 8.429 ⬚ 8.427

2. 28.1470 ⬚ 28.147

3. 0.06183 ⬚ 0.06184

Set E pages 22–23

Round 1,627.485 to the nearest hundred. The digit 6 is in the hundreds place. Since the digit in the tens place is less than 5, the hundreds place stays the same.

Therefore, round 1,627.485 to 1,600.

Remember to round up when the digit to the right of the place to be rounded is 5 or more.

Round 6,350.8485 to the nearest

1. thousandth.   **2.** ten.   **3.** one.

Set F pages 24–27

Estimate the sum by rounding to the nearest tenth.

$$\begin{array}{r} 6.0583 \rightarrow 6.1 \\ + 3.6439 \rightarrow + 3.6 \\ \hline 9.7 \end{array}$$

Remember to round each number to the same place.

1. Estimate $5.0832 + 8.2519$ by rounding to the nearest tenth.

Set G pages 28–29

The commutative and the associative properties of addition can help you find a sum using mental math.

$$\begin{aligned} 1.8 + 7.5 + 0.2 &= 1.8 + 0.2 + 7.5 \\ &= 2.0 + 7.5 \\ &= 9.5 \end{aligned}$$

Remember that you can add numbers in any order.

Use mental math to find each sum.

1. $1.5 + 3.7 + 0.5$ **2.** $2.3 + 6.1 + 0.7$

3. $3.5 + 10.0 + 6.5$ **4.** $0.6 + 0.3 + 0.4$

Set H pages 30–31

Estimate. Then subtract.

$48,342 - 7,691$

Round to the nearest thousand.

$48,000 - 8,000 = 40,000$

$$\begin{array}{r} {\scriptstyle 7\,1214} \\ 4\,\cancel{8},\cancel{3}\,\cancel{4}\,2 \\ - 7,6\,9\,1 \\ \hline 4\,0,6\,5\,1 \end{array}$$

Remember to align the decimal points when you add or subtract decimals.

Estimate. Then subtract.

1.
$$\begin{array}{r} 30,862 \\ - 9,406 \\ \hline \end{array}$$
   2.
$$\begin{array}{r} 316.4 \\ - 185.76 \\ \hline \end{array}$$

3. $409,613 - 27,348$

Set I pages 32–33

Use subtraction to solve the following equation because subtraction is the inverse of addition.

$$\begin{aligned} k + 89 &= 147 \\ k + 89 - 89 &= 147 - 89 \\ k + 0 &= 58 \\ k &= 58 \end{aligned}$$

Remember to add or subtract the same number from both sides of the equation.

Solve each equation.

1. $n + 4 = 9$ **2.** $7 + k = 18$

3. $41 + h = 107$ **4.** $m + 128 = 206$

More Practice

Set A   pages 4–5

Decide what kind of number to use in each situation.

1. Measuring your weight on a scale

2. Measuring the length of a mosquito

Set B   pages 8–9

Draw a 10-by-10 grid on paper. Label the *x*- and *y*-axes.
Graph and label these points on your grid.

1. *A* (0, 3)   **2.** *B* (3, 0)   **3.** *C* (5, 8)

4. *D* (8, 5)   **5.** *E* (7, 7)   **6.** *F* (7, 6)

Write the coordinates of each point.

7. *G*   **8.** *H*   **9.** *I*

10. *J*   **11.** *K*   **12.** *L*

13. *M*   **14.** *N*   **15.** *O*

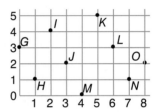

Set C   pages 14–15

Write each number in words.

1. 8,762,903,654,003   **2.** 0.8324   **3.** 407.079   **4.** 2.000849

Write each number in standard form.

5. Eighteen billion, fourteen million, seventeen thousand

6. Nine hundred trillion, six million, seventeen thousand, twelve

7. Two and three hundred sixty-four millionths

8. Eighty-four and one thousand twenty-five millionths

Set D   pages 16–19

Compare. Use >, <, or =.

1. 8,031 ▦ 4,846   **2.** 4.776 ▦ 4.777   **3.** 4.86 ▦ 4.860

4. 26.9 ▦ 26.89   **5.** 0.401 ▦ 0.399   **6.** 0.04813 ▦ 0.04812

Write the numbers in order from least to greatest.

7. 0.07, 0.007, 0.7, 7.070

8. 306,403; 304,603; 403,036

9. 37.28; 37.3; 37.82; 37.828

10. 302.7; 513; 87.888; 8.7888

Set E pages 22–23

Round 4,076.3805 to the nearest

1. thousandth. **2.** tenth. **3.** one. **4.** hundred. **5.** thousand.

Round 0.06425 to the nearest

6. hundredth. **7.** tenth. **8.** thousandth. **9.** ten-thousandth. **10.** one.

Set F pages 24–27

Estimate each sum or difference by rounding to the nearest tenth.

1. 9.05837	**2.** 54.6403	**3.** 1.9247	**4.** 409.16384
− 6.30712	+ 19.50169	+ 8.1006	− 40.916384

Estimate each sum or difference. Then add or subtract.
Is your estimate greater than or less than the exact answer?

5. 3,941.82	**6.** 791.4	**7.** 6,108.4	**8.** 9.004
+ 803.4	− 53.6	+ 831.5	− 1.461

Set G pages 28–29

For Exercises 1–4, tell whether you would use mental
math, paper and pencil, or a calculator. Then add.

1. 3.65	**2.** 7.001	**3.** 32.71	**4.** 46.8
+ 2.35	+ 2.991	+ 82.91	+ 53.2

Mental Math Use mental math to find each sum.

5. 4.5 + (5.0 + 0.5) **6.** (2.75 + 2.25) + 1.0 **7.** (4 + 6) + (3.2 + 6.8)

Set H pages 30–31

Estimate. Then subtract.

1. 368,049	**2.** 25.19	**3.** 43,205	**4.** 826.7
− 57,604	− 14.03	− 9,506	− 483.07

Mixed Practice Tell whether you would use mental
math, paper and pencil, or a calculator. Then find each answer.

5. 3.47 + 8.09 + 6.305 **6.** 68.07 − 38.06 **7.** 664.39 − 24.16

Set I pages 32–33

Solve each equation.

1. $n + 6 = 35$ **2.** $18 + k = 41$ **3.** $d + 4 = 27$ **4.** $9 + d = 21$

5. $149 + e = 183$ **6.** $r + 130 = 287$ **7.** $253 = 84 + m$

Enrichment

History of Numeration

The ancient Romans used these letters as numerals. The table shows the value in the decimal system of each Roman numeral.

Symbol	I	V	X	L	C	D	M
Decimal Value	1	5	10	50	100	500	1,000

You can add or subtract the values of these symbols to show any number.

If the value of a symbol is greater than or equal to the value of the symbol to its right, add the values.

Symbol	XX	LX	VIII	LXXXVI
Decimal Value	10 + 10 = 20	50 + 10 = 60	5 + 1 + 1 + 1 = 8	50 + 10 + 10 + 10 + 5 + 1 = 86

If the value of the symbol is less than the value of the symbol on its right, subtract the values.

Symbol	IV	IX	XL	CD	XC
Decimal Value	5 − 1 = 4	10 − 1 = 9	50 − 10 = 40	500 − 100 = 400	100 − 10 = 90

Many numbers require both adding and subtracting.

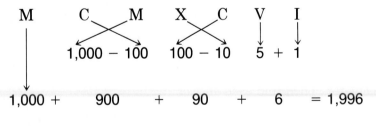

M   C   M   X   C   V   I

1,000 − 100   100 − 10   5 + 1

1,000 +   900   +   90   +   6   = 1,996

Write the decimal value.

1. XIV   **2.** CCXLIX   **3.** MMCMIV   **4.** CCCXXXVII   **5.** MCMLXX

Write a Roman numeral.

6. 33   **7.** 71   **8.** 243   **9.** 1,995   **10.** 3,700

Chapter 1 Review/Test

Tell whether you would use a whole number, a decimal, or a fraction to

1. measure the length of a table in feet.

2. count the students in your class who are on the swim team.

3. Choose the best measure for the length of a carrot.

20 mm   20 cm   20 m

4. Choose the most sensible temperature for an icicle.

0°C   20°C   100°C

Write the coordinates of each point.

5. P **6.** R **7.** U

8. Find the rule for calculating y. Then write the three missing numbers in the table.

x	1	2	3	4	5	6
y	9	8	7			

9. Write this number in standard form.

93 billion, 682 million, 385 thousand, 7

10. Write the decimal for three hundred six thousandths.

Compare. Use <, >, or =.

11. 8,271 ▦ 8,732

12. 48.276 ▦ 48.265

Round to the nearest tenth.

13. 2.463   **14.** 3.03   **15.** 7.96

Estimate each sum or difference. Round to the nearest tenth.

16. 66.008 − 40.8   **17.** 5.07 + 3.98

Add or subtract.

18. 42.7 + 4.036 + 8   **19.** 831 − 227

20. What number plus 10 is 35? Write and solve an equation.

Read the problem below. Then answer the question.

Of the 735 runners who began a marathon, only 546 finished the race. How many dropped out along the way?

21. What do you want to find out?

    a. The number who dropped out
    b. The number who finished
    c. The number who started
    d. The length of the race

22. Write About Math Is the ordered pair (2, 3) the same as the ordered pair (3, 2)? Why is giving the coordinates in order important?

Multiplying Whole Numbers and Decimals 2

Did You Know: July 20, 1994, marks the 25th anniversary of man's first walk on the moon and Neil Armstrong's words, "That's one small step for a man, one giant leap for mankind." Neil Armstrong's weight with space suit was 60 pounds on the moon and 350 pounds on earth.

Number-Sense Project

Estimate
How much do you think a person who weighs 100 pounds on earth would weigh on the moon?

Gather Data
When the gravity on the earth is 1, the number 0.17 gives the gravity on the moon. Find the numbers that give the gravity on the other planets.

Analyze and Report
Tell if a 100-pound person would weigh more than or less than 100 pounds on each of the other planets.

Multiplying by a One-Digit Multiplier

Build Understanding

At a cultural fair, Janet and Eduardo saw a Guatemalan craftsman make "worry doll" pins. The artist used 3 figures to make each pin. How many figures were used to make the 2 rows of pins on display, if each row had 24 pins?

Some Guatemalans share their worries with these dolls to relieve their concerns.

A. Both students multiplied $2 \times 3 \times 24$ to find the answer.

Janet multiplied 24 by 3 and then multiplied that product by 2.

Eduardo multiplied 2×3 mentally and then multiplied 24 by 6.

$$\begin{array}{r} {}^{1}\\ 24 \\ \times\ 3 \\ \hline 72 \end{array}$$

$3 \times 4 = 12$
$12 = 1$ ten 2 ones
3×2 tens $= 6$ tens
6 tens + 1 ten = 7 tens

$$\begin{array}{r} 72 \\ \times\ 2 \\ \hline 144 \end{array}$$

$$2 \times 3 = 6$$

$$\begin{array}{r} {}^{2}\\ 24 \\ \times\ 6 \\ \hline 144 \end{array}$$ ← Factors
← Product

Both methods give the same result, 144 figures.

$2 \times (3 \times 24) = (2 \times 3) \times 24$ $2 \times (3 \times 24)$ is read "2 times the product 3 times 24." The parentheses show which operation to do first.

The ***associative*** (or ***grouping***) ***property of multiplication*** states that three or more factors can be grouped in any way without affecting the product.

B. Compare $(2 \times 3) \times 24$ and $(3 \times 2) \times 24$.

$$\begin{array}{ccc} (2 \times 3) \times 24 & \text{▦} & (3 \times 2) \times 24 \\ 6\ \ \times 24 & = & 6\ \ \times 24 \\ (2 \times 3) \times 24 & = & (3 \times 2) \times 24 \end{array}$$

$2 \times 3 = 6$ and $3 \times 2 = 6$.
Both multiplications become 6×24.

The ***commutative*** (or ***order***) ***property of multiplication*** states that changing the order of the factors does not affect the product.

■ **Write About Math** Choose three numbers and multiply each by 1. Multiply the same three numbers by 0. Write two statements, one called the *multiplication property of one*, and the other called the *multiplication property of zero*.

Check Understanding

For another example, see Set A, pages 80–81.

Complete each exercise.

1. $58 \times (2 \times 9) = (\text{\rule{0.5cm}{0.3cm}} \times \text{\rule{0.5cm}{0.3cm}}) \times 9$ **2.** $83 \times \text{\rule{0.5cm}{0.3cm}} = 0$ **3.** $\text{\rule{0.5cm}{0.3cm}} \times 1 = 94$

Practice

For More Practice, see Set A, pages 82–83.

Multiply.

4. 17	**5.** 37	**6.** 83	**7.** 36	**8.** 325	**9.** 481
× 4	× 8	× 9	× 5	× 3	× 6

10. 4×327 **11.** 7×53 **12.** 3×11 **13.** 7×44 **14.** 8×69

15. 3×741 **16.** 8×912 **17.** $3 \times 2 \times 46$ **18.** $2 \times 2 \times 38$ **19.** 5×301

Find the missing number without computing. Write which property is shown.

20. $(6 \times 8) \times 4 = 6 \times (\text{\rule{0.5cm}{0.3cm}} \times 4)$ **21.** $20 \times \text{\rule{0.5cm}{0.3cm}} = 0$ **22.** $\text{\rule{0.5cm}{0.3cm}} \times 77 = 77$

23. $24 \times 8 = 8 \times \text{\rule{0.5cm}{0.3cm}}$ **24.** $0 = 35 \times \text{\rule{0.5cm}{0.3cm}}$ **25.** $14 \times 9 = \text{\rule{0.5cm}{0.3cm}} \times 14$

Problem Solving

Solve each problem.

26. Each African Zulu doll was decorated with 215 glass beads. How many packages with 100 beads in each package were needed to decorate 5 dolls?

27. Mr. Umoki sold 7 Japanese netsuke. Each figure was worth $28. How much money did he collect?

Japanese netsuke are miniature sculptures made of ivory, wood, metal, or ceramic.

Critical Thinking What is the greatest possible product when multiplying a 1-digit number and a

28. 2-digit number?   **29.** 3-digit number?   **30.** 4-digit number?

Exponents and Powers

Build Understanding

A. The Power of Folding
Groups: Work with a partner.

a. Copy the table below.

b. Fold a sheet of paper in half and record the number of layers. Continue folding the paper in half until it has been folded 5 times. Record the number of layers. Copy and complete the table.

Number of Folds	Number of Layers	Number of Times 2 Is a Factor	Powers of 2
1	2	1	2^1
2	4 or (2×2)	2	2^2
3	▦ or (▦ × ▦ × ▦)	3	2^3
4	▦ or (▦ × ▦ × ▦ × ▦)	▦	2^4
5	▦ or (▦ × ▦ × ▦ × ▦ × ▦)	▦	2^5

c. How many layers will there be after 6 folds? 7 folds?

B. Write 3^4 in *standard form*.

3^4 is read "3 to the fourth *power*."

The *exponent* tells how many times the *base* is used as a factor.

$$\overset{\text{exponent}}{3^{4}} = 3 \times 3 \times 3 \times 3$$

base

$3^4 = 81$ standard form

C. Write $5 \times 5 \times 2 \times 2 \times 2$ using exponents.

$$5 \times 5 = 5^2 \qquad 2 \times 2 \times 2 = 2^3$$

5^2 is read "5 to the second power" or "5 *squared*."

2^3 is read "2 to the third power" or "2 *cubed*."

$$5 \times 5 \times 2 \times 2 \times 2 = 5^2 \times 2^3$$

■ **Talk About Math**   Why would you write a number using exponents rather than in standard form?

Check Understanding

For another example, see Set B, pages 80–81.

1. In 5^4 the base is ▦ and the exponent is ▦.

2. Write 7^3 in standard form.

3. Write $4 \times 4 \times 4 \times 9 \times 9 \times 9 \times 9$ using exponents.

Practice

For More Practice, see Set B, pages 82–83.

Write in standard form.

4. 3^2 5. 4^3 6. 2^4 7. 4^2 8. 0^5

9. $2^2 \times 3^3$ 10. $2^5 \times 4^2$ 11. $2^3 \times 4^2$ 12. $3^2 \times 5^3$ 13. $2^2 \times 3^2$

14. 3×9^3 15. $1^8 \times 7^4$ 16. $2^4 \times 4^2$ 17. $0^9 \times 5^3$ 18. $9^1 \times 9^1$

19. $6^2 \times 3^2$ 20. $2^3 \times 7^2$ 21. $3^4 \times 4^1$ 22. $8^2 \times 3^2$ 23. $9^2 \times 1^3 \times 5^2$

Write each product using exponents and in standard form.

24. $7 \times 7 \times 7 \times 7$ 25. $4 \times 4 \times 4$ 26. $2 \times 2 \times 2 \times 2 \times 2$

27. $1 \times 1 \times 1$ 28. $2 \times 2 \times 5 \times 5 \times 5$ 29. $4 \times 3 \times 3 \times 4$

30. $9 \times 9 \times 4 \times 9 \times 5$ 31. $6 \times 4 \times 6 \times 6 \times 6$ 32. $8 \times 2 \times 8 \times 2 \times 8$

33. $4 \times 5 \times 4 \times 5 \times 4$ 34. $(4 \times 5) \times (5 \times 4)$ 35. $(7 \times 1) \times (7 \times 1) \times 7$

Problem Solving

Solve each problem.

36. **Critical Thinking** Does $2^4 = 4^2$? Will this pattern be true for any two numbers? Try 2^3 and 3^2, and then 5^2 and 2^5. Explain why $2^4 = 4^2$ is or is not true.

37. **Calculator** You can press 8 ⊗ ⊜ to find 8^2, 8 ⊗ ⊜ ⊜ to find 8^3, and so on. Find 8^8. What happens when you try 8^9? Why?

Write each set of numbers in order from greatest to least.

38. 5^2 135 5^3 15 5^4 39. 2^5 9^2 4^3 1^9 3^3

Patterns with Exponents

Build Understanding

Scientists use exponents to express large numbers.

A. Study the table. Compare each exponent with the number of zeros in standard form.

What pattern do you see?

Powers of 10	Standard Form
10^1	10
10^2	100
10^3	1,000
10^4	10,000
10^5	100,000
10^6	1,000,000

B. You know how to write a number in expanded form this way.

52,038 = 50,000 + 2,000 + 30 + 8

To write a number in expanded form using exponents, think of each number as the product of a 1-digit number and a power of 10.

$$52,038 = (5 \times 10,000) + (2 \times 1,000) + (3 \times 10) + 8$$
$$= (5 \times 10^4) + (2 \times 10^3) + (3 \times 10^1) + 8$$

■ **Write About Math** Write a statement about the pattern in Example A.

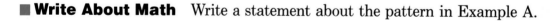

Check Understanding

For another example, see Set C, pages 80–81.

1. Write 100,000,000,000 as a power of 10.

2. Write 3^1 and 5^1 in standard form.

3. A *googol* is 10^{100}. In standard form, how many zeros is that?

4. In Example B, why doesn't the expanded form include 10^2?

5. Complete the expanded form of 356,042 using powers of 10.
356,042 = 300,000 + 50,000 + 6,000 +   40   + 2
= $(3 \times 10^{⋮}) + (5 \times 10^{⋮}) + (6 \times 10^{⋮}) + (4 \times 10^{⋮}) + 2$

6. Write in standard form:
$(2 \times 10^6) + (3 \times 10^4) + (7 \times 10^3) + (3 \times 10^2) + (4 \times 10^1) + 9$

Practice

For More Practice, see Set C, pages 82–83.

Write each number in expanded form using exponents.

7. 452   **8.** 1,356   **9.** 101   **10.** 20,256   **11.** 25,749   **12.** 96,080

13. 799   **14.** 9,205   **15.** 162   **16.** 73,285   **17.** 3,400   **18.** 85,310

19. 935   **20.** 7,528   **21.** 368   **22.** 60,102   **23.** 8,907   **24.** 92,183

Write each number in standard form.

25. $(3 \times 10^2) + (5 \times 10^1) + 2$

26. $(7 \times 10^3) + (4 \times 10^1) + 7$

27. $(9 \times 10^3) + (7 \times 10^2) + (2 \times 10^1)$

28. $(5 \times 10^6) + (3 \times 10^4) + 9$

29. $(5 \times 10^4) + (6 \times 10^2) + (8 \times 10^1)$

30. $(6 \times 10^5) + (3 \times 10^2) + 8$

 Calculator Write the numbers with exponents and in standard form.

31. The powers of 3 from 3^1 through 3^9 **32.** The powers of 5 from 5^1 through 5^9

Problem Solving

33. The interior temperature of the sun is about 35,000,000° F. Write this temperature in expanded form using exponents.

Critical Thinking Use your lists from Exercises 31 and 32 to help you answer the questions.

34. Describe the pattern of the ones digits in the powers of 3.

35. In standard form, what is the ones digit in 3^{11}? in 3^{45}?

36. Liang said that $3^{13} = 1,594,327$. Can this be correct? Explain.

37. In standard form, what are the last three digits of 5^{347}?

Explore ———— **Math**

38. Copy and complete. Write each answer as a power of 10. Use paper and pencil or a calculator.

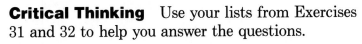
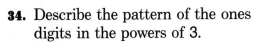

$10^1 \times 10^1 = $ $10^2 \times 10^1 = $ $10^3 \times 10^1 = $ $10^4 \times 10^1 = $
$10^1 \times 10^2 = $ $10^2 \times 10^2 = $ $10^3 \times 10^2 = $ $10^4 \times 10^2 = $

39. Write a statement about finding products such as $10^2 \times 10^5$.

Mental Math: Multiples of 10

Build Understanding

A. If a plane travels at a speed of 300 miles per hour for 4 hours, how far will it travel?

Find 4 × 300.

Think: 4 × 300 = 4 × (3 × 100)
$$= (4 × 3) × 100 \quad \text{Use the associative property of multiplication.}$$
$$= 12 × 100$$
$$= 1,200$$

The plane will travel 1,200 miles.

> The distance between Chicago, Illinois, and Sarasota, Florida, is about 1,200 miles.

B. Find 20 × 20 × 50.

20 × 20 × 50 ← First, multiply the factors without considering the ending zeros.
2 × 2 × 5 = 20

20 × 20 × 50 ← Then write as many ending zeros in the product as there are in all the factors.

20 × 20 × 50 = 20,000

C. You can use the ***distributive property*** to help you multiply mentally. Find 6 × 24 mentally.

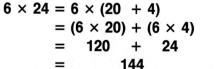

6 × 24 = 6 × (20 + 4)   Think of 24 as 20 + 4.
$$= (6 × 20) + (6 × 4) \quad \text{Multiply 6 times each addend.}$$
$$= \quad 120 \quad + \quad 24 \quad \text{Then add the products.}$$
$$= \quad\quad 144$$

■ **Talk About Math** How could you use the distributive property with subtraction to find 7 × 99 mentally? 4 × 38?

Check Understanding

For another example, see Set D, pages 80–81.

Write the number of ending zeros
in each product and multiply.

1. 20 × 30   **2.** 30 × 500

Copy and complete using the
distributive property.

3. 5 × 21 = 5 × (▦ + ▦)
    = (5 × ▦) + (5 × ▦)

Practice

For More Practice, see Set D, pages 82–83.

Multiply. Use mental math.

4. 20 × 100   **5.** 20 × 30   **6.** 500 × 70   **7.** 40 × 8,000   **8.** 50 × 60

9. 30 × 30   **10.** 70 × 10   **11.** 80 × 600   **12.** 10,000 × 3   **13.** 20 × 5,000

14. 50 × 40   **15.** 80 × 30   **16.** 40 × 200   **17.** 60,000 × 2   **18.** 50 × 3,000

Use the distributive property to multiply mentally.

19. 4 × 59   **20.** 6 × 14   **21.** 8 × 51   **22.** 2 × 20   **23.** 5 × 43

24. 5 × 37   **25.** 8 × 43   **26.** 6 × 27   **27.** 5 × 96   **28.** 3 × 63

29. 3 × 45   **30.** 9 × 61   **31.** 7 × 53   **32.** 4 × 82   **33.** 2 × 150

34. 6 × 15   **35.** 7 × 39   **36.** 3 × 304   **37.** 9 × 160   **38.** 8 × 495

Problem Solving

Solve. Use mental math.

39. Tom flew 2,000 miles one week on
business trips. If the next week he flew
three times that distance, how many
miles did he travel the second week?

40. Four people bought tickets to Little
Rock for $109. Find the total cost
of the tickets.

Be flexible. If you get
stuck, try another idea.

41. Estimation   At the airport,
Chico spent $6.95 on lunch, $2.35
on a magazine, and $7 on a T-shirt.
About how much did he spend?

42. Number Sense   If one factor
ends in 2 zeros and the other ends
in 3 zeros, how many zeros can
appear at the end of the product?

Estimating Products

Build Understanding

A. The Alvarez Medical Supply Corporation needs to buy 43 new cars for their sales representatives. Each car costs $9,905. About how much will be spent for these new cars?

Estimate 43 × 9,905.
Round each factor so that *only the first digit is not zero*.
Then multiply mentally.

43 × 9,905   Round.

  ↓   ↓   ↓

40 × 10,000 = 400,000   Multiply mentally.

About $400,000 will be spent for the cars.

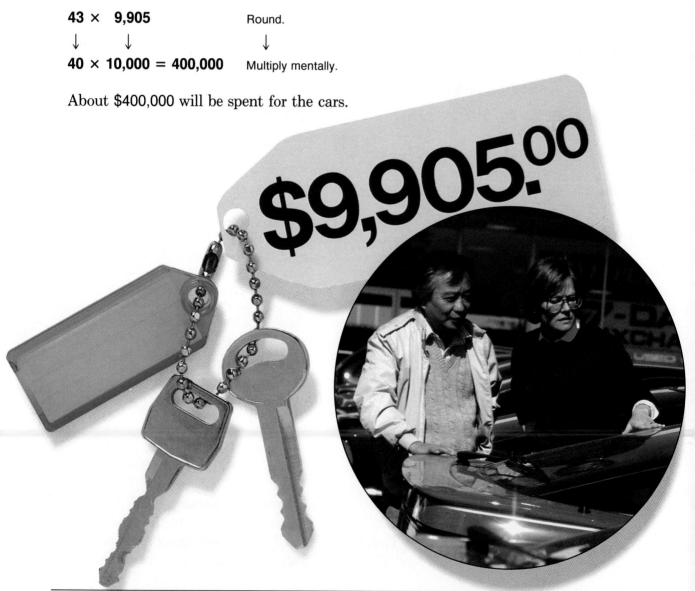

54

B. Estimate 56 × 20 by finding a range.

Determine which multiples of 10 or 100 this factor lies between. 56 is between 50 and 60.

↓
56 × 20
↑

This factor is a multiple of 10 already.

The product is between 50 × 20 and 60 × 20.

             ↓   ↓

       1,000   1,200

56 × 20 is between 1,000 and 1,200.

c. Estimate 24 × 4 by using compatible numbers.

24 × 4   Think of numbers that are close to 24 and that can be mentally multiplied by 4.

23 × 4 = ?   **25 × 4 = 100**

25 and 4 are compatible numbers because they can be easily multiplied.

24 × 4 is about 100.

■ **Talk About Math** In Example C, can you decide whether 24 × 4 is greater than 100? In Example A, can you decide whether 43 × 9,905 is greater than 400,000? Explain your answers.

Check Understanding

For another example, see Set E, pages 80–81.

Choose the best estimate for each product.

1. 113 × 66
  a. 700   **b.** 7,000   **c.** 70,000

2. 494 × 410
  a. 2,000   **b.** 20,000   **c.** 200,000

3. Find a range for the product 72 × 26 by rounding both factors up and both factors down.

4. Estimate 18 × 52 by using compatible numbers.

5. Number Sense When can you be sure an estimate is greater than the actual product?

Practice

For More Practice, see Set E, pages 82–83.

Estimate each product by rounding each factor so that only the first digit is not zero. **Remember** to round up when the second digit is 5 or greater.

6. 48 × 67   **7.** 23 × 84   **8.** 76 × 16   **9.** 21 × 52

10. 57 × 177   **11.** 93 × 326   **12.** 411 × 937   **13.** 295 × 491

14. 67 × 177   **15.** 36 × 1,507   **16.** 559 × 2,276   **17.** 267 × 4,195

Estimate each product by finding a range.

18. 44 × 40   **19.** 30 × 68   **20.** 21 × 80   **21.** 33 × 600

22. 288 × 300   **23.** 200 × 348   **24.** 35 × 56   **25.** 17 × 83

26. 51 × 845   **27.** 72 × 248   **28.** 97 × 325   **29.** 93 × 768

Estimate each product using compatible numbers.

30. 6 × 24   **31.** 2 × 73   **32.** 36 × 2   **33.** 21 × 3

34. 76 × 20   **35.** 46 × 21   **36.** 12 × 455   **37.** 15 × 226

38. 27 × 820   **39.** 23 × 4,109   **40.** 55 × 2,047   **41.** 77 × 4,187

Mixed Practice   Estimate using any method. Tell which method you chose.

42. 6 × 26   **43.** 21 × 38   **44.** 65 × 25   **45.** 46 × 85

46. 34 × 94   **47.** 87 × 96   **48.** 41 × 6,951   **49.** 58 × 408

50. 307 × 592   **51.** 432 × 985   **52.** 217 × 7,942   **53.** 255 × 4,095

Problem Solving

54. Critical Thinking Look at Exercises 6–17. In which did you round both factors up? both factors down?

55. Critical Thinking How could you round to get a better estimate for a product like 76 × 16? like 56 × 35?

56. Debby Williams bought a car with a basic price of $12,405. She ordered air conditioning and an AM/FM radio. What was the total cost of the car?

57. Which is more expensive, an automatic transmission and bucket seats, or a sun roof and air conditioning?

New Car	
Option	Price
Air conditioning	$550
AM/FM radio	$145
Bucket seats	$490
Automatic transmission	$550
Sun roof	$305

Basic price: $12,405

58. A $500 rebate is offered by the manufacturer if all the options listed above are purchased. Find the total cost of the car with all the options.

59. If the Alvarez Corporation in Example A buys 43 cars that are $1,050 cheaper, about how much will the company save?

60. The Alvarez Corporation decided to buy 18 cars at the $9,905 price and 25 cars that cost $8,495 apiece. About how much was the total amount spent on the cars?

Skills _____ Review   pages 28–29

Add.

1. 801 + 138	**2.** 7.46 + 3.03	**3.** 505 + 891	**4.** 2.9 + 0.85	**5.** 12.4 + 7.1	**6.** 8.79 + 6.5

7. 8.037 + 5.21   **8.** 392 + 79.5   **9.** 27 + 451 + 507

10. 2,417 + 7,217   **11.** 3.6 + 0.5 + 0.41   **12.** 271 + 658 + 4,662

Multiplying by Multiples of 10 or 100

Build Understanding

A. Camp Multi-Fun charges $30 per person each day for room and board. What is the total income per day for 247 people?

Multiply 247 by 30.

$$\begin{array}{r} 247 \\ \times\ 30 \\ \hline 0 \end{array}$$

$247 \times 30 = 247 \times (3 \times 10)$
$\qquad\qquad = (247 \times 3) \times 10$
Since 10 is a factor, you know that the last digit in the product is 0.

$$\begin{array}{r} 247 \\ \times\ 30 \\ \hline 7{,}410 \end{array}$$

Now multiply by 3, the other factor.

The camp receives $7,410 per day to serve 247 people.

B. Find 400×129.

$$\begin{array}{r} 129 \\ \times 400 \\ \hline 51{,}600 \end{array}$$

$129 \times 400 = 129 \times (4 \times 100)$
$\qquad\qquad = (129 \times 4) \times 100$
$\qquad\qquad = 516 \times 100$

C. Mental Math   Find $50 \times 9 \times 4$ mentally.

$50 \times 9 \times 4 = 50 \times 4 \times 9$
$\qquad\qquad = 200 \times 9$
$\qquad\qquad = 1{,}800$

■ **Write About Math**   Write a statement for multiplying by multiples of 10 and 100.

Check Understanding

For another example, see Set F, pages 80–81.

Multiply.

1.	2.	3.	4.	
24 × 10	24 × 100	762 × 20	762 × 200	**5.** What pattern do you see in Exercises 1 and 2? 3 and 4?

Tell which two factors you would multiply first. Then multiply.

6. $2 \times 7 \times 5$ **7.** $6 \times 3 \times 5$ **8.** $7 \times 5 \times 4 \times 3$ **9.** $2 \times 3 \times 5 \times 3$

Practice

For More Practice, see Set F, pages 82–83.

Multiply. Use mental math when you can.

10.	11.	12.	13.	14.	15.
36 × 7	36 × 70	79 × 8	79 × 80	87 × 400	870 × 400

16.	17.	18.	19.	20.	21.
53 × 20	53 × 200	794 × 6	794 × 600	429 × 300	586 × 700

22. 94×50 **23.** 59×80 **24.** 103×9 **25.** 295×500

26. 70×6 **27.** 6×700 **28.** 39×40 **29.** 60×502

30. 60×20 **31.** 7×99 **32.** 400×13 **33.** 820×6

34. $40 \times 30 \times 5$ **35.** $8 \times 5 \times 9$ **36.** 245×80 **37.** $4 \times 30 \times 5 \times 40$

Problem Solving

Solve each problem.

38. Estimation A camper spent $3.56, $2.10, and $1.65 on craft items. Did this cost more than $8.00? Write the steps you used to arrive at an answer.

39. The camp charges $100 for a family to stay 3 days. How much will the camp collect if 62 families each stay 3 days?

40. In Example A, how much less would the camp collect if the charge per day was lowered to $20?

41. Last summer the camp served an average of 200 people for 10 full weeks. Find the total collected by the camp at $30 per person per day.

Multiplying by a Multi-Digit Number

Build Understanding

A. A class of 28 students is raising money for a trip to Washington, D.C. Transportation costs $96 per person. How much money does the class need to raise?

Think: 28 groups, with $96 in each group. You can use multiplication to solve the problem.

Find 28 × 96.　　　Estimate: 28 × 96

$$30 \times 100 = 3,000$$

$$
\begin{array}{r}
96 \\
\times 28 \\
\hline
768 \\
1920 \\
\hline
2,688
\end{array}
$$

Think: 28 = 20 + 8

768 ← 8 × 96
1920 ← 20 × 96

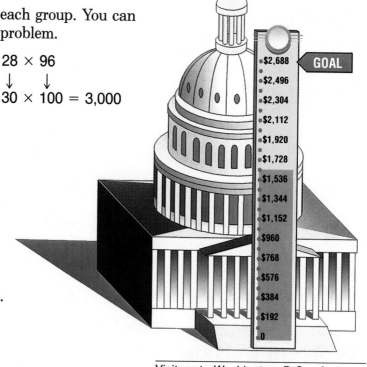

Compare the product (2,688) with the estimate (3,000). The product is reasonable.

The class needs to raise $2,688.

B. Find 247 × 596.
First, estimate: 200 × 600 = 120,000.

Visitors to Washington, D.C., often tour the United States Capitol.

Paper and Pencil

$$
\begin{array}{r}
596 \\
\times 247 \\
\hline
4172 \\
23840 \\
119200 \\
\hline
147,212
\end{array}
$$

Think: 247 = 200 + 40 + 7

4172 ← 7 × 596
23840 ← 40 × 596
119200 ← 200 × 596

Calculator

Press:　247 ⊗ 596 ⊜

Display: *147212.*

247 × 596 = 147,212

■ **Talk About Math**　In Example A, how do you know before computing that the cost of transportation is less than $3,000? Can you make the same kind of decision in Example B? Explain.

Check Understanding

For another example, see Set G, pages 80–81.

Estimate. Then choose the exact product from those given.

1. 68×97

    a. 13,396
    b. 6,596
    c. 5,372

2. 234×528

    a. 54,752
    b. 235,522
    c. 123,552

Complete the exercise below.

3.
$$\begin{array}{r} 314 \\ \times\,206 \\ \hline \end{array}$$
▓▓▓▓ ← 6×314
62800 ← ▓▓▓▓ $\times\ 314$
▓▓▓▓

Practice

For More Practice, see Set G, pages 82–83.

Multiply. Be sure to estimate first.

4. 46×32 **5.** 836×63 **6.** 317×56 **7.** 529×83

8. 692×49 **9.** 832×93 **10.** 438×217 **11.** 827×535

12. 754×430 **13.** 637×905 **14.** $1,447 \times 266$ **15.** $2,394 \times 462$

Calculator Multiply. **Remember** to estimate to be sure your answer is reasonable.

16. 624×976 **17.** 389×848 **18.** $478 \times 5,656$ **19.** $724 \times 9,739$

20. $822 \times 2,482$ **21.** $572 \times 3,982$ **22.** $425 \times 4,953$ **23.** $803 \times 6,008$

Mixed Practice Multiply.

24. 5×38 **25.** 2×707 **26.** $7 \times 4,101$ **27.** 60×61 **28.** 3×900

29. 40×333 **30.** 400×81 **31.** 600×85 **32.** $432 \times 6,890$

Problem Solving

Use the table to solve each problem.

Advance Ticket Purchase	Cost for Round Trip
4 weeks	$308
2 weeks	$358
7 days or less	$569

33. What is the cost of 3 round-trip tickets with 2-week advance purchase?

34. How much would you save on a ticket if you purchased it 4 weeks in advance instead of 3 days in advance?

Choose a Computation Method

Build Understanding

Hana and her brother Tani are selling old toys and books at the local flea market.

A. They have 32 books for sale at 50¢ each. How much money will they get if they sell all of the books?

Tani used *paper and pencil*.

$$\begin{array}{r} 50 \\ \times 32 \\ \hline 100 \\ 1500 \\ \hline 1600 \end{array}$$ 1600¢ = $16.00

They will get $16.00.

Hana used *mental math*. She knew that 50¢ is $\frac{1}{2}$ of a dollar, so she divided 32 by 2.

32 ÷ 2 = 16

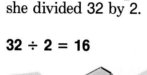

B. Mrs. Lugo bought these three toys and paid with a $20 bill. How much change should she receive?

▦ Calculator   1.75 ⊕ 2.5 ⊕ 1.95 ⊜ 6.2

M+ 20 ⊖ MRC ⊜ 13.8

Mrs. Lugo should receive $13.80 in change.

■ Talk About Math   When is it a good idea to use a calculator? When is mental math helpful?

Check Understanding

1. How could you use mental math to find the cost of 28 articles at $0.25 each?

2. How could you use your calculator to answer Example B if you started by entering 20?

Practice

For Exercises 3–30, tell whether you would use mental math,
paper and pencil, or a calculator. Then find each answer.

3. $20 + 15$ **4.** $6{,}013 - 3{,}979$ **5.** 84×5 **6.** $400 + 600$ **7.** 96×8

8. 54×6 **9.** $513 + 87$ **10.** $735 - 135$ **11.** 47×2 **12.** 800×30

13. $\begin{array}{r} 70 \\ \times\, 20 \\ \hline \end{array}$ **14.** $\begin{array}{r} 837 \\ \times\ 33 \\ \hline \end{array}$ **15.** $\begin{array}{r} 129 \\ +\,802 \\ \hline \end{array}$ **16.** $\begin{array}{r} 701 \\ -\,121 \\ \hline \end{array}$ **17.** $\begin{array}{r} 2{,}620 \\ -\,1{,}620 \\ \hline \end{array}$ **18.** $\begin{array}{r} 906 \\ -\,487 \\ \hline \end{array}$

19. 676×82 **20.** $10{,}331 - 1{,}879$ **21.** 512×10 **22.** $7{,}000 + 400$

23. $314 - 24$ **24.** 928×100 **25.** $45 + 7{,}418$ **26.** $7{,}734 \times 872$

27. $70 \times 3 \times 2$ **28.** 736×197 **29.** $(859 + 242) \times 5$ **30.** $7 \times (495 + 863)$

Problem Solving

Solve each problem.

31. Jenny bought a used keyboard for $35.00. She paid with two $20 bills. How much change did she receive?

32. Manuel sold 35 old record albums for $0.30 each. How much money did he receive for the albums?

33. How much was collected at the market from 119 tables rented at $9 each?

Midchapter ✓ Checkup

1. Write $2 \times 2 \times 3 \times 3 \times 4$ using exponents. Then multiply.

2. Use standard form to write $(7 \times 10^4) + (3 \times 10^2) + 1$.

Estimate each product.

3. 76×95 **4.** 12×609 **5.** 870×476 **6.** $43 \times 1{,}972$

Tell whether you would use mental math, paper and pencil, or a calculator. Then find each answer.

7. 64×606 **8.** 200×42 **9.** 70×509 **10.** $15 \times 2{,}983$ **11.** 6×90

Explore as a Team

A palindrome is a number which reads the same forward and backward. Some examples of palindromes are 121, 4,004, 6, and 3,333.

Calculator   Any of the numbers in the chart at the right can be changed into a palindrome by reversing the digits and adding, and repeating this procedure until you get a palindrome.

101
101: 0 step

110
110 + 011 = 121
110: 1 step

195
195 + 591 = 786
786 + 687 = 1,473
1,473 + 3,741 = 5,214
5,214 + 4,125 = 9,339

195: 4 steps

1. Make a chart listing the numbers 100 through 195.

2. Have each member of the team choose a row or column of numbers in the chart and use a calculator to find how many steps are needed to turn each number into a palindrome. Record the number of steps required and the palindrome in the chart. Continue to pick rows and columns of numbers until all numbers are tested.

3. Which number required the most steps?

4. Discuss patterns you noticed with your team.

Palindrome Chart

100	132	164
101	133	165
102	134	166
103	135	167
104	136	168
105	137	169
106	138	170
107	139	171
108	140	172
109	141	173
110	142	174
111	143	175
112	144	176
113	145	177
114	146	178
115	147	179
116	148	180
117	149	181
118	150	182
119	151	183
120	152	184
121	153	185
122	154	186
123	155	187
124	156	188
125	157	189
126	158	190
127	159	191
128	160	192
129	161	193
130	162	194
131	163	195

Real-Life Decision Making

Suppose you are at a store and need to pay the cashier $6.47 for your purchases. This is the money you have in your wallet.

1. What bills and coins would you use to pay for your purchases?

2. Could you pay for your purchases in a different way?

3. How would you pay for your purchases so that you would receive a 5 dollar bill as your exact change?

Number-Sense Project

Look back at pages 44-45.

Calculator Since the gravity on the moon is 0.17 of earth's gravity, multiply each weight by 0.17 to find moon weight. On each Apollo moon landing, the astronauts brought back rock samples. The earth weight of these samples is given below. Find their moon weight.

1. Apollo 11: 48.5 lb

2. Apollo 12: 74.7 lb

3. Apollo 14: 96 lb

4. Apollo 15: 170 lb

5. Apollo 16: 213 lb

6. Apollo 17: 243 lb

Make a Table

Build Understanding

Two planes left Washington, D.C., for the 3,600-mile flight to London. Flight 614 left at 1:00 and averaged 450 miles per hour. Flight 508 left at 3:00 and averaged 1,000 miles per hour. When Flight 508 passed Flight 614, about what time was it in Washington?

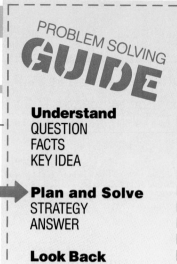

PROBLEM SOLVING
GUIDE

Understand
QUESTION
FACTS
KEY IDEA

Plan and Solve
STRATEGY
ANSWER

Look Back
SENSIBLE ANSWER
ALTERNATE APPROACH

Understand   Flight 508 overtook Flight 614 when they were both the same distance from Washington. List times and distances traveled until the distances are about the same.

Plan and Solve   STRATEGY   Make a table to list the times and distances.

Time	Miles from Washington	
	Flight 614	Flight 508
1:00	0	0
2:00	450	0
3:00	900	0
4:00	1,350	1,000
5:00	1,800	2,000

4:00	1,350	1,000
4:30	1,575	1,500
5:00	1,800	2,000

Flight 508 passed Flight 614 between 4:00 and 5:00. Try 4:30.

In the half hour after 4:00, Flight 614 traveled $\frac{1}{2} \times (450)$, or 225 more miles. In that same time Flight 508 traveled $\frac{1}{2} \times (1,000)$, or 500, more miles.

At 4:30, Flight 508 was only 75 miles behind Flight 614.

ANSWER   Flight 508 passed Flight 614 shortly after 4:30.

Look Back   When Flight 508 left, Flight 614 had gone 900 miles. Flight 508 traveled 500 miles per hour faster, so it would make up 900 miles in less than 2 hours.

■ **Talk About Math**   Discuss how to find a closer estimate of when Flight 508 passed Flight 614.

Check Understanding

1. What was the time in Washington when Flight 508 landed in London?

2. How much longer was Flight 614 in the air than Flight 508?

3. If Flight 614 had averaged 500 miles per hour, when would Flight 508 have passed it?

Practice

Solve each problem. Ashton is 400 miles from Lyons by bus, train, or car.

4. Maxine left Ashton for Lyons at noon, driving at an average speed of 45 miles per hour. Chen followed at 1:00, driving at 55 miles per hour. How far from Ashton was Chen when he passed Maxine?

5. A bus left Ashton at 4:00 P.M. for Lyons and averaged 50 miles per hour. A train from Ashton, which averaged 80 miles per hour, arrived in Lyons at the same time as the bus. When did the train leave Ashton?

6. When the bus in Exercise 5 left Ashton for Lyons, another bus left Lyons for Ashton. If this bus averaged 30 miles per hour, at what time did the buses meet?

7. The train in Exercise 5 left Lyons and completed a 489-mile ride from Lyons to Barrington. How many miles did the train travel?

8. Tom can rent a car for $25 a day plus 20¢ a mile or for $30 a day with no mileage fee. How many miles per day must he drive to make the $30-a-day car more worthwhile?

Choose a **Strategy**

9. A kit used to weigh gold includes a pan balance, a 1-ounce weight, a 3-ounce weight, a 9-ounce weight, and a 27-ounce weight. The instructions claim that *all* whole-number amounts of gold from 1 oz through 40 oz can be measured with some or all of these four weights on the balance. Are the kit instructions correct? Explain your answer.

Multiplying Decimals

Build Understanding

A. Decimal Models

Materials: Grid paper

Groups: Small groups of 3 or 4 students

a. Make 4 decimal models like the ones shown.

b. Shade 8 tenths of each whole.

c. Count to find the number of tenths that are shaded in all.

4 × 8 tenths = ▦ tenths

d. Remember that multiplication is the same as repeated addition.

4 × 0.8 = 0.8 + 0.8 + 0.8 + 0.8 = ▦

e. Look at your two answers. Are they the same?

f. In 4 × 0.8, how many decimal places are in the factors? How many are in the product?

g. Find 0.6 × 0.3.

First shade 3 tenths of a whole.
Then shade 0.6 of that amount.

The answer is the part that has been shaded twice.

h. 0.6 × 0.3 = 18 ▦

Rewrite the product as a decimal.

i. In 0.6 × 0.3, how many places are in the factors? How many are in the product?

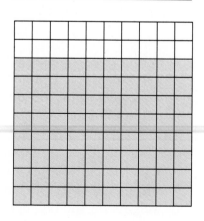

68

B. Find 3 × 1.5.

The factor 1.5 is between 1 and 2.
Estimate by finding a range.
3 × 1 = 3, and 3 × 2 = 6.
The product is between 3 and 6.

$$
\begin{array}{r}
1.5 \leftarrow \text{1 decimal place} \\
\times\ \ 3 \leftarrow \text{0 decimal places} \\
\hline
4.5 \leftarrow \text{1 + 0, or 1, decimal place}
\end{array}
$$

To multiply with decimals, first multiply as with whole numbers. Then count the total number of decimal places in the factors and show that number of decimal places in the product.

C. Find 3.95 × 12.5.

Estimate by rounding each factor to the nearest whole number.

4 × 13 = 52   Since both factors were rounded up, the product will be less than 52.

Multiply.

Paper and Pencil

$$
\begin{array}{r}
1\,2.5 \leftarrow \text{1 decimal place} \\
\times\,3.9\,5 \leftarrow \text{2 decimal places} \\
\hline
6\,2\,5 \\
1\,1\,2\,5\,0 \\
3\,7\,5\,0\,0 \\
\hline
4\,9.3\,7\,5 \leftarrow \text{2 + 1, or 3, decimal places}
\end{array}
$$

▦ Calculator

Press: 12.5 ⌈×⌉ 3.95 ⌈=⌉

Display: *49.375*

12.5 × 3.95 = 49.375

■ **Talk About Math**   In Example C, how can the estimate help you place the decimal point in the product?

Check Understanding

For another example, see Set H, pages 80–81.

Complete the following.

1.

0.1 × 0.9 = ▦

2.

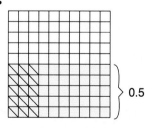

▦ × 0.5 = ▦

3. There are ▦ decimal places in 0.091 and ▦ decimal place in 39.3. The product of 0.091 and 39.3 has ▦ decimal places.

Number Sense   Copy each equation. Place a decimal point in each underlined number so that the product is reasonable.

4. 3.1 × 56 = <u>1736</u>   **5.** 0.87 × <u>209</u> = 1.8183   **6.** 0.5 × 0.7 = <u>35</u>

Practice

For More Practice, see Set H, pages 82–83.

Complete the following.

7. 1.4

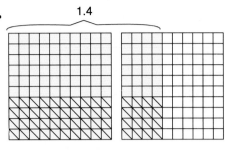

1.4 × ▦ = 0.56

8.

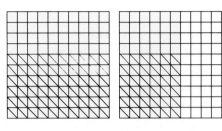

▦ × ▦ = 0.96

Estimate each product. Then find the product.

9. 5.2 × 6.04   **10.** 9.3 × 3.1   **11.** 9.05 × 8.4

12. 3.4 × 6.9   **13.** 81.3 × 2.3   **14.** 0.89 × 18.7

Multiply. **Remember** to place a decimal point in your answer.

15. 2.2 × 8	**16.** 4.96 × 6	**17.** 0.25 × 7.8	**18.** 4.93 × 1.5	**19.** 0.99 × 0.6
20. 8.4 × 3.2	**21.** 8.81 × 7.1	**22.** 2.3 × 0.61	**23.** 4.9 × 0.54	**24.** 6.71 × 0.08
25. 7.9 × 3.3	**26.** 3.89 × 5.9	**27.** 0.38 × 5.2	**28.** 4.68 × 0.67	**29.** 9.42 × 0.13

30. 7 × 6.3   **31.** 0.67 × 5.6   **32.** 0.3 × 6.26   **33.** 9.1 × 1.51

34. 8 × 9.2   **35.** 0.82 × 3.4   **36.** 0.9 × 7.35   **37.** 4.6 × 2.39

38. 0.54 × 1.03   **39.** 0.07 × 9.17   **40.** 0.34 × 64.3   **41.** 5.05 × 53.2

Mixed Practice   Tell whether you would use paper and pencil, mental math, or a calculator. Then find each product.

42. 5 × 46   **43.** 75 × 17   **44.** 10 × 89   **45.** 0.31 × 27

46. 0.5 × 4.08   **47.** 30 × 500   **48.** 0.48 × 601   **49.** 0.9 × 0.3

50. 3^2 × 5.2   **51.** 4^3 × 0.25   **52.** 2^5 × 0.29   **53.** 9^2 × 0.83

Problem Solving

Solve each problem.

54. A small box of raisins has 1.5 milligrams of iron. How much iron is in 6 small boxes? in 1.5 boxes?

Cheese Type	Amount	Calcium
Cheddar	1 ounce	211 mg
Cottage (1% fat)	1 cup	138
Ricotta (whole milk)	$\frac{1}{2}$ cup	257
Ricotta (part skim)	$\frac{1}{2}$ cup	337

55. Roberta makes a dip for vegetables with $\frac{1}{2}$ cup of cottage cheese and $\frac{1}{2}$ cup of part-skim-milk ricotta cheese. How much calcium is in the dip?

56. How many milligrams of calcium are in 1.35 pounds of cheddar cheese? (Hint: There are 16 ounces in 1 pound.)

Skills _____ **Review**   pages 16–19, 28–31

Estimate. Then find the sum or difference.

1. 644 + 439   **2.** 606 − 109   **3.** 427 − 345

4. 3,966 + 4,907   **5.** 6,750 − 2,181   **6.** 5,200 + 3,114

7. 42,314 − 36,670   **8.** 22,744 − 14,792   **9.** 75,420 + 85,705

Compare. Use <, >, or =.

10. 1,767 ⊞ 17,607   **11.** 0.82 ⊞ 0.820   **12.** 89,403 ⊞ 809,403

13. 0.505 ⊞ 0.5505   **14.** 10.06 ⊞ 10.006   **15.** 89.05 ⊞ 98.05

Multiplying Decimals: Zeros in the Product

Build Understanding

Estelle's restaurant sells salads. Estelle needs to know the cost of the ingredients for a single serving. The costs are shown in the table.

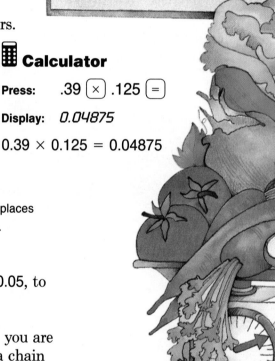

Item	Cost Per Pound	Amount Needed for One Serving
Lettuce	$0.41	1 oz = 0.063 lb
Tomato	$0.89	2 oz = 0.125 lb
Cucumber	$0.39	2 oz = 0.125 lb
Grated Carrot	$0.45	0.4 oz = 0.025 lb
Onion	$0.32	2 oz = 0.125 lb

Find the cost of the cucumber to the nearest cent.

Multiply as with whole numbers.

Paper and Pencil

Place the decimal point in the product.

$$
\begin{array}{r}
0.39 \leftarrow \text{2 decimal places} \\
\times 0.125 \leftarrow \text{3 decimal places} \\
\hline
195 \\
780 \\
3900 \\
\hline
0.04875 \leftarrow \text{2 + 3, or 5, decimal places}
\end{array}
$$

Write a zero to show 5 decimal places.

$0.04875 \approx 0.05$

The cost of the cucumber is $0.05, to the nearest cent.

Calculator

Press: .39 $\times$ .125 $=$

Display: *0.04875*

$0.39 \times 0.125 = 0.04875$

■ **Talk About Math** Suppose you are ordering salad ingredients for a chain of restaurants. How would all the decimal places be useful to you?

Check Understanding

For another example, see Set I, pages 80–81.

Number Sense Copy each equation. Place a decimal point in each underlined number so that the product is reasonable.

1. $0.04 \times 1.23 = \underline{492}$ **2.** $0.05 \times \underline{673} = 0.03365$ **3.** $\underline{5} \times 0.113 = 0.0565$

Practice

For More Practice, see Set I, pages 82–83.

Multiply. **Remember** to count the decimal places in both factors.

4.	5.	6.	7.	8.
0.0 5 7 × 0.4 3	0.0 9 2 ×0.0 8 6	0.1 2 5 × 2.3	0.0 0 4 7 × 8.1 3	0.0 5 9 ×0.3 0 7

9.	10.	11.	12.	13.
0.1 0 3 ×0.0 0 5	0.0 1 7 × 0.1 7	0.0 0 9 6 × 0.8 7	0.0 3 1 × 0.0 2 2	0.0 5 1 × 1.2 3

14.	15.	16.	17.	18.
0.083 × 0.067	0.118 × 0.079	0.027 × 0.635	0.083 × 0.49	8.0854 × 0.123

19. 6.1×0.0024 **20.** 0.026×1.004 **21.** 0.0703×0.052 **22.** 5.08×0.099

23. 0.035×1.2 **24.** 0.004×2.5 **25.** 0.033×0.54 **26.** 0.015×0.066

27. 3.3×0.0238 **28.** 0.486×0.032 **29.** 0.082×0.67 **30.** 11.06×0.038

Calculator Multiply.

31. 0.0245×6.69 **32.** 0.728×84.9 **33.** 0.0799×0.224 **34.** 23.0376×3.91

35. 0.0719×0.84 **36.** 38.475×2.6 **37.** 11.275×0.35 **38.** 8.0854×8.24

Problem Solving

Use the information in the example. For one serving,
find the cost of

39. the lettuce. **40.** the tomato. **41.** the carrot. **42.** the whole salad.

Critical Thinking Solve each problem.

43. Jeffrey wrote $0.35 \times 0.29 = 1.015$. How can you tell,
without multiplying, that Jeffrey's answer is incorrect?

44. When you multiply two numbers,
each of which is greater than 1, the
product is greater than either of the
factors. Show two examples of this
statement and explain why the
statement is reasonable.

45. When you multiply two numbers,
each of which is less than 1, the
product is less than either of the
factors. Show two examples of this
statement and explain why the
statement is reasonable.

Mental Math: Multiplying Decimals by Powers of 10

Build Understanding

Americans eat an average of 81.4 pounds of fresh vegetables a year. How many pounds of vegetables would 10 people eat?

Find 10 × 81.4.

$$\begin{array}{r} 8\,1.4 \\ \times\ \ 1\,0 \\ \hline 8\,1\,4.0 \end{array}$$

Multiply as with whole numbers. Then place the decimal point in the quotient.

Ten people would eat about 814 pounds of vegetables.

■ **Talk About Math** When you multiply 23.47 by 100, why doesn't a decimal point have to be written in the answer? When 0.29 is multiplied by 1,000, why is there a zero at the end of the product?

Check Understanding

For another example, see Set J, pages 80–81.

Complete the following sentences.

1. To multiply 10 and 3.9 mentally, move the decimal point ▦ places to the ___?___.

2. To multiply 10,000 and 0.8 mentally, move the decimal point ▦ places to the ___?___.

3. The product of 100 and 81.4 is ▦.

4. The product of 0.6 and 1,000 is ▦.

Practice

For More Practice, see Set J, pages 82–83.

Multiply. Use mental math.

5. 0.36×10 **6.** 6.02×100 **7.** 100×0.003 **8.** 73.4×100

9. $3.2 \times 1{,}000$ **10.** $521.62 \times 1{,}000$ **11.** $0.00059 \times 10{,}000$

12. $0.0062 \times 1{,}000$ **13.** $10{,}000 \times 81.4$ **14.** $100{,}000 \times 0.705$

Copy and complete the table.

n	2.891	23.08	**16.**		0.857	0.0243	**19.**	**20.**
$100 \times n$	289.1	**15.**	70.5	**17.**	**18.**		6.88	0.0007

Mixed Practice   For Exercises 21–29, tell whether you would use mental math, paper and pencil, or a calculator. Then find the product.

21. 2×42 **22.** 34×633 **23.** 3.16×5.5 **24.** 0.03×9 **25.** 6.8×0.19

26. 10×31 **27.** 80×14 **28.** 9.9×100 **29.** $1{,}000 \times (2.10 + 0.03)$

Problem Solving

Copy and complete the table.

Number of Pounds of Food Eaten Per Year

Type of Food	1 Person	10 Persons	100 Persons	1,000 Persons
Fish	14.5	**30.**	**31.**	**32.**
Milk	245	**33.**	**34.**	**35.**
Fresh Fruit	**36.**	882	**37.**	**38.**

Place the decimal point in each underlined number.

39. $0.63 \times 10^1 = \underline{0630}$ **40.** $10.35 \times 10^2 = \underline{010350}$ **41.** $3.06 \times 10^3 = \underline{03060}$

42. Write a statement for multiplying a decimal by a power of 10.

43. Use Data   Use the table on page 72. How many pounds of lettuce would be needed to make 1,000 servings of salad?

Deciding When an Estimate Is Enough

PROBLEM SOLVING GUIDE

Understand
QUESTION
FACTS
KEY IDEA

Plan and Solve
STRATEGY
ANSWER

Look Back
SENSIBLE ANSWER
ALTERNATE APPROACH

Build Understanding

There is $85 in the sixth-grade activity fund. The students want to buy 28 tickets to "Pirate's Cave." The tickets cost $2.90 each. Brian estimated the total cost to be 30 × $3, or $90. Do the students have enough money for the tickets?

Understand QUESTION Does the estimate of $90 definitely mean that $85 is not enough for 28 tickets?

FACTS The tickets cost $2.90 each. The students have $85 to pay for 28 tickets. The estimate is $90.

KEY IDEA The estimate is sufficient only if it shows that the *exact* cost of the 28 tickets is less than $85.

Plan and Solve Brian used 30 × $3.00 for his estimate. He rounded both factors up, so 28 × $2.90 is less than 30 × $3.00.

28 × 2.90 = a number less than 90

↓   ↓

30 × 3.00 = 90.00

Brian's estimate shows only that *the exact cost of the tickets is less than $90.00.* It does not show whether the exact cost is also less than $85.00.

ANSWER Brian's estimate is not sufficient. To make a decision, he should find 28 × $2.90.

Look Back Find the exact answer: 28 × 2.90 = 81.20. The actual cost is less than $85.

■ **Talk About Math** If $100 was in the activity fund for the 28 tickets, would Brian's estimate be enough to answer the question?

Check Understanding

Ellen has $21. She estimates that 5 tickets to Dinosaur Valley will cost $20. Tell whether Ellen's estimate is enough to be sure she can buy 5 tickets if each ticket costs

1. $3.75.   **2.** $4.40.   **3.** $3.95.

Practice

For Exercises 4–7, decide whether an estimate is sufficient to answer the question. Explain why. If an exact answer is needed, find the answer.

4. The Sky Ride costs $2.20. If 204 people ride it, will the owner receive more than $450?

5. The Log Ride lasts for 11 minutes. Can Oliver take the ride 3 times in half an hour?

6. A school bus seats 52 people. Will 7 buses be enough to take 350 students to Merry Marvels Amusement Park?

7. Mr. Hansen has $25. Is this enough money to buy souvenirs that cost $3.50, $4.25, $11.00, $3.00, and $1.75?

8. Write a problem for which you can estimate to find the answer.

9. Write a problem for which you cannot estimate to find the answer.

Choose a ——— Strategy

10. *Calendar Shuffle* Michelle owns a company that employs 7 salespeople. She wants to hold a meeting of all 7 salespeople. Because of their travel schedules, the salespeople are in the office only on certain days.

Alani is in the office every day. Bernie is there every second day, Chuck every third day, Debra every fourth day, Ellen every fifth day, Frank every sixth day, and Gordon every seventh day.

If all the salespeople were in the office yesterday, how long will it be before they can meet again?

Skills Review

Multiply. Use mental math if you can.

1. 35
    × 40

2. 6.7
    × 8

3. 27
    × 4

4. 6.2 × 100

5. 0.26 × 0.15

6. 2.7 × 3.04

7. 80 × 50 × 2

8. 1,000 × 0.52

9. 87 × 83

10. 58 × 372

11. 30 × 70

Estimate. Then multiply.

12. 41 × 49

13. 465 × 98

14. 78 × 67

15. 18 × 93

Write in standard form.

16. 4^3

17. $2^5 × 3^2$

18. $(6 × 10^4) + (2 × 10^3) + (7 × 10^1)$

Write in expanded form using exponents.

19. 248

20. 3,000

21. 4,679

22. 47,202

Write using exponents and in standard form.

23. 9 × 9 × 9

24. 5 × 5 × 7

25. 2 × 2 × 2 × 2 × 4 × 4

Find the missing number. Which property is shown?

26. 27 × ▦ = 27

27. 3,295 × 0 = ▦

28. 87 × 93 = ▦ × 87

Problem-Solving Review

Solve each problem.

29. Alice bought a set of paints for $6.50 and sketching paper for $2.95. The sales tax was $0.66. How much did she spend?

30. Mr. O'Hara flew 5,000 miles on business trips in April. He flew three times as many miles in May. How many miles did he fly in May?

31. Fred wants to buy 4 paperback books for $3.95 each and another book for $7.25. Is $20 enough to pay for the books?

32. Velvet earned $15 baby-sitting. Her brother earned $3.50 an hour for 4 hours doing yard work. Who earned more money?

33. Philip is buying a new car that costs $13,575. He made a down payment of $2,000. How much does he still owe on the car?

34. The Empire State Building in New York City is 1,250 feet tall. Write this number in expanded notation using powers of ten.

35. Data File Use the data on pages 124–125. How much would you weigh on each planet? Remember, weight depends on surface gravity.

36. Make a Data File Record the high and low temperatures each day for a week. Display the data in a table.

Estimate. Then compute.

1. $\begin{array}{r} 42 \\ \times\, 23 \\ \hline \end{array}$ **2.** $\begin{array}{r} 793 \\ -\, 289 \\ \hline \end{array}$ **3.** $\begin{array}{r} 6.72 \\ +\, 47.6 \\ \hline \end{array}$ **4.** $\begin{array}{r} 468 \\ \times\, 72 \\ \hline \end{array}$ **5.** $\begin{array}{r} 27 \\ \times\, 4 \\ \hline \end{array}$

6. 6.2×0.4 **7.** $7.003 - 4.417$ **8.** 0.26×0.15 **9.** 30×700

10. $5.107 + 0.452$ **11.** 40×35 **12.** 4.06×0.79 **13.** $2{,}341.6 + 29.7$

14. $27.6 - 13.04$ **15.** 158×327 **16.** 2.7×8.6 **17.** $36.02 + 3.875$

Use mental math to compute.

18. $2.5 + 3.6 + 0.5$ **19.** 0.0036×10 **20.** $1{,}000 \times 0.32$ **21.** 70×60

22. $3 \times 20 \times 5$ **23.** $4.3 + 2.7 + 2$ **24.** 0.671×100 **25.** $56 \times 1{,}000$

Solve each equation.

26. $n + 9 = 46$ **27.** $d + 92 = 178$ **28.** $39 = 18 + x$ **29.** $68 + m = 471$

Compare. Use $>$, $<$, or $=$.

30. $42.7 \; \blacksquare \; 42.68$ **31.** $3.001 \; \blacksquare \; 2.99$ **32.** $0.37 \; \blacksquare \; 0.37$ **33.** $0.07 \; \blacksquare \; 0.071$

Round 0.04258 to the nearest

34. hundredth.   **35.** tenth.   **36.** thousandth.   **37.** ten-thousandth.

Write in standard form.

38. 4^3 **39.** $2^5 \times 3^2$ **40.** $(2 \times 10^3) + (1 \times 10^2) \times (7 \times 10^1)$

Write using exponents and in standard form.

41. $7 \times 7 \times 7$ **42.** $9 \times 9 \times 3 \times 3$ **43.** $2 \times 2 \times 2 \times 2 \times 2 \times 4 \times 4$

Find the missing numbers. Write which property is shown.

44. $8 \times \blacksquare = 8$ **45.** $3 \times 0 = \blacksquare$ **46.** $(3 \times 7) \times 5 = (\blacksquare \times 3) \times 5$

Write in order from least to greatest.

47. 0.122, 0.012, 0.102, 0.21   **48.** 0.033, 0.0333, 0.03, 0.3

49. Find the rule for calculating y. Then complete the table.

x	1	2	3	4	5	6
y	▦	6	9	12	▦	▦

Reteaching

Set A   pages 46–47

Find the missing number.

$(3 \times 9) \times 5 = 3 \times (\boxed{} \times 5)$

Applying the associative property of multiplication, the number is 9.

Remember that the order of the factors does not affect the product.

Find the missing number.

1. $(4 \times 7) \times 3 = 4 \times (7 \times \boxed{})$

2. $5 \times 9 \times 2 = 5 \times \boxed{} \times 9$

Set B   pages 48–49

Write this product using exponents.

$3 \times 3 \times 3 \times 5 \times 5$
$3 \times 3 \times 3 \times 5 \times 5 = 3^3 \times 5^2$

Remember that an exponent tells how many times the base is a factor.

Write each product using exponents.

1. $6 \times 6 \times 6$ **2.** $4 \times 4 \times 5 \times 5$

Set C   pages 50–51

Write 20,476 in expanded form using exponents.

$20{,}476 = 20{,}000 + 400 + 70 + 6$
$\phantom{20{,}476} = (2 \times 10{,}000) + (4 \times 100) +$
$\phantom{20{,}476 = } (7 \times 10) + 6$
$\phantom{20{,}476} = (2 \times 10^4) + (4 \times 10^2) +$
$\phantom{20{,}476 = } (7 \times 10^1) + 6$

Remember to think of each number as the product of a one-digit number and a power of 10.

Write each number in expanded form using exponents.

1. 782   **2.** 22,869   **3.** 107,546

Set D   pages 52–53

Use the distributive property to find 6×56.

$6 \times 56 = 6 \times (50 + 6)$
$ = (6 \times 50) + (6 \times 6)$
$ = 300 + 36$
$ = 336$

Remember to think of one factor as a sum of two numbers that are easy to multiply.

Multiply mentally.

1. 8×27 **2.** 7×53 **3.** 97×4

Set E   pages 54–57

Estimate $56 \times 8{,}526$.
Round each factor so that only the first digit is not zero.

$56 \times 8{,}526$
$\downarrow \downarrow$
$60 \times 9{,}000 = 540{,}000$

Remember to write as many zeros in the product as there are in the factors.

Estimate the product by rounding each factor so that only the first digit is not zero.

1. 53×26 **2.** $42 \times 3{,}985$

3. 38×12 **4.** 63×487

Set F pages 58–59

Find $50 \times 23 \times 4$.

$$50 \times 23 \times 4 = (50 \times 4) \times 23$$
$$= 200 \times 23$$
$$= 4{,}600$$

Remember to look for multiples of 10 or 100 when multiplying several factors.

Multiply.

1. $78 \times 5 \times 2$ **2.** $5 \times 16 \times 20$

3. $4 \times 53 \times 25$ **4.** $250 \times 84 \times 4$

Set G pages 60–61

Find 334×621.

First, estimate:

$300 \times 600 = 180{,}000$

$$
\begin{array}{r}
334 \\
\times\, 621 \\
\hline
334 \\
6\,680 \\
200\,400 \\
\hline
207{,}414
\end{array}
$$

Remember to round so that you can estimate mentally.

Estimate. Then multiply.

1. 32×23 **2.** 38×29

3. 905×44 **4.** 295×166

Set H pages 68–71

Find 4.86×11.3.

$$
\begin{array}{r}
4.8\,6 \leftarrow \text{2 decimal places} \\
\times\, 1\,1.3 \leftarrow \text{1 decimal place} \\
\hline
1\,4\,5\,8 \\
4\,8\,6\,0 \\
4\,8\,6\,0\,0 \\
\hline
5\,4.9\,1\,8 \leftarrow \text{2 + 1, or 3 decimal places}
\end{array}
$$

Remember to place a decimal point in the product.

Multiply.

1. $\begin{array}{r} 3.4 \\ \times\ 6 \\ \hline \end{array}$ **2.** $\begin{array}{r} 5.32 \\ \times\ 7 \\ \hline \end{array}$ **3.** $\begin{array}{r} 0.6\,1 \\ \times\ 2.9 \\ \hline \end{array}$

4. 0.82×3.4 **5.** 8.6×2.95

Set I pages 72–73

Find 0.25×0.33.

$$
\begin{array}{r}
0.2\,5 \leftarrow \text{2 decimal places} \\
\times\, 0.3\,3 \leftarrow \text{2 decimal places} \\
\hline
7\,5 \\
7\,5\,0 \\
\hline
0.0\,8\,2\,5 \leftarrow \text{4 decimal places}
\end{array}
$$

Remember that you may have to write extra zeros when you place the decimal point in the product.

Multiply.

1. $\begin{array}{r} 0.0\,4\,3 \\ \times\ 0.2\,7 \\ \hline \end{array}$ **2.** $\begin{array}{r} 0.0\,8\,6 \\ \times\, 0.5\,0\,9 \\ \hline \end{array}$

Set J pages 74–75

Find 100×0.49.

Since there are two zeros in 100, move the decimal point two places to the right.

$100 \times 0.49 = 49$

Remember that you may have to write zeros in the product when multiplying a number by 10, 100, or 1,000.

Multiply.

1. 10×8.7 **2.** $1{,}000 \times 0.39$

More Practice

Set A pages 46–47

Multiply.

1.	18	2.	49	3.	75	4.	28	5.	453	6.	817
	× 3		× 6		× 9		× 4		× 5		× 7

Find the missing number without computing. Tell which property is shown.

7. $(8 \times 3) \times 7 = 8 \times (\blacksquare \times 7)$ **8.** $89 \times 5 = 5 \times \blacksquare$

Set B pages 48–49

Write in standard form.

1. 3^3 **2.** 5^3 **3.** $4^3 \times 3^2$ **4.** $2^4 \times 6^2$ **5.** $4^2 \times 5^2$

Write using exponents and in standard form.

6. $8 \times 8 \times 8$ **7.** $3 \times 3 \times 3 \times 3$ **8.** $3 \times 3 \times 4 \times 4 \times 4 \times 4$

Set C pages 50–51

Write each number in expanded form using exponents.

1. 638   **2.** 1,985   **3.** 210   **4.** 22,189   **5.** 26,547

Write each number in standard form.

6. $(4 \times 10^3) + (7 \times 10^2) + (9 \times 10^1)$ **7.** $(6 \times 10^4) + (8 \times 10^2) + (3 \times 10^1)$

Set D pages 52–53

Multiply. Use mental math.

1. $30 \times 1,000$ **2.** 5×300 **3.** 40×600 **4.** 6×48 **5.** 9×15

Set E pages 54–57

Estimate the product by rounding each factor so that only the first digit is not zero.

1. 35×42 **2.** 26×71 **3.** 18×224 **4.** 318×728

Estimate the product by finding a range.

5. 34×40 **6.** 26×70 **7.** 246×200 **8.** 41×63

Estimate the product using compatible numbers.

9. 47×2 **10.** 4×26 **11.** 21×52 **12.** 18×157

Set F   pages 58–59

Multiply. Use mental math when you can.

1. $\begin{array}{r} 86 \\ \times\ 9 \\ \hline \end{array}$	**2.** $\begin{array}{r} 86 \\ \times 90 \\ \hline \end{array}$	**3.** $\begin{array}{r} 47 \\ \times 20 \\ \hline \end{array}$	**4.** $\begin{array}{r} 47 \\ \times 200 \\ \hline \end{array}$	**5.** $\begin{array}{r} 52 \\ \times 300 \\ \hline \end{array}$

6. 80×7 **7.** 7×800 **8.** 19×50 **9.** $6 \times 5 \times 8$

Set G   pages 60–61

Estimate. Then multiply.

1. 27×43 **2.** 641×52 **3.** 428×61 **4.** 535×704

Calculator   Multiply.

5. 749×836 **6.** 496×327 **7.** $298 \times 1,409$ **8.** $814 \times 2,376$

Mixed Practice   Multiply.

9. 5×49 **10.** 4×505 **11.** 300×72 **12.** 64×50

Set H   pages 68–71

Multiply.

1. $\begin{array}{r} 4.3 \\ \times\ 9 \\ \hline \end{array}$	**2.** $\begin{array}{r} 5.38 \\ \times\ 6 \\ \hline \end{array}$	**3.** $\begin{array}{r} 0.49 \\ \times\ 3.8 \\ \hline \end{array}$	**4.** $\begin{array}{r} 6.7 \\ \times 0.83 \\ \hline \end{array}$	**5.** $\begin{array}{r} 9.54 \\ \times\ 6.2 \\ \hline \end{array}$

6. 8×5.4 **7.** 0.76×9.3 **8.** 0.45×81.2 **9.** 9.06×1.17

Set I   pages 72–73

Multiply.

1. $\begin{array}{r} 0.36 \\ \times 0.25 \\ \hline \end{array}$	**2.** $\begin{array}{r} 0.29 \\ \times 0.074 \\ \hline \end{array}$	**3.** $\begin{array}{r} 0.0047 \\ \times\ 0.6 \\ \hline \end{array}$	**4.** $\begin{array}{r} 0.052 \\ \times\ 1.34 \\ \hline \end{array}$	**5.** $\begin{array}{r} 0.091 \\ \times 0.91 \\ \hline \end{array}$

6. 3.1×0.042 **7.** 0.62×2.3 **8.** 0.09×0.05 **9.** 6.03×0.88

Calculator   Multiply.

10. 0.5259×3.66 **11.** 0.828×65.7 **12.** 0.0943×0.335 **13.** 87.9×0.6877

Set J   pages 74–75

Multiply. Use mental math.

1. 10×0.98 **2.** 7.06×100 **3.** $436.29 \times 1,000$

4. $0.0084 \times 1,000$ **5.** $0.00076 \times 10,000$ **6.** $10,000 \times 49.3$

Enrichment

Square Roots

When you multiply a number by itself, the result is called the **square** of the number.

Since $3 \times 3 = 9$, 9 is the square of 3.
Since $7 \times 7 = 49$, 49 is the square of 7.

The **square root** of a number is the number which when multiplied by itself yields the given number. The symbol $\sqrt{}$ means "the square root of."

3 is the square root of 9, since $3 \times 3 = 9$. $\sqrt{9} = 3$
7 is the square root of 49, since $7 \times 7 = 49$.
$\sqrt{49} = 7$

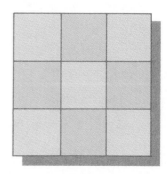

The area of this square is 9 square units.

The length of a side of this square is 3 units.

1. ▦ **Calculator** Make a list of squares by squaring the numbers from 1 through 25.

Refer to the list of square numbers you made in Exercise 1 to find the following square roots.

2. $\sqrt{16}$ 3. $\sqrt{36}$ 4. $\sqrt{81}$ 5. $\sqrt{4}$ 6. $\sqrt{25}$

7. $\sqrt{225}$ 8. $\sqrt{144}$ 9. $\sqrt{400}$ 10. $\sqrt{625}$ 11. $\sqrt{196}$

12. $\sqrt{169}$ 13. $\sqrt{289}$ 14. $\sqrt{256}$ 15. $\sqrt{361}$ 16. $\sqrt{121}$

17. $\sqrt{441}$ 18. $\sqrt{576}$ 19. $\sqrt{529}$ 20. $\sqrt{324}$ 21. $\sqrt{484}$

Find the following.

22. $\sqrt{9} \times \sqrt{4}$ 23. $\sqrt{9} \times \sqrt{9}$ 24. $\sqrt{16} + \sqrt{9}$

Write *true* or *false*.

25. $\sqrt{9} \times \sqrt{4} = \sqrt{36}$ 26. $\sqrt{9} \times \sqrt{9} = \sqrt{81}$ 27. $\sqrt{16} + \sqrt{9} = \sqrt{25}$

Chapter 2 Review/Test

Multiply.

1. $\begin{array}{r} 637 \\ \times \quad 5 \\ \hline \end{array}$ **2.** $\begin{array}{r} 5{,}406 \\ \times \quad 8 \\ \hline \end{array}$

Write each number in standard form.

3. 6^3

4. $2^2 \times 3^4$

5. Write $2 \times 2 \times 2 \times 2 \times 5 \times 5$ using exponents.

Write each number in expanded form using exponents.

6. 987

7. 45,206

Write each number in standard form.

8. $(6 \times 10^3) + (8 \times 10^2) + (1 \times 10^1) + 3$

9. $(5 \times 10^4) + (2 \times 10^2) + (7 \times 10^1)$

Estimate each product.

10. 48×51 **11.** 602×416

Multiply. Use mental math.

12. $82 \times 1{,}000$

13. 700×30

14. 10×2.8

15. 72.3×100

16. $1{,}000 \times 0.7$

Multiply.

17. $\begin{array}{r} 327 \\ \times \quad 60 \\ \hline \end{array}$ **18.** $\begin{array}{r} 327 \\ \times \quad 54 \\ \hline \end{array}$

19. $\begin{array}{r} 0.54 \\ \times \quad 29 \\ \hline \end{array}$ **20.** $\begin{array}{r} 0.36 \\ \times \quad 2.7 \\ \hline \end{array}$

21. $\begin{array}{r} 0.3 \\ \times 0.2 \\ \hline \end{array}$ **22.** $\begin{array}{r} 0.037 \\ \times \quad 0.25 \\ \hline \end{array}$

23. 80.2×59.3 **24.** 0.05×0.07

Use these facts to solve Problem 25.

Bus One leaves Coogan at 7:15 A.M. and reaches Fremont at 7:57 A.M.

25. Does Bus One travel from Coogan to Fremont in less than half an hour? Did you need an exact answer to solve this problem?

Read the problem below. Then answer the question.

If pecans sold for $2.15 a pound, how much did the Simpsons receive for their harvest of 7,263 pounds of pecans?

26. Which computation method would you use to solve the problem?

   a. Multiply using mental math.
   b. Divide using mental math.
   c. Multiply using a calculator.
   d. Divide using a calculator.

27. **Write About Math** How can you use the distributive property to help you find 3×590 mentally?

Dividing Whole Numbers

3

Did You Know:
People can wait in line for up to an hour to ride on The American Eagle roller coaster at Six Flags Great America in Gurnee, Illinois. The ride, which features a 147-foot drop and speeds of 66 miles per hour, lasts for 2 minutes 23 seconds. The roller coaster structure is covered with 9,000 gallons of white paint, and contains 1,360,000 board feet of lumber, almost 130,000 bolts, and over 15 tons of nails.

Photo at right: The Tidal Wave® Ride, Six Flags Great America, Gurnee, IL

Number-Sense Project

Estimate
About how many minutes do you estimate you spend waiting in line each day?

Gather Data
List the places that you wait in line. Keep track of the number of minutes you wait in line each day for a week.

Analyze and Report
How many minutes did you spend waiting in line for the week? Compare your results with those of your classmates. List the 3 places you and your classmates spend the most time waiting in line.

Dividing to Find Missing Factors

Build Understanding

You know that multiplication means bringing together groups of the same size and that division means separating into groups of equal size.

A. Divide and Conquer

Materials: About 60 cubes or other small objects for each group, containers

Groups: An even number of groups of at least three people

a. Groups pair off to form opposing teams, A and B. Team A spills some of the cubes on a desktop and counts them.

b. Team B forms equal groups of cubes and writes a multiplication sentence and a division sentence for their arrangement. Team B forms any other equal groups that are possible and writes the appropriate multiplication and division sentences.

c. Team A then forms equal groups of cubes and writes a multiplication and a division sentence for each arrangement Team B did not form.

d. Each team gets a point for each correct sentence. Teams reverse roles and repeat the steps above.

B. Multiplying and dividing by the same number does not change the original number. Multiplication and division are *inverse operations*.

Complete these sentences.

$(15 \div 5) \times 5 = $ ▦
$(10 \times 4) \div 4 = $ ▦
$(n \times 7) \div 7 = $ ▦

c. 🖩 **Calculator**   Solve $s \times 13 = 156$.

$$s \times 13 = 156$$
$$s \times 13 \div \mathbf{13} = 156 \div \mathbf{13}$$
$$s = 156 \div 13$$

$156 \,\boxed{\div}\, 13 \,\boxed{=}\, 12$

$$s = 12$$

Check: $12 \times 13 = 156$

■ **Write About Math**   Write four pairs of equations to illustrate the fact that multiplication and division are inverse operations.

Check Understanding

For another example, see Set A, pages 118–119.

Complete each set of equations.

1. $7 \times 6 = $ ▦
    ▦ $\div 6 = 7$

2. ▦ $\times 9 = 72$
    $72 \div 9 = $ ▦

Solve each equation.

3. $z \times 7 = 56$

4. $6 \times m = 90$

Practice

For More Practice, see Set A, pages 120–121.

Tell whether you would use mental math or a calculator. Then solve each equation. **Remember** to get the variable by itself.

5. $2 \times e = 14$

6. $3 \times c = 30$

7. $4 \times m = 12$

8. $3 \times v = 24$

9. $a \times 6 = 72$

10. $50 \times t = 500$

11. $g \times 8 = 64$

12. $k \times 137 = 137$

13. $x \times 12 = 144$

14. $7 \times z = 84$

15. $b \times 15 = 90$

16. $w \times 6 = 126$

17. $5 \times s = 85$

18. $f \times 20 = 100$

19. $8 \times r = 88$

20. $c \times 25 = 200$

21. $h \times 6 = 150$

22. $13 \times t = 65$

23. $d \times 80 = 400$

24. $7 \times n = 343$

Number Sense Complete the following sentences. Assume $n \neq 0$.

25. $3 \div 1 = $ ▦

26. $372 \div 1 = $ ▦

27. $n \div 1 = $ ▦

28. $6 \div 6 = $ ▦

29. $244 \div 244 = $ ▦

30. $n \div n = $ ▦

31. $0 \div 4 = $ ▦

32. $0 \div n = $ ▦

Problem Solving

Choose a _____ Strategy

Plan to Save Savemore State Bank has two checking account plans. Plan A charges $0.20 for each check written, plus a monthly service charge of $2.50. Plan B charges $0.15 for each check written, plus a monthly service charge of $3.10.

33. With each plan, what is the monthly cost if one check is written? If 20 checks are written?

34. What is the minimum number of checks that must be written each month in order to save money with Plan B?

Mental Math: Division

Build Understanding

A. Evelyn had a part-time job and earned $2,400 in six months. She earned the same amount each month. What were her monthly earnings?

You need to separate 2,400 into 6 equal parts. Find 2,400 ÷ 6. Remember that division is the inverse of multiplication.

6 × 4 = 24, so 24 ÷ 6 = 4.
6 × 40 = 240, so 240 ÷ 6 = 40.
6 × 400 = 2,400, so 2,400 ÷ 6 = 400.

Evelyn earned $400 each month.

B. Divide mentally to find 3,600 ÷ 90.

Study these pairs of equations.

36 ÷ 9 = 4

3,600 ÷ 90   **4 × 10**

100 ÷ 10 = 10

3,600 ÷ 90 = 40

C. Divide mentally to find 4,000 ÷ 500.

40 ÷ 5 = 8

4,000 ÷ 500   **8 × 1**

100 ÷ 100 = 1

4,000 ÷ 500 = 8

■ **Write About Math** Look at Examples B and C. Describe a method of dividing when both the divisor and dividend end in at least one zero.

Check Understanding

For another example, see Set B, pages 118–119.

Copy and complete each group of equations.

1. $20 \div \blacksquare = 10$
$200 \div \blacksquare = 100$
$2{,}000 \div \blacksquare = 1{,}000$

2. $300 \div 5 = \blacksquare$
$300 \div 50 = \blacksquare$
$3{,}000 \div \blacksquare = 6$

3. $90 \div 5 = 18$
$900 \div 5 = \blacksquare$
$9{,}000 \div 5 = \blacksquare$

Practice

For More Practice, see Set B, pages 120–121.

Find each quotient mentally.

4. $54 \div 9$ **5.** $540 \div 9$ **6.** $5{,}400 \div 9$ **7.** $5{,}400 \div 90$

8. $63 \div 7$ **9.** $630 \div 7$ **10.** $630 \div 70$ **11.** $6{,}300 \div 70$

12. $350 \div 5$ **13.** $900 \div 3$ **14.** $4{,}500 \div 9$ **15.** $420 \div 60$

16. $1{,}200 \div 60$ **17.** $350 \div 50$ **18.** $2{,}400 \div 12$ **19.** $3{,}200 \div 8$

20. $3{,}200 \div 400$ **21.** $7{,}700 \div 110$ **22.** $6{,}000 \div 120$ **23.** $9{,}000 \div 150$

Mixed Practice   Find each answer mentally.

24. 2×6 **25.** $40 \div 5$ **26.** 8×10 **27.** 15×100 **28.** $900 \div 30$

29. 8×1 **30.** $60 \div 10$ **31.** 7×0 **32.** 6×6 **33.** 50×40

34. $66 \div 6$ **35.** $28 \div 7$ **36.** $12 \times 1{,}000$ **37.** $90 \div 9$ **38.** 25×12

Problem Solving

Solve.

39. Evelyn worked 80 hours every month. Use the result of Example A to find how much she earned per hour.

40. **Estimation**   Han earns $6.45 per hour as an assistant to a veterinarian. Does she earn more than $180 for 32 hours of work?

41. Mr. Fuller paid his son Brian $10 each time he mowed the lawn. If Brian mowed the lawn 12 times, how much did he earn?

42. Mr. Torres earned a total of $682.50 one week. For the first 35 hours he works each week he earns $15 per hour. How much did he earn in overtime?

Estimating Quotients

Build Understanding

The Gregorian calendar, which uses features of ancient Roman and Egyptian calendars, is the one generally used by Western nations. It, too, has been officially adopted by other countries such as China, Egypt, Turkey, Japan, and India. The Hebrew calendar, the official calendar of Israel, is also used all over the world.

A. About how many weeks are there in 198 days?

Estimate $198 \div 7$.
One way to estimate is with **compatible numbers**. Choose numbers that can be divided mentally and that are close to the numbers in the problem.

$198 \div 7$
$\downarrow$

Choose a multiple of 7 that is close to 198.

$210 \div 7 = 30$
$198 \div 7 \approx 30$

There are about 30 weeks in 198 days.

B. Estimate $315 \div 52$.

$315 \div 52$
$\downarrow \qquad \downarrow$

Multiples of 52 are difficult to find mentally, so change both 315 and 52 to compatible numbers.

$300 \div 50 = 6$
$315 \div 52 \approx 6$

The quotient is about 6.

C. Sometimes you estimate by finding a **range** for the quotient. Estimate $267 \div 8$.

Think: $240 \div 8 = 30$ and $320 \div 8 = 40$

Since 267 is between 240 and 320,
$267 \div 8$ is between 30 and 40.

■ **Talk About Math** In Example C, is the actual quotient closer to 30 or 40? How do you know?

Check Understanding

For another example, see Set C, pages 118–119.

Choose a reasonable range for each quotient.

1. 656 ÷ 8
  a. 80 to 90   **b.** 8 to 9

2. 593 ÷ 3
  a. 10 to 20   **b.** 100 to 200

Practice

For More Practice, see Set C, pages 120–121.

Estimate each quotient by using compatible numbers.
For Exercises 3–6, tell whether your estimate is
less than or greater than the actual quotient.

3. 609 ÷ 9   **4.** 869 ÷ 6   **5.** 610 ÷ 5   **6.** 1,343 ÷ 8

7. 887 ÷ 72   **8.** 584 ÷ 49   **9.** 1,253 ÷ 24   **10.** 6,772 ÷ 35

Estimate each quotient by finding a range.

11. 642 ÷ 3   **12.** 293 ÷ 7   **13.** 986 ÷ 5   **14.** 569 ÷ 8

15. 758 ÷ 9   **16.** 5,136 ÷ 3   **17.** 9,112 ÷ 40   **18.** 6,765 ÷ 50

Estimate. **Remember** to choose numbers that can be
divided mentally.

19. 661 ÷ 7   **20.** 490 ÷ 8   **21.** 552 ÷ 5   **22.** 1,783 ÷ 9

23. 3,941 ÷ 40   **24.** 2,051 ÷ 29   **25.** 6,455 ÷ 83   **26.** 8,292 ÷ 52

Problem Solving

Weeks of different lengths were used in ancient
cultures. Estimate how many weeks there would
be in a 365-day year based on

27. Assyria's 6-day week.

28. West Africa's 4-day week.

29. Rome's 8-day week.

30. Peruvian Inca's 10-day week.

Solve each problem.

31. Some Islamic years have six
29-day months and six 30-day
months. How many days are there
in these years?

32. In the Hebrew calendar, an hour is
divided into 1,080 equal parts.
About how many seconds long
would each part be?

One-Digit Divisors

Build Understanding

The sixth-grade students at McKinley School are planning a class trip to Monterey and San Francisco. The table shows the number of students in each sixth-grade class.

Teacher	Number of Students
Mr. Baca	35
Ms. Cipriano	37
Mr. Debarian	36
Ms. Harris	34
Mr. Lundgren	33
Total	175

A. Mrs. Toyan, the school principal, would like to organize the students into groups of no more than 8 students. How many groups of 8 students will there be? Will any students be in a group of fewer than 8 students?

To separate 175 into equal groups, divide.
Find 175 ÷ 8.
Estimate: 160 ÷ 8 = 20.

```
     2
8)175
  16
   1
```

Divide. How many 8s in 17? 2
Multiply 8 and 2.
Subtract and compare. 1 is less than 8.

```
    21 R 7
8)175
  16↓
   15
    8
    7
```

Bring down the 5.
How many 8s in 15? 1
Multiply 8 and 1.
Subtract and compare.
7 is less than 8, the divisor.
You have no more digits to bring down.
The remainder is 7.

Check:

```
    21  ← Quotient
×    8  ← Divisor
   168
+    7  ← Remainder
   175  ← Dividend
```

The students will be organized into 21 groups of 8 students and 1 group of 7 students.

B. If 32 yards of banner paper are used for a sign on each of the three buses, what is the maximum length of each banner?

To find the size of each of the three equal parts, divide. Find 32 ÷ 3.

$$
\begin{array}{r}
10\frac{2}{3} \\
3\overline{)32} \\
30 \\
\hline
2 \\
0 \\
\hline
2
\end{array}
$$

Does it make sense to say that each banner is 10 R2 yards long? No.

Write the remainder and the divisor as a fraction.

Check: 10 × 3 = 30, 30 + 2 = 32.

Each banner can be $10\frac{2}{3}$ yards long.

c.  **Calculator** Find 3,937 ÷ 6.

Express the quotient as a decimal rounded to the nearest tenth. Estimate: 3,600 ÷ 6 = 600.

Press: 3937 ÷ 6 = **Display:** *656.16666*

656.16666 ≈ 656.2

■ **Talk About Math** Why do you think the remainder in Example A is shown as a whole number and the remainder in Example B is shown as part of a fraction?

San Francisco is noted for its Golden Gate Bridge and the San Francisco Bay Bridge (below and left).

Check Understanding

For another example, see Set D, pages 118–119.

Complete each division exercise.

1.
```
     ▦5 R▦
  3)7 6
    6
   ─
    1 6
    1 5
    ─
     ▦
```

2.
```
        5
   1 2▦ ▦
 8)9 7 3
   8
   ─
   1 6
   1 6
   ─
     1 3
       ▦
     ─
       5
```

3.
```
      8▦9 R▦
 4)3,4 7 9
   3 2
   ──
     2 7
     
       3 9
       3 6
       ─
         ▦
```

4.
```
      ▦▦8 R▦
 7)1,6 6 9
   1 4
   ──
     ▦ 6
     
       ▦ 9
       ▦ 6
       ─
         ▦
```

5.
```
    ▦▦▦ R▦
 6)8 3 5
   ▦
   ─
   ▦▦
   ▦▦
   ──
     ▦
     ▦
     ─
     ▦
```

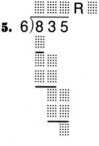

Practice

For More Practice, see Set D, pages 120–121.

Divide. Show remainders as whole numbers.

6. 9)86   **7.** 5)48   **8.** 8)980   **9.** 6)2,921   **10.** 8)1,234   **11.** 9)5,375

12. 345 ÷ 6   **13.** 728 ÷ 3   **14.** 974 ÷ 8   **15.** 392 ÷ 5   **16.** 461 ÷ 7

17. 691 ÷ 2   **18.** 587 ÷ 9   **19.** 158 ÷ 6   **20.** 774 ÷ 8   **21.** 846 ÷ 7

22. 461 ÷ 7   **23.** 289 ÷ 6   **24.** 4,132 ÷ 5   **25.** 8,983 ÷ 8   **26.** 7,491 ÷ 6

Divide. Show remainders as fractions.

27. 2)57   **28.** 7)675   **29.** 9)698   **30.** 3)5,918   **31.** 7)2,178

32. 9)3,908   **33.** 8)3,908   **34.** 6)3,908   **35.** 5)3,908   **36.** 4)3,908

37. 85 ÷ 3   **38.** 718 ÷ 6   **39.** 6,580 ÷ 9   **40.** 5,062 ÷ 7

41. 3,617 ÷ 8   **42.** 7,545 ÷ 9   **43.** 5,482 ÷ 6   **44.** 1,748 ÷ 7

 Calculator Use a calculator to divide. Express quotients as decimals rounded to the nearest tenth.

45. 6)92   **46.** 9)473   **47.** 6)367

48. 9)1,096   **49.** 7)9,510   **50.** 4)7,323

51. 743 ÷ 3   **52.** 513 ÷ 4   **53.** 4,217 ÷ 6

54. 4,312 ÷ 6   **55.** 5,773 ÷ 4   **56.** 9,634 ÷ 7

Problem Solving

Solve.

57. During their three-day trip the students will buy their lunches. The cost of each lunch is estimated at $2.75. Alfonso has $10.00 for lunch money. Does he have enough?

58.  **Calculator** Mr. Baca's class had a school button sale to raise money for the class trip. They sold 153 buttons for $0.30 each. How much money did they raise?

TIPS FOR PROBLEM SOLVERS

Take risks. Try your hunches. They often work.

59. In Example A students were assigned to groups of 8 students or less. Suppose all the groups must have an equal number of 9 students or less. How many students would be in each group?

60. **Critical Thinking** Look at Exercises 32–36. As you increase the divisor, what happens to the quotient? As you decrease the divisor, what happens to the quotient? What should happen to the quotient if the divisor is doubled?

Skills 📖 **Review**   pages 46–47

Multiply.

1. $\begin{array}{r}59\\ \times\ 6\end{array}$	**2.** $\begin{array}{r}35\\ \times\ 2\end{array}$	**3.** $\begin{array}{r}21\\ \times\ 8\end{array}$	**4.** $\begin{array}{r}75\\ \times\ 4\end{array}$	**5.** $\begin{array}{r}145\\ \times\ 3\end{array}$	**6.** $\begin{array}{r}537\\ \times\ 5\end{array}$
7. $\begin{array}{r}291\\ \times\ 5\end{array}$	**8.** $\begin{array}{r}108\\ \times\ 4\end{array}$	**9.** $\begin{array}{r}389\\ \times\ 6\end{array}$	**10.** $\begin{array}{r}725\\ \times\ 7\end{array}$	**11.** $\begin{array}{r}299\\ \times\ 9\end{array}$	**12.** $\begin{array}{r}486\\ \times\ 8\end{array}$

13. 1×78 **14.** 0×709 **15.** 6×278 **16.** 9×180 **17.** 836×7

One-Digit Divisors: Zeros in the Quotient

Build Understanding

The Kwan family drove from Cincinnati, Ohio, to Houston, Texas. Dan Kwan kept the chart shown at the right to show the distance they drove each day. What was the average distance they drove each day?

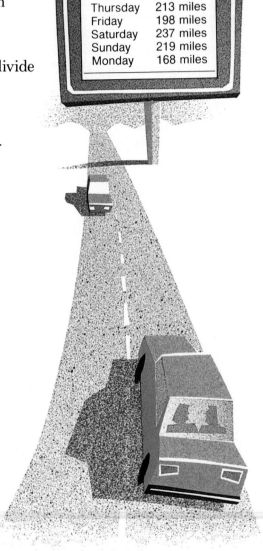

Distances Driven	
Thursday	213 miles
Friday	198 miles
Saturday	237 miles
Sunday	219 miles
Monday	168 miles

To find the average, add the five distances and divide the sum by 5.

$213 + 198 + 237 + 219 + 168 = 1{,}035$

Now find $1{,}035 \div 5$. Estimate: $1{,}000 \div 5 = 200$.

$$\begin{array}{r} 2 \\ 5\overline{)1{,}0\,3\,5} \\ \underline{1\,0} \\ 0 \end{array}$$

Divide.
How many 5s are in 10? 2
Write 2 in the quotient.
Subtract and compare.

$$\begin{array}{r} 2\,0 \\ 5\overline{)1{,}0\,3\,5} \\ \underline{1\,0}\downarrow \\ 0\,3 \\ \underline{0} \\ 3 \end{array}$$

Bring down the 3.
Divide.
How many 5s are in 3? 0
Write 0 in the quotient.
Subtract and compare.

$$\begin{array}{r} 2\,0\,7 \\ 5\overline{)1{,}0\,3\,5} \\ \underline{1\,0} \\ 0\,3 \\ \underline{0} \\ 3\,5 \\ \underline{3\,5} \\ 0 \end{array}$$

Bring down the 5.
Divide.
How many 5s in 35? 7
Write 7 in the quotient.
Subtract and compare.
The remainder is 0.

Check:

$$\begin{array}{r} 2\,0\,7 \\ \times 5 \\ \hline 1{,}0\,3\,5 \end{array}$$

The Kwan family drove an average of 207 miles per day.

■ **Talk About Math** Why should you record zeros in a quotient?

Check Understanding

For another example, see Set E, pages 118–119.

Copy and complete.

$$\begin{array}{c} 4\ \blacksquare\ R\ \blacksquare \\ \textbf{1. } 5)\overline{2\ 0\ 6} \end{array} \qquad \begin{array}{c} 1\ \blacksquare\ 1\ R\ \blacksquare \\ \textbf{2. } 4)\overline{4\ 8\ 6} \end{array} \qquad \begin{array}{c} \blacksquare\ 0\ 4 \\ \textbf{3. } 6)\overline{3{,}0\ 2\ 4} \end{array} \qquad \begin{array}{c} 7\ \blacksquare\ \blacksquare\ R\ \blacksquare \\ \textbf{4. } 7)\overline{4{,}9\ 6\ 4} \end{array} \qquad \begin{array}{c} \blacksquare\ \blacksquare\ \blacksquare\ R\ \blacksquare \\ \textbf{5. } 9)\overline{5{,}4\ 7\ 7} \end{array}$$

Practice

For More Practice, see Set E, pages 120–121.

Estimate and then divide. **Remember** to place zeros in the quotient when needed. Show remainders as whole numbers.

6. $4)\overline{163}$ **7.** $5)\overline{101}$ **8.** $3)\overline{420}$ **9.** $2)\overline{213}$ **10.** $3)\overline{602}$

11. $6)\overline{1{,}853}$ **12.** $9)\overline{1{,}881}$ **13.** $7)\overline{1{,}120}$ **14.** $9)\overline{1{,}716}$ **15.** $8)\overline{3{,}845}$

16. $7{,}025 \div 7$ **17.** $7{,}207 \div 8$ **18.** $6{,}186 \div 6$ **19.** $20{,}403 \div 4$

Mixed Practice   Find each answer. Use mental math when possible. Show remainders as fractions.

20. 10×14 **21.** $547 \div 5$ **22.** 4×70 **23.** 300×93

24. $7{,}775 \div 7$ **25.** $2{,}505 \times 2$ **26.** $9{,}608 \div 8$ **27.** 450×55

28. $210 \div 3$ **29.** $5{,}400 \div 60$ **30.** $3{,}152 \div 8$ **31.** $3{,}233 \div 4$

Number Sense   What remainders are possible when you divide a

32. number by 6?   **33.** number by 9?   **34.** number by 4?

Problem Solving

Solve each problem.

35. Use Data   What is the average size of the sixth-grade classes listed on page 94?

36. If Dan had driven 50 miles farther on one day, what would happen to the average distance?

37. Dan's car gets 30 miles per gallon, and he estimates that gasoline will cost about $1.20 per gallon. How much should he budget for gasoline for the 919-mile trip to Austin?

38. Which plan is less costly for four people? By how much? Motel A: Two rooms at $55 each; breakfast included. Motel B: One room at $75 with two cots; breakfast costs $4.95 each.

Two-Digit Divisors: One-Digit Quotient

Build Understanding

A. Mr. Molina's social studies class has been studying contrasts between rural and urban living. Albert is writing a report for the class about cities. He has gathered some information about cities with at least 100,000 people. He found a total of **169** large cities. To the nearest whole number, what is the average number of large cities per state?

Find 169 ÷ 50.   Estimate: 150 ÷ 50 = 3.

$$
\begin{array}{r}
3\,\text{R}\,19 \\
50\overline{)169} \\
150 \\
\hline
19
\end{array}
$$

Divide.
Think: How many 50s are in 169? 3
Multiply 3 and 50.
Subtract and compare.
The remainder is 19.

The average number of large cities per state is a little more than 3 large cities per state.

B. 🖩 **Calculator**   Find 612 ÷ 85 and record the remainder as a whole number.

612 ÷ 85 = *7.2*

To write the remainder as a whole number:

7 × 85 = *595.*

612 − 595 = *17.*

612 ÷ 85 = 7 R17

Talk About Math   In Example B, what other key sequences could you use to determine the remainder as a whole number?

Would you consider the area around which you live rural or urban?

Check Understanding

For another example, see Set F, pages 118–119.

Copy and complete each exercise.

Find the error in each exercise.

1.
$$
\begin{array}{r}
8\ \text{R}24 \\
46\overline{)392} \\
3\ \blacksquare\blacksquare \\
\hline
24
\end{array}
$$

2.
$$
\begin{array}{r}
4\ \text{R}\ \blacksquare\blacksquare \\
67\overline{)284} \\
\blacksquare\blacksquare 8 \\
\hline
\blacksquare\blacksquare
\end{array}
$$

3.
$$
\begin{array}{r}
2\ \text{R}9 \\
32\overline{)689} \\
64 \\
\hline
9
\end{array}
$$

4.
$$
\begin{array}{r}
60\ \text{R}2 \\
53\overline{)320} \\
318 \\
\hline
2
\end{array}
$$

5. **Number Sense** Explain how estimating can help you avoid the errors in Exercises 3 and 4.

Practice

For More Practice, see Set F, pages 120–121.

Divide. Write each remainder as a whole number.

6. $32\overline{)97}$ 　　7. $23\overline{)97}$ 　　8. $18\overline{)86}$ 　　9. $41\overline{)89}$ 　　10. $37\overline{)116}$

11. $78\overline{)648}$ 　　12. $61\overline{)499}$ 　　13. $97\overline{)390}$ 　　14. $77\overline{)351}$ 　　15. $54\overline{)327}$

16. $766 \div 85$ 　　17. $448 \div 56$ 　　18. $144 \div 27$ 　　19. $120 \div 34$ 　　20. $846 \div 62$

21. $450 \div 59$ 　　22. $777 \div 78$ 　　23. $97 \div 13$ 　　24. $297 \div 48$ 　　25. $483 \div 92$

26. $412 \div 65$ 　　27. $398 \div 72$ 　　28. $548 \div 91$ 　　29. $675 \div 91$ 　　30. $939 \div 95$

For Exercises 31–55, tell whether you would use mental math, paper and pencil, or a calculator. Then find each quotient. Record each remainder as a whole number.

31. $42\overline{)339}$ 　　32. $90\overline{)630}$ 　　33. $62\overline{)500}$ 　　34. $90\overline{)360}$ 　　35. $53\overline{)371}$

36. $42\overline{)412}$ 　　37. $80\overline{)320}$ 　　38. $72\overline{)390}$ 　　39. $70\overline{)420}$ 　　40. $25\overline{)775}$

41. $210 \div 30$ 　　42. $122 \div 35$ 　　43. $318 \div 47$ 　　44. $450 \div 50$ 　　45. $267 \div 30$

46. $350 \div 70$ 　　47. $420 \div 60$ 　　48. $256 \div 27$ 　　49. $124 \div 14$ 　　50. $545 \div 15$

51. $423 \div 60$ 　　52. $500 \div 20$ 　　53. $295 \div 32$ 　　54. $689 \div 87$ 　　55. $290 \div 48$

Mixed Practice　Divide. Write each remainder as a fraction.

56. $7,042 \div 9$ 　　57. $5,872 \div 7$ 　　58. $4,350 \div 4$ 　　59. $628 \div 3$

60. $4,886 \div 8$ 　　61. $3,879 \div 5$ 　　62. $1,259 \div 9$ 　　63. $2,587 \div 8$

Problem Solving

Solve.

64. How many cities have populations of 100,000 people or more, but less than 1 million people?

For Exercises 65 and 66, round each answer to the nearest whole number.

U.S. Urban Areas

Population Size	Number of Cities
1,000,000 or more	6
500,000–999,999	16
250,000–499,999	33
100,000–249,999	114
50,000–99,999	250
25,000–49,999	526

65. What is the average number of cities per state with populations between 50,000 and 99,999?

66. What is the average number of cities per state with populations between 100,000 and 499,999?

67. Number Sense There are 9,326 towns in the United States with populations under 1,000 people. Are there more or fewer than 10 million people in the United States living in towns with populations under 1,000 people?

68. Critical Thinking Refer to Example A. Do you think that every state has 3 cities with populations of at least 100,000 people? Why or why not?

Reading ———— Math

Numbers and Symbols
Copy and complete each equation.

1. 125 ▦ 25 = 5

2. 32.4 ▦ 4.4 = 28

3. 628 ▦ 9 = 5,652

4. 8,775 ▦ 5 = 1,755

5. 1,064 ▦ 84 = 980

6. 21.63 ▦ 21.82 = 43.45

7. 73.5 ▦ 20 = 1,470

8. 4,245 ▦ 5 = 4,250

Midchapter Checkup

For Exercises 1–4, tell whether you would use mental math or
a calculator. Then solve each equation for n.

1. $n \times 9 = 63$ **2.** $n \times 4 = 44$ **3.** $n \times 15 = 105$ **4.** $16 \times n = 96$

Find each quotient mentally.

5. $450 \div 5$ **6.** $1,400 \div 7$ **7.** $2,700 \div 30$ **8.** $7,200 \div 800$

Estimate each quotient.

9. $5\overline{)526}$ **10.** $3\overline{)257}$ **11.** $32\overline{)128}$ **12.** $63\overline{)3,102}$

Divide. Show remainders as whole numbers.

13. $6\overline{)89}$ **14.** $3\overline{)83}$ **15.** $8\overline{)1,234}$ **16.** $6\overline{)4,351}$

17. $194 \div 8$ **18.** $623 \div 2$ **19.** $2,565 \div 4$ **20.** $8,983 \div 8$

Divide. Write quotients using fractions.

21. $367 \div 9$ **22.** $235 \div 8$ **23.** $846 \div 4$ **24.** $191 \div 3$

25. $2,261 \div 3$ **26.** $1,618 \div 7$ **27.** $1,158 \div 6$ **28.** $5,175 \div 8$

Divide. Show remainders as whole numbers.

29. $43\overline{)331}$ **30.** $32\overline{)119}$ **31.** $21\overline{)185}$ **32.** $65\overline{)627}$

33. $31\overline{)124}$ **34.** $79\overline{)201}$ **35.** $68\overline{)357}$ **36.** $79\overline{)431}$

Problem-Solving Workshop

Number-Sense Project

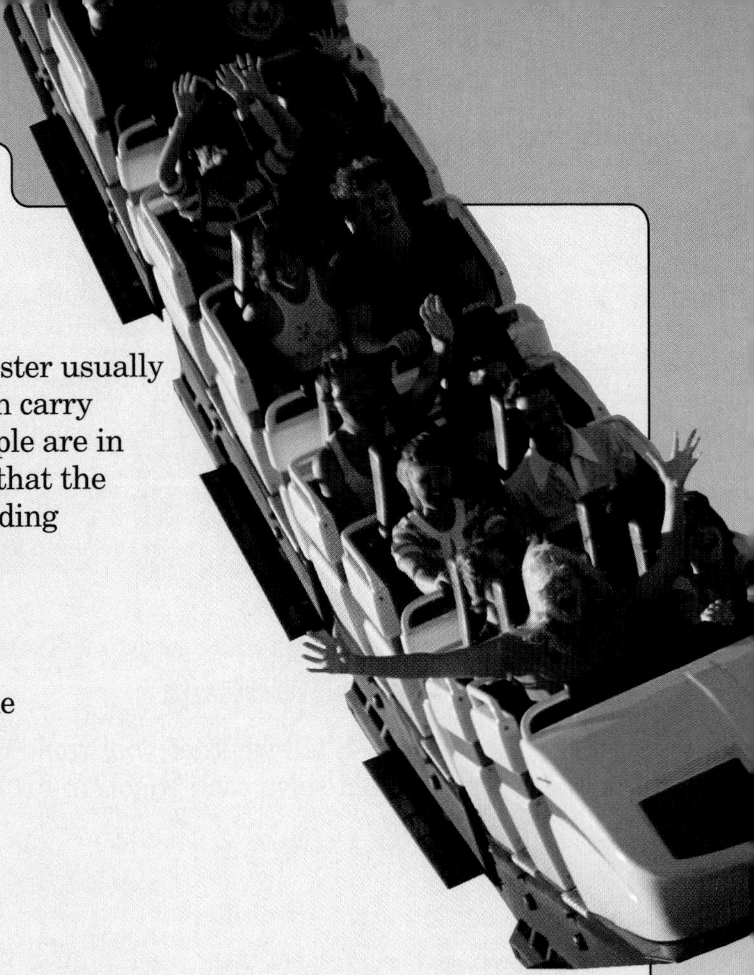

Look back at pages 86–87.

1. The American Eagle roller coaster usually operates 4 trains, each of which can carry 30 people. Suppose that 1,200 people are in line waiting to get on the ride and that the ride takes 4 minutes, including loading and unloading.

a. How many people can be on the ride at one time?

b. How many times would the ride have to run so that 1,200 people could take the ride?

c. About how long would it take before all of the people have had a ride?

2. Tell whether the wait would be longer or shorter than your answer to Exercise 1c.

a. if less than 1,200 people are in line.

b. if 150 people can ride each time.

c. if the times between rides, loading and unloading, is 5 minutes.

Visual-Thinking Activity

Replace each symbol with a digit from 0-9. One digit is missing. Which one is it?

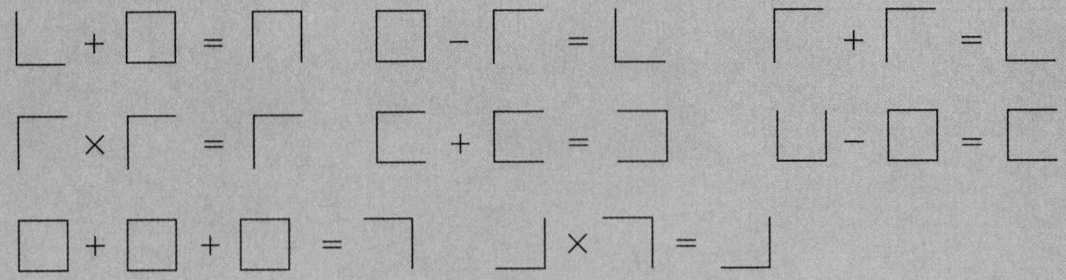

$$\llcorner + \square = \sqcap \qquad \square - \ulcorner = \llcorner \qquad \ulcorner + \ulcorner = \llcorner$$

$$\ulcorner \times \ulcorner = \ulcorner \qquad \lfloor + \lfloor = \rfloor \qquad \sqcup - \square = \lfloor$$

$$\square + \square + \square = \sqcap \qquad \lrcorner \times \sqcap = \lrcorner$$

Math-at-Home Activity

1. Play the "Remainder Game" with your family. You will need to write the digits 1 to 6 on index cards and put them in a bag.

Make a playing board like the one shown below.

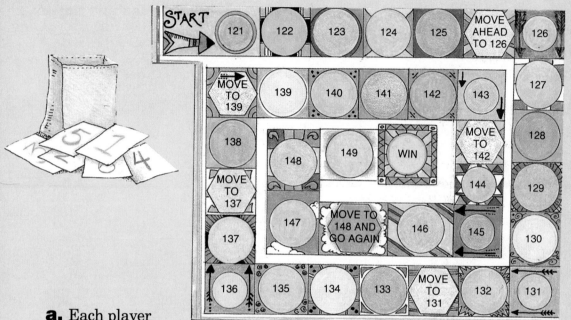

a. Each player starts the game by placing a marker on space 121.

b. The first player draws a card from the bag and divides 121 by the number on the card. The remainder shows how many spaces the player can move.

c. Players take turns drawing a card, dividing the number on the space their marker is on by the number on the card, and moving their markers.

d. The first player to land exactly on 150 is the winner.

My science teacher says amoebas divide in order to multiply. Well, they certainly won't do very well in a math class!

Interpret the Remainder

Build Understanding

Sometimes in division problems you have to decide how to interpret the remainder.

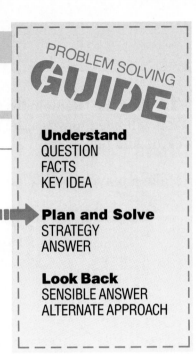

PROBLEM SOLVING
GUIDE

Understand
QUESTION
FACTS
KEY IDEA

▐▌▶ **Plan and Solve**
STRATEGY
ANSWER

Look Back
SENSIBLE ANSWER
ALTERNATE APPROACH

A. On Tuesday a sports announcer mentioned that the baseball season would open in 60 days. Maria can go to the opening game only if it is on a Saturday or a Sunday. Will she be able to go to the game?

Understand   Find the number of weeks and days in 60 days.

▐▌▶ **Plan and Solve**

STRATEGY   Divide 60 by 7 to find the number of weeks and days in 60 days.

$$\begin{array}{r} 8\ R\ 4 \\ 7)\overline{6\ 0} \\ \underline{5\ 6} \\ 4 \end{array}$$

60 days is 8 weeks, 4 days.

ANSWER   Eight weeks from Tuesday is a Tuesday. Four days after that is a Saturday. Maria can go to the game.

Look Back   Eight weeks is 7×8, or 56, days. $56 + 4 = 60$ days

B. How many $7 box-seat tickets can you buy with $60?

Only 8 tickets can be purchased.

C. If a boxed section of seats holds 7 people, how many boxes are needed for 60 people?

Eight boxes are not enough, so **9** boxes are needed.

D. Sixty days is about how many weeks?

60 days is $8\frac{4}{7}$ weeks, or about $8\frac{1}{2}$ weeks.

■ **Talk About Math** For each of Examples A–D, the computation is the same. Explain how the remainder affects the answer. Why can a mixed number be the answer for Example D but not for Examples A, B, or C?

Check Understanding

Write a problem that uses 15 ÷ 2 and has an answer of

1. 7 teams.　　　**2.** 8 packages.　　　**3.** $1.　　　**4.** $7\frac{1}{2}$ feet.

Practice

Give each answer.

5. Tennis balls are sold in cans of 3 balls each. How many cans should Rose buy if the team needs 35 tennis balls?

6. Jack drove 133 miles to the hockey tournament on 6 gallons of gasoline. This is an average of how many miles per gallon?

7. A 100-foot running track is marked in 8 equal sections. How long is each section?

8. The soccer team has a jug that holds 18 quarts of water. How many gallons of water is this?

9. Kim bought as many $7 box-seat tickets as she could with $25. How many tickets could she buy?

10. Manuel bought 5 baseball tickets. Each ticket cost $12.95. How much money did he spend?

11. Today is Monday. If the soccer season starts in 45 days, on what day of the week will the season start?

12. Ashley found 50 golf balls near the golf course. If she puts them in packages of 12 each, how many balls will not be in a package?

13. The ticket office offered a free ticket for each $15 ticket bought. How much would each of 5 friends pay, if they were to share the total cost of 5 tickets?

14. Stan bought as many $3 general admission tickets as he could with $20. How much money did he have left?

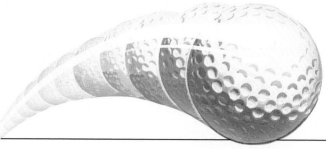

Adjusting Quotients

Build Understanding

A. Beverly Goh sells plants and flower bulbs. As a special offer she sells the Spring Sampler with an assortment of 84 bulbs. How many Spring Samplers can she make from 325 bulbs? How many bulbs will she have left?

Find $325 \div 84$.
Estimate using compatible numbers: $320 \div 80 = 4$.

$$\begin{array}{r} 4 \\ 84\overline{)325} \\ 336 \end{array}$$

Divide.
Think: How many 8s in 32? 4
Multiply.
336 is greater than 325, so 4 is too large.

$$\begin{array}{r} 3\ R73 \\ 84\overline{)325} \\ 252 \\ \hline 73 \end{array}$$

Try 3 instead.
Multiply.
Subtract and compare.
The remainder is 73.

Check:
$$\begin{array}{r} 84 \\ \times\ 3 \\ \hline 252 \\ +\ 73 \\ \hline 325 \end{array}$$

Beverly can make 3 Spring Samplers. She will have 73 bulbs left.

B. Find $238 \div 47$.

$$\begin{array}{r} 4 \\ 47\overline{)238} \\ 188 \\ \hline 50 \end{array}$$

Divide.
Think: 47 rounds to 50.
How many 5s in 23? 4
Multiply.
Subtract and compare.
50 is greater than 47, so 4 is too small.

$$\begin{array}{r} 5\ R3 \\ 47\overline{)238} \\ 235 \\ \hline 3 \end{array}$$

Try 5 instead.
Multiply.
Subtract and compare.
The remainder is 3.

Talk About Math Show two different ways to estimate $238 \div 47$ before dividing. How would these two results influence your choice of a quotient?

Check Understanding

For another example, see Set G, pages 118–119.

Decide whether each quotient needs to be adjusted.

1. $89\overline{)462}$ → 5
2. $72\overline{)305}$ → 8
3. $46\overline{)416}$ → 8
4. $52\overline{)421}$ → 8
5. $31\overline{)181}$ → 6
6. $68\overline{)459}$ → 7

Practice

For More Practice, see Set G, pages 120–121.

Estimate and then divide. Write each remainder as a whole number.

7. $76\overline{)196}$
8. $54\overline{)496}$
9. $36\overline{)149}$
10. $59\overline{)367}$
11. $13\overline{)104}$

12. $27\overline{)201}$
13. $52\overline{)155}$
14. $32\overline{)256}$
15. $94\overline{)370}$
16. $48\overline{)185}$

17. $153 \div 39$
18. $197 \div 20$
19. $442 \div 49$
20. $740 \div 83$

21. $144 \div 16$
22. $500 \div 63$
23. $362 \div 57$
24. $682 \div 69$

Mixed Practice   Find each answer. **Remember** to watch the signs.

25. 29×406
26. $261 + 444$
27. $9,258 \div 6$
28. $568 - 254$

29. $5,964 \times 30$
30. $392 \div 42$
31. $9,129 + 840$
32. $7,289 - 4,001$

33. $4,025 \div 8$
34. $7,442 - 1,816$
35. $6,426 + 1,695$
36. $564 \div 82$

Problem Solving

Solve.

37. Beverly Goh has a money-back guarantee on the bulbs she sells. A customer asked for a refund for a narcissus bulb that didn't sprout. How much money should Beverly send as a refund?

Price List	
Narcissus	3 for $ 2.50
Crocus	12 for $ 3.00
Tulip	3 for $ 2.00
Two-tone Iris	6 for $ 2.00
Jumbo Daffodil Set	36 for $19.00

38. Beverly received 500 tulip bulbs from a supplier. How many packages of 3 tulip bulbs can she make?

39. A customer ordered 9 narcissus, 36 crocus, and 24 two-tone iris bulbs. What is the total cost for these bulbs?

Two-Digit Divisors: Two or More Digits in the Quotient

Build Understanding

A. At the zoo, a tour bus leaves as soon as it is full. Each bus holds 29 people. On Saturday 1,840 people took the bus trip. How many tour buses were filled on Saturday?

Find 1,840 ÷ 29. Estimate: 1,800 ÷ 30 = 60.

```
        6
  29)1,840
     174
  ─────────
      10
```
Round 29 to 30.
How many 3s in 18? 6
Multiply. Subtract and compare.

```
       63 R13              Check:    63
  29)1,840                         ×29
     174↓                          ───
  ───────                           567
     100                           1260
      87                          ─────
  ───────                         1,827
      13                            +13
                                  ─────
                                  1,840
```
Bring down the 0.
How many 3s in 10? 3
Multiply 3 and 29.
Subtract and compare.
The remainder is 13.

On Saturday 63 buses were filled.

B. Find 825 ÷ 42.

```
       2
  42)825
     84
```
Round 42 to 40.
How many 4s in 8? 2
Multiply. 84 is greater than 82, so 2 is too large.

```
     19 R27
  42)825
     42
  ──────
     405
     378
  ──────
      27
```
Try 1 instead.
Multiply 1 and 42.
Subtract and compare.
How many 4s in 40? 10
Since 10 cannot be a digit in the quotient, try 9.
Multiply. Subtract and compare. The remainder is 27.

■ **Talk About Math** In Example A, what does the remainder mean? How many tour buses were needed for the 1,840 people?

110

Check Understanding

For another example, see Set H, pages 118–119.

Copy and complete each exercise.   Estimate. Then divide.

1.
```
     1 ▦ R46
7 3)8 4 9
   ▦▦▦
   ‾‾‾‾‾
   1 1 9
     ▦▦
     ‾‾‾
     4 6
```

2.
```
     ▦ 5 R ▦▦
3 7)9 4 6
   ▦▦▦
   ‾‾‾‾
   2 0 6
     ▦▦▦▦
     ‾‾‾‾
     2 1
```

3. 45)958

4. 53)966

Practice

For More Practice, see Set H, pages 120–121.

Divide. Write each remainder as a whole number.

5. 32)596

6. 72)829

7. 51)730

8. 18)939

9. 56)6,283

10. 74)9,120

11. 81)2,196

12. 44)3,956

13. 12)763

14. 37)8,018

15. 15)4,512

16. 85)6,434

17. 7,665 ÷ 48

18. 2,907 ÷ 29

19. 1,682 ÷ 22

20. 1,838 ÷ 54

21. 9,999 ÷ 90

22. 8,703 ÷ 62

23. 2,643 ÷ 19

24. 5,281 ÷ 74

25. 89,472 ÷ 94

26. 1,450 ÷ 23

27. 4,595 ÷ 68

28. 68,297 ÷ 98

Problem Solving

Explore ———— Math

▦ Calculator Use repeated subtraction to find 486 ÷ 32. Use tally marks to keep track of how many times you subtract 32.

486 ⊟ 32 ═ 454   ⊟ 32 ═   } Repeat this step until the display is less than 32.

Mark one tally mark.   Mark one tally mark.

29. How many times did you subtract? How much was left over?

30. Divide using your calculator and compare your answers. How is division related to subtraction?

Two-Digit Divisors: Zeros in the Quotient

Build Understanding

Mercedes is using a graphics scanner to copy a picture of the Statue of Liberty. The picture covers 53 square inches and contains an estimated 8,000 dots. About how many dots per square inch must the scanner be able to read to get a picture of similar quality?

Find 8,000 ÷ 53.   Estimate: 8,000 ÷ 50 = 160.

```
      1
53)8,0 0 0      Round 53 to 50.
   5 3          How many 5s in 8? 1
   ───          Multiply.
   2 7          Subtract and compare.
```

```
      1 5
53)8,0 0 0
   5 3 ↓        Bring down 0 tens.
   ───          How many 5s in 27? 5
   2 7 0        Multiply.
   2 6 5        Subtract and compare.
   ─────
       5
```

```
    1 5 0  R50
53)8,0 0 0
   5 3 │
   ─── │
   2 7 0│
   2 6 5↓        Bring down 0 ones.
   ───── │        How many 53s in 50? 0
       5 0       Multiply. Subtract and compare.
         0       The remainder is 50.
       ───
       5 0
```

Check: (150 × 53) + 50 = 7,950 + 50
                        = 8,000

The scanner must be able to read about 150 dots per square inch.

■ **Talk About Math** How would the estimate be affected if 10,000 and 50 were chosen as the compatible numbers? How close could you expect the estimate to be to the actual answer?

Check Understanding

For another example, see Set I, pages 118–119.

1. Look at Exercises 7–10. Which will have the greatest quotient?

2. Look at Exercises 23–26. How many digits will each quotient have?

Tell whether you would use mental math or paper and pencil. Then divide.

3. 4,410 ÷ 45   4. 5,490 ÷ 90   5. 2,432 ÷ 38   6. 8,888 ÷ 22

Practice

For More Practice, see Set I, pages 120–121.

Mental Math   Try to use mental math to divide.

7. 21)4,200   8. 40)16,040   9. 90)18,090   10. 50)35,000

11. 1,240 ÷ 31   12. 2,500 ÷ 25   13. 54,039 ÷ 60   14. 12,003 ÷ 30

15. 1,500 ÷ 75   16. 60,030 ÷ 15   17. 6,308 ÷ 21   18. 2,600 ÷ 52

19. 1,890 ÷ 63   20. 492 ÷ 12   21. 8,789 ÷ 87   22. 6,560 ÷ 32

Tell whether you would use paper and pencil or a calculator.
Then divide. Round calculator quotients to the nearest tenth.

23. 25)2,659   24. 49)9,817   25. 67)5,360   26. 74)3,705

27. 59)53,607   28. 74)28,886   29. 30)12,003   30. 87)26,448

31. 2,780 ÷ 91   32. 4,678 ÷ 42   33. 1,340 ÷ 96   34. 87,910 ÷ 42

35. 32,167 ÷ 55   36. 42,850 ÷ 63   37. 61,000 ÷ 58   38. 88,172 ÷ 37

Problem Solving

Solve.

39. If the picture of the Statue of Liberty contained an estimated 9,000 dots, how many dots per square inch would the scanner need to read?

40. An inexpensive scanner can read only 72 dots per square inch. How many dots can it read in a picture covering 32 square inches?

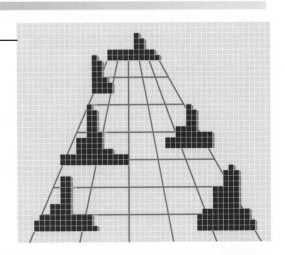

PROBLEM SOLVING **GUIDE**

Write an Equation

A
L
G
E
B
R
A

Build Understanding

An ostrich egg is about 156 mm long. This is 12 times as long as a hummingbird egg. How long is a hummingbird egg?

Understand   156 mm is 12 times as long as a hummingbird egg.

Plan and Solve   STRATEGY   *Write an equation* which says 12 times some number is 156. 12 times a number equals 156.

$$12 \times w = 156$$

$$\frac{12w}{12} = \frac{156}{12}$$

$$w = 13$$

ANSWER   A hummingbird egg is about 13 mm long.

Look Back $12 \times 13 = 156$, so 156 mm is 12 times as long as 13 mm.

■ **Write About Math**   Write a problem that can be solved using the equation $24 \times w = \$624$.

PROBLEM SOLVING GUIDE

Understand
QUESTION
FACTS
KEY IDEA

Plan and Solve
STRATEGY
ANSWER

Look Back
SENSIBLE ANSWER
ALTERNATE APPROACH

Check Understanding

Choose the correct equation for each problem. Then solve the equation and give the answer.

1. One day 12 new birds were put into the aviary to make a total of 60 birds. How many birds were in the aviary before the 12 birds were added?

$b + 12 = 60$ $b - 12 = 60$

2. After the students from Ashland School paid $12 to enter the zoo, they had $60 left in the class treasury. How much did they have before entering the zoo?

$m + 60 = 12$ $m - 12 = 60$

3. In the zoo museum a collection of bird models is divided equally among 12 display areas. If there are 60 models in each area, how many models are in the collection?

$$\frac{s}{12} = 60 \qquad \frac{s}{60} = 60$$

4. Last year 12 wild geese settled in the zoo pond. This year 60 geese arrived. The number of geese this year is how many times the number that came last year?

$$n + 12 = 60 \qquad n \times 12 = 60$$

Practice

Write an equation. Then give the answer.

5. A hummingbird's wings can beat as many as 4,500 times per minute. This is an average of how many times per second?

6. A snail moves at about 2.5 feet per minute. How far can a snail travel in an hour?

7. At birth, Earl the elephant weighed 175 pounds. At nine months he weighed 700 pounds. His weight at nine months was how many times his birth weight?

8. A migrating duck can travel up to 11,200 kilometers per week. This is an average of how many kilometers per day?

9. An ostrich egg weighs over 5,000 times as much as a hummingbird's egg. A hummingbird egg weighs about 0.3 grams. Estimate the weight of an ostrich egg.

10. For short distances, an elephant can run about 36.6 feet per second and a cheetah can run about 102 feet per second. How much farther can a cheetah run in a second than an elephant?

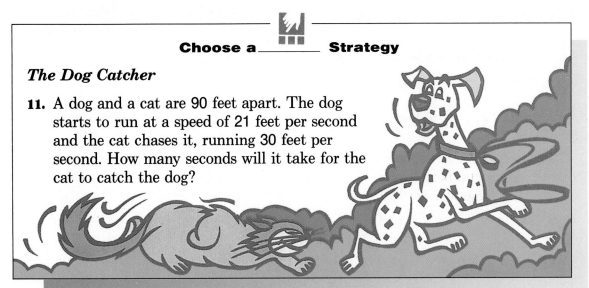

Choose a ———— Strategy

The Dog Catcher

11. A dog and a cat are 90 feet apart. The dog starts to run at a speed of 21 feet per second and the cat chases it, running 30 feet per second. How many seconds will it take for the cat to catch the dog?

Skills Review

Tell whether you would use mental math or a calculator. Then solve for n.

1. $3 \times n = 15$ **2.** $n \times 14 = 98$

Find each quotient mentally.

3. $320 \div 40$ **4.** $2,400 \div 3$

5. $3,600 \div 12$ **6.** $4,800 \div 600$

Estimate each quotient.

7. $637 \div 8$ **8.** $207 \div 5$

9. $442 \div 15$ **10.** $8,892 \div 9$

Divide. Show remainders as whole numbers.

11. $8\overline{)75}$ **12.** $6\overline{)2,720}$

13. $834 \div 8$ **14.** $1,612 \div 7$

15. $72\overline{)289}$ **16.** $65\overline{)328}$

17. $450 \div 90$ **18.** $144 \div 28$

19. $26\overline{)134}$ **20.** $74\overline{)496}$

21. $678 \div 13$ **22.** $2,566 \div 42$

Divide. Show remainders as fractions.

23. $7\overline{)621}$ **24.** $5\overline{)5,432}$

25. $490 \div 4$ **26.** $6,093 \div 2$

Tell whether you would use mental math, paper and pencil, or a calculator. Then divide.

27. $15\overline{)30,000}$ **28.** $46\overline{)4,784}$

29. $2,165 \div 20$ **30.** $42,000 \div 18$

Problem-Solving Review

Solve each problem.

31. Ten members of the Drama Club each bought a ticket to a play. Each ticket costs $4.75. What was the total cost of the tickets?

32. Manuel knows that his car averages about 22.5 miles per gallon of gasoline. If the 12-gallon gas tank is at least half full, does Manuel have enough gas to travel 100 miles? Is an estimate enough in this case?

33. How many days are there in 250 hours? How many hours are left over?

34. How many $5 movie tickets can be bought with $28?

35. Emma, Linda's little sister, was born exactly 9 years after Linda. Linda is 12 years old. Write and solve an equation to find Emma's age.

36. **Data File** Use the data on pages 124–125. How many regular field goals did Michael Jordan make in the 1986–1987 season?

37. **Make a Data File** Use an encyclopedia or other references to find the wingspan of 10 different birds. Display the data in a table. List the birds from smallest to largest.

Write each number in standard form.

1. Four hundred thousand, six hundred two and eighteen hundredths

2. 5^3

3. $2^4 \times 3^2$

4. $(3 \times 10^3) + (7 \times 10^2) + 4$

Estimate. Then find each answer.

5.
$$\begin{array}{r} 325 \\ \times\ \ \ 4 \\ \hline \end{array}$$

6.
$$\begin{array}{r} 6.052 \\ +\ 2.939 \\ \hline \end{array}$$

7.
$$\begin{array}{r} 0.25 \\ \times\ 6.4 \\ \hline \end{array}$$

8.
$$\begin{array}{r} 76.8 \\ -\ 3.25 \\ \hline \end{array}$$

9.
$$\begin{array}{r} 507 \\ \times\ 450 \\ \hline \end{array}$$

10. $9\overline{)75}$

11. $6\overline{)455}$

12. 48×76

13. $5\overline{)3{,}657}$

14. $7\overline{)730}$

15. $8\overline{)6{,}403}$

16. $5\overline{)5{,}155}$

17. 3.45×0.06

18. $53\overline{)373}$

19. $18.3 - 4.6$

20. $77\overline{)453}$

21. $89\overline{)881}$

Write in expanded form using exponents.

22. 425

23. 808

24. 6,987

25. 4,006

26. 21,654

Use mental math to find each answer.

27. 30×200

28. $63 \div 9$

29. $4.52 + 2.48$

30. $800 \div 4$

31. $450 \div 90$

32. 7.9×100

33. $5{,}600 \div 70$

34. $12{,}080 \div 40$

Solve each equation.

35. $3 \times c = 24$

36. $r \times 20 = 80$

37. $14 + t = 35$

38. $104 = 8 \times y$

Find the missing number. Write which property is shown.

39. $24 \times 8 = \text{▦} \times 24$

40. $(2 \times 4) \times 6 = 2 \times (\text{▦} \times 6)$

41. $\text{▦} \times 63 = 63$

42. $725 \times \text{▦} = 0$

Write the coordinates of each point.

43. A

44. B

45. C

46. Move A to a new location by adding 2 to the x-coordinate and 1 to the y-coordinate. What are the new coordinates?

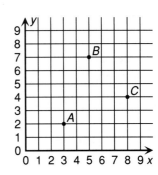

Reteaching

Use division to solve the following equation, because division is the inverse of multiplication.

$$n \times 16 = 176$$
$$n \times 16 \div 16 = 176 \div 16$$
$$n = 176 \div 16$$
$$n = 11$$

Remember that you can multiply or divide both sides of an equation by the same non-zero number without changing the answer.

Solve each equation.

1. $p \times 4 = 32$ **2.** $8 \times x = 72$

3. $d \times 6 = 144$ **4.** $5 \times m = 90$

Set B   pages 90–91

Divide mentally to find $2,000 \div 40$.

$$20 \div 4 = 5$$
$$2,000 \div 40$$
$$100 \div 10 = 10$$
$$5 \times 10 = 50$$

Remember that dividing both the dividend and divisor by 10 or 100 does not change the quotient.

Find each quotient mentally.

1. $7,200 \div 80$ **2.** $4,800 \div 600$

Set C   pages 92–93

Estimate $310 \div 8$.

Choose a multiple of 8 close to 310.

$$320 \div 8 = 40$$
$$310 \div 8 \approx 40$$

Remember to change the divisor and dividend to compatible numbers.

Estimate each quotient.

1. $260 \div 9$ **2.** $1,560 \div 8$

Set D   pages 94–97

Find $343 \div 6$.

```
   57 R1
6)343      There are 5 sixes in 34.
- 30  ← 6 × 5
  43       There are 7 sixes in 43.
- 42  ← 6 × 7
   1  ← Remainder
```

Remember to check the division by multiplying the quotient and divisor and then adding the remainder.

Divide and show the remainder as a whole number. Check the answer.

1. $2)\overline{37}$ **2.** $5)\overline{57}$ **3.** $7)\overline{489}$

Set E   pages 98–99

Find $123 \div 4$

```
   3              30 R3
4)123          4)123
- 12           - 12
  03             03
                - 0
                 3
```
There are 0 fours in 3. Write 0 in the quotient.

Remember to place zeros in the quotient when needed.

Estimate and then divide.

1. $4)\overline{833}$ **2.** $6)\overline{657}$ **3.** $7)\overline{760}$

4. $3)\overline{620}$ **5.** $5)\overline{532}$ **6.** $8)\overline{2,459}$

Set F   pages 100–103

Find 189 ÷ 62.

Estimate 180 ÷ 60 = 3

```
        3 R3
62)189  ← There are 3 60s in 189.
  − 186  ← 62 × 3
      3  ← Remainder
```

Remember to write the answer as a quotient and a remainder.

Divide.

1. 16)66   2. 31)98

3. 68)283   4. 52)315

Set G   pages 108–109

Find 251 ÷ 43.

Estimate. Use compatible numbers.

240 ÷ 40 = 6

```
     6      6 is too large          5 R36
43)251      because 258      43)251
 − 258      is greater than    − 215
            251. Try 5.            36
```

Remember that if you cannot subtract, try a smaller quotient.

Estimate and then divide.

1. 58)355   2. 75)450

3. 63)495   4. 95)655

5. 753 ÷ 82   6. 271 ÷ 94

Set H   pages 110–111

Find 2,387 ÷ 72

Estimate: 2,100 ÷ 70 = 30

```
      33 R11
72)2,387    Round 72 to 70.
  − 2 16    There are 3 sevens in 23.
    227     There are 3 sevens in 22.
  − 216
     11  ← Remainder
```

Remember to estimate with numbers that you can divide mentally.

Estimate. Then divide.

1. 21)489   2. 29)464

3. 34)728   4. 52)884

5. 37)2,368   6. 62)8,318

Set I   pages 112–113

Find 4,177 ÷ 32.

Round 32 to 30.

```
     130 R17
32)4,177    There is 1 three in 4.
  − 3 2
     97     There are 3 threes in 9.
  − 96
     17     There are 0 threes in 1.
  −  0      Write 0 in the quotient.
     17
```

Remember to check your answer.

Tell whether you would use paper and pencil or a calculator. Then divide.

1. 21)639   2. 18)725

3. 63)3,163   4. 56)3,375

5. 37)8,912   6. 43)5,615

More Practice

Set A   pages 88–89

For Exercises 1–4, tell whether you would use mental math or a calculator. Then solve each equation.

1. $3 \times c = 27$ **2.** $5 \times s = 65$ **3.** $6 \times y = 132$ **4.** $7 \times w = 56$

Number Sense   Complete the following sentences.

5. $86 \div 1 = \blacksquare$ **6.** $47 \div 47 = \blacksquare$ **7.** $0 \div 62 = \blacksquare$ **8.** $h \div 1 = \blacksquare$

Set B   pages 90–91

Find each quotient mentally.

1. $56 \div 7$ **2.** $560 \div 7$ **3.** $5,600 \div 7$ **4.** $5,600 \div 70$

5. $4,800 \div 12$ **6.** $2,100 \div 30$ **7.** $3,600 \div 12$ **8.** $4,200 \div 600$

Mixed Practice   Find each answer mentally.

9. 3×8 **10.** $80 \div 8$ **11.** 12×100 **12.** $45 \div 9$

Set C   pages 92–93

Estimate each quotient by using compatible numbers. For Exercises 1–4, tell whether your estimate is less than or greater than the actual quotient.

1. $117 \div 3$ **2.** $224 \div 8$ **3.** $375 \div 9$ **4.** $1,362 \div 48$

Estimate each quotient by finding a range.

5. $649 \div 5$ **6.** $251 \div 8$ **7.** $438 \div 7$ **8.** $757 \div 8$

Set D   pages 94–97

Divide. Show remainders as whole numbers.

1. $8)\overline{75}$ **2.** $6)\overline{51}$ **3.** $5)\overline{722}$ **4.** $7)\overline{858}$ **5.** $8)\overline{9,237}$

Divide. Show remainders as fractions.

6. $2)\overline{43}$ **7.** $8)\overline{665}$ **8.** $6)\overline{685}$ **9.** $3)\overline{4,369}$ **10.** $4)\overline{3,430}$

Calculator   Use a calculator to divide. Express quotients as decimals rounded to the nearest tenth.

11. $7)\overline{95}$ **12.** $8)\overline{499}$ **13.** $3)\overline{587}$ **14.** $6)\overline{1,348}$ **15.** $9)\overline{4,699}$

Independent Study MORE PRACTICE

Set E   pages 98–99

Estimate and then divide.

1. $6\overline{)125}$
2. $8\overline{)166}$
3. $7\overline{)764}$
4. $9\overline{)1,869}$
5. $4\overline{)2,431}$

6. $3\overline{)1,513}$
7. $6\overline{)1,844}$
8. $9\overline{)2,885}$
9. $7\overline{)3,646}$
10. $4\overline{)2,123}$

Set F   pages 100–103

Divide. Write each remainder as a whole number.

1. $42\overline{)91}$
2. $76\overline{)575}$
3. $64\overline{)341}$
4. $24\overline{)103}$

For Exercises 5–8, tell whether you would use mental math, paper and pencil, or a calculator. Then find each quotient. Record each remainder as a whole number.

5. $72\overline{)638}$
6. $80\overline{)480}$
7. $45\overline{)359}$
8. $60\overline{)540}$

Set G   pages 108–109

Estimate and then divide. Write each remainder as a whole number.

1. $13\overline{)117}$
2. $29\overline{)221}$
3. $47\overline{)276}$
4. $62\overline{)488}$
5. $53\overline{)312}$

Mixed Practice   Find each answer.

6. 37×608
7. $6,482 - 1,614$
8. $8,047 + 2,162$
9. $291 \div 24$

Set H   pages 110–111

Divide. Write each remainder as a whole number.

1. $27\overline{)642}$
2. $25\overline{)377}$
3. $42\overline{)512}$
4. $61\overline{)740}$

5. $21\overline{)1,197}$
6. $65\overline{)7,815}$
7. $54\overline{)3,672}$
8. $43\overline{)2,659}$

Set I   pages 112–113

Mental Math   Try to use mental math to divide.

1. $32\overline{)6,400}$
2. $60\overline{)36,060}$
3. $3,900 \div 30$
4. $32,035 \div 40$

For Exercises 5–8, tell whether you would use paper and pencil or a calculator. Then estimate and divide.

5. $29\overline{)2,788}$
6. $48\overline{)7,438}$
7. $7,815 \div 65$
8. $39,521 \div 72$

Enrichment

Order of Operations

Julio and Michelle were asked to compute $7 + 8 \times 5$. Julio said the answer was 75. Michelle said that the answer was 47. Who was right? The answer depends on whether you add first or multiply first.

Where more than one operation is involved and more than one answer is possible, mathematicians have agreed to use a standard *order of operations.*

1. First, do all operations within parentheses.

2. Next, multiply and divide in order from left to right.

3. Next, add and subtract in order from left to right.

$$5 + (7 \times 4) \div 2 - (20 - 7) =$$
$$5 + 28 \div 2 - 13 =$$
$$5 + 14 - 13 =$$
$$19 - 13 =$$
$$6$$

You can omit multiplication signs when parentheses are used. Thus 8×5 may be written as $8(5)$, $(8)5$, or $(8)(5)$.

A fraction, or division, bar indicates division. Therefore, $24 \div 8$ can be written as $\frac{24}{8}$, and $(7 + 5) \div (5 - 1)$ can be written as $\frac{(7 + 5)}{(5 - 1)}$.

A division bar acts as a grouping symbol. Both the numerator and the denominator should be treated as if there were parentheses around them. Thus, any operation in the numerator or the denominator must be performed before the division.

$$20 - \frac{16 + 4}{12 - 8} = 20 - \frac{(16 + 4)}{(12 - 8)} = 20 - \frac{20}{4} = 20 - 5 = 15$$

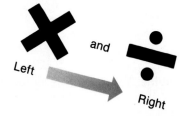

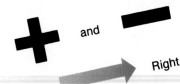

Find each answer.

1. $7 + 8 \times 6$ **2.** $40 - 8 \div 2$ **3.** $24 \div 3 \times 8$ **4.** $3 \times 5 + 16 \div 4$

5. $6 \times 6 \div 2$ **6.** $7(9 - 4)$ **7.** $8(5 + 7)$ **8.** $3(7) + 2(8)$

9. $\frac{9 + 9}{5 - 3}$ **10.** $10 - \frac{4 + 5}{3}$ **11.** $\frac{4(9 - 6)}{3}$ **12.** $\frac{2(5 + 7)}{3(6 - 4)}$

Chapter 3 Review/Test

Find *n*.

1. $n \times 12 = 72$

2. $40 \times n = 880$

Estimate each quotient by finding a range.

3. $230 \div 9$

4. $453 \div 7$

5. $1,460 \div 3$

Divide.

6. $8\overline{)40}$

7. $7\overline{)61}$

8. $4\overline{)984}$

9. $8\overline{)9,893}$

10. $9\overline{)2,738}$

11. $6\overline{)6,162}$

12. $52\overline{)327}$

13. $73\overline{)628}$

14. $19\overline{)161}$

15. $48\overline{)347}$

16. $27\overline{)962}$

17. $62\overline{)4,647}$

18. $81\overline{)9,978}$

19. $35\overline{)29,606}$

20. $24\overline{)9,619}$

21. $93\overline{)28,746}$

Find each quotient mentally.

22. $480 \div 60$

23. $6,300 \div 90$

Write whether each quotient needs to be adjusted.

24. $67\overline{)432}$ with quotient 6

25. $58\overline{)394}$ with quotient 7

26. $21\overline{)176}$ with quotient 7

27. $43\overline{)392}$ with quotient 9

28. *Sputnik I* circled the earth every 90 minutes. How many times did it circle the earth in one day? (1 day = 1,440 minutes)

29. Pedro needs 195 tiles for the floor of the family room. There are 8 tiles in each carton. How many cartons should Pedro buy?

Read the problem below. Then answer the question.

It takes 52 centimeters of canvas to make a book bag. How many book bags can be made from 340 centimeters of canvas?

30. Which answer is most sensible?

   a. 8 book bags   b. 6 book bags
   c. 28 cm   d. 60 book bags

31. **Write About Math** What fact about multiplication and division is illustrated by these equations?

   $4 \times 5 = 20 \qquad 20 \div 5 = 4$

DATA FILE

1. Table

PLANET	SIDEREAL DAY	GRAVITY
	(one rotation)	(Earth =1)
Mercury	58.7 days	0.38
Venus	243 days (backwards)	0.91
Earth	23 h 56 min	1.00
Mars	24 h 37 min	0.38
Jupiter	9 h 55 min	2.54
Saturn	10 h 40 min	1.08
Uranus	15 h 36 min	0.91
Neptune	18 h 28 min	1.19
Pluto	6.37 days (backwards)	0.05

1. Table: A *sidereal day* is the length of time it takes a planet to rotate on its axis once. The surface gravity for each planet is compared to the surface gravity on Earth.

2. Sports Report: This report shows how Michael Jordan, NBA star, scored his points during the 1986-87 season.

3. Magazine Ad: This listing gives the item numbers and prices for various rocket models, accessories, pamphlets, and books that can be ordered.

4. Mileage Guide: Mileage between various cities in southern California is given. Mileage guides assume that you will use the shortest, most commonly used route.

2. Sports Report

Michael Jordan's Points
1986-87 Season

	Points
Regular field goals	2,172
Three-point field goals	36
Free throws	833

3. Magazine Ad

Model Rockets

No.	Model	Price
801	Mosquito	$1.60
870	Pulsar	2.40
871	Yector	2.40
872	Sparrow	2.40
873	Hawkeye	2.40
1377	Hercules	7.50
1380	Phoenix	13.50
1381	Yankee	2.90
1906	Sizzler	5.80
1917	Zinger	2.40
1933	X-16	5.80

Model Rocket Accessories

Code No.	Item	Price
1672	Blast Off Flight Pack	$19.20
2205	Safety Cap Key	0.90
2220	Electron Beam Launcher	12.70
2231	Fin Alignment Guide	11.20
2233	Emergency Repair Kit	3.80
2241	Blast Deflector Plate	2.00
2247	Micro Clips (2 per pack)	1.20
2262	Parachute 10-inch	1.60
2264	Parachute 12-inch	1.60
2267	Parachute 18-inch	2.00
2271	Parachute 24-inch	2.00

Pamphlets and Books

Code No.	Title	Price
2817	Guide for Aerospace Clubs	$0.90
2819	Model Rocket Technical Manual	0.60
2845	The Classic Collection	3.00
2859	The Rocket Book	12.90
2860	Handbook of Model Rocketry	10.90
2861	Advanced Model Rocketry	8.50

4. Mileage Guide

	Los Angeles	Santa Barbara	Palm Springs	San Diego	Anaheim/Orange
Los Angeles	0				
Santa Barbara	97	0			
Palm Springs	105	206	0		
San Diego	121	225	149	0	
Anaheim/Orange County	29	105	88	90	0

San Francisco

Santa Barbara
Los Angeles
Anaheim/Orange County
Palm Springs
San Diego

125

Give the letter for the correct answer.

1. What is 2,046 in expanded form?

　a. 2,000 + 400 + 60
　b. 2,000 + 40 + 6
　c. 2 + 4 + 6
　d. 200 + 40 + 6

2. Which numbers are written in order from least to greatest?

　a. 12,506　12,078　12,320
　b. 12,078　12,506　12,320
　c. 12,078　12,320　12,506
　d. 12,320　12,078　12,506

3. Round 4,628 to the nearest thousand.

　a. 4,000　　**b.** 5,600
　c. 4,700　　**d.** 5,000

4. Which statement is true?

　a. 1.06 > 1.60
　b. 1.06 < 1.061
　c. 1.06 > 1.08
　d. 1.06 < 1.006

5. What is three hundredths written as a decimal?

　a. 0.3　　**b.** 0.03
　c. 0.003　**d.** 300.0

6. Round 16.271 to the nearest tenth.

　a. 16.3　　**b.** 20
　c. 16.27　**d.** 16.2

7. Estimate the sum. First round both numbers to the nearest hundred.

538 + 261

　a. 800　　**b.** 700
　c. 900　　**d.** 600

8. Add.

4,763
+ 5,856

　a. 9,519　　**b.** 9,619
　c. 10,619　**d.** 10,519

9. Subtract.

8,237
− 4,562

　a. 4,775　　**b.** 4,675
　c. 3,775　　**d.** 3,675

10. Estimate the product.

37 × 43

　a. 1,200　**b.** 160
　c. 120　　**d.** 1,600

11. Multiply.

3.9
× 4.3

　a. 167.7　**b.** 13.26
　c. 132.6　**d.** 16.77

12. Multiply.

$$\begin{array}{r} 0.07 \\ \times\ 0.5 \\ \hline \end{array}$$

a. 3.5   **b.** 0.035
c. 0.35   **d.** 0.00035

13. Walton is 300 miles from Leeds by bus, train, or car. A bus left Walton at 2 P.M. for Leeds and averaged 50 miles per hour. A train from Walton, which averaged 75 miles per hour, arrived in Leeds at the same time as the bus. When did the train leave Walton?

a. 3 P.M.   **b.** 5 P.M.
c. 4 P.M.   **d.** 6 P.M.

14. Divide.

$3\overline{)1,521}$

a. 507   **b.** 57
c. 570   **d.** 500 R7

15. Divide.

$124 \div 19$

a. 6   **b.** 5 R14
c. 5 R4   **d.** 6 R10

16. Divide.

$80\overline{)36,572}$

a. 432 R82   **b.** 457 R12
c. 407 R82   **d.** 456 R92

17. Divide.

$25\overline{)7,538}$

a. 310 R13   **b.** 300 R13
c. 301 R13   **d.** 31 R13

18. Estimate this quotient by using compatible numbers.

$1,202 \div 29$

a. 30   **b.** 400
c. 300   **d.** 40

19. Choose the equation that should be used to solve this problem. Then solve the problem.

The store had 125 cartons of eggs at the start of the day. When the store closed, there were 37 cartons left. How many cartons of eggs were sold?

a. $135 + 37 = n$; 172 cartons
b. $125 - 37 = n$; 88 cartons
c. $172 - 125 = n$; 37 cartons
d. $n + 37 = 75$; 38 cartons

Read the problem below. Then answer the question.

If oats sold for $6 per bushel, how much did the Williamses receive for their harvest of 4,267 bushels?

20. Which operation would you use to solve the problem?

a. Multiplication; $4,267 \times 6$
b. Division; $4,267 \div 6$
c. Addition; $4,267 + 6$
d. Subtraction; $4,267 - 6$

Dividing Decimals

4

Did You Know: When Kareem Abdul-Jabbar retired in 1989 after 20 years in the National Basketball Association he had a career total of 44,149 points and had played in a total of 1,797 games.

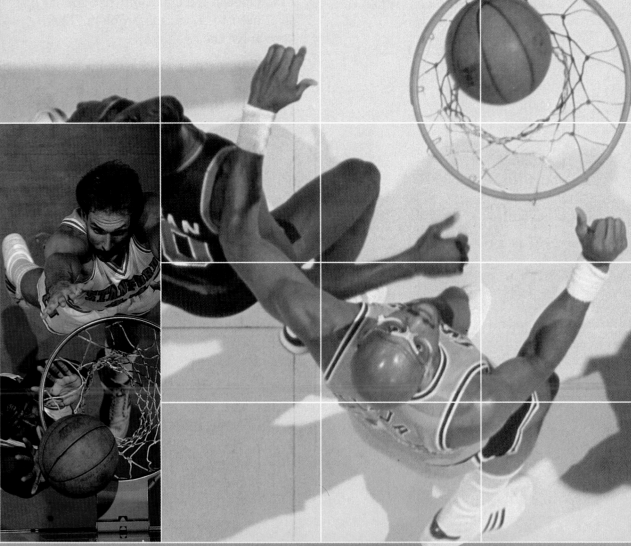

Number-Sense Project

Estimate

Select a person that is playing in a sport this time of year. Predict the number of points this player will score in his or her next game.

Gather Data

Find the total number of points "your person" has scored in past games. Try to get data for at least 5 games.

Analyze and Report

Find the average number of points "your person" scored per game based on the data you collected. Is your prediction for the next game close to the average?

Estimating Quotients

Build Understanding

A. Bob bought 12 golf balls for $14.98. Did each golf ball cost more or less than $1.00?

$14.98 \div 12$

If the divisor is less than the dividend, the quotient is greater than one.
If the divisor is greater than the dividend, the quotient is less than one.

The dividend, $14.98, is larger than the divisor, 12, so the quotient is greater than 1.

Each golf ball costs more than $1.00.

B. Use compatible numbers to estimate $523.6 \div 23$. Compatible numbers make the division easier to do mentally.

$523.6 \div 23$ Choose numbers close to the dividend and the divisor that are easy to use.

$525 \div 25 = 21$

The quotient is about 21.

C. Estimate $62.5 \div 8$. Find a range to estimate the quotient.

$62.5 \div 8$

Think: $8 \times 8 = 64$
$8 \times 7 = 56$

Since 62.5 is between 56 and 64, $62.5 \div 8$ is between 7 and 8.

■ **Talk About Math** In Example C, will the actual quotient be closer to 7 or 8? How can you tell without dividing?

Check Understanding

For another example, see Set A, pages 154–155.

Choose the best estimate.

1. $154.16 \div 46$
   a. 0.3   **b.** 3   **c.** 30

2. $6,247.7 \div 8$
   a. 8   **b.** 80   **c.** 800

Between which two numbers will the quotient be found?

3. $41.6 \div 6$
   a. 2 and 3 **b.** 4 and 5 **c.** 6 and 7

4. $18.92 \div 9$
   a. 1 and 2 **b.** 2 and 3 **c.** 3 and 4

Practice

For More Practice, see Set A, pages 156–157.

Without dividing, tell whether the quotient is greater than 1 or less than 1.

5. $4.05 \div 5$ **6.** $25.2 \div 14$ **7.** $97.7 \div 123$ **8.** $8.19 \div 24$

9. $106\overline{)74.2}$ **10.** $83\overline{)141.1}$ **11.** $13\overline{)10.4}$ **12.** $36\overline{)36.72}$

Estimate the quotient.

13. $80.1 \div 4$ **14.** $27.99 \div 5$ **15.** $515.3 \div 53$ **16.** $146 \div 6$

17. $45.16 \div 7$ **18.** $867 \div 84$ **19.** $940.8 \div 32$ **20.** $98.1 \div 25$

21. $700 \div 19$ **22.** $13.4 \div 4$ **23.** $28.8 \div 14$ **24.** $557.8 \div 48$

25. $61\overline{)245}$ **26.** $18\overline{)208.5}$ **27.** $9\overline{)66.2}$ **28.** $26\overline{)76.7}$

29. $9\overline{)162}$ **30.** $39\overline{)788.7}$ **31.** $98\overline{)694.2}$ **32.** $6\overline{)58.2}$

33. $57\overline{)128}$ **34.** $2\overline{)13.86}$ **35.** $18\overline{)608.7}$ **36.** $68\overline{)695.7}$

Problem Solving

Solve each problem.

37. The track team is having sweatshirts made with the team name on them. If 12 sweatshirts cost $99.50, about how much will each sweatshirt cost?

38. Critical Thinking Eduardo bought 4 cans of tennis balls for $10.95. Each can holds 3 balls. If he sells the balls to his friends for $1 each, will he lose money?

Skills _____ **Review** pages 68–71

Multiply.

1. $\begin{array}{r} 9.9 \\ \times\ 6 \end{array}$ **2.** $\begin{array}{r} 60.3 \\ \times\ 5.5 \end{array}$ **3.** $\begin{array}{r} 6.7 \\ \times 4.4 \end{array}$ **4.** $\begin{array}{r} 1.83 \\ \times 42.7 \end{array}$ **5.** $\begin{array}{r} 282.5 \\ \times\ 74.1 \end{array}$ **6.** $\begin{array}{r} 6.89 \\ \times 0.47 \end{array}$

Dividing a Decimal by a Whole Number

Build Understanding

 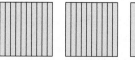

A. How Many Tenths?
Materials: 3 ten-by-ten grids, scissors
Groups: Work with a partner or in a small group.

Find 2.7 ÷ 3.

a. How many tenths are in one square?

b. How many tenths are in two squares?

c. How many tenths are in 2.7? Shade 27 tenths in the models.

d. Cut apart the shaded tenths strips. How many shaded tenths strips are there?

e. Form three equal groups of tenths strips. How many tenths are in each group?

2.7 ÷ 3 = 0.9

B. A swim team was timed at 9.2 minutes for the 800-meter freestyle relay. Each team has four swimmers. What was the average time per swimmer?

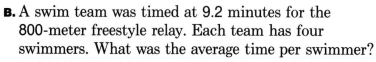

$$4\overline{)9.2}$$ The divisor is a whole number. Place the decimal point in the quotient directly above the decimal point in the dividend.

$$\begin{array}{r} 2.3 \\ 4\overline{)9.2} \\ 8 \\ \hline 1\,2 \\ 1\,2 \\ \hline 0 \end{array}$$ Then divide the same way you divide whole numbers.

The average time per swimmer was 2.3 minutes.

c. 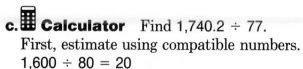 **Calculator** Find 1,740.2 ÷ 77.
First, estimate using compatible numbers.
1,600 ÷ 80 = 20

Press: 1740.2 ÷ 77 =

Display: *22.6*

Look back at the estimate. The answer is reasonable. 1,740.2 ÷ 77 = 22.6

■ **Write About Math** Write a sentence telling why it is important to estimate when using a calculator.

Check Understanding

For another example, see Set B, pages 154–155.

Use decimal models to solve.

1. $2 \div 4$ **2.** $1.5 \div 5$ **3.** $4.2 \div 6$ **4.** $3.6 \div 2$ **5.** $2.4 \div 3$ **6.** $3.5 \div 7$

7. $19.44 \div 27$

a. 0.72   **b.** 7.2   **c.** 72

8. $324.8 \div 14$

a. 0.232   **b.** 2.32   **c.** 23.2

Practice

For More Practice, see Set B, pages 156–157.

9. Number Sense Look at Exercises 10–21.
Tell which quotients will be less than 1.

Divide. **Remember** to place the decimal point in the quotient.

10. $5\overline{)4.85}$ **11.** $3\overline{)13.65}$ **12.** $14\overline{)148.4}$ **13.** $9\overline{)27.09}$

14. $6\overline{)75.6}$ **15.** $13\overline{)106.6}$ **16.** $5\overline{)95.5}$ **17.** $32\overline{)258.24}$

18. $264.6 \div 84$ **19.** $16.68 \div 4$ **20.** $42.56 \div 76$ **21.** $2.464 \div 11$

For Exercises 22–37, tell whether you would use paper
and pencil or a calculator. Then find each quotient.

22. $9\overline{)58.5}$ **23.** $61\overline{)7.93}$ **24.** $35\overline{)117.6}$ **25.** $13\overline{)35.49}$

26. $12\overline{)494.4}$ **27.** $6\overline{)144.54}$ **28.** $19\overline{)2,331.3}$ **29.** $68\overline{)33.388}$

30. $464.24 \div 8$ **31.** $99.36 \div 27$ **32.** $337.8 \div 4$ **33.** $382.7 \div 43$

34. $260.4 \div 7$ **35.** $38.25 \div 85$ **36.** $24.03 \div 89$ **37.** $431.08 \div 52$

Problem Solving

Solve each problem.

38. The Blue Hill swim team
swam the relay in
11.6 minutes. If each of
their times was the same,
how long did each of the
four team members swim?

39. Estimation Arturo paid $10.50
for a season pass for school
sporting events. If he attends
6 events, does it cost more or
less than $1.50 per event?

Writing Zeros in the Quotient

Build Understanding

The energy used in light bulbs is measured in watts. Sound energy can also be measured in watts. A trombone can produce 80 times as much sound energy as a piccolo. What is the energy output of a piccolo?

Instrument	Energy Output
Piano	0.440 watt
Trombone	6.40 watts
Snare drum	12 watts
Human voice	0.000024 watt

Find 6.40 ÷ 80.

Place the decimal point in the quotient directly above the decimal point in the dividend.

$$\begin{array}{r} . \quad \\ 80\overline{)6.40} \end{array}$$

There are no 80s in 6. Write a zero above the 6.

$$\begin{array}{r} 0. \quad \\ 80\overline{)6.40} \end{array}$$

There are no 80s in 64. Write a zero above the 4. Then continue to divide.

$$\begin{array}{r} 0.08 \\ 80\overline{)6.40} \\ \underline{640} \\ 0 \end{array}$$

The energy output of a piccolo is 0.08 watt.

■ **Talk About Math** Explain why the zeros after the decimal point are not necessary in the number 0.1500 but are necessary in the number 0.0031.

Check Understanding

For another example, see Set C, pages 154–155.

Copy and complete.

1.
$$\begin{array}{r} 0.\blacksquare 9 \\ 5\overline{)0.45} \\ \underline{45} \\ 0 \end{array}$$

2.
$$\begin{array}{r} 0.\blacksquare\blacksquare 9 \\ 17\overline{)0.153} \\ \underline{\blacksquare\blacksquare 3} \\ 0 \end{array}$$

3.
$$\begin{array}{r} 0.0\blacksquare\blacksquare \\ 92\overline{)0.552} \\ \underline{\blacksquare\blacksquare 2} \\ \blacksquare \end{array}$$

4.
$$\begin{array}{r} \blacksquare\blacksquare\blacksquare\blacksquare \\ 4\overline{)0.208} \\ \underline{\blacksquare} \\ 0\blacksquare \\ \blacksquare \\ \underline{\blacksquare} \end{array}$$

5.
$$\begin{array}{r} \blacksquare\blacksquare\blacksquare\blacksquare \\ 6\overline{)3.006} \\ \underline{\blacksquare} \\ \blacksquare\blacksquare \\ \blacksquare \\ \underline{\blacksquare} \end{array}$$

Mental Math Without dividing, choose the correct quotient.

6. 0.36 ÷ 9

    a. 4.0   **b.** 0.4   **c.** 0.04

7. 0.006 ÷ 3

    a. 0.2   **b.** 0.002   **c.** 0.0002

Practice

For More Practice, see Set C, pages 156–157.

Find each quotient.

8. $4\overline{)2.8}$ **9.** $7\overline{)0.56}$ **10.** $2\overline{)0.018}$ **11.** $3\overline{)0.21}$

12. $6\overline{)0.096}$ **13.** $9\overline{)0.63}$ **14.** $8\overline{)0.072}$ **15.** $5\overline{)0.455}$

16. $24\overline{)4.8}$ **17.** $41\overline{)28.7}$ **18.** $84\overline{)2.52}$ **19.** $65\overline{)1.95}$

20. 18.24 ÷ 38   **21.** 0.174 ÷ 29   **22.** 0.0923 ÷ 71   **23.** 0.6417 ÷ 31

24. 19.6 ÷ 49   **25.** 94.5 ÷ 27   **26.** 1.947 ÷ 59   **27.** 0.6205 ÷ 73

Mixed Practice   For Exercises 28–43, tell whether you would use paper and pencil or a calculator. Then find each quotient.

28. 67.8 ÷ 3   **29.** 9.12 ÷ 6   **30.** 0.81 ÷ 9   **31.** 129.6 ÷ 18

32. 19.72 ÷ 29   **33.** 2.88 ÷ 36   **34.** 2,053.9 ÷ 47   **35.** 0.1178 ÷ 62

36. 65.05 ÷ 5   **37.** 5.746 ÷ 17   **38.** 269.8 ÷ 19   **39.** 44.85 ÷ 23

40. 0.325 ÷ 13   **41.** 0.429 ÷ 26   **42.** 7.812 ÷ 63   **43.** 89.79 ÷ 73

Problem Solving

Use the table on page 134 to solve Problems 44–48.

44. What is the energy output of 1 million voices?

45. How many trombones would produce 1,280 watts of energy?

46. A piano can produce 8 times as much sound energy as a flute. How much energy does a flute produce?

47. If a snare drum, a piano, and a trombone all play at once, what is the combined energy output of the instruments?

48. Critical Thinking Find a combination of instruments that can produce at least as much energy as a 40-watt bulb uses.

Mental Math: Dividing by 10, 100, 1,000

Build Understanding

A. The bar graph shows the number of radios, televisions, and telephones per 100 persons in the United States in 1987. For every 100 persons there were 212 radios. How many radios is that per person?

Find 212 ÷ 100.

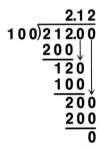

```
      2.12
100)212.00
    200↓
    120
    100↓
      200
      200
        0
```

There were about 2 radios per person.

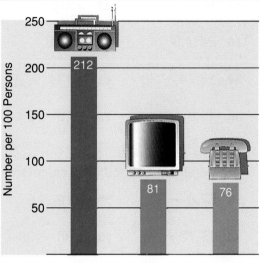

Number per 100 Persons

Radios   Televisions   Telephones

B. Look for a pattern in the division exercises.

483.2 ÷ 1 = 483.2	50.3 ÷ 1 = 50.3
483.2 ÷ 10 = 48.32	50.3 ÷ 10 = 5.03
483.2 ÷ 100 = 4.832	50.3 ÷ 100 = 0.503
483.2 ÷ 1,000 = 0.4832	50.3 ÷ 1,000 = 0.0503

To divide a number by 10, 100, or 1,000, move the decimal point one place to the left for each zero in the divisor.

■ **Talk About Math** Tell a way to remember in which direction you should move the decimal point when dividing by 10, 100, or 1,000.

Check Understanding

For another example, see Set D, pages 154–155.

Choose the correct answer.

1. 0.21 ÷ 10
    a. 2.10   **b.** 0.021   **c.** 0.0021

2. 82.4 ÷ 1,000
    a. 0.0824   **b.** 0.824   **c.** 8.24

Number Sense Arrange the quotients from least to greatest.

3. a. 22.4 ÷ 100   **b.** 22.4 ÷ 10   **c.** 22.4 ÷ 1,000   **d.** 224 ÷ 10

4. a. 813.6 ÷ 10   **b.** 8.136 ÷ 100   **c.** 8,136 ÷ 1,000   **d.** 81.36 ÷ 100

Practice

For More Practice, see Set D, pages 156–157.

Use mental math to divide by moving the decimal point. **Remember** to count the zeros in the divisor.

5. 40.5 ÷ 100 **6.** 2.5 ÷ 1,000 **7.** 70.3 ÷ 100 **8.** 0.03 ÷ 10

9. 983 ÷ 100 **10.** 90.9 ÷ 100 **11.** 4,518 ÷ 100 **12.** 38,693 ÷ 100

13. 88.56 ÷ 10 **14.** 0.009 ÷ 100 **15.** 0.75 ÷ 1,000 **16.** 0.057 ÷ 100

17. 7.03 ÷ 1,000 **18.** 74.41 ÷ 10 **19.** 2.301 ÷ 100 **20.** 320.16 ÷ 1,000

21. 9.125 ÷ 10 **22.** 6,392 ÷ 100 **23.** 7,452 ÷ 1,000 **24.** 25,125 ÷ 100

25. 478.5 ÷ 1,000 **26.** 0.235 ÷ 10 **27.** 45.42 ÷ 100 **28.** 3.667 ÷ 10

A L G E B R A

Critical Thinking Copy and complete. Some exercises have more than one answer.

29. $g ÷ 10 = 95.38$ **30.** $432 ÷ t = 4.32$ **31.** $9,385 ÷ b = 9.385$

32. $a ÷ 1,000 = 4.251$ **33.** $p ÷ r = 9.351$ **34.** $x ÷ y = 0.0843$

Problem Solving

Use the bar graph on page 136 to solve Problems 35–39.

35. Is there more than one television set for each person in the United States?

36. What is the average number of televisions owned by 50 people?

37. How many telephones are there for each person in the United States?

38. If you counted the radios that were owned by 200 persons in the United States, how many radios would you expect to count?

TIPS FOR PROBLEM SOLVERS

Take risks. Try your hunches. They often work.

39. Use Data The average number of radios per household in the U.S. was 5.6 in 1990. Find the total number of households in Example A on page 430. What was the total number of radios in U.S. households in 1990?

Expressing Fractions as Decimals

Build Understanding

When Reuben practiced shooting baskets last Saturday, he made a basket $\frac{5}{8}$ of the time. Write $\frac{5}{8}$ as a decimal rounded to the nearest hundredth.

$$\frac{5}{8} = 5 \div 8$$

To write a fraction as a decimal, divide the numerator by the denominator.

```
    0.6 2 5
8)5.0 0 0
  4 8 ↓
    2 0
    1 6 ↓
      4 0
      4 0
        0
```

Remember that you may need to add zeros to carry out the division.

Round 0.625 to 0.63.

$\frac{5}{8}$ as a decimal rounded to the nearest hundredth is 0.63.

■ **Write About Math** Why must you divide to 3 places after the decimal point in order to round to hundredths?

Many disabled youth can participate in competitive and recreational wheelchair sports.

Check Understanding

For another example, see Set E, pages 154–155.

Number Sense Choose the division statement that has the same meaning as the fraction.

1. $\frac{1}{4}$ **a.** $1 \div 4$ **b.** $4 \div 1$ **2.** $\frac{11}{12}$ **a.** $11 \div 12$ **b.** $12 \div 11$

Write each fraction as a decimal. For Exercises 6 and 7, round your answer to the nearest hundredth.

3. $\frac{1}{4}$ **4.** $\frac{3}{10}$ **5.** $\frac{1}{5}$ **6.** $\frac{7}{8}$ **7.** $\frac{13}{16}$

Practice

For More Practice, see Set E, pages 156–157.

Write each fraction as a decimal. **Remember** to divide the numerator by the denominator.

8. $\frac{4}{5}$ **9.** $\frac{1}{2}$ **10.** $\frac{7}{10}$ **11.** $\frac{3}{8}$ **12.** $\frac{3}{5}$ **13.** $\frac{9}{15}$ **14.** $\frac{19}{25}$

15. $\frac{17}{20}$ **16.** $\frac{1}{25}$ **17.** $\frac{9}{40}$ **18.** $\frac{18}{25}$ **19.** $\frac{91}{100}$ **20.** $\frac{3}{16}$ **21.** $\frac{111}{200}$

22. $\frac{9}{10}$ **23.** $\frac{5}{16}$ **24.** $\frac{45}{200}$ **25.** $\frac{73}{100}$ **26.** $\frac{8}{25}$ **27.** $\frac{19}{40}$ **28.** $\frac{9}{12}$

29. $\frac{11}{16}$ **30.** $\frac{44}{100}$ **31.** $\frac{4}{8}$ **32.** $\frac{87}{200}$ **33.** $\frac{3}{25}$ **34.** $\frac{9}{20}$ **35.** $\frac{39}{40}$

Calculator Write each fraction as a decimal rounded to the nearest hundredth.

36. $\frac{1}{8}$ **37.** $\frac{365}{1,000}$ **38.** $\frac{3}{16}$ **39.** $\frac{9}{200}$ **40.** $\frac{29}{500}$ **41.** $\frac{3}{400}$ **42.** $\frac{654}{2,000}$

43. $\frac{57}{400}$ **44.** $\frac{1}{16}$ **45.** $\frac{421}{500}$ **46.** $\frac{117}{200}$ **47.** $\frac{7}{125}$ **48.** $\frac{411}{625}$ **49.** $\frac{99}{2,500}$

Problem Solving

Solve each problem.

50. The sixth-grade classes at Wayne Middle School raised $102.75, $250.39, and $152.85 for the Junior Wheelchair Games. How much did they raise altogether?

51. Amelia and José practiced for a wheelchair race every day for ten days. José was faster $\frac{6}{10}$ of the time. Write $\frac{6}{10}$ as a decimal.

Midchapter **Checkup**

Estimate.

1. $67.5 \div 5$ **2.** $8.51 \div 17$ **3.** $9.502 \div 35$ **4.** $75.9 \div 67$

Divide. Use mental math whenever possible.

5. $36.6 \div 6$ **6.** $0.189 \div 27$ **7.** $29.9 \div 10$ **8.** $97.22 \div 1,000$

9. Write $\frac{1}{5}$ as a decimal.   **10.** Write $\frac{7}{8}$ as a decimal.

Real-Life Decision Making

$3.75
Bits
(3 Pieces)

$8.47
Box
(10 Pieces)

$11.25
Bucket
(15 Pieces)

$28.54
Barrel
(50 Pieces)

1. Which is the best buy in terms of price?

2. Which would be the best buy for your family? Explain your answer.

3. Describe a situation in which it would make the most sense to buy

   a. the Bits.   **b.** the Box.

   c. the Bucket.   **d.** the Barrel.

Critical-Thinking Activity

Lisa said to Sarah, "My classroom number is 328. What is yours?" Sarah replied, "My room number is less than yours and when it is divided by 2, 3, 4, 5, or 6 the remainder is one but when it is divided by 7, it has no remainder." What is Sarah's room number?

Problem Solving WORKSHOP

Explore with a Computer

Use the *Spreadsheet Workshop Project* with this activity.

1. Suppose you saved 5 nickels, 5 dimes, and 5 quarters in a week. At the computer, type the number of coins saved.

2. The table will calculate how much you saved that week. How much would you have saved if you continued to save the same amount for 10 weeks? How much would you have in a year?

3. What if you saved more than 5 of each coin each week? Set a total amount of money you would like to save in a year. Find how many coins you would need to save each week to reach your total.

```
File  Edit  Forms  Change  Extras  Help
Saving Coins
        A        B      C      D      E
                Coins   $    $ per    $
  1             per    per    10     per
  2             week   week  weeks   year
  3
  4  Nickels     5     0.25   2.50  13.00
  5  Dimes
  6  Quarters
  7  TOTAL
  8
  9
B5                                      ◲

Use arrows to move the highlight.
Press Return for menus.
```

Number-Sense Project

Calculator *Look back at pages 128-129.* Use a calculator to find each answer.

1. Find the average number of points Kareem Abdul-Jabbar scored per game. Round to the nearest tenth.

2. Find the average number of games he played per year. Round to the nearest whole number.

Repeating Decimals

Build Understanding

A. North America covers about $\frac{1}{6}$ of the earth's land area. Write the fraction as a decimal.

Find $1 \div 6$.

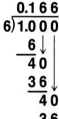

```
     0.1 6 6
  6)1.0 0 0
    6↓
    4 0
    3 6↓        Continue to divide until you
      4 0       see a pattern.
      3 6
         4
```

$\frac{1}{6}$ is a ***repeating decimal***. The pattern will repeat over and over again. To write the decimal, put a bar over the digit or digits that repeat.

$\frac{1}{6} = 0.166\ldots = 0.1\overline{6}$

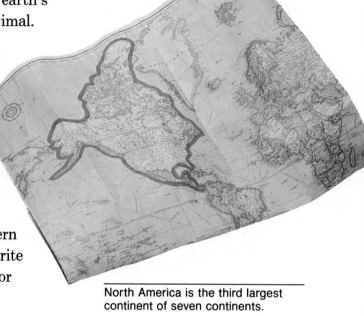

North America is the third largest continent of seven continents.

B. Write $\frac{4}{11}$ as a repeating decimal. Find $4 \div 11$.

Paper and Pencil

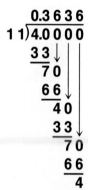

```
     0.3 6 3 6
 11)4.0 0 0 0
    3 3↓
      7 0
      6 6↓
        4 0
        3 3↓
          7 0
          6 6
             4
```

If you continue, the remainder will always be 7 or 4, and you will continue to get 3 followed by 6 in the quotient.

🖩 Calculator

Press: 4 ÷ 11 =

Display: *0.3636363*

The calculator can only show 8 places. To write the decimal, put a bar over the digits that repeat.

$\frac{4}{11} = 0.3636\ldots = 0.\overline{36}$

■ **Talk About Math** Does $0.1\overline{6} = 0.\overline{16}$? Explain your answer.

Check Understanding

For another example, see Set F, pages 154–155.

1. Write 0.010101 . . . with a bar over the digits that repeat.

2. Write the next five digits of the decimal $0.1\overline{23}$.

Write each fraction as a repeating decimal. **Remember** to put a bar over the digit or digits that repeat.

3. $\frac{1}{3}$ **4.** $\frac{11}{12}$ **5.** $\frac{2}{15}$ **6.** $\frac{7}{11}$ **7.** $\frac{5}{18}$ **8.** $\frac{7}{33}$ **9.** $\frac{6}{22}$ **10.** $\frac{7}{18}$

Practice

For More Practice, see Set F, pages 156–157.

Write each fraction as a repeating decimal.

11. $\frac{2}{3}$ **12.** $\frac{5}{6}$ **13.** $\frac{11}{15}$ **14.** $\frac{1}{11}$ **15.** $\frac{13}{18}$ **16.** $\frac{10}{33}$ **17.** $\frac{1}{9}$ **18.** $\frac{5}{22}$

19. $\frac{41}{99}$ **20.** $\frac{8}{9}$ **21.** $\frac{2}{11}$ **22.** $\frac{22}{33}$ **23.** $\frac{10}{11}$ **24.** $\frac{15}{33}$ **25.** $\frac{4}{15}$ **26.** $\frac{3}{54}$

Tell whether you would use paper and pencil or a calculator. Then write each fraction as a repeating decimal.

27. $\frac{4}{11}$ **28.** $\frac{7}{30}$ **29.** $\frac{5}{36}$ **30.** $\frac{50}{99}$ **31.** $\frac{13}{15}$ **32.** $\frac{17}{180}$ **33.** $\frac{7}{66}$

34. $\frac{7}{15}$ **35.** $\frac{17}{22}$ **36.** $\frac{5}{12}$ **37.** $\frac{5}{111}$ **38.** $\frac{9}{220}$ **39.** $\frac{11}{600}$ **40.** $\frac{15}{11}$

Problem Solving

Solve each problem.

41. Europe covers $\frac{1}{15}$ of the earth's land area. Write $\frac{1}{15}$ as a decimal.

42. Australia covers $\frac{1}{18}$ of the earth's land area. Write $\frac{1}{18}$ as a decimal.

Explore _____ Math

Calculator   Use a calculator to write each fraction as a repeating decimal.

43. $\frac{1}{9}$ **44.** $\frac{2}{9}$ **45.** $\frac{3}{9}$ **46.** $\frac{4}{9}$

Use the pattern you discovered to write each fraction as a repeating decimal. Then use your calculator to check.

47. $\frac{5}{9}$ **48.** $\frac{6}{9}$ **49.** $\frac{7}{9}$ **50.** $\frac{8}{9}$

Give Sensible Answers

Build Understanding

Suppose you bought a 3-pound bag of oranges and wanted to know the cost per pound. Would you want to know the cost per pound to the nearest dollar? to the nearest cent? to the nearest tenth of a cent?

A. Three pounds of oranges cost $2. What is the price per pound?

Understand Since prices are given in dollars and cents, divide until the quotient is in thousandths. Then round to the nearest hundredth (cent).

Plan and Solve

$$0.6\,6\,6 \approx 0.6\,7$$
$$3\overline{)2.0\,0\,0}$$

$$\frac{1\,8}{2\,0}\downarrow$$
$$\frac{1\,8}{2\,0}\downarrow$$
$$\frac{1\,8}{2}$$

Write the dividend in thousandths. Divide. Then round the quotient to the nearest hundredth.

The oranges cost about $0.67 a pound.

Look Back SENSIBLE ANSWER
$3 \times \$0.67 = \$2.01$
Since $0.67 was rounded up, the answer is reasonable.

■ **Talk About Math** A package of 200 napkins costs $1.09. What is the best description of the cost: 1 for $0.0055, 10 for $0.055, or 100 for $0.55?

PROBLEM SOLVING GUIDE

Understand
QUESTION
FACTS
KEY IDEA

Plan and Solve
STRATEGY
ANSWER

Look Back
SENSIBLE ANSWER
ALTERNATE APPROACH

Check Understanding

Select the most sensible answer.

1. If a milk truck traveled 625 miles in 13 hours, it averaged about how many miles per hour (mph)?

a. 48.076 mph **b.** 48.1 mph **c.** 48 mph

2. If one gallon of milk (16 cups) costs $1.99, what is the price of the milk per cup?

a. $0.1244 **b.** $0.1 **c.** $0.12

Practice

Solve each problem.

3. An 8-ounce bottle of lemon juice costs $1.49. What is the cost per ounce?

4. A $2.49 can of lemonade mix will make 64 cups of lemonade. What is the cost per cup?

5. A train pulling refrigerated cars travels at an average speed of 62 miles per hour. How long will it take to travel 2,400 miles?

6. About 0.95 of the weight of a watermelon is water. How much does the water weigh in a 20-pound watermelon?

7. A whole watermelon costs $3.50. Cut wedges are sold for $0.20 per pound. Would it be cheaper to buy a 22-pound watermelon or 22 pounds of wedges?

Reading ———— **Math**

Numbers and Symbols For each word expression below, find the number in the box that has the same meaning. One number will not be used.

0.9	$0.8\overline{6}$
0.86	0.188
1.88	0.09

1. $\frac{3}{16}$ written as a decimal and rounded to the nearest thousandth

2. The quotient 3.44 divided by 4

3. The quotient 0.27 divided by 3

4. The quotient 18.8 divided by 10

5. $\frac{13}{15}$ written as a decimal

Dividing by a Decimal

Build Understanding

A. New Problem, Same Quotient
Groups: Work with a partner.

a. Use paper and pencil or a calculator to solve:

8 ÷ 2   80 ÷ 20   800 ÷ 200

What do you notice about the quotients?

b. Use paper and pencil or a calculator to solve:

250 ÷ 50   25 ÷ 5

What do you think the quotient will be for 2.5 ÷ 0.5?

B. Find 1.23 ÷ 0.15.

Paper and Pencil

$$0.15\overline{)1.230}$$

So that you can divide by a whole number, multiply both the dividend and the divisor by 100. Place the decimal point in the quotient.

$$0.15\overline{)1.230}$$
$$\begin{array}{r} 8.2 \\ \underline{120}\downarrow \\ 30 \\ \underline{30} \\ 0 \end{array}$$

Divide as with whole numbers.

Calculator   Will the quotient be less than or greater than 1?

The dividend is greater than the divisor, so the quotient will be greater than 1.

Press: 1.23 ÷ 0.15 =

Display: *8.2*

■ **Talk About Math**   In Example B, what would happen to the quotient if you multiplied the divisor by 100 but did not multiply the dividend?

Check Understanding

For another example, see Set G, pages 154–155.

Place the decimal point correctly in each quotient.

1. $0.4\overline{)0.92}$ quotient 23

2. $1.67\overline{)13.36}$ quotient 8

Find each quotient.

3. $2.9\overline{)11.89}$

4. $0.59\overline{)0.0649}$

146

Practice

For More Practice, see Set G, pages 156–157.

Number Sense Without dividing, choose which exercise has the same quotient.

5. 2.6 ÷ 1.3
   a. 260 ÷ 13   **b.** 0.26 ÷ 0.13

6. 25.9 ÷ 6.2
   a. 2.59 ÷ 62   **b.** 259 ÷ 62

Divide.

7. 0.6)‾5.4‾

8. 0.9)‾0.18‾

9. 1.4)‾13.86‾

10. 0.86)‾0.688‾

11. 1.7)‾10.54‾

12. 2.4)‾16.8‾

13. 0.07)‾0.035‾

14. 0.96)‾0.144‾

15. 0.015 ÷ 0.005

16. 13.76 ÷ 3.2

17. 0.441 ÷ 0.63

18. 0.0258 ÷ 0.086

Tell whether you would use paper and pencil or a calculator. Then find each quotient. Round each quotient to the nearest tenth.

19. 0.4)‾0.856‾

20. 2.8)‾2.716‾

21. 0.37)‾0.3108‾

22. 0.65)‾0.1105‾

23. 0.1785 ÷ 0.51

24. 0.55576 ÷ 0.082

25. 1.515 ÷ 0.25

26. 0.2498 ÷ 7.8

Problem Solving

Critical Thinking Using a divisor of 0.8, write a division exercise so that the quotient will be

27. less than 1.

28. greater than 1.

29. For Exercises 15–18, write an exercise that has the same quotient and a whole-number divisor.

Choose a ___ Strategy

Getting Mileage from Decimals
The table shows Mrs. Sheng's gasoline purchases and her car's odometer readings at each purchase during May. She filled the tank each time she bought gas. To the nearest tenth, how many miles per gallon did her car get from

Date	Odometer	Amount
May 1	4,468.2 mi	Full tank
May 9	4,738.0 mi	8.3 gal
May 14	4,939.3 mi	6.8 gal
May 22	5,228.3 mi	9.6 gal
May 31	5,509.1 mi	9.0 gal

30. May 1 to May 9?

31. May 14 to May 31?

Zeros in the Dividend

Build Understanding

Whole and ground chilies, coriander seeds, ground turmeric, and nuts are sold at this Indian shop.

Many of the spices we use are imported from India and Indonesia. Besides adding flavor to foods, some spices, such as turmeric and saffron, are used as dyes.

A. A small container can hold 0.75 ounce of ground saffron. How many containers can be filled with 10.5 ounces of ground saffron?

Find $10.5 \div 0.75$.

$$0.7\,5\,\overline{)1\,0.5\,0}\qquad\cdot$$

Multiply the divisor and the dividend by 100. Place the decimal point in the quotient.

$$\begin{array}{r} 1\,4. \\ 0.7\,5\,\overline{)1\,0.5\,0} \\ 7\,5 \\ \hline 3\,0\,0 \\ 3\,0\,0 \\ \hline 0 \end{array}$$

Divide 1,050 by 75.

14 containers can be filled.

B. Divide 127 by 75.3. Round the quotient to the nearest hundredth.

Estimate: $140 \div 70 = 2$

Paper and Pencil

$$\begin{array}{r} 1.6\,8\,6 \approx 1.6\,9 \\ 7\,5.3\,\overline{)1\,2\,7.0\,0\,0\,0} \\ 7\,5\,3\downarrow \\ \hline 5\,1\,7\,0 \\ 4\,5\,1\,8\downarrow \\ \hline 6\,5\,2\,0 \\ 6\,0\,2\,4\downarrow \\ \hline 4\,9\,6\,0 \\ 4\,5\,1\,8 \\ \hline 4\,4\,2 \end{array}$$

Multiply the divisor and the dividend by 10.

Carry out the division to thousandths, in order to round to hundredths.

▦ Calculator

Press: 127 ⊡÷⊡ 75 ⊡.⊡ 3 ⊡=⊡

Display: *1.6865869*

■ **Talk About Math** How can you decide whether an estimate is close enough to the actual answer to be reasonable?

Check Understanding

For another example, see Set H, pages 154–155.

Choose the most reasonable value for each quotient.

1. 33 ÷ 1.5
   a. 22   b. 2.2   c. 0.22

2. 9 ÷ 0.6
   a. 1.5   b. 15   c. 150

Divide. **Remember** to add zeros to the dividend as needed.

3. 4.8 ÷ 0.16   4. 33 ÷ 0.6   5. 1.85 ÷ 0.074   6. 204 ÷ 2.4

Practice

For More Practice, see Set H, pages 156–157.

Divide.

7. 0.6)78   8. 0.04)4.04   9. 3.5)245   10. 6.2)248

11. 0.018)0.09   12. 0.022)0.11   13. 0.5)75   14. 0.72)46.8

15. 154 ÷ 0.7   16. 16.4 ÷ 0.05   17. 8 ÷ 0.25   18. 14.3 ÷ 0.65

Tell whether you would use paper and pencil or a calculator.
Then divide. Round to the nearest hundredth.

19. 3.1)10.7   20. 0.072)0.69   21. 0.61)27   22. 1.2)12.7

23. 0.46)15.8   24. 5.67)364.7   25. 7.52)67.08   26. 3.04)7.002

Problem Solving

Solve each problem.

27. It takes about 2,500 blossoms to make 0.5 ounce of saffron, the world's most expensive spice. About how many blossoms would make 6 ounces of saffron?

28. The cinnamon tree, which is native to Sri Lanka, yields long sticks of cinnamon bark. How many 5.5-inch sticks can be cut from a 44-inch stick of cinnamon bark?

The inner bark of the cinnamon branch is peeled and rolled into long sticks. The sticks are dried, smoked, and bundled together before selling them as cinnamon.

Choose an Operation

Build Understanding

A. Mr. Blackstone paid $8.75 for 5 movie theater tickets. The price of each ticket was the same amount. How much did he pay for each ticket?

Understand Think of separating $8.75 into 5 equal groups, each representing the price of one ticket.

Plan and Solve STRATEGY The problem suggests separating a total into equal groups, and finding the numbers of groups, so *choose the operation* of *division*.

Divide $8.75 by 5.

8 ⬚.⬚ 75 ⬚÷⬚ 5 ⬚=⬚ *1.75*

ANSWER Each ticket costs $1.75.

Look Back 5 × $1.75 = $8.75.
The answer checks.

B. Adults pay $3.25 for tickets and students pay $1.75. How much more do adults pay per ticket than students?
To compare numbers, *subtract*.

C. Popcorn costs $1.25 a box. How much do 5 boxes cost?
To find a total when the groups are equal, *multiply*.

D. Lorie spent $1.25, $0.75, and $0.60 for refreshments. How much did she spend?
To find the total when the groups are not equal, *add*.

■ **Write About Math** Write a problem that is solved by dividing.

Understand
QUESTION
FACTS
KEY IDEA

Plan and Solve
STRATEGY
ANSWER

Look Back
SENSIBLE ANSWER
ALTERNATE APPROACH

Check Understanding

Tell what operation you would use to find each answer.

1. Each of XX rows in a theater has 00 seats. How many seats does the theater have?

2. XX tickets were sold this morning and 00 tickets were sold this afternoon. How many tickets were sold in all?

3. After Shelly paid XX for popcorn, she had 00 left. How much money did she have to begin with?

4. If XX tickets were sold in 00 days, what is the average number of tickets sold per day?

Practice

Tell what operation you would use. Then find the answer.

5. A theater has 1,264 seats. This includes 386 seats in the balcony. How many seats are not in the balcony?

6. Mrs. Kelly paid for $3.66 worth of refreshments with a $10 bill. How much change did she receive?

7. Beth turned in money for 32 play tickets that cost $2.25 each. How much money did she turn in?

8. Kevin earned $26.10 for working 6 hours as an usher in a theater. How much did he earn per hour?

9. The least expensive movie tickets cost $1.75, and the most expensive cost 3 times this amount. What do the most expensive tickets cost?

10. It cost $1,350 for a movie theater to rent a movie that was shown 15 times. What was the rental cost per showing?

Choose a ———— Strategy

Dollars and Sense

11. Senior citizens can pay $20 a year for a card that enables them to buy theater tickets for $3.25 each. Without the card, the tickets cost $6.00. How many movies a year would a person have to see before buying the senior-citizen card would make sense?

PROBLEM SOLVING
STRATEGIES

Choose an Operation
Write an Equation
Make a Table

Skills Review

Without dividing, tell whether each quotient is greater than 1 or less than 1.

1. 5.75 ÷ 6   **2.** 113.2 ÷ 82

3. 7)8.53   **4.** 225)202.5

Estimate each quotient.

5. 44.3 ÷ 9   **6.** 312 ÷ 29

7. 4)18.3   **8.** 9)67.8

Divide.

9. 16.25 ÷ 5   **10.** 57.12 ÷ 7

11. 16)172.8   **12.** 78)26.52

13. 0.64 ÷ 8   **14.** 0.296 ÷ 37

15. 0.4)4.8   **16.** 2.5)22.5

17. 4.16 ÷ 3.2   **18.** 0.056 ÷ 0.008

19. 4.3)344   **20.** 0.8)250

Use mental math to divide.

21. 35.5 ÷ 10   **22.** 0.45 ÷ 100

23. 782 ÷ 100   **24.** 3.61 ÷ 1,000

Write each fraction as a decimal. Use a bar to write repeating decimals.

25. $\frac{2}{5}$ **26.** $\frac{1}{3}$ **27.** $\frac{5}{9}$

28. $\frac{7}{8}$ **29.** $\frac{1}{2}$ **30.** $\frac{3}{11}$

Divide. Round the quotient to the nearest hundredth.

31. 6.8)6.92   **32.** 0.55)13.4

Problem-Solving Review

Solve each problem.

33. Sal has $127 in his savings account. He plans to save $10 each month for the next three months. How much will his total savings be at the end of the three months?

34. Three brothers bought a stereo for $355.95. They shared the cost equally. About how much did each brother pay?

35. A package of 1,000 sheets of paper costs $5.00. What is the cost per sheet?

36. Together Anthony and James made 78 party favors. Anthony made 44 of them. Write and solve an equation to find the number of party favors that James made.

37. If the average food consumption of wheat flour is 123 pounds per person per year, how many pounds would you expect 1,000 people to consume in a year?

38. **Data File** Use the data on pages 266–267. For which road is the auto toll cost per mile the greatest?

39. **Make a Data File** Take a survey of your friends' favorite foods. Give 20 people the choice of three foods. Ask which is their favorite of three foods, such as pizza, tacos, or chicken. Record your results in a table.

Write each product using exponents.

1. $5 \times 5 \times 5$ **2.** $1 \times 1 \times 1 \times 1 \times 1$ **3.** $3 \times 3 \times 7 \times 7 \times 7$

Use mental math to find each answer.

4. $240 \div 60$ **5.** $6.056 \div 100$ **6.** $30 \times 7,000$ **7.** $12 + 29 + 8$

8. $21\overline{)1,470}$ **9.** $20 \times 30 \times 50$ **10.** $31\overline{)31,000}$ **11.** $3.96 \div 1,000$

Write the numbers in order from least to greatest.

12. 65.02; 65.20; 6.205; 602.5   **13.** 1.0598; 1.5098; 1.0958; 0.1895

Write the next five digits of each decimal.

14. $0.\overline{5}$ **15.** $0.\overline{18}$ **16.** $0.4\overline{6}$ **17.** $0.8\overline{3}$ **18.** $0.4\overline{09}$

Estimate. Then find each answer.

19. $\begin{array}{r} 7,605 \\ \times \quad 8 \\ \hline \end{array}$ **20.** $\begin{array}{r} 2,407.1 \\ - \quad 384.5 \\ \hline \end{array}$ **21.** $\begin{array}{r} 3.85 \\ \times 1.22 \\ \hline \end{array}$ **22.** $\begin{array}{r} 85.25 \\ + \quad 7.75 \\ \hline \end{array}$

23. $7\overline{)53}$ **24.** $5\overline{)3,226}$ **25.** 485×97 **26.** $43\overline{)93}$

27. $72 \times 1,086$ **28.** $1,395 \div 24$ **29.** $124.47 \div 27$ **30.** $16.12 \div 3.1$

Solve each equation.

31. $3 \times n = 27$ **32.** $n + 27 = 50$ **33.** $n \times 10 = 70$ **34.** $225 = n \times 5$

Write in standard form.

35. Two and five thousand twenty-four millionths

36. 4^3 **37.** $0^5 \times 2^4$ **38.** $3^2 \times 4^2$

Find the rule for calculating y in each table. Then copy and complete each table.

39.

x	4	8	12	16	20	24
y	1	2	3			

40.

x	1	2	3	4	5	6
y	3	4	5			

Write each fraction as a decimal. Use a bar for repeating decimals.

41. $\frac{3}{4}$ **42.** $\frac{5}{8}$ **43.** $\frac{5}{6}$ **44.** $\frac{3}{25}$ **45.** $\frac{2}{3}$

Reteaching

Set A pages 130–131

Estimate $316.5 \div 42$.

Use compatible numbers. Choose numbers close to the dividend and the divisor that you can divide easily.

$$316.5 \div 42$$
$$\downarrow \qquad \downarrow$$
$$320 \div 40 = 8$$

The quotient is about 8.

Remember to estimate by using compatible numbers.

Estimate the quotient.

1. $43\overline{)158}$ **2.** $27\overline{)119}$

3. $61.7 \div 6$ **4.** $165 \div 8$

5. $589 \div 12$ **6.** $922 \div 33$

Set B pages 132–133

Find $10.8 \div 3$.

The divisor is a whole number. Place the decimal point in the quotient directly above the decimal point in the dividend.

$$\begin{array}{r} 3.6 \\ 3\overline{)10.8} \\ -9 \\ \hline 1\,8 \\ -1\,8 \\ \hline 0 \end{array}$$

Remember that after you place the decimal point in the quotient, you divide decimals the same way you divide whole numbers.

Divide.

1. $19.6 \div 7$ **2.** $3.54 \div 6$

3. $96.1 \div 31$ **4.** $20.47 \div 23$

Set C pages 134–135

Find $1.984 \div 32$.

$$\begin{array}{r} 0. \\ 32\overline{)1.984} \end{array}$$ There are no 32s in 1.
Write a zero above the 1.

$$\begin{array}{r} 0.062 \\ 32\overline{)1.984} \\ 1\,92 \\ \hline 64 \\ 64 \\ \hline 0 \end{array}$$ There are no 32s in 19.
Write a zero above the 9.
Now continue to divide.

Remember that after the decimal point there must be a digit in the quotient above each digit in the dividend.

Find each quotient.

1. $3\overline{)2.7}$ **2.** $8\overline{)0.32}$

3. $6\overline{)0.042}$ **4.** $7\overline{)0.035}$

5. $4\overline{)0.06}$ **6.** $9\overline{)0.729}$

Set D pages 136–137

Find $3.7 \div 100$.

Since there are two zeros in 100, move the decimal point two places to the left.

$$3.7 \div 100 = 0.037$$

A zero was written before the 3 when the decimal point was moved.

Remember to move the decimal point one place to the left for each zero in the divisor.

Divide by moving the decimal point.

1. $32.6 \div 100$ **2.** $8.7 \div 1,000$

3. $3,692 \div 100$ **4.** $0.6 \div 10$

Set E pages 138–139

Write $\frac{7}{8}$ as a decimal.

$\frac{7}{8}$ means $7 \div 8$.

$$8\overline{)7.000} \quad \begin{array}{r} 0.875 \\ \hline \end{array}$$

Write zeros in the dividend as needed.

```
   0.875
8)7.000
  6 4
  ----
   60
   56
   ----
    40
    40
    ----
     0
```

$\frac{7}{8} = 0.875$

Remember that you may need to add zeros in the dividend as you divide.

Write each fraction as a decimal.

1. $\frac{2}{5}$ 2. $\frac{3}{4}$ 3. $\frac{9}{10}$

4. $\frac{13}{20}$ 5. $\frac{47}{100}$ 6. $\frac{7}{25}$

7. $\frac{5}{8}$ 8. $\frac{65}{400}$ 9. $\frac{163}{200}$

Set F pages 142–143

Write $\frac{7}{15}$ as a repeating decimal.

```
    0.466
15)7.000
   6 0
   ----
   1 00
     90
   ----
    100
     90
    ----
     10
```

$\frac{7}{15}$ means $7 \div 15$.

$\frac{7}{15} = 0.466...$

$= 0.4\overline{6}$

Remember to divide until you see a pattern.

Write each fraction as a repeating decimal.

1. $\frac{1}{3}$ 2. $\frac{7}{18}$ 3. $\frac{1}{6}$

4. $\frac{3}{11}$ 5. $\frac{4}{15}$ 6. $\frac{20}{33}$

Set G pages 146–147

Find $6.12 \div 1.8$.

To make the divisor a whole number, multiply the divisor and dividend by 10.

```
        3.4
1.8)6.12
    5 4
    ----
     72
     72
     ----
      0
```

Remember to multiply a decimal by 10, 100, or 1,000, move the decimal point one place to the right for each zero.

Divide.

1. $0.08\overline{)0.96}$ 2. $2.3\overline{)10.58}$

3. $1.6\overline{)4.48}$ 4. $5.7\overline{)22.23}$

Set H pages 148–149

Find $18.2 \div 0.07$.

To make the divisor a whole number, multiply the divisor and dividend by 100.

```
           2 60.
0.07)18.20
     14
     ----
      4 2
      4 2
      ----
       00
       00
       ----
        0
```

Remember to move the decimal point the same number of places in the divisor and dividend.

Divide.

1. $0.4\overline{)64}$ 2. $0.08\overline{)4.08}$

3. $0.9\overline{)78.3}$ 4. $0.06\overline{)14.1}$

More Practice

Set A   pages 130–131

Without dividing, tell whether the quotient is greater than
1 or less than 1.

1. 8.09 ÷ 9 **2.** 36.4 ÷ 32 **3.** 86.7 ÷ 94 **4.** 31.6 ÷ 31

Estimate the quotient.

5. 48.6 ÷ 5 **6.** 392.7 ÷ 40 **7.** 235 ÷ 8 **8.** 591 ÷ 7

9. $17\overline{)331}$ **10.** $3\overline{)26.3}$ **11.** $29\overline{)614}$ **12.** $78\overline{)629}$

Set B   pages 132–133

Divide.

1. $3\overline{)15.9}$ **2.** $6\overline{)404.4}$ **3.** $8\overline{)23.28}$ **4.** $4\overline{)12.24}$

5. 17.28 ÷ 12 **6.** 5.481 ÷ 27 **7.** 2.047 ÷ 23 **8.** 35.97 ÷ 33

For Exercises 9–12, tell whether you would use paper and
pencil or a calculator. Then find each quotient.

9. $5\overline{)37.5}$ **10.** $49\overline{)287.63}$ **11.** $6\overline{)24.36}$ **12.** $38\overline{)36.48}$

Set C   pages 134–135

Find each quotient.

1. $8\overline{)0.48}$ **2.** $4\overline{)0.352}$ **3.** $15\overline{)0.45}$ **4.** $23\overline{)0.92}$

5. 1.54 ÷ 22 **6.** 1.325 ÷ 25 **7.** 1.278 ÷ 71 **8.** 0.0585 ÷ 9

Mixed Practice   For Exercises 9–12, tell whether you
would use paper and pencil or a calculator. Then find
each quotient.

9. 86.4 ÷ 4 **10.** 2.43 ÷ 27 **11.** 79.2 ÷ 44 **12.** 0.867 ÷ 17

Set D   pages 136–137

Use mental math to divide by moving the decimal point.

1. 29.4 ÷ 10 **2.** 3.2 ÷ 100 **3.** 90.1 ÷ 1,000 **4.** 0.09 ÷ 10

5. 762 ÷ 100 **6.** 3.206 ÷ 100 **7.** 42.192 ÷ 100 **8.** 76.41 ÷ 1,000

9. 39.04 ÷ 10 **10.** 3.09 ÷ 1,000 **11.** 5.62 ÷ 100 **12.** 480.23 ÷ 1,000

Set E   pages 138–139

Write each fraction as a decimal.

1. $\frac{1}{4}$ **2.** $\frac{1}{5}$ **3.** $\frac{1}{20}$ **4.** $\frac{7}{25}$ **5.** $\frac{31}{100}$ **6.** $\frac{7}{20}$

▦ **Calculator**   Write each fraction as a decimal rounded to the nearest hundredth.

7. $\frac{9}{40}$ **8.** $\frac{7}{16}$ **9.** $\frac{11}{200}$ **10.** $\frac{182}{1,000}$ **11.** $\frac{27}{40}$ **12.** $\frac{27}{400}$

Set F   pages 142–143

Write each fraction as a repeating decimal.

1. $\frac{1}{18}$ **2.** $\frac{5}{9}$ **3.** $\frac{7}{30}$ **4.** $\frac{9}{11}$ **5.** $\frac{11}{18}$ **6.** $\frac{13}{36}$

For Exercises 7–12, tell whether you would use paper and pencil or a calculator. Then write each fraction as a repeating decimal.

7. $\frac{1}{9}$ **8.** $\frac{7}{12}$ **9.** $\frac{11}{15}$ **10.** $\frac{7}{18}$ **11.** $\frac{11}{30}$ **12.** $\frac{25}{36}$

Set G   pages 146–147

Divide.

1. $0.7\overline{)6.3}$ **2.** $0.8\overline{)1.12}$ **3.** $0.16\overline{)2.56}$ **4.** $0.36\overline{)0.288}$

Tell whether you would use paper and pencil or a calculator. Then find each quotient. Round each quotient to the nearest tenth.

5. $6.8\overline{)0.2312}$ **6.** $8.3\overline{)27.307}$ **7.** $55.1\overline{)23.142}$ **8.** $0.002\overline{)0.002698}$

Set H   pages 148–149

Divide.

1. $0.7\overline{)42}$ **2.** $7.2\overline{)216}$ **3.** $1.6\overline{)0.84}$ **4.** $3.6\overline{)5.94}$

5. $0.08\overline{)0.576}$ **6.** $0.48\overline{)40.8}$ **7.** $0.04\overline{)146.8}$ **8.** $3.8\overline{)8.74}$

For Exercises 9–12, tell whether you would use paper and pencil or a calculator. Then divide.

9. $8.4\overline{)31.5}$ **10.** $3.6\overline{)5.94}$ **11.** $1.5\overline{)8.79}$ **12.** $4.2\overline{)35.07}$

Enrichment

Foreign Currencies

Suppose you are going to travel on a trip around the world. You will have to exchange your U.S. money for the currency used in each country that you visit. The exchange rates vary from day to day, depending upon the economy. In order to find how much a certain currency is worth in terms of dollars, you can look in a daily newspaper. The following exchange rates were published recently.

1 U.S. dollar = 4.8 francs (France)
1 U.S. dollar = 0.50 pounds (Great Britain)
1 U.S. dollar = 3,125 pesos (Mexico)
1 U.S. dollar = 125 yen (Japan)

Change $50 to francs.
Find the exchange rate.
$1 = 4.8 francs
Estimate: $1 is about 5 francs, so $50 is about 50 × 5, or 250, francs. To find the exact amount, multiply 50 by 4.8.
50 × 4.8 = 240 francs

Change 6,000 Mexican pesos to U.S. dollars.
$1 = 3,125 pesos
Estimate: $1 is about 3,000 pesos.
6,000 ÷ 3,000 = 2, so 6,000 pesos is about $2.
To find the exact amount, divide 6,000 by 3,125.
6,000 ÷ 3,125 = 1.92 dollars

Change each dollar amount to the given currency.
Round answers to the nearest hundredth.

1. $100 to yen   **2.** $75 to pesos   **3.** $20 to pounds   **4.** $27.95 to francs

Change each foreign currency to U.S. dollars.

5. 50 pounds   **6.** 10,000 yen   **7.** 500 francs   **8.** 25,000 pesos

9. Change 50 francs to pounds. Hint: First change francs to dollars. Then change dollars to pounds.

Chapter 4 Review/Test

Without dividing, tell whether the quotient is greater than 1 or less than 1.

1. 2.7 ÷ 27

2. 55 ÷ 14.8

3. Find a range for the quotient 43.7 ÷ 9.

Divide.

4. $9\overline{)5.4}$ **5.** $12\overline{)4.44}$

6. $7\overline{)0.84}$ **7.** $52\overline{)71.24}$

8. 40.72 ÷ 8   **9.** 26.39 ÷ 13

10. 0.144 ÷ 48   **11.** 0.1591 ÷ 43

Divide by moving the decimal point. Use mental math.

12. 9.56 ÷ 10

13. 18.9 ÷ 100

14. 88.2 ÷ 1,000

Write each fraction as a decimal. Use a bar to write any repeating decimals.

15. $\frac{3}{10}$ **16.** $\frac{7}{8}$ **17.** $\frac{13}{15}$

18. $\frac{5}{33}$ **19.** $\frac{7}{25}$ **20.** $\frac{7}{60}$

Divide.

21. $0.7\overline{)0.028}$ **22.** $0.43\overline{)0.645}$

23. $0.4\overline{)72}$ **24.** $0.16\overline{)4}$

25. Tell what operation you will use to find the answer. Then solve.

Nancy ran in four races. She ran 6.4 miles, 12.5 miles, 10.6 miles, and 9.3 miles. What is the total distance she ran?

26. An 11-ounce bottle of shampoo costs $6.47. What is the cost per ounce?

Read the problem below. Then answer the question.

Juan walked 5 miles in a charity walk. He took pledges of $0.20 per mile. How much did Juan earn for the charity by finishing the walk?

27. Which fact do you need to know to solve the problem?

  a. The winner of the race
  b. Juan's race time
  c. The number of runners
  d. The number of pledges Juan received

28. **Write About Math** In the decimal $0.\overline{45}$ what does the bar mean?

Using Geometry

5

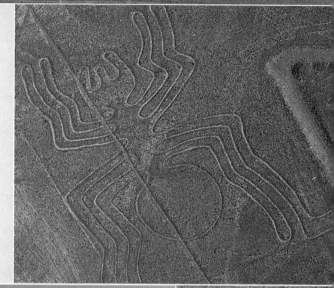

Number-Sense Project

Estimate
How might the Nasca Indians have drawn such long straight lines so accurately?

Gather Data
The Nascans may have drawn the lines by aligning three poles. Work in groups and try to devise methods to draw long lines on the ground between two given endpoints.

Analyze and Report
Discuss the methods used by each group. Which do you think would result in the most accurate drawing?

161

Basic Geometric Ideas

Build Understanding

The following terms are commonly used in geometry.

Term	Description	Diagram	Symbol
Point	An exact location in space	A •	A a capital letter
Line	A straight path of points continuing in both directions	K L M (line)	$\overleftrightarrow{KL}$, $\overleftrightarrow{LK}$, $\overleftrightarrow{LM}$, $\overleftrightarrow{ML}$, $\overleftrightarrow{KM}$, or $\overleftrightarrow{MK}$ (Two points name a line.)
Ray	A straight path of points continuing in one direction having only one *endpoint*	H I J	$\overrightarrow{JH}$ or $\overrightarrow{JI}$ (Endpoint must be first.)
Line segment	A straight path of points between two points	B C	$\overline{BC}$ or $\overline{CB}$ (endpoints B and C)
Congruent line segments	Segments with the same length	D $\frac{1}{2}$ in. E; F $\frac{1}{2}$ in. G	$\overline{DE} \cong \overline{FG}$ (read: line segment DE is congruent to line segment FG)
Intersecting lines	Lines that meet at a point	O N P	$\overleftrightarrow{ON}$ and $\overleftrightarrow{NP}$ intersect at point N.
Plane	A flat surface that extends without end in all directions	$\mathcal{R}$ O N P	plane $\mathcal{R}$
Parallel lines	Lines in a plane that never meet	S T; U V	$\overleftrightarrow{ST} \parallel \overleftrightarrow{UV}$ (read: line ST is parallel to line UV)
Skew lines	Lines that do not lie in the same plane	$\mathcal{L}$ P N; $\mathcal{R}$ S T	$\overleftrightarrow{ST}$ and $\overleftrightarrow{NP}$ lie in planes $\mathcal{R}$ and $\mathcal{L}$.

■ **Talk About Math** What is the intersection of two lines? two planes?

Check Understanding
For another example, see Set A, pages 192–193.

Tell what geometric figure is suggested by each of the following.

1. The edge of a book   **2.** The sharp end of a pencil   **3.** A beam of light

Use the figure at the right for Exercises 4 and 5.

4. Name the rays on $\overleftrightarrow{AC}$.

5. Name the intersecting lines.

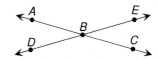

Practice
For More Practice, see Set A, pages 194–195.

Use the figure at the right for Exercises 6–14.

6. Give two other names for $\overleftrightarrow{AC}$.

7. Name four rays on $\overleftrightarrow{PQ}$.

8. Give another name for $\overrightarrow{AC}$.

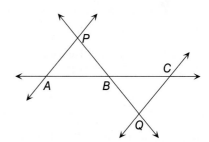

9. Name four rays with endpoint B.

10. Name two lines containing B.

11. Name three points on $\overleftrightarrow{AC}$.

12. Name three line segments on $\overleftrightarrow{PQ}$.

13. Name the lines which intersect $\overleftrightarrow{AC}$ and name the points of intersection.

14. If possible, draw a line that intersects all four lines shown in the figure.

Copy the figure at the right for Exercises 15–16.

15. Draw skew lines and label their planes $\mathcal{W}$ and $\mathcal{X}$.

16. How many line segments are there in the figure?

Problem Solving

Complete the following.

17. Draw points X and Y. How many lines can you draw through both points X and Y?

18. Draw $\overleftrightarrow{FG}$ parallel to $\overleftrightarrow{HI}$ and $\overleftrightarrow{HI}$ parallel to $\overleftrightarrow{KL}$. What do you notice about $\overleftrightarrow{KL}$ and $\overleftrightarrow{FG}$?

163

Angles and Angle Measurement

Build Understanding

A. Folding Angles

a. Start with a square sheet of paper. Fold it in half so that the left edge meets the right edge. Next fold the paper in half so that the bottom edge meets the top edge. Finally, fold the paper in half diagonally so that the bottom edge meets the left edge.

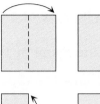

b. Open the paper and draw eight rays with a common endpoint (the center). Label the rays as shown in the diagram.

c. An *angle* is formed by two rays that have the same endpoint. *I* is the endpoint of ray *IH* and ray *IA*. The endpoint is the *vertex* of the angle. The rays are the *sides* of the angle.

Name as many other angles as you can find in the diagram.

The angle formed by rays *IH* and *IA* is ∠*HIA*, read "angle *HIA*." The vertex is always the middle letter.

B. A *protractor* is a tool for measuring angles. It is divided into units called *degrees*. Your Math Sketcher contains a protractor.

To measure an angle, place the center mark of the protractor on the vertex of the angle and the zero mark on a side of the angle.

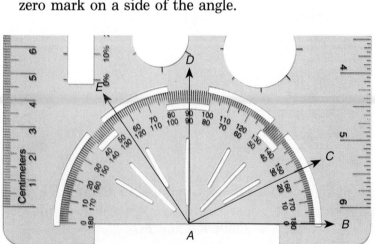

An *acute angle* is an angle with a measure less than 90°. ∠*BAC* is an acute angle.

A *right angle* is an angle with a measure of 90°. ∠*BAD* is a right angle. The symbol ⌐ is used to show a right angle. Rays *AB* and *AD* are *perpendicular.* The symbol ⊥ is read "is perpendicular to."

An *obtuse angle* is an angle with a measure greater than 90° and less than 180°. ∠*BAE* is an obtuse angle.

c. Sometimes instead of using a protractor you **construct** a figure using a **straightedge** and a **compass**. Construct an angle congruent to ∠M.

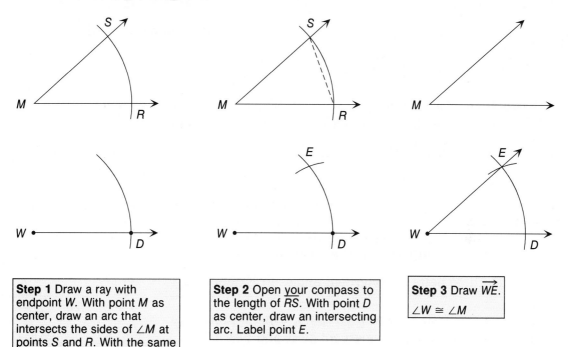

Step 1 Draw a ray with endpoint W. With point M as center, draw an arc that intersects the sides of ∠M at points S and R. With the same opening, draw an arc intersecting the ray at point D.

Step 2 Open your compass to the length of $\overline{RS}$. With point D as center, draw an intersecting arc. Label point E.

Step 3 Draw $\overrightarrow{WE}$.
∠W ≅ ∠M

D. A **bisector** divides an angle into two congruent parts. Follow these steps to construct the bisector of ∠RST.

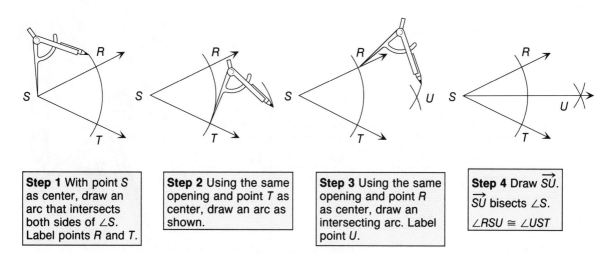

Step 1 With point S as center, draw an arc that intersects both sides of ∠S. Label points R and T.

Step 2 Using the same opening and point T as center, draw an arc as shown.

Step 3 Using the same opening and point R as center, draw an intersecting arc. Label point U.

Step 4 Draw $\overrightarrow{SU}$.
$\overrightarrow{SU}$ bisects ∠S.
∠RSU ≅ ∠UST

■ **Talk About Math** Explain how a right angle can help you determine whether another angle is acute or obtuse.

Check Understanding

For another example, see Set B, pages 192–193.

Fill in each blank.

1. The vertex of ∠*ABC* is ___?___.

2. Another name for ∠*GHI* is ___?___.

3. The sides of ∠*DEF* are ___?___ and ___?___.

Estimation Use Example A on page 164. Estimate the measure of the following angles. Are the angles acute, right, or obtuse?

4. ∠*HIA*   5. ∠*EIH*   6. ∠*EIC*   7. ∠*GIA*   8. ∠*EIF*   9. ∠*FIA*

Practice

For More Practice, see Set B, pages 194–195.

Two angles are ***congruent*** if they have the same measure.

10. Name three pairs of congruent angles in Example A.

Draw an angle with the given measure, using a protractor. Then construct an angle congruent to it and bisect it.

11. 25°   12. 70°   13. 120°   14. 150°

Use the figure below for Exercises 15–35.

15. Name all acute angles.

16. Name all right angles.

17. Name all obtuse angles.

Complete the table.

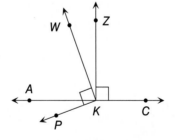

Angle	Vertex	Sides	Estimate of the Measure	Actual Measure
∠AKP	18.	$\overrightarrow{KA}$, $\overrightarrow{KP}$	19.	20.
21.	K	$\overrightarrow{KP}$, $\overrightarrow{KW}$	22.	23.
∠AKW	24.	25.	26.	27.
∠WKZ	28.	29.	30.	31.
32.	33.	$\overrightarrow{KP}$, $\overrightarrow{KZ}$	34.	35.

Problem Solving

Copy and complete the table.

Number of Rays	**36.**	**37.**	**38.**	**39.**
Number of Angles	**40.**	**41.**	**42.**	**43.**

44. Number Sense   How many angles are formed by 6 rays? 7 rays?

45. Critical Thinking   How many angles are formed by *n* rays?

ALGEBRA

Explore —————— Math

Two angles are ***complementary*** if the sum of their measures is 90°. The corner of a piece of paper forms a 90° angle. Fold a piece of paper so that the corner is the vertex of complementary angles.

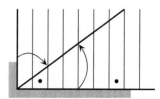

46. Find the measure of each angle.

Two angles are ***supplementary*** if the sum of their angle measures is 180°. Draw point *X* on the edge of a piece of paper. Fold the paper so that point *X* is the vertex of supplementary angles.

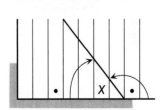

47. Give the measure of each angle.

48. Can two obtuse angles be supplementary? Explain.

49. Can two acute angles be supplementary? Explain.

50. Can two acute angles be complementary? Explain.

51. Bradley looked at the diagram at the right and found the measure of each angle without measuring. How did he do this? What is the measure of each angle?

52. Which angles in the diagram are congruent?

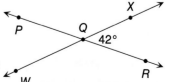

Polygons

Build Understanding

A. Alicia looked up the meanings of the following words in a dictionary:

> **tricycle** a three-wheeled vehicle
>
> **quadriceps** the muscle of the front of the thigh, divided into four parts
>
> **pentathlon** an athletic contest involving five events
>
> **hexapod** six-footed
>
> **octet** a musical composition for eight voices or instruments

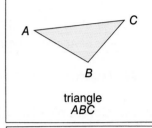

triangle
ABC

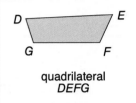

quadrilateral
DEFG

B. A *polygon* is a closed figure made up of three or more line segments called sides.

The definitions in Example A can be used to name each polygon to the right. Polygons are named using their vertices.

A *regular polygon* is a polygon with all sides congruent and all angles the same size.

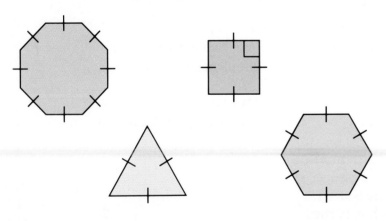

pentagon
HIJKL

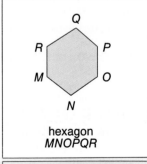

hexagon
MNOPQR

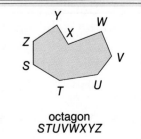

octagon
STUVWXYZ

■ **Write About Math** Define *triangle, quadrilateral, pentagon, hexagon,* and *octagon* using the word *polygon.*

168

Check Understanding

For another example, see Set C, pages 192–193.

Use the examples on page 168. Name a polygon with

1. six sides. **2.** four sides. **3.** five sides. **4.** eight sides.

Name each polygon.

5.

6.

7.

Practice

For More Practice, see Set C, pages 194–195.

Name each polygon.

8.   **9.**   **10.**   **11.**

12.   **13.**   **14.**  **15.**

16. Which polygons in Exercises 8–15 are regular polygons?

Sketch the following.

17. A triangle with a right angle

18. Two triangles with a common side

19. A quadrilateral with only one pair of parallel sides

20. A quadrilateral with two pairs of equal sides and no right angles

Problem Solving

Solve each problem.

21. A decade is a period of ten years. What is a ten-sided polygon called?

22. *Dodecaphonic* means "twelve-tone." How many sides does a dodecagon have?

23. How many vertices does a polygon with *n* sides have?

24. **Critical Thinking** What is the fewest number of vertices a polygon can have? Name the polygon.

Types of Triangles

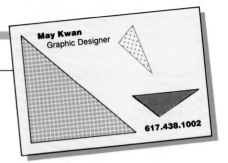

Build Understanding

May Kwan is a graphics designer. She often uses geometric figures in her work. The design at the right is made from three triangles.

May knows that the sum of the measures of the angles of a triangle is 180°.

If you tear off the angles of a triangle and put them together, they form a straight line. A straight line measures 180°.

A. Find the measure of ∠C or ∠ACB.

Add the known measures.　　**40 + 83 = 123**

Subtract the sum from 180.　**180 − 123 = 57**

The measure of ∠C is 57°.

B. Triangles are classified according to the measures of their angles.

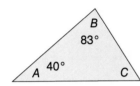

An **acute triangle** has three acute angles.

A **right triangle** has one right angle.

An **obtuse triangle** has one obtuse angle.

C. Triangles can also be classified according to the lengths of their sides. The slash marks show congruent sides.

A **scalene triangle** has no congruent sides.

An **isosceles triangle** has at least two congruent sides.

An **equilateral triangle** has three congruent sides.

■ **Talk About Math** Is an equilateral triangle a regular polygon? Explain.

Check Understanding

For another example, see Set D, pages 192–193.

Use triangle *PQR*.

1. Is triangle *PQR* acute, right, or obtuse?

2. Is triangle *PQR* scalene, isosceles, or equilateral?

3. Find the measure of ∠*R*.

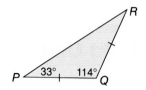

Practice

For More Practice, see Set D, pages 194–195.

For Exercises 4–11, tell whether you would use mental math, paper and pencil, or a calculator to find the measure of angle *A*. Then find the measure.

4.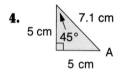

5.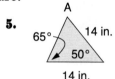

6.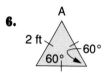

7.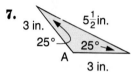

8.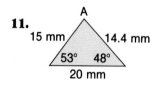

9.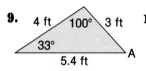

10.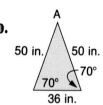

11.

12. Tell whether each triangle in Exercises 4–11 is acute, obtuse, or right.

13. Tell whether each triangle in Exercises 4–11 is scalene, isosceles, or equilateral.

Problem Solving

Number Sense Use triangle *PQR* above.

14. Could a triangle larger than triangle *PQR* have angles with the same measures as ∠*P*, ∠*Q*, and ∠*R*?

Critical Thinking Try to draw triangles that fit the classifications listed. Mark congruent sides and right angles. If the triangle cannot be drawn, write X.

15. Acute, scalene

16. Acute, isosceles

17. Acute, equilateral

18. Obtuse, scalene

19. Obtuse, isosceles

20. Obtuse, equilateral

21. Right, scalene

22. Right, isosceles

23. Right, equilateral

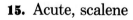

TIPS FOR PROBLEM SOLVERS

Think about your own thinking. Pause to ask, "How is this going to help me solve the problem?"

Solve a Simpler Problem

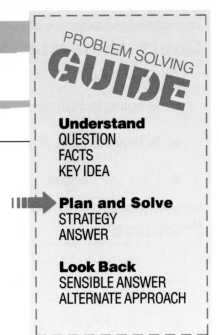

PROBLEM SOLVING GUIDE

Understand
QUESTION
FACTS
KEY IDEA

▶ **Plan and Solve**
STRATEGY
ANSWER

Look Back
SENSIBLE ANSWER
ALTERNATE APPROACH

Build Understanding

Find the sum of the measures of the angles in an octagon.

Understand   QUESTION   What is the sum of the angle measures in an octagon?

FACTS   There are 8 angles in an octagon.

KEY IDEA   The sum of the measures of the angles in a triangle is 180°.

▶ **Plan and Solve**   STRATEGY   Try a simpler problem. Find the sum of the angle measures in a quadrilateral and a pentagon. Try to find a pattern.

A quadrilateral can be divided into two triangles. The sum of the angle measures is 2 × 180°, or 360°.

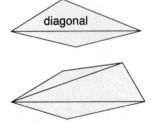

diagonal

A pentagon can be divided into three triangles. The sum of the angle measures is 3 × 180°, or 540°.

Notice that the number of triangles is two less than the number of sides in the polygon. Use this pattern to complete the table.

Name of figure	Triangle	Quadrilateral	Pentagon	Hexagon	Heptagon	Octagon
Number of sides	3	4	5	6	7	8
Number of triangles	1	2	3	4	5	6
Sum of angle measures	1x180° 180°	2x180° 360°	3x180° 540°	4x180° 720°	5x180° 900°	

ANSWER   The angle measures in an octagon total 1,080°.

Look Back   SENSIBLE ANSWER   As the number of sides increases by 1, the number of triangles increases by 1, and the sum of the angle measures increases by 180°. The table shows this pattern.

■ **Talk About Math**   What is the measure of each angle of a regular octagon?

Check Understanding

 Calculator   Use the table in the example for Exercises 1–4.

1. Find the sum of the angle measures of a decagon (10-sided polygon).

2. Find the measure of one angle in a regular decagon.

3. If the sum of the angle measures in a polygon is 720°, into how many triangles was it divided?

4. Name the polygon described in Exercise 3.

Practice

 Calculator   Find each answer.

5. Find the sum of the angle measures in a dodecagon (12-sided polygon).

6. Find the measure of one angle of a regular quadrilateral.

Find the total number of square units in a square that measures

7. 1 unit by 1 unit.   **8.** 2 units by 2 units.   **9.** 3 units by 3 units.

How many more units are in a square

10. 2 units by 2 units than in a square 1 unit by 1 unit?

11. 3 units by 3 units than in a square 2 units by 2 units?

12. What pattern do you notice in Exercises 7–9?

13. Use the pattern to find the number of squares in a square 4 units by 4 units.

| Skills | Review | pages 94–99, 132–135 |

Divide.

1. 705 ÷ 7   **2.** 964 ÷ 6   **3.** 3,011 ÷ 2   **4.** 4,821 ÷ 8

5. 9,020 ÷ 3   **6.** 4,507 ÷ 9   **7.** 1,250 ÷ 5   **8.** 1,255 ÷ 6

9. $11\overline{)72.93}$ **10.** $5\overline{)3.75}$ **11.** $6\overline{)3.114}$ **12.** $18\overline{)93.6}$

13. $9\overline{)57.6}$ **14.** $26\overline{)0.9386}$ **15.** $17\overline{)7.922}$ **16.** $23\overline{)21.298}$

Quadrilaterals

Build Understanding

A. Four Sides, Four Angles
Materials: Dot paper, rulers, protractors
Groups: Small groups of 3 to 6 students

a. A *quadrilateral* is a four-sided polygon. Here are
several types of quadrilaterals.

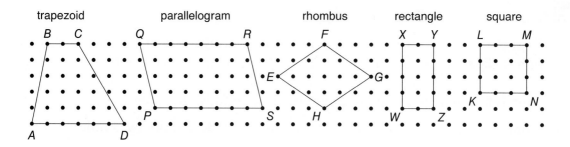

b. Measure the sides of each quadrilateral above and
record the lengths in centimeters.

c. For each quadrilateral, name the pairs of parallel sides.

d. Measure the angles of each quadrilateral. Which angles
are equal in measure? Which are right angles?

e. Describe a trapezoid. Is it a quadrilateral?

f. Describe a parallelogram. How is it like a trapezoid?
How is it different?

g. Describe a rhombus. How is it like a parallelogram?
How is it different?

h. Describe a rectangle. How is it like a rhombus? How is
it different?

i. Describe a square. How is it like a rectangle? How is it
different?

B. The properties of various types of quadrilaterals are summarized below.

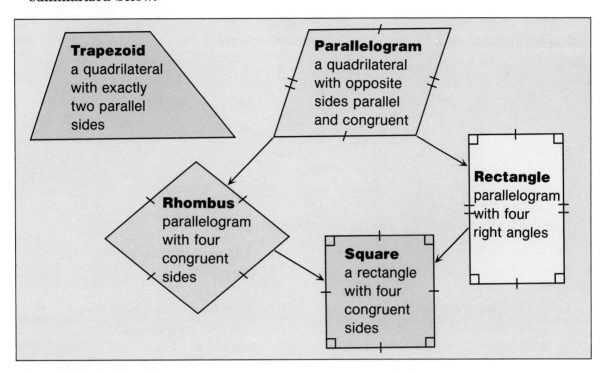

Trapezoid
a quadrilateral with exactly two parallel sides

Parallelogram
a quadrilateral with opposite sides parallel and congruent

Rhombus
parallelogram with four congruent sides

Rectangle
parallelogram with four right angles

Square
a rectangle with four congruent sides

■ **Talk About Math**   Is every square a rectangle? Is every rectangle a square? Why or why not?

Check Understanding

Use the information on pages 174 and 175 to complete each sentence.

1. A trapezoid is a quadrilateral with ___?___ .

2. A parallelogram is a quadrilateral with ___?___ .

3. A rectangle is a parallelogram with ___?___ .

4. A rhombus is a parallelogram with ___?___ .

5. A square is a rectangle with ___?___ .

6. A square is a rhombus with ___?___ .

Practice

Give all of the names that apply to each figure. Use trapezoid, parallelogram, rhombus, rectangle, square.

7. 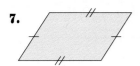 **8.** 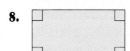 **9.**   **10.**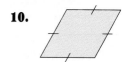

11. 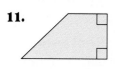 **12.** 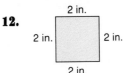 **13.** 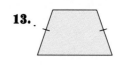 **14.**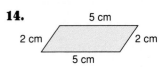

Use dot paper to draw figures that fit the descriptions.

15. A trapezoid with two congruent sides

16. A trapezoid with no congruent sides

17. A parallelogram with four congruent sides that is not a square

18. A rectangle with two sides twice as long as the other two sides

Mixed Practice   Use the information on pages 168–171 and 174–175. Give all names that apply to each figure.

19.  **20.** 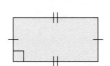 **21.**   **22.**

23.   **24.**   **25.**   **26.**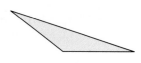

Problem Solving

Critical Thinking   Answer the following questions.

27. What characteristics are needed in a rectangle to make it a square?

28. Can a rhombus have only one pair of parallel sides?

29. Can a trapezoid have two right angles? Can a trapezoid have four right angles? Why or why not?

30. If a rhombus has one right angle, what do you know about the other three angles? What is another name for this figure?

Reading ——— Math

Vocabulary   Match each item in the second column
with the word in the first column which best names it.

1. Point   **a.** A beam of light from a searchlight

2. Line   **b.** A new pencil

3. Line segment   **c.** End of a straight pin

4. Ray   **d.** The floor in your classroom

5. Plane   **e.** A long straight road

6. Intersecting planes **f.** Adjacent walls in a room

Midchapter ——— Checkup

Refer to the diagram for Exercises 1–3.

1. Give two other names for $\overleftrightarrow{DF}$.

2. Name four rays on $\overleftrightarrow{DH}$.

3. Name four rays with endpoint E.

4. Name a polygon with 3 sides.   **5.** Name a polygon with 5 sides.

Identify each triangle as *acute, obtuse,* or *right.* Then
identify each triangle as *scalene, isosceles,* or *equilateral.*

6.   **7.**   **8.**

Give all the names that apply to each figure. Use *trapezoid,*
parallelogram, rhombus, rectangle, and *square.*

9.   **10.** 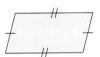   **11.**   **12.**

Number-Sense Project

Look back at pages 160–161.

1. Let one inch represent a mile. Draw a line and mark off 8 one-mile segments. Label them *AB, BC, CD,* and so on. Put point *X* one mile above point *C* and draw line *AX* to represent a line that deviates from the original line by 1 mile in every 2 miles. Measure to determine how much line *AX* deviates from the original line.

a. In 8 miles   **b.** In 6 miles   **c.** In 4 miles   **d.** In 1 mile

2. Now put point *Y* one mile above point *E* and draw line *AY.* Determine how much line *AY* deviates from the original line.

a. In 8 miles

b. In 4 miles

c. In 2 miles

d. In 1 mile

e. How much did the Nascan lines deviate per mile? At this rate, how much would they deviate in 5 miles?

f. If you have noticed a pattern in these exercises, try to determine how much the Nascan lines deviated per foot.

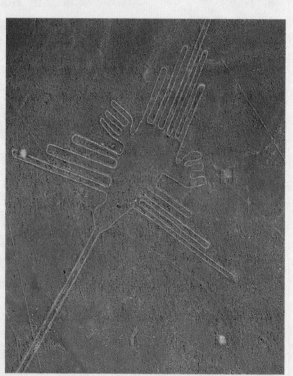

Visual-Thinking Activity

For each exercise, compare the letters. Then decide which number compares to the number in the shaded column in the same way.

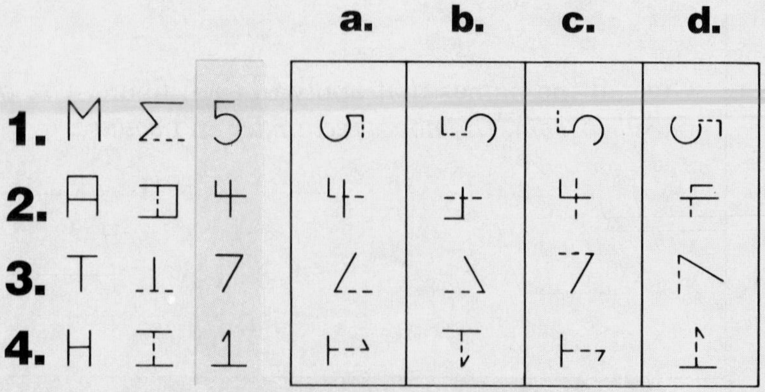

			a.	**b.**	**c.**	**d.**
1. M	Σ	5	�५	५	५	५
2. A	⊟	4	4	4	4	4
3. T	⊥	7	∠	⅃	7	↗
4. H	⊥	1	⊢	⊤	⊢	⊥

Explore with a Computer

Use the *Geometry Workshop Project* for this activity.

1. Look at the angles displayed on the screen. Estimate the measure of each angle.

2. Use the **Angle** option under **Measure** to find the actual measures of the angles. Make a chart like the one on page 166.

3. Bisect angles *DBC* and *CBI*. Are the angles divided into two congruent parts?

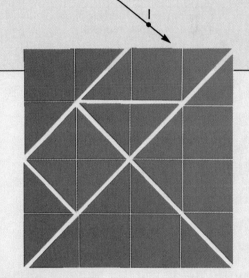

Math-at-Home Activity

An ancient Chinese puzzle, called a tangram, consists of seven pieces which are cut from a square.

1. Work with one or more members of your family. See how many of the figures shown below you can make using tangrams.

2. Use all seven pieces to make three of the following geometric shapes: triangle, rectangle, trapezoid, parallelogram, pentagon, or hexagon.

Circles

Build Understanding

A *polar map* is a map that is centered on the North Pole or the South Pole. The lines running outward like the spokes of a wheel are called meridians of longitude. The **circles** are called parallels of latitude.

Polar maps are used by pilots on flights over polar regions.

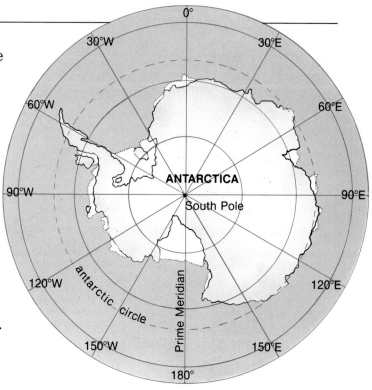

A. All the points on a circle are the same distance from its **center**. A circle is named by its center. Circle O is shown in the diagram.

The distance around a circle is the **circumference**.

A **chord** is any line segment with endpoints on the circle.

A **diameter** is a line segment through the center of the circle with both endpoints on the circle.

A **radius** is a line segment from the center to a point on the circle.

B. The two diameters shown in circle X are perpendicular and form right angles.

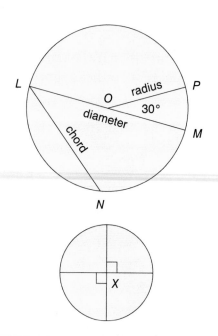

A **central angle** is an angle with its vertex at the center of a circle. $\angle MOP$ is a central angle.

The sum of the central angle measures in a circle is $4 \times 90°$, or $360°$.

■ **Talk About Math** Is a diameter also a chord? Is a chord also a diameter?

Check Understanding

For another example, see Set E, pages 192–193.

Refer to circle O on page 180.

1. Name each radius shown in circle O.

2. What is the measure of $\angle POL$?

3. Is radius $\overline{OP}$ also a chord? Explain.

Practice

For More Practice, see Set E, pages 194–195.

Use the circle at the right.

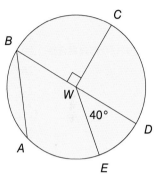

4. Name the circle.

5. Name a diameter.

6. Name each radius.

7. Name two chords.

8. What is the measure of $\angle CWD$?

9. What is the measure of $\angle EWB$?

Mental Math What is the diameter of a circle with a radius of

10. 2 inches?

11. 1 inch?

12. $1\frac{1}{2}$ inches?

Refer to the polar map on page 180. Use a protractor to measure each angle. **Remember** to align one ray with 0° on the protractor.

13. Find the angle between the prime meridian and the meridian labeled 60° E.

14. Find the angle formed by the meridians labeled 30° W and 90° E.

Problem Solving

15. Critical Thinking How are the radius and the diameter of a circle related?

Explore ———— Math

16. Draw two circles with the same center that do not intersect.

17. Draw two circles that intersect in exactly one point.

18. Draw two circles that intersect in exactly two points.

19. Can the circles in Exercise 18 have the same center? Explain.

Use Logical Reasoning

Build Understanding

Ann, Bill, Ceil, Derek, Edna, and Frank are sales managers for Goode and Company. Each day, each manager must talk by phone with each of the other managers. Either person can make the call. What is the fewest telephone calls that can occur?

PROBLEM SOLVING
GUIDE

Understand
QUESTION
FACTS
KEY IDEA

▌▌▶ **Plan and Solve**
STRATEGY
ANSWER

Look Back
SENSIBLE ANSWER
ALTERNATE APPROACH

Understand   QUESTION   What is the fewest possible calls?

FACTS   Six people are talking with each other each day. A call from Ann to Bill is the same as a call from Bill to Ann.

▌▌▶ **Plan and Solve**   STRATEGY   Use logical reasoning. Think of each person as a point on a circle and each telephone call as a segment between two points. Find the total number of segments needed to connect all six points to each other.

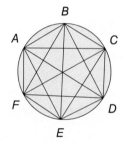

From point A, you can draw five segments.

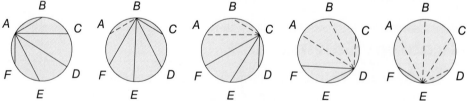

From point B, you can draw four different segments. $\overline{BA}$ is the same as $\overline{AB}$. From point C there are three new segments, from point D two new segments, and from point E one new segment. There are a total of 5 + 4 + 3 + 2 + 1, or 15, segments.

ANSWER   The fewest telephone calls that can take place is 15 calls.

Look Back   ALTERNATE APPROACH   You could list and count the calls: (A–B, A–C, A–D, etc.).

■ **Talk About Math**   Suppose that rather than making telephone calls, each manager gave each other manager a gift. How many gifts would be exchanged?

Check Understanding

At a sales meeting four sales managers shook hands with each other. Let *A, B, C,* and *D* stand for the managers. A handshake between *A* and *B* is the same as one between *B* and *A.*

1. How many segments can you draw from point *A* to the other three points?

2. How many new segments can you draw from point *B* to the other points?

3. How many different segments can you draw from point *C* to each of the other points?

4. How many segments are there in all? How many handshakes?

Practice

Tell if you would use paper and pencil, mental math, or a calculator. Then answer each question.

5. How many calls are made if five managers talk with each other once? if ten managers talk with each other?

6. An office has seven computers. There is one connection between each pair of computers. How many connections are there?

Choose a ———— Strategy

Meeting Halfway   Gail and Juan live 4 miles apart. In how many places could they meet that are exactly 3 miles from Gail's house and 3 miles from Juan's house? Use the scale *1 inch equals 1 mile.*

7. Use dots to show where each person lives. How far apart are the dots?

8. What geometric figure shows all of the points 3 miles from Gail's house? Draw the figure.

9. Show all points that are 3 miles from Juan's house. In how many places could Gail and Juan meet?

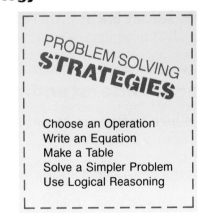

PROBLEM SOLVING
STRATEGIES

Choose an Operation
Write an Equation
Make a Table
Solve a Simpler Problem
Use Logical Reasoning

Congruent and Similar Figures

Build Understanding

Fernando ordered 2 large pictures and 4 smaller pictures. The large pictures are both the same size and shape. The small pictures are the same shape, but not the same size as the larger pictures.

A. *Congruent figures* are the same size and shape. You can decide if two figures are congruent by tracing one of the figures and trying to fit it on the other. Are these pairs of figures congruent? Explain.

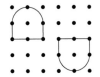 Yes; they are the same size and shape.

 No; they are not the same shape.

 No; they are not the same size.

B. *Similar figures* have the same shape but may differ in size. Are the pairs of figures similar?

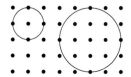 Yes; both circles are the same shape.

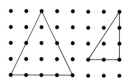 No; the triangles are not the same shape.

■ **Talk About Math** Are all congruent figures similar? Are all similar figures congruent?

Check Understanding

For another example, see Set F, pages 192–193.

1. Which pictures in Fernando's package are similar?

2. Which pictures in Fernando's package are congruent?

Use the figures at the right for Exercises 3–8. Are the figures congruent?

3. *A* and *B*   4. *B* and *C*   5. *B* and *D*

Are the figures similar?

6. *A* and *B*   7. *B* and *C*   8. *B* and *D*

Practice

For More Practice, see Set F, pages 194–195.

Are the figures *congruent, similar,* or *neither?*

9. *P* and *Q*   **10.** *R* and *S*   **11.** *T* and *V*

12. *T* and *U*   **13.** *V* and *Y*   **14.** *W* and *X*

15. *N* and *Z*   **16.** *W* and *Z*   **17.** *O* and *W*

Use dot paper.

18. Sketch a figure that is congruent to rectangle *Z*.

19. Sketch a figure that is similar to but not congruent to triangle *T*.

20. Sketch a figure that is congruent to polygon *R*.

21. Sketch a figure that is similar to triangle *Y*.

22. Sketch a figure that is congruent to square *X*.

23. Critical Thinking   What is the width of a rectangle that is 8 units long and is similar to a rectangle that is 4 units long and 3 units wide?

Are the figures *always* similar, *never* similar, or *sometimes* similar? Sketch figures to explain your answers.

24. Two circles   **25.** Two triangles   **26.** Two squares

27. A rectangle and a triangle   **28.** A rectangle and a trapezoid

Problem Solving

A $\frac{1}{4}$-inch grid has been drawn on the picture at the right.

29. Use inch grid paper. Copy the part of the picture shown in each square onto the corresponding square in your grid. Is your picture similar to the one shown?

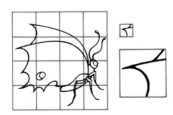

30. How can you make a picture that is congruent to the one shown?

31. How can you make a picture that is similar, but smaller than the one shown?

Transformations

Build Understanding

Iranian families have been making rugs for hundreds of years. Each rug-weaving family uses its own type of pattern.

Many patterns for rugs are made by moving geometric figures in various ways. The figures in this rug have the same size and shape but are in various positions. If you fold the rug in half lengthwise, the two halves of the pattern match. The pattern is *symmetric.*

A *slide, turn,* and *flip* are ways figures can be moved on a plane. These movements are called *transformations.*

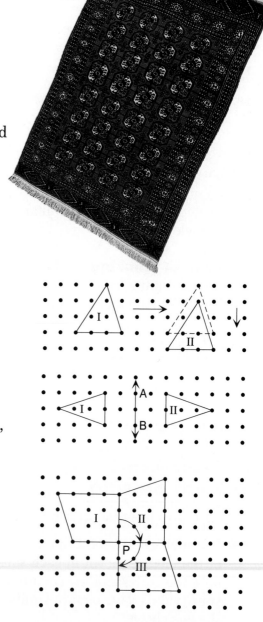

A. A slide moves a figure right, left, up, or down. Triangle II is a result of sliding triangle I six units to the right and one unit down.

B. A flip is a mirror image of a figure. When triangle I is flipped over $\overleftrightarrow{AB}$, the result is triangle II. If you folded the dot paper at $\overleftrightarrow{AB}$, the parts of the triangles would fit exactly.

C. Figures can be turned about a given point. A $\frac{1}{4}$ clockwise turn of figure I about point P results in figure II. A $\frac{1}{4}$ turn is a 90° turn.

A 90° clockwise turn of figure II about point P results in figure III. A $\frac{1}{2}$, or 180° clockwise turn of figure I also results in figure III.

A 180° clockwise turn of a figure is not the same as a mirror image.

■ **Talk About Math**   What happens if you turn a figure 180° and then turn it 180° again about the same point?

Check Understanding

For another example, see Set G, pages 192–193.

Use Examples A, B, and C for Exercises 1–3.

1. A ___?___ moves a figure up, down, left, or right.

2. A $\frac{1}{4}$ clockwise turn is a ___?___° turn.

3. A ___?___ is a mirror image of a figure.

Practice

For More Practice, see Set G, pages 194–195.

In Exercises 4–9, describe how to move from figure I to figure II. Write *slide, flip,* or *turn.* The figures in Exercises 7–9 are used by some Iranian rug weavers.

4.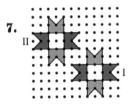

5.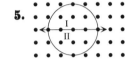

6.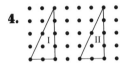

7.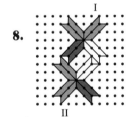

8.

9.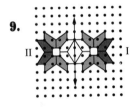

Use dot paper.

10. Draw triangle *ABC.* Show a flip over $\overline{BC}$.

11. Draw triangle *LMN.* Show a slide 2 units right and 3 units down.

Problem Solving

Solve each problem.

12. **Use Data** Copy trapezoid *ABCD* in Example A on page 174 on dot paper. Turn it 180° clockwise about point *A* and show the result.

13. **Critical Thinking** Use the Navajo rug shown at the right. Give two examples of how transformations are used in the rug's pattern.

14. Start with a geometric figure and use slides, flips, and turns to create your own rug pattern. Explain how you used transformations to make your pattern.

Navajo tradition states that the Navajo people have always made rugs and blankets like this one.

Three-Dimensional Figures

Build Understanding

Mark Weinberg makes paperweights in the shape
of various three-dimensional figures. Several are
shown below.

a. **b.** **c.** **d.** 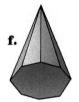 **e.** **f.**

A. A *polyhedron* is a three-dimensional figure made
up of flat surfaces called *faces*. The faces are
polygons. The polyhedron at the right has 6 faces,
12 *edges* (segments where two faces meet), and
8 *vertices* (points where three or more edges meet).

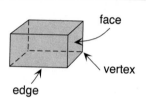

face

vertex

edge

B. A *prism* is a polyhedron with two
parallel and congruent *bases*.
A prism is named by the
shape of its bases.

Triangular prism   Square prism   Pentagonal prism

C. A *pyramid* is a polyhedron with
one base. A pyramid is named by the
shape of its base.

Triangular pyramid   Rectangular pyramid   Hexagonal pyramid

D. Three-dimensional figures with curved surfaces are *not* polyhedrons.

A *cylinder* has two circular
bases which are parallel and
congruent.

A *cone* has one circular
base. The curved surface
meets in a point.

A *sphere* has no base. Every point
on a sphere is the same distance
from the center.

■ **Talk About Math**   In a prism, what is the shape of the faces
that are not bases? Answer the same question about pyramids.

188

Check Understanding

For another example, see Set H, pages 192–193.

Give the name of the three-dimensional figure suggested by each paperweight on page 188.

1. a   **2.** b   **3.** c   **4.** d   **5.** e   **6.** f

Practice

For More Practice, see Set H, pages 194–195.

Use the figure at the right for Exercises 7–10.

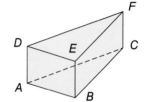

7. Name the faces.   **8.** Name the edges.

9. Name the vertices.   **10.** Name the figure.

Copy and complete the table. **Remember** that prisms and pyramids are named by the shape of their bases.

	Triangular prism	Rectangular prism	Pentagonal prism	Triangular pyramid	Rectangular pyramid	Pentagonal pyramid
Number of faces	**11.**	**12.**	**13.**	**14.**	**15.**	**16.**
Number of vertices	**17.**	**18.**	**19.**	**20.**	**21.**	**22.**
Number of edges	**23.**	**24.**	**25.**	**26.**	**27.**	**28.**

Use the table above.

29. How is the number of faces of a prism related to the number of sides of a base?

30. How is the number of faces of a pyramid related to the number of sides of the base?

Problem Solving

Solve each problem.

31. Susan bought a paperweight in the shape of a hexagonal pyramid. How many faces, vertices, and edges does the paperweight have?

32. Mark made a paperweight in the shape of a prism with nine faces. How many sides does each base of the paperweight have?

33. Critical Thinking What is the least number of faces a prism can have? a pyramid?

34. A cube is a prism in which all faces are squares. Is a square prism always a cube?

Skills Review

1. Name two rays with endpoint *C*.

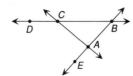

2. Give the measure of ∠*CAB*.

3. Draw an angle of 80°.

Name each polygon.

4.

5.

6. Is triangle *MNP* acute, right, or obtuse?

7. Is triangle *MNP* scalene, isosceles, or equilateral?

Give all the names for each figure. Use *trapezoid*, *parallelogram*, *rhombus*, *rectangle*, and *square*.

8.

9.

10. What is the diameter of a circle with a radius of 3 meters?

11. Are figures *a* and *c* congruent, similar, or neither?

12. Which figure is a slide of figure *a*?

Name each figure.

13.

14.

15.

Problem-Solving Review

Solve each problem.

16. The ingredients for each enchilada cost Mrs. Rodriguez $0.29. Find the cost of the ingredients for 36 enchiladas.

17. Sam drove to his uncle's farm and back, 143 miles each way. How many miles did he drive in all?

18. A triangle has two angles with a measure of 35° each. What is the measure of the third angle?

19. Jeff works after school at a grocery store. He earns $5.36 per hour. How much does he earn in 10 hours?

20. The photography club sold peanuts to raise money for equipment. They sold 115 bags for 35 cents each. How much money did they raise?

21. A can of tomato juice costs $1.39 and contains 48 ounces. To the nearest cent, how much does 1 ounce of tomato juice cost?

22. **Data File** Use the data on pages 266–267. Trace the pattern and make an octahedron. How many faces, edges, and vertices does an octahedron have?

23. **Make a Data File** Use an encyclopedia or other reference book to find the distance from earth to five stars. Make a table listing the stars in order, starting with the closest one to the earth.

1. Give two other names for $\overleftrightarrow{AC}$.

2. Name two lines which intersect $\overleftrightarrow{AC}$.

3. Name two rays with endpoint C.

4. Name an acute angle.

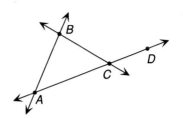

Find each answer.

5. $8\overline{)969}$	**6.** $3.05 + 79.9$	**7.** $5\overline{)4,258}$	**8.** $6\overline{)1,502}$
9. $342 \div 56$	**10.** $1,598 \div 38$	**11.** $3.28 \div 4$	**12.** 268×76
13. $8\overline{)0.064}$	**14.** $25\overline{)5.125}$	**15.** $7.5 - 4.28$	**16.** $0.7\overline{)0.35}$
17. $25.6 \div 32$	**18.** 0.0044×0.6	**19.** $3.03 \div 0.03$	**20.** $264 \div 4.4$

Write each number in standard form.

21. $(6 \times 10^3) + (4 \times 10^1) + 9$

22. Six and five millionths

Name each figure.

23. 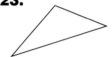 **24.**   **25.**   **26.**   **27.**

Compare. Use >, <, or =.

28. $5.09 \;▦\; 3.99$ **29.** $0.597 \;▦\; 0.5795$ **30.** $4.605 \;▦\; 46.05$

Use mental math to find each answer.

31. 400×30	**32.** $8,000 \div 4$	**33.** $20 \times 1,000$	**34.** $12,060 \div 60$
35. $63.25 \div 10$	**36.** 21×80	**37.** $0.02 \div 100$	**38.** 0.0087×100

Are the figures *always* similar, *never* similar, or *sometimes* similar?

39. Two squares   **40.** Two triangles   **41.** A circle and a square

Solve each equation.

42. $d + 50 = 96$ **43.** $4 \times q = 48$ **44.** $99 = f + 55$ **45.** $168 = h \times 6$

Reteaching

Set A   pages 162–163

A line is named by two points, but a line has no endpoints.

A ray is named by two points, but only one of these is an endpoint.

Remember that two lines in a plane are parallel if they never meet.

Use this figure for Exercises 1 and 2.

1. Name two rays with endpoint *A*.

2. Name two lines that pass through *C*.

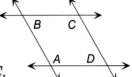

Set B   pages 164–167

All angles are one of three types.

a. Acute: measure is less than 90°
b. Obtuse: measure is greater than 90°
c. Right: measure is 90°

Remember that the symbol ⊥ means "is perpendicular to."

1. Name all acute angles.

2. Name all right angles.

3. Name all obtuse angles.

Set C   pages 168–169

This polygon is a quadrilateral with two pairs of equal sides and four right angles.

Remember that a polygon with all sides congruent and all angles the same size is a regular polygon.

Match each description in Exercises 1 and 2 with quadrilateral *a, b,* or *c.*

1. A quadrilateral with two right angles and two parallel sides

2. A quadrilateral whose opposite sides are parallel

Set D   pages 170–171

The sum of the measures of the angles of a triangle is 180°. Find the measure of ∠*DEF*.

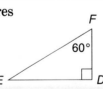

Add the known measures.

∠*EDF* is a right angle → 90 + 60 = 150

Subtract this sum from 180 to find the unknown measure.

180 − 150 = 30 → The measure of ∠*DEF* is 30°.

Remember that an acute triangle has three acute angles.

Find the measure of angle *A*.

1.

2.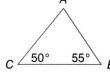

Set E   pages 180–181

Why isn't segment AB
a diameter of this
circle?

The endpoints of segment AB are on the
circle, but segment AB does not go through
the center of the circle.

Remember that a radius of a circle has
endpoints at the center and on the circle.

This circle has
more than
one diameter.
Name the diameters.

Set F   pages 184–185

Are these figures congruent, similar, or
neither?

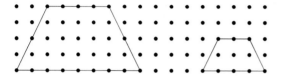

They are similar because they have the
same shape. They are not congruent
because they are not the same size.

Remember that congruent figures are
also similar, but similar figures are not
necessarily congruent.

Which triangles are congruent to
triangle ABC?

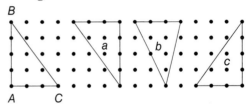

Set G   pages 186–187

There are three ways to move a polygon.

Slide: the polygon moves right, left, up, or
down.

Flip: The polygon is flipped over a line and
forms a mirror image of itself.

Turn: The polygon turns on a point.

Remember that two consecutive
turns of 180° returns a figure to its
original position.

Is polygon II formed by a flip, slide,
or turn?

Set H   pages 188–189

In a rectangular pyramid the base is a
rectangle.

The pyramid has eight
edges: $\overline{AB}$, $\overline{BC}$, $\overline{CD}$,
$\overline{DA}$, $\overline{EA}$, $\overline{EB}$, $\overline{EC}$, $\overline{ED}$;
and five vertices: A,
B, C, D, E.

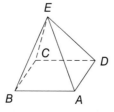

Remember that prisms and pyramids are
named by the shape of their bases.

Use the figure below for Exercises 1–3.

1. Name the figure.

2. Name the vertices.

3. Name the edges.

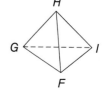

More Practice

Set A   pages 162–163

Use the figure at the right for Exercises 1–5.

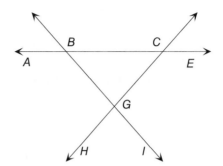

1. Name $\overleftrightarrow{AE}$ in three different ways.

2. Name two lines that contain G.

3. Give another name for $\overrightarrow{BE}$.

4. Name three line segments on $\overleftrightarrow{HC}$.

5. Name three rays with endpoint B.

Set B   pages 164–167

Draw an angle with the given measure. Bisect it.

1. 35°   **2.** 80°   **3.** 130°   **4.** 160°

Use the figure at the right for Exercises 5–7.

5. Name all acute angles.

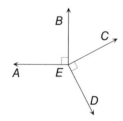

6. Name all right angles.

7. Name all obtuse angles.

Set C   pages 168–169

Name each polygon.

1.   **2.**   **3.**   **4.**

Sketch the following.

5. A quadrilateral with one right angle   **6.** A quadrilateral with two right angles

Set D   pages 170–171

Tell whether you would use mental math, paper and pencil, or
a calculator to find the measure of angle A. Then find the measure.

1. 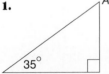   **2.**    **3.** 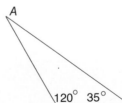   **4.**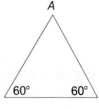

Set E pages 180–181

Use the circle at the right.

1. Name the circle.   2. Name a diameter.

3. Name each radius.   4. Name two chords.

5. What is the measure of $\angle RST$?

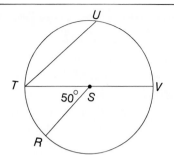

Answer each question.

6. Use a compass to draw a circle with a diameter of 3 inches.

7. Draw three circles with the same center that do not intersect.

Set F pages 184–185

Tell whether the figures are congruent, similar, or neither.

1. A and J 2. B and H 3. C and G

4. D and I 5. E and K 6. F and L

Use dot paper.

7. Sketch a figure congruent to quadrilateral I.

8. Sketch a figure similar to, but not congruent to rectangle A.

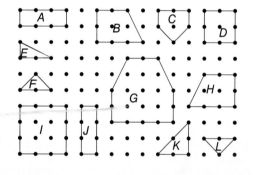

Set G pages 186–187

Describe how to move from figure I to figure II. Write slide, flip, or turn.

1.   2.   3.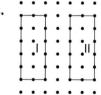

Use dot paper.

4. Draw right triangle ABC. Show a turn of 90°.

5. Draw triangle XYZ. Show a slide 4 units down and 4 units right.

Set H pages 188–189

Use the figure at the right for Exercises 1–4.

1. Name the faces.   2. Name the edges.

3. Name the vertices.   4. Name the figure.

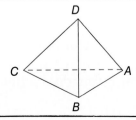

Enrichment

Constructing the Perpendicular Bisector of a Line Segment

A bisector of a line segment divides the segment into two congruent parts. A **perpendicular bisector** bisects a segment and is perpendicular to it. In the diagram at the right, $\overleftrightarrow{CD}$ and $\overleftrightarrow{GH}$ are bisectors of $\overline{XY}$. The perpendicular bisector of $\overline{XY}$ is $\overleftrightarrow{GH}$.

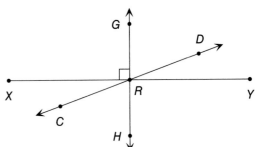

Follow these steps to construct the perpendicular bisector of $\overline{ST}$.

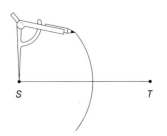

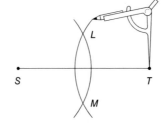

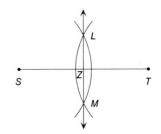

| **Step 1** With point S as center, open your compass more than halfway to point T. Then draw an arc that intersects $\overline{ST}$. | **Step 2** Using the same opening and point T as center, draw an arc that intersects the first arc. Label points L and M. | **Step 3** Draw $\overleftrightarrow{LM}$. Line LM is the perpendicular bisector of $\overline{ST}$. $\overline{SZ} \cong \overline{ZT}$ |

Draw segment JK so that it is 3 inches long. Use your drawing to answer Exercises 1–5.

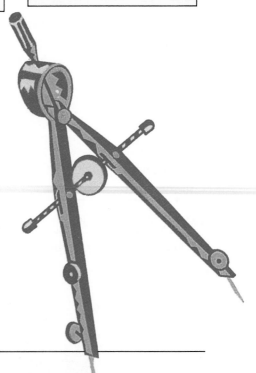

1. Use the steps above to construct $\overleftrightarrow{AB}$, the perpendicular bisector of $\overline{JK}$. Label the point where $\overline{JK}$ intersects $\overleftrightarrow{AB}$ as N.

2. Without measuring, give the length of $\overline{JN}$. Use your ruler to check your answer.

3. Use a protractor to measure $\angle ANK$ and $\angle JNA$. Is $\overleftrightarrow{AB}$ perpendicular to $\overline{JK}$?

4. Draw another bisector of $\overline{JK}$.

5. How many bisectors does a line segment have?

Chapter 5 Review/Test

1. Name two rays on $\overleftrightarrow{PR}$.

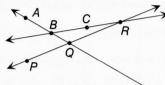

2. Which lines intersect at point Q?

3. Are lines BC and PQ parallel?

4. Measure the angle and tell whether it is right, acute, or obtuse.

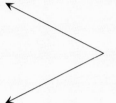

5. Draw an angle of 100°.

6. A triangle has angles of 30°, 40°, and 110°. Is the triangle right, acute, or obtuse?

7. Two angles of a triangle have measures of 50° and 70°. What is the measure of the third angle?

8. What kind of polygon does this appear to be? Use all terms that apply.

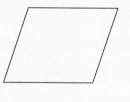

9. Is this triangle equilateral, isosceles, or scalene?

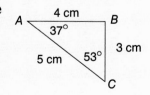

10. Name each radius shown of circle P.

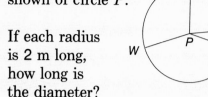

11. If each radius is 2 m long, how long is the diameter?

Use the diagram.

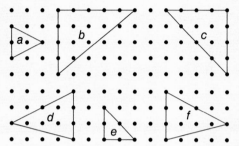

12. Which figure is similar to figure c?

13. Which figure is a flip of figure d?

14. A pyramid has a base with 7 sides. How many faces, edges, and vertices does it have?

15. Find the measure of one angle of a regular pentagon.

Read the problem below. Then answer the question.

There are 9 people in a room. Each person shakes hands with each of the other people in the room. How many handshakes are there in all?

16. Choose the most sensible answer.

    a. 9   b. 36   c. 90

17. **Write About Math** In Problem 9, how do you know that the triangle is a right triangle?

Relating Number Theory and Fraction Concepts

Did You Know:
The Federal government owns about 1,200,000 square miles of the land in the United States. Several famous national parks are shown here.

Number-Sense Project

Estimate

Guess the total area of the United States. What fraction of the total area do you think is owned by the federal government?

Gather Data

Find the total area of the United States, including land and water. Round to the nearest hundred thousand square miles.

Analyze and Report

How many square miles make up one half of the United States? Does the government own more or less than this amount? About what fraction of the total area is owned by the government?

Divisibility Rules

Build Understanding

A teacher pairs 115 students for tennis and assigns teams of five for basketball. Will any students be left over after each assignment?

A. Teamwork

Groups: With a partner

a. If you divide any whole number by 2 and there is a remainder of zero, the number is ***divisible*** by 2. Use division to test each of the following numbers for divisibility by 2, 3, 5, and 10:

12, 20, 27, 33, 38, 46, 54, 63, 65, 72, 85, 93, 100, 115

b. Make a table like this one. Record your results.

Divisible by 2	
Divisible by 3	
Divisible by 5	
Divisible by 10	

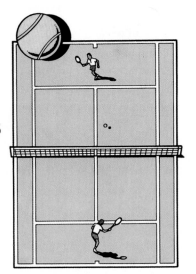

c. Without dividing, how can you tell that a number is divisible by 2?

d. Without dividing, how can you tell that a number is divisible by 5? by 10?

e. For each number that is divisible by 3, find the sum of the digits. How can you tell without dividing that a number is divisible by 3?

B. 🖩 **Calculator** A calculator shows divisibility by giving a whole-number quotient.

Divide 23,450 by 7.

23450 ÷ 7 = *3350*

23,450 is divisible by 7.

Divide 23,450 by 6.

23450 ÷ 6 = *3908.3333*

23,450 is not divisible by 6.

■ **Talk About Math** If a number is divisible by 10, must it be divisible by 5? If a number is divisible by 5, must it be divisible by 10? Explain your thinking.

Check Understanding

For another example, see Set A, pages 226–227.

Give the missing words.

1. If a number is divisible by 3, the sum of its digits is __?__.

2. If a number is divisible by 2, the number is __?__.

3. If a number is divisible by 5, its ones digit is ▦ or ▦.

Practice

For More Practice, see Set A, pages 228–229.

Complete the chart.

Number	Divisible by 2	3	5	10
105	4.	5.	6.	7.
480	8.	9.	10.	11.
1,306	12.	13.	14.	15.
3,892	16.	17.	18.	19.
6,999	20.	21.	22.	23.

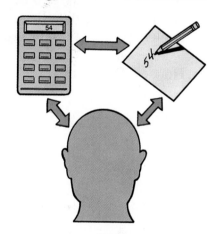

Use your head before grabbing a calculator.

For Exercises 24–35, tell whether you would use paper and pencil, mental math, or a calculator. Then tell whether the number is divisible by 6.

24. 54   25. 900   26. 1,799   27. 1,500   28. 63   29. 420

30. 123   31. 182   32. 4,332   33. 9,006   34. 1,542   35. 998

36. Look at Exercises 24–35. Which numbers are divisible by 2? by 3?

37. **Number Sense** Write a way to determine divisibility by 6.

Problem Solving

Solve each problem.

38. If 115 students enrolled in physical education are assigned to teams of nine students for baseball, will any students be left over after the assignments are made?

39. If 113 students attended class on Monday and Friday, 110 on Tuesday, 114 on Wednesday, and 115 on Thursday, find the average attendance for the week.

Prime and Composite Numbers

Build Understanding

An American Indian folk tale tells of a young warrior who wanted to paint a picture of the sunset. The warrior was unable to match the colors of the sunset until the Great Spirit created bright, colorful wild flowers to be used as paintbrushes. These flowers became known as "Indian paintbrushes."

A. How can 8 Indian paintbrushes be arranged in equal rows?

2 rows of 4
$2 \times 4 = 8$

4 rows of 2
$4 \times 2 = 8$

1 row of 8
$1 \times 8 = 8$

8 rows of 1
$8 \times 1 = 8$

Since $8 = 2 \times 4$ and $8 = 1 \times 8$, the *factors* of 8 are 1, 2, 4, and 8. When 8 is divided by any of its factors the remainder is 0.

B. Find all the factors of 12.

$12 = 1 \times 12$ $12 = 2 \times 6$ $12 = 3 \times 4$

The factors of 12 are 1, 2, 3, 4, 6, and 12.

C. Find all the factors of 17.

$17 = 1 \times 17$

The factors of 17 are 1 and 17.

A *prime number* is a whole number greater than 1 that has exactly two factors: the number itself and 1. A *composite number* is a whole number greater than 0 that has more than two factors.

D. Use a factor tree to write 60 as a product of prime numbers.

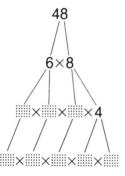

In a factor tree the branches lead to factors.

60 = 2 × 30

60 = 2 × 2 × 15

60 = 2 × 2 × 3 × 5

The **_prime factorization_** of 60 is $2 \times 2 \times 3 \times 5$, or $2^2 \times 3 \times 5$.

E. Write the prime factorization of 200 using exponents.

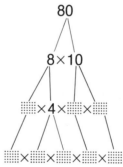

Remember that the order of factors can be changed because of the commutative property.

The prime factorization of 200 is $2 \times 2 \times 2 \times 5 \times 5$, or $2^3 \times 5^2$.

■ **Talk About Math** What number is a factor of all whole numbers? Why is it not used in writing prime factorizations or in factor trees?

Check Understanding

For another example, see Set B, pages 226–227.

Copy and complete each factor tree.

1.

48

6×8

▦×▦×▦×4

▦×▦×▦×▦×▦

2.

110

2×▦

2×5×▦

3.

80

8×10

▦×4×▦

▦×▦×▦×▦×▦

4.

252

6×42

▦×▦×7×▦

▦×▦×▦×▦×▦

5. Give the prime factorization using exponents for Exercises 1–4.

Practice

For More Practice, see Set B, pages 228–229.

Although the Dutch and Belgians grow over 10,000 varieties of tulips, this flower also thrives in Iran, Armenia, Turkey, and North Africa. Using as many vases as needed, draw dots to show all the ways the given number of tulips can be placed so that each vase has the same number of tulips.

6. 15 tulips   **7.** 20 tulips   **8.** 36 tulips

9. 23 tulips   **10.** 31 tulips   **11.** 27 tulips

Netherlands' traditional costumes include wooden shoes, full trousers for men, and skirts and lace caps for women.

Tell if each number is prime or composite.

12. 89   **13.** 67   **14.** 51   **15.** 107   **16.** 227   **17.** 159   **18.** 132

19. 235   **20.** 173   **21.** 127   **22.** 592   **23.** 103   **24.** 1,111   **25.** 6,855

Give a factor tree for each number. **Remember** to use
divisibility rules to help you.

26. 28   **27.** 125   **28.** 180   **29.** 84   **30.** 220   **31.** 216   **32.** 945

For each number, write the prime factorization using exponents.

33. 252   **34.** 450   **35.** 108   **36.** 500   **37.** 400   **38.** 375   **39.** 343

40. 105   **41.** 92   **42.** 160   **43.** 189   **44.** 1,024   **45.** 299   **46.** 4,123

▦ Calculator Write the prime factorization for each number
using exponents.

47. 22,720   **48.** 386,100   **49.** 163,800   **50.** 372,708   **51.** 381,150

Problem Solving

Find all the prime numbers from 1 to 100.

52. List all the numbers from 1 to 100.
Cross out 1 because it is neither prime nor
composite.
Circle 2 and cross out all the even numbers.
Circle 3 and cross out the numbers divisible by 3.
Circle 5 and cross out the numbers divisible by 5.
Circle 7 and cross out the numbers divisible by 7.
Any numbers not crossed out should be circled.
These are the prime numbers from 1 to 100.

Organize your work
to help you think clearly.

▶ Write an equation. Then give the answer.

A
L
G
E
B
R
A

53. The dandelion, the best known flower in
the world, probably originated in central
Asia. Each flower is really a cluster of
about 200 tiny flowers, or florets. About
how many florets would there be in 150
dandelions?

The word *dandelion* comes
from the French *dent de lion*—
"lion's tooth."

Don't Sleep, Count Sheep A sheepherder designed the corral pictured below to separate sheep into holding pens A, B, C, and D. The sheep enter the corral at the top. As they approach each triangular obstacle, half of the sheep turn left and half of the sheep turn right.

If 760 sheep enter the corral, about how many will arrive at each pen?

54. If 16 sheep enter the corral, will the same number of sheep arrive at each pen?

55. If there are 64 sheep in the herd, how many will arrive at each pen?

56. How many sheep will be in each pen if the herd contains 128 sheep? 760 sheep?

Greatest Common Factor

Build Understanding

A. Find all the factors of 12 and all the factors of 18. Remember that factors of 12 are numbers that can be multiplied to give 12.

Think: What numbers can be multiplied to give 12?

1 × 12
2 × 6
3 × 4
4 × 3 ⎫
6 × 2 ⎬ The factors repeat
12 × 1 ⎭ after 3 × 4.

The factors of 12 are
1, 2, 3, 4, 6, and 12.

Think: What numbers can be multiplied to give 18?

1 × 18
2 × 9
3 × 6
6 × 3 ◄——Stop when factors
           begin to repeat.

The factors of 18 are
1, 2, 3, 6, 9, and 18.

B. Look at the lists of factors of 12 and 18. Factors of both 12 and 18 are 1, 2, 3, and 6. Therefore, 1, 2, 3, and 6 are *common factors* of 12 and 18.

```
                                              ——— common factors
Factors of 12:  (1) (2) (3)  4  (6)      12
Factors of 18:  (1) (2) (3)     (6)  9       18
                                              ——— greatest common factor
```

The *greatest common factor*, or GCF, of 12 and 18 is 6.

C. Use prime factorizations to find the GCF of 84 and 120.

84 = 2 × 2 × 3 × 7   Find the product of the
120 = 2 × 2 × 2 × 3 × 5   common prime numbers.

2 × 2 × 3 = 12
The GCF of 84 and 120 is 12.

■ **Talk About Math**   If two numbers have a GCF of 10, what can you say about their ones digits? If two numbers have a GCF of 2, what else do you know about these numbers?

The greatest common factor of 24 and 60 is also 12.

Check Understanding

For another example, see Set C, pages 226–227.

Copy and complete.

1. The factors of 30 are 1, ▦, ▦, 5, ▦, ▦, ▦, and 30.

2. The common factors of 30 and 45 are 1, ▦, ▦, and ▦.

3. The GCF of 30 and 45 is ▦.

4. The GCF of 60 and 72 is ▦.

Practice

For More Practice, see Set C, pages 228–229.

Find the GCF for each set of numbers.

5. 8, 12 **6.** 10, 25 **7.** 8, 11 **8.** 15, 50 **9.** 12, 32

10. 27, 66 **11.** 21, 35 **12.** 24, 60 **13.** 18, 48 **14.** 120, 180

15. 225, 150 **16.** 100, 200 **17.** 6, 12, 30 **18.** 16, 80, 48

19. 14, 42, 49 **20.** 8, 16, 20 **21.** 6, 16, 30 **22.** 114, 133, 209

Calculator Find the GCF for each set of numbers.

23. 115, 230, 345 **24.** 102, 85, 34 **25.** 120, 84, 60

26. 138, 140, 198 **27.** 104, 152, 168 **28.** 165, 198, 154

Problem Solving

Solve each problem.

29. Critical Thinking A company must design boxes to hold 12 bars of soap in a single layer. Each bar is 3 in. long and 2 in. wide. Sketch boxes of every size that can hold 12 bars. Show all arrangements of the bars in each box.

30. Number Sense Which number between 1 and 28 has the greatest number of factors? List the factors.

Skills	Review	pages 46–47

Multiply.

1. 1×78 **2.** 0×709 **3.** 6×278 **4.** 9×180 **5.** 7×698

Try and Check

PROBLEM SOLVING
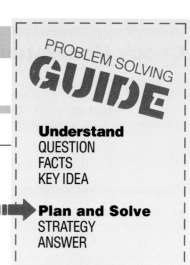
GUIDE

Understand
QUESTION
FACTS
KEY IDEA

▶ **Plan and Solve**
STRATEGY
ANSWER

Look Back
SENSIBLE ANSWER
ALTERNATE APPROACH

Build Understanding

Brenda makes square plaques out of square mirrors. She notices that the length of one side of a plaque is an odd number. She wonders if the whole perimeter will be an odd number. How can she decide?

Understand A square has four equal sides. The perimeter is the distance around the square. To find the perimeter, multiply the length of a side by 4.

▶ **Plan and Solve** STRATEGY Try and check whole numbers for the length of a side. See if the perimeter is an even or an odd number.

Length of a side (s)	1	2	3	6	10	25	36
Perimeter (4 × s)	4	8	12	24	40	100	144

ANSWER In each case, the perimeter is an even number.

Look Back ALTERNATE APPROACH Since the length of a side of a square is multiplied by 4 to find the perimeter, the perimeter has a factor of 4, or two factors of 2. It is always an even number.

■ **Talk About Math** All the sides of a regular polygon are equal. How do you find the perimeter of a regular polygon with three sides? with five sides?

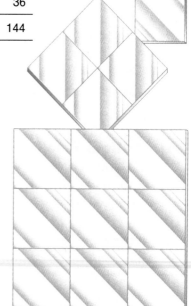

Check Understanding

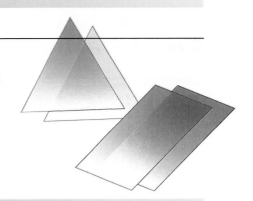

1. If the lengths of the sides of an equilateral triangle are whole numbers, can the perimeter be an odd number? a prime number?

2. If the lengths of the sides of a rectangle are whole numbers, can the perimeter be an odd number? a prime number?

Practice

A
L
G
E
B
R
A

▶ **Number Sense**   For Exercises 3–14, try and check to determine if the resulting number is always even, is always odd, or can be either even or odd. Write *Always even*, *always odd*, or *even or odd*.

3. The sum of two even numbers

4. The sum of two odd numbers

5. The sum of an even and an odd number

6. The product of two even numbers

7. The product of two odd numbers

8. The product of an even and an odd number.

9. $b + 1$ 10. $2z$ 11. $2r + 1$ 12. $3h + 1$ 13. $5n$ 14. m^2

Solve each problem.

15. Brenda sells her plaques for $3.95 a square foot. How much will she charge for a square plaque with a 4-foot side?

16. Brenda will make a rectangular plaque from 35 square mirrors. In how many different ways can she arrange the squares? Sketch each arrangement.

Reading ——— Math

Vocabulary   Write *true* or *false*. If false, correct the sentence by replacing the underlined part.

1. Even numbers are divisible by <u>5</u>.

2. The prime factorization of 30 is <u>5 × 6</u>.

3. A number that has exactly two factors is a <u>prime</u> number.

4. The numbers 25 and 50 are <u>composite</u> numbers.

Equal Fractions

Build Understanding

A carpenter must be able to read fractions of an inch on a ruler quickly.

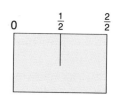

A. Nailing Down Fractions
Materials: Ruler, paper, scissors
Groups: With a partner

a. Use your ruler to make inch models like the ones on this page. Cut out your inch models.

b. Name the other two marks on the fourths model. Name all the marks on the other models.

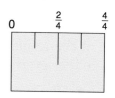

c. Locate $\frac{2}{8}$. Use your inch models to find two other fractions equal to $\frac{2}{8}$. By lining up the zero points on your models, you can see which fractions are equal to each other. Repeat for $\frac{6}{8}$.

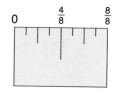

d. List all the fractions shown on the models that are equal to: $\frac{1}{2}$, $\frac{1}{4}$, $\frac{3}{8}$, $\frac{5}{8}$, $\frac{3}{4}$, $\frac{7}{8}$, and $\frac{2}{2}$.

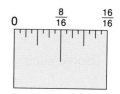

e. What is the most common name for $\frac{2}{2}$, $\frac{4}{4}$, $\frac{8}{8}$, and $\frac{16}{16}$? Name some other fractions that are equal to them.

B. You can multiply or divide the numerator and denominator of a fraction by the same nonzero number to find equal fractions.

$$\frac{6}{8} = \frac{6 \times \boxed{3}}{8 \times \boxed{3}} = \frac{18}{24}$$ You are multiplying by a name for 1.

$$\frac{6}{8} = \frac{6 \div \boxed{2}}{8 \div \boxed{2}} = \frac{3}{4}$$ You are dividing by a name for 1.

C. Use common factors to write $\frac{12}{18}$ in lowest terms. A fraction is in **lowest terms** when 1 is the greatest common factor of the numerator and denominator.

$$\frac{12}{18} = \frac{12 \div \boxed{2}}{18 \div \boxed{2}} = \frac{6}{9}$$ The greatest common factor of 6 and 9 is 3.

$$\frac{6}{9} = \frac{6 \div \boxed{3}}{9 \div \boxed{3}} = \frac{2}{3}$$ The greatest common factor of 2 and 3 is 1.

The fractions $\frac{12}{18}$ and $\frac{6}{9}$ are not in lowest terms, but $\frac{2}{3}$ is in lowest terms.

D. Use the greatest common factor to write $\frac{8}{12}$ in lowest terms.

The greatest common factor of 8 and 12 is 4. Two different methods are shown.

$$\frac{8}{12} = \frac{8 \div \boxed{4}}{12 \div \boxed{4}} = \frac{2}{3} \qquad \frac{8}{12} = \frac{\boxed{2 \times 2} \times 2}{\boxed{2 \times 2} \times 3} = \frac{2}{3}$$
$$\qquad\quad\uparrow \qquad\qquad\qquad\qquad \uparrow$$
$$\qquad\quad \text{GCF} \qquad\qquad\qquad\quad \text{GCF}$$

The fraction $\frac{8}{12}$ in lowest terms is $\frac{2}{3}$.

■ **Talk About Math** How many fractions are equal to $\frac{9}{15}$? How many of these fractions are in lowest terms?

Check Understanding

For another example, see Set D, pages 226–227.

Find the missing numbers.

1. $\frac{2}{5} = \frac{2 \times \blacksquare}{5 \times \blacksquare} = \frac{10}{25}$ **2.** $\frac{3}{4} = \frac{3 \times \blacksquare}{4 \times \blacksquare} = \frac{9}{12}$ **3.** $\frac{12}{15} = \frac{2 \times 2 \times 3}{3 \times 5} = \frac{\blacksquare}{\blacksquare}$

4. $\frac{2}{3} = \frac{\blacksquare}{9}$ **5.** $\frac{3}{5} = \frac{\blacksquare}{30}$ **6.** $\frac{18}{3} = \frac{\blacksquare}{1}$ **7.** $\frac{3}{12} = \frac{1}{\blacksquare}$ **8.** $\frac{15}{18} = \frac{5}{\blacksquare}$

Give the greatest common factor of the numerator and denominator.

9. $\frac{2}{9}$ **10.** $\frac{2}{4}$ **11.** $\frac{10}{24}$ **12.** $\frac{13}{15}$ **13.** $\frac{8}{14}$ **14.** $\frac{7}{8}$ **15.** $\frac{25}{30}$ **16.** $\frac{18}{24}$

17. Which fractions in Exercises 9–16 are in lowest terms?

Practice

For More Practice, see Set D, pages 228–229.

Find the missing numbers.

18. $\frac{2}{3} = \frac{\blacksquare}{6} = \frac{6}{\blacksquare} = \frac{\blacksquare}{12}$ **19.** $\frac{3}{12} = \frac{\blacksquare}{4} = \frac{2}{\blacksquare} = \frac{\blacksquare}{16}$ **20.** $\frac{1}{5} = \frac{\blacksquare}{20} = \frac{2}{\blacksquare} = \frac{6}{\blacksquare}$

21. $\frac{2}{8} = \frac{\blacksquare}{4} = \frac{\blacksquare}{32} = \frac{6}{\blacksquare}$ **22.** $\frac{3}{7} = \frac{21}{\blacksquare} = \frac{42}{\blacksquare} = \frac{\blacksquare}{84}$ **23.** $\frac{5}{9} = \frac{10}{\blacksquare} = \frac{15}{\blacksquare} = \frac{\blacksquare}{36}$

Write three fractions equal to the given fraction.

24. $\frac{1}{2}$ **25.** $\frac{7}{9}$ **26.** $\frac{3}{8}$ **27.** $\frac{2}{6}$ **28.** $\frac{15}{20}$ **29.** $\frac{6}{10}$ **30.** $\frac{18}{22}$ **31.** $\frac{6}{7}$

32. $\frac{4}{9}$ **33.** $\frac{5}{15}$ **34.** $\frac{1}{6}$ **35.** $\frac{2}{9}$ **36.** $\frac{12}{16}$ **37.** $\frac{3}{20}$ **38.** $\frac{16}{38}$ **39.** $\frac{33}{36}$

Write each fraction in lowest terms. **Remember** to use the GCF.

40. $\frac{12}{15}$ **41.** $\frac{12}{36}$ **42.** $\frac{9}{16}$ **43.** $\frac{11}{22}$ **44.** $\frac{14}{49}$ **45.** $\frac{21}{30}$ **46.** $\frac{48}{72}$ **47.** $\frac{66}{88}$

48. $\frac{30}{85}$ **49.** $\frac{18}{34}$ **50.** $\frac{24}{108}$ **51.** $\frac{36}{132}$ **52.** $\frac{26}{78}$ **53.** $\frac{24}{56}$ **54.** $\frac{54}{63}$ **55.** $\frac{14}{35}$

56. $\frac{50}{75}$ **57.** $\frac{18}{20}$ **58.** $\frac{40}{60}$ **59.** $\frac{4}{44}$ **60.** $\frac{43}{90}$ **61.** $\frac{124}{155}$ **62.** $\frac{121}{132}$ **63.** $\frac{91}{105}$

Problem Solving

Solve each problem.

64. If Mr. Hazen cuts a piece of lumber 54 inches long from a board that is 75 inches long, how long will the remaining piece be?

65. Ralph spent 6 hours building bookshelves. He earns $7.35 per hour. What amount did he earn?

Number Sense Write each answer in lowest terms. What fraction of the whole numbers

66. from 1 to 100 are even numbers?

67. from 1 to 100 are square numbers?

68. from 1 to 50 are prime numbers?

69. from 1 to 30 are composite numbers?

Midchapter ———— Checkup

Complete the chart.

Divisible by

Number	2	3	5	10
62	**1.**	**2.**	**3.**	**4.**
297	**5.**	**6.**	**7.**	**8.**
315	**9.**	**10.**	**11.**	**12.**
1,500	**13.**	**14.**	**15.**	**16.**

Tell if each number is prime or composite.

17. 62   **18.** 103   **19.** 249

For each number, write the prime factorization using exponents.

20. 80   **21.** 202   **22.** 420

Find the GCF for each set of numbers.

23. 39, 26   **24.** 49, 21   **25.** 90, 76   **26.** 400, 360   **27.** 16, 24, 50

28. When is the product of two numbers a prime number?

29. When is the product of two numbers an even number?

30. Write $\frac{28}{49}$ in lowest terms.

31. Write $\frac{25}{125}$ in lowest terms.

Problem-Solving Workshop

Real-Life Decision Making

Suppose you want to phone your cousin who lives in another state. The cost to call her long distance depends on the time of day you call and how long you talk.

	11:00 P.M. to 8:00 A.M.	8:00 A.M. to 5:00 P.M.	5:00 P.M. to 11:00 P.M.
Cost of First Minute	$0.25	$0.62	$0.38
Cost for Each Additional Minute	$0.18	$0.43	$0.26

1. How much will it cost to make a 1-minute call at 2 P.M.? at 6 P.M.? at midnight?

2. Would it be better to talk for 3 minutes at 2 P.M., at 6 P.M., or at midnight? Why?

Number-Sense Project

Look back at pages 198-199.

1. About how many square miles of land in the United States is owned by the federal government?

2. About $\frac{1}{2}$ of the federal land is controlled by the Bureau of Land Management. About how many square miles is this?

3. About $\frac{1}{4}$ of the federal land is controlled by the Forest Service. About how many square miles is this?

4. About $\frac{1}{12}$ of the federal land is controlled by the National Park Service. About how many square miles is this?

Explore with a Computer

Use the *Fractions Workshop Project* for this activity.

1. At the computer, you will see a circle that has been marked and shaded.

2. Find all the equivalent fractions the computer model can show. Select the **Mark** option and find how else you can mark the model. What other equal parts can be selected to divide the circle? How many of each of these new parts are shaded? Try out all the combinations and record the results.

3. Make a new model that shows $\frac{6}{8}$. Repeat Step 2 to find all the equivalent fraction models the computer can show.

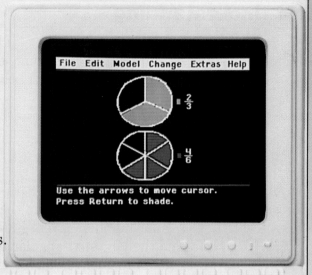

Explore as a Team

In 1742, a mathematician named Christian Goldbach proposed that every even number greater than 2 could be written as the sum of two primes.

In this activity you will work as a team on Goldbach's Conjecture.

1. Begin by making a list of prime numbers less than 100.

2. Make a chart of the even numbers 2-100.

3. Divide the numbers among the members of your team. Each member should write each number as the sum of two primes. Work as a team on the numbers for which a sum of primes could not be found.

4. Discuss any patterns and strategies that were helpful in completing the task.

5. Which prime numbers did you use the most? Were there any prime numbers you never used as addends?

TIPS FOR WORKING TOGETHER

Involve your whole group. Help everyone to participate.

Find a Pattern

Build Understanding

Tina has 58 sequins to decorate the back of a blouse. How many rows of sequins can be in a triangle? The first four **triangular numbers** are shown below..

First: 1

Second: 3

Third: 6

Fourth: 10

PROBLEM SOLVING GUIDE

Understand
QUESTION
FACTS
KEY IDEA

▶ **Plan and Solve**
STRATEGY
ANSWER

Look Back
SENSIBLE ANSWER
ALTERNATE APPROACH

Understand   Find a relationship among the triangular numbers given. Extend it to find the largest triangular number less than or equal to 58.

 Plan and Solve   STRATEGY   Looking for a relationship among numbers suggests the strategy *find a pattern*. Look for a way to get from each triangular number to the next.

Try adding 2. 1 + 2 = 3, but 3 + 2 ≠ 6. Try adding other numbers. 1 + 2 = 3, 3 + 3 = 6, 6 + 4 = 10.

Notice the pattern. To find the next triangular number, add 5. Use the pattern to find the next few triangular numbers:

$$1 \longrightarrow 3 \longrightarrow 6 \longrightarrow 10 \longrightarrow 15 \longrightarrow 21 \longrightarrow 28 \longrightarrow 36 \longrightarrow 45 \longrightarrow 55 \longrightarrow 66$$
$$+2 \quad +3 \quad +4 \quad +5 \quad +6 \quad +7 \quad +8 \quad +9 \quad +10 \quad +11$$

ANSWER   Tina can make a triangle with 10 rows.

Look Back   ALTERNATE APPROACH   Write the numbers in the following way:

1st: 1	2nd: 3	3rd: 6	4th: 10	5th: 15	6th: 21
$\frac{1 \times 2}{2}$	$\frac{2 \times 3}{2}$	$\frac{3 \times 4}{2}$	$\frac{4 \times 5}{2}$	$\frac{5 \times 6}{2}$	$\frac{6 \times 7}{2}$

■ **Talk About Math** Which approach would you use to find the twenty-fifth triangular number? What is that number?

Check Understanding

1. The first three square numbers are shown at the right. Use dots to show the next two square numbers.

column

← row

1   4   9

2. If you were to draw the 50th square number, how many rows and columns would you make? What is that number?

3. Write a method for finding square numbers.

Practice

Solve each problem.

4. Three rectangular numbers are shown. Use dots to show the next two rectangular numbers for this set.

2   6   12

5. Look for a pattern in the rectangular numbers. Then find the sixth rectangular number.

6. Find the tenth rectangular number and the fiftieth rectangular number.

7. Write a rule to find any rectangular number.

8. Write a rule to find any triangular number.

Explore ———— Math

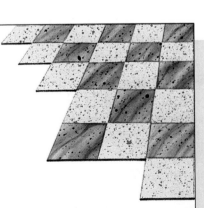

Suppose you want to tile a rectangular floor area that is 40 in. long and 24 in. wide. Square tiles come with sides 1, 2, 3, 5, 8, 10, and 12 inches long. Use grid paper to explore ways of placing tiles on the floor.

9. Find the largest size of tile that could be used to cover the floor without cutting any tiles.

Multiples and Least Common Multiple

Build Understanding

A. The band is practicing for a concert. In one song the bass drum player beats the drum every fourth beat, and the triangle player strikes the triangle every fifth beat. When will the bass drum and the triangle be played on the same beat?

List some multiples of 4 and 5.

The first six multiples of 4 are:

4 × 1 = 4	4 × 4 = 16
4 × 2 = 8	4 × 5 = 20
4 × 3 = 12	4 × 6 = 24

Multiples of 4: 4, 8, 12, 16, 20, 24, . . .

The first six multiples of 5 are:

5 × 1 = 5	5 × 4 = 20
5 × 2 = 10	5 × 5 = 25
5 × 3 = 15	5 × 6 = 30

Multiples of 5: 5, 10, 15, 20, 25, 30, . . .

On the 20th beat the triangle and the bass drum will both be played.

B. Find the least common multiple of 12 and 15. The *least common multiple (LCM)* of 12 and 15 is the least number that is a multiple of 12 and 15.

List the multiples of 12 and 15.

	× 1	× 2	× 3	× 4	× 5	× 6	× 7
12	12	24	36	48	60	72	84
15	15	30	45	60	75	90	105

The LCM of 12 and 15 is 60.

c. ▦ **Calculator** You can use a calculator to help you find multiples. To find multiples of 12 using a calculator, use this key sequence:

Press: 12 ⊞ ⌷=⌷ ⌷=⌷ 24 ⌷=⌷ 36 ⌷=⌷ 48 ⌷=⌷ 60 ⌷=⌷ 72 ⌷=⌷

Display: *84.*

■ **Write About Math** Write a problem to find the least common multiple of three numbers. Solve.

218

Check Understanding

For another example, see Set E, pages 226–227.

Which of the following numbers are

1. factors of 6? 12, 1, 3, 24, 2, 6

2. multiples of 12? 6, 2, 12, 24, 48, 4

3. **Number Sense** How many common multiples of 6 and 8 are there? Is there a greatest common multiple of 6 and 8? Explain.

Practice

For More Practice, see Set E, pages 228–229.

For Exercises 4–27, tell whether you would use mental math or paper and pencil. Then find the LCM.

4. 16, 12   5. 14, 35   6. 33, 35   7. 7, 20   8. 16, 24   9. 30, 10

10. 36, 15   11. 13, 18   12. 6, 20   13. 5, 18   14. 24, 30   15. 36, 72

16. 15, 39   17. 10, 17   18. 18, 27   19. 65, 20   20. 28, 16   21. 64, 32

22. 15, 40   23. 26, 39   24. 4, 18   25. 24, 48   26. 14, 63   27. 40, 7

Mixed Practice Write the GCF and LCM.

28. 15, 25   29. 12, 30   30. 7, 10   31. 21, 35   32. 11, 33   33. 51, 60

34. 18, 45   35. 9, 23   36. 14, 42   37. 16, 52   38. 32, 128   39. 8, 108

40. 20, 26   41. 24, 66   42. 28, 24   43. 39, 52   44. 30, 48   45. 40, 25

Problem Solving

Solve each problem.

46. **Calculator** In the song in Example A, how many times in the first 100 beats will the bass drum and triangle play together?

47. Ruth spent $162.50 for flute lessons. Each lesson cost $12.50. How many lessons did Ruth have?

48. **Estimation** Barbara and Paula spent $9.50 on a book of piano duets and $3.95 on other sheet music. Barbara paid $6.50. Did Paula pay more than or less than Barbara? Explain.

Common Denominators

Build Understanding

A. After a party $\frac{1}{3}$ of one pizza and $\frac{5}{6}$ of another pizza were left. How could the pizza be cut into equal pieces?

Any Way You Slice It
Materials: Ruler, scissors
Groups: Small groups of 3 or 4 students

a. To represent whole pizzas, draw and cut out two rectangles 5 cm by 12 cm.

b. To represent the parts of the pizzas that are left, cut out two more rectangles, each 5 cm wide. How long should the rectangle be for $\frac{1}{3}$ of a pie? for $\frac{5}{6}$?

c. Use paper folding or a ruler to divide the two smaller rectangles into equal pieces. What fraction of a whole is each of your pieces?

d. How would you cut the $\frac{5}{6}$ pizza? How would you cut the $\frac{1}{3}$ pizza?

e. A ***common denominator*** for two fractions is a common multiple of the denominators.

B. Write $\frac{3}{4}$ and $\frac{1}{6}$ using the ***least common denominator***, or ***LCD***.

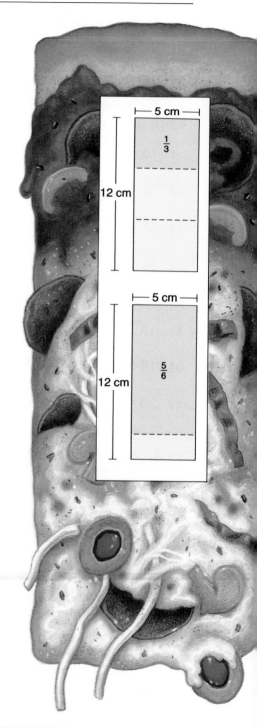

Find the least common multiple of the denominators.

Multiples of 4: 4   8   12   12 is the least common multiple,
Multiples of 6: 6   12   18   or LCM, of 4 and 6.

$$\frac{3}{4} = \frac{}{12} \qquad \frac{1}{6} = \frac{}{12}$$ Multiply each fraction by 1.

$$\frac{3}{4} \times \frac{3}{3} = \frac{9}{12} \qquad \frac{1}{6} \times \frac{2}{2} = \frac{2}{12}$$ Remember that multiplying by 1 does not change the value of the number.

$\frac{3}{4}$ and $\frac{1}{6}$ can be written as $\frac{9}{12}$ and $\frac{2}{12}$.

■ **Talk About Math** Can the least common denominator
of two fractions be equal to one of the denominators?
Give two examples to support your answer.

Check Understanding

For another example, see Set F, pages 226–227.

Complete each exercise.

1. $\frac{1}{4} = \frac{1 \times \blacksquare}{4 \times \blacksquare} = \frac{\blacksquare}{36}$ **2.** $\frac{8}{9} = \frac{8 \times \blacksquare}{9 \times \blacksquare} = \frac{\blacksquare}{36}$ **3.** $\frac{3}{7} = \frac{3 \times \blacksquare}{7 \times \blacksquare} = \frac{\blacksquare}{35}$

Write each pair of fractions using the least common denominator.
Remember to find the least common multiple of the denominators.

4. $\frac{3}{5}, \frac{1}{2}$ **5.** $\frac{3}{4}, \frac{5}{11}$ **6.** $\frac{7}{9}, \frac{2}{3}$ **7.** $\frac{1}{12}, \frac{5}{24}$ **8.** $\frac{2}{7}, \frac{5}{6}$ **9.** $\frac{4}{7}, \frac{3}{21}$ **10.** $\frac{1}{4}, \frac{3}{7}$

Practice

For More Practice, see Set F, pages 228–229.

Write each pair of fractions using the least common denominator.

11. $\frac{3}{4}, \frac{3}{8}$ **12.** $\frac{2}{5}, \frac{7}{10}$ **13.** $\frac{3}{4}, \frac{1}{5}$ **14.** $\frac{5}{12}, \frac{2}{3}$ **15.** $\frac{1}{3}, \frac{3}{10}$ **16.** $\frac{3}{5}, \frac{1}{4}$ **17.** $\frac{5}{8}, \frac{7}{12}$

18. $\frac{5}{6}, \frac{5}{7}$ **19.** $\frac{3}{6}, \frac{3}{8}$ **20.** $\frac{11}{12}, \frac{3}{4}$ **21.** $\frac{9}{10}, \frac{7}{8}$ **22.** $\frac{5}{6}, \frac{1}{2}$ **23.** $\frac{3}{20}, \frac{7}{25}$ **24.** $\frac{5}{9}, \frac{11}{21}$

25. $\frac{7}{8}, \frac{5}{12}$ **26.** $\frac{3}{10}, \frac{8}{15}$ **27.** $\frac{3}{4}, \frac{2}{15}$ **28.** $\frac{1}{16}, \frac{5}{24}$ **29.** $\frac{8}{9}, \frac{5}{6}$ **30.** $\frac{6}{7}, \frac{1}{28}$ **31.** $\frac{3}{5}, \frac{7}{21}$

32. $\frac{3}{5}, \frac{2}{3}$ **33.** $\frac{4}{5}, \frac{7}{15}$ **34.** $\frac{1}{2}, \frac{2}{3}$ **35.** $2, \frac{5}{8}$ **36.** $4, \frac{5}{6}$ **37.** $5, \frac{12}{13}$ **38.** $9, \frac{11}{20}$

39. Write the fractions in Exercises 11–17 with a common
denominator that is not the least common denominator.

Problem Solving

Four friends shared a pizza. Mary ate $\frac{1}{3}$ of the pizza,
Alicia and Martha each ate $\frac{1}{4}$, and Beth ate $\frac{1}{6}$.

40. Into how many equal slices did they
need to cut the pizza?

41. How many slices of the pizza did
each girl eat?

42. Use Data Beth made a dessert that served three people and
contained 1 cup of whole-milk ricotta cheese. How many milligrams
of calcium did each serving have? Use the table on page 71.

Comparing and Ordering Fractions

Build Understanding

The Highland Middle School newspaper surveyed 96 sixth-grade students about how they listen to music. They used a circle graph to display the results.

A. Do more students listen to tapes or to CDs?

Compare $\frac{1}{3}$ and $\frac{1}{4}$.

Find the least common denominator of 3 and 4.

$$\frac{1}{3} = \frac{4}{12} \qquad \frac{1}{4} = \frac{3}{12}$$

Write $\frac{1}{3}$ and $\frac{1}{4}$ using 12 as the new denominator. Compare the numerators.

$$\frac{4}{12} > \frac{3}{12}, \text{ so } \frac{1}{3} > \frac{1}{4}.$$

More students listen to tapes than listen to CDs.

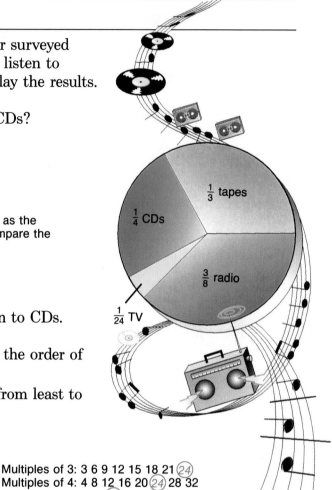

$\frac{1}{3}$ tapes

$\frac{1}{4}$ CDs

$\frac{3}{8}$ radio

$\frac{1}{24}$ TV

B. Starting with the least popular, what is the order of popularity of radio, tapes, and CDs?
Write the fractions $\frac{1}{3}$, $\frac{1}{4}$, and $\frac{3}{8}$ in order from least to greatest.

Find the least common denominator for the fractions.

Multiples of 3: 3 6 9 12 15 18 21 (24)
Multiples of 4: 4 8 12 16 20 (24) 28 32
Multiples of 8: 8 16 (24) 32 40

The LCD is 24.

$$\frac{1 \times 8}{3 \times 8} = \frac{8}{24} \qquad \frac{1 \times 6}{4 \times 6} = \frac{6}{24} \qquad \frac{3 \times 3}{8 \times 3} = \frac{9}{24}$$

$$\frac{6}{24} < \frac{8}{24} < \frac{9}{24}, \text{ so } \frac{1}{4} < \frac{1}{3} < \frac{3}{8}.$$

Starting with the least popular, the order is CDs, tapes, and radio.

■ **Write About Math** Compare $\frac{1}{5}$ and $\frac{1}{6}$. Write a method to compare fractions mentally when both numerators are 1.

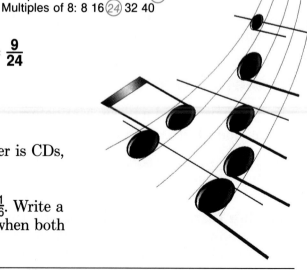

Check Understanding

For another example, see Set G, pages 226–227.

1. Explain how to compare fractions when the denominators are the same.

Copy and complete. Replace ▦ with <, >, or =.

2. $\frac{5 \times 2}{6 \times 2} = $ ▦; $\frac{1 \times 3}{4 \times 3} = $ ▦; $\frac{5}{6}$ ▦ $\frac{1}{4}$

3. $\frac{2}{15} = $ ▦; $\frac{3}{10} = $ ▦; $\frac{2}{15}$ ▦ $\frac{3}{10}$

Practice

For More Practice, see Set G, pages 228–229.

Mental Math Compare the fractions. Use <, >, or =.

4. $\frac{3}{5}$ ▦ $\frac{4}{5}$ **5.** $\frac{5}{5}$ ▦ $\frac{6}{6}$ **6.** $\frac{1}{3}$ ▦ $\frac{1}{2}$ **7.** $\frac{1}{9}$ ▦ $\frac{1}{3}$ **8.** $\frac{2}{5}$ ▦ $\frac{2}{7}$ **9.** $\frac{4}{9}$ ▦ $\frac{4}{5}$

Compare the fractions. Use <, >, or =.

10. $\frac{5}{6}$ ▦ $\frac{4}{6}$ **11.** $\frac{3}{4}$ ▦ $\frac{3}{5}$ **12.** $\frac{2}{7}$ ▦ $\frac{1}{4}$ **13.** $\frac{3}{8}$ ▦ $\frac{2}{5}$ **14.** $\frac{3}{10}$ ▦ $\frac{1}{4}$ **15.** $\frac{9}{16}$ ▦ $\frac{7}{12}$

16. $\frac{8}{12}$ ▦ $\frac{2}{3}$ **17.** $\frac{5}{8}$ ▦ $\frac{2}{3}$ **18.** $\frac{9}{10}$ ▦ $\frac{7}{9}$ **19.** $\frac{15}{20}$ ▦ $\frac{3}{4}$ **20.** $\frac{10}{35}$ ▦ $\frac{4}{5}$ **21.** $\frac{7}{40}$ ▦ $\frac{9}{25}$

22. $\frac{5}{8}$ ▦ $\frac{8}{10}$ **23.** $\frac{3}{7}$ ▦ $\frac{7}{14}$ **24.** $\frac{8}{32}$ ▦ $\frac{2}{8}$ **25.** $\frac{14}{22}$ ▦ $\frac{6}{8}$ **26.** $\frac{8}{9}$ ▦ $\frac{20}{26}$ **27.** $\frac{5}{45}$ ▦ $\frac{9}{81}$

Write the fractions in order from least to greatest.

28. $\frac{3}{8}, \frac{3}{4}, \frac{2}{5}$ **29.** $\frac{1}{2}, \frac{1}{3}, \frac{1}{5}$ **30.** $\frac{5}{6}, \frac{3}{4}, \frac{1}{2}$ **31.** $\frac{2}{5}, \frac{3}{10}, \frac{1}{6}$ **32.** $\frac{5}{12}, \frac{4}{9}, \frac{2}{5}$ **33.** $\frac{13}{16}, \frac{9}{10}, \frac{17}{20}$

34. $\frac{2}{3}, \frac{4}{9}, \frac{3}{5}$ **35.** $\frac{9}{19}, \frac{5}{8}, \frac{1}{2}$ **36.** $\frac{11}{12}, \frac{13}{14}, \frac{8}{9}$ **37.** $\frac{1}{9}, \frac{2}{19}, \frac{4}{27}$ **38.** $\frac{7}{18}, \frac{3}{8}, \frac{4}{9}$ **39.** $\frac{10}{17}, \frac{7}{10}, \frac{13}{20}$

Problem Solving

Solve each problem.

40. In a survey, $\frac{3}{4}$ of the sixth-grade students said they have a radio and $\frac{5}{8}$ said they have a TV. Do more of the students have radios or TVs?

41. Mavis spent $9.95 on a tape and $12.95 on a CD. How much did she spend?

42. Of Jamie's tapes, $\frac{1}{15}$ are blues, $\frac{1}{2}$ are folk, and $\frac{13}{30}$ are country. What music does he have the most of?

Skills Review

Is each number divisible by 2? by 3? by 5? by 10?

1. 40 **2.** 432 **3.** 360 **4.** 141

Tell if each number is prime or composite.

5. 19 **6.** 24 **7.** 216 **8.** 23

9. 171 **10.** 85 **11.** 47 **12.** 92

13. Write the prime factorization of 120 using exponents.

Find the greatest common factor for each set of numbers.

14. 12, 18 **15.** 55, 33 **16.** 36, 63

Write three fractions equal to the given fraction.

17. $\frac{1}{3}$ **18.** $\frac{2}{5}$ **19.** $\frac{3}{15}$ **20.** $\frac{4}{6}$

Write each fraction in lowest terms.

21. $\frac{4}{8}$ **22.** $\frac{8}{12}$ **23.** $\frac{16}{48}$ **24.** $\frac{9}{15}$

Find the least common multiple for each set of numbers.

25. 8, 12 **26.** 35, 20 **27.** 7, 10

Write the fractions using the least common denominator.

28. $\frac{2}{3}, \frac{3}{4}$ **29.** $\frac{2}{5}, \frac{5}{6}$

Compare. Use $<$, $>$, or $=$.

30. $\frac{4}{5} \blacksquare \frac{2}{3}$ **31.** $\frac{3}{10} \blacksquare \frac{1}{4}$

32. $\frac{1}{2} \blacksquare \frac{3}{6}$ **33.** $\frac{5}{6} \blacksquare \frac{6}{7}$

Problem-Solving Review

Solve each problem.

34. Ace Rental offers a car for $99 per week with 500 free miles. After the first 500 miles, the cost is 21¢ per mile. Best Buy Rentals offers a car for $21 per day and 21¢ cents per mile. Which would you choose for a 5-day, 1,000-mile trip?

35. It took Mr. Kohl 7 hours and 43 minutes to drive 357 miles. Estimate the average rate of speed in miles per hour.

36. What fraction of the numbers from 1 to 25 are prime numbers?

37. The ages of five cousins can be written as 5^2, 2^3, 3^3, 3^2, and 4^2. Write their ages in order from youngest to oldest.

38. On a test, Jason answered $\frac{9}{11}$ of the questions correctly, and Mark answered $\frac{8}{9}$ of the questions correctly. Write each score as a decimal to the nearest hundredth. Which boy had a higher score?

39. **Data File** Use the data on pages 266–267. List seven animals in order from slowest runner to fastest runner.

40. **Make a Data File** Use your local telephone book to compare the cost of making a 1-minute call to each of 5 other countries. What does it cost for a 3-minute call to the place that is the farthest away?

Write each fraction as a decimal. Use a bar for repeating decimals.

1. $\frac{1}{4}$ **2.** $\frac{5}{8}$ **3.** $\frac{1}{6}$ **4.** $\frac{4}{9}$ **5.** $\frac{4}{5}$ **6.** $\frac{7}{12}$

Describe how to move from figure I to figure II. Write *slide, flip,* or *turn.*

7.    **8.**   **9.**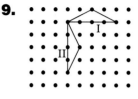

Estimate. Then find each answer.

10. 29×50 **11.** $33.8 - 2.94$ **12.** 4.3×0.44 **13.** $7.5 \times 1,000$

14. $546 \div 5$ **15.** $1,765 \div 45$ **16.** $13.72 \div 4$ **17.** $4.5 + 7.0 + 3.8$

Round 125.6085 to the nearest

18. thousandth.   **19.** tenth.   **20.** one.   **21.** hundred.

Write each fraction in lowest terms.

22. $\frac{5}{10}$ **23.** $\frac{6}{8}$ **24.** $\frac{10}{25}$ **25.** $\frac{12}{18}$ **26.** $\frac{8}{32}$ **27.** $\frac{20}{30}$

28. What is the diameter of a circle with a radius of 3 inches?

Write each number in standard form.

29. $2^5 \times 3^2$ **30.** $1^8 \times 8^2$ **31.** $2^3 \times 5^2$ **32.** $3^2 \times 4^2 \times 0^2$

Solve each equation.

33. $4 \times r = 64$ **34.** $s \times 9 = 9$ **35.** $12 = t \times 2$ **36.** $45 = 15 \times u$

37. Find the measure of angle A in triangle ABC.

38. Is triangle ABC acute, right, or obtuse?

39. Is triangle ABC scalene, isosceles, or equilateral?

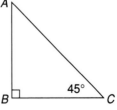

40. How many faces, edges, and vertices does a square prism have?

Write the fractions in order from least to greatest.

41. $\frac{1}{2}, \frac{1}{3}, \frac{1}{4}$ **42.** $\frac{3}{5}, \frac{3}{4}, \frac{2}{3}$ **43.** $\frac{7}{10}, \frac{1}{2}, \frac{3}{5}$ **44.** $\frac{2}{3}, \frac{3}{4}, \frac{5}{8}$

Reteaching

Set A   pages 200–201

The number 720 is divisible by:
2 because 720 is an even number;
3 because 7 + 2 + 0 = 9 and 9 is divisible by 3;
5 because 720 ends in 0;
10 because 720 ends in 0.

Remember that a number divisible by 5 is not divisible by 10 unless the number ends in 0.

Which of these numbers is divisible by

117	920
834	507

1. 2?   **2.** 3?   **3.** 5?   **4.** 10?

Set B   pages 202–205

Use a factor tree to write the prime factorization of 54.

$$54$$
$$6 \times 9$$
$$2 \times 3 \times 3 \times 3$$

$$54 = 6 \times 9$$
$$= 2 \times 3 \times 3 \times 3$$

Prime factorization: ⟶ = 2 × 3 × 3 × 3
Using exponents: ⟶ = 2 × 3³

Remember that an exponent tells how many times a number is multiplied by itself.

Write the prime factorization for each number using exponents.

1. 150   **2.** 204   **3.** 455

4. 176   **5.** 351   **6.** 600

Set C   pages 206–207

Find the greatest number that is a factor of both 12 and 20. This is the greatest common factor, or GCF.
Factors of 12: 1, 2, 3, 4, 6, 12
Factors of 20: 1, 2, 4, 5, 10, 20
Common factors of 12 and 20: 1, 2, 4
GCF of 12 and 20: 4

Remember that the GCF of two numbers is less than or equal to the smaller of the two numbers.

Find the GCF for each set of numbers.

1. 6, 15   **2.** 20, 32   **3.** 15, 32

4. 14, 49   **5.** 25, 40   **6.** 12, 48, 54

Set D   pages 210–213

Write two fractions equal to $\frac{8}{12}$. Divide the numerator and denominator by a common factor.

$\frac{8}{12} = \frac{8 \div 4}{12 \div 4} = \frac{2}{3}$ You are dividing by $\frac{4}{4}$ or 1.

You can also multiply the fraction by 1.

$\frac{8}{12} = \frac{8 \times 2}{12 \times 2} = \frac{16}{24}$

Both $\frac{2}{3}$ and $\frac{16}{24}$ equal $\frac{8}{12}$.

Remember that to find an equal fraction, multiply or divide the numerator and denominator by the same nonzero number.

Write three fractions equal to the given fraction.

1. $\frac{6}{15}$ **2.** $\frac{5}{8}$ **3.** $\frac{15}{20}$

4. $\frac{1}{3}$ **5.** $\frac{24}{32}$ **6.** $\frac{50}{75}$

Set E   pages 218–219

Find the least common multiple (LCM) of 6 and 10.

List some multiples of 6 and 10.

	× 1	× 2	× 3	× 4	× 5
6	6	12	18	24	30
10	10	20	30	40	50

The LCM of 6 and 10 is 30.

Remember that a multiple of a number is the product of the number and any nonzero whole number.

Find the LCM for each pair of numbers.

1. 6, 15   2. 5, 7   3. 4, 10

4. 16, 20   5. 18, 8   6. 21, 6

7. 25, 15   8. 40, 30   9. 100, 35

Set F   pages 220–221

A common denominator for two fractions is a common multiple of the denominators. The least common denominator, LCD, is the least common multiple.

Write $\frac{7}{8}$ and $\frac{1}{12}$ using the LCD.

The LCM of 8 and 12 is 24.

Since $8 \times 3 = 24, \frac{7}{8} \times \frac{3}{3} = \frac{21}{24}$.

Since $12 \times 2 = 24, \frac{1}{12} \times \frac{2}{2} = \frac{2}{24}$.

Remember that multiplying a fraction by 1 does not change the value of the fraction.

Write each pair of fractions using the least common denominator.

1. $\frac{2}{5}, \frac{1}{6}$ 2. $\frac{1}{3}, \frac{1}{6}$ 3. $\frac{7}{12}, \frac{3}{4}$

4. $\frac{7}{10}, \frac{5}{6}$ 5. $\frac{4}{5}, \frac{5}{8}$ 6. $\frac{1}{2}, \frac{21}{100}$

7. $\frac{4}{5}, \frac{2}{3}$ 8. $\frac{3}{8}, \frac{9}{10}$ 9. $\frac{5}{12}, \frac{7}{18}$

Set G   pages 222–223

To compare fractions that have different denominators, write the fractions using the LCD.

Compare $\frac{5}{6}$ and $\frac{7}{8}$.

$\frac{5}{6} = \frac{5 \times 4}{6 \times 4} = \frac{20}{24}$

$\frac{7}{8} = \frac{7 \times 3}{8 \times 3} = \frac{21}{24}$

Since $\frac{20}{24} < \frac{21}{24}, \frac{5}{6} < \frac{7}{8}$.

Remember that the symbols $>$ and $<$ open toward the greater number. For example, $\frac{5}{6} < \frac{7}{8}$ and $\frac{7}{8} > \frac{5}{6}$.

Compare the fractions. Use $<$, $>$, or $=$.

1. $\frac{4}{10}$ ⬚ $\frac{50}{100}$ 2. $\frac{3}{4}$ ⬚ $\frac{1}{2}$

3. $\frac{3}{8}$ ⬚ $\frac{5}{12}$ 4. $\frac{5}{8}$ ⬚ $\frac{25}{40}$

5. $\frac{3}{4}$ ⬚ $\frac{5}{6}$ 6. $\frac{7}{10}$ ⬚ $\frac{5}{16}$

Write the fractions in order from least to greatest.

7. $\frac{3}{5}, \frac{1}{2}, \frac{4}{7}$ 8. $\frac{2}{9}, \frac{1}{12}, \frac{3}{8}$

More Practice

Set A   pages 200–201

Complete the table.

Divisible by

Number	2	3	5	10
195	**1.**	**2.**	**3.**	**4.**
330	**5.**	**6.**	**7.**	**8.**
435	**9.**	**10.**	**11.**	**12.**

Tell whether the number is divisible by 6.

13. 72   **14.** 1,200   **15.** 2,019   **16.** 1,800   **17.** 96   **18.** 690

Set B   pages 202–205

Tell if the number is prime or composite.

1. 345   **2.** 119   **3.** 59   **4.** 121   **5.** 31   **6.** 1,011

Give a factor tree for each number.

7. 32   **8.** 80   **9.** 120   **10.** 96   **11.** 210   **12.** 224

For each number, write the prime factorization using exponents.

13. 126   **14.** 242   **15.** 135   **16.** 400   **17.** 600   **18.** 264

Set C   pages 206–207

Find the GCF of each set of numbers.

1. 15, 18   **2.** 20, 30   **3.** 9, 25   **4.** 45, 75   **5.** 27, 36

6. 16, 60   **7.** 40, 24   **8.** 36, 24   **9.** 18, 72   **10.** 16, 48, 72

Set D   pages 210–213

Write three fractions equal to the given fraction.

1. $\frac{1}{4}$ **2.** $\frac{5}{9}$ **3.** $\frac{7}{8}$ **4.** $\frac{4}{6}$ **5.** $\frac{25}{30}$ **6.** $\frac{30}{100}$

7. $\frac{8}{10}$ **8.** $\frac{6}{18}$ **9.** $\frac{1}{7}$ **10.** $\frac{4}{9}$ **11.** $\frac{4}{16}$ **12.** $\frac{7}{20}$

Write each fraction in lowest terms.

13. $\frac{9}{15}$ **14.** $\frac{13}{26}$ **15.** $\frac{12}{36}$ **16.** $\frac{7}{15}$ **17.** $\frac{28}{40}$ **18.** $\frac{50}{55}$ **19.** $\frac{96}{116}$ **20.** $\frac{48}{144}$

Set E   pages 218–219

Find the LCM.

1. 3, 10   2. 2, 3   3. 6, 15   4. 4, 13   5. 7, 12   6. 25, 5

7. 6, 21   8. 5, 14   9. 8, 12   10. 18, 54   11. 35, 10   12. 4, 9

13. 13, 6   14. 35, 20   15. 18, 5   16. 82, 41   17. 24, 9   18. 16, 12

Mixed Practice   Write the GCF and LCM for each pair of numbers.

19. 4, 14   20. 15, 40   21. 13, 39   22. 9, 10   23. 16, 20   24. 21, 30

Set F   pages 220–221

Write each pair of fractions using the least common denominator.

1. $\frac{1}{4}, \frac{5}{8}$ 2. $\frac{3}{5}, \frac{3}{20}$ 3. $\frac{4}{9}, \frac{2}{3}$ 4. $\frac{3}{10}, \frac{1}{6}$ 5. $\frac{1}{2}, \frac{2}{5}$ 6. $\frac{3}{4}, \frac{1}{10}$

7. $\frac{1}{12}, \frac{3}{8}$ 8. $\frac{9}{10}, \frac{1}{3}$ 9. $\frac{2}{5}, \frac{3}{4}$ 10. $\frac{4}{8}, \frac{4}{5}$ 11. $\frac{7}{12}, \frac{1}{5}$ 12. $\frac{5}{6}, \frac{8}{9}$

13. $\frac{4}{5}, \frac{1}{2}$ 14. $\frac{4}{15}, \frac{1}{3}$ 15. $\frac{3}{10}, \frac{1}{4}$ 16. $\frac{5}{16}, \frac{1}{2}$ 17. $\frac{3}{10}, \frac{1}{8}$ 18. $\frac{13}{20}, \frac{5}{7}$

Set G   pages 222–223

Mental Math   Compare the fractions. Use $<$, $>$, or $=$.

1. $\frac{5}{12} \boxplus \frac{7}{12}$ 2. $\frac{1}{5} \boxplus \frac{1}{6}$ 3. $\frac{4}{4} \boxplus \frac{5}{5}$ 4. $\frac{1}{8} \boxplus \frac{1}{4}$ 5. $\frac{2}{3} \boxplus \frac{2}{9}$

Compare the fractions. Use $<$, $>$, or $=$.

6. $\frac{3}{5} \boxplus \frac{4}{5}$ 7. $\frac{3}{10} \boxplus \frac{2}{10}$ 8. $\frac{5}{6} \boxplus \frac{5}{7}$ 9. $\frac{1}{4} \boxplus \frac{2}{5}$ 10. $\frac{8}{9} \boxplus \frac{9}{10}$

11. $\frac{5}{8} \boxplus \frac{3}{4}$ 12. $\frac{12}{16} \boxplus \frac{3}{4}$ 13. $\frac{7}{10} \boxplus \frac{5}{9}$ 14. $\frac{4}{5} \boxplus \frac{20}{25}$ 15. $\frac{29}{100} \boxplus \frac{3}{10}$

Write the fractions in order from least to greatest.

16. $\frac{1}{6}, \frac{1}{8}, \frac{1}{7}$ 17. $\frac{5}{8}, \frac{3}{4}, \frac{2}{3}$ 18. $\frac{7}{10}, \frac{4}{8}, \frac{3}{4}$ 19. $\frac{5}{6}, \frac{4}{5}, \frac{2}{3}$ 20. $\frac{1}{2}, \frac{4}{7}, \frac{3}{5}$

21. $\frac{7}{10}, \frac{2}{3}, \frac{3}{5}$ 22. $\frac{1}{6}, \frac{3}{8}, \frac{1}{4}$ 23. $\frac{2}{5}, \frac{5}{9}, \frac{7}{15}$ 24. $\frac{7}{10}, \frac{8}{9}, \frac{2}{3}$ 25. $\frac{5}{8}, \frac{7}{12}, \frac{5}{6}$

Enrichment

Perfect, Abundant, and Deficient Numbers

A prime number has only two factors, one and the number itself. For example, 5 is a prime number since its only factors are 1 and 5.

If a whole number greater than 1 is not prime, it is composite. The **proper factors** of a number are all the factors except the number itself. A composite number is either a **perfect number,** an **abundant number,** or a **deficient number.**

Perfect numbers

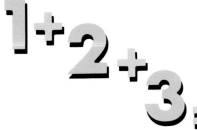

	Perfect Numbers	Abundant Numbers	Deficient Numbers
Meaning	The sum of the proper factors is equal to the number itself.	The sum of the proper factors is greater than the number itself.	The sum of the proper factors is less than the number itself.
Example	6	18	9
Proper factors	1, 2, 3	1, 2, 3, 6, 9	1, 3
Sum of the proper factors	$1 + 2 + 3 = 6$	$1 + 2 + 3 + 6 + 9 > 18$	$1 + 3 < 9$

Deficient numbers

Determine if each number is perfect, abundant, or deficient.

1. 50   2. 15   3. 100   4. 58   5. 24

6. 496   7. 256   8. 400   9. 225   10. 297

11. Only one perfect number other than 6 is less than 100. See if you can find it.

Abundant numbers

Chapter 6 Review/Test

Is the number divisible by 2? by 3? by 5? by 10?

1. 45

2. 120

3. 164

List all the factors of each number. Then tell if the number is prime, composite, or neither.

4. 39

5. 37

6. List all the factors of 40.

Find the common factors of each pair of numbers. Then name the greatest common factor.

7. 6; 10

8. 24; 28

Write each fraction in lowest terms.

9. $\frac{3}{6}$ **10.** $\frac{8}{12}$ **11.** $\frac{30}{36}$

12. List the first six multiples of 8.

13. Find the least common multiple of 4 and 10.

Write the fractions using the least common denominator.

14. $\frac{2}{9}$ $\frac{1}{3}$ **15.** $\frac{2}{5}$ $\frac{1}{4}$

Compare. Use $<$, $>$, or $=$.

16. $\frac{4}{7}$ ⬚ $\frac{5}{7}$ **17.** $\frac{2}{3}$ ⬚ $\frac{5}{8}$

18. Write whether 5 more than an odd number is always even or always odd.

19. Choose the rule for this list of numbers:
1, 3, 5, 7, 9, 11
a. $\frac{1}{n}$ **b.** $2n - 1$ **c.** $n - 2$

Read the problem below. Then answer the question.

How can you tell when the product of five numbers is zero?

20. What is the key idea that you would use to solve the problem?

a. The average of five numbers is found by dividing the sum of the numbers by 5.
b. The least common multiple of five numbers is always greater than zero.
c. A number whose ones digit is zero is divisible by 5.
d. Any number multiplied by zero is zero.

21. **Write About Math**   Is a number divisible by 6 divisible by 3? Explain.

Adding and Subtracting Fractions

Did You Know: The Columbus Zoo contains over 7500 animals, representing about 680 different species. About $\frac{1}{10}$ of the species are mammals, $\frac{1}{3}$ are fish, $\frac{3}{10}$ are reptiles, and $\frac{1}{8}$ are birds.

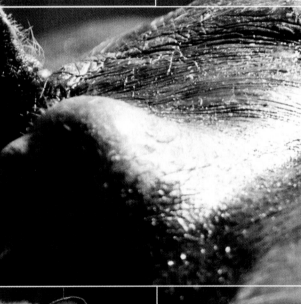

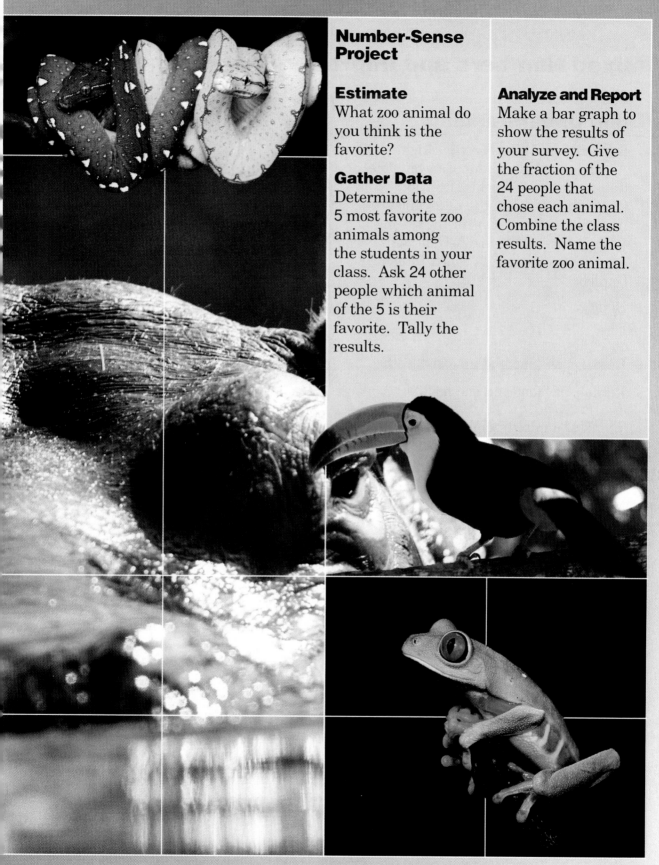

Number-Sense Project

Estimate
What zoo animal do you think is the favorite?

Gather Data
Determine the 5 most favorite zoo animals among the students in your class. Ask 24 other people which animal of the 5 is their favorite. Tally the results.

Analyze and Report
Make a bar graph to show the results of your survey. Give the fraction of the 24 people that chose each animal. Combine the class results. Name the favorite zoo animal.

Mixed Numbers and Improper Fractions

Build Understanding

Ken and Enid hiked on the Bright Angel Trail at the Grand Canyon. The trail leads to the Bright Angel Campground, a distance of $9\frac{2}{5}$ miles from the trailhead. One of the resting spots is called Mile-and-a-Half House. Another resting spot is called Indian Gardens.

Bright Angel Trail	Distance from Trailhead
Mile-and-a-Half House	$1\frac{9}{16}$ mi
Indian Gardens	$4\frac{1}{2}$ mi
Bright Angel Campground	$9\frac{2}{5}$ mi
Phantom Ranch	$9\frac{3}{5}$ mi

Read $1\frac{9}{16}$ as "one and nine sixteenths."

Read $4\frac{1}{2}$ as "four and one half."

A. Think of a mixed number as the sum of a whole number and a fraction, without the addition sign.

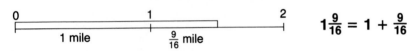

$$1\frac{9}{16} = 1 + \frac{9}{16}$$

B. Any mixed number can be written as an **_improper fraction_**. The numerator of an improper fraction is greater than or equal to the denominator.

Write $4\frac{1}{2}$ as an improper fraction.

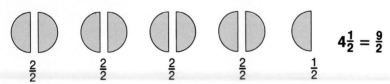

$$4\frac{1}{2} = \frac{9}{2}$$

$\frac{2}{2}$ $\frac{2}{2}$ $\frac{2}{2}$ $\frac{2}{2}$ $\frac{1}{2}$

You can use a shortcut to write a mixed number as an improper fraction.

Multiply the denominator by the whole number. Add the numerator.

$$4\frac{1}{2} = \frac{(2 \times 4) + 1}{2} = \frac{9}{2}$$

The denominator stays the same.

234

The Grand Canyon was formed by the Colorado River.

c. Write the improper fraction $\frac{47}{5}$ as a mixed number.

$$\frac{47}{5} = 47 \div 5$$

Divide the numerator by the denominator.

$$\begin{array}{r} 9\frac{2}{5} \\ 5{\overline{)47}} \\ 45 \\ \hline 2 \end{array}$$

$$\frac{47}{5} = 9\frac{2}{5}$$

D. Compare the mixed numbers $1\frac{3}{16}$ and $1\frac{1}{4}$.

$1\frac{3}{16}$ ⬚ $1\frac{1}{4}$ The whole numbers are the same.

$1\frac{3}{16}$ ⬚ $1\frac{4}{16}$ Use a common denominator.

$1\frac{3}{16} < 1\frac{4}{16}$ Compare the fractions.

$1\frac{3}{16} < 1\frac{1}{4}$

■ **Talk About Math** Use Example B to explain how to write 4 as an improper fraction.

Check Understanding

For another example, see Set A, pages 260–261.

Write each exercise as a mixed number. Draw a sketch to represent each.

1. One and one third **2.** Three and seven eighths **3.** Two and one fifth

Complete the table.

Mixed Number	Sum	Rename Whole Number	Improper Fraction
$3\frac{2}{3}$	**4.**	$\frac{9}{3} + \frac{2}{3}$	**5.**
$4\frac{3}{4}$	$4 + \frac{3}{4}$	**6.**	**7.**

Give each missing number.

8. $2 = \frac{⬚}{4}$ **9.** $⬚ = \frac{16}{4}$ **10.** $3\frac{⬚}{5} = \frac{19}{5}$ **11.** $8\frac{4}{7} = \frac{⬚}{7}$ **12.** $9\frac{⬚}{8} = \frac{77}{8}$

Practice

For More Practice, see Set A, pages 262–263.

Complete the table.

Picture	Mixed Number	Sum	Rename Whole Number	Improper Fraction	Quotient
	$2\frac{1}{3}$	$2 + \frac{1}{3}$	$\frac{6}{3} + \frac{1}{3}$	$\frac{7}{3}$	$7 \div 3$
	13.	$1 + \frac{5}{6}$	**14.**	**15.**	**16.**
17.	**18.**	**19.**	$\frac{4}{2} + \frac{1}{2}$	**20.**	**21.**
	22.	**23.**	**24.**	$\frac{5}{4}$	**25.**

Write each number as an improper fraction.

26. $4\frac{3}{4}$ **27.** $8\frac{1}{5}$ **28.** $10\frac{1}{8}$ **29.** $1\frac{2}{13}$ **30.** $6\frac{3}{7}$ **31.** 5

Write each improper fraction as a mixed number.

32. $\frac{25}{7}$ **33.** $\frac{13}{4}$ **34.** $\frac{19}{2}$ **35.** $\frac{43}{8}$ **36.** $\frac{36}{5}$ **37.** $\frac{60}{11}$

Compare. Use <, >, or =.

38. $2\frac{3}{5} \ \blacksquare \ 2\frac{5}{6}$ **39.** $8\frac{6}{10} \ \blacksquare \ 8\frac{3}{5}$ **40.** $1\frac{9}{10} \ \blacksquare \ 2\frac{1}{10}$ **41.** $\frac{10}{3} \ \blacksquare \ \frac{15}{4}$ **42.** $6\frac{5}{8} \ \blacksquare \ 6\frac{3}{4}$

43. $2\frac{5}{6} \ \blacksquare \ 3\frac{1}{6}$ **44.** $6\frac{1}{6} \ \blacksquare \ \frac{37}{6}$ **45.** $\frac{16}{4} \ \blacksquare \ \frac{12}{6}$ **46.** $7\frac{1}{4} \ \blacksquare \ \frac{28}{4}$ **47.** $\frac{30}{4} \ \blacksquare \ \frac{15}{2}$

48. $\frac{15}{5} \ \blacksquare \ \frac{27}{9}$ **49.** $9\frac{1}{8} \ \blacksquare \ 8\frac{3}{16}$ **50.** $12 \ \blacksquare \ \frac{24}{2}$ **51.** $6\frac{3}{10} \ \blacksquare \ 6\frac{33}{100}$

Write the numbers in order from least to greatest.

52. $4\frac{1}{5}, 4\frac{7}{10}, 4\frac{1}{2}$ **53.** $2\frac{1}{4}, 1\frac{1}{5}, 3\frac{1}{6}$ **54.** $\frac{7}{8}, \frac{4}{3}, 1\frac{1}{4}$ **55.** $5\frac{4}{5}, 5\frac{3}{4}, \frac{27}{5}$

56. $7\frac{1}{8}, \frac{50}{8}, 6\frac{7}{8}$ **57.** $\frac{17}{6}, \frac{17}{8}, \frac{17}{10}$ **58.** $\frac{18}{3}, 1\frac{5}{8}, \frac{7}{4}$ **59.** $9\frac{2}{7}, \frac{48}{5}, \frac{19}{2}$

Problem Solving

Solve each problem.

60. The distance from the trailhead to the Colorado River is $7\frac{5}{8}$ miles. Write the distance as an improper fraction.

61. Mr. Martinez walked $\frac{6}{4}$ miles from the Indian Gardens to Plateau Point. Write as a mixed number the distance he walked.

62. Heta hiked 1 mile from Plateau Point to the Colorado River, and another $\frac{4}{5}$ mile to the Phantom Ranch. How far did she hike in all?

63. Estimation Akio Osaka spent 5 days at the Grand Canyon. Akio hiked about the same amount each day, and he kept track of the distances he hiked. Altogether he hiked $41\frac{1}{2}$ miles. About how many miles did he hike each day?

64. Critical Thinking Write 4.5 and 3.2 as mixed numbers.

Skills **Review** pages 170–171

Find the third measure in each triangle. Tell whether the triangle is acute, right, or obtuse.

1.

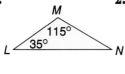

2.

3.

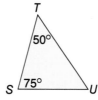

4.

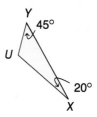

5.

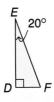

6.

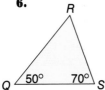

7.

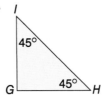

8.

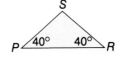

Estimating Sums and Differences

Build Understanding

To do math mentally, sometimes it is easier to compare numbers to a reference point.

A. Compare each fraction below to $\frac{1}{2}$.

Use fraction pieces or draw a picture to compare each fraction to $\frac{1}{2}$.

$\frac{3}{10}$ $\frac{1}{2}$ $\frac{4}{8}$ $\frac{1}{2}$ $\frac{2}{3}$ $\frac{1}{2}$

$\frac{3}{10}$ $<$ $\frac{1}{2}$ $\frac{4}{8}$ $=$ $\frac{1}{2}$ $\frac{2}{3}$ $>$ $\frac{1}{2}$

B. Estimate $\frac{1}{3} + \frac{5}{12}$.

Compare each fraction to $\frac{1}{2}$.

$\frac{1}{3}$ 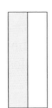 $\frac{1}{2}$ $\longrightarrow$ $\frac{1}{3}$ $<$ $\frac{1}{2}$

$\frac{5}{12}$  $\frac{1}{2}$ $\longrightarrow$ $\frac{5}{12}$ $<$ $\frac{1}{2}$

$\frac{1}{3} < \frac{1}{2}$ and $\frac{5}{12} < \frac{1}{2}$, so $\frac{1}{3} + \frac{5}{12} < \frac{1}{2} + \frac{1}{2}$, or < 1.

C. Estimate $\frac{7}{12} + \frac{3}{4}$.

$\frac{7}{12} > \frac{1}{2}$ and $\frac{3}{4} > \frac{1}{2}$, so $\frac{7}{12} + \frac{3}{4} > \frac{1}{2} + \frac{1}{2}$, or > 1.

238

D. Is $\frac{3}{10} + \frac{5}{8}$ greater than 1, less than 1, or equal to 1?

Compare each fraction to $\frac{1}{2}$.

$\frac{3}{10}$ ⬚ $\frac{1}{2}$ $\frac{3}{10} < \frac{1}{2}$.

$\frac{5}{8}$ ⬚ $\frac{1}{2}$ $\frac{5}{8} > \frac{1}{2}$.

$\frac{3}{10} + \frac{5}{8} > \frac{5}{8}$ It can only be determined that the sum is greater than the greater fraction.

E. Estimate $5\frac{3}{8} - 2\frac{1}{2}$.

$$5\frac{3}{8} - 2\frac{1}{2}$$ Round to the nearest whole number.

$$\downarrow \qquad \downarrow$$

$$5 \; - \; 3 \; = 2$$ If the fractional part is less than $\frac{1}{2}$, round down. If the fractional part is $\frac{1}{2}$ or greater, round up.

$$5\frac{3}{8} - 2\frac{1}{2} \approx 2$$ $\approx$ means "is approximately equal to."

F. Estimate $3\frac{3}{8} + 4\frac{3}{4}$.

$$3\frac{3}{8} + 4\frac{3}{4}$$
$$\downarrow \qquad \downarrow$$
$$3 \; + \; 4 \; = 7$$ Use only the whole-number parts.

$$3\frac{3}{8} + 4\frac{3}{4} \approx 7$$

■ **Talk About Math** You can also compare a fraction to $\frac{1}{2}$ by looking at its numerator and denominator. Discuss how you would do this.

Check Understanding

For another example, see Set B, pages 260–261.

Use fraction pieces or draw a picture to compare each fraction to $\frac{1}{2}$.

1. $\frac{1}{6}$ **2.** $\frac{5}{10}$ **3.** $\frac{1}{5}$ **4.** $\frac{6}{12}$ **5.** $\frac{3}{10}$ **6.** $\frac{15}{16}$ **7.** $\frac{3}{7}$ **8.** $\frac{5}{9}$

Name three fractions that

9. are less than $\frac{1}{2}$.   **10.** are greater than $\frac{1}{2}$.   **11.** are equal to $\frac{1}{2}$.

Choose the letter of the correct answer.

12. $3\frac{5}{8} - $ ⬚ ≈ 1

a. $2\frac{3}{4}$ **b.** $2\frac{1}{3}$ **c.** $1\frac{7}{8}$

13. ⬚ $- 3\frac{7}{8} \approx 4$,

a. $7\frac{2}{3}$ **b.** $8\frac{4}{5}$ **c.** $8\frac{2}{3}$

Choose the *best* estimate by comparing each fraction to $\frac{1}{2}$. Is the sum: (a) greater than 1, (b) less than 1, or (c) greater than the greater fraction in the exercise?

14. $\frac{3}{8} + \frac{5}{6}$ **15.** $\frac{5}{8} + \frac{4}{7}$ **16.** $\frac{1}{2} + \frac{7}{9}$ **17.** $\frac{2}{9} + \frac{1}{3}$ **18.** $\frac{4}{10} + \frac{5}{9}$

239

Choose the *best* estimate by comparing each fraction to $\frac{1}{2}$.
Is the sum: (a) greater than 1, (b) less than 1, or (c) greater
than the greater fraction in the exercise?

19. $\frac{2}{3} + \frac{4}{5}$ **20.** $\frac{6}{7} + \frac{1}{4}$ **21.** $\frac{1}{2} + \frac{5}{7}$ **22.** $\frac{3}{10} + \frac{2}{3}$ **23.** $\frac{1}{3} + \frac{2}{5}$ **24.** $\frac{3}{8} + \frac{4}{7}$

25. $\frac{5}{9} + \frac{5}{18}$ **26.** $\frac{3}{5} + \frac{6}{7}$ **27.** $\frac{1}{12} + \frac{4}{5}$ **28.** $\frac{2}{3} + \frac{3}{5}$ **29.** $\frac{7}{10} + \frac{4}{7}$ **30.** $\frac{1}{4} + \frac{1}{3}$

Round each mixed number to the nearest whole number.
Remember to look at the fractional part of each mixed
number.

31. $8\frac{1}{2}$ **32.** $6\frac{4}{5}$ **33.** $3\frac{5}{6}$ **34.** $7\frac{3}{8}$ **35.** $6\frac{5}{12}$ **36.** $17\frac{5}{16}$ **37.** $9\frac{7}{15}$

38. $21\frac{11}{14}$ **39.** $6\frac{3}{4}$ **40.** $16\frac{5}{12}$ **41.** $9\frac{7}{8}$ **42.** $3\frac{2}{5}$ **43.** $14\frac{1}{2}$ **44.** $19\frac{3}{7}$

Estimate each sum or difference. Round mixed numbers to
the nearest whole number. **Remember** to watch the signs.

45. $9\frac{5}{6}$ **46.** $4\frac{2}{5}$ **47.** $5\frac{7}{8}$ **48.** $6\frac{5}{12}$ **49.** $6\frac{1}{10}$ **50.** $8\frac{3}{8}$
  $\underline{-3\frac{1}{3}}$ $\underline{-1\frac{2}{3}}$ $\underline{+8\frac{3}{4}}$ $\underline{+2\frac{3}{10}}$ $\underline{+3\frac{5}{6}}$ $\underline{-5\frac{7}{10}}$

51. $8\frac{4}{5} - 2\frac{1}{3}$ **52.** $4\frac{3}{5} + 8\frac{1}{8}$ **53.** $7\frac{9}{10} - 2\frac{1}{5}$ **54.** $8\frac{1}{8} - 6\frac{3}{10}$ **55.** $9\frac{7}{16} + 2\frac{5}{8}$

Estimate each sum or difference. Use only the
whole-number parts.

56. $8\frac{2}{3}$ **57.** $4\frac{1}{2}$ **58.** $10\frac{1}{6}$ **59.** $11\frac{2}{5}$ **60.** $5\frac{73}{100}$ **61.** $8\frac{13}{20}$
  $\underline{-7\frac{11}{16}}$ $\underline{+2\frac{5}{12}}$ $\underline{-5\frac{5}{8}}$ $\underline{-2\frac{7}{10}}$ $\underline{+6\frac{1}{4}}$ $\underline{+9\frac{5}{12}}$

62. $14\frac{7}{12} - 9\frac{2}{5}$ **63.** $12\frac{3}{4} + 2\frac{2}{5}$ **64.** $5\frac{7}{8} + \frac{1}{3}$ **65.** $7\frac{3}{4} + \frac{5}{6}$ **66.** $\frac{6}{11} + 9\frac{3}{7}$

67. $32\frac{11}{21} + 12\frac{1}{9}$ **68.** $105\frac{3}{8} + 55\frac{1}{2}$ **69.** $13\frac{1}{7} - 8\frac{1}{12}$ **70.** $85 - 42\frac{1}{3}$

Problem Solving

Solve each problem.

71. Sarah Yoder bought $\frac{3}{8}$ yard of red fabric and $\frac{1}{4}$ yard of blue fabric for a quilt she is making. Did she buy more than a yard of fabric?

72. Samuel Lapp planted $2\frac{1}{2}$ acres of sweet corn and $3\frac{3}{4}$ acres of other vegetables to sell at his farm stand. About how many acres did he plant for his farm stand?

Critical Thinking   Find two different mixed numbers

73. that round to 3.   **74.** with an estimated difference of 2.

75. with an estimated sum of 5.

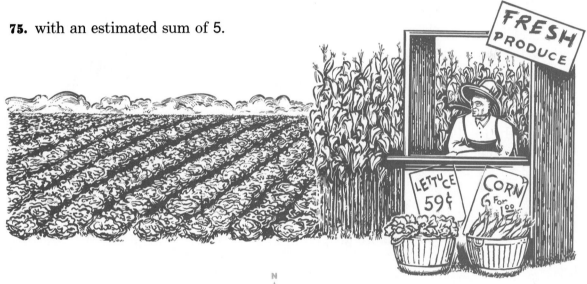

Explore ———— Math

Look at these two pairs of fractions.

$\frac{7}{8}$ and $\frac{5}{6}$ $\frac{11}{12}$ and $\frac{15}{16}$

Notice that each numerator is one less than each denominator.

76. For each pair of fractions, which fraction is closer to 1?

77. Write a statement for deciding which fraction is closer to 1 when each numerator is one less than the denominator.

Use your statement to decide which fraction is closer to 1.

78. $\frac{3}{4}$ or $\frac{2}{3}$ **79.** $\frac{7}{8}$ or $\frac{9}{10}$ **80.** $\frac{11}{12}$ or $\frac{9}{10}$ **81.** $\frac{19}{20}$ or $\frac{24}{25}$ **82.** $\frac{59}{60}$ or $\frac{54}{55}$

Adding Fractions

Build Understanding

Cassandra is working on a report about the climate in the southwestern United States. She found this table showing typical rainfall in Phoenix, Arizona, during the period April through July.

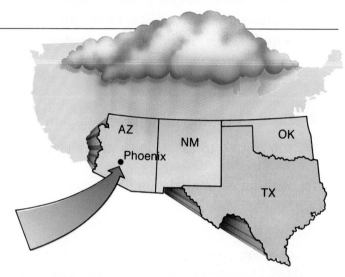

April	May	June	July
$\frac{3}{10}$ in.	$\frac{1}{10}$ in.	$\frac{1}{5}$ in.	$\frac{3}{4}$ in.

A. Find the total amount of rainfall in June and July.

Find $\frac{1}{5} + \frac{3}{4}$.

Estimate: $\frac{1}{5} < \frac{1}{2}$ and $\frac{3}{4} > \frac{1}{2}$, so you can tell only that the sum will be greater than $\frac{3}{4}$.

$$\begin{aligned}\frac{1}{5} &= \frac{4}{20}\\ +\frac{3}{4} &= \frac{15}{20}\\ \hline &\ \ \frac{19}{20}\end{aligned}$$

Write the fractions with a common denominator. Then add.

The total amount of rainfall in June and July was $\frac{19}{20}$ inch.

B. Find the total amount of rainfall for April through July.

Find $\frac{3}{10} + \frac{1}{10} + \frac{1}{5} + \frac{3}{4}$.

$$\begin{aligned}\frac{3}{10} &= \frac{6}{20}\\ \frac{1}{10} &= \frac{2}{20}\\ \frac{1}{5} &= \frac{4}{20}\\ +\frac{3}{4} &= \frac{15}{20}\\ \hline &\ \ \frac{27}{20} = 1\frac{7}{20}\end{aligned}$$

Use a common denominator.

The total amount of rainfall for April through July was $1\frac{7}{20}$ inches.

■ **Write About Math** Find the total amount of rainfall in April and May. Then write the fractions for rainfall in these months as decimals and find the sum. Are your answers the same?

Check Understanding

For another example, see Set C, pages 260–261.

Find the missing numbers.

1. $\dfrac{1}{3} = \dfrac{4}{}$
$+\dfrac{5}{12} = \dfrac{5}{12}$
$\overline{}$
$\dfrac{}{12} = \dfrac{3}{4}$

2. $\dfrac{3}{5} = \dfrac{}{40}$
$+\dfrac{3}{8} = \dfrac{}{40}$
$\overline{}$
$\dfrac{}{40}$

3. $\dfrac{5}{8} = \dfrac{15}{}$
$+\dfrac{2}{3} = \dfrac{16}{}$
$\overline{}$
$\dfrac{}{} = 1\dfrac{7}{}$

4. $\dfrac{9}{10} = \dfrac{}{20}$
$+\dfrac{3}{4} = \dfrac{}{}$
$\overline{}$
$\dfrac{}{} = 1\dfrac{}{}$

Mental Math Add mentally. Notice that one denominator is twice the other.

5. $\dfrac{2}{5} + \dfrac{3}{10}$
6. $\dfrac{1}{2} + \dfrac{1}{4}$
7. $\dfrac{2}{3} + \dfrac{5}{6}$
8. $\dfrac{5}{6} + \dfrac{3}{12}$
9. $\dfrac{3}{8} + \dfrac{3}{4}$
10. $\dfrac{8}{15} + \dfrac{13}{30}$

11. **Estimation** Look at Exercises 12–14. Tell which exercises will have answers greater than 1.

Practice

For More Practice, see Set C, pages 262–263.

Tell whether you would use mental math or paper and pencil.
Then find each sum. Write your answers in lowest terms.

12. $\dfrac{2}{3}$
$+\dfrac{4}{5}$

13. $\dfrac{5}{8}$
$+\dfrac{3}{4}$

14. $\dfrac{1}{6}$
$+\dfrac{5}{12}$

15. $\dfrac{3}{5}$
$\dfrac{1}{2}$
$+\dfrac{7}{10}$

16. $\dfrac{3}{10}$
$\dfrac{4}{5}$
$+\dfrac{31}{100}$

17. $\dfrac{2}{3}$
$\dfrac{11}{12}$
$+\dfrac{9}{16}$

18. $\dfrac{3}{4} + \dfrac{1}{6}$
19. $\dfrac{1}{3} + \dfrac{9}{10}$
20. $\dfrac{1}{12} + \dfrac{3}{8}$
21. $\dfrac{3}{5} + \dfrac{11}{15} + \dfrac{2}{3}$
22. $\dfrac{3}{16} + \dfrac{1}{8} + \dfrac{5}{6}$

Complete each table. Write your answers in lowest terms.

+	$\frac{1}{4}$	$\frac{2}{3}$	$\frac{3}{4}$	$\frac{5}{12}$
$\frac{1}{4}$	$\frac{1}{2}$	**23.**	1	**24.**

+	$\frac{4}{5}$	$\frac{2}{5}$	$\frac{3}{10}$	$\frac{4}{25}$
$\frac{1}{5}$	**25.**	**26.**	$\frac{1}{2}$	**27.**

+	$\frac{1}{4}$	$\frac{1}{8}$	$\frac{5}{6}$	$\frac{2}{6}$
$\frac{1}{6}$	**28.**	**29.**	**30.**	**31.**

Problem Solving

Solve each problem.

32. Phoenix typically gets $\frac{7}{10}$ inches of rainfall in January. Use decimals to find out how much more rain falls in January than in April.

33. April, May, June, and July are the driest months of the year in Phoenix. In which month is rainfall the least?

Subtracting Fractions

Build Understanding

Spider	Average Body Length
Black widow	$\frac{3}{8}$ inch
Daddy longlegs	$\frac{1}{4}$ inch
Garden spider	$\frac{7}{8}$ inch

Black widow

Daddy longlegs

Garden spider

A. What is the difference in the lengths of the bodies of the black widow and the daddy longlegs?

Find $\frac{3}{8} - \frac{1}{4}$.

$$\frac{3}{8} = \frac{3}{8}$$
$$-\frac{1}{4} = \frac{2}{8}$$
$$\frac{1}{8}$$

The denominators are different. Write the fractions with a common denominator.

The body of the black widow is $\frac{1}{8}$ inch longer than the body of the daddy longlegs.

B. Find $\frac{7}{8} - \frac{1}{3}$.

$$\frac{7}{8} = \frac{21}{24}$$
$$-\frac{1}{3} = \frac{8}{24}$$
$$\frac{13}{24}$$

Check to make sure that the difference is less than the first fraction.

$$\frac{13}{24} < \frac{21}{24} \text{ or } \frac{7}{8}$$

$$\frac{7}{8} - \frac{1}{3} = \frac{13}{24}$$

■ **Talk About Math** Tell how you would find how much larger the garden spider is than the black widow.

Check Understanding

For another example, see Set D, pages 260–261.

Find the missing numbers.

1. $\frac{}{10} - \frac{1}{10} = \frac{6}{10} = \frac{}{5}$ **2.** $\frac{}{12} - \frac{1}{4} = \frac{}{12} = \frac{1}{6}$ **3.** $\frac{6}{7} - \frac{2}{3} = \frac{}{21} - \frac{}{} = \frac{}{}$

4. What did you rename in Exercise 2? How did you do it?

Practice

For More Practice, see Set D, pages 262–263.

Subtract. **Remember** to give your answer in lowest terms.

5. $\frac{7}{8} - \frac{3}{8}$ **6.** $\frac{7}{10} - \frac{1}{10}$ **7.** $\frac{7}{16} - \frac{1}{8}$ **8.** $\frac{11}{15} - \frac{2}{5}$ **9.** $\frac{2}{3} - \frac{1}{6}$ **10.** $\frac{3}{4} - \frac{1}{16}$

11. $\frac{5}{6} - \frac{1}{6}$ **12.** $\frac{3}{4} - \frac{1}{4}$ **13.** $\frac{11}{12} - \frac{5}{6}$ **14.** $\frac{5}{6} - \frac{1}{3}$ **15.** $\frac{3}{4} - \frac{2}{5}$ **16.** $\frac{9}{10} - \frac{2}{3}$

17. $\frac{11}{16} - \frac{1}{2}$ **18.** $\frac{7}{10} - \frac{2}{5}$ **19.** $\frac{7}{8} - \frac{5}{12}$ **20.** $\frac{7}{12} - \frac{1}{4}$ **21.** $\frac{17}{20} - \frac{5}{6}$ **22.** $\frac{17}{25} - \frac{5}{8}$

23. $\frac{7}{9} - \frac{1}{2}$ **24.** $\frac{3}{10} - \frac{1}{4}$ **25.** $\frac{9}{16} - \frac{1}{12}$ **26.** $\frac{7}{8} - \frac{1}{6}$ **27.** $\frac{1}{2} - \frac{3}{16}$ **28.** $\frac{5}{7} - \frac{1}{5}$

Mixed Practice   Find each answer.

29. $\frac{3}{8} - \frac{1}{6}$ **30.** $\frac{4}{5} + \frac{2}{3}$ **31.** $\frac{1}{2} - \frac{5}{12}$ **32.** $\frac{7}{10} + \frac{2}{3}$ **33.** $\frac{5}{18} + \frac{3}{4}$ **34.** $\frac{15}{16} - \frac{2}{3}$

35. $\frac{8}{9} - \frac{5}{12}$ **36.** $\frac{1}{3} + \frac{7}{8}$ **37.** $\frac{1}{2} + \frac{7}{10}$ **38.** $\frac{14}{15} - \frac{3}{5}$ **39.** $\frac{5}{6} - \frac{1}{5}$ **40.** $\frac{2}{3} + \frac{3}{10}$

41. Rewrite Exercises 1, 12, and 18 using decimals.

Problem Solving

Use the table to find the difference between the shortest and longest body length.

42. Aphid   **43.** Firefly   **44.** Ladybird beetle

45. Number Sense   Which insects could be the same length?

Insect	Range of Body Length
Aphid	$\frac{1}{16}$ to $\frac{1}{8}$ inch
Firefly	$\frac{1}{4}$ to $\frac{7}{8}$ inch
Ladybird beetle	$\frac{1}{10}$ to $\frac{3}{8}$ inch

Midchapter Checkup

Compare. Use <, >, or =.   Estimate each sum or difference.

1. $1\frac{1}{6} \, \begin{smallmatrix}\blacksquare\end{smallmatrix} \, \frac{7}{6}$ **2.** $6\frac{7}{12} \, \begin{smallmatrix}\blacksquare\end{smallmatrix} \, \frac{13}{2}$ **3.** $\frac{1}{4} + \frac{1}{5}$ **4.** $18\frac{5}{6} - 7\frac{11}{12}$

Find each answer.

5. $\frac{1}{3} + \frac{1}{5}$ **6.** $\frac{3}{8} - \frac{1}{4}$ **7.** $\frac{5}{6} + \frac{1}{2}$ **8.** $\frac{7}{12} - \frac{1}{3}$ **9.** $\frac{2}{3} - \frac{1}{10}$ **10.** $\frac{6}{7} + \frac{3}{5}$

Explore as a Team

Each team member should mark a 10-by-10 grid using colored pencils or markers. Use at least four different markings or colors. Describe the square and ask a question about it.

The following describes the square shown.

a. $\frac{1}{5}$ of the square is striped.

b. $\frac{1}{10}$ of the square is dotted.

c. Of the part that is neither striped nor dotted, $\frac{2}{5}$ is red and $\frac{1}{7}$ is blue.

d. The rest of the square has wavy lines.

What fraction of the square has wavy lines?

Real-Life Decision Making

1. Choose a magazine. Determine the total number of pages used for advertising in that magazine.

2. What fractional part of the magazine is advertising?

3. Compare your results with others. What should an advertiser consider before buying an ad? What should a consumer consider before subscribing?

Explore with a Computer

Use the *Fractions Workshop Project* for this activity.

1. Suppose you were reading a recipe for a cereal mix. At the computer, manipulate the model to find if $\frac{2}{3}$ cup nuts, $\frac{3}{4}$ cup oats, and $\frac{1}{2}$ cup raisins would fit into a 2-cup container.

2. How much would you have left in the container if you ate $\frac{3}{4}$ cup of the mixture?

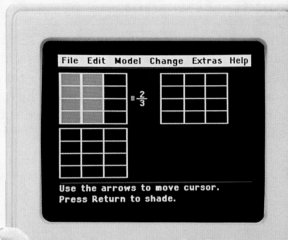

Number-Sense Project

Look back at pages 232-233.

The table tells about how many of each kind of animal are in the Columbus Zoo. Use this data for Exercises a-f.

What fraction of the total number of animals are

    a. mammals?

    b. birds?

    c. reptiles?

    d. fish?

    e. mammals and birds ?

    f. reptiles and fish?

Kind of Animal	Number
Mammals	300
Birds	200
Reptiles	1,000
Fish	5,000
Other	1,000
Total	7,500

Work Backward

Build Understanding

Much of what we know about ancient Egyptian mathematics comes from the Rhind Papyrus, a document that is over 3,600 years old. From this document we learned that the ancient Egyptians wrote most fractions as **unit fractions** or as the sum of unit fractions with different denominators. Unit fractions have numerators of 1.

For example, they wrote

$\frac{2}{15}$ as $\frac{1}{10} + \frac{1}{30}$ and $\frac{3}{5}$ as $\frac{1}{3} + \frac{1}{5} + \frac{1}{15}$.

Write $\frac{7}{8}$ as the sum of unit fractions.

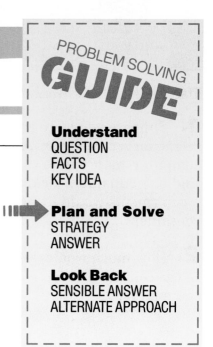

PROBLEM SOLVING GUIDE

Understand
QUESTION
FACTS
KEY IDEA

→ **Plan and Solve**
STRATEGY
ANSWER

Look Back
SENSIBLE ANSWER
ALTERNATE APPROACH

Understand   QUESTION   How can you write $\frac{7}{8}$ as the sum of fractions with numerators of 1?

→ **Plan and Solve**   STRATEGY   You can solve this problem by *working backward*. The greatest unit fraction less than $\frac{7}{8}$ is $\frac{1}{2}$. Subtract $\frac{1}{2}$ from $\frac{7}{8}$.

$\frac{7}{8} - \frac{1}{2} = \frac{7}{8} - \frac{4}{8} = \frac{3}{8}$, so

$\frac{7}{8} = \frac{1}{2} + \frac{3}{8}$. Now write $\frac{3}{8}$ as the sum of unit fractions.

$\frac{3}{8} - \frac{1}{4} = \frac{3}{8} - \frac{2}{8} = \frac{1}{8}$, so $\frac{3}{8} = \frac{1}{4} + \frac{1}{8}$.

ANSWER $\frac{7}{8} = \frac{1}{2} + \frac{1}{4} + \frac{1}{8}$

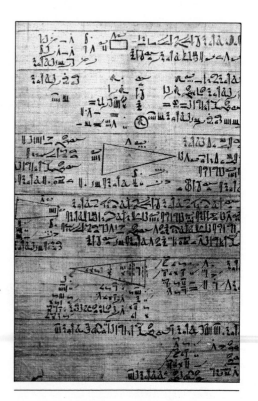

Look Back   Check your work.
$\frac{1}{2} + \frac{1}{4} + \frac{1}{8} = \frac{4}{8} + \frac{2}{8} + \frac{1}{8} = \frac{7}{8}$

■ **Write About Math**   Write $\frac{7}{8}$ as the sum of unit fractions in another way. Start with $\frac{1}{3}$ instead of $\frac{1}{2}$.

Check Understanding

Find the greatest unit fraction less than each of the following fractions.

1. $\frac{5}{6}$ **2.** $\frac{3}{8}$ **3.** $\frac{2}{5}$ **4.** $\frac{3}{10}$ **5.** $\frac{7}{25}$ **6.** $\frac{3}{16}$ **7.** $\frac{7}{30}$ **8.** $\frac{9}{50}$ **9.** $\frac{3}{100}$

Find the missing numbers. Write each fraction as a sum of different unit fractions.

10. $\frac{5}{6}$ $\frac{5}{6} - \boxed{}$

$\frac{5}{6} - \frac{3}{6} = \boxed{} = \frac{1}{3}$

$\frac{5}{6} = \boxed{} + \frac{1}{3}$

11. $\frac{3}{4}$ $\frac{3}{4} - \frac{1}{2}$

$\frac{3}{4} - \boxed{} = \boxed{}$

$\frac{3}{4} = \frac{1}{2} + \boxed{}$

12. $\frac{8}{15}$ $\frac{8}{15} - \frac{1}{3}$

$\frac{8}{15} - \boxed{} = \frac{3}{15} = \boxed{}$

$\frac{8}{15} = \boxed{} + \boxed{}$

Practice

Write each fraction as the sum of unit fractions with different denominators.

13. $\frac{2}{3}$ **14.** $\frac{2}{5}$ **15.** $\frac{3}{8}$ **16.** $\frac{7}{10}$ **17.** $\frac{3}{5}$ **18.** $\frac{7}{12}$

19. $\frac{3}{10}$ **20.** $\frac{4}{5}$ **21.** $\frac{11}{12}$ **22.** $\frac{9}{10}$ **23.** $\frac{7}{9}$ **24.** $\frac{6}{7}$

25. The Rhind Papyrus contains a table in which fractions with 10 as the denominator are written as the sum of unit fractions or as the sum of unit fractions and the fraction $\frac{2}{3}$. Write the fraction $\frac{n}{10}$ in this format if $n = 4$, 6, and 7.

Choose a ———— Strategy

Forming Fractions   Use four of the digits 1, 3, 4, 5, 7, and 8 in this form: $\boxed{} + \boxed{}$. Write two fractions that

26. have the greatest possible sum.

27. have the greatest possible sum that is less than 1.

28. are both less than 1 and have the greatest possible sum.

29. are both less than 1 and have the least possible sum.

Adding Mixed Numbers

Build Understanding

Rosa and her family took a trip to Spain. Their first stop was Madrid, the capital of Spain. They visited an ancient city called Avila, which is $1\frac{1}{4}$ hours from Madrid, and Salamanca, which is $1\frac{3}{4}$ hours from Avila.

A. Find the total travel time from Madrid to Salamanca.

Find $1\frac{1}{4} + 1\frac{3}{4}$.

$$1\frac{1}{4}$$
$$+\,1\frac{3}{4}$$

The denominators are the same, so add the numerators.

$$2\frac{4}{4} = 2 + 1$$
$$= 3$$

Write the answer in lowest terms.

The total travel time from Madrid to Salamanca is 3 hours.

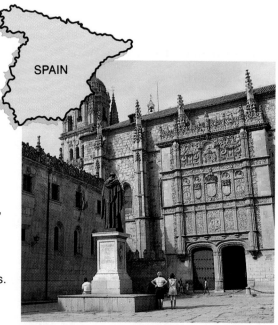

SPAIN

Spain is part of the Iberian Peninsula.

B. Find $2\frac{1}{6} + 1\frac{1}{3}$.

Estimate: $2\frac{1}{6} \approx 2$, $1\frac{1}{3} \approx 1$, $2 + 1 = 3$.

$$2\frac{1}{6} = 2\frac{1}{6}$$
$$+\,1\frac{1}{3} = 1\frac{2}{6}$$
$$3\frac{3}{6} = 3\frac{1}{2}$$

Write the fractions with a common denominator. Then add.

$$2\frac{1}{6} + 1\frac{1}{3} = 3\frac{1}{2}$$

C. **Calculator** You can use a calculator to add mixed numbers when the fractional parts can be changed to decimals.

Find $3\frac{9}{10} + 2\frac{1}{2}$.

Estimate: $3\frac{9}{10} \approx 4$, $2\frac{1}{2} \approx 3$, $4 + 3 = 7$.

Think: $3\frac{9}{10} = 3.9$, $2\frac{1}{2} = 2.5$

Press: 3.9 $+$ 2.5 $=$

Display: *6.4*

$$6.4 = 6\frac{4}{10} = 6\frac{2}{5}$$

■ **Talk About Math** Explain why the answer to Example B is more than the estimate and why the answer to Example C is less than the estimate.

Check Understanding

For another example, see Set E, pages 260–261.

Find the missing numbers.

1. $1\frac{1}{2}$
$+2\frac{}{2}$
$\overline{3\frac{2}{2}} = \blacksquare$

2. $6\frac{1}{3} = 6\frac{\blacksquare}{9}$
$+1\frac{2}{9} = 1\frac{2}{9}$
$\overline{7\frac{\blacksquare}{9}}$

Estimate each sum. Then add.

3. $2\frac{1}{5}$
$+4\frac{3}{10}$

4. $3\frac{2}{5}$
$+2\frac{3}{4}$

5. $5\frac{2}{3}$
$+7\frac{7}{8}$

Practice

For More Practice, see Set E, pages 262–263.

Estimate each sum. Then add.

6. $8\frac{1}{6}$
$+1\frac{1}{3}$

7. $2\frac{3}{8}$
$+5\frac{3}{8}$

8. $1\frac{5}{6}$
$+9\frac{1}{12}$

9. 6
$+2\frac{2}{3}$

10. $9\frac{3}{5}$
$+\ \frac{1}{8}$

11. $6\frac{1}{6}$
$+4\frac{7}{10}$

12. $7\frac{3}{4} + 9$

13. $2\frac{1}{2} + 4\frac{5}{12}$

14. $4\frac{1}{5} + 13\frac{7}{8}$

15. $12\frac{1}{5} + 9\frac{1}{6}$

16. $8\frac{5}{7} + 3\frac{2}{3}$

17. $4\frac{1}{2} + 5\frac{2}{3}$

18. $1\frac{3}{10} + \frac{8}{9}$

19. $7\frac{1}{4} + \frac{5}{6}$

20. $\frac{7}{12} + 3\frac{4}{5}$

21. $18\frac{7}{11} + 4\frac{1}{6}$

Match each exercise with the correct key sequence.

22. $2\frac{1}{2} + 3\frac{3}{4}$

23. $2\frac{1}{4} + 3\frac{3}{10}$

24. $2\frac{1}{5} + 3\frac{3}{100}$

25. $2\frac{1}{20} + 3\frac{7}{10}$

a. $2.2 \boxed{+} 3.03$

b. $2.25 \boxed{+} 3.3$

c. $2.5 \boxed{+} 3.75$

d. $2.05 \boxed{+} 3.7$

Calculator Use a calculator to find each sum. **Remember** to change each mixed number to a decimal.

26. $8\frac{7}{10} + 1\frac{1}{4}$

27. $2\frac{3}{5} + 4\frac{1}{2}$

28. $6\frac{1}{10} + 3\frac{3}{4}$

29. $7\frac{3}{10} + 5\frac{3}{16}$

30. $4\frac{5}{8} + 3\frac{11}{20}$

Problem Solving

Critical Thinking On Sunday Rosa's family plans to spend time in Retiro Park. They plan to spend 2 hours rowing on a lake, $\frac{3}{4}$ hour having lunch at an outdoor café, and $1\frac{1}{2}$ hours listening to a band concert.

31. The band concert is at 2:00 P.M. What are three possible schedules if the present time is 10:30 A.M.?

32. For each schedule, what is the total time from 10:30 A.M. until the end of the last activity?

Subtracting Mixed Numbers

Build Understanding

A. Shades of Subtraction
Materials: Fraction pieces
Groups: Four students

Find $1\frac{1}{2} - \frac{5}{8}$ using fraction pieces.

a. Place fraction pieces representing $1\frac{1}{2}$ on your desk. Trace around each piece. What pieces did you use?

b. Next use fraction pieces to help you shade a part of your drawing that represents $\frac{5}{8}$. What pieces did you use?

c. What fraction is represented by the unshaded part of your drawing? Use fraction pieces, if needed, to find out. What is $1\frac{1}{2} - \frac{5}{8}$?

d. Now find $1\frac{2}{5} - \frac{1}{2}$ by tracing around fraction pieces. Describe the steps you used to solve the problem.

B. Rename $4\frac{2}{5}$ as $3\frac{\boxed{}}{5}$.

$$4\frac{2}{5} = 4 + \frac{2}{5}$$

$$= 3 + 1 + \frac{2}{5}$$

$$= 3 + \frac{5}{5} + \frac{2}{5}$$

$$= 3\frac{7}{5}$$

c. Find $2\frac{2}{3} - 1\frac{3}{4}$ using fraction pieces. First estimate: $3 - 2 = 1$.

Trace around pieces representing $2\frac{2}{3}$.

Rename $2\frac{2}{3}$ and $1\frac{3}{4}$ using a common denominator. Show the $2\frac{8}{12}$ in your drawing.

Rename $2\frac{8}{12}$ as $1\frac{20}{12}$. Show this in your drawing. Shade $1\frac{9}{12}$.

$$2\frac{2}{3}$$
$$-1\frac{3}{4}$$

$=$

$$2\frac{8}{12}$$
$$1\frac{9}{12}$$

$=$

$$1\frac{20}{12}$$
$$1\frac{9}{12}$$
$$\overline{\frac{11}{12}}$$

D. Find $12\frac{1}{4} - 5\frac{7}{8}$.

Estimate: $12 - 6 = 6$.

Use a common denominator. Rename $12\frac{2}{8}$.

$$12\frac{1}{4} = 12\frac{2}{8} = 11\frac{10}{8}$$
$$-\ 5\frac{7}{8} =\ \ 5\frac{7}{8} =\ \ 5\ \frac{7}{8}$$
$$\overline{6\ \frac{3}{8}}$$

■ **Write About Math** Describe the steps you would perform to find $4 - 2\frac{3}{10}$ using fraction pieces. How did you rename 4?

Check Understanding

For another example, see Set F, pages 260–261.

Subtract. Use fraction pieces to help you.

1. 3
$-1\frac{1}{3}$

2. $2\frac{1}{4}$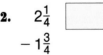
$-1\frac{3}{4}$

Rename each mixed number.

3. $2\frac{1}{8} = 1\frac{}{8}$ **4.** $5\frac{3}{4} = 4\frac{}{4}$

Find the missing numbers.

5. $5 = 4\frac{}{3}$
$-1\frac{1}{3} = 1\frac{1}{3}$
$\overline{3\frac{}{3}}$

6. $9\frac{4}{5} = 9\frac{}{15}$
$-5\frac{1}{3} = 5\frac{}{}$
$\overline{4\frac{}{15}}$

Practice

For More Practice, see Set F, pages 262–263.

Subtract. You may use fraction pieces or pictures to help you.

7. $5\frac{2}{3}$
$-4\frac{1}{3}$

8. 4
$-2\frac{2}{3}$

9. 3
$-1\frac{5}{8}$

10. $3\frac{1}{5}$
$-\frac{3}{5}$

11. $3\frac{1}{6}$
$-2\frac{5}{6}$

12. $4\frac{3}{8}$
$-1\frac{7}{8}$

13. $6\frac{3}{8}$
$-4\frac{3}{4}$

14. $7\frac{1}{5}$
$-4\frac{3}{5}$

15. 9
$-7\frac{1}{2}$

16. $5\frac{7}{10}$
$-4\frac{9}{10}$

17. $8\frac{1}{8}$
$-3\frac{1}{2}$

18. 8
$-7\frac{1}{4}$

Tell whether you would use mental math or paper and pencil. Then find each difference.

19. $5\frac{3}{4} - 2\frac{1}{4}$ **20.** $16 - 5\frac{1}{5}$ **21.** $10\frac{7}{8} - 5\frac{1}{16}$ **22.** $8\frac{1}{2} - 5\frac{2}{3}$ **23.** $9\frac{2}{3} - 6\frac{11}{12}$

24. $6\frac{1}{2} - 4\frac{1}{2}$ **25.** $12 - 2\frac{7}{9}$ **26.** $11\frac{3}{8} - 8\frac{5}{6}$ **27.** $7\frac{1}{2} - 4\frac{3}{10}$ **28.** $3 - 2\frac{4}{5}$

🖩 **Calculator** Use your calculator to find each difference or sum.

29. $37\frac{1}{10} - 32\frac{3}{4}$ **30.** $20 - 6\frac{1}{2}$ **31.** $8\frac{1}{2} + 6\frac{1}{4}$ **32.** $9\frac{3}{4} + 16\frac{3}{4}$ **33.** $7\frac{5}{8} - 4\frac{4}{5}$

Mixed Practice Find each answer. **Remember** to give your answer in lowest terms.

34. $12\frac{2}{5} + 7\frac{3}{5}$ **35.** $\frac{1}{6} + \frac{5}{8}$ **36.** $\frac{3}{8} - \frac{1}{16}$ **37.** $10\frac{1}{4} + \frac{1}{2}$ **38.** $\frac{3}{4} - \frac{1}{6}$

39. $2\frac{3}{4} + 6\frac{5}{6}$ **40.** $\frac{3}{5} - \frac{1}{6}$ **41.** $\frac{2}{3} + 4\frac{1}{4}$ **42.** $8\frac{1}{2} - 3\frac{7}{12}$ **43.** $7\frac{1}{3} + 5\frac{3}{10}$

Problem Solving

Critical Thinking Solve each problem.

44. Find a whole number and a fraction having a difference of $2\frac{1}{5}$.

45. The sum of two mixed numbers is $34\frac{3}{5}$. One of the numbers is $15\frac{1}{2}$. Find the other number.

In the Northern Hemisphere the shortest day of the year occurs in December, with an average of $9\frac{3}{4}$ hours of daylight. The longest day, in June, has an average of $14\frac{1}{2}$ hours of sunlight.

46. How much more sunlight does the longest day have than the shortest day?

47. In Bangor, Maine, the shortest day of the year has $8\frac{7}{10}$ hours of daylight. How much less daylight is this than the average daylight for the Northern Hemisphere in December?

48. In San Diego, California, the shortest day of the year has 10 hours of daylight. How much more daylight does San Diego have on the shortest day than Bangor?

49. Use Data Refer to the Bright Angel Trail signpost on page 234.

On the longest day of the year, Mr. Eaton started hiking at dawn. He hiked from the trailhead to the Phantom Ranch at the rate of 1 mile every 25 minutes. How much daylight was left when he reached the ranch?

Compare problems to help you relate new problems to ones you've solved before.

Reading ——— Math

Equal Values Match equal values.

1. One half

2. One minus one fourth

3. Two thirds subtracted from four

4. Three fifths

5. Three and three eighths

6. Three sixths plus five tenths

a. Six tenths

b. One

c. Two and eleven eighths

d. Four eighths

e. Three and one third

f. Three fourths

Too Much or Too Little Information

PROBLEM SOLVING
GUIDE

IIII➡ **Understand**
QUESTION
FACTS
KEY IDEA

Plan and Solve
STRATEGY
ANSWER

Look Back
SENSIBLE ANSWER
ALTERNATE APPROACH

Build Understanding

Shadow puppetry was enjoyed in China over a thousand years ago. Today, it is performed throughout the world. Shadow puppets are flat figures held by a rod or wire against a white screen. As a light shines behind the figures, the audience sees only their shadows.

Lena plans to make a bird shadow puppet. What is the total length of rod she will need?

IIII➡ **Understand**   QUESTION   What is the total length of the rod she will need?

FACTS   The three rods must measure $2\frac{1}{4}$ ft, $2\frac{1}{4}$ ft, and $1\frac{3}{4}$ ft.

KEY IDEA   Add the lengths of the three rods. The other information is not needed.

Plan and Solve   Estimate: $2 + 2 + 2 = 6$

$2\frac{1}{4} + 2\frac{1}{4} + 1\frac{3}{4}$

$4\frac{1}{2} + 1\frac{3}{4} = 6\frac{1}{4}$

ANSWER   Lena will need $6\frac{1}{4}$ ft of rod.

Look Back   The answer is close to the estimate.

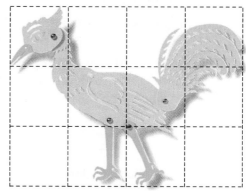

DIRECTIONS FOR CHINESE BIRD SHADOW PUPPET

1. Cut head, body, tail, and legs out of cardboard.
2. Cut slits to show decorations.
3. Hinge pieces at Xs with paper fasteners.
4. Cut three rods: $2\frac{1}{4}$ ft, $2\frac{1}{4}$ ft, and $1\frac{3}{4}$ ft.
5. Attach longer rods to top of head and tail; shorter rod to middle of body.

■ **Talk About Math**   Make up a problem about the puppet directions that cannot be solved because there is *too little information*.

Check Understanding

Use the puppet directions on page 256. If there is not enough information given, write *too little information*. Otherwise, solve the problem.

1. How much will the rod cost?

Think: How many feet of rod are needed altogether? What is the cost per foot? Can you find the answer with facts that are given?

2. How long is the shortest rod in inches?

Think: Is the number of inches in a foot given? Do you know this fact? Can you find it elsewhere?

Practice

Use the puppet directions on page 256. If there is not enough information given, write *too little information*. Otherwise, solve the problem.

3. How much longer is the rod for the head than the rod for the body?

4. Lena bought fasteners for $0.25, cardboard for $1.25, and the dowel rod. How much did she spend?

Each of these two Turkish puppets represents a character in a story.

Lena bought the materials needed for *Wayang*, a type of shadow puppetry done in Indonesia. She purchased 18 feet of dowel rod for $3.96, 4 sheets of cardboard at $1.25 a piece, 3 dozen fasteners, a hobby knife, and $1\frac{7}{8}$ yards of white fabric for the screen.

5. How much did Lena pay for the hobby knife?

6. How much did Lena pay for the cardboard?

7. Lena used $1\frac{1}{4}$ yards of the fabric. How much was left?

8. Lena needs 26 fasteners. Did she buy enough?

9. Lena used $2\frac{2}{3}$ sheets of cardboard. How much is left?

10. How much did all supplies cost?

Shadow puppets are popular forms of entertainment in many parts of the world, including Indonesia.

Skills Review

Write an improper fraction for each mixed number.

1. $3\frac{1}{3}$ **2.** $2\frac{3}{8}$ **3.** $4\frac{5}{6}$

Write a mixed number or whole number for each improper fraction.

4. $\frac{9}{3}$ **5.** $\frac{27}{8}$ **6.** $\frac{35}{10}$

Write the fractions in order from least to greatest.

7. $2\frac{2}{3}, 2\frac{3}{4}, 2\frac{3}{5}$ **8.** $1\frac{1}{6}, \frac{5}{8}, \frac{3}{4}$

Estimate each sum as greater than or less than 1.

9. $\frac{3}{5} + \frac{5}{8}$ **10.** $\frac{2}{9} + \frac{1}{4}$ **11.** $\frac{1}{2} + \frac{3}{7}$

Estimate each sum or difference.

12. $2\frac{1}{3} + 4\frac{5}{6}$ **13.** $5\frac{3}{4} - 2\frac{1}{8}$

14. $4\frac{5}{6} + 1\frac{4}{5}$ **15.** $8\frac{1}{3} - 2\frac{2}{9}$

Add or subtract.

16. $\frac{3}{4} + \frac{5}{8}$ **17.** $\frac{5}{6} + \frac{7}{8}$

18. $\frac{7}{12} + \frac{1}{3}$ **19.** $\frac{2}{5} + \frac{1}{2} + \frac{7}{10}$

20. $\frac{7}{10} - \frac{2}{5}$ **21.** $\frac{3}{4} - \frac{1}{6}$

22. $\frac{7}{12} - \frac{3}{8}$ **23.** $\frac{2}{3} - \frac{3}{10}$

24. $3\frac{2}{3}$ **25.** $5\frac{5}{6}$ **26.** $2\frac{2}{3}$

    $+ 2\frac{1}{6}$ $- 1\frac{3}{4}$ $+ \frac{4}{5}$

27. $5\frac{7}{8}$ **28.** $6\frac{5}{6}$ **29.** $8\frac{1}{2}$

    $- 2\frac{3}{8}$ $- 1\frac{1}{4}$ $- 2\frac{5}{7}$

Problem-Solving Review

Solve each problem.

30. How many 0.75-ounce slices of cheese are in a 24-ounce package?

31. Jon's yearly car expenses were $1,309. Mark's expenses were twice as much. What were Mark's yearly car expenses?

32. Robin has 1 yard of ribbon. She needs pieces measuring $\frac{5}{6}$ of a foot, $1\frac{1}{3}$ feet, and $\frac{3}{4}$ of a foot. Does she have enough ribbon?

33. It is about 300 miles from City A to City B. The Audete family left City A and drove for 6 hours at an average speed of 47 miles per hour. Did they reach City B?

34. The officers in the photo club are president, secretary, and treasurer. Jan is not the secretary. Alex does not deal with money. Mark holds the highest office. Which person holds each office?

35. **Data File** Use the data on pages 266–267. What size nail would you use to nail a $\frac{3}{4}$-inch thickness of plywood to a $1\frac{1}{2}$-inch board?

36. **Make a Data File** Find the ads for homes in the newspaper. Compare the prices of homes. What are some reasons for the difference in prices of homes?

Write each number in words.

1. 1,560,302,040　　**2.** 50.01045

Write each number in expanded form using exponents.

3. 5,234　　**4.** 23,050　　**5.** 70,302

Estimate. Then compute.

6.　23.765　　**7.**　45.20　　**8.**　3.98
　　+ 18.029　　　− 11.964　　　× 2.4

9. 45.6 + 1.698　　**10.** 7.2 − 4.185

Solve each equation for n.

11. $4 \times n = 64$　　**12.** $32 + n = 99$

13. $53 = n + 25$　　**14.** $n \times 3 = 87$

Write the coordinates of each point.

15. A　　**16.** B

17. Give the letter that names the point located by (2, 4).

Multiply or divide. For Exercises 20-21, show remainders as whole numbers.

18. 0.77×1.35　　**19.** 0.056×0.094

20. $645 \div 76$　　**21.** $2,845 \div 58$

22. $6\overline{)135.66}$　　**23.** $45\overline{)3.15}$

Solve each problem.

24. Name 2 lines containing B.

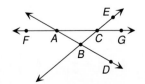

25. Name an obtuse angle.

Write each fraction as a decimal. Use a bar to write repeating decimals.

26. $\frac{4}{5}$　**27.** $\frac{1}{6}$　**28.** $\frac{5}{8}$　**29.** $\frac{7}{9}$

Tell if the number is prime or composite.

30. 37　　**31.** 225　　**32.** 123

Name each figure.

33. 　**34.** 　**35.**

Write three fractions equal to the given fraction.

36. $\frac{2}{3}$　**37.** $\frac{1}{5}$　**38.** $\frac{6}{12}$　**39.** $\frac{10}{30}$

Write the fractions in order from least to greatest.

40. $\frac{1}{6}, \frac{1}{4}, \frac{1}{5}$　　　**41.** $\frac{5}{8}, \frac{7}{12}, \frac{3}{4}$

Write an improper fraction for each mixed number.

42. $5\frac{1}{3}$　　**43.** $3\frac{5}{6}$　　**44.** $10\frac{2}{5}$

Estimate each sum as greater than or less than 1.

45. $\frac{3}{4} + \frac{2}{3}$　**46.** $\frac{1}{5} + \frac{2}{9}$　**47.** $\frac{1}{2} + \frac{7}{9}$

Add or subtract.

48. $\frac{5}{6} + \frac{5}{8}$　　　**49.** $4\frac{2}{3} + 2\frac{5}{12}$

50. $\frac{7}{10} - \frac{1}{4}$　　　**51.** $3\frac{1}{6} - 2\frac{2}{9}$

Reteaching

Set A pages 234–237

Write $2\frac{3}{5}$ as an improper fraction.

$2\frac{3}{5} = 2 + \frac{3}{5}$

$\qquad = \frac{10}{5} + \frac{3}{5}$

$\qquad = \frac{13}{5}$

To find the numerator, multiply 2 times the denominator, 5. Then add the numerator, 3, to the product.

Remember that the numerator of an improper fraction is greater than or equal to the denominator.

Copy and complete the table.

Mixed Number	Sum	Rename Whole Number	Improper Fraction
$2\frac{2}{5}$	**1.**	$\frac{10}{5} + \frac{2}{5}$	**2.**
$3\frac{2}{3}$	$3 + \frac{2}{3}$	**3.**	**4.**

Set B pages 238–241

Estimate $\frac{3}{5} + \frac{1}{8}$.

Compare each fraction to $\frac{1}{2}$.

$\frac{3}{5} > \frac{1}{2}$

$\frac{1}{8} < \frac{1}{2}$

Since one fraction is greater than $\frac{1}{2}$ and another is less than $\frac{1}{2}$, then the sum is greater than the greater fraction.

Remember that the sum is > 1 if both fractions are $> \frac{1}{2}$ and the sum is < 1 if both fractions are $< \frac{1}{2}$.

Choose the *best* estimate by comparing each fraction to $\frac{1}{2}$. Is the sum: (a) greater than 1, (b) less than 1, or (c) greater than the greater fraction in the exercise?

1. $\frac{5}{6} + \frac{5}{8}$ **2.** $\frac{1}{3} + \frac{3}{5}$ **3.** $\frac{9}{10} + \frac{1}{6}$

4. $\frac{3}{8} + \frac{1}{4}$ **5.** $\frac{7}{10} + \frac{4}{5}$ **6.** $\frac{5}{12} + \frac{3}{4}$

7. $\frac{3}{10} + \frac{2}{3}$ **8.** $\frac{7}{12} + \frac{5}{6}$ **9.** $\frac{3}{8} + \frac{1}{5}$

Set C pages 242–243

Find the sum: $\frac{3}{10} + \frac{3}{4}$

Write the fractions with a common denominator. Then add.

$\begin{aligned} \frac{3}{10} &= \frac{6}{20} \\ + \frac{3}{4} &= \frac{15}{20} \\ \hline &\ \ \frac{21}{20} = 1\frac{1}{20} \end{aligned}$

Remember that if the sum is an improper fraction, write it as a mixed number.

Add. Give answers in lowest terms.

1. $\frac{1}{3}$ $+ \frac{5}{6}$ **2.** $\frac{3}{8}$ $+ \frac{5}{16}$ **3.** $\frac{1}{6}$ $\frac{5}{12}$ $+ \frac{7}{24}$

4. $\frac{7}{10} + \frac{1}{3}$ **5.** $\frac{7}{8} + \frac{1}{2} + \frac{4}{5}$

Set D   pages 244–245

Subtract.

$\frac{5}{6} - \frac{4}{9}$

Write the fractions with a common denominator. Then subtract.

$\frac{5}{6} = \frac{15}{18}$

$-\frac{4}{9} = \frac{8}{18}$

$\overline{\phantom{-\frac{4}{9} =} \frac{7}{18}}$

Remember to check to make sure that the difference is less than the first number.

Subtract. Give answers in lowest terms.

1. $\frac{4}{5} - \frac{2}{5}$ **2.** $\frac{7}{10} - \frac{3}{5}$ **3.** $\frac{2}{3} - \frac{1}{4}$

4. $\frac{11}{12} - \frac{5}{6}$ **5.** $\frac{5}{8} - \frac{1}{6}$ **6.** $\frac{4}{5} - \frac{7}{12}$

Set E   pages 250–251

Estimate the sum. Then add.

$6\frac{2}{5} + 3\frac{1}{4}$

Estimate.

$6\frac{2}{5} \approx 6,\ 3\frac{1}{4} \approx 3,\ 6 + 3 = 9$

Write the fraction with a common denominator. Then add.

$6\frac{2}{5} = 6\frac{8}{20}$

$+ 3\frac{1}{4} = 3\frac{5}{20}$

$\overline{\phantom{+ 3\frac{1}{4} =} 9\frac{13}{20}}$

Remember that the answer will be less than the estimate if both addends are rounded up.

Estimate each sum. Then add.

1. $3\frac{1}{6}$ **2.** 5 **3.** $7\frac{1}{3}$

$+ 4\frac{5}{6}$ $+ 2\frac{1}{4}$ $+ 4\frac{2}{5}$

4. $8\frac{2}{3} + 7\frac{3}{8}$ **5.** $10\frac{1}{5} + 4\frac{5}{6}$

6. $9\frac{3}{4} + 6\frac{7}{10}$ **7.** $5\frac{4}{9} + 3\frac{11}{12}$

Set F   pages 252–255

Subtract.

$4 - 2\frac{1}{5}$

Estimate. $4 - 2 = 2$

Rename 4 so you can subtract.

$4 = 3 + 1 = 3 + \frac{5}{5} = 3\frac{5}{5}$

$4 = 3\frac{5}{5}$

$- 2\frac{1}{5} = 2\frac{1}{5}$

$\overline{\phantom{- 2\frac{1}{5} =} 1\frac{4}{5}}$

Remember that renaming a mixed number as a whole number and an improper fraction does not change the number.

Subtract. Use fraction pieces if needed.

1. 6 **2.** 5 **3.** 8

$- 3\frac{1}{4}$ $- 2\frac{1}{10}$ $- 4\frac{5}{8}$

4. $9 - 7\frac{5}{6}$ **5.** $12 - 3\frac{3}{5}$

6. $3\frac{1}{5} - 1\frac{2}{3}$ **7.** $8\frac{3}{10} - 4\frac{1}{2}$

More Practice

Set A pages 234–237

Compare. Use $<$, $>$, or $=$.

1. $1\frac{7}{10}$ ⬚ $1\frac{9}{10}$
2. $7\frac{3}{8}$ ⬚ $7\frac{3}{4}$
3. $4\frac{3}{7}$ ⬚ $4\frac{9}{21}$
4. $\frac{11}{4}$ ⬚ $\frac{9}{2}$
5. $\frac{9}{8}$ ⬚ $\frac{10}{9}$

Write in order from least to greatest.

6. $3\frac{1}{3}, 3\frac{3}{5}, 3\frac{1}{2}$
7. $4\frac{1}{6}, 3\frac{7}{8}, 2\frac{11}{12}$
8. $\frac{5}{6}, \frac{8}{7}, 1\frac{1}{3}$
9. $2\frac{1}{2}, 2\frac{5}{8}, 2\frac{2}{5}$
10. $\frac{10}{7}, \frac{10}{6}, \frac{10}{5}$

Set B pages 238–241

Choose the *best* estimate by comparing each fraction to $\frac{1}{2}$.
Is the sum: (a) greater than 1, (b) less than 1, or (c) greater
than the greater fraction in the exercise?

1. $\frac{2}{5} + \frac{7}{16}$
2. $\frac{7}{10} + \frac{3}{4}$
3. $\frac{5}{8} + \frac{5}{9}$
4. $\frac{1}{3} + \frac{5}{6}$
5. $\frac{3}{8} + \frac{7}{10}$
6. $\frac{8}{9} + \frac{11}{12}$

Round each mixed number to the nearest whole number.

7. $9\frac{3}{4}$
8. $2\frac{7}{8}$
9. $4\frac{2}{5}$
10. $6\frac{7}{13}$
11. $3\frac{5}{9}$
12. $8\frac{7}{18}$
13. $1\frac{5}{8}$
14. $5\frac{3}{7}$

Estimate each sum or difference. Round mixed numbers
to the nearest whole number. Then find each sum or difference.

15. $3\frac{3}{8} - 2\frac{1}{3}$
16. $7\frac{5}{6} - 4\frac{1}{4}$
17. $9\frac{3}{5} + 5\frac{1}{8}$
18. $4\frac{1}{2} + 2\frac{7}{10}$
19. $8\frac{3}{4} + 9\frac{2}{3}$

Set C pages 242–243

For Exercises 1–9, tell whether you would use mental math or paper
and pencil. Then find each sum. Give answers in lowest terms.

1. $\begin{array}{r} \frac{1}{4} \\ +\frac{5}{6} \\ \hline \end{array}$
2. $\begin{array}{r} \frac{3}{10} \\ +\frac{4}{5} \\ \hline \end{array}$
3. $\begin{array}{r} \frac{5}{9} \\ +\frac{3}{18} \\ \hline \end{array}$
4. $\begin{array}{r} \frac{2}{3} \\ +\frac{3}{8} \\ \hline \end{array}$
5. $\begin{array}{r} \frac{1}{4} \\ \frac{5}{8} \\ +\frac{7}{16} \\ \hline \end{array}$
6. $\begin{array}{r} \frac{1}{2} \\ \frac{2}{3} \\ +\frac{11}{12} \\ \hline \end{array}$

7. $\frac{9}{10} + \frac{3}{10} + \frac{7}{10}$
8. $\frac{3}{4} + \frac{1}{3} + \frac{1}{2}$
9. $\frac{5}{6} + \frac{7}{8} + \frac{2}{3}$

Complete each function table. Give answers in lowest terms.

10.

+	$\frac{1}{3}$	$\frac{1}{2}$	$\frac{2}{5}$	$\frac{2}{9}$	$\frac{5}{12}$
$\frac{1}{3}$	$\frac{2}{3}$				

11.

+	$\frac{3}{8}$	$\frac{5}{16}$	$\frac{7}{24}$	$\frac{2}{5}$	$\frac{5}{6}$
$\frac{1}{8}$	$\frac{1}{2}$				

Set D pages 244–245

Subtract.

1. $\frac{5}{8} - \frac{3}{8}$ **2.** $\frac{11}{12} - \frac{5}{12}$ **3.** $\frac{7}{8} - \frac{3}{4}$ **4.** $\frac{7}{16} - \frac{1}{8}$ **5.** $\frac{9}{10} - \frac{1}{2}$

6. $\frac{3}{10} - \frac{1}{5}$ **7.** $\frac{13}{24} - \frac{1}{2}$ **8.** $\frac{5}{6} - \frac{2}{5}$ **9.** $\frac{5}{12} - \frac{1}{4}$ **10.** $\frac{17}{20} - \frac{2}{3}$

Mixed Practice Find each answer.

11. $\frac{3}{5} + \frac{1}{4}$ **12.** $\frac{5}{6} - \frac{3}{8}$ **13.** $\frac{1}{3} - \frac{1}{12}$ **14.** $\frac{3}{10} + \frac{1}{2}$ **15.** $\frac{5}{6} - \frac{4}{5}$

Set E pages 250–251

Estimate each sum. Then add.

1. $\begin{array}{r} 3\frac{2}{5} \\ + 8\frac{3}{10} \\ \hline \end{array}$ **2.** $\begin{array}{r} 4\frac{1}{2} \\ + 2\frac{1}{6} \\ \hline \end{array}$ **3.** $\begin{array}{r} 5\frac{3}{10} \\ + 4\frac{3}{10} \\ \hline \end{array}$ **4.** $\begin{array}{r} 9 \\ + 1\frac{3}{4} \\ \hline \end{array}$ **5.** $\begin{array}{r} 7\frac{3}{5} \\ + \frac{5}{6} \\ \hline \end{array}$ **6.** $\begin{array}{r} 2\frac{7}{8} \\ + 3\frac{1}{3} \\ \hline \end{array}$

7. $6\frac{3}{8} + 10$ **8.** $4\frac{1}{3} + 5\frac{7}{12}$ **9.** $3\frac{1}{8} + 9\frac{1}{6}$ **10.** $11\frac{2}{3} + 8\frac{3}{5}$ **11.** $2\frac{3}{4} + 6\frac{9}{10}$

Set F pages 252–255

Subtract. You may use fraction pieces to help you work
Exercises 1–6.

1. $\begin{array}{r} 7\frac{5}{6} \\ - 1\frac{1}{6} \\ \hline \end{array}$ **2.** $\begin{array}{r} 5 \\ - 3\frac{3}{4} \\ \hline \end{array}$ **3.** $\begin{array}{r} 7 \\ - 2\frac{5}{8} \\ \hline \end{array}$ **4.** $\begin{array}{r} 8\frac{1}{6} \\ - \frac{5}{6} \\ \hline \end{array}$ **5.** $\begin{array}{r} 9\frac{1}{4} \\ - \frac{3}{4} \\ \hline \end{array}$ **6.** $\begin{array}{r} 6\frac{5}{8} \\ - 2\frac{7}{8} \\ \hline \end{array}$

For Exercises 7–12, tell whether you would use mental
math or paper and pencil. Then find each difference.

7. $\begin{array}{r} 5\frac{3}{8} \\ - 2\frac{3}{16} \\ \hline \end{array}$ **8.** $\begin{array}{r} 6 \\ - 3\frac{2}{3} \\ \hline \end{array}$ **9.** $\begin{array}{r} 12\frac{5}{6} \\ - 8\frac{1}{6} \\ \hline \end{array}$ **10.** $\begin{array}{r} 11\frac{3}{4} \\ - 8\frac{1}{8} \\ \hline \end{array}$ **11.** $\begin{array}{r} 4\frac{3}{8} \\ - 1\frac{1}{2} \\ \hline \end{array}$ **12.** $\begin{array}{r} 7\frac{1}{6} \\ - 3\frac{2}{5} \\ \hline \end{array}$

Mixed Practice Find each answer.

13. $13\frac{1}{8} + 9\frac{3}{4}$ **14.** $\frac{5}{6} - \frac{5}{12}$ **15.** $\frac{1}{6} + \frac{3}{5}$ **16.** $12\frac{3}{8} + \frac{3}{4}$ **17.** $8 - 3\frac{7}{12}$

Enrichment

Egyptian Numeration

The ancient Egyptians used numerals based on everyday objects.

1	10	100	1,000	10,000	100,000
Stroke	Arch	Coiled Rope	Lotus Flower	Finger	Tadpole

You can use a series of these symbols to express any number.

$12,301 = 10,000 + 2(1,000) + 3(100) + 1$

Write each of the following numbers in Egyptian numerals.

1. 22

2. 101

3. 150

4. 304

5. 610

6. 12,030

7. 5,050

8. 20,000

9. 300,000

10. 201,000

Chapter 7 Review/Test

Write a fraction for each mixed number.

1. $2\frac{1}{3}$ **2.** $4\frac{3}{8}$ **3.** $6\frac{3}{5}$

Write a mixed number or whole number for each fraction.

4. $\frac{23}{7}$ **5.** $\frac{52}{8}$ **6.** $\frac{14}{2}$

Estimate by determining whether the sum is greater than 1 or less than 1.

7. $\frac{7}{8} + \frac{5}{6}$ **8.** $\frac{5}{10} + \frac{7}{9}$

9. $\frac{3}{13} + \frac{1}{5}$ **10.** $\frac{3}{5} + \frac{9}{10}$

Add.

11. $\begin{array}{r} \frac{1}{5} \\ + \frac{3}{5} \\ \hline \end{array}$ **12.** $\begin{array}{r} \frac{3}{8} \\ + \frac{7}{8} \\ \hline \end{array}$

13. $\begin{array}{r} \frac{2}{3} \\ + \frac{2}{5} \\ \hline \end{array}$ **14.** $\begin{array}{r} 9\frac{2}{3} \\ + 1\frac{1}{3} \\ \hline \end{array}$

15. $\begin{array}{r} 2\frac{1}{2} \\ + 2\frac{3}{5} \\ \hline \end{array}$ **16.** $\begin{array}{r} 7\frac{5}{8} \\ + 6\frac{3}{4} \\ \hline \end{array}$

Subtract.

17. $\begin{array}{r} \frac{5}{6} \\ - \frac{1}{6} \\ \hline \end{array}$ **18.** $\begin{array}{r} \frac{5}{8} \\ - \frac{1}{4} \\ \hline \end{array}$ **19.** $\begin{array}{r} \frac{11}{12} \\ - \frac{4}{5} \\ \hline \end{array}$

20. $\begin{array}{r} 5\frac{1}{8} \\ - 3\frac{7}{8} \\ \hline \end{array}$ **21.** $\begin{array}{r} 6\frac{4}{9} \\ - 1\frac{2}{3} \\ \hline \end{array}$ **22.** $\begin{array}{r} 8\frac{1}{4} \\ - 3\frac{5}{6} \\ \hline \end{array}$

23. Joanne bought a piece of wood $45\frac{1}{4}$ inches long for $39.25. She cut off a $23\frac{3}{8}$-inch piece. How much was left?

Read the problem below. Then answer the question.

Write $\frac{4}{5}$ as the sum of unit fractions with different denominators.

24. Which of the following statements tells the first step in working backward to solve the problem?

   a. Subtract $\frac{4}{5}$ from 1.

   b. Find the greatest unit fraction less than $\frac{4}{5}$ and subtract it from $\frac{4}{5}$.

   c. Write $\frac{4}{5}$ as the sum of $\frac{2}{5}$ and $\frac{3}{5}$.

   d. Add $\frac{1}{5}$ to $\frac{4}{5}$.

25. **Write About Math** In Exercises 7–10, explain how you can tell if the sum of the fractions is greater than 1.

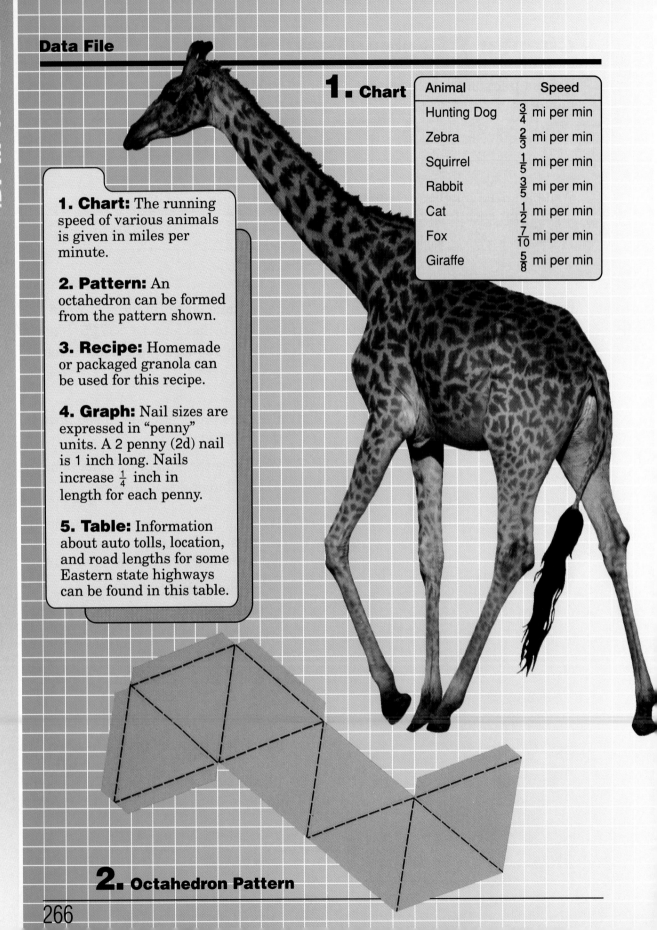

DATA FILE

1. **Chart**

Animal	Speed
Hunting Dog	$\frac{3}{4}$ mi per min
Zebra	$\frac{2}{3}$ mi per min
Squirrel	$\frac{1}{5}$ mi per min
Rabbit	$\frac{3}{5}$ mi per min
Cat	$\frac{1}{2}$ mi per min
Fox	$\frac{7}{10}$ mi per min
Giraffe	$\frac{5}{8}$ mi per min

1. Chart: The running speed of various animals is given in miles per minute.

2. Pattern: An octahedron can be formed from the pattern shown.

3. Recipe: Homemade or packaged granola can be used for this recipe.

4. Graph: Nail sizes are expressed in "penny" units. A 2 penny (2d) nail is 1 inch long. Nails increase $\frac{1}{4}$ inch in length for each penny.

5. Table: Information about auto tolls, location, and road lengths for some Eastern state highways can be found in this table.

2. **Octahedron Pattern**

3. Recipe

Honey-Granola Chicken

$2\frac{1}{2}$ to $3\frac{1}{2}$ pound chicken, cut up

Salt and pepper

$\frac{1}{2}$ cup honey

1 egg

2 cups granola, crushed

Heat oven to 350. Sprinkle chicken with salt and pepper. Beat honey and egg in shallow dish. Dip chicken into honey mixture, then coat with granola. Bake in ungreased baking pan for $1\frac{1}{4}$ to $1\frac{3}{4}$ hours. Serves 6.

4. Graph

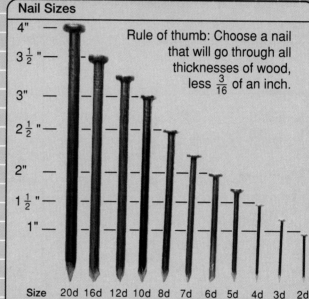

Nail Sizes

Rule of thumb: Choose a nail that will go through all thicknesses of wood, less $\frac{3}{16}$ of an inch.

| Size | 20d | 16d | 12d | 10d | 8d | 7d | 6d | 5d | 4d | 3d | 2d |

(vertical scale: 4", $3\frac{1}{2}$", 3", $2\frac{1}{2}$", 2", $1\frac{1}{2}$", 1")

5. Table

Toll Road Information

State	Road Name	Location	Miles	Auto Toll
New Jersey	Atlantic City Expressway	Turnersville to Atlantic City	44	$ 1.25
	Garden State Parkway	Montvale to Cape May	173	3.75
	New Jersey Turnpike	Delaware Memorial Bridge to George Washington Bridge	113	2.70
New York	New York Thruway:			
	Eastbound	PA state line to New York City	496	$18.05
	Westbound	New York City to PA state line	496	15.55
	Berkshire Section	Selkirk to MA Turnpike	24	1.20
	New England Section	New York City to CT Turnpike	15	0.50
	Niagara Section	Buffalo to Niagara Falls	21	1.50
Ohio	James W. Shocknessy Ohio Turnpike	PA state line to IN state line	241	$ 4.90
Pennsylvania	Pennsylvania Turnpike	NJ state line to Ohio state line	358	$11.30
	Northeast section, PA Turnpike	Norristown to Scranton	110	3.20

Cumulative Review/Test

Give the letter for the correct answer.

1. What does the 7 mean in 14.2376?

  a. 7 hundredths
  b. 7 tenths
  c. 7 hundreds
  d. 7 thousandths

2. Round 13,628 to the nearest thousand.

  a. 13,000   **b.** 10,000
  c. 14,000   **d.** 13,600

3. Add.

$$\begin{array}{r} 4,687 \\ +\ \ \ 369 \end{array}$$

  a. 5,046   **b.** 5,056
  c. 4,956   **d.** 4,946

4. Subtract.

$$\begin{array}{r} 7,348 \\ -\ 2,653 \end{array}$$

  a. 4,795   **b.** 5,695
  c. 5,795   **d.** 4,695

5. Add.

$$\begin{array}{r} 13.45 \\ +24.86 \end{array}$$

  a. 38.21   **b.** 38.41
  c. 38.11   **d.** 38.31

6. Subtract.

$$\begin{array}{r} 36.73 \\ -12.96 \end{array}$$

  a. 24.87   **b.** 24.23
  c. 23.77   **d.** 23.23

7. Choose the equation that should be used to solve this problem. Then solve the problem.

A greeting card store has 2,435 cards in stock. A shipment of 939 cards is received. How many cards does the store have now?

  a. $2,435 + 939 = n$; 3,374 cards
  b. $2,435 - 939 = n$; 1,496 cards
  c. $2,435 - 1,496 = n$; 939 cards
  d. $n + 939 = 2,435$; 1,496 cards

8. Estimate the product.

63×58

  a. 3,000   **b.** 360
  c. 30   **d.** 3,600

9. Multiply.

307×90

  a. 2,763   **b.** 28,530
  c. 27,630   **d.** 24,540

10. Multiply.

$$\begin{array}{r} 343 \\ \times\ \ 46 \end{array}$$

  a. 15,778   **b.** 21,952
  c. 19,742   **d.** 14,468

11. Multiply.

   0.03
× 0.4

a. 0.12   **b.** 0.012
c. 1.2   **d.** 12

12. Divide.

$13\overline{)10,579}$

a. 806 R1   **b.** 813 R10
c. 713 R10   **d.** 926 R1

13. Divide.

8.82 ÷ 9

a. 0.098   **b.** 9.8
c. 98   **d.** 0.98

14. Divide.

$0.08\overline{)0.032}$

a. 4   **b.** 0.4
c. 0.04   **d.** 12

15. Choose the most sensible measure for the area of a living room floor.

a. 96 cu ft   **b.** 96 sq ft
c. 96 ft   **d.** 96 sq mi

16. Which term describes this figure?

a. Rectangle   **b.** Square
c. Parallelogram **d.** Rhombus

17. What is $\frac{8}{10}$ written in lowest terms?

a. $\frac{4}{5}$ **b.** $\frac{1}{2}$
c. $\frac{3}{4}$ **d.** $\frac{16}{20}$

18. What is the least common multiple of 6 and 8?

a. 14   **b.** 48   **c.** 36   **d.** 24

19. What is $\frac{17}{3}$ written as a mixed number?

a. $2\frac{2}{3}$ **b.** $7\frac{1}{3}$
c. $5\frac{2}{3}$ **d.** $14\frac{1}{3}$

20. Add.

$\frac{2}{3} + \frac{1}{6} + \frac{7}{12}$

a. $1\frac{5}{12}$ **b.** $\frac{5}{6}$
c. $1\frac{9}{24}$ **d.** $1\frac{7}{12}$

Read the problem below. Then answer the question.

Becky worked 5.6 hours painting the porch. She used 4.3 gallons of blue paint and 1.7 gallons of white paint. How many gallons of paint did she use?

21. Which fact is not needed?

a. Becky worked 5.6 hours.
b. She used 4.3 gallons of blue paint.
c. She used 1.7 gallons of white paint.

Multiplying and Dividing Fractions

8

Did You Know: The "snowflakes" on the right began with an equilateral triangle. Then on each of the 3 sides of the figure an equilateral triangle was drawn with sides one-third as long. The pattern was repeated to form the last two figures.

Number-Sense Project

Estimate
If the length of each side in the first figure is 1, estimate the length of each side in the second figure. Estimate the perimeter of the second figure.

Gather Data
If the third figure began with a triangle with side lengths of 1, what fraction gives the length of each side of the third figure? How many sides does it have?

Analyze and Report
If all four figures below began with an equilateral triangle with side lengths of 1, find the perimeter of each figure.

271

Meaning of Multiplication of Fractions

Build Understanding

A. Brian lives on a farm in Ireland. He must get water from his well by turning a crank. For each complete turn of the crank, the water bucket rises 6 feet. This table shows how much the bucket rises with different numbers of turns of the crank.

Number of turns	0	1	2	3
Number of feet bucket rises	0	6	12	18

Since 1 turn causes a rise of 6 feet, you can write the result of 2 turns as $2 \times 6 = 12$.

B. If Brian cranks half a turn, the bucket will rise half of 6 feet, or 3 feet. Similarly, the bucket rises 3 feet for each half turn, as shown in this table.

Number of turns	0	$\frac{1}{2}$	1	$1\frac{1}{2}$	2	$2\frac{1}{2}$	3
Number of feet bucket rises	0	3	6	9	12	15	18

You can write the results of $\frac{1}{2}$ turn and $1\frac{1}{2}$ turns using multiplication sentences.

$\frac{1}{2}$ of 6 = 3 $1\frac{1}{2}$ of 6 = 9

$\downarrow \downarrow \downarrow$ $\downarrow \;\; \downarrow \;\; \downarrow$

$\frac{1}{2} \times 6 = 3$ $1\frac{1}{2} \times 6 = 9$

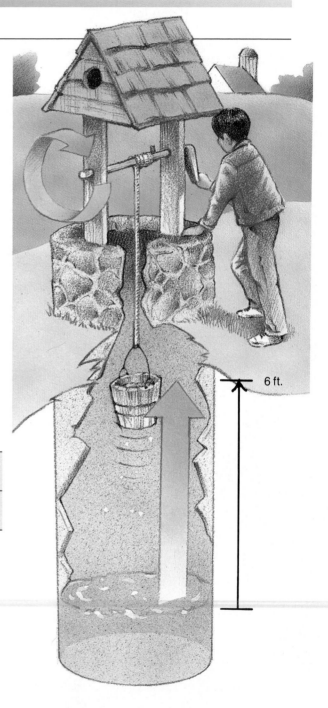

6 ft.

The rope and crank of a well act like a simple pulley system to raise or lower a bucket.

c. Each turn of the crank on Janet's well raises the bucket half a foot. If one turn raises the bucket $\frac{1}{2}$ foot, then how far will the bucket rise for $\frac{1}{3}$ turn? First mark the rope every $\frac{1}{2}$ foot. Then mark $\frac{1}{2}$ ft into thirds.

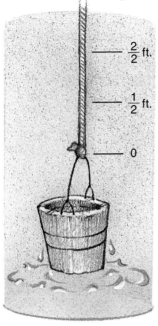
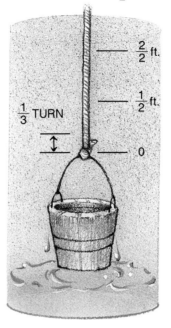
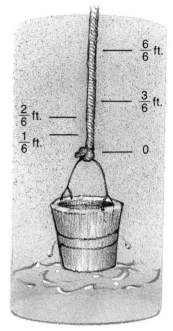

$$\frac{1}{3} \times \frac{1}{2} = \frac{1}{6}$$

The bucket will rise $\frac{1}{6}$ foot for each $\frac{1}{3}$ turn, as shown in the next table.

Number of turns	0	$\frac{1}{3}$	$\frac{2}{3}$	1	$1\frac{1}{3}$	$1\frac{2}{3}$	2	$2\frac{1}{3}$	$2\frac{2}{3}$	3
Number of feet bucket rises	0	$\frac{1}{6}$	$\frac{2}{6}$	$\frac{3}{6}$	$\frac{4}{6}$	$\frac{5}{6}$	1	$1\frac{1}{6}$	$1\frac{2}{6}$	$1\frac{3}{6}$

■ **Write About Math**
Write a multiplication sentence to show that $\frac{2}{3}$ turn of $\frac{1}{2}$ foot causes a rise of $\frac{2}{6}$ foot.

Check Understanding

For another example, see Set A, pages 298–299.

Answer each question.

1. If one turn of a crank raises a bucket $\frac{1}{3}$ foot, how high will the bucket rise for $\frac{1}{7}$ turn? $\frac{3}{7}$ turn?

2. If one turn of a crank raises a bucket $\frac{1}{5}$ foot, how high will the bucket rise for $\frac{1}{3}$ turn? $\frac{2}{3}$ turn?

Write each statement as a multiplication sentence.

3. $\frac{2}{3}$ turn of 6 feet causes a rise of 4 feet.

4. $1\frac{1}{3}$ turns of 6 feet cause a rise of 8 feet.

Make a table for each.

5. Thirds of a turn on Brian's well, from 3 to 5 turns

6. Sixths of a turn on Brian's well, from 2 to 4 turns

7. Thirds of a turn on Janet's well, from 3 to 5 turns

8. Sixths of a turn on Janet's well, from 2 to 4 turns

9. Half turns on Brian's well, from 3 to 6 turns

10. Half turns on Janet's well, from 3 to 6 turns

Mental Math   Use mental math to complete each table for the number of turns and the number of feet a bucket rises.

11.

Turns	0	1	2	3	4	5	6
Feet	0	$\frac{1}{2}$					

12.

Turns	0	$\frac{1}{2}$	1	$1\frac{1}{2}$	2	$2\frac{1}{2}$	3
Feet	0	$\frac{1}{4}$	$\frac{1}{2}$				

13.

Turns	0	$\frac{1}{2}$	1	$1\frac{1}{2}$	2	$2\frac{1}{2}$	3
Feet	0		8				

14.

Turns	0	$\frac{1}{3}$	$\frac{2}{3}$	1	$1\frac{1}{3}$	$1\frac{2}{3}$	2
Feet	0	4		12			

15.

Turns	0	$\frac{1}{2}$	1	$1\frac{1}{2}$	2	$2\frac{1}{2}$	3
Feet	0		10				

16.

Turns	0	$\frac{1}{4}$	$\frac{2}{4}$	$\frac{3}{4}$	1	$1\frac{1}{4}$	$1\frac{2}{4}$
Feet	0				12		

17.

Turns	0	$\frac{1}{2}$	1	$1\frac{1}{2}$	2	$2\frac{1}{2}$	$7\frac{1}{2}$
Feet	0				$\frac{4}{5}$		

18.

Turns	0	$\frac{1}{5}$	$\frac{2}{5}$	$\frac{3}{5}$	$\frac{4}{5}$	1	$2\frac{2}{5}$	$3\frac{4}{5}$
Feet	0				$\frac{1}{2}$			

19.

Turns	0	$\frac{1}{4}$	$\frac{2}{4}$	$\frac{3}{4}$	1	$1\frac{1}{4}$	$1\frac{2}{4}$
Feet	0		4				

20.

Turns	0	$\frac{1}{2}$	1	$1\frac{1}{2}$	2	$2\frac{1}{2}$	3	$3\frac{1}{2}$
Feet	0		$\frac{1}{4}$					

21.

Turns	0	$\frac{1}{6}$	$\frac{2}{6}$	$\frac{3}{6}$	$\frac{4}{6}$	$\frac{5}{6}$	1	$1\frac{1}{6}$
Feet	0						6	

22.

Turns	0	$\frac{1}{2}$	1	$1\frac{1}{2}$	2	$2\frac{1}{2}$	3
Feet	0		$1\frac{1}{2}$				

Problem Solving

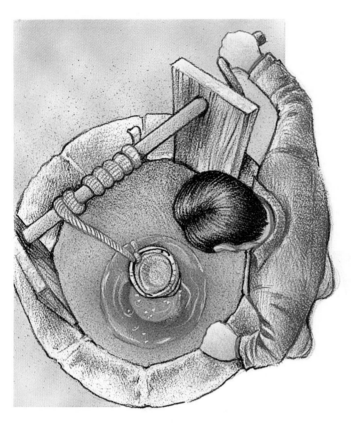

Each turn of the crank on Jonathan's well raises the bucket 2 feet.

23. How far does $\frac{1}{4}$ of a turn raise the bucket?

24. How many feet would the bucket rise in 12 turns?

25. How many turns would it take to raise the bucket $8\frac{1}{2}$ feet?

26. How many feet would the bucket rise in $2\frac{1}{2}$ turns?

27. How many turns would it take to raise the bucket all the way up, if it takes $16\frac{5}{8}$ turns to raise it to the half-way mark?

Explore ——— Math

You can show multiplication of fractions by folding paper.

28. To show $\frac{1}{2} \times \frac{1}{3}$, fold a piece of paper in half and then fold the half into thirds.

29. Unfold the paper and shade one of the sections formed by the fold lines.

30. What fraction of the original piece did you shade?

Use this method to fold and shade each fraction of a piece of paper.

31. $\frac{1}{2} \times \frac{1}{4}$ **32.** $\frac{1}{3} \times \frac{1}{3}$ **33.** $\frac{3}{4} \times \frac{2}{3}$ **34.** $\frac{1}{8} \times \frac{1}{2}$ **35.** $\frac{2}{3} \times \frac{1}{4}$ **36.** $\frac{5}{8} \times \frac{3}{4}$

Multiplying Fractions

Build Understanding

A. Garden Delight
Materials: Paper, ruler
Groups: Small groups of 3 to 5 students each

Mr. Grant raises herbs, flowers, and vegetables to sell to restaurants and in a stand at the local farmers' market. Flowers and herbs make up $\frac{1}{4}$ of the garden, and $\frac{1}{3}$ of that section is for herbs. How much of the total garden is for herbs?

Find $\frac{1}{3}$ of $\frac{1}{4}$ or $\frac{1}{3} \times \frac{1}{4}$.

a. Draw a square with 4-inch sides.

b. Show the second fraction by dividing the square into four equal parts.

c. Shade one of the four equal parts.

d. What fraction of the square is shaded?

e. Now show the first fraction by dividing the square into three equal parts, drawing lines going in the other direction.

f. Draw diagonal lines to indicate $\frac{1}{3}$ of the shaded section.

g. What fraction of the square is shaded and has diagonal lines?

h. What fraction of Mr. Grant's garden is used to grow herbs?

B. Find $\frac{1}{4} \times \frac{3}{5}$.

To multiply fractions, multiply the numerators and multiply the denominators.

$$\frac{1}{4} \times \frac{3}{5} = \frac{1 \times 3}{4 \times 5} = \frac{3}{20}$$

c. Find $\frac{3}{4} \times \frac{5}{6}$.

$$\frac{3}{4} \times \frac{5}{6} = \frac{3 \times 5}{4 \times 6} = \frac{15}{24}$$

Give your answer in lowest terms.

$$\frac{15}{24} = \frac{3 \times 5}{3 \times 8} = \frac{5}{8}$$

↑
Another name for 1

D. You can often use a shortcut to multiply fractions. Look for common factors in the numerators and denominators.

3 is a factor of 6 and 9. Divide the numerator and the denominator by 3.

$$\frac{6}{7} \times \frac{5}{9} = \frac{\overset{2}{\cancel{6}} \times 5}{7 \times \underset{3}{\cancel{9}}} = \frac{10}{21}$$

■ **Talk About Math** Explain why your answer is already in lowest terms when you use the shortcut shown in Example D.

Check Understanding

For another example, see Set B, pages 298–299.

Tell what multiplication of fractions is shown by each model.

1. **2.** 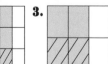 **3.** **4.** **5.** **6.**

Draw a model for each multiplication.

7. $\frac{1}{3} \times \frac{2}{3}$ **8.** $\frac{1}{5} \times \frac{1}{3}$ **9.** $\frac{3}{4} \times \frac{1}{2}$ **10.** $\frac{5}{8} \times \frac{7}{10}$ **11.** $\frac{4}{5} \times \frac{1}{8}$ **12.** $\frac{1}{6} \times \frac{3}{4}$

Practice

For More Practice, see Set B, pages 300–301.

Multiply. Write your answers in lowest terms.
Remember to use the shortcut method when possible.

13. $\frac{1}{4} \times \frac{1}{2}$ **14.** $\frac{3}{4} \times \frac{2}{5}$ **15.** $\frac{5}{6} \times \frac{3}{5}$ **16.** $\frac{1}{10} \times \frac{2}{3}$ **17.** $\frac{3}{8} \times \frac{2}{5}$ **18.** $\frac{1}{4} \times \frac{3}{4}$

19. $\frac{4}{5} \times \frac{7}{8}$ **20.** $\frac{1}{3} \times \frac{3}{10}$ **21.** $\frac{3}{4} \times \frac{5}{6}$ **22.** $\frac{1}{2} \times \frac{1}{2}$ **23.** $\frac{7}{10} \times \frac{1}{4}$ **24.** $\frac{3}{8} \times \frac{1}{3}$

25. $\frac{9}{10} \times \frac{5}{6}$ **26.** $\frac{1}{2} \times \frac{7}{8}$ **27.** $\frac{2}{3} \times \frac{4}{5}$ **28.** $\frac{1}{5} \times \frac{1}{5}$ **29.** $\frac{1}{6} \times \frac{9}{10}$ **30.** $\frac{1}{3} \times \frac{1}{3}$

31. $\frac{1}{2} \times \frac{2}{3}$ **32.** $\frac{1}{6} \times \frac{2}{3}$ **33.** $\frac{4}{5} \times \frac{5}{8}$ **34.** $\frac{1}{6} \times \frac{2}{5}$ **35.** $\frac{5}{8} \times \frac{2}{3}$ **36.** $\frac{2}{5} \times \frac{5}{6}$

For Exercises 37–52, tell whether you would use
mental math or paper and pencil. Then multiply.
Write your answer in lowest terms.

37. $\frac{1}{4} \times \frac{1}{5}$ **38.** $\frac{1}{3} \times \frac{2}{3}$ **39.** $\frac{2}{3} \times \frac{2}{3}$ **40.** $\frac{3}{4} \times \frac{2}{3}$

41. $\frac{1}{4} \times \frac{3}{5}$ **42.** $\frac{4}{5} \times \frac{1}{6}$ **43.** $\frac{3}{10} \times \frac{7}{10}$ **44.** $\frac{9}{10} \times \frac{47}{100}$

45. $\frac{11}{12} \times \frac{2}{3}$ **46.** $\frac{5}{6} \times \frac{2}{3}$ **47.** $\frac{5}{12} \times \frac{3}{10}$ **48.** $\frac{5}{6} \times \frac{3}{10}$

49. $\frac{5}{8} \times \frac{18}{100}$ **50.** $\frac{7}{10} \times \frac{5}{16}$ **51.** $\frac{2}{5} \times \frac{5}{16}$ **52.** $\frac{5}{12} \times \frac{72}{100}$

▦ Calculator Multiply. **Remember** to change
the fractions to decimals before you multiply.

53. $\frac{1}{2} \times \frac{1}{10}$ **54.** $\frac{1}{4} \times \frac{2}{5}$ **55.** $\frac{7}{10} \times \frac{7}{10}$ **56.** $\frac{1}{8} \times \frac{1}{5}$

57. $\frac{2}{5} \times \frac{3}{10}$ **58.** $\frac{9}{10} \times \frac{1}{4}$ **59.** $\frac{1}{2} \times \frac{1}{4}$ **60.** $\frac{1}{5} \times \frac{3}{10}$

61. $\frac{3}{4} \times \frac{7}{10}$ **62.** $\frac{3}{5} \times \frac{1}{2}$ **63.** $\frac{1}{4} \times \frac{5}{8}$ **64.** $\frac{3}{8} \times \frac{1}{2}$

Problem Solving

Solve each problem.

65. How much of Mr. Grant's garden contains flowers?

66. Mr. Grant raises several varieties of tomatoes. One quarter of the total garden is planted with tomatoes, and $\frac{2}{5}$ of the tomatoes are cherry tomatoes. How much of his total garden is planted with cherry tomatoes?

67. Use Data   Mr. Grant sells his lettuce for $0.75 a pound and his tomatoes for $0.50 a pound. How much would a single serving of salad made with lettuce and tomatoes cost? Use information on page 72 to solve.

Be confident so you can do your best.

68. A restaurant buys 10 bunches of basil and 5 bunches of parsley from Mr. Grant each week. The basil costs $0.85 a bunch and the parsley costs $0.40 a bunch. What is the total amount the restaurant pays Mr. Grant each week?

Number Sense   Draw a model to support each answer.

69. Is $\frac{2}{3} \times \frac{1}{4}$ more or less than $\frac{1}{4}$? than $\frac{2}{3}$?

70. Is $\frac{2}{3} + \frac{1}{4}$ more or less than $\frac{1}{4}$? than $\frac{2}{3}$?

71. Does $\frac{2}{3} + \frac{5}{6} = \frac{5}{6} + \frac{2}{3}$?

72. Does $\frac{2}{3} \times \frac{5}{6} = \frac{5}{6} \times \frac{2}{3}$?

Skills _____ **Review**   pages 242–245

Add or subtract. **Remember** to write your answer in lowest terms.

1. $\frac{2}{5}$ $+ \frac{2}{5}$ **2.** $\frac{7}{10}$ $+ \frac{3}{10}$ **3.** $\frac{2}{3}$ $- \frac{1}{3}$ **4.** $\frac{5}{6}$ $- \frac{1}{3}$ **5.** $\frac{5}{12}$ $- \frac{1}{8}$ **6.** $\frac{2}{3}$ $+ \frac{3}{5}$

7. $\frac{1}{5} + \frac{1}{2} + \frac{1}{10}$ **8.** $\frac{83}{100} - \frac{7}{10}$ **9.** $\frac{27}{100} + \frac{9}{10} + \frac{1}{2}$ **10.** $\frac{23}{30} - \frac{2}{3}$

Multiplying Mixed Numbers

Build Understanding

A. Find the area of Veterans Park. Remember to multiply length by width to find the area of a rectangle.

City park	Length	Width
Veterans	3 blocks	$\frac{1}{2}$ block
Washington	4 blocks	$3\frac{1}{2}$ blocks
Martin Luther King	$4\frac{1}{2}$ blocks	$2\frac{1}{2}$ blocks

Find $3 \times \frac{1}{2}$.

$3 \times \frac{1}{2}$ Write 3 as a fraction. Then multiply.

$$\frac{3}{1} \times \frac{1}{2} = \frac{3 \times 1}{1 \times 2} = \frac{3}{2} = 1\frac{1}{2}$$

The area of Veterans Park is $1\frac{1}{2}$ square blocks.

B. Find the area of Martin Luther King Park. Estimate the area by finding a range.

$4\frac{1}{2}$ is between 4 and 5.

$2\frac{1}{2}$ is between 2 and 3.

The range is between 8 (4×2) and 15 (5×3).

Now find $4\frac{1}{2} \times 2\frac{1}{2}$.

$$\frac{9}{2} \times \frac{5}{2} = \frac{9 \times 5}{2 \times 2} = \frac{45}{4} = 11\frac{1}{4}$$

$11\frac{1}{4}$ is between 8 and 15, so the answer is reasonable.

The area of the park is $11\frac{1}{4}$ square blocks.

■ **Talk About Math** How would you estimate the area of Washington Park?

Check Understanding

For another example, see Set C, pages 298–299.

Find the missing numbers.

1. $6 \times \frac{1}{5} = \frac{\boxed{}}{1} \times \frac{1}{5} = \frac{\boxed{}}{5} = \boxed{}\frac{\boxed{}}{5}$

2. $\frac{1}{2} \times 4\frac{1}{2} = \frac{1}{2} \times \frac{\boxed{}}{2} = \frac{\boxed{}}{4} = \boxed{}\frac{1}{4}$

3. $10 \times 6\frac{1}{3} = \frac{10}{1} \times \frac{\boxed{}}{3} = \frac{\boxed{}}{3} = 63\boxed{}$

4. $2\frac{1}{3} \times 2\frac{1}{5} = \frac{\boxed{}}{3} \times \frac{\boxed{}}{5} = \frac{\boxed{}}{\boxed{}} = 5\frac{\boxed{}}{15}$

Practice

For More Practice, see Set C, pages 300–301.

Multiply. **Remember** to change the mixed numbers
and whole numbers to fractions.

5. $3 \times \frac{3}{5}$ **6.** $\frac{1}{2} \times 6\frac{3}{4}$ **7.** $8\frac{1}{2} \times \frac{1}{6}$ **8.** $1\frac{1}{8} \times \frac{3}{4}$ **9.** $5\frac{1}{4} \times \frac{2}{7}$

10. $\frac{4}{5} \times 3\frac{1}{3}$ **11.** $\frac{5}{6} \times 3$ **12.** $7\frac{1}{5} \times \frac{5}{6}$ **13.** $1\frac{1}{2} \times \frac{1}{3}$ **14.** $6\frac{2}{3} \times \frac{1}{5}$

15. $2\frac{1}{4} \times \frac{3}{4}$ **16.** $3\frac{2}{3} \times \frac{3}{10}$ **17.** $2\frac{1}{2} \times \frac{1}{6}$ **18.** $2\frac{3}{5} \times \frac{1}{2}$ **19.** $4\frac{4}{5} \times \frac{1}{3}$

Estimation   Find a range. Then multiply.

20. $6 \times 5\frac{1}{2}$ **21.** $5\frac{1}{8} \times 9\frac{3}{4}$ **22.** $4 \times 6\frac{3}{10}$ **23.** $10 \times 2\frac{43}{100}$ **24.** $8\frac{1}{2} \times 6\frac{2}{3}$

25. $6\frac{3}{5} \times 9\frac{7}{12}$ **26.** $2\frac{2}{3} \times 5\frac{1}{8}$ **27.** $8\frac{1}{6} \times 3\frac{9}{10}$ **28.** $10\frac{1}{2} \times 1\frac{4}{5}$ **29.** $9\frac{1}{5} \times 6\frac{2}{3}$

30. $6\frac{2}{3} \times 2\frac{1}{4}$ **31.** $2\frac{1}{6} \times 1\frac{4}{5}$ **32.** $4\frac{1}{8} \times 2\frac{2}{3}$ **33.** $2\frac{5}{8} \times 6$ **34.** $7\frac{1}{2} \times 1\frac{7}{10}$

Mixed Practice   Tell whether you would use
mental math or pencil and paper. Then multiply.

35. $\frac{4}{5} \times \frac{1}{2}$ **36.** $\frac{5}{6} \times \frac{2}{3}$ **37.** $6\frac{7}{8} \times 4\frac{1}{12}$ **38.** $8\frac{5}{16} \times 5$ **39.** $12 \times \frac{3}{4}$

Problem Solving

Solve each problem.

40. A playground in the Martin Luther
King Park is $50\frac{1}{2}$ feet by $25\frac{1}{4}$ feet.
Find the area of the playground.

41. A sandbox at the Martin Luther
King Park is $6\frac{1}{3}$ feet by $6\frac{1}{3}$ feet.
Find the area of the sandbox.

42. Critical Thinking   Is the
product of two mixed numbers less
than or greater than each factor?
Explain your answer.

43. Visual Thinking   Draw models
that explain the answers for
Exercises 35 and 39.

Use Alternate Strategies

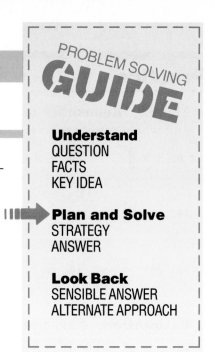

PROBLEM SOLVING
GUIDE

Understand
QUESTION
FACTS
KEY IDEA

Plan and Solve
STRATEGY
ANSWER

Look Back
SENSIBLE ANSWER
ALTERNATE APPROACH

Build Understanding

At the Fun Fair there was a prize for guessing how many quarters would be in a stack as high as the ceiling. Kevin found that a stack of 11 quarters is about $\frac{3}{4}$ inch high. If the ceiling is 8 feet high, how many quarters would be in the stack?

Understand   Think: If 11 quarters are $\frac{3}{4}$ inch thick, how many quarters are 8 feet, or 96 inches, high?

Plan and Solve

STRATEGY   You can make a table to solve this problem.

Inches	Quarters
$\frac{3}{4}$	11
$1\frac{1}{2}$	22
3	44
12	176
96	1,408

STRATEGY   You can solve this problem by working backward. How many $\frac{3}{4}$-inch stacks of quarters make 96 inches?

96 ÷ 0.75 = 128

How many quarters are in 128 stacks that are each $\frac{3}{4}$ high?

128 × 11 = 1,408

ANSWER   There would be 1,408 quarters in the stack.

ANSWER   There would be 1,408 quarters in the stack.

Look Back   SENSIBLE ANSWER   Since 11 quarters make a stack that is not quite an inch high, a stack of 96 × 11, or 1,056, quarters will be less than 96 inches high. Since 1,408 quarters is more than 1,056 quarters, the answer is reasonable.

Write About Math   Describe another way to do the problem.

Check Understanding

Reuben has $1.25 in dimes and nickels. He wants to use all the dimes to play the basketball toss game. If he has 16 coins, how many times can he play this game?

1. Try and check combinations of the 16 dimes and nickels to find one that totals $1.25.

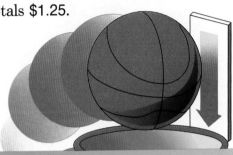

2. Is there another way to solve the problem? Are there an even or odd number of nickels? What is the greatest number of dimes there could be? the least number of nickels? the least number of dimes? How does answering these questions help you solve the problem?

Practice

The length of a row of 15 pennies placed side by side is about $11\frac{1}{4}$ inches. Use this fact to solve Exercises 3 and 4.

3. Make a table to find the number of pennies in a row 90 feet long.

4. Show how to solve Exercise 3 using another strategy.

The weight of 100 pennies is about $\frac{5}{8}$ pound. Use this fact to solve Exercises 5 and 6.

5. Work backward to find the number of pennies in 65 pounds of pennies.

6. Show how to solve Exercise 5 using another strategy.

7. Melika has $1.85 in quarters and dimes. She has a total of 14 coins. How many quarters and dimes does Melika have?

8. Show how to solve Exercise 7 using another strategy.

9. A stack of 5 dimes is about $\frac{1}{4}$ inch high. How high is a stack of 200 dimes?

10. A stack of 5 nickels is about $\frac{3}{8}$ inch high. How many nickels are in a stack that is 2 feet high?

Midchapter _____ Checkup

Multiply.

1. $\frac{5}{8} \times \frac{1}{2}$ 2. $\frac{2}{5} \times 9$ 3. $3\frac{3}{8} \times \frac{1}{3}$ 4. $4\frac{5}{6} \times 3\frac{1}{3}$ 5. $\frac{7}{9} \times \frac{27}{28}$

Critical Thinking Activity

The coach wants order on the court!

She wants her players to line up from shortest to tallest.

Heidi is $2\frac{1}{2}$ inches taller than Lois.

Veronica is $3\frac{1}{4}$ inches shorter than Heidi.

Lois is 1 inch taller than Talia but 4 inches shorter than Sally.

The tallest player is 5 feet $5\frac{1}{2}$ inches tall.

1. Draw a diagram to help arrange the players in order from shortest to tallest.

2. Find the height of each player.

MATH
laugh

There are four houses in a row. They are green, white, yellow, and red. If the yellow house is to the right of the white and red one, and it's next to the green one, where is the white house?

ANSWER
(In Washington, D.C.!)

Math-at-Home Activity

1. Talk with your family and decide on a meal you would like to prepare together.

2. Write the menu and choose the recipes you want to use. If necessary, change the recipes to serve the number of people in your family.

3. Make a list of the ingredients you will need.

4. After the ingredients have been purchased, prepare the food, eat, and enjoy!

Number-Sense Project

Look back at pages 270-271.
Suppose the length of each side of the triangle in the first figure is 1 unit and that the length of a new side is one-third the length of a side in the previous figure.

	1st Figure	2nd Figure	3rd Figure	4th Figure	5th Figure
Length of a Side	1	$\frac{1}{3}$	$\frac{1}{9}$	**1.**	**2.**
Number of Sides	3	12	48	**3.**	**4.**
Perimeter	3	4	$5\frac{1}{3}$	**5.**	**6.**

A
L
G
E
B
R
A

Mental Math: Properties

Build Understanding

People around the world use masks in festivals, celebrations, and theater. In some cultures masks are considered art forms or religious symbols.

Northwest
Coast
Indian

A. These masks were made for religious ceremonies. It took $2\frac{3}{4}$ hours to make the Kachina mask, $3\frac{1}{2}$ hours to make the Tibetan mask, and $2\frac{1}{4}$ hours to make the Northwest Coast Indian mask. What is the total length of time it took to make the three masks?

$2\frac{3}{4} + \left(3\frac{1}{2} + 2\frac{1}{4}\right)$

$2\frac{3}{4} + \left(2\frac{1}{4} + 3\frac{1}{2}\right)$

$\left(2\frac{3}{4} + 2\frac{1}{4}\right) + 3\frac{1}{2}$

$\quad 5 \quad + \quad 3\frac{1}{2} \quad = \quad 8\frac{1}{2}$

Remember that you are using the **commutative property** when you change the **order** of numbers.

Remember that you are using the **associative property** when you change **groups.**

It took $8\frac{1}{2}$ hours to make the three masks.

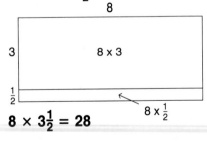

Hopi kachina

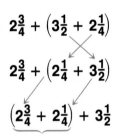

Tibetan

The word *mask* may come from the Arabic word "maskhara" which means buffoon or clown.

B. Find $8 \times 3\frac{1}{2}$. Use the **distributive property.**

$8 \times 3\frac{1}{2} = 28$

$8 \times \left(3 + \frac{1}{2}\right) = \left(8 \times 3\right) + \left(8 \times \frac{1}{2}\right)$

$\qquad\qquad\qquad = \quad 24 \quad + \quad 4$

$\qquad\qquad\qquad = \qquad 28$

Two numbers whose product is 1 are **reciprocals** of each other. Recognizing reciprocals can make multiplication easier.

C. Find $\frac{3}{2} \times \frac{3}{4} \times \frac{2}{3}$.

$\frac{3}{2}$ and $\frac{2}{3}$ are reciprocals. $\frac{3}{2} \times \frac{2}{3} = \frac{6}{6} = 1$

$\frac{3}{2} \times \frac{3}{4} \times \frac{2}{3} = \frac{3}{4} \times 1 = \frac{3}{4}$

D. Write the reciprocal of $8\frac{3}{4}$.

$8\frac{3}{4} = \frac{35}{4} \qquad \frac{35}{4} \times \frac{4}{35} = 1$

$\frac{4}{35}$ is the reciprocal of $8\frac{3}{4}$.

■ **Talk About Math** When is the reciprocal of a number greater than the number? less than the number?

Check Understanding

For another example, see Set D, pages 298–299.

Write the letter of the correct answer.

1. $6\frac{3}{8} + 2\frac{1}{3} + 1\frac{5}{8}$ **2.** $2 \times 3\frac{1}{5}$ **3.** $6\frac{2}{3} + 1\frac{1}{3}$ **4.** $\frac{6}{7} \times \frac{7}{6} \times 4$ **5.** $9\frac{5}{8} \times 5 \times \frac{8}{77}$

a. 8 **b.** 4 **c.** $10\frac{1}{3}$ **d.** $9\frac{5}{8}$ **e.** $6\frac{2}{5}$ **f.** 5

Practice

For More Practice, see Set D, pages 300–301.

Use mental math to find each answer. **Remember** to look for reciprocals.

6. $1\frac{3}{4} + 3\frac{1}{2} + 2\frac{1}{4}$ **7.** $\frac{7}{10} \times \frac{3}{4} \times \frac{4}{3}$ **8.** $2 \times 4\frac{3}{10}$ **9.** $3\frac{1}{5} \times 10$

10. $2\frac{3}{8} + 1\frac{5}{8} - 2$ **11.** $1\frac{2}{5} + 3\frac{1}{5} + 6\frac{2}{5}$ **12.** $\frac{2}{5} \times \frac{3}{8} \times 4\frac{1}{2}$ **13.** $4 \times 3\frac{1}{4}$

14. $\frac{1}{6} \times \frac{2}{5} \times 6$ **15.** $6 \times 6\frac{1}{6}$ **16.** $3\frac{1}{3} \times \frac{3}{10} \times \frac{7}{10}$ **17.** $4\frac{3}{4} + 5\frac{1}{4} - 10$

18. $2\frac{1}{3} + 1\frac{3}{4} + 1\frac{2}{3}$ **19.** $3\frac{7}{8} \times 2\frac{1}{2} \times \frac{2}{5}$ **20.** $2\frac{1}{8} + 3\frac{7}{8} + 1\frac{3}{8}$ **21.** $2 \times 4\frac{3}{10} + 2 \times \frac{7}{10}$

Problem Solving

Ancient Greeks were the first to use masks in theater. Japanese, Chinese, and Italian cultures have also used masks in drama. Solve the following problems about theatrical masks.

22. Seth wants to cut foot-long pieces of wire from wires $5\frac{1}{2}$ feet, $2\frac{3}{4}$ feet, and $1\frac{3}{4}$ feet to hang masks used in a Japanese drama. How many foot-long pieces can he cut?

23. If a Nigerian theatrical mask has a height of $6\frac{3}{4}$ inches, could three copies of this mask be displayed vertically on a $1\frac{1}{2}$-foot-long banner?

Noh is a type of Japanese play in which actors wear masks to represent different emotions.

Choose an Operation

PROBLEM SOLVING
GUIDE

Understand
QUESTION
FACTS
KEY IDEA

Plan and Solve
STRATEGY
ANSWER

Look Back
SENSIBLE ANSWER
ALTERNATE APPROACH

Build Understanding

Dirk works as a graphic artist for a nature magazine. Part of his job is fitting photographs on the pages. To make them fit, he can either enlarge, reduce, or trim off portions of the photographs. Dirk has a picture of a moose that is $11\frac{1}{2}$ inches long and $8\frac{3}{4}$ inches wide. He needs to reduce it to one half the length and width. Find the length of the reduced photograph.

Understand The reduced size is one half of the original size. The original size is $11\frac{1}{2}$ inches. Find $\frac{1}{2}$ of $11\frac{1}{2}$.

 **Plan and Solve**

STRATEGY Choose the operation of multiplication. Find $\frac{1}{2} \times 11\frac{1}{2}$.

$$\frac{1}{2} \times 11\frac{1}{2} = \frac{1}{2} \times \frac{23}{2} = \frac{23}{4} = 5\frac{3}{4}$$

ANSWER The reduced picture is $5\frac{3}{4}$ inches long.

Look Back Since $2 \times 5\frac{3}{4} = 11\frac{1}{2}$, the original is twice the length of the reduced photograph.

■ **Talk About Math** Find the width of the reduced photograph.

When a graphic artist only wants to use part of a photograph, he usually *crops* it.

Check Understanding

For Exercises 1–4, tell which operation is used and why.

1. Exercise 5   **2.** Exercise 6   **3.** Exercise 7   **4.** Exercise 8

Practice

Solve.

5. One day Dirk started work $\frac{3}{4}$ hour early and stayed $1\frac{1}{2}$ hours late to finish working on the March issue. How much extra time did he work?

6. A page is separated into 4 columns, each $2\frac{1}{2}$ inches wide. How wide is the page?

7. Four pictures, each $2\frac{7}{8}$ inches wide, are placed side by side. How wide is the resulting display?

8. A picture that was $8\frac{3}{4}$ inches long was trimmed to $6\frac{1}{2}$ inches. How much was trimmed off?

Tell which operation to use. Then solve.

9. Koko cut $\frac{11}{16}$ inch off the bottom of a picture that was $9\frac{1}{2}$ inches long. How long is the picture now?

10. A page 14 inches wide is divided into 8 equal columns. How wide is each column?

11. Dirk has three pictures that measure $4\frac{1}{4}$ inches, 4 inches, and 7 inches in width. If they are each reduced to be one half as wide and then placed side by side, how wide will the resulting display be?

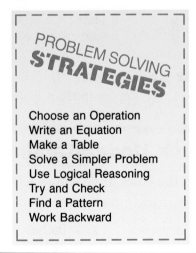

Choose a Strategy

A copy machine can reduce a picture to $\frac{2}{3}$ of its length and width, and enlarge a picture $1\frac{1}{2}$ times its length and width.

12. To reduce the length of a picture from 12 inches to about 5 inches, how many times will it have to be reduced?

13. To enlarge the width of a picture from 2 inches to about 10 inches, how many times will it have to be enlarged?

PROBLEM SOLVING
STRATEGIES

Choose an Operation
Write an Equation
Make a Table
Solve a Simpler Problem
Use Logical Reasoning
Try and Check
Find a Pattern
Work Backward

Meaning of Division of Fractions

Build Understanding

A. For an art project, Maria cuts pieces from several ribbons. How many $\frac{1}{2}$-inch pieces can she cut from this 5-inch red ribbon?

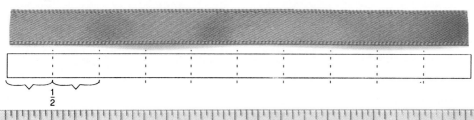

$\frac{1}{2}$

You can use a paper model to illustrate this situation.
Ten $\frac{1}{2}$-inch pieces of paper can be placed alongside a 5-inch piece.

$$5 \div \frac{1}{2} = 10$$ A 5-inch length of ribbon can be divided into ten $\frac{1}{2}$-inch pieces.

B. How many $\frac{3}{8}$-inch pieces can be cut from a $\frac{3}{4}$-inch piece of ribbon?

In the paper model, two $\frac{3}{8}$-inch pieces fit alongside the $\frac{3}{4}$-inch piece.

$$\frac{3}{4} \div \frac{3}{8} = 2$$ A $\frac{3}{4}$-inch piece of ribbon can be divided into two $\frac{3}{8}$-inch pieces.

■ **Talk About Math** In Example A explain why there are more than 5 pieces of ribbon.

Check Understanding

For another example, see Set E, pages 298–299.

Use the ruler in Example A to answer the following questions.
How many $\frac{1}{2}$-inch pieces can be cut from each length of ribbon?

1. 3 inches   **2.** 4 inches   **3.** $1\frac{1}{2}$ inches   **4.** $3\frac{1}{2}$ inches   **5.** $9\frac{1}{2}$ inches

6. Write division sentences for Exercises 1–5.

Practice

For More Practice, see Set E, pages 300–301.

Find each quotient. Use a ruler if you wish.

7. $1\frac{1}{4} \div \frac{1}{4}$ **8.** $\frac{3}{4} \div \frac{1}{8}$ **9.** $1\frac{1}{4} \div \frac{5}{8}$ **10.** $1\frac{1}{2} \div \frac{3}{8}$ **11.** $2\frac{3}{4} \div \frac{1}{16}$

12. $3\frac{1}{2} \div \frac{7}{8}$ **13.** $\frac{1}{2} \div \frac{1}{4}$ **14.** $2\frac{1}{2} \div \frac{1}{2}$ **15.** $2 \div \frac{1}{4}$ **16.** $1\frac{1}{8} \div \frac{1}{8}$

17. $2\frac{1}{4} \div \frac{3}{8}$ **18.** $2\frac{5}{8} \div \frac{1}{8}$ **19.** $2\frac{1}{4} \div \frac{3}{4}$ **20.** $2\frac{1}{8} \div \frac{1}{8}$ **21.** $3\frac{1}{2} \div \frac{1}{2}$

Calculator Find each quotient. **Remember** to change the mixed numbers and fractions to decimals.

22. $7\frac{1}{2} \div 2\frac{1}{2}$ **23.** $6\frac{3}{4} \div 2\frac{1}{4}$ **24.** $3 \div \frac{3}{4}$ **25.** $5 \div \frac{1}{7}$ **26.** $9 \div \frac{1}{8}$

27. $2\frac{1}{2} \div 1\frac{1}{4}$ **28.** $8\frac{1}{4} \div 2\frac{3}{4}$ **29.** $9 \div 2\frac{1}{4}$ **30.** $8 \div \frac{4}{5}$ **31.** $6 \div \frac{3}{8}$

Mixed Practice Find each answer.

32. $1\frac{1}{2} \times \frac{3}{4}$ **33.** $\frac{3}{8} \div \frac{1}{8}$ **34.** $2\frac{1}{2} \times \frac{5}{8}$ **35.** $3 \div \frac{3}{8}$ **36.** $3\frac{1}{3} \times \frac{3}{10}$

37. $3\frac{5}{6} \div \frac{1}{6}$ **38.** $\frac{1}{4} \times \frac{2}{3}$ **39.** $5\frac{1}{5} \div \frac{2}{5}$ **40.** $4 \div \frac{2}{3}$ **41.** $4\frac{4}{7} \times \frac{7}{8}$

42. $4\frac{4}{5} \div \frac{1}{5}$ **43.** $3\frac{1}{3} \times \frac{3}{5}$ **44.** $9\frac{1}{3} \times \frac{3}{4}$ **45.** $7 \div \frac{1}{4}$ **46.** $7\frac{1}{2} \times \frac{2}{3}$

Problem Solving

Solve each problem.

47. How many pieces of ribbon would Maria have if she cut a $1\frac{1}{2}$-inch piece of ribbon into $\frac{1}{8}$-inch pieces?

48. Maria has a 4-inch piece of ribbon. Will she be able to cut eight $\frac{1}{2}$-inch pieces from it?

Number Sense Find each answer.

49. Find $\frac{1}{2} \div \frac{1}{6}$ and $\frac{1}{2} \times 6$. Compare your answers. What do you notice?

50. How are 6 and $\frac{1}{6}$ related?

51. Critical Thinking Look at your answers to Problems 49 and 50. How are multiplication and division of fractions related? Give examples to support your answer.

Dividing Fractions and Mixed Numbers

Build Understanding

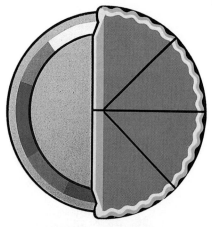

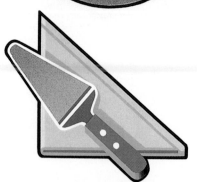

A. Divide $\frac{1}{2}$ by $\frac{1}{8}$.

Estimation First estimate whether the quotient will be less than or greater than 1.

Observe these divisions by whole numbers.

$$6 \div 3 = 2 \qquad\qquad 3 \div 4 = \frac{3}{4}$$

Dividend Divisor Quotient   Dividend Divisor Quotient

$$6 > 3, \text{ so } 2 > 1. \qquad 3 < 4, \text{ so } \frac{3}{4} < 1.$$

$$\frac{1}{2} \div \frac{1}{8} = \text{▦}$$

$\frac{1}{2}$ (the dividend) $> \frac{1}{8}$ (the divisor), **so** ▦ (the quotient) **> 1.**

The quotient will be greater than 1.

Now study whole numbers to learn how to divide by fractions.

$$6 \div 3 = 2 \qquad\qquad 3 \div 4 = \frac{3}{4}$$

$$6 \times \frac{1}{3} = 2 \qquad\qquad 3 \times \frac{1}{4} = \frac{3}{4}$$

3 and $\frac{1}{3}$ are reciprocals.   4 and $\frac{1}{4}$ are reciprocals.

Dividing by a number is the same as multiplying by its reciprocal.

$$\frac{1}{2} \div \frac{1}{8} = \text{▦} \qquad \text{Multiply by the reciprocal of } \tfrac{1}{8}.$$

$$\frac{1}{2} \times 8 = \text{▦} \qquad \text{The reciprocal of } \tfrac{1}{8} \text{ is 8.}$$

$$\frac{1}{2} \div \frac{1}{8} = \frac{1}{2} \times 8 = \frac{1 \times \overset{4}{\cancel{8}}}{\underset{1}{\cancel{2}} \times 1} = 4 \qquad \text{Check: } 4 > 1.$$

B. Find $3 \div \frac{3}{10}$.

Estimate whether the quotient will be greater than or less than 1.

$3 > \frac{3}{10}$, so the quotient will be greater than 1.

$$3 \div \frac{3}{10} = \frac{3}{1} \times \frac{10}{3} = \frac{\cancel{3}}{1} \times \frac{10}{\cancel{3}} = 10$$

Multiply 3 by the **reciprocal** of $\frac{3}{10}$.

C. Find $2\frac{5}{8} \div 7$.

First estimate.

$2\frac{5}{8} < 7$, so the quotient will be less than 1.

$$2\frac{5}{8} \div 7 = \frac{21}{8} \div \frac{7}{1} \quad \text{Write as fractions.}$$

$$= \frac{21}{8} \times \frac{1}{7} \quad \text{Multiply } \frac{21}{8} \text{ by the reciprocal of 7.}$$

$$= \frac{\overset{3}{\cancel{21}}}{8} \times \frac{1}{\underset{1}{\cancel{7}}}$$

$$= \frac{3}{8}$$

D. Find $5\frac{2}{3} \div 2\frac{1}{3}$.

Estimation Estimate by rounding to whole numbers. $6 \div 2 = 3$

$$5\frac{2}{3} \div 2\frac{1}{3} = \frac{17}{3} \div \frac{7}{3} \quad \text{Write as fractions.}$$

$$= \frac{17}{3} \times \frac{3}{7} \quad \text{Multiply } \frac{17}{3} \text{ by the reciprocal of } \frac{7}{3}.$$

$$= \frac{17}{\cancel{3}} \times \frac{\overset{1}{\cancel{3}}}{7}$$

$$= \frac{17}{7}$$

$$= 2\frac{3}{7}$$

■ **Talk About Math** Write $3 \div 3$ as a multiplication problem and solve. Write $3 \div \frac{1}{3}$ as a multiplication problem and solve.

Check Understanding

For another example, see Set F, pages 298–299.

Find the missing numbers.

1. $\frac{3}{8} \div \frac{1}{8} = \frac{3}{8} \times \boxed{} = \frac{\boxed{}}{8} = 3$ **2.** $5 \div \frac{1}{2} = 5 \times \boxed{} = \boxed{}$

3. $\frac{1}{4} \div \frac{1}{2} = \boxed{} \times \frac{2}{1} = \frac{2}{4} = \frac{\boxed{}}{2}$ **4.** $2\frac{1}{5} \div \frac{1}{3} = \frac{\boxed{}}{5} \times \frac{\boxed{}}{1} = \frac{\boxed{}}{\boxed{}} = 6\frac{\boxed{}}{5}$

5. Is $\frac{3}{8} \div \frac{5}{6}$ equal to $\frac{5}{6} \div \frac{3}{8}$? Then multiply by the reciprocal of each divisor to verify your answer.

Practice

For More Practice, see Set F, pages 300–301.

Estimation Tell whether the quotient will be less than or greater than 1.

6. $6 \div \frac{5}{8}$ **7.** $\frac{1}{3} \div \frac{13}{16}$ **8.** $9\frac{1}{2} \div 6$ **9.** $5\frac{1}{4} \div 8$ **10.** $\frac{4}{5} \div \frac{5}{6}$ **11.** $4\frac{1}{2} \div 3\frac{1}{4}$

Find the quotient. **Remember** to multiply by the reciprocal of the divisor.

12. $\frac{3}{8} \div \frac{5}{12}$ **13.** $1\frac{1}{4} \div 6$ **14.** $9 \div \frac{3}{16}$ **15.** $6 \div 3\frac{1}{2}$ **16.** $5\frac{1}{4} \div \frac{3}{8}$

17. $\frac{5}{6} \div \frac{5}{12}$ **18.** $2\frac{7}{10} \div 4$ **19.** $1\frac{3}{10} \div \frac{1}{2}$ **20.** $3 \div \frac{3}{5}$ **21.** $8\frac{1}{4} \div 3\frac{2}{3}$

Estimation Find the estimated quotient by rounding to whole numbers.

22. $4\frac{1}{2} \div 1\frac{2}{5}$ **23.** $11\frac{2}{3} \div 2\frac{7}{8}$ **24.** $8\frac{2}{3} \div 2\frac{1}{6}$ **25.** $7\frac{1}{5} \div 6\frac{3}{4}$ **26.** $9\frac{5}{8} \div 2\frac{2}{7}$

Find the quotient. **Remember** to estimate first.

27. $9\frac{3}{4} \div 5$ **28.** $2\frac{4}{5} \div 10$ **29.** $3\frac{1}{6} \div 6\frac{1}{3}$ **30.** $3\frac{1}{4} \div 1\frac{3}{10}$ **31.** $4\frac{3}{8} \div 2$

32. $2\frac{2}{3} \div 6\frac{1}{4}$ **33.** $14\frac{3}{8} \div 2\frac{1}{12}$ **34.** $6\frac{2}{5} \div 5\frac{3}{10}$ **35.** $1\frac{5}{6} \div 7\frac{1}{2}$ **36.** $9\frac{3}{5} \div 12$

ALGEBRA ▶ Complete each table.

37.

n	$\frac{1}{8}$	$\frac{1}{4}$	$\frac{2}{5}$	$\frac{1}{6}$	$\frac{5}{12}$
$n \div \frac{1}{2}$					

38.

x	$3\frac{1}{2}$	5	10	$9\frac{2}{3}$	$6\frac{4}{5}$
$x \div \frac{2}{5}$					

39.

s	$2\frac{3}{5}$	$7\frac{1}{2}$	$4\frac{5}{6}$	$3\frac{7}{12}$	$8\frac{7}{8}$
$s \div 5$					

40.

t	$2\frac{1}{6}$	$3\frac{2}{5}$	$1\frac{2}{3}$	$7\frac{7}{10}$	$10\frac{3}{4}$
$t \div 3\frac{1}{3}$					

41.

b	$\frac{1}{2}$	$\frac{5}{8}$	$1\frac{2}{3}$	$2\frac{1}{12}$	$9\frac{3}{5}$
$b \div 8$					

42.

a	$\frac{7}{10}$	$1\frac{1}{5}$	$2\frac{3}{8}$	$3\frac{4}{5}$	$7\frac{4}{5}$
$a \div 6\frac{1}{2}$					

Mixed Practice Find each answer.

43. $7 \times 1\frac{1}{3}$ **44.** $\frac{2}{3} \times \frac{1}{12}$ **45.** $1\frac{1}{5} \div \frac{1}{6}$ **46.** $6\frac{1}{4} \times 4\frac{2}{3}$

47. $\frac{5}{6} \div \frac{1}{10}$ **48.** $5 \div \frac{7}{8}$ **49.** $10 \times \frac{4}{5}$ **50.** $10\frac{1}{2} \div 4\frac{2}{3}$

51. $9\frac{1}{4} \times 2\frac{1}{4}$ **52.** $10\frac{1}{3} \times 6$ **53.** $4 \div \frac{1}{5}$ **54.** $8\frac{2}{3} \div \frac{1}{9}$

Problem Solving

For a party of ten people, 3 pepperoni pizzas, 2 mushroom pizzas, and 1 half pepperoni and half mushroom pizza were ordered. All the pizzas were cut into sixths.

55. How many pizzas were ordered?

56. How many slices of pepperoni pizza were there?

57. How many slices of mushroom pizza were there?

58. How will you divide 36 pieces by nine people? by ten people?

59. If a cheese pizza costs $6.50 and toppings cost $0.75 for whole or half pizzas, how much did the pizzas cost?

Reading _____ Math

Vocabulary Complete the paragraph using some of the words below to fill in the blanks. Each word may be used more than once:

reciprocal, divisor, greater, dividend, quotient, less

If five is divided by one third, five is the **1.** ? and one third is the **2.** ? . You would estimate the **3.** ? as **4.** ? than one, because the **5.** ? is greater than the **6.** ? . To divide, you must multiply by the **7.** ? of one third.

Skills Review

1. One turn of a wagon wheel moves the wagon 12 inches. Use mental math to complete this table.

Turns	0	$\frac{1}{2}$	1	$1\frac{1}{2}$	2	$2\frac{1}{2}$
Inches			12			

Multiply.

2. $\frac{1}{3} \times \frac{1}{5}$ **3.** $\frac{5}{6} \times \frac{2}{3}$

4. $\frac{7}{12} \times \frac{3}{8}$ **5.** $\frac{3}{10} \times \frac{7}{10}$

6. $5 \times 2\frac{1}{4}$ **7.** $2\frac{1}{3} \times 4\frac{2}{5}$

8. $3\frac{3}{8} \times 1\frac{1}{12}$ **9.** $2\frac{5}{6} \times 2\frac{5}{17}$

Find each answer. Use mental math if you can. Look for reciprocals.

10. $\frac{7}{9} \times \frac{3}{2} \times \frac{2}{3}$ **11.** $1\frac{2}{7} + 2\frac{4}{7} + \frac{1}{7}$

How many $\frac{1}{4}$-inch pieces of paper can be cut from each length?

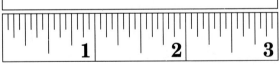

12. 1 in.   **13.** 2 in.   **14.** $2\frac{3}{4}$ in.

15. Write a division sentence for Exercise 14.

Divide.

16. $\frac{3}{4} \div \frac{1}{8}$ **17.** $\frac{7}{12} \div \frac{2}{3}$

18. $3\frac{4}{5} \div 10$ **19.** $5 \div \frac{1}{4}$

20. $2\frac{1}{2} \div 1\frac{3}{8}$ **21.** $12 \div 1\frac{2}{3}$

22. $4\frac{3}{5} \div \frac{1}{2}$ **23.** $3\frac{1}{6} \div 2\frac{3}{8}$

Problem-Solving Review

Solve each problem.

24. Samuel is making two shelves. Each shelf will be $4\frac{1}{3}$ feet long. How much lumber does he need to make the two shelves?

25. Jay is using pebbles to show the square numbers. How many pebbles does he need to show the sixth square number?

26. Mrs. Casteline made 6 cheese pizzas and 5 pepper pizzas. She cut each pizza into fourths. How many sections did she have?

27. Diego used $\frac{2}{3}$ of a can of paint to paint the doghouse. Cesar needs $\frac{1}{4}$ of a can of paint for a sign. Is there enough paint left for Cesar?

28. Shana will spend 30 minutes on homework for each of 3 classes. Ann will spend 20 minutes on homework for each of 4 classes. Make a table to find what time each girl must start her work to be finished by 6:00.

29. Data File Use the data on pages 410–411. How much of each ingredient do you need to make enough Citrus Fruit Juice for 12 people? for 2 people?

30. Make a Data File Use reference books to research 7 facts about your state and present them in a table. Possible facts to research are: population, land area, and amounts of different crops produced in the state.

Write each number in standard form.

1. Three hundred forty billion, six million, twenty-four thousand, eighty.

2. Two and seventy-five millionths.

3. 5^3 **4.** 4^2 **5.** $2^4 \times 3^3$

Estimate. Tell which method you used.

6. $\begin{array}{r} 6.457 \\ +\,3.72 \\ \hline \end{array}$ **7.** $\begin{array}{r} 52.076 \\ -\,14.952 \\ \hline \end{array}$ **8.** $\begin{array}{r} 8.753 \\ -\,4.82 \\ \hline \end{array}$

9. 24×4 **10.** 19×737

11. $248 \div 61$ **12.** $80{,}632 \div 89$

13. $32\overline{)95.4}$ **14.** $58\overline{)593.6}$

Name each polygon.

15.   **16.**   **17.**

Multiply or divide.

18. 346×179 **19.** 23.97×3.006

20. $5{,}473 \div 7$ **21.** $685 \div 26$

22. $75.67 \div 23$ **23.** $148.8 \div 3.1$

Write the prime factorization using exponents.

24. 72   **25.** 124   **26.** 550

Write the fractions using the least common denominator.

27. $\frac{2}{3}, \frac{3}{8}$ **28.** $\frac{5}{12}, \frac{5}{6}$

Are the figures listed *always* similar, *never* similar, or *sometimes* similar?

29. Two squares

30. A square and a pentagon

Write a mixed number or whole number for each improper fraction.

31. $\frac{28}{8}$ **32.** $\frac{32}{4}$ **33.** $\frac{55}{9}$

Write the numbers in order from least to greatest.

34. $\frac{7}{8}, 1\frac{1}{4}, \frac{5}{6}$ **35.** $2\frac{3}{5}, 2\frac{3}{4}, 2\frac{2}{3}$

Add or subtract.

36. $\frac{4}{5} - \frac{1}{3}$ **37.** $\frac{5}{6} + \frac{5}{8}$

38. $10 - 3\frac{3}{4}$ **39.** $\frac{1}{2} + \frac{3}{4} + \frac{2}{3}$

40. $4\frac{1}{4} + 1\frac{5}{6}$ **41.** $3\frac{1}{3} - 1\frac{3}{4}$

Give the reciprocal of each number.

42. $\frac{5}{6}$ **43.** 8   **44.** $2\frac{2}{3}$

Use mental math to find each answer.

45. $\frac{2}{3} \times \frac{4}{5} \times \frac{3}{2}$ **46.** $4\frac{1}{2} \times 10$

Multiply or divide.

47. $\frac{3}{4} \times \frac{1}{2}$ **48.** $\frac{2}{5} \times \frac{5}{6}$

49. $2\frac{2}{3} \times 2\frac{1}{4}$ **50.** $\frac{3}{8} \div \frac{1}{4}$

51. $6 \div \frac{1}{3}$ **52.** $3\frac{1}{2} \div 1\frac{5}{6}$

Set A pages 272–275

One turn of a tricycle wheel moves it 12 inches. Therefore,

$\frac{1}{2}$ of a turn moves it 6 inches.

$\frac{1}{3}$ of a turn moves it 4 inches.

$\frac{1}{4}$ of a turn moves it 3 inches.

$\frac{1}{6}$ of a turn moves it 2 inches.

Remember that finding a fraction of a number suggests multiplication.

Make a table for each.

1. Thirds of a turn of the tricycle wheel, from 0 to 4 turns

2. Fourths of a turn of the tricycle wheel, from 0 to 3 turns

3. Sixths of a turn of the tricycle wheel, from 0 to 2 turns

Set B pages 276–279

To multiply fractions, multiply the numerators and multiply the denominators.

$\frac{5}{8} \times \frac{2}{3} = \frac{5 \times 2}{8 \times 3} = \frac{10}{24}$

Give your answer in lowest terms.

$\frac{10}{24} = \frac{\boxed{2} \times 5}{\boxed{2} \times 12} = \frac{5}{12}$

↑
Another name for 1

Remember to look for common factors in the numerator and denominator.

Multiply. Write your answer in lowest terms.

1. $\frac{1}{2} \times \frac{1}{10}$ 2. $\frac{5}{6} \times \frac{3}{8}$ 3. $\frac{4}{5} \times \frac{5}{8}$

4. $\frac{3}{5} \times \frac{10}{21}$ 5. $\frac{8}{9} \times \frac{12}{13}$ 6. $\frac{7}{10} \times \frac{4}{35}$

Set C pages 280–281

Find $2\frac{2}{3} \times 3\frac{1}{2}$.

To multiply with mixed numbers write fractions for the mixed numbers.

$2\frac{2}{3} \times 3\frac{1}{2} = \frac{\overset{4}{\cancel{8}}}{3} \times \frac{7}{\underset{1}{\cancel{2}}}$

$= \frac{28}{3}$

$= 9\frac{1}{3}$

Remember to change whole numbers and mixed numbers to improper fractions before you multiply.

Multiply.

1. $5 \times 4\frac{1}{3}$ 2. $4\frac{1}{2} \times 1\frac{3}{5}$

3. $2\frac{1}{5} \times 3\frac{1}{8}$ 4. $6\frac{1}{5} \times 3\frac{3}{4}$

5. $7\frac{3}{10} \times 2\frac{1}{2}$ 6. $8\frac{1}{6} \times 3\frac{1}{7}$

7. $9\frac{3}{5} \times 1\frac{7}{8}$ 8. $2\frac{7}{10} \times 4\frac{4}{9}$

Set D   pages 286–287

Rearranging the order of the addends can help to make addition easier.

$$3\frac{1}{5} + \left(4\frac{1}{3} + 2\frac{4}{5}\right) = 3\frac{1}{5} + \left(2\frac{4}{5} + 4\frac{1}{3}\right)$$
$$= \left(3\frac{1}{5} + 2\frac{4}{5}\right) + 4\frac{1}{3}$$
$$= 6 + 4\frac{1}{3}$$
$$= 10\frac{1}{3}$$

Recognizing reciprocals can make multiplication easier.

$$\frac{5}{6} \times \frac{4}{9} \times \frac{6}{5} = \left(\frac{5}{6} \times \frac{6}{5}\right) \times \frac{4}{9}$$
$$= \quad 1 \quad \times \frac{4}{9}$$
$$= \frac{4}{9}$$

Remember that you are using the commutative property when you change the order of numbers.

Use mental math to find each answer.

1. $2\frac{1}{2} + 6\frac{1}{5} + 1\frac{1}{2}$ **2.** $\frac{4}{5} \times \frac{2}{3} \times \frac{3}{2}$

3. $\frac{1}{5} + \frac{3}{5} + \frac{4}{5}$ **4.** $4\frac{1}{2} + 3\frac{3}{8} + 1\frac{1}{8}$

5. $5\frac{1}{6} + 3\frac{3}{6} - 1$ **6.** $\frac{5}{6} \times \frac{3}{4} \times \frac{6}{5}$

7. $5\frac{1}{3} + 4\frac{1}{2} + 1\frac{2}{3}$ **8.** $\frac{8}{9} \times \frac{4}{5} \times \frac{9}{8}$

Set E   pages 290–291

How many $\frac{1}{4}$-inch pieces can be cut from a $2\frac{1}{2}$-inch piece of ribbon?

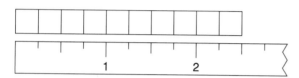

Counting the pieces shows that
$2\frac{1}{2} \div \frac{1}{4} = 10$.

Remember that a ruler is a good model to help you divide a number by fractions whose denominators are 2, 4, 8, and 16.

Find each quotient.

1. $\frac{3}{4} \div \frac{1}{4}$ **2.** $\frac{1}{2} \div \frac{1}{4}$ **3.** $\frac{1}{4} \div \frac{1}{8}$

4. $1\frac{1}{2} \div \frac{1}{2}$ **5.** $1\frac{1}{4} \div \frac{1}{4}$ **6.** $1\frac{1}{2} \div \frac{1}{8}$

7. $1\frac{3}{4} \div \frac{1}{16}$ **8.** $1\frac{1}{2} \div \frac{3}{16}$ **9.** $1\frac{7}{8} \div \frac{5}{8}$

Set F   pages 292–295

Find $2 \div \frac{1}{5}$.

Dividing by a number is the same as multiplying by its reciprocal.

$$2 \div \frac{1}{5} = 2 \times 5$$
$$= 10$$

Remember to write mixed numbers as fractions when dividing.

Find the quotient.

1. $6 \div \frac{1}{10}$ **2.** $3 \div \frac{3}{8}$

3. $4\frac{2}{3} \div \frac{2}{3}$ **4.** $2\frac{1}{4} \div 3\frac{1}{8}$

5. $8\frac{3}{4} \div 2\frac{1}{12}$ **6.** $5\frac{3}{5} \div 1\frac{2}{5}$

More Practice

Set A pages 272–275

One turn of a tricycle wheel moves the tricycle 15 inches.

Make a table for each.

1. Thirds of a turn of the tricycle wheel, from 0 to 4 turns

2. Fifths of a turn of the tricycle wheel, from 0 to 2 turns

Mental Math Use mental math to complete each table for the number of turns of the wheel and the number of inches the tricycle moves.

3.

Turns	0	$\frac{1}{2}$	1	$1\frac{1}{2}$	2	$2\frac{1}{2}$	3
Inches	0		10				

4.

Turns	0	$\frac{1}{3}$	$\frac{2}{3}$	1	$1\frac{1}{3}$	$1\frac{2}{3}$	2
Inches	0	3		9			

5.

Turns	0	$\frac{1}{5}$	$\frac{2}{5}$	$\frac{3}{5}$	$\frac{4}{5}$	1	$1\frac{1}{5}$
Inches	0				10		

6.

Turns	0	$\frac{1}{4}$	$\frac{1}{2}$	$\frac{3}{4}$	1	$1\frac{1}{4}$	$1\frac{1}{2}$
Inches	0				16		

Set B pages 276–279

For Exercises 1–10, tell whether you would use mental math or paper and pencil. Then multiply. Write your answer in lowest terms.

1. $\frac{1}{3} \times \frac{1}{5}$

2. $\frac{1}{4} \times \frac{3}{4}$

3. $\frac{3}{4} \times \frac{1}{5}$

4. $\frac{7}{8} \times \frac{2}{7}$

5. $\frac{5}{12} \times \frac{4}{15}$

6. $\frac{4}{5} \times \frac{1}{8}$

7. $\frac{5}{6} \times \frac{3}{4}$

8. $\frac{3}{4} \times \frac{2}{3}$

9. $\frac{3}{5} \times \frac{1}{3}$

10. $\frac{7}{20} \times \frac{16}{21}$

Calculator Multiply.

11. $\frac{1}{5} \times \frac{3}{10}$

12. $\frac{3}{4} \times \frac{3}{5}$

13. $\frac{3}{10} \times \frac{3}{10}$

14. $\frac{1}{2} \times \frac{4}{5}$

15. $\frac{9}{10} \times \frac{1}{4}$

Set C pages 280–281

Multiply.

1. $4 \times \frac{3}{8}$

2. $\frac{1}{4} \times 5\frac{2}{5}$

3. $6\frac{1}{3} \times \frac{1}{2}$

4. $2\frac{3}{8} \times \frac{1}{6}$

5. $5\frac{1}{4} \times \frac{6}{7}$

Estimation Find a range. Then multiply.

6. $8 \times 3\frac{1}{4}$

7. $6\frac{3}{8} \times 4\frac{1}{2}$

8. $5 \times 3\frac{1}{10}$

9. $7\frac{1}{6} \times 4\frac{3}{10}$

10. $9\frac{1}{3} \times 2\frac{1}{4}$

Set D   pages 286–287

Use mental math to find each answer.

1. $2\frac{1}{3} + 5\frac{1}{4} + 4\frac{2}{3}$ **2.** $\frac{3}{5} \times \frac{5}{6} \times \frac{5}{3}$ **3.** $6 \times 9\frac{1}{10}$ **4.** $\frac{1}{8} \times \frac{3}{5} \times 8\frac{1}{3}$

5. $7\frac{1}{6} + 5\frac{5}{6} - 3$ **6.** $8\frac{1}{4} \times 10$ **7.** $3\frac{2}{7} + 1\frac{4}{7} + 3\frac{1}{7}$ **8.** $4 \times 1\frac{1}{4} \times \frac{1}{5}$

Set E   pages 290–291

Find each quotient. Use a ruler if you need to.

1. $\frac{1}{2} \div \frac{1}{2}$ **2.** $\frac{3}{8} \div \frac{1}{8}$ **3.** $1\frac{3}{4} \div \frac{1}{8}$ **4.** $1\frac{7}{8} \div \frac{3}{8}$ **5.** $2\frac{1}{2} \div \frac{5}{16}$

 **Calculator**   Find each quotient.

6. $8\frac{1}{2} \div 1\frac{7}{10}$ **7.** $5\frac{1}{4} \div 1\frac{3}{4}$ **8.** $6 \div \frac{1}{4}$ **9.** $7\frac{1}{5} \div 4\frac{1}{2}$ **10.** $4\frac{3}{5} \div 1\frac{1}{4}$

Set F   pages 292–295

Estimation   Tell whether the quotient will be less than or greater than 1.

1. $4 \div \frac{5}{6}$ **2.** $\frac{1}{5} \div \frac{1}{6}$ **3.** $6\frac{3}{8} \div 6$ **4.** $3\frac{1}{4} \div 4\frac{1}{3}$ **5.** $2\frac{3}{8} \div 1\frac{1}{4}$

Find the quotient.

6. $\frac{3}{5} \div \frac{7}{10}$ **7.** $3\frac{1}{2} \div 4$ **8.** $8 \div \frac{4}{5}$ **9.** $5\frac{3}{10} \div 3$ **10.** $9 \div 2\frac{1}{4}$

Estimation   Estimate each quotient by rounding to whole numbers.

11. $8\frac{1}{3} \div 2\frac{1}{4}$ **12.** $11\frac{1}{2} \div 1\frac{7}{8}$ **13.** $6\frac{3}{4} \div 2\frac{1}{8}$ **14.** $10\frac{2}{5} \div \frac{7}{8}$ **15.** $12\frac{1}{5} \div 3\frac{7}{8}$

Find the quotient.

16. $5\frac{1}{4} \div 2$ **17.** $8\frac{1}{3} \div 4\frac{1}{6}$ **18.** $1\frac{1}{10} \div 4\frac{1}{5}$ **19.** $7\frac{1}{8} \div 3\frac{3}{4}$ **20.** $5\frac{3}{5} \div 1\frac{1}{3}$

Complete each table.

21.

x	$\frac{1}{3}$	$\frac{3}{5}$	$\frac{1}{6}$	$\frac{5}{8}$	$\frac{7}{12}$
$x \div \frac{1}{3}$					

22.

n	$2\frac{4}{5}$	$1\frac{1}{2}$	$5\frac{1}{6}$	$4\frac{3}{10}$	$8\frac{4}{5}$
$n \div 4$					

Enrichment

Betweenness Property of Numbers

One day a rabbit didn't eat enough carrots. With each hop the rabbit could only jump half as far as it did on the preceding hop. How long would it take the rabbit to reach a carrot patch **60 feet** away?

1. Complete the following table:

Hop	1st	2nd	3rd	4th	5th	6th
Distance covered	30 ft	15 ft				
Fraction of total distance covered	$\frac{1}{2}$	$\frac{1}{4}$	$\frac{1}{8}$			

2. After six hops, will the rabbit reach the carrot patch?

3. If the rabbit keeps hopping, will it reach its goal by the 12th hop? Write fractions for the parts of the 60 feet covered by the 7th through 12th hops.

4. If the rabbit could keep hopping shorter and shorter distances each time, would it ever reach the carrot patch?

Exercise 4 illustrates an important fact. For any two numbers, there is another number between them. This is the ***betweenness property.***

To find a number halfway between $\frac{1}{100}$ and $\frac{1}{1000}$, find the average of the numbers.

$$\frac{1}{100} + \frac{1}{1,000} = \frac{10}{1,000} + \frac{1}{1,000} = \frac{11}{1,000}$$

$$\frac{11}{1,000} \div 2 = \frac{11}{1,000} \times \frac{1}{2} = \frac{11}{2,000}$$

To find the average of any two numbers, add the numbers and divide the sum by 2.

Therefore, $\frac{11}{2,000}$ is a number that is halfway between $\frac{1}{100}$ and $\frac{1}{1,000}$.

Find a number that is halfway between each pair of numbers.

5. $\frac{3}{16}; \frac{1}{4}$ **6.** $\frac{1}{10}; \frac{1}{100}$ **7.** $\frac{15}{24}; \frac{16}{24}$ **8.** $\frac{1}{7}; \frac{1}{8}$ **9.** $\frac{99}{100}; 1$

Chapter 8 Review/Test

Use the picture to find each answer.

1. $6 \times \frac{1}{4}$

2. $2 \div \frac{1}{3}$

Multiply.

3. $\frac{3}{4} \times \frac{1}{4}$ **4.** $\frac{3}{5} \times \frac{3}{4}$

5. $\frac{5}{6} \times \frac{9}{10}$ **6.** $\frac{3}{4} \times 20$

7. $\frac{4}{9} \times 18$ **8.** $40 \times \frac{5}{6}$

9. $2\frac{1}{2} \times \frac{4}{5}$ **10.** $4\frac{5}{6} \times 2\frac{2}{5}$

Give the reciprocal for each number.

11. $\frac{2}{3}$ **12.** 5   **13.** $1\frac{3}{4}$

Use mental math to find each answer.

14. $3 \times 2\frac{1}{4}$ **15.** $\frac{5}{6} \times \frac{3}{4} \times \frac{6}{5}$

Divide.

16. $\frac{6}{7} \div \frac{2}{3}$ **17.** $\frac{3}{10} \div \frac{4}{5}$

18. $\frac{5}{8} \div 5$ **19.** $3\frac{2}{3} \div 1\frac{5}{8}$

20. $3 \div 1\frac{4}{5}$ **21.** $2\frac{1}{5} \div 1\frac{5}{6}$

Read each problem below. Then answer the question that follows it.

Phil wants to put up a picket fence. Each picket is $2\frac{1}{4}$ inches wide. How many pickets, side by side, must he use to put up a fence 90 feet long? Phil worked backward to solve the problem.

22. What other strategy could he have used?

    a. Find a pattern.
    b. Make a table.
    c. Use logical reasoning.

Mona has exercise class 2 times a week. Each class is $1\frac{1}{2}$ hours long and costs $5 per hour. How many hours does she spend in class each week?

23. Which equation would you use to solve the problem?

    a. $\$5 \times 2$
    b. $2 \times 1\frac{1}{2}$ hours
    c. $1\frac{1}{2}$ hours $\times \$5$
    d. $2 \times 1\frac{1}{2}$ hours $\times \$5$

24. **Write About Math** Under what condition would the reciprocal of a number be larger than the number?

Using Measurement

9

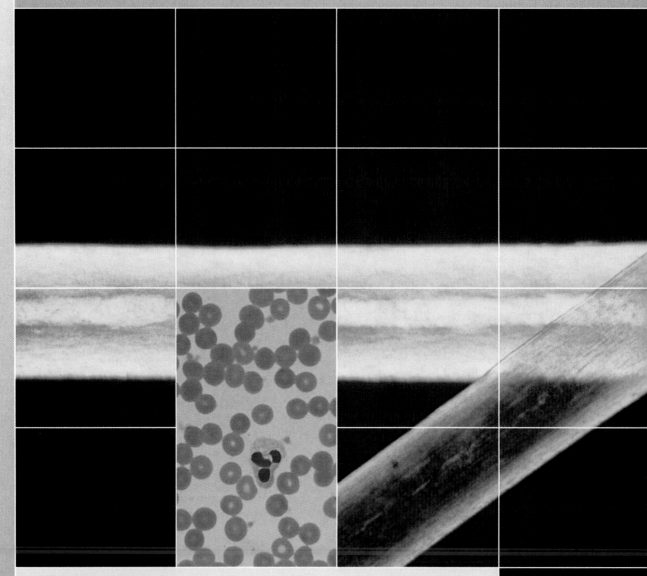

Did You Know: A living cell can be seen only under a microscope. There are three basic kinds of microscopes, a light microscope, which can magnify an object up to 2,000 times, an electron microscope, which can magnify up to 1 million times, and an ion microscope, which can magnify up to 2 million times with extreme clarity.

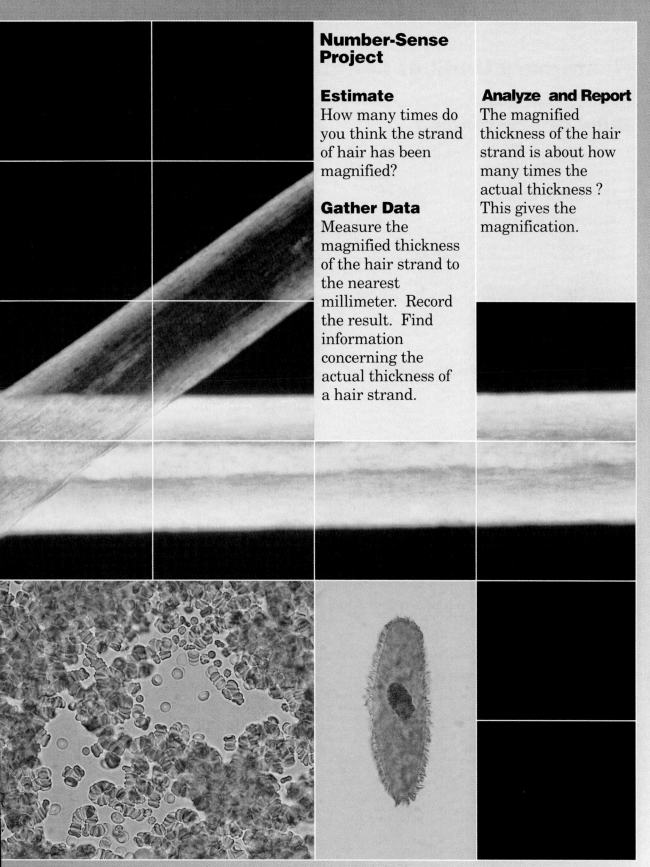

Number-Sense Project

Estimate
How many times do you think the strand of hair has been magnified?

Gather Data
Measure the magnified thickness of the hair strand to the nearest millimeter. Record the result. Find information concerning the actual thickness of a hair strand.

Analyze and Report
The magnified thickness of the hair strand is about how many times the actual thickness? This gives the magnification.

305

Customary Units of Length, Area, and Volume

Build Understanding

A. Mira Vuksan is a landscape designer. She often plants sycamores as shade trees. She knows they can grow to a height of 100 feet.

Customary Units

Length	Area	Volume
inches (in.) feet (ft) yards (yd) miles (mi)	square inches (sq in.) square feet (sq ft) square yards (sq yd) square miles (sq mi)	cubic inches (cu in.) cubic feet (cu ft) cubic yards (cu yd)

B. Mira has enough seeds to plant an *area* of 100 square feet with flowers. The area of a figure is measured in square units.

C. Mira installs a planter that holds 27 cubic feet of dirt. The planter has a *volume* of 27 cubic feet. Volume is measured in cubic units.

D. Write 67 inches as feet and inches.

To change to a **larger** unit, **divide**.

12 in. = 1 ft
67 ÷ 12 = 5 R7
67 in. = 5 ft 7 in.

12 in. = 1 ft
3 ft = 1 yd
36 in. = 1 yd
5,280 ft = 1 mi
1,760 yd = 1 mi

E. Write 1 yard 2 feet 1 inch as inches.

1 yd = 3 ft
3 × 12 = 36 in.
2 ft = 24 in.
36 in. + 24 in. + 1 in. = 61 in.
1 yd 2 ft 1 in. = 61 in.

To change to a **smaller** unit, **multiply**.

■ **Talk About Math**   Why do you divide 67 by 12 in Example D?

Check Understanding

For another example, see Set A, pages 334–335.

Estimation   Choose the most sensible measure.

1. Width of a sidewalk
   3 in.   3 ft   30 yd

2. Height of a bush
   24 in.   40 ft   75 yd

3. Area of a backyard
   30 sq in.   50 sq yd   50 sq mi

4. Volume of a flowerpot
   100 cu in.   100 cu ft   100 cu yd

Practice

For More Practice, see Set A, pages 336–337.

Would you use units of length, of area, or of volume to compare the sizes of

5. two playgrounds?   **6.** two refrigerators?   **7.** two pieces of string?

Find each missing number. **Remember** to use the correct operation.

8. 120 in. = ⬚ ft   **9.** 8 ft = ⬚ in.   **10.** 17 yd = ⬚ ft

11. 2 mi = ⬚ ft   **12.** 93 ft = ⬚ yd   **13.** 144 in. = ⬚ yd

14. 9 ft 7 in. = ⬚ in.   **15.** 5 yd 2 ft = ⬚ in.   **16.** 6 mi = ⬚ yd

17. 500 ft = ⬚ yd ⬚ ft   **18.** $2\frac{7}{8}$ mi = ⬚ ft   **19.** 1 cu yd = ⬚ cu ft

For Exercises 20–29, tell whether you would use paper and pencil, mental math, or a calculator. Then find each missing number.

20. 504 in. = ⬚ yd   **21.** 7 ft 5 in. = ⬚ in.   **22.** 1 mi 200 ft = ⬚ ft

23. 9 ft 8 in. = ⬚ in.   **24.** 10 mi = ⬚ ft   **25.** 37 yd 2 ft = ⬚ ft

26. 782 in. = ⬚ yd ⬚ ft ⬚ in.   **27.** 7,486 ft = ⬚ mi ⬚ yd ⬚ ft

28. 10,456 ft = ⬚ mi ⬚ yd ⬚ ft   **29.** 1 cu yd = ⬚ cu in.

Problem Solving

30. A magnolia tree Mira planted has grown to be 16 feet tall. Write this height in yards and feet.

Explore ———— Math

You can use a model to explore how many square inches are in a square foot.

31. Use grid paper to draw a square with sides 12 units long. Think of each grid unit as 1 inch long.

32. How many grid squares are in each row? How many rows are there?

33. How many grid squares are in your large square? How many square inches are in 1 square foot?

34. Explain how you could determine the number of square inches in a square yard.

Estimating and Measuring in the Customary System

Build Understanding

A. Closer and Closer
Materials: Math Sketcher or ruler
Groups: With a partner

You can measure lengths to the nearest inch, half inch, quarter inch, and eighth inch with a ruler. Smaller units are used to get measures closer to the actual length.

a. Lay the inch ruler of your Math Sketcher along the red line segment at the left. Is the length closer to 3 inches or to 4 inches?

b. What is the length of the red segment to the nearest inch?

c. Is the length of the red segment closer to 3 inches or to $3\frac{1}{2}$ inches? What is the length to the nearest half inch?

d. Is the length of the red segment closer to 3 inches or to $3\frac{1}{4}$ inches? What is the length to the nearest quarter inch?

e. Measure the length of the blue segment to the nearest quarter inch.

B. Measure the length of the pencil to the nearest eighth inch.

The length is between $4\frac{2}{8}$ inches and $4\frac{3}{8}$ inches, but it is closer to $4\frac{3}{8}$ inches. To the nearest eighth inch, it is $4\frac{3}{8}$ inches long.

■ **Talk About Math** If a pencil is $4\frac{3}{8}$ inches long to the nearest eighth inch, can it be longer than the one pictured? shorter? Explain.

Check Understanding

For another example, see Set B, pages 334–335.

1. For the segments in Example A, what unit of measure can be used to determine which segment is longer?

2. Using a ruler, draw three line segments of different lengths that are all 2 inches long to the nearest inch.

Practice

For More Practice, see Set B, pages 336–337.

Refer to the line segments below for Exercises 3–22.
Give the measure of each segment to the unit indicated.

A ——————————— B   C ——————————————— D
E ————————————————— F
G ——————————————————— H
J ————————————————————— K

To nearest	$\overline{AB}$	$\overline{CD}$	$\overline{EF}$	$\overline{GH}$	$\overline{JK}$
inch	3.	4.	5.	6.	7.
half inch	8.	9.	10.	11.	12.
quarter inch	13.	14.	15.	16.	17.
eighth inch	18.	19.	20.	21.	22.

23. **Estimation**   Without using your ruler, draw a segment about $1\frac{1}{2}$ inches long. Then measure your segment. Is it too long? too short? How close was your estimate?

Problem Solving

Solve each problem.

24. **Critical Thinking**   Ami's pen is $5\frac{1}{2}$ inches long to the nearest half inch. What is the shortest possible actual length? Could the actual length be $5\frac{13}{16}$ inches?

25. **Use Data**   Find circle O on page 180. Measure the diameter $\overline{LM}$ and the chord $\overline{LN}$ to the nearest eighth inch. Which line segment is longer?

26. **Number Sense**   The length of a pencil to the nearest inch is 3 inches. Complete the following: If x represents the actual length of the pencil, ▦ $\leq x$ and $x <$ ▦.

ALGEBRA

Customary Units of Capacity and Weight

Build Understanding

In his catering business, Juan Delgado prepares food in large quantities. To do so, he must know equivalent units of capacity and weight.

A. When Juan triples a pudding recipe, he finds he needs 6 teaspoons of vanilla. How many tablespoons of vanilla should he pour?

$6 \div 3 = 2$ To change to a **larger** unit, **divide**.

Juan needs 2 tablespoons of vanilla.

B. Juan uses 4 pounds 8 ounces of carrots for a stew. How many ounces do the carrots weigh?

$4 \times 16 = 64$ To change to a **smaller** unit, **multiply**.

$64 + 8 = 72$ Add the remaining ounces.

The carrots weigh 72 ounces.

■ **Talk About Math** If a juice bottle is labeled "16 oz," do you think it holds 1 pound of juice? Explain.

Units of Capacity

3 teaspoons (tsp) = 1 tablespoon (T)
2 tablespoons = 1 fluid ounce (fl oz)
8 fluid ounces = 1 cup (c)
2 cups = 1 pint (pt)
2 pints = 1 quart (qt)
4 quarts = 1 gallon (gal)

Units of Weight

16 ounces (oz) = 1 pound (lb)
2,000 pounds = 1 ton

Check Understanding

For another example, see Set C, pages 334–335.

Find each missing number.

1. 24 qt = (24 ÷ ▦) = ▦ gal

2. 5 lb = (5 × ▦) = ▦ oz

3. 20 fl oz = 2 c ▦ fl oz

4. 9 T = ▦ fl oz 1 T

5. 2 lb 20 oz = ▦ lb 4 oz

6. 3 gal 7 qt = 4 gal ▦ qt

Practice

For More Practice, see Set C, pages 336–337.

Estimation Choose the more sensible measure.

7. Capacity of a mug
1 c or 1 gal

8. Weight of a freezer
300 lb or 3 tons

9. Salt in a pot of soup
1 tsp or 1 c

10. It takes fewer pounds than ounces to measure a weight, so ___?___ by 16 to change 48 ounces to pounds.

11. Because it takes more cups than pints to measure a capacity, ___?___ by 2 to change 8 pints to cups.

Find each missing number. **Remember** to use the correct operation.

12. 4 pt = ▦ qt   **13.** 7 tons = ▦ lb   **14.** 6 lb = ▦ oz   **15.** 12 tsp = ▦ T

16. 14 qt = ▦ pt   **17.** 3 qt = ▦ fl oz   **18.** 5 gal = ▦ pt   **19.** 24 qt = ▦ gal

20. 2 tons = ▦ oz   **21.** 72 fl oz = ▦ c   **22.** 22 c = ▦ pt   **23.** 8,000 lb = ▦ tons

24. 2,456 lb = ▦ ton ▦ lb   **25.** 43 fl oz = ▦ c ▦ fl oz

26. 5 gal 3 qt = ▦ qt   **27.** 1,248 tsp = ▦ gal ▦ qt ▦ c

Mental Math Choose the greater capacity or weight.

28. 16 qt or 33 pt   **29.** 17 tsp or 6 T   **30.** $\frac{1}{2}$ lb or 5 oz   **31.** 17 pt or 2 gal

---

Problem Solving

Complete the table to show the amount of each ingredient which will be needed for 16, 24, and 48 servings.

Amount Needed for Number of Servings

	8	16	24	48
beef shank	3 lb	**32.**	**33.**	**34.**
water	1 qt	**35.**	**36.**	**37.**
sliced carrots	1 c	**38.**	**39.**	**40.**
tomatoes	1 lb	**41.**	**42.**	**43.**

TIPS FOR PROBLEM SOLVERS

Don't give up. Some problems take longer than others.

▦ **Calculator** Find each capacity or weight.

44. How many teaspoons of water does a 50-gallon tank hold?

45. How many ounces does a $2\frac{1}{2}$-ton van weigh?

Choose an Operation

Build Understanding

The students at Lincoln Middle School are planning a picnic.

PROBLEM SOLVING
GUIDE

Understand
QUESTION
FACTS
KEY IDEA

Plan and Solve
STRATEGY
ANSWER

Look Back
SENSIBLE ANSWER
ALTERNATE APPROACH

A. Dawn needs 5 tablecloths, each 3 ft 10 in. long. Will an 18-foot roll contain enough paper?

Understand Find the total length of paper needed. Compare this length to 18 ft.

 Plan and Solve STRATEGY   All 5 tablecloths will have the same length. *Choose the operation* of multiplication.

$$\begin{array}{r} 3 \text{ ft } 10 \text{ in.} \\ \times \qquad 5 \\ \hline 15 \text{ ft } 50 \text{ in.} = 19 \text{ ft } 2 \text{ in.} \end{array}$$

ANSWER   Dawn needs 19 ft 2 in. of paper, so an 18-ft roll is not enough.

Look Back Each tablecloth will be 2 in. shorter than 4 ft, so Dawn needs 10 in. less than 20 ft, or 19 ft 2 in. of paper.

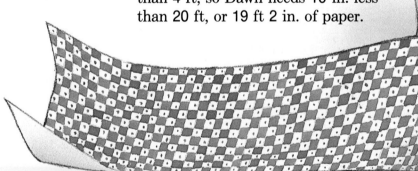

B. If Dawn uses a 25-ft roll of paper, how much will be left?

$$\begin{array}{r} 25 \text{ ft} \\ - 19 \text{ ft } 2 \text{ in.} \end{array} \longrightarrow \begin{array}{r} 24 \text{ ft } 12 \text{ in.} \\ - 19 \text{ ft } 2 \text{ in.} \\ \hline 5 \text{ ft } 10 \text{ in.} \end{array}$$

Five ft 10 in. will be left.

■ **Talk About Math**   Three tables of different lengths are placed together. If you know the length of each table, what operation would you use to find the total length of the tables?

Check Understanding

Solve.

1. If three tables with lengths of 3 ft 6 in., 2 ft 10 in., and 3 ft are placed together, what is their total length?

2. If 25 cups of lemonade are taken from a full 12-quart bowl, how many cups of lemonade will be left in the bowl?

Practice

Solve each problem. **Remember** to use an appropriate operation.

3. Find the total amount of fruit juice needed for a punch recipe that uses 4 c of lemon juice, 6 c of pineapple juice, and 1 qt of orange juice.

4. Fifty-seven people will be at a picnic. If each person drinks 2 cups of punch, how much punch will be used?

5. Liz filled a 5-qt pitcher with lemonade from a 6-gal jug. How much lemonade was left in the jug?

6. Alan planned to serve one 4-oz hamburger to each of the 57 people at the picnic. How much meat will be needed?

7. Kele bought boxes of tomatoes weighing 4 lb 9 oz, 3 lb 8 oz, and 4 lb 7 oz. Find the total weight of the tomatoes.

8. Jill bought 3 containers of potato salad, each weighing 2 lb 6 oz. What was the total weight of the potato salad?

Choose a _____ Strategy

What's the Total?

9. Larry paid $18.00 for 10 lb of meat. He bought a whole number of pounds of each kind of meat shown at the right. How much of each kind did he buy?

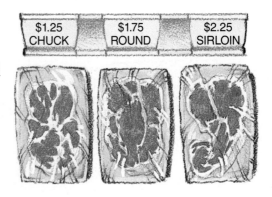

Metric Units of Length, Area, and Volume

Build Understanding

A. Sue Wong plays baseball at a field that is 12 city blocks from her home. This distance is about 1 kilometer (km).

Her baseball bat is about 1 meter long.

She uses a baseball sewn with thread about 1 millimeter (mm) thick.

The cleats on Sue's shoes are about 1 centimeter (cm) high.

The metric system of measurements is based on powers of 10.

Prefix	kilo-	hecto-	deka-		deci-	centi-	milli-
Meaning	1,000 m	100 m	10 m	1 m	0.1 m	0.01 m	0.001 m
Symbol	km	hm	dam	m	dm	cm	mm

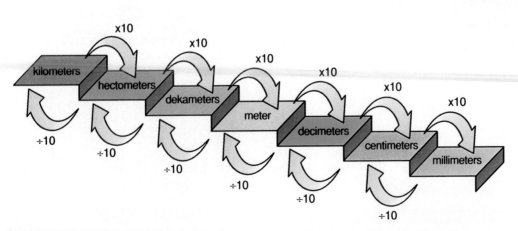

314

B. Change 3.2 m to centimeters.

1 m = 100 cm
3.2 × 100 = 320
3.2 m = 320 cm

To change to a **smaller** unit, **multiply**.
To multiply by 100, move the decimal point 2 places to the right.

C. Change 9 millimeters to meters.

1 mm = 0.001 m
9 ÷ 1,000 = 0.009
9 mm = 0.009 m

To change to a **larger** unit, **divide**.
To divide by 1,000, move the decimal point 3 places to the left.

D. In the metric system, area is usually measured in square centimeters (cm^2) or square meters (m^2).

1 square centimeter
1 cm^2
(actual size)

E. In the metric system, volume is usually measured in cubic centimeters (cm^3) or cubic meters (m^3).

1 cubic centimeter
1 cm^3
(actual size)

■ **Talk About Math**   Explain why changing from one unit of length to another is easier in the metric system than in the customary system.

Check Understanding

For another example, see Set D, pages 334–335.

Complete.

1. One kilometer is the same as ▦ meters.

2. One decimeter is the same as ▦ millimeters.

3. To change 6 meters to kilometers, ___?___ by 1,000.

4. To change 500 meters to centimeters, ___?___ by 100.

5. To change 21 centimeters to ___?___, multiply by 10.

6. To change 150 millimeters to meters, divide 150 by ▦.

Estimation   Choose the most sensible measure.

7. Distance from home plate to first base
27.4 cm   27.4 m   27.4 km

8. Area of the baseball playing field
5,000 cm^2 5,000 m^2 0.5 m^2

9. Width of home plate
43 cm   43 m   4.3 km

10. Volume of a popcorn box
1 m^3 1,000 cm^3 1 m^2

Practice

For More Practice, see Set D, pages 336–337.

Estimation Choose the most sensible measure.

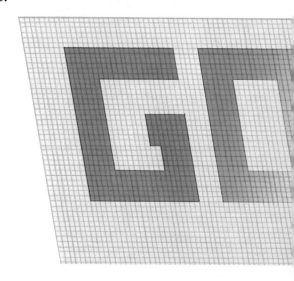

11. Length of a pen

14 cm   14 mm   14 m

12. Length of a river

1,000 km   1,000 m   1,000 mm

13. Area of a stamp

40 cm²   4 mm²   400 mm²

14. Thickness of a coin

2 cm   2 mm   2 dm

15. Area of a chair seat

900 cm²   9 cm²   90 m²

Find each missing number.

16. 6 m = ▦ cm

17. 180 mm = ▦ cm

18. 3 km = ▦ m

19. 7,000 m = ▦ km

20. 15 cm = ▦ m

21. 4 cm = ▦ m

22. 3.2 m = ▦ mm

23. 876 m = ▦ km

24. 19 m = ▦ dm

25. 400 m = ▦ hm

26. 150 hm = ▦ m

27. 20 m = ▦ dam

28. 5.7 dm = ▦ m

29. 7.2 hm = ▦ m

30. 24.3 cm = ▦ mm

31. 62.7 km = ▦ m

32. 90 mm = ▦ m

33. 5 cm = ▦ mm

34. 355 m = ▦ km

35. 29 mm = ▦ cm

36. 48.19 m = ▦ dm

Mental Math Which is shorter?

37. 7 m or 70 cm

38. 25 km or 2,500 m

39. 0.04 m or 40 cm

40. 1.2 km or 120 hm

41. 900 mm or 9 cm

42. 80,000 mm or 0.08 hm

Give three other measures equivalent to the given measure.

43. 15 km

44. 1,400 mm

45. 38 hm

46. 900 cm

47. 12 dm

48. 450 mm

49. 7 m

50. 97 dam

51. 6.2 km

52. 0.14 m

Problem Solving

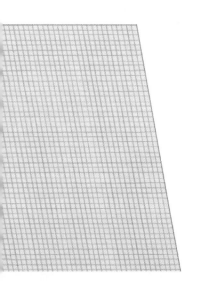

Critical Thinking Solve each problem.

53. Sue made a poster with an area of 1 m² from grid paper that has 1-cm squares. Did she use more or fewer than 1,000 of the 1-cm² squares?

54. Ned's locker has a volume of 1 m³. If the locker were filled with 1-cm cubes, would more or fewer than 10,000 cubes be needed?

55. Three men are 2 m, 175 cm, and 19 dm tall. Write these heights from shortest to tallest.

Midchapter **Checkup**

Estimation Choose the most sensible measure.

1. Length of a hammer
12 in.   12 ft   12 yd

2. Area of a porch
100 sq in.   100 sq ft   100 sq mi

3. Volume of a closet
2 cu in.   2 cu ft   2 cu yd

4. Area of a city park
100 sq in.   100 sq ft   1 sq mi

5. Capacity of a paint bucket
1 tsp   1 c   1 gal

6. Capacity of a cereal bowl
1 tsp   1 c   1 gal

Find each missing number.

7. 180 in. = ▓ ft

8. 5 mi = ▓ ft.

9. 1,850 mm = ▓ m

10. 8 ft 7 in. = ▓ in.

11. 19 yd 1 ft = ▓ ft

12. 2.4 km = ▓ m

Give the measure of each segment to the nearest half inch.

13. _____   **14.** _____

Give the measure of each segment to the nearest quarter inch.

15. _____   **16.** _____   **17.** _____

Problem Solving WORKSHOP

Real-Life Decision Making

1. Suppose you are having a party and want to make some confetti holders. Use two rectangular pieces of paper of the same size. Make one tall tube by taping together the longer sides of the paper and one short tube by taping together the shorter sides of the paper.

2. Will both tubes hold the same amount of confetti?

3. Fill one tube with puffed cereal, foam packing pellets, or dry beans. Pour the contents into the other cylinder. Compare and decide which tube will hold more confetti.

4. Which tube would you make to hold the confetti? Why?

Number-Sense Project

Look back at pages 304–305.

1. Very small objects are often measured in microns. One micron is one millionth of a meter. The actual length of the objects below is given in millimeters. Write each length in microns.

    a. Red blood cell: 0.007 mm

    b. Pox virus: 0.0004 mm

    c. Paramecium: 0.075 mm

    d. Muscle cell: 0.05 mm

    e. Protein molecule: 0.000009 mm

    f. Water molecule: 0.0000003 mm

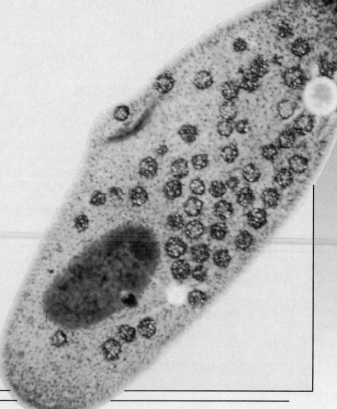

Paramecium: Magnified 160 X

Explore with a Computer

Use the *Geometry Workshop Project* for this activity.

Students in the Photography Club are learning about enlarging pictures. They start with a picture 2 units long and 3 units wide, and then double the length of each side.

1. What is the area of the original picture? At the computer, size the picture to double the length of each side. What is the area of the enlarged picture?

2. Double the length of each side again. What is the area of the enlarged picture?

3. When you double the lengths of both sides of a rectangle, how does the area change?

Critical-Thinking Activity

A 3-cup, a 5-cup, and an 8-cup pitcher are on the table. The 8-cup pitcher is full of punch and the other two are empty.

1. Describe the steps it would take to pour the punch from one pitcher to another so that the punch is divided equally between two of the pitchers.

2. How many steps did it take?

3. Can it be done in fewer steps?

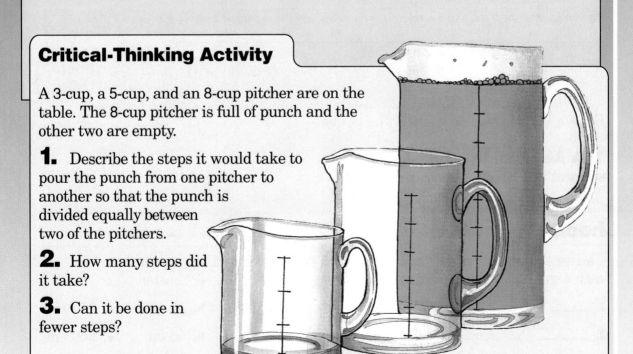

Estimating and Measuring in the Metric System

Build Understanding

All around the globe, men, women, and children have worn some type of jewelry for thousands of years. Jewelry is often fashioned out of metal, bones, fabric, shells, wood, gems, glass, and synthetic materials.

Since 1291, much of the world's beautiful glass jewelry has come from the island of Murano, near Venice, Italy. Until the 18th century, the master glassblowers were expected to keep their skills a secret from outsiders.

A. Measure the length of this string of Murano beads to the nearest millimeter.

The string of beads is 145 mm long.

B. Draw a segment that is 11.4 cm long.

Place a point at the 0 mark of the ruler. Draw another point at the mark for 11.4 cm.

Draw a line segment to connect the points.

■ **Talk About Math**   What are some other ways to draw a segment of length 11.4 cm using a ruler?

Check Understanding

For another example, see Set E, pages 334–335.

Choose the best estimate for the length of each segment. Then measure each segment to the nearest millimeter and to the nearest centimeter.

1. _____   **a.** 2.5 mm   **b.** 25 mm   **c.** 25 cm

2. _____   **a.** 56 mm   **b.** 56 cm   **c.** 560 cm

3. _____   **a.** 7 mm   **b.** 700 mm   **c.** 7 cm

Practice

For More Practice, see Set E, pages 336–337.

Estimate the length of each segment in centimeters. Then measure to find the length to the nearest centimeter.

4. ────────────── **5.** ─────── **6.** ──────────────

Estimate the length of each segment in millimeters. Then measure to find the length to the nearest millimeter.

7. ──── **8.** ───────── **9.** ──────────────

Draw a segment that has the given length.

10. 6 mm **11.** 46 mm **12.** 6 cm **13.** 2.5 cm **14.** 8.2 cm **15.** 12.6 cm

16. Draw three line segments of different lengths that are all 8 cm long to the nearest centimeter.

African trading beads are made in many parts of the world, including Venice and the island of Murano in Italy. The section of the African necklace shown represents only $\frac{1}{10}$ of its actual length.

17. Determine the length of the necklace to the nearest centimeter.

18. Suppose the pattern repeats. About how many striped beads would the necklace have?

Problem Solving

Explore ───── Math

In China, jade is considered the most precious gem stone. While green jade is the most common, the Chinese prefer some of the stone's more rare colors.

19. Why is it hard to measure the length of this string of jade beads?

20. How could a piece of string be helpful in finding the length?

21. Use a piece of string and a ruler to find the length to the nearest centimeter.

Metric Units of Capacity and Mass

Build Understanding

A. The basic unit of capacity in the metric system is the *liter (L)*. Another common unit is the *milliliter (mL)*.

A large thermos bottle holds about 1 L of soup.

A tablespoon holds about 15 mL of soup.

| 1 liter = 1,000 milliliters |

B. The basic unit of mass in the metric system is the *gram (g)*. Other common units are the *kilogram (kg)* and *milligram (mg)*.

A raisin has a mass of about 1 g.

Two loaves of bread have a mass of about 1 kg.

A few grains of salt have a mass of about 1 mg.

| 1 kilogram = 1,000 grams |
| 1 gram = 1,000 milligrams |

C. Change 3,185 milliliters to liters.

1 L = 1,000 mL
3,185 ÷ 1,000 = 3.185
3,185 mL = 3.185 L

D. Change 4.3 grams to milligrams.

1 g = 1,000 mg
4.3 × 1,000 = 4,300
4.3 g = 4,300 mg

■ **Talk About Math** What operation do you use to change from a smaller unit to a larger unit?

Check Understanding

For another example, see Set F, pages 334–335.

Complete.

1. To change 18 kg to grams, __?__ 18 by 1,000.

2. To change 285 mL to liters, __?__ 285 by 1,000.

3. Number Sense For which of Exercises 4–12 will you need to divide?

Practice

For More Practice, see Set F, pages 336–337.

Find each missing number. **Remember** to move the decimal point
to the left or the right.

4. 8 kg = ▦ g **5.** 7,000 mL = ▦ L **6.** 1.5 g = ▦ mg

7. 2,220 g = ▦ kg **8.** 0.45 g = ▦ mg **9.** 175 mL = ▦ L

10. 9.2 kg = ▦ g **11.** 240 mL = ▦ L **12.** 0.03 g = ▦ mg

13. 12 L = ▦ mL **14.** 675 mg = ▦ g **15.** 4,200 g = ▦ kg

Mixed Practice Find each missing number.

16. 2.3 km = ▦ m **17.** 150 mm = ▦ m **18.** 19 g = ▦ mg

19. 279 cm = ▦ m **20.** 52 mL = ▦ L **21.** 450 kg = ▦ g

22. 8,200 g = ▦ kg **23.** 7.1 L = ▦ ml **24.** 18 m = ▦ cm

Problem Solving

Critical Thinking Which is the better buy?

25.

$1.49 300 g $0.55 100 g

26.

$4.29 1 kg $0.89 200 g

27. Would two 650-milliliter cans of stew fit in a 1-liter container?

Choose a _____ Strategy

Water, Water, Everywhere Do you use more water for a
shower or for a bath? Suppose you always use 250 L of water
for a bath and your shower uses 15 L of water per minute.

28. How many minutes would a 150-L shower take?

29. What is the greatest whole number of minutes you can shower
and still use less water than you would use taking a bath?

Time

Build Understanding

Units of Time

60 seconds (sec) = 1 minute (min)
60 minutes = 1 hour (h)
24 hours = 1 day (da)
365 days = 1 year (y)
366 days = 1 leap year
100 years = 1 century

A. While shopping, Mr. Ozawa left his car at a parking garage from 3:45 P.M. to 5:03 P.M. How long was his car in the garage?

5:03 ⟶ ending time
− 3:45 ⟶ starting time

4:63	To subtract, rewrite 5:03.
− 3:45	Since 1 h = 60 min, add
1:18	60 min to 3 min.

The car was in the garage for 1 hour 18 minutes.

B. Mrs. Ozawa parked her car from 10:10 A.M. to 2:20 P.M. How long was her car parked?

On a **24-hour clock** time is expressed in relationship to midnight. Write the times on a 24-hour clock and subtract.

12-hour clock	24-hour clock
2:20 P.M.	14:20
− 10:10 A.M.	− 10:10
	4:10

The car was parked for 4 hours 10 minutes.

■ **Talk About Math**   Describe another way to do Example B.

Check Understanding

For another example, see Set G, pages 334–335.

Complete.

1. 9 min = ▦ sec

2. 150 min = 2 h ▦ min

3. 36 h = ▦ da 12 h

4. On a 12-hour clock, 14:00 would be ___?___.

5. On a 24-hour clock, 1:00 P.M. would be ___?___.

6.
    4 h 30 min
  + 2 h 40 min
    6 h ▦ min = 7 h ▦ min

7.
    5 h 20 min →   4 h ▦ min
  − 1 h 50 min → − 1 h 50 min
                    3 h ▦ min

Practice

For More Practice, see Set G, pages 336–337.

Find each missing number.

8. 23 min = ▦ sec   **9.** 360 min = ▦ h   **10.** 5 da = ▦ h

Express each time on a 12-hour clock. **Remember** to write A.M. or P.M.

11. 15:25   **12.** 19:01   **13.** 23:00   **14.** 9:25   **15.** 13:45   **16.** 11:15

Express each time on a 24-hour clock.

17. 7:00 P.M.   **18.** 3:15 P.M.   **19.** 6:22 A.M.   **20.** 10:52 P.M.   **21.** 1:30 P.M.

Find each time.

22. 4 h 45 min after 11:30 P.M.   **23.** 13 h 47 min after 11:30 A.M.

Solve.

24.   2 h 15 min
      $\underline{+\ 6\ h\ 20\ min}$

25.   12 h 10 min
      $\underline{-\ 5\ h\ 35\ min}$

26.   3 h 42 min
      $\underline{+\ 4\ h\ 25\ min}$

27. ▦ **Calculator** Compute the number of minutes in a
year (not a leap year).

Problem Solving

Solve.

28. Boris drives a delivery truck for the Floor Store. At 8:05 A.M., before beginning his drive, Boris punched a time clock. After finishing, he punched out at 5:20 P.M. If he took 30 minutes for lunch, how long did Boris work?

29. On one day, Mr. Ozawa parked his car until 3:40 P.M. Parking costs $2.00 for the first hour and $0.75 for each additional half hour or part of a half hour. If he paid $4.25 for parking, what is the earliest time Mr. Ozawa could have left his car?

Skills _____ **Review**   pages 28–31, 68–71, 146–147

Find each answer.

1. 1.8 × 2.7   **2.** 7.5 − 1.38   **3.** 0.6)0.42   **4.** 2.76 + 5.04

Use Data from a Table

Build Understanding

Nell's flight left Boston at 12:00 noon and arrived in Denver at 2:20 P.M. local time. How long did the flight take?

The world is divided into 24 *time zones*. The time zones for North America are shown below.

Understand   QUESTION   How long was the flight?

FACTS   Nell left at 12:00 noon Boston time and arrived at 2:20 P.M. Denver time.

KEY IDEA   Denver time is 2 hours earlier than Boston time.

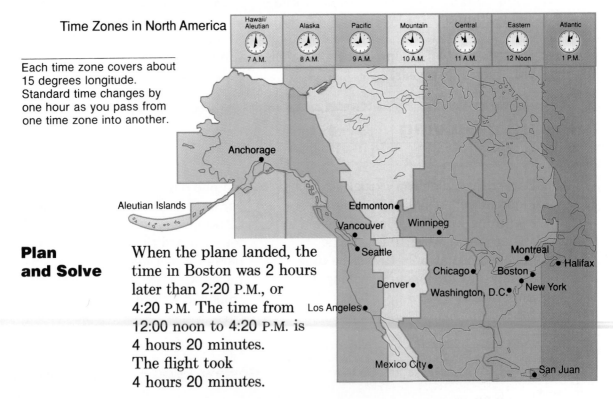

Time Zones in North America

Each time zone covers about 15 degrees longitude. Standard time changes by one hour as you pass from one time zone into another.

Plan and Solve   When the plane landed, the time in Boston was 2 hours later than 2:20 P.M., or 4:20 P.M. The time from 12:00 noon to 4:20 P.M. is 4 hours 20 minutes. The flight took 4 hours 20 minutes.

Look Back   The flight lasted from 10:00 A.M. Denver time to 2:20 P.M. Denver time, or 4 hours 20 minutes.

■**Talk About Math**   If you travel from west to east, should you set your watch ahead or back?

Understand
QUESTION
FACTS
KEY IDEA

Plan and Solve
STRATEGY
ANSWER

Look Back
SENSIBLE ANSWER
ALTERNATE APPROACH

Check Understanding

When it is 10:45 A.M. in Winnipeg, what time is it in

1. Los Angeles? **2.** Montreal? **3.** San Juan? **4.** Anchorage?

A flight left Winnipeg at 1:15 P.M. local time
and landed in Seattle 4 hours 20 minutes later.

5. What time was it in Winnipeg when the plane landed?

6. What was the local time in Seattle when the plane landed?

Practice

Solve each problem. All times are local times.
Remember to use the table of time zones on page 326.

7. A plane left Mexico City at 7:55 A.M. and arrived in Los Angeles at 10:30 A.M. How long was the flight?

8. A plane left Los Angeles at 1:20 P.M. and arrived in Boston at 9:09 P.M. How long did the flight take?

9. A plane took 1 hour 35 minutes to fly from Halifax to Montreal. If the flight left at 5:50 P.M., what time did it reach Montreal?

10. A flight from Seattle to Chicago took 3 hours 25 minutes. If the plane landed at 5:30 P.M., at what time did it leave Seattle?

Use the table at the right. When it is 6:00 P.M. on Tuesday in New York, what time is it in

11. London? **12.** Bangkok? **13.** Sydney?

Use the table to solve.

14. Harry left New York at 10:15 A.M. on Friday and arrived in Los Angeles 6 hours later. He continued his trip and arrived in Tokyo 14 hours after reaching Los Angeles. What was the time in Tokyo when he arrived?

Times Around the World

New York	12:00 noon Tues.
London	5:00 P.M. Tues.
Cairo	7:00 P.M. Tues.
Calcutta	11:00 P.M. Tues.
Bangkok	12:00 midnight
Tokyo	2:00 A.M. Wed.
Sydney	3:00 A.M. Wed.

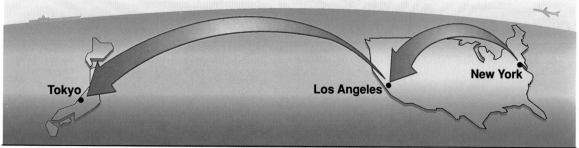

Temperature

Build Understanding

A. On a spring day, a weather forecaster's thermometer gave the temperature as 59 degrees **Fahrenheit** (59°F), which is 15 degrees **Celsius** (15°C).

B. If the weather forecast calls for very hot weather, would a sensible temperature be 50°F or 95°F?

From this thermometer, you can see that 95°F is more sensible for a very hot day.

C. A meteorologist made the graph below to record the temperature changes throughout the day on November 1. At what time was the temperature the lowest?

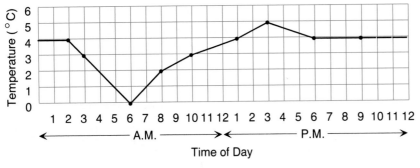

The temperature was lowest at 6:00 A.M.

■ **Talk About Math** What might you enjoy doing outside when the temperature is 25°F? 25°C?

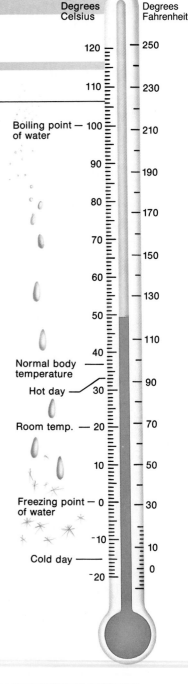

Check Understanding

For another example, see Set H, pages 334–335.

Refer to the thermometer shown above.

1. What are the freezing point and boiling point of water in degrees Celsius? in degrees Fahrenheit?

2. The temperature changed from −2°C to 7°C. Tell if the temperature fell or rose and by how many degrees.

Practice

For More Practice, see Set H, pages 336–337.

Estimation   Choose the most sensible temperature.
You may refer to the thermometer shown on page 328.

3. A snowy day
   22°F   22°C   62°C

4. A warm day
   35°F   26°C   72°C

5. A glass of cold juice
   8°F   38°C   38°F

6. A cup of hot tea
   85°C   85°F   32°C

7. A block of ice
   32°C   100°C   32°F

8. Body temperature
   99°F   99°C   140°C

For each change, tell whether the temperature has fallen
or risen and by how much. **Remember** to specify degrees
Celsius or Fahrenheit.

9. From 43°F to 2°F

10. From −1°C to 18°C

11. From −5°C to −23°C

12. From 7°F to −7°F

13. From −12°F to 4°F

14. From −6°C to 0°C

15. From −18°F to −4°F

16. From 82°F to 64°F

17. From 0°C to 13°C

Use the graph in Example C to find

18. the rise in temperature from
10:00 A.M. to 1:00 P.M.

19. the drop in temperature from
2:00 A.M. to 6:00 A.M.

Problem Solving

The thermometer below shows temperatures for a 12-hour period.

20. Make a graph similar to the
one in Example C showing
the temperatures from
6:00 A.M. to 6:00 P.M.

21. At what time was the
temperature the highest?
the lowest?

22. By how much did the
temperature increase from
6:00 A.M. to noon?

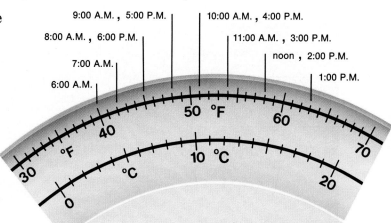

Give Sensible Answers

Build Understanding

When Alejandra Montero visited France, she made the chart shown at the bottom of the page.

Alejandra saw a sign that said "Paris, 50 km." Which is the most sensible estimate for the distance to Paris?

a. 80 mi   **b.** 10 mi   **c.** 30 mi   **d.** 100 mi

Understand You know that 1 km is a little more than $\frac{1}{2}$ mi. Choose the number of miles closest to 50 km.

Plan and Solve Since 1 km is a little more than $\frac{1}{2}$ mi, 50 km is a little more than 25 mi. Choice b is too small. Since 1 km is less than 1 mi, 50 km is less than 50 mi. Choices a and d are too large. The most sensible choice is 30 mi.

Look Back SENSIBLE ANSWER Of all the choices, 30 mi is the closest to being a little more than 25 mi.

Understand
QUESTION
FACTS
KEY IDEA

Plan and Solve
STRATEGY
ANSWER

Look Back
SENSIBLE ANSWER
ALTERNATE APPROACH

Metric to Customary
1 cm—a little less than $\frac{1}{2}$ inch
1 m—a little more than a yard
1 km—a little more than $\frac{1}{2}$ mile
1 L—a little more than a quart
1 kg—a little more than 2 pounds
28 g—about 1 ounce
450 g—about 1 pound
4 L—about 1 gallon
250 mL—about 1 cup
5 cm—about 2 inches

Several boulevards in Paris converge at the Arc de Triomphe.

■ Talk About Math If Alejandra realizes that 1 km is a little more than $\frac{1}{2}$ mi, will her estimate be closer to an exact answer for shorter distances or for longer distances?

Check Understanding

Number Sense Find the answers.

1. Can a 3-L pitcher hold more or less than a 3-qt pitcher?

2. Is a 100-m dash longer or shorter than a 100-yard dash?

3. Is a 40-cm ribbon longer or shorter than a 40-in. ribbon?

Estimation Choose the most sensible estimate for each measure.

4. 50 cm is about ▦ inches.
   10   20   100

5. 1,000 mL is about ▦ cups.
   4   9   16

6. 80 g is about ▦ ounces.
   3   5   40

7. 65 m is about ▦ yards.
   59   71   100

Practice

Solve each problem. **Remember** to compare customary and metric units in Exercises 8–11.

8. Alejandra flew 4,998 km to Paris. Was this more or less than 4,000 miles?

9. Alejandra read that the Eiffel Tower is 300 m tall. Is this taller or shorter than a 900-foot building?

10. Alejandra mailed a 14-kg package. Was it lighter or heavier than a 28-lb package?

11. Alejandra's father bought 40 L of gasoline for the car. At home he usually buys 10 gallons. Did he buy more or less gas than usual?

12. **Critical Thinking** Alejandra bought some post cards. She gave $\frac{1}{4}$ of them to her sister. On Tuesday she mailed twice as many cards as she mailed on Monday. On Tuesday she sent 8 cards and still had 3 cards left. How many cards did Alejandra buy?

Skills Review

Find each missing number.

1. 60 in. = ▦ ft

2. 3 yd 2 ft = ▦ ft

3. 10 qt = ▦ pt

4. 35 fl oz = ▦ c ▦ fl oz

5. 450 cm = ▦ mm

6. 3,500 g = ▦ kg

7. 0.75 L = ▦ mL

Choose the best estimate for the length of each segment.

8. $\frac{1}{2}$ in.   3 in.   1 ft

9. 5 mm   5 cm   5 m

Measure the rope to the nearest

10. quarter inch.   **11.** millimeter.

Solve.

12. What time will it be 3 hr 45 min after 10:30 P.M.?

13.   2 h 45 min   **14.**   10 min 15 sec
      + 1 h 30 min   − 2 min 35 sec

For each change, tell whether the temperature has fallen or risen and by how much.

15. From −5°F   **16.** From 15°C
     to 2°F   to −3°C

Problem-Solving Review

Solve each problem.

17. A playground measures $75\frac{1}{2}$ feet by $50\frac{1}{2}$ feet. What is the area of the playground?

18. The length of a row of five nickels placed side by side is about $4\frac{1}{4}$ inches. Make a table to find the number of nickels in a row 10 feet long.

19. During one week, Marvin practiced guitar for $\frac{1}{2}$ hour on Monday, $\frac{1}{4}$ hour on Tuesday, 1 hour on Wednesday, $\frac{3}{4}$ hour on Thursday, and $\frac{1}{2}$ hour on Friday. How many hours did he practice that week?

20. Mrs. Olmstead used $4\frac{1}{8}$ yards of blue fabric and $2\frac{3}{4}$ yards of red fabric to make costumes. How much more blue fabric than red fabric did she use?

21. Which is the better buy, 12 ounces of peanut butter for $1.89 or 1 pound of peanut butter for $2.05?

22. **Data File** Use the data on pages 410–411. How many 1-liter bottles of grapefruit juice would you need to make citrus fruit juice for 12 people?

23. **Make a Data File** Look through the grocery advertisements in a newspaper. Make a table comparing the prices of three different items at two different stores.

Write the numbers in order from least to greatest.

1. 0.6, 1.06, 0.06, 1.116, 1.16

2. 39.4, 3.94, 3.49, 34.09, 34.90

Solve each equation for b.

3. $5 \times b = 100$ **4.** $5 + b = 100$

5. $42 = b \times 6$ **6.** $72 = 58 + b$

Multiply or divide. Use mental math.

7. 600×20 **8.** $30 \times 7,000$

9. $0.56 \times 1,000$ **10.** $10,000 \times 3.6$

11. $4,500 \div 90$ **12.** $240 \div 8$

13. $24.5 \div 100$ **14.** $0.63 \div 1,000$

Solve each problem.

15. Name a radius of the circle.

16. Name the diameter.

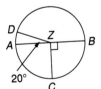

17. What is the measure of $\angle CZD$?

Find the GCF for each set of numbers.

18. 8, 12   **19.** 30, 45

Compare. Use $<$, $>$, or $=$.

20. $\frac{3}{7}$ ▦ $\frac{5}{7}$ **21.** $\frac{5}{8}$ ▦ $\frac{5}{9}$

22. $\frac{12}{4}$ ▦ 3 **23.** $1\frac{5}{12}$ ▦ $\frac{19}{12}$

Estimate by finding a range.

24. $5\frac{3}{4} \times 3\frac{1}{2}$ **25.** $6\frac{2}{5} \times 8\frac{2}{3}$

Estimate the quotient by rounding to the nearest whole number.

26. $8\frac{1}{3} \div 1\frac{5}{8}$ **27.** $14\frac{3}{4} \div 4\frac{5}{7}$

Compute.

28. $\frac{3}{5} + \frac{1}{2}$ **29.** $\frac{5}{12} \times \frac{2}{10}$

30. $\frac{7}{8} \div \frac{3}{4}$ **31.** $\frac{7}{9} - \frac{2}{3}$

32. $4\frac{5}{7} - 2\frac{1}{2}$ **33.** $1\frac{2}{3} \times 2\frac{1}{4}$

34. $4\frac{1}{2} \div 3$ **35.** $3\frac{2}{5} + 2\frac{2}{3}$

Measure the segment above to the nearest

36. quarter inch.   **37.** centimeter.

Find each missing number.

38. 50 in. = ▦ ft ▦ in.

39. 5 pt = ▦ qt ▦ pt

40. 6 m = ▦ cm

41. 3.5 kg = ▦ g

42. 240 min = ▦ h

Choose the most sensible measure.

43. Length of a pencil

   7 in.   7 ft   7 yd

44. Area of a bedroom

   120 sq in.   120 sq ft   120 sq mi

45. Volume of a shoe box

   3,000 cm³   3,000 m³   3,000 km³

Reteaching

You know the following facts:

12 in. = 1 ft, 3 ft = 1 yd, 36 in. = 1 yd.

Change 706 inches to yards, feet, and inches.

706 ÷ 36 = 19 R22
706 in. = 19 yd 22 in.

Since 22 in. = 1 ft 10 in.,
706 in. = 19 yd 1 ft 10 in.

Remember to divide when you are changing to a larger unit of measure.

Find each missing number.

1. 19 in. = ▦ ft ▦ in.

2. 216 in. = ▦ yd

3. 480 in. = ▦ yd ▦ ft

Measure the length of this pencil to the nearest eighth inch.

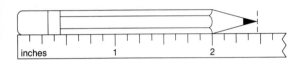

The length is close to $2\frac{4}{8}$ inches.

To the nearest eighth inch, it is $2\frac{4}{8}$, or $2\frac{1}{2}$ inches.

Remember that the smaller the unit of measurement on a ruler, the more exact is the measurement.

Measure the line segment below to the nearest

1. half inch.

2. quarter inch.

A ———————————————— B

You know the following facts:

2 pints = 1 quart
4 quarts = 1 gallon

Change 32 quarts to
a. gallons   **b.** pints

32 ÷ 4 = 8 gallons
32 × 2 = 64 pints

Remember to multiply when you change to a smaller unit of measure.

Find each missing number.

1. 20 qt = ▦ gal   **2.** 18 qt = ▦ pt

3. 10 gal = ▦ qt   **4.** 8 gal = ▦ pt

You know the following fact:

1,000 m = 1 km

Change 685 meters to kilometers.

685 ÷ 1,000 = 0.685
685 m = 0.685 km

Remember to move the decimal point to the left when you divide by 10, 100, or 1,000.

Find each missing number.

1. 793 m = ▦ km   **2.** 5.2 km = ▦ m

Independent Study **RETEACHING**

Set E   pages 320–321

Measure the length of this nail to the nearest millimeter.

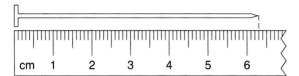

The tip of the nail is closer to **63 mm** than to **64 mm**.

The nail is **63 millimeters** long.

Remember that the smaller the unit of measurement that you use, the more exact will be your measurement.

Measure to find the length to the nearest millimeter.

1. ————————————

2. ————————

3. ——————————————

Set F   pages 322–323

You know the following fact.

1,000 grams = 1 kilogram

Change 3,255 grams to kilograms. To change from a smaller unit of measure to a larger unit, you divide.

3,255 ÷ 1,000 = 3.255
3,255 g = 3.255 kg

Remember to move the decimal point to the right when you multiply by 10, 100, or 1,000.

Find each missing number.

1. 2,560 g = ▦ kg

2. 6.4 kg = ▦ g

Set G   pages 324–325

Express 5:20 A.M. and 5:20 P.M. on a 24-hour clock.

For A.M. time, you rewrite the time without the A.M.
5:20 A.M. is 5:20 on the 24-hour clock.

For P.M. time, you add 12 to the hours.
5:20 P.M. is 17:20 on the 24-hour clock.

Remember that on a 24-hour clock time is expressed in relationship to midnight.

Express each time on a 24-hour clock.

1. 6:00 P.M.   **2.** 8:45 A.M.

3. 1:40 P.M.   **4.** 9:52 P.M.

Set H   pages 328–329

By how much did the temperature change from Monday to Tuesday?

Monday's high: 22°C
Tuesday's high: 26°C

The temperature rose from 22°C to 26°C. This is a rise of 4°C.

Remember to always specify degrees as Celsius or Fahrenheit.

For each change in temperature, tell whether it has fallen or risen and by how much.

1. From 18°C to 11°C

2. From −3°C to 18°C

More Practice

Set A pages 306–307

Find each missing number.

1. 144 in. = ▦ ft

2. 18 yd = ▦ ft

3. 4 mi = ▦ ft

4. 11 ft 6 in. = ▦ in.

5. 400 ft = ▦ yd ▦ ft

For Exercises 6–7, tell whether you would use paper and pencil, mental math, or a calculator. Then find each missing number.

6. 6,598 ft = ▦ mi ▦ yd ▦ ft

7. 967 in. = ▦ yd ▦ ft ▦ in.

Set B pages 308–309

Refer to the line segments below for Exercises 1–16. Give the measure of each segment to the unit indicated.

A ————————— B   C ————————————————————— D

E ———————————————————— F

G —————————————————————————— H

To nearest	$\overline{AB}$	$\overline{CD}$	$\overline{EF}$	$\overline{GH}$
inch	**1.**	**2.**	**3.**	**4.**
half inch	**5.**	**6.**	**7.**	**8.**
quarter inch	**9.**	**10.**	**11.**	**12.**
eighth inch	**13.**	**14.**	**15.**	**16.**

Set C pages 310–311

Find each missing number.

1. 4 qt = ▦ fl oz

2. 6 gal = ▦ pt

3. 3 tons = ▦ oz

4. 7 lb = ▦ oz

5. 18 tsp = ▦ T

6. 2,344 lb = ▦ ton ▦ lb

Mental Math Choose the greater capacity or weight.

7. 11 qt or 3 gal

8. $\frac{1}{4}$ lb or 6 oz

9. $\frac{1}{2}$ lb or 6 oz

Set D pages 314–317

Find each missing number.

1. 5 m = ▦ cm

2. 290 mm = ▦ cm

3. 275 cm = ▦ m

4. 4.6 m = ▦ mm

5. 6.3 hm = ▦ m

6. 47 dm = ▦ m

Set E pages 320–321

Estimate the length of each segment in centimeters. Then measure to find the length to the nearest centimeter.

1. _____ **2.** _____ **3.** _____

Estimate the length of each segment in millimeters. Then measure to find the length to the nearest millimeter.

4. _____ **5.** _____ **6.** _____

Draw a segment that has the given length.

7. 10 mm **8.** 36 mm **9.** 3.1 cm **10.** 7.8 cm

Set F pages 322–323

Find the missing number.

1. 12 kg = ▒ g **2.** 2.8 g = ▒ mg **3.** 250 mL = ▒ L

Mixed Practice Find each missing number.

4. 275 mm = ▒ m **5.** 88 mL = ▒ L **6.** 37 g = ▒ mg

Set G pages 324–325

Find each missing number.

1. 34 min = ▒ sec **2.** 480 min = ▒ hr **3.** 7 da = ▒ h **4.** 12 h = ▒ min

Express each time on a 12-hour clock.

5. 17:45 **6.** 10:50 **7.** 14:20 **8.** 23:35

Express each time on a 24-hour clock.

9. 6:30 P.M. **10.** 2:10 P.M. **11.** 11:50 A.M. **12.** 11:10 P.M.

Solve.

13. 3 h 25 min
     + 8 h 17 min

14. 11 h 20 min
     − 4 h 47 min

15. 5 h 36 min
     + 6 h 45 min

Set H pages 328–329

For each change in temperature, tell whether it has fallen or risen and by how much.

1. From 68°F to 10°F **2.** From −5°C to 20°C **3.** From −8°C to 30°C

4. From 9°C to −9°C **5.** From −18°F to 8°F **6.** From −3°C to 3°C

Enrichment

Measuring Instruments

A variety of measuring instruments are used in daily life. Common measuring instruments are rulers, bathroom scales, tape measures, and speedometers.

However, other measuring instruments are not as common.

See how many of the measuring instruments listed in Column A you can match with the person in Column B who is most likely to use that measuring instrument. You will probably need to use a dictionary or some other reference book to help you match items. Be sure to note how the word is pronounced.

Column A	Column B
1. sphygmomanometer	**a.** surveyor
2. gap gauge	**b.** graphic artist
3. altimeter	**c.** photographer
4. light meter	**d.** mechanic
5. measuring cup	**e.** chemist
6. tachometer	**f.** chef
7. micrometer	**g.** electrician
8. ammeter	**h.** pilot
9. graduated cylinder	**i.** meteorologist
10. metronome	**j.** pharmacist
11. barometer	**k.** race car driver
12. T square	**ℓ.** machinist
13. transit	**m.** musician
14. apothecary scale	**n.** doctor
15. sextant	**o.** ship's navigator

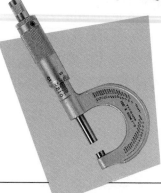

Chapter 9 Review/Test

Find each missing number.

1. 63 ft = ▦ yd

2. 49 in. = ▦ ft ▦ in.

3. 5 tons = ▦ lb

4. 5 pt 3 c = ▦ c

Choose the best estimate for the length of each segment.

5. _____

$\frac{1}{2}$ in.   2 in.   2 ft

6. _____

3 mm   3 m   3 cm

Find each missing number.

7. 250 mm = ▦ cm

8. 0.56 hm = ▦ m

9. 3.8 g = ▦ mg

10. 672 mL = ▦ L

11. 15 min = ▦ sec

12. 3 da 18 h = ▦ h

13. What time is 6 h 35 min after 9:25 A.M.?

For each change in temperature, tell whether it has fallen or risen and by how much.

14. From −4°C to −1°C

15. From 18°F to −9°F

Add or subtract.

16.   7 h 15 min
      − 2 h 35 min

17.   1 h 52 min
      + 3 h 14 min

Use the table below for Exercise 18.

Date	Temperature at Noon	
	(Celsius)	(Fahrenheit)
Mar. 15	0°C	32°F
Apr. 15	10°C	50°F
May 15	20°C	68°F
June 15	30°C	86°F

18. At 6:00 P.M. on March 15, the temperature was −7°C. How much did the temperature fall between noon and 6:00 P.M.?

19. Choose the operation needed. Then solve the problem.

Mary bought two boxes of cucumbers. One weighed 3 lb 8 oz, and the other weighed 2 lb 9 oz. How much did both boxes weigh?

Read the problem below. Then answer the question.

Henri was visiting America. He saw a road sign that said, "Boston, 100 miles." In kilometers, how far was Boston?

20. Choose the most sensible estimate.

a. About 200 km

b. About 20 km

c. About 50 km

21. **Write About Math**   Is it easier to convert from one unit to another in the customary or in the metric system? Explain.

Relating Geometry and Measurement

Did You Know: The lush rain forests in the Amazon region of Brazil receive an average of 160 inches of rainfall a year. This amount of rain falling over a one square mile area would fill almost 50 million bathtubs. One inch of water falling on a one square mile area amounts to over 170 million gallons of water.

Number-Sense Project

Estimate
How much water do you think would drip from a leaking faucet in one day? In one year?

Gather Data
Put a measuring cup under a dripping faucet and collect water for 15 minutes.

Analyze and Report
Combine your results with that of your classmates to estimate the amount of water that is wasted if a faucet drips for 1 hour. If each of an estimated 90 million households in the United States had at least one faucet that leaked at this rate, how much water would be wasted in a year?

341

Perimeter

Build Understanding

A. Many schools are named after important people. Cyrus attends Du Sable school which was named after Jean Baptiste Pointe Du Sable, the first Haitian settler in the Chicago area. Cyrus wants to find the **perimeter,** or distance around his classroom at Du Sable school. A drawing of the classroom is shown below.

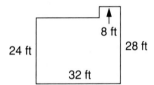

Add the length of all the sides to find the perimeter.

$P = 32 + 24 + 24 + 4 + 8 + 28$ Let P stand for
$P = 120$ the perimeter.

The perimeter of the classroom is 120 feet.

Jean Baptiste Pointe Du Sable built a trading post on the bank of the Chicago River about 1779.

B. Find the perimeter of the tennis court at Du Sable school. The court is a rectangle. The perimeter *(P)* is equal to 2 times the length *(l)* plus 2 times the width *(w)*.

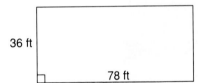

$P = 2 \times (l + w)$
$P = 2 \times (78 + 36)$
$P = 2 \times 114$
$P = 228$

The perimeter of the tennis court is 228 feet.

■ **Write About Math**   Write a formula for the perimeter of a regular hexagon.

Check Understanding

For another example, see Set A, pages 368–369.

Find the perimeter for each figure.

1.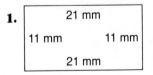

2.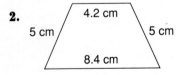

3.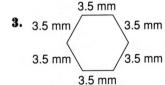

Practice

For More Practice, see Set A, pages 370–371.

Find the perimeter of each polygon described below.

4. A rectangle whose sides measure $3\frac{1}{2}$ in. and $9\frac{1}{4}$ in.

5. A triangle with sides of length $1\frac{7}{8}$ in., $2\frac{1}{4}$ in., and $3\frac{1}{2}$ in.

6. A parallelogram whose sides measure $6\frac{3}{4}$ in. and $8\frac{1}{4}$ in.

7. A parallelogram with sides 3.6 cm and 4.2 cm long

8. A quadrilateral with sides of 3.5 m, 4 m, 2.7 m, and 3.7 m

9. A triangle with sides of length 6 cm, 8 cm, and 10 cm

10. A regular hexagon, 7.5 in. on a side

11. A regular octagon, each side 6 cm long

12. A square, 3.4 m on a side

13. A pentagon with sides of 1.92 m, 3.5 m, 6 m, 4.83 m, and 3.59 m

14. A rhombus with sides of 3.5 m

15. A rectangle whose sides measure 23.5 m and 12 m

16.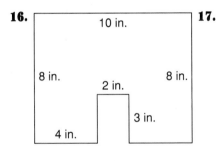

17.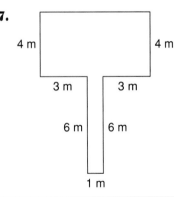

18.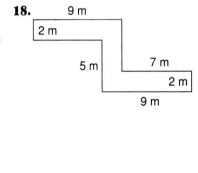

Problem Solving

Solve each problem.

19. On grid paper, sketch three different rectangular classrooms, each with a perimeter of 120 feet. Which classroom seems the largest? Explain.

20. Critical Thinking The perimeter of a rectangular wall mural at Benito Juárez school is 48 feet. The length of one of the sides is 16 feet. Find the length of the other sides.

Benito Juárez school is named after Benito Juárez, a Zapotec Indian who became president of Mexico in 1861. A series of four wall murals at the school depicts the history of Mexico.

Circumference

Build Understanding

The distance around a circle is called the ***circumference.***

Object	Circumference (C)	Diameter (d)	$\frac{C}{d}$ to nearest hundredth
Bicycle wheel	191.0 cm	61.1 cm	191 ÷ 61.1 = 3.13
Bicycle headlight	32.0 cm	10.1 cm	32.0 ÷ 10.1 = 3.17
Bicycle gear	39.9 cm	12.6 cm	39.9 ÷ 12.6 = 3.17
Reflector	15.9 cm	5.1 cm	15.9 ÷ 5.1 = 3.12

A. What pattern appears in the chart? In each case, the circumference divided by the diameter is a number that is a little greater than 3.1. This quotient is named by the Greek letter π (pi). The decimal for π never ends and never repeats. Two approximations that are often used for π are 3.14 and $\frac{22}{7}$.

$\pi \approx$ **3.1415926 . . .**   The symbol ≈ means "is approximately equal to."

B. Find the circumference of a circle with a diameter of 7 in. Use $\frac{22}{7}$ for π.

$C = \pi \times d$ Estimate: 3 × 7 = 21

$C \approx \frac{22}{7} \times 7$

$C \approx 22$

The circumference is about 22 inches.

C. Find the circumference of a circle with a radius of 5 cm. Use 3.14 for π.

$C = \pi \times d$ Estimate: 3 × 10 = 30

$C \approx 3.14 \times 10$ Since the radius is 5, the diameter is 10.

$C \approx 31.4$

The circumference is about 31.4 cm.

■ **Talk About Math** Why do you think $\frac{22}{7}$ was used for π in Example B and 3.14 was used for π in Example C?

Check Understanding

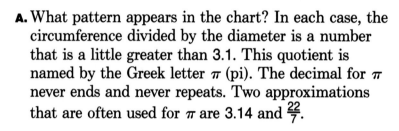

For another example, see Set B, pages 368–369.

Estimation Estimate each of the following.

1. d when $C = 15$ cm   **2.** r when $C = 15$ cm   **3.** C when $d = 4$ cm

4. C when $r = 5$ in.   **5.** d when $C = 27$ in.   **6.** r when $C = 36$ in.

Practice

For More Practice, see Set B, pages 370–371.

Find the circumference of each circle. **Remember** to
check if your answer is reasonable.

7.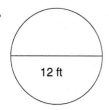
12 ft

8.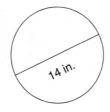
14 in.

9.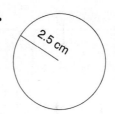
2.5 cm

10.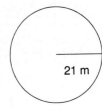
21 m

11.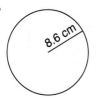
8.6 cm

12.
20 cm

13.
10.5 in.

14.
1 in.

15. r = 35 cm   **16.** d = 35 cm   **17.** r = 7.5 m   **18.** d = 1.2 ft

19. r = 42 in.   **20.** d = 9.8 cm   **21.** r = 5 cm   **22.** d = 6.3 cm

Find the perimeter of each figure.

23.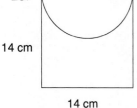
14 cm   14 cm
14 cm

24.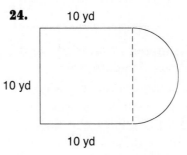
10 yd
10 yd
10 yd

25.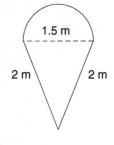
1.5 m
2 m   2 m

Problem Solving

Solve each problem.

26. **Calculator** The circumference
of a unicycle wheel is 75.36 in. Find
the diameter.

27. The circumference of a dirt-bike
wheel is 62.8 in. Find the radius.

Critical Thinking How does the circumference
of a circle change if you

28. double the diameter?

29. double the radius?

Make a Table

Build Understanding

Find the perimeter of a chain of 50 equilateral triangles if the triangles are joined side to side. Each side is 1 decimeter long.

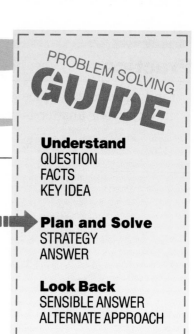

PROBLEM SOLVING
GUIDE

Understand
QUESTION
FACTS
KEY IDEA

IIII➤ **Plan and Solve**
STRATEGY
ANSWER

Look Back
SENSIBLE ANSWER
ALTERNATE APPROACH

Understand   Find the perimeter of a chain of 50 triangles that have been joined side to side.

IIII➤**Plan and Solve**   STRATEGY   Make a table starting with one triangle. Try to find a pattern.

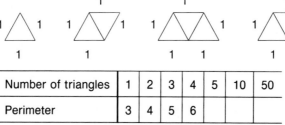

Number of triangles	1	2	3	4	5	10	50
Perimeter	3	4	5	6			

Study the number of triangles and the perimeters. How are they related? The perimeter is always two more than the number of triangles. A chain of 10 triangles will have a perimeter of 12 decimeters.

ANSWER   A chain of 50 triangles will have a perimeter of 52 decimeters.

Look Back   SENSIBLE ANSWER   As each triangle is added, two new sides are added to the perimeter and one old side is covered. The net gain is 1 side, or 1 unit. Thus, adding 49 triangles will give a perimeter of $(50 \times 1) + 2$, or 52 dm.

■ **Talk About Math**   Use the table to find the perimeter of a chain of 100 triangles; of n triangles.

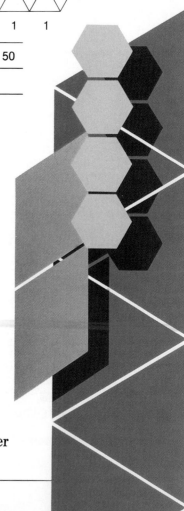

346

Check Understanding

A chain of rectangles is formed when 50 squares are joined side to side. Each side of a square is 1 decimeter long.

1. What is the perimeter of a chain made from 1 square? 2 squares? 3 squares?

2. By how much does the perimeter increase as the number of squares increases by 1?

3. Does simply adding 2 to the number of squares give the perimeter?

4. Does multiplying the number of squares by 2 and then adding 2 give the perimeter?

Practice

Make a table and look for a pattern to solve each problem.

5. Find the perimeter of a chain of 50 parallelograms. Each side is 1 in. long.

6. Find the perimeter of a chain of 50 hexagons. Each side is 1 decimeter long.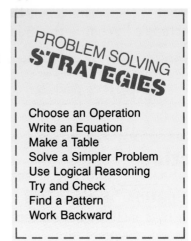

7. Find the perimeter of a chain of 50 equilateral triangles. Each side is 2 cm long.

8. Find the perimeter of a chain of 50 squares. Each side is 2 in. long.

Choose a _____ Strategy

How Far, How Fast?   José likes to climb palm trees. However, as he goes up 3 feet every 20 seconds, he slips back 1 foot. He wants to pick a coconut at the top of an 18-foot-tall palm tree.

9. At the end of 40 seconds, how high off the ground is he?

10. What is José's net gain for every 20 seconds?

11. How long will it take José to achieve a net gain of 12 feet?

12. How long will it take him to pick the coconut?

PROBLEM SOLVING
STRATEGIES

Choose an Operation
Write an Equation
Make a Table
Solve a Simpler Problem
Use Logical Reasoning
Try and Check
Find a Pattern
Work Backward

A
L
G
E
B
R
A

Area of Rectangles and Squares

Build Understanding

Jeanne works for a ceramic tile company. Sometimes Jeanne has to tile a floor that has an irregular shape like the one shown. Each square represents 1 square foot.

By counting, you can see that the area is 24 square feet. Another way to find the area is to divide the figure into two parts, a rectangle and a square. Then find the area of each part.

$A = \ell \times w$	Multiply the length and width.	$A = s^2$	For a square, $\ell = s$ and $w = s$.

$A = \ell \times w$ Multiply the $A = s^2$ For a square,
$A = 4 \times 2$ length and $A = 4^2$ $\ell = s$ and $w = s$.
$A = 8$ width. $A = 16$

The total area is $16 + 8$, or 24, square feet.

■ **Write About Math** How are the formulas for finding the area of a square and a rectangle alike? How are they different?

Check Understanding

For more examples, see Set C, pages 368–369.

1. What is the perimeter of this rectangle? What is the area?

13 m

2 m

2. Find the area of a square that measures 7 ft on a side. Find its perimeter. How do the units compare?

Practice

For More Practice, see Set C, pages 370–371.

Estimation Estimate the area of each figure. Then find each area. **Remember** that area is always expressed in square units.

3. A rectangle, $11\frac{1}{2}$ yd by 5 yd

4. A square, 9.25 m on a side

5. A rectangle, 10.7 mm by 6.8 mm

Find the area of each shaded region.

6.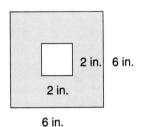
5.1 cm
7.8 cm

7.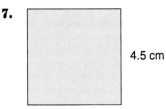
4.5 cm
4.5 cm

8.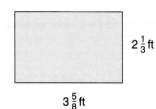
$2\frac{1}{3}$ ft
$3\frac{5}{8}$ ft

9.
2 in.   6 in.
2 in.
6 in.

10.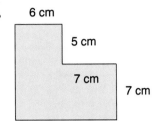
6 cm
5 cm
7 cm
7 cm

11.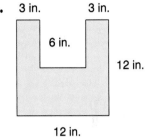
3 in.   3 in.
6 in.
12 in.
12 in.

Problem Solving

Solve each problem.

12. Jeanne must cover a bathroom floor with tiles that are 1-inch square. The floor is 4 feet by 7 feet. How many tiles are needed?

13. Jeanne must cover a bathroom wall with square tiles that are 4 inches on a side. The wall is 7 feet by 8 feet. How many tiles are needed?

Explore ——— Math

On the Double

14. Draw a rectangle that is 3 inches by 4 inches. What is the area?

15. Double the dimensions of the rectangle in Exercise 14. What is the area?

16. Draw another rectangle with different dimensions. Find the area. Then double the dimensions and find the area.

17. How does doubling the dimensions of a rectangle affect the area?

18. What effect would tripling the dimensions have on the area of a rectangle?

Area of Parallelograms and Triangles

Build Understanding

A. Slicing Figures
Materials: 1-cm grid paper, scissors
Groups: With a partner

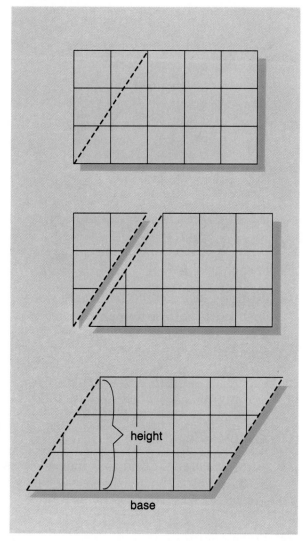

a. Copy the rectangle on a sheet of grid paper. What formula can you use to find the area of a rectangle? What is the area of the rectangle?

b. Draw a dashed line as shown and cut out the rectangle. Then cut along the dashed line to make two pieces.

c. Move the triangular piece as shown in the third diagram. What type of figure is formed?

d. What can you say about the area of the rectangle and the area of the parallelogram?

e. The dimensions used to find the area of a parallelogram are the **base** and the height. The **height** is the distance between two parallel sides. Which dimensions of the rectangle correspond to the base and the height of the parallelogram?

f. The squares on the grid paper have sides 1 centimeter long. What are the lengths of the base and the height of the parallelogram?

g. How can you use the base and the height to find the area of a parallelogram? What is the area of the parallelogram?

The area of a parallelogram is equal to the base times the height. $A = b \times h$

B. a. What is the area of this rectangle?

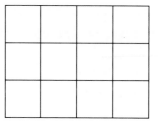

b. Copy the rectangle on grid paper. Draw the diagonal and shade the bottom part. Cut the rectangle and place the unshaded part over the shaded part. What part of the rectangle does the triangle represent?

c. What is the area of the triangle?

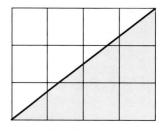

d. Next, copy the third rectangle at the right. Cut out the unshaded parts and see if they fit on top of the shaded part. What is the area of the shaded triangle?

The area (A) of a triangle is equal to $\frac{1}{2}$ the base (b) times the height (h).

$A = \frac{1}{2} \times b \times h$

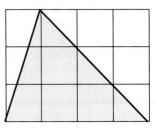

c. Find the area of this parallelogram.

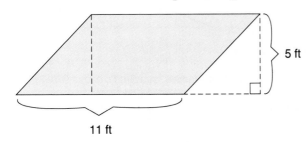

11 ft

$A = b \times h$
$A = 5 \times 11 = 55$

The area is 55 sq ft.

D. Find the area of this triangle.

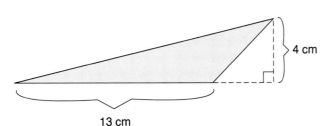

13 cm

$A = \frac{1}{2} \times b \times h$

$A = \frac{1}{2} \times 13 \times 4$

$A = \frac{1}{2} \times 52 = 26$

The area is 26 cm².

■ **Talk About Math**   Refer to step d in Example B. Suppose you separate the figure as shown at the right. How could you find the area of the shaded region?

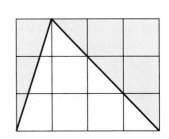

Check Understanding

For another example, see Set D pages 368–369.

Complete the following.

1.

7 in.

18 in.

$A = b \times h$
$A = \text{▦} \times \text{▦}$
$A = \text{▦}$
The area is ▦ sq in.

2.
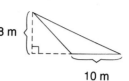
8 m

10 m

$A = \frac{1}{2} \times b \times h$
$A = \frac{1}{2} \times \text{▦} \times \text{▦}$
$A = \text{▦}$
The area is ▦ m².

Find the area of each shaded triangle. Each square represents 1 cm².

3. **4.** **5.**
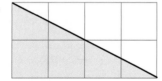 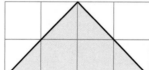 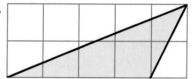

Practice

For More Practice, see Set D, pages 370–371.

Find the area of each figure. **Remember** to give
your answer in square units.

6.

8 in.

6 in.

7.

7 ft

4 ft   4 ft

8.
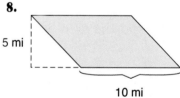
5 mi

10 mi

9.
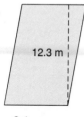
12.3 m

8.1 m

10.
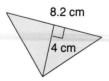
8.2 cm

4 cm

11.
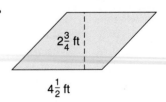
$2\frac{3}{4}$ ft

$4\frac{1}{2}$ ft

12. A triangle with base
$\frac{7}{8}$ in. and height 2 in.

13. A parallelogram with
base 4.3 cm and
height 5.7 cm

14. A triangle with base
12.5 m and height
6.8 m

Mixed Practice   Find the area of each figure.

15.

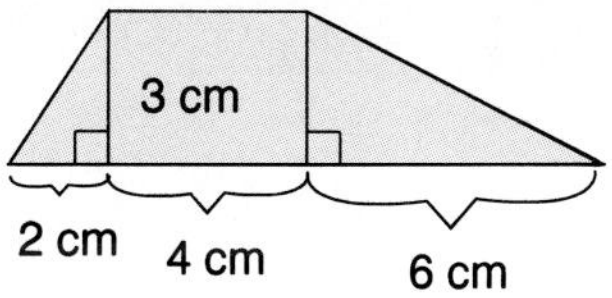

2 cm   4 cm   6 cm   3 cm

16.

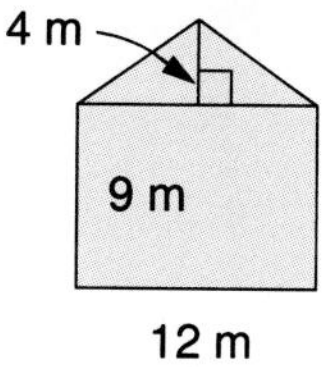

4 m

9 m

12 m

17.

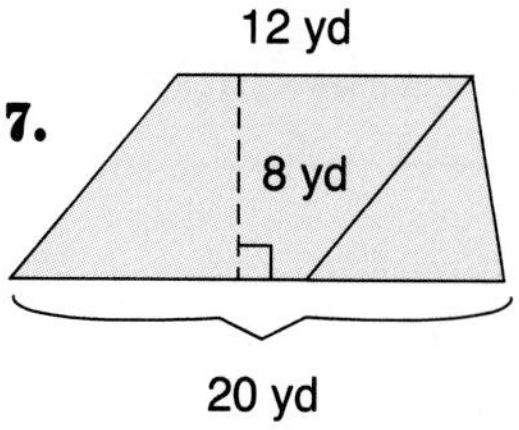

12 yd

8 yd

20 yd

18.

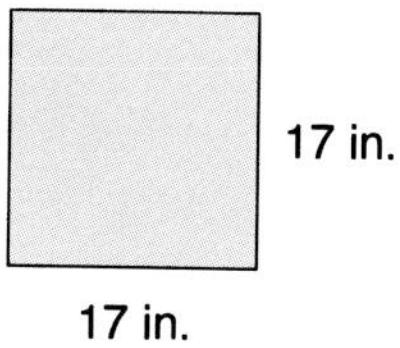

17 in.

17 in.

19.

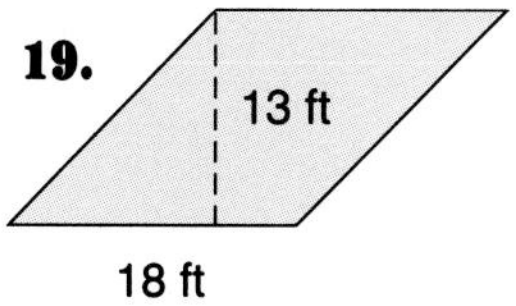

13 ft

18 ft

20.

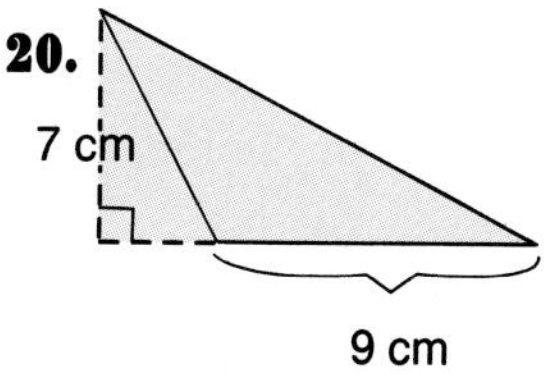

7 cm

9 cm

21.

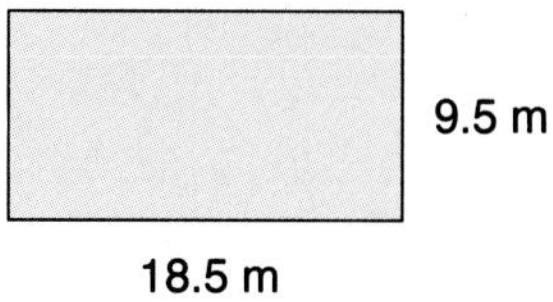

9.5 m

18.5 m

22. A parallelogram with base 3 ft and height 1.5 ft

23. A triangle with base 12 cm and height 4 cm

24. A square with sides of length $8\frac{1}{2}$ in.

Problem Solving

Complete the following.

25. Use grid paper. Draw three different parallelograms, each with an area of 12 square units.

26. Use grid paper. Draw three different triangles, each with an area of 12 square units.

Use Data   Refer to page 343. Find the area of the figure in

27. Exercise 4.   **28.** Exercise 12.   **29.** Exercise 15.   **30.** Exercise 16.

Midchapter ✓ **Checkup**

Find the perimeter or circumference.

1.

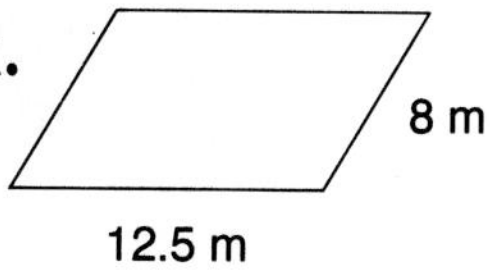

8 m

12.5 m

2.

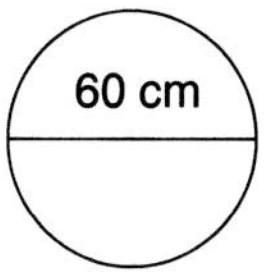

60 cm

3.

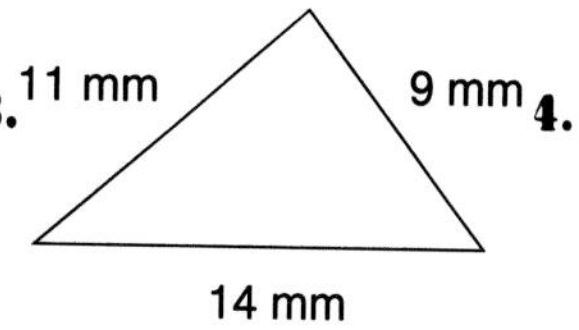

11 mm   9 mm

14 mm

4.

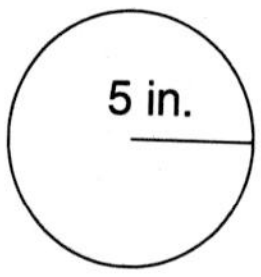

5 in.

For Exercises 5–7 find the area of each figure.

5. $1\frac{1}{2}$ in.

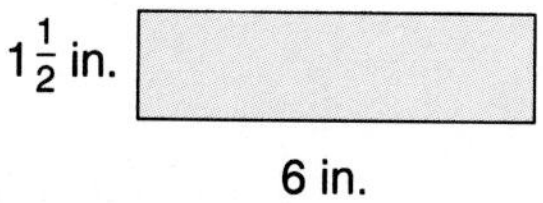

6 in.

6.

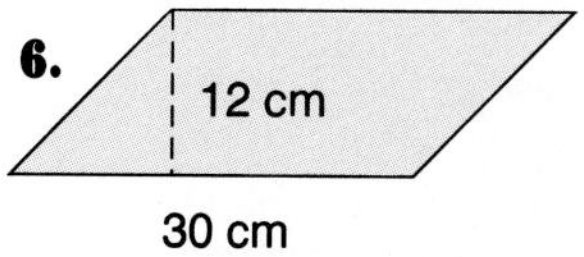

12 cm

30 cm

7. A triangle with base 10 in. and height 5 in.

Visual-Thinking Activity

Copy the patterns below on a sheet of graph paper. Cut out the shapes, fold, and tape into cubes.

Place the four cubes next to each other so that along the top, bottom, front, and back there are four different geometric shapes.

Number-Sense Project

Look back at pages 340-341.

1. About 12,000,000 square miles of the earth's surface is rain forest. About $\frac{1}{3}$ of the rain forests in the world are in Brazil. How many square miles of rain forest are in Brazil?

2. If one inch of rain fell on the forests of Brazil, about how many gallons of water would this be?

3. During one year an average of 160 inches of rain falls on the rain forests of Brazil. About how many quadrillion gallons of water in this?

Problem Solving WORKSHOP

Explore with a Computer

Use the *Geometry Workshop Project* for this project.

1. Design a piece of furniture for yourself using geometric shapes. Sketch a plan of your design on paper.

2. At the computer, use the **Draw** option to make geometric shapes. Use the options in the **Extras** and **Edit** menus to arrange the shapes and make a picture of your piece of furniture.

File Edit Draw Measure Extras Help

3. Suppose you wanted to cover your piece of furniture with material. What are the dimensions of the piece of furniture? Use the options under **Measure** to find the perimeter and area of the piece of furniture you have drawn.

4. How much material do you need?

Real-Life Decision Making

Suppose you want to build a rectangular dog pen in your back yard. Your yard is 28 feet wide and 32 feet long and you want to use 72 feet of fencing.

1. What different sizes could you possibly make the pen if you only used whole number dimensions? Remember, the pen has to fit in the yard.

2. Which of the possible rectangles would you choose to build? Explain your answer.

Area of Circles

Build Understanding

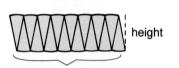

base · height

A. Circle Slicing
Materials: Paper, scissors
Groups: With a partner

a. Draw a circle with a radius of 4 inches. Then draw 8 diameters as shown. Cut out the circle and then cut it into wedges.

b. Rearrange the wedges to form a shape that looks somewhat like a parallelogram.

c. How does the circumference of the circle compare with the base of the parallelogram? How does the radius of the circle compare with the height of the parallelogram?

d. Explain the steps given below to find the formula for the area of a circle.

$$A = \quad b \quad \times \quad h$$
$$\downarrow \qquad \downarrow$$
$$A = (\tfrac{1}{2} \times C) \times \quad r$$
$$A = \tfrac{1}{2} \times (2 \times \pi \times r) \times r \qquad C = 2 \times \pi \times r$$
$$A = \pi \times r^2$$

B. Find the area of a circle that has a radius of 4 cm. Use 3.14 for π.

Estimate: $3 \times 4^2 = 3 \times 16 = 48.$

Paper and Pencil
$A = \pi \times r^2$
$A \approx 3.14 \times (4)^2$
$A \approx 3.14 \times 16 = 50.24$

▥ Calculator
Press: 3.14 ⎡×⎤ 4 ⎡×⎤ 4 ⎡=⎤

Display: *50.24*

The area of the circle is approximately 50.24 cm².

■ **Talk About Math** Explain how to find the area of a circle if you know its diameter.

Check Understanding

For another example, see Set E, pages 368–369.

Estimation Estimate the area of each circle.
Then complete the following. Use 3.14 for π.

1. $A = \pi \times r^2$
   $A \approx \text{▦} \times (\text{▦})^2$
   $A \approx \text{▦}$

15 m

2. $A = \pi \times r^2$
   $A \approx 3.14 \times (\text{▦})^2$
   $A \approx \text{▦}$

3.5 cm

Practice

For More Practice, see Set E, pages 370–371.

Estimation Estimate the area of each circle.
Then find each area. **Remember** that area is
measured in square units.

3.

28 in.

4.

49 ft

5.

6 cm

6.

16 in.

For Exercises 7–18, tell whether you would use paper and pencil
or a calculator. Then find the area of each circle.

7. Radius: 26 in.   8. Radius: 1.5 cm   9. Diameter: 9 in.   10. Diameter: 8.4 m

11. Radius: 14 in.   12. Radius: 15 cm   13. Diameter: 3 ft   14. Diameter: 24 in.

15. Radius: 100 cm   16. Radius: 30 in.   17. Diameter: 20 cm 18. Diameter: 11 ft

Problem Solving

Solve each problem.

19. **Critical Thinking** If the side of
   a square is the same length as the
   radius of a circle, which shape will
   have the greater area? Explain.

20. Julio must find the area of a
   circular window that has a
   12-in. radius. What is the area?

21. A circular frame that is 1 in. wide
   surrounds a circular window that
   has a diameter of 12 in. (not
   including the frame). What is the
   area of the frame?

22. Alan must replace the glass in a
   circular porthole that is 16 in.
   in diameter. He will cut the glass
   from a 16-in. square. How much
   glass will be wasted?

Use a Formula

Build Understanding

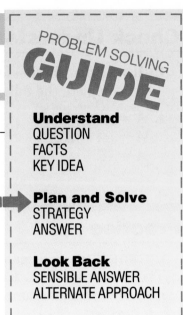

Patricia wants to wallpaper one wall that measures 8 feet by 10 feet. How many 25-foot rolls of wallpaper must she buy if the paper is 2 feet wide?

Understand   QUESTION   How many rolls of wallpaper will have an area that is equal to or greater than the area of the wall?

FACT   The dimensions of the wall are 8 feet by 10 feet. The paper comes in rolls 2 feet by 25 feet.

▶**Plan and Solve**   STRATEGY   The walls are rectangular. Use the formula for the area of a rectangle to find the area of the wall.

10 ft

8 ft

$A = \ell \times w$
$A = 8 \times 10$
$A = 80$

Find the number of square feet on each roll of wallpaper.

$A = \ell \times w$ 25 ft
$A = 25 \times 2$
$A = 50$ 2 ft

Find the number of 50-square-foot rolls needed to cover 80 square feet.

ANSWER   Each roll contains 50 square feet. Patricia will need to buy 2 rolls of paper.

Look Back   SENSIBLE ANSWER   The answer is sensible because 80 is greater than 50 and less than 100. Therefore, Patricia will need between one and two rolls of wallpaper.

■ **Talk About Math**   What information would you need to know to find the amount of wallpaper needed to paper Patricia's entire room?

Check Understanding

Choose a formula from the table to solve each problem.

	Square	Rectangle	Triangle
Area	$A = s^2$	$A = \ell \times w$	$A = \frac{1}{2} \times b \times h$
Perimeter	$P = 4 \times s$	$P = 2 \times (\ell + w)$	$P = x + y + z$

1. The length and width of a room are 20 feet and 12 feet. What is the perimeter?

2. The base and height of a triangle are 12 inches and 8 inches. What is the area?

3. The side of a square is 2.5 cm. What is the area?

Practice

Solve each problem.

4. Patricia's bedroom is 10 feet wide and 12 feet long. How many 25-foot-long rolls of border will she need to border the room?

5. Patricia has a triangular window in her closet. How tall is the window if the area of the window is 600 cm² and the base is 30 cm?

6. Patricia wants to cover a bulletin board with mirrors. The board is 16 inches on each side. How many mirrors will she need if each mirror is 4 inches on a side?

7. Patricia is adding a 2-inch border to a bedspread that measures 84 inches by $96\frac{1}{2}$ inches. What dimensions will the finished spread have?

Choose a _____ Strategy

A Tight Fit A hallway in Patricia's house is shown at the right. She wants to bring a cabinet with a base 2 feet by 4 feet through the turn in the hallway without tilting it or turning it on its side.

8. Cut out a rectangle to represent the cabinet. Will it pass through the hallway? Try rectangles with other whole-number dimensions.

9. What are the area and dimensions of the largest rectangle that will pass through the hallway?

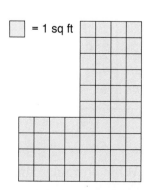

= 1 sq ft

A
L
G
E
B
R
A

Surface Area of Prisms

Build Understanding

Anna Laslo is a cabinet maker. She must find the surface area of a cabinet to determine how much wood is needed. The *surface area* of a prism is the sum of the areas of its faces. Find the surface area of the cabinet shown at the right.

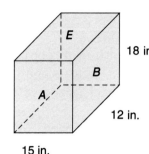

18 in.

12 in.

15 in.

Cabinets are usually rectangular prisms although they can also be other shapes.

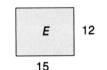

Face	Area of Face (in square inches)
A	15 × 18 = 270
B	12 × 18 = 216
C	15 × 18 = 270
D	12 × 18 = 216
E	15 × 12 = 180
F	15 × 12 = 180
	Total area: 1,332 sq in.

■ **Talk About Math** How could you quickly find the surface area of a cube?

Check Understanding

For another example, see Set F, pages 368–369.

Find the surface area of the triangular prism by completing the table.

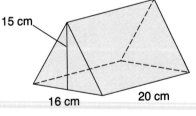

Face	Area of Figure (in cm²)
P	**1.** 17 × 20 = ▦
Q	**2.** ▦ × ▦ = ▦
R	**3.** ▦ × ▦ = ▦
S	**4.** $\frac{1}{2}$ × 16 × 15 = ▦
T	**5.** $\frac{1}{2}$ × ▦ × 15 = ▦
	6. Total area: ▦ cm²

7. What formulas did you use to find the surface area of the prism in Exercises 1–6?

Practice

For More Practice, see Set F, pages 370–371.

Tell how many faces each prism has. Then draw and label the faces of the prism in Exercise 9.

8.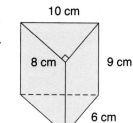
5 in.
6 in.
3 in.

9.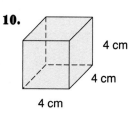
10 cm
8 cm
9 cm
6 cm

10.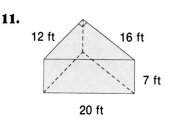
4 cm
4 cm
4 cm

11.
12 ft
16 ft
7 ft
20 ft

Find the surface area of the prism in

12. Exercise 8.   **13.** Exercise 9.   **14.** Exercise 10.   **15.** Exercise 11.

Problem Solving

Solve the problem.

16. Critical Thinking Suppose you have a block made of cubes glued together. It is 3 cubes wide, 3 cubes high, and 3 cubes deep. If you dip the entire block in a bucket of paint, how many cubes will have no paint on them? How many will have one face painted? two faces? three faces? four or more faces?

TIPS FOR PROBLEM SOLVERS

Visualize the problem in your mind to help you understand it better.

Explore ————— Math

Prisms and Cubes

17. Make a rectangular prism by arranging 8 cubes as shown. What is its surface area?

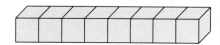

18. Make another prism that is 8 cubes long by 1 cube wide. What is its surface area?

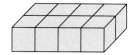

19. Find another arrangement for a rectangular prism that has a smaller surface area than the arrangements in Exercises 17 and 18. Describe the figure. What is its surface area?

361

Volume of Prisms

Build Understanding

A. Cubes and More Cubes
Materials: Unit cubes
Groups: 4 students

A box is 3 units by 2 units by 4 units. How many unit cubes will it take to fill the box?

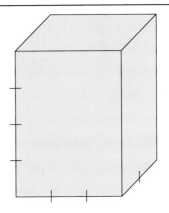

a. Use unit cubes. Make a row of 3 unit cubes as shown. Use enough cubes to cover the bottom. How many cubes did you use? How many rows?

b. How many layers will it take to fill the box? Make a model with unit cubes showing the total number of cubes needed to fill the box.

c. What is the total number of cubes needed?

d. Notice the following relationship.

cubes per row	×	number of rows	×	number of layers	=	total number of cubes
↓		↓		↓		↓
(3	×	2)	×	4	=	24
↓		↓		↓		↓
length	×	width	×	height	=	volume

To find the volume of a rectangular prism, multiply the length (ℓ) times the width (w) times the height (h).

$$V = \ell \times w \times h$$

B. Find the volume of this prism.

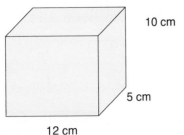

10 cm

5 cm

12 cm

$V = \ell \times w \times h$
$V = 12 \times 5 \times 10$
$V = 600$

The volume is 600 cm³.

c. Find the volume of this cube.

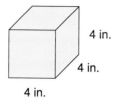

4 in.

4 in.

4 in.

$V = s \times s \times s$ or s^3
$V = 4 \times 4 \times 4$, or 4^3
$V = 64$

The volume is 64 cu in.

■ **Talk About Math** If the length, width, and height of a prism are measured in inches, in what unit will the volume be measured?

Check Understanding

For another example, see Set G, pages 368–369.

Find the number of cubes in each shape.

1.

2.

3.

Mental Math Use mental math to find the volume of each prism.

4. $\ell = 10$ cm
$w = 3.7$ cm
$h = 10$ cm

5. $\ell = 20$ in.
$w = 5$ in.
$h = 7$ in.

6. $\ell = 6.5$ m
$w = 2$ m
$h = 5$ m

7. $\ell = 25$ m
$w = 4$ m
$h = 68$ m

Number Sense Choose which is larger.

8. 1 cm³ or 1 cu in.

9. 10 cu in. or 1 cu ft

10. 2 cu ft or 1 cu yd

Practice

For More Practice, see Set G, pages 370–371.

Find the volume of each prism. **Remember** to use cubic units in your answer.

11.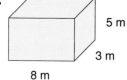

5 m

3 m

8 m

12.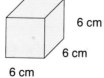

6 cm

6 cm

6 cm

13.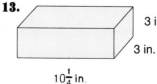

3 in.

3 in.

$10\frac{1}{4}$ in.

14.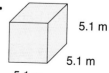

5.1 m

5.1 m

5.1 m

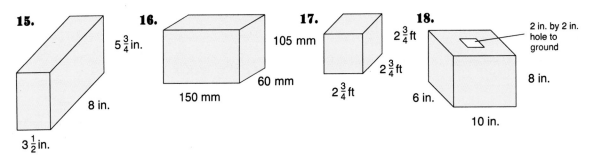

15. $5\frac{3}{4}$ in. 8 in. $3\frac{1}{2}$ in.

16. 105 mm 60 mm 150 mm

17. $2\frac{3}{4}$ ft $2\frac{3}{4}$ ft $2\frac{3}{4}$ ft

18. 2 in. by 2 in. hole to ground 8 in. 6 in. 10 in.

Find the volume of each prism.

19. $\ell = 7$ in.
$w = 7$ in.
$h = 7$ in.

20. $\ell = 10.5$ mm
$w = 6$ mm
$h = 2$ mm

21. $\ell = 9$ cm
$w = 6$ cm
$h = 12$ cm

22. $\ell = 15$ in.
$w = 15$ in.
$h = 10$ in.

23. $\ell = 1$ in.
$w = 8.5$ in.
$h = 3$ in.

24. $\ell = 2.6$ cm
$w = 4.1$ cm
$h = 5.4$ cm

25. $\ell = 2.5$ ft
$w = 2.5$ ft
$h = 2.5$ ft

26. $\ell = 10$ cm
$w = 12$ cm
$h = 20$ cm

27. Which of the prisms in Exercises 19–26 are cubes?

Problem Solving

Solve each problem.

28. A rectangular gerbil cage has a volume of 960 cubic inches with a length of 12 inches and a width of 8 inches. How high is the cage?

29. **Calculator** A fish tank measures 55 cm by 35 cm by 45 cm. What is the volume of the tank?

30. A doghouse is 3 feet by 4 feet by 4 feet. Find the volume. Is the volume greater or less than a doghouse with a volume of 1 cubic yard?

31. A birdfeeder is 16 cm by 20 cm by 12 cm. A sack of birdseed has a volume of 4 dm³. Is this enough birdseed to fill the feeder?

| Skills | Review | pages 110–113 |

Divide.

1. $46\overline{)1,865}$ **2.** $3,132 \div 29$ **3.** $80\overline{)1,679}$ **4.** $4,159 \div 69$

5. $16\overline{)3,248}$ **6.** $5,440 \div 45$ **7.** $35\overline{)2,830}$ **8.** $53\overline{)48,277}$

Vocabulary Complete the paragraphs below using the following words or formulas.

perimeter	circumference	$A = \ell \times w$
area	radius	$P = 2 \times (\ell + w)$
volume	$A = \pi \times r^2$	$V = \ell \times w \times h$
		$C = \pi \times d$

Marla works in a building supplies store. Frequently she must work with customers in figuring out how much of an item is needed.

1. Mr. Petrillo wants to buy paneling to cover a wall. Marla says, "You must find the ___?___ of the rectangle. You can use the formula ___?___."

2. Mrs. Wong wants to figure the length of the molding that is needed to go around the ceiling of a room. Marla says, "You must find the ___?___ of the rectangle. You can use the formula ___?___."

3. Mr. Hicks wants to find how much space is contained in a portable storage shed. Marla says, "You must find the ___?___ of a rectangular prism. You can use the formula ___?___."

4. Miss Stein wants to put edging around a circular flower bed. Marla says, "You must find the ___?___ of a circle. You can use the formula ___?___."

5. Mr. Evans is buying a plastic cover for a circular pool. Marla says, "You must find the ___?___ of the circle. You can use the formula ___?___. If you know the diameter, you can find the ___?___ by dividing the diameter by 2."

Skills Review

Find the perimeter of each polygon.

1. A regular pentagon, each side 7 inches long

2. A rectangle with a length of 12 cm and a width of 5 cm

Find the circumference. Use 3.14 for π.

3. 14 ft

4. 5 cm

Find the area of the shaded region.

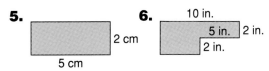

5. 2 cm 5 cm

6. 10 in. 5 in. 2 in. 2 in.

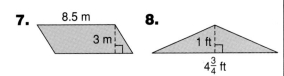

7. 8.5 m 3 m

8. 1 ft $4\frac{3}{4}$ ft

Find the area of the circle in

9. Exercise 3.   **10.** Exercise 4.

Find the surface area of each prism.

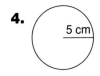

11. 5 m 5 m 5 m

12. 6 ft 8 ft 4 ft 10 ft

Find the volume of each prism.

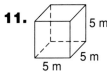

13. 5 m 5 m 5 m

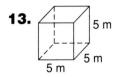

14. 4 in. 5 in. 15 in.

Problem-Solving Review

Solve each problem.

15. Mrs. Fuller paid $8.95 for 25 pounds of dog food. To the nearest cent, what was the cost per pound for the dog food?

16. A rectangular garden has a width of 25 feet and a length of 40 feet. What is the perimeter of the garden?

17. A game circle painted on a playground has a radius of 8 feet. Find its circumference.

18. Will the contents of four 1-liter containers fit into a gallon container?

19. On February 2, the high temperature for the day was reported as 78°F. Would you expect that this weather report was from Wisconsin or Florida?

20. The land area of Tennessee is 41,328 square miles. The land area of Rhode Island is 1,049 square miles. About how many times could Rhode Island fit into Tennessee?

21. **Data File** Use the data on pages 410–411. How much greater is the area of the doubles court than the area of the singles court?

22. **Make a Data File** Measure the length and width of each room in your house. Calculate the area of each room and record your findings in a table.

Round 63,451.9335 to the nearest

1. hundred.

2. thousandth.

Find each answer.

3. 407.6 − 295.55

4. 6.45 + 3.892

5. 8.634 × 2.8

6. 329 × 488

7. 4.93 × 8.75

8. 4,365 ÷ 7

9. 65,360 ÷ 82

10. 75)247.5

11. 2.3)6.9

Use triangle *ABC* to solve each problem.

12. Is triangle *ABC* acute, right, or obtuse?

13. Is triangle *ABC* scalene, isosceles, or equilateral?

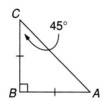

14. Find the measure of angle *A*.

Write each fraction in lowest terms.

15. $\frac{5}{20}$

16. $\frac{10}{12}$

17. $\frac{6}{9}$

18. $\frac{10}{50}$

Estimate by rounding each mixed number to the nearest whole number.

19. $4\frac{3}{8} + 2\frac{2}{3}$

20. $10\frac{1}{6} - 2\frac{3}{4}$

21. $3\frac{4}{5} \times 2\frac{2}{7}$

22. $8\frac{7}{8} \div 2\frac{5}{6}$

For each change, tell whether the temperature has fallen or risen and by how much.

23. From 75°F to 50°F

24. From −4°C to 4°C

Compute.

25. $\frac{3}{5} + \frac{3}{10}$

26. $4\frac{1}{3} - 2\frac{1}{2}$

27. $2\frac{3}{8} \times 1\frac{1}{6}$

28. $\frac{3}{4} \div \frac{1}{8}$

Solve.

29. 4 h 45 min + 3 h 30 min

30. 5 h 15 min − 1 h 20 min

31. Estimate the length of each side of the triangle in millimeters.

Find each missing number.

32. 14 qt = ▦ gal ▦ qt

33. 350 mL = ▦ L

Find the perimeter of each figure.

34. 20 in. 15 in.

35. 2.6 m / 2 m / 2.6 m

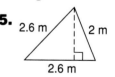

Find the area of the figure in

36. Exercise 34.

37. Exercise 35.

Solve.

38. Find the area of a circle with a radius of 10 cm. Use 3.14 for π.

Use the prism for Exercises 39 and 40.

39. Find the surface area.

40. Find the volume.

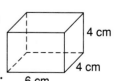

4 cm
4 cm
6 cm

Reteaching

Set A   pages 342–343

Find the perimeter
of this figure.
Add:
15 + 9 + 9 + 9 + 9
= 51 cm

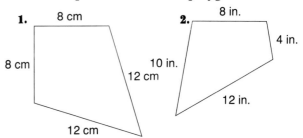

Notice that 4 sides are 9 centimeters and
one side is 15 centimeters.
(4 × 9) + 15 = 36 + 15
= 51 ←Perimeter is 51 cm.

Remember that perimeter is the distance
around a figure.

Find the perimeter of each polygon.

1.   8 cm   **2.**   8 in.

8 cm   10 in.   4 in.
12 cm
12 cm   12 in.

Set B   pages 344–345

Find the circumference of each circle.

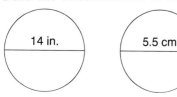

Use $\frac{22}{7}$ for π.   Use 3.14 for π.

$C = \pi \times d$ $C = \pi \times d$

$C \approx \frac{22}{7} \times 14$ $C \approx 3.14 \times 5.5$

$C \approx 44$ in. $C \approx 17.27$ cm

Remember to use 3 for π when you
estimate the circumference.

Estimate and find each circle's
circumference.

1.   **2.**

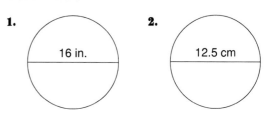

16 in.   12.5 cm

Set C   pages 348–349

Find the area of this figure.
Divide the figure into two parts.
Find the area of each part.

II   6 in.

12 in.

12 in.   6 in.

6 in.
6 in.

6 in.   6 in.

I   12 in.

6 in.

Part I: $A = \ell \times w$ Part 2: $A = s^2$
$A = 12 \times 6$ $A = 6^2$
$A = 72$ $A = 36$

The total area is 72 + 36, or 108 sq in.

Remember that the area of a figure is the
number of square units needed to cover the
figure.

Find the area of the shaded region.

1.   8.2 cm

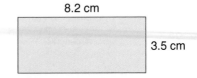

3.5 cm

2.   7 in.

2 in.   4 in.

2 in.

Set D   pages 350–353

Find the area of this triangle.

$A = \frac{1}{2} \times$ base $\times$ height

$A = \frac{1}{2} \times 14 \times 3$

$A = \frac{1}{2} \times 42 = 21 \leftarrow 21$ cm²

Remember to give your answer in square units.

Find the area of each figure.

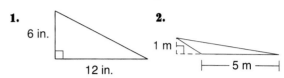

1. 6 in. 12 in.   **2.** 1 m 5 m

Set E   pages 356–357

Find the area of this circle.
Use 3.14 for π.
$A = \pi \times r^2$
$A \approx 3.14 \times (6)^2$
$A \approx 3.14 \times 36 \approx 113.04$
The area is approximately 113.04 cm².

6 cm

Remember that the area of a circle is an approximation.

Estimate the area of each circle. Then find each area.

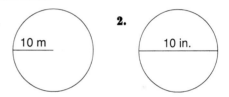

1. 10 m   **2.** 10 in.

Set F   pages 360–361

Find the surface area of this triangular prism.
The area of each face:

A: $\frac{1}{2} \times 8 \times 6 = 24$
B: $6 \times 6 \quad = 36$
C: $6 \times 8 \quad = 48$
D: $\frac{1}{2} \times 8 \times 6 = 24$
E: $6 \times 10 \quad = 60$

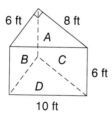

Total area: 192 sq ft

Remember to include the area of each face when you find total surface area.

Find the surface area of each prism.

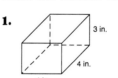

1. 3 in. 4 in. 4 in.   **2.** 10 cm 8 cm 6 cm 3 cm

Set G   pages 362–365

Find the volume of this prism.

Multiply the length, the width, and the height.

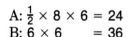

3 cm 4 cm 3 cm

Length   Width   Height   Volume
4 cm × 3 cm × 3 cm = 36 cm³

Remember that volume is the measure of the amount of space inside a solid figure.

Find the volume of each prism.

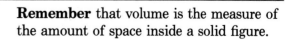

1. 2 cm 5 cm 3 cm   **2.** 3 cm 4 cm 4 cm

More Practice

Set A pages 342–343

Find the perimeter of each polygon described below.

1. A rectangle whose sides measure $4\frac{1}{4}$ in. and $8\frac{1}{2}$ in.

2. A parallelogram with sides 6.3 cm and 5.4 cm long

3. A regular hexagon, each side 7 cm long

4. A square, 8.7 m on a side

5. A triangle with sides $1\frac{3}{8}$ in., $2\frac{1}{2}$ in., and $4\frac{1}{4}$ in.

6. A pentagon with sides of 2.1 m, 4.2 m, 7.4 m, 5.36 m, and 3.62 m

Set B pages 344–345

Find the circumference of each circle.

1. 20 in.

2. 18 in.

3. 4.2 cm

4. 11 m

5. $r = 45$ cm

6. $d = 45$ cm

7. $r = 9.5$ m

8. $d = 24$ ft

Find the perimeter of each figure.

9.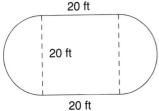

20 ft

20 ft

20 ft

10.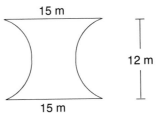

15 m

15 m

12 m

Set C pages 348–349

Estimation Estimate the area of each figure. Then find each area.

1. A rectangle, 18 in. by 9 in.

2. A square, 11.5 cm on a side

3. A rectangle, 21.2 m by 17.5 m

Find the area of the shaded region.

4.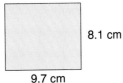

8.1 cm

9.7 cm

5.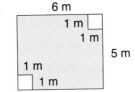

6 m

1 m

1 m

5 m

1 m

1 m

6.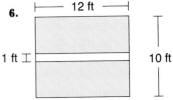

12 ft

1 ft

10 ft

370

Set D   pages 350–353

Find the area of each figure.

1.
12 ft
12 ft

2.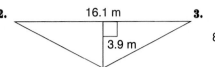
16.1 m
3.9 m

3.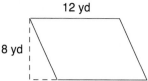
12 yd
8 yd

4. A triangle with base $1\frac{1}{2}$ ft and height 4 ft

5. A parallelogram with base 6.5 cm and height 8.3 cm

6. A triangle with base 10.6 m and height 8.4 m

Set E   pages 356–357

Estimation   Estimate the area of each circle. Then find each area.

1.
20 in.

2.
25 m

3.
32 ft

4.
52 in.

For Exercises 5–8, tell whether you would use paper and pencil or a calculator. Then find the area of each circle.

5. Radius: 7 in.   **6.** Radius: 3.7 m   **7.** Diameter: 11 ft   **8.** Diameter: 42 cm

Set F   pages 360–361

Find the surface area of each prism.

1.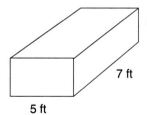
3 ft
7 ft
5 ft

2.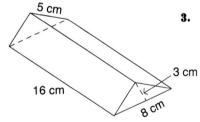
5 cm
16 cm
3 cm
8 cm

3.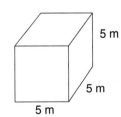
5 m
5 m
5 m

Set G   pages 362–365

Find the volume of each prism.

1.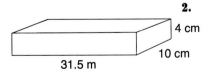
4 cm
10 cm
31.5 m

2.
$4\frac{1}{2}$ yd
6 yd
6 yd

3.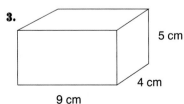
5 cm
4 cm
9 cm

371

Enrichment

Volumes of Cylinders, Cones, and Spheres

Three common types of solid geometric figures are the cylinder, the cone, and the sphere. The formulas for the volumes of each of these figures are given. In each figure, r stands for the radius, and h stands for the height.

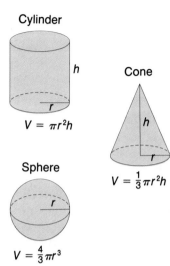

Cylinder

$V = \pi r^2 h$

Cone

$V = \frac{1}{3}\pi r^2 h$

Sphere

$V = \frac{4}{3}\pi r^3$

Over 2,000 years ago, the Greek mathematician Archimedes discovered a very interesting relationship between the volumes of the cylinder, cone, and sphere when the radius and height of each are the same, as in the figures at the right.

Use the formulas for volume to answer these questions. Leave answers in terms of π.

1. Find the volume of the cylinder below.

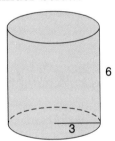

6

3

2. Find the volume of the cone below.

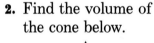

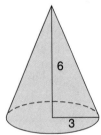

6

3

3. Find the volume of the sphere below.

3

4. Add the volumes of the cone and the sphere. What relationship do you find between this sum and the volume of the cylinder?

5. What is the relationship between the volume of the cylinder and the volume of the cone?

6. Find the volume of the cylinder with a radius of 5 feet and a height of 10 feet.

7. Now find the volume of a cone with radius 5 feet and height 10 feet.

8. Use your answer to Exercises 6 and 7 to find the volume of a sphere with diameter 10 feet. Check your answer by using the formula.

Chapter 10 Review/Test

Find the area of each circle. (Use 3.14 for π.)

1.
8 cm

2.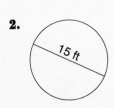
15 ft

3. Find the perimeter of a pentagon whose sides are 6 ft, 8 ft, 12 ft, 10 ft, and 12 ft long.

4. If the diameter of a circle is 6 in., what is the circumference? (Use 3.14 for π.)

5. Find the area of a rectangle 11 in. long and $8\frac{1}{2}$ in. wide.

6. Find the area of a triangle with base 31 cm and height 16 cm.

7. Find the area of the striped part of the flag of the Bahamas.

├─ 26 cm ─┤
22 cm
├─────── 45 cm ───────┤

Find the area of each parallelogram.

8.
4 cm
├── 6 cm ──┤

9.
3 in.
├── 4 in. ──┤

10. Find the total surface area of this prism.

11. Find the volume of this prism.

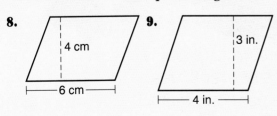
2 m
5 m
4 m

12. A baking dish has a circumference of 80 cm. To the nearest tenth, what is the diameter of the dish? (Use 3.14 for π.)

Make a table and look for a pattern to solve Problems 13 and 14.

13. Find the perimeter of a chain of 40 parallelograms. Each side is 3 in. long.

14. Find the perimeter of a chain of 30 equilateral triangles. Each side is 8 cm long.

Read the problem below. Then answer the question.

You want to build a tree house. For the floor and ceiling you have two square boards with sides 4 meters long. You want the walls to be 2 meters high. How much more wood do you need to finish your house?

15. Choose the most sensible answer.

   a. 10 m   **b.** 10 m^2
   c. 30 m^2 **d.** 300 m^2

16. **Write About Math** Explain why the surface area of a prism is measured in square units and the volume of a prism is measured in cubic units.

Understanding Ratios, Proportions, and Percents

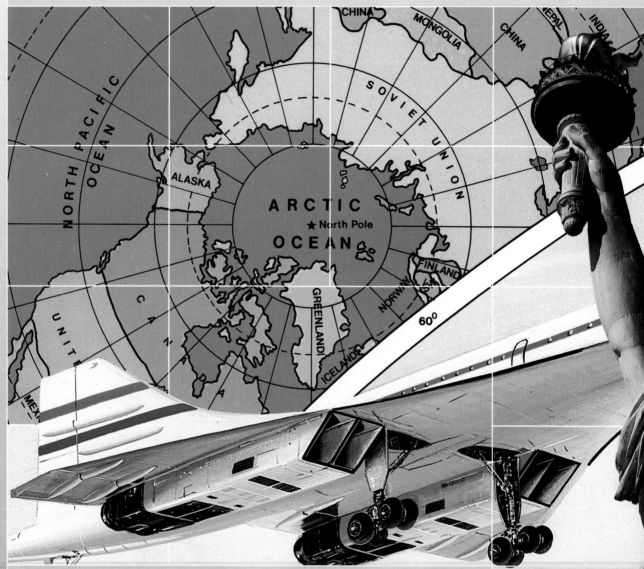

Did You Know: The Concorde supersonic airplane is about 204 feet long and has a wingspace of over 83 feet. The plane can average over 1,000 miles per hour (mph). Passengers on the Concorde can travel the 3,600 miles between Paris and New York City in less than 4 hours.

374

Number-Sense Project

Estimate
Name a location that is about 1,000 miles from your home. If you could drive, how many hours of non-stop driving would it take?

Gather Data
About how fast can a car travel on a highway? What is a reasonable speed for a train? Find the average speed of a subsonic jet.

Analyze and Report
Graph the speed of each method of transportation. How long would it take to travel 1,000 miles using each method?

Ratios

Build Understanding

1990-91 FOOTBALL SEASON					
Mustangs	7	Lawton	6	Mustangs	7	St. Rita	13
Mustangs	12	Jones	3	Mustangs	12	Sawyer	6
Mustangs	14	M.L. King	12	Mustangs	28	Taft	21
Mustangs	0	St. Rita	6	Mustangs	14	M.L. King	20
Mustangs	21	Sawyer	14	Mustangs	13	Kaplan	10

A. A *ratio* compares two quantities. Examine the display above. Compare the games won to the games lost.

games won → ooooooo → $\frac{7}{3}$ **The ratio of games won to**
games lost → xxx → $\frac{7}{3}$ **games lost is read "7 to 3."**

The ratio 7 to 3 can be written $\frac{7}{3}$ or 7:3. The ***first term*** in the ratio is 7, and the ***second term*** is 3.

B. What is the ratio of games lost to games won?

games lost → xxx → $\frac{3}{7}$ **The ratio is read**
games won → ooooooo → $\frac{3}{7}$ **"3 to 7."**

This ratio also tells about the Mustangs' wins and losses, but in reverse order. The ratios $\frac{3}{7}$ and $\frac{7}{3}$ are not the same.

■ **Talk About Math**   How do you decide which number to give as the first term of a ratio?

Check Understanding

For another example, see Set A, pages 404–405.

1. What does the ratio $\frac{3}{10}$ tell about the Mustangs' season?

Which of the ratios at the right could compare

$\frac{5}{4}$	$\frac{4}{9}$	$\frac{9}{5}$	$\frac{9}{4}$	$\frac{5}{9}$	$\frac{10}{10}$

2. wins to total games played?

3. wins to losses?

Practice

For More Practice, see Set A, pages 406–407.

Use the picture. Write a ratio for

4. footballs to baseballs.

5. baseballs to basketballs.

6. basketballs to all the balls shown.

Suppose you added 3 soccer balls and 1 golf ball to the picture above. Write a ratio for

7. golf balls to soccer balls.

8. soccer balls to footballs.

9. basketballs and soccer balls to all the balls.

The enrollment of Madison Middle School is given at the right. What is the ratio of

	Grade 6	Grade 7	Grade 8
Girls	60	82	65
Boys	67	59	68

10. sixth-grade girls to sixth-grade boys?

11. sixth-grade girls to eighth-grade girls?

12. sixth-grade boys to sixth-grade girls?

13. seventh graders to sixth graders?

14. eighth graders to the total number of students?

Problem Solving

Four teams make up the Southtown Basketball League. This season the teams played no games out of the league.

15. Which team won the most games? the fewest games?

16. For which team was the ratio of wins to losses 10 to 2?

17. Which team won $\frac{1}{6}$ of its games?

18. How many games were played in the Southtown League this season?

School	Wins	Losses
Rosen	10	2
Davis	7	5
Kowalski	5	7
Adams	2	10

Equal Ratios

Build Understanding

A. Mr. Chen told his class: "Your assignment is to find a ratio that compares a number of people in Wyoming to land area."

Some students made this display:

Mr. Chen wrote:

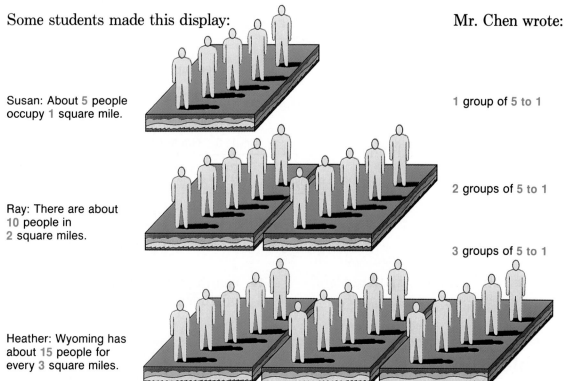

Susan: About **5** people occupy **1** square mile.

1 group of **5** to **1**

Ray: There are about **10** people in **2** square miles.

2 groups of **5** to **1**

3 groups of **5** to **1**

Heather: Wyoming has about **15** people for every **3** square miles.

The students used different pairs of numbers, but each diagram features the same number of people per square mile. Equal ratios are shown.

$$\frac{\text{people}}{\text{square miles}} \longrightarrow \frac{5}{1} = \frac{10}{2} = \frac{15}{3}$$

B. Describe these examples.

$$\frac{5 \times 2}{1 \times 2} = \frac{10}{2} \qquad \frac{5 \times 3}{1 \times 3} = \frac{15}{3} \qquad \frac{10 \div 2}{2 \div 2} = \frac{5}{1} \qquad \frac{15 \div 3}{3 \div 3} = \frac{5}{1}$$

If you multiply or divide both terms of a ratio by the same nonzero number, you will get a ratio that is equal to the original ratio.

c. Find other ratios for $\frac{6}{9}$.

There are endless possibilities.

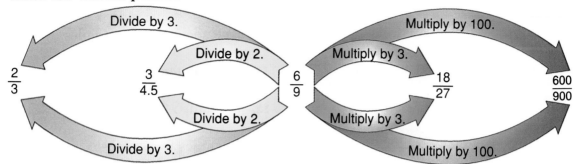

A *rate* is a ratio that compares one quantity to a different kind of quantity. Examples are people to square miles, miles per gallon, and feet per second. Equal ratios express the same rate.

D. Complete the table.

people	32				
square miles	1	2	3	4	5

people	32	64	96	128	160
square miles	1	2	3	4	5

■ **Talk About Math** Are equal ratios always obtained when you add the same number to both terms of a ratio? Are equal ratios obtained when you subtract the same number from both terms? Give examples to support your opinion.

Check Understanding

For another example, see Set B, pages 404–405.

1. Does a population density of 1 person per 5 square miles match the ratios in Example A? Make a diagram to support your answer.

2. Make diagrams of $\frac{4}{6}$ and of three ratios that are equal to $\frac{4}{6}$.

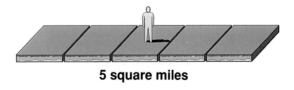

5 square miles

Mental Math Complete each equation.

3. $\frac{7 \times \blacksquare}{8 \times \blacksquare} = \frac{14}{16}$ **4.** $\frac{12 \times \blacksquare}{10 \times \blacksquare} = \frac{36}{30}$ **5.** $\frac{5 \div \blacksquare}{25 \div \blacksquare} = \frac{1}{5}$ **6.** $\frac{36 \div \blacksquare}{16 \div \blacksquare} = \frac{\blacksquare}{\blacksquare}$

Practice

For More Practice, see Set B, pages 406–407.

Make a diagram of each ratio.

7. 3 people per square mile

8. 1 person in 2 square miles

9. 5 teachers for 100 students

10. 8 people for 2 cars

11. 10 students for 1 bus

12. 13 stamps for $4.00

13. 10 postcards for $2.00

14. 5 pennies for 1 nickel

15. 4 nickels for 2 dimes

16. 3 maps for $7.00

Find three ratios that are equal to the given ratio.
In Exercises 17–22, use multiplication.
In Exercises 23–28, use division.

17. $\frac{1}{2}$ **18.** $\frac{7}{3}$ **19.** $\frac{3}{7}$ **20.** $\frac{1}{5}$ **21.** $\frac{5}{6}$ **22.** $\frac{3}{4}$

23. $\frac{16}{24}$ **24.** $\frac{8}{8}$ **25.** $\frac{50}{20}$ **26.** $\frac{80}{40}$ **27.** $\frac{24}{32}$ **28.** $\frac{40}{200}$

Copy and complete each table to show equal ratios.

29.

feet	88	176	264	440	880
seconds	1	2	▦	▦	▦

30.

miles	45	90	180	360	▦	1,440
gallons	2	4	8	▦	10	▦

31.

kilometers	22	44	▦	88	110	154	▦	286	▦
hours		3	6	9	▦	15	▦	30	▦	60

32.

tickets	6	▦	18	24	▦	102	▦	300	▦
dollars	5	10	15	▦	30	▦	120	▦	500

33.

first term		15	25	▦	50	80	▦	▦	500	1,000
second term	▦	▦	▦	64	▦	▦	160	240	800	▦

▦ **Calculator** Divide both terms of $\frac{5}{1}$ by the following.

34. 2 **35.** 5 **36.** 8 **37.** 10 **38.** 25 **39.** 100

40. 125 **41.** 200 **42.** 250 **43.** 500 **44.** 800 **45.** 1,000

Problem Solving

Solve each problem.

46. The Wyoming Office of Tourism is advertising a job that pays $450 for a 37.5-hour work week. What does the job pay per hour? What would the pay be for working 10 hours?

47. Alaska has about 14 people per 20 square miles. Is this rate greater than or less than 1 person per square mile? About how many Alaskans live in 100 square miles?

48. Critical Thinking Refer to the scale drawings of North Carolina and Connecticut. Which state has more people? How would you know? Which state is more densely populated? How would you know?

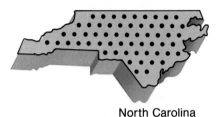

North Carolina

Trace the following drawings. The given populations are rounded to the nearest hundred thousand. Place a dot for every 100,000 people in each state.

Connecticut

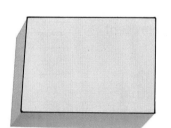

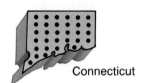

49. Georgia
5,500,000 people

50. Colorado
2,900,000 people

51. Maryland
4,200,000 people

52. Critical Thinking Use your pictures to rank the three states in order from the greatest number of people per square mile to the least.

Skills ———— **Review**   pages 218–219, 206–207

List the first six multiples of

1. 5   **2.** 14   **3.** 8   **4.** 7

List all the common factors of

5. 2 and 6   **6.** 30 and 12

Solve each equation.

7. $7 \times n = 14$ **8.** $3 \times t = 39$ **9.** $6r = 24$ **10.** $9s = 54$

A
L
G
E
B
R
A

Proportions

Build Understanding

A. Two equal ratios form a *proportion*.

Do the ratios $\frac{2}{3}$ and $\frac{8}{12}$ form a proportion?

Try to use multiplication or division to get one ratio from the other.

Multiply both terms of $\frac{2}{3}$ by 4.

$$\frac{2 \times 4}{3 \times 4} = \frac{8}{12} \qquad \frac{2}{3} = \frac{8}{12}$$

The ratios are equal. Therefore, they do form a proportion.

B. In a scale model of the solar system, a 6-inch-diameter sphere represents Earth. Set up a proportion to find what size sphere will be needed to represent the sun.

	Approximate diameter
Earth	8,000 mi
Sun	800,000 mi

In this scale model the ratio of the model size of the Earth to its actual size is equal to the ratio of the model size of the sun to its actual size.

$$\frac{\text{model size of Earth}}{\text{actual size of Earth}} = \frac{\text{model size of the sun}}{\text{actual size of the sun}}$$

Substitute the known quantities: $\dfrac{6}{8,000} = \dfrac{}{800,000}$

■ **Talk About Math** What other proportions could correctly describe the information in Example B?

Check Understanding   For another example, see Set C, pages 404–405.

1. In Example A, start with the ratio 8 to 12 and obtain the ratio 2 to 3.

Show whether each ratio forms a proportion with $\frac{5}{4}$.

2. $\frac{10}{8}$ **3.** $\frac{500}{400}$ **4.** $\frac{4}{5}$ **5.** $\frac{57}{47}$ **6.** $\frac{25}{24}$ **7.** $\frac{125}{100}$ **8.** $\frac{30}{29}$

Practice

For More Practice, see Set C, pages 406–407.

Mental Math Tell whether each pair of ratios forms a proportion.

9. $\frac{1}{5}, \frac{2}{10}$ **10.** $\frac{6}{3}, \frac{10}{8}$ **11.** $\frac{4}{11}, \frac{2}{22}$ **12.** $\frac{18}{36}, \frac{3}{6}$ **13.** $\frac{5}{7}, \frac{7}{9}$ **14.** $\frac{20}{25}, \frac{16}{20}$

15. $\frac{3}{8}, \frac{9}{32}$ **16.** $\frac{6}{4}, \frac{30}{20}$ **17.** $\frac{16}{21}, \frac{20}{35}$ **18.** $\frac{3}{11}, \frac{11}{3}$ **19.** $\frac{10}{18}, \frac{25}{45}$ **20.** $\frac{5}{9}, \frac{25}{40}$

Set up a proportion that describes each situation.
Remember to write terms in the correct order.

21. Nine oranges for $1.20 is the same price as three oranges for $0.40.

22. Traveling 88 ft per second means going 880 ft in 10 seconds.

23. If a telescope costs $115, our school will pay $1,380 for a dozen.

24. A 4-in. by 5-in. picture of Mars is enlarged to 16 in. by 20 in.

25. Double a recipe using 3 drops of food coloring per 8 ounce glass.

26. If you read 5 books each month, you will read 60 books in a year.

Problem Solving

Write a proportion that would give the size of the model for each planet. In the model, 6 inches represents 8,000 miles.

Planet	Approximate diameter
Jupiter	88,000 mi
Saturn	75,000 mi
Neptune	28,000 mi
Mars	4,000 mi

27. Mars **28.** Jupiter

29. Saturn **30.** Neptune

Critical Thinking Use each set of four numbers to form two proportions.

31. 3, 4, 24, 32 **32.** 1, 7, 2, 14 **33.** 50, 20, 5, 2 **34.** 7, 6, 30, 35

Choose a _____ Strategy

Number Lock-Up Ray won't tell his locker number, but he gives these clues: The first digit is greater than 8 and the second digit is even.

35. What might Ray's locker number be?

A▶
L
G
E
B
R
A

Solving Proportions

Build Understanding

A. Woodcarvers from the Oaxaca valley of southern Mexico are known for their colorful figures which are carved with simple tools.

Mr. Jiménez completed an order for 5 figures, 3 of which were deer. The next order for 15 figures has a proportional number of deer. How many deer will there be in the new order?

Write a proportion. Let n be the number of deer in the new order.

In the Oaxaca valley there are about 200 families who carve wooden figures for a living.

$$\begin{array}{cc} \text{Current} & \text{New} \\ \text{order} & \text{order} \end{array}$$

$$\frac{\text{deer}}{\text{all figures}} \begin{array}{c} \to \\ \to \end{array} \frac{3}{5} = \frac{n}{15}$$

Estimation Since 3 is more than half of 5, the answer should be more than half of 15.

$$\frac{3}{5} \overset{\times 3}{\underset{\times 3}{=}} \frac{n}{15}$$

Mental Math Think: 15 is 5×3, so n must be 3×3, or 9.

$$n = 9$$

Of the new order of 15 carved figures, 9 will be deer.

Oaxaca woodcarving has been in existence for hundreds of years.

B. Study these proportions. Multiply each pair of terms that are shown within the same loop. You will be finding **cross-products**.

$$\frac{2}{3} = \frac{4}{6}$$ 2 × 6 = 12 $\qquad$ $$\frac{7}{12} = \frac{3.5}{6}$$ 7 × 6 = 42
$\qquad\qquad\quad$ 3 × 4 = 12 $\qquad\qquad\qquad\qquad\qquad$ 12 × 3.5 = 42

What pattern do you see? Write three more proportions and multiply pairs of terms in the same way. What happens?

In a proportion, the cross-products are equal. If the cross-products of two ratios are equal, then the ratios form a proportion.

C. Solve $\frac{4}{5} = \frac{30}{n}$.

The terms in the numerators of the proportion are known, but 30 is not a multiple of 4. Neither ratio can be simplified. Try using the cross-products instead.

Paper and pencil

$\frac{4}{5} = \frac{30}{n}$ $\qquad$ Write the cross-products.

$4 \times n = 5 \times 30$ $\qquad$ Multiply.
$4n = 150$

$n = 150 \div 4$ $\qquad$ Divide both sides of
$n = 37.5$ $\qquad\quad$ the equation by 4.

Check: $\qquad$ $\frac{4}{5} \overset{?}{=} \frac{30}{37.5}$ $\qquad$ Substituting 37.5 for n results in equal cross-products. Therefore, 37.5 is the correct answer.

$4 \times 37.5 \overset{?}{=} 5 \times 30$

$150 = 150$

▦ Calculator This key sequence shows how to solve the proportion.

Press: $\quad 5 \; \boxed{\times} \; 30 \; \boxed{\div} \; 4 \; \boxed{=}$

Display: $\quad 37.5$

■ Write About Math Write a problem involving the proportion $\frac{4}{5} = \frac{30}{n}$.

Check Understanding

For another example, see Set D, pages 404–405.

Solve each proportion. **Remember** to check your answers.

1. $\frac{5}{8} = \frac{a}{16}$ $\qquad$ **2.** $\frac{18}{90} = \frac{2}{b}$ $\qquad$ **3.** $\frac{15}{25} = \frac{33}{n}$ $\qquad$ **4.** $\frac{27}{63} = \frac{y}{35}$ $\qquad$ **5.** $\frac{36}{60} = \frac{x}{20}$

Number Sense For Exercises 6–9, decide whether $r = 55$ is a reasonable answer. Explain how you decided.

6. $\frac{270}{450} = \frac{33}{r}$ $\qquad$ **7.** $\frac{270}{450} = \frac{r}{33}$ $\qquad$ **8.** $\frac{33}{270} = \frac{450}{r}$ $\qquad$ **9.** $\frac{270}{33} = \frac{450}{r}$

Practice

For More Practice, see Set D, pages 406–407.

Solve each proportion. **Remember** to estimate so that you will know if your answer is reasonable.

10. $\frac{9}{10} = \frac{c}{50}$ **11.** $\frac{n}{18} = \frac{30}{20}$ **12.** $\frac{25}{100} = \frac{d}{20}$ **13.** $\frac{n}{30} = \frac{7}{10}$ **14.** $\frac{a}{36} = \frac{21}{27}$

15. $\frac{10}{40} = \frac{x}{24}$ **16.** $\frac{3}{4} = \frac{b}{60}$ **17.** $\frac{r}{10} = \frac{12}{5}$ **18.** $\frac{3}{51} = \frac{p}{68}$ **19.** $\frac{12}{16} = \frac{t}{28}$

Calculator Solve each proportion by using cross-products. Check your answers.

20. $\frac{3}{14} = \frac{k}{21}$ **21.** $\frac{15}{18} = \frac{4}{f}$ **22.** $\frac{10}{8} = \frac{35}{h}$ **23.** $\frac{32}{c} = \frac{80}{50}$

24. $\frac{16}{12} = \frac{24}{g}$ **25.** $\frac{13}{n} = \frac{32.5}{16}$ **26.** $\frac{p}{18} = \frac{81}{54}$ **27.** $\frac{4}{6} = \frac{m}{3.3}$

Mixed Practice For Exercises 28–43, tell whether you would use paper and pencil, a calculator, or mental math to solve the proportion. Then solve.

28. $\frac{a}{36} = \frac{8}{32}$ **29.** $\frac{b}{27} = \frac{1}{12}$ **30.** $\frac{7}{10} = \frac{r}{12}$ **31.** $\frac{s}{39} = \frac{9}{27}$

32. $\frac{0.15}{t} = \frac{35}{7}$ **33.** $\frac{2.8}{u} = \frac{4.8}{6.0}$ **34.** $\frac{0.2}{14} = \frac{0.03}{v}$ **35.** $\frac{0.4}{11} = \frac{0.6}{w}$

36. $\frac{4}{10} = \frac{c}{26}$ **37.** $\frac{6}{10} = \frac{24}{d}$ **38.** $\frac{0.5}{1} = \frac{c}{20}$ **39.** $\frac{7}{3.5} = \frac{f}{50}$

40. $\frac{5}{7} = \frac{4}{g}$ **41.** $\frac{12}{h} = \frac{3}{11}$ **42.** $\frac{2.75}{11} = \frac{i}{9}$ **43.** $\frac{6.2}{k} = \frac{5}{8}$

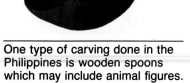

Problem Solving

44. Use Data Refer to the previous lesson. In Example B, page 382, and Exercises 27–30, page 383, solve the proportions you set up.

One type of carving done in the Philippines is wooden spoons which may include animal figures.

Solve each problem.

45. Marcos, a Philippine carver, works 8 hours a day, 6 days a week. How many hours does he work each week?

46. Estimation Marcos can complete 1,200 figures a year. About how many figures does he carve each week?

The animal woodcarvings of the Native Indians of the northwest coast symbolized clans, and supernatural or historical events in their lives. Suppose an Alaskan museum has 110 woodcarvings including 20 totem poles and 30 masks. The museum plans to collect a total of 385 woodcarvings in the same proportion as the original number of items.

47. How many totem poles will the museum collect?

48. How many masks will the museum collect?

49. The new collection will have 35 rattles. How many rattles were there previously?

50. How many woodcarvings in the new collection will *not* be totem poles?

51. Can you determine whether the museum's original collection included other carvings besides totem poles, masks, and rattles? Explain your answer.

TIPS FOR PROBLEM SOLVERS

Be flexible. If you get stuck, try another idea.

Although the carving styles among the different Indian groups are similar, the way each group uses color in their carvings is unique.

Midchapter ✓ Checkup

At the end of the summer, the My Bag Shop had sold 25 red tote bags, 5 white tote bags, and 11 blue tote bags. Find each ratio.

1. Red tote bags to white tote bags

2. Blue tote bags to red ones

Draw a diagram of each ratio.

3. 1 person per square mile

4. 2 square miles per person

5. Write four ratios that are equal to $\frac{12}{8}$.

Tell whether each pair of ratios forms a proportion.

6. $\frac{25}{36}, \frac{3}{6}$ **7.** $\frac{4}{10}, \frac{30}{75}$ **8.** $\frac{14}{7}, \frac{12}{5}$ **9.** $\frac{8}{15}, \frac{48}{90}$ **10.** $\frac{45}{54}, \frac{60}{72}$

Solve each proportion.

11. $\frac{1}{4} = \frac{4}{x}$ **12.** $\frac{w}{24} = \frac{5}{60}$ **13.** $\frac{t}{30} = \frac{3}{9}$ **14.** $\frac{25}{8} = \frac{x}{12}$ **15.** $\frac{10}{a} = \frac{15}{12}$

Problem-Solving Workshop

Math-at-Home Activity

1. Rearranging the furniture in a room can give any room a completely new look. Decide with your family on one room in your home where you might like to rearrange the furniture.

2. Together, measure the dimensions of the floor. Then use $\frac{1}{2}$-inch graph paper to make a large scale drawing of the area. Make sure to show the placement of the windows and doors on the drawing.

3. Measure each piece of furniture in the room. Then use a second piece of graph paper and make and cut out scale drawings for the furniture.

4. With your family, move the pieces around the scale drawing to see how rearranging the furniture would change the room.

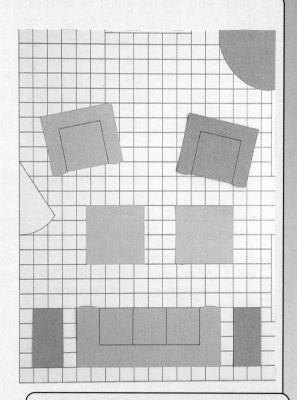

Visual Thinking Activity

Which is a top view drawing of the room full of furniture?

a.

b.

c.

d.

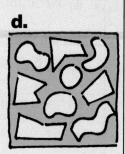

Explore with a Computer

Use a *Spreadsheet Workshop* for this activity.

1. Of the students in the sixth grade at Marist School, 42 students have pets and 18 do not have pets. At the computer type these numbers into the spreadsheet. What is the ratio of students with pets to students without pets?

2. Suppose half the students in the 6th grade are boys. If boys have the same ratio of students with pets to students without pets, how many boys do not have pets? Use the spreadsheet to find the proportion.

3. The entire school has 400 students. If the ratio of students with pets to students without pets is the same as in the 6th-grade class, about how many students in the school have pets?

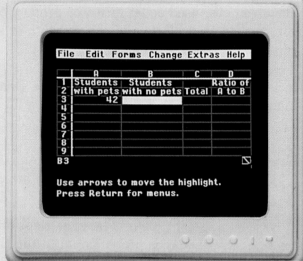

Number-Sense Project

Look back at pages 374-375. The table gives maximum speeds of animals on foot over short distances.

1. Give the following ratios using the data given. Then write an equal ratio in which the second number is one.

Example:
Antelope to human: 60 to 25 or 2.4 to 1

    a. Lion to human   **b.** Rabbit to human

    c. Bear to human   **d.** Cheetah to human

    e. Dog to human

Animal	Speed
Cheetah	70 mph
Antelope	60 mph
Lion	50 mph
Dog	45 mph
Rabbit	35 mph
Bear	30 mph
Human	25 mph
Turkey	15 mph
Chicken	10 mph
Snail	0.03 mph

Write an Equation

Build Understanding

Have you ever used equal ratios or proportions when you worked on projects and experiments in science class?

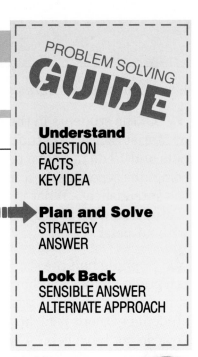

A. If a person sleeps an average of 8 hours a day, how many years would that person sleep in a lifetime of 72 years?

Understand   FACTS   There are 24 hours in a day, and a person sleeps an average of 8 hours a day.

KEY IDEA   The time slept during a day is proportional to the time slept during a lifetime.

▶ **Plan and Solve**   STRATEGY   Set up and solve a proportion.

Hours in a day   Years in a lifetime

$$\text{Time sleeping} \rightarrow \atop \text{Total time} \rightarrow \quad \frac{8}{24} = \frac{w}{72}$$

You might solve the proportion mentally.

$$\frac{8}{24} = \frac{w}{72}$$ $72 = 24 \times 3,$ so $w = 8 \times 3.$

$$\frac{8}{24} = \frac{24}{72}$$

You could also use cross-products.

$$\frac{8}{24} = \frac{w}{72}$$
$$8 \times 72 = 24 \times w$$
$$576 = 24w$$
$$24 = w$$

ANSWER   The person would sleep about 24 years in a lifetime.

Look Back   Since 8 hours is one third of a day, it seems logical that a person sleeps about one third of a lifetime.

B. Ron found that a dripping faucet filled one cup every 15 minutes. At this rate, how many cups of water would drip from the faucet in one day (24 hours)?

Mental Math   Think of equal ratios.

Think: 1 cup in 15 minutes;   15 min = $\frac{1}{4}$ hr
4 cups in 1 hour; $4 \times 24 = 96$
96 cups in 24 hours.

■ **Write About Math**   Show how you would solve Example B by using a proportion.

Check Understanding

1. Complete this set of equal rates.

$$\frac{44 \text{ ft}}{1 \text{ sec}} = \frac{\text{▦ ft}}{60 \text{ sec}} = \frac{\text{▦ ft}}{1 \text{ min}} = \frac{\text{▦ mi}}{1 \text{ min}} = \frac{\text{▦ mi}}{60 \text{ min}} = \frac{\text{▦ mi}}{1 \text{ hr}}$$

2. If you spend 5 minutes a day brushing your teeth, about how many days would you spend brushing your teeth in a year?

Practice

If a lifetime is 72 years, how much time would you spend on the activities described in Exercises 3–6?

3. Sleeping: 7 hours a day

4. Eating: $2\frac{1}{2}$ hours a day

5. Exercising: 30 minutes a day

6. Sleeping, eating, and exercising

Solve each problem.

7. At 3 miles per hour, how far could you walk in 5 hours?

8. At 5 miles in 2 hours, how far could you hike in 5 hours?

9. An ant can lift 50 times its weight. If human strength were proportional to that of ants, how much could a 92-pound person lift?

10. A grasshopper can jump 20 times its own length. If the jumping ability of humans were proportional to that of a grasshopper, how far could a 6-foot-tall person jump?

11. Mary can walk or take the bus to school. The 2-mile bus ride to school takes 5 minutes. Mary can walk 3 miles per hour. How much longer does it take her to get to school when she walks?

Similar Figures

Build Understanding

The rectangles in Figures 1 and 2 have the same shape. Figures with the same shape are **similar**.

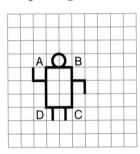

Figure 1

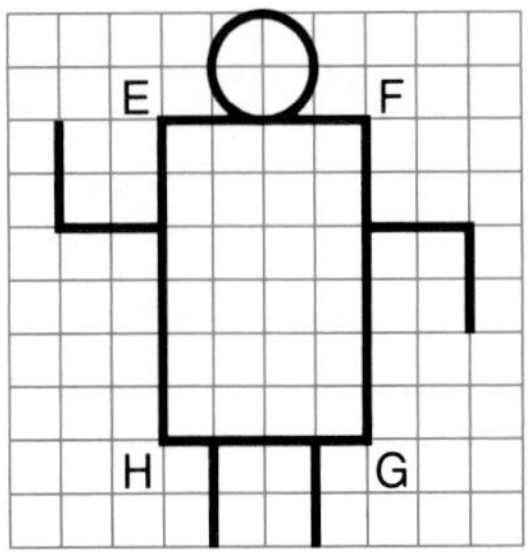

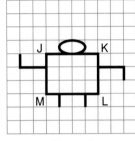

Figure 2

Figure 3

Only when figures are similar are corresponding sides proportional: when you compare the length of each side of one figure to the length of its corresponding side in the other figure, the ratios you get are equal.

A. Show that the rectangles in Figures 1 and 2 are similar.

$$\frac{\textbf{width}}{\textbf{width}} = \frac{\textbf{length}}{\textbf{length}}$$ Rectangle *ABCD*
Rectangle *EFGH*

$$\frac{2}{4} \overset{?}{=} \frac{3}{6}$$

Both ratios can be simplified to the ratio $\frac{1}{2}$, so they are equal.

You could also use cross-products.

$$\frac{2}{4} \overset{?}{=} \frac{3}{6}$$ Find 2 × 6 and 4 × 3.

12 = 12   The cross-products are equal, so the ratios are equal.

You have seen two ways to show that the ratios of corresponding sides are equal. Either way proves that rectangle *ABCD* is similar to rectangle *EFGH*.

B. Show that the rectangles in Figures 1 and 3 are *not* similar.

$$\frac{\textbf{width}}{\textbf{width}} = \frac{\textbf{length}}{\textbf{length}}$$ Rectangle *ABCD*
Rectangle *JKLM*

$$\frac{2}{4} \overset{?}{=} \frac{3}{3}$$

The ratios cannot be shown to be equal to the same ratio.

Try using the cross-products.

$$\frac{2}{4} \overset{?}{=} \frac{3}{3}$$ Find 2 × 3 and 4 × 3.

6 ≠ 12   The cross-products are not equal, so the ratios are not equal.

Either way—simplifying or using cross-products—shows that the ratios of corresponding sides are not equal. Rectangle *ABCD* is not similar to rectangle *JKLM*.

c. When figures are similar, you can use a proportion to find the unknown length of a side.

The two triangles at the right are similar. The corresponding sides are $\overline{QR}$ and $\overline{XY}$, $\overline{RS}$ and $\overline{YZ}$, and $\overline{SQ}$ and $\overline{ZX}$. Use a proportion to find z, the length of $\overline{XY}$.

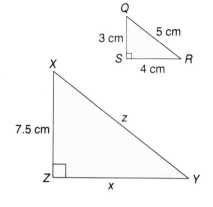

■ **Estimation** 3 corresponds to 7.5. $2 \times 3 < 7.5 < 3 \times 3$
5 corresponds to z. $2 \times 5 < z < 3 \times 5$
Therefore, z is between 10 and 15.

$$\frac{\text{length of } \overline{SQ}}{\text{length of } \overline{ZX}} = \frac{\text{length of } \overline{QR}}{\text{length of } \overline{XY}}$$

$$\frac{3}{7.5} = \frac{5}{z}$$

$3 \times z = 7.5 \times 5$ Use cross-products.

$$\frac{3z}{3} = \frac{37.5}{3}$$

$$z = 12.5$$

The length of $\overline{XY}$ is 12.5 centimeters.

■ **Talk about Math** If two triangles are congruent, must they be similar? Why or why not? If two triangles are similar, must they be congruent? Why or why not?

Check Understanding

For another example, see Set E, pages 404–405.

1. Which proportion could be used to find the length of side YZ in Example C? Solve the proportion.

$\frac{3}{7.5} = \frac{5}{x}$ $\frac{7.5}{4} = \frac{5}{x}$ $\frac{4}{x} = \frac{5}{12.5}$

2. Trace triangle QRS above. At each angle of triangle XYZ, try to fit the tracing on triangle XYZ so that a pair of angles match. Can this be done? Make three diagrams to show the results and label the angles.

3. Triangles DEF and GHJ are similar. Name the three pairs of corresponding sides.

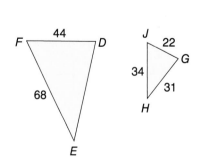

4. Find the length of side DE in triangle DEF.

Practice

For More Practice, see Set E, pages 406–407.

Are the pairs of figures similar? If so, list three equal ratios to show how the sides correspond.

5.
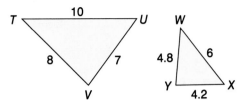

6.
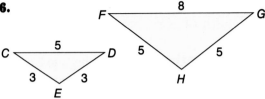

Figures in each pair below are similar. List the pairs of corresponding sides.

7.
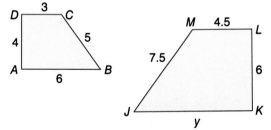

8.
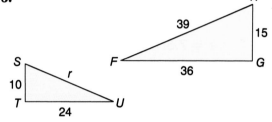

9. Find the length of side $\overline{JK}$.

10. Find the length of side $\overline{SU}$.

For each pair of similar figures below, tell whether you would use paper and pencil, a calculator, or mental math to find x. Then find the value of x.

11.
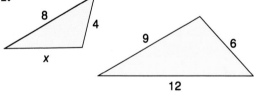

12.
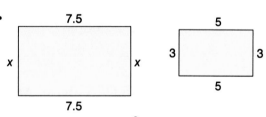

13.
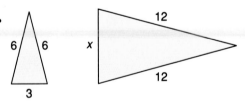

14.
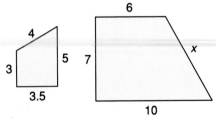

15.
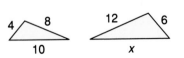

16.
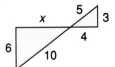

Problem Solving

Which of the following rectangular screens are similar to a
computer monitor that measures 5 in. by 7 in.? Explain.

17. A miniature TV
screen 2 in. by 3 in.

18. A TV monitor
17.5 in. by 24.5 in.

19. A movie screen 20 ft
by 28 ft

When Mary Lou drew Figures 1 and 2 on page 392,
she used a ratio of 1 to 2. A length of 1 in the first
picture became a length of 2 in the second picture.

For each exercise, use grid paper to draw a figure
similar to the given figure. Use the ratio given.

20. 1 to 2   **21.** 1 to 3   **22.** 2 to 1

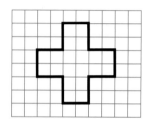

23. 1 to 3   **24.** 2 to 1   **25.** 6 to 7

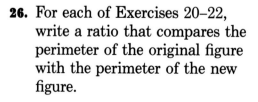

Explore ———— Math

26. For each of Exercises 20–22,
write a ratio that compares the
perimeter of the original figure
with the perimeter of the new
figure.

27. For each of Exercises 20–22,
write a ratio comparing the area
of the original figure to the area
of the new figure.

28. How is the perimeter of a figure
affected when the length of each
side is doubled? tripled? halved?

29. How is the area of a figure
affected when the length of each
side is doubled? tripled? halved?

Use Data from a Diagram

Build Understanding

Archaeologists often make "digs" in search of artifacts from the past. They make accurate *scale drawings* to show where objects are found.

A. This scale drawing shows where a statue (S) and its base (B) were found. How far apart are these locations?

Understand   QUESTION   What is the actual distance between S and B?

FACTS   A distance of 1 centimeter anywhere on the drawing means an actual distance of 4 meters. A ruler placed on the drawing shows S and B drawn 3.5 cm apart.

KEY IDEA   Distance in the drawing is proportional to actual distance.

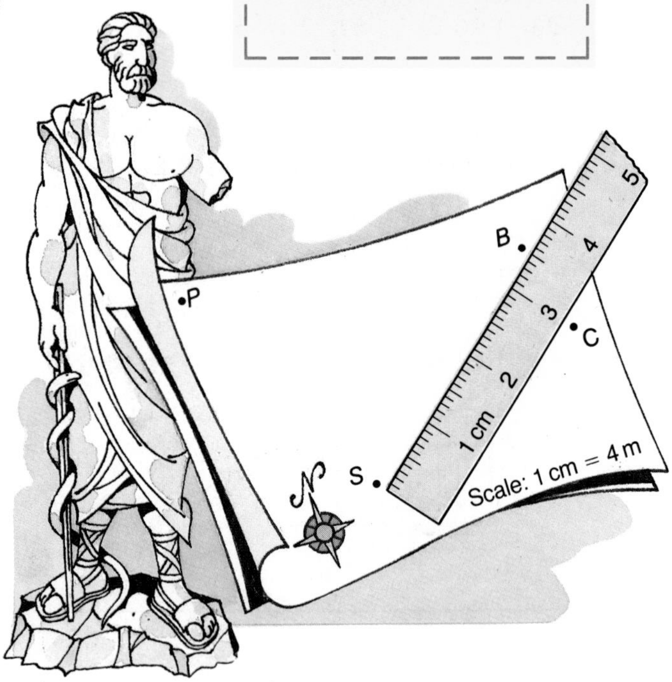

Plan and Solve   Write and solve a proportion.

Distance on drawing (cm) →
―――――――――――――――――――   → $\dfrac{1}{4} = \dfrac{3.5}{d}$
Actual distance (m)

$$1 \times d = 4 \times 3.5$$

$$d = 14$$

The statue and its base were found 14 meters apart.

Look Back   Be sure the ruler is positioned directly below the correct points, in this case, S and B.

PROBLEM SOLVING
GUIDE

Understand
QUESTION
FACTS
KEY IDEA

Plan and Solve
STRATEGY
ANSWER

Look Back
SENSIBLE ANSWER
ALTERNATE APPROACH

B. Estimation   Determine the approximate distance from Paris to Munich in kilometers.

On the edge of an index card, mark off the map locations of Paris and Munich. Place the card against the bar scale with one mark at the zero point. The actual distance from Paris to Munich is nearly 700 km.

■ **Talk About Math**   How would you estimate the distance from Paris to Munich in miles?

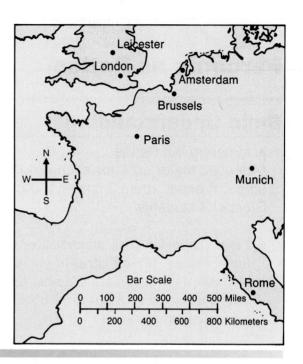

The air distance between New York and Los Angeles is 2,451 miles—over $3\frac{1}{2}$ times greater than the 690 air miles between Paris and Rome.

Check Understanding

1. If 1 cm represents 50 km, what length represents 25 km?

2. A store has maps of Asia with scales of 1 cm = 200 km and 1 cm = 400 km. Which map requires more paper?

Practice

Use the scale drawing in Example A.

3. How far were the coins (C) found from the pottery (P)?

4. A jug was found 10 meters from the statue. How far apart would these items be on the drawing?

A map has a scale of 1 in. to 200 in.

5. What actual length does 10 inches on the map represent?

6. What length on the map represents 5 feet?

Use the map on this page. Estimate these distances in miles and kilometers.

7. Amsterdam to London   8. Leicester to Paris   9. Brussels to Munich

Percents as Ratios

Build Understanding

A. Metering out Ratios
Materials: Meter stick for each group; strips of paper about 3 cm by 100 cm
Groups: 4 students

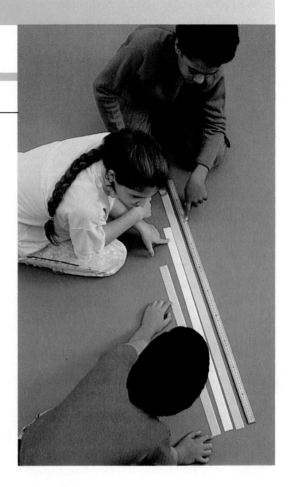

a. Place the meter stick on a desk or the floor. Place a 100-cm strip of paper just above the meter stick. Label the strip segment *AB*. Align it with the zero mark on the stick.

b. Take turns. Each group member cuts off a shorter strip and places it above the previous strip. All strips should be lined up with the zero mark.

c. For each strip in your group, write a ratio that compares its length to the length *AB*. How are the ratios alike? How are they different?

B. The number 100 is a convenient number in our number system. It is used as the second term in ratios called **percents**. The word *percent* means "for every hundred." You can refer to 42 out of 100 in these ways:

As a ratio: $\frac{42}{100}$ "42 out of 100"   **As a percent:** 42%   "42 percent"

c. Write the ratio $\frac{1}{4}$ as a percent. Write a proportion using 100 as the second term of one ratio.

$$\frac{1}{4} = \frac{x}{100}$$
$$\frac{1}{4} = \frac{25}{100}$$

$$\overset{\times 25}{\frac{1}{4} = \frac{x}{100}}\underset{\times 25}{}$$

Therefore, $\frac{1}{4} = \frac{25}{100} = 25\%$.

D. Write the ratio $\frac{2}{3}$ as a percent.

$$\begin{array}{r} 0.6\,6\frac{2}{3} \\ 3\overline{)2.0\,0} \\ \underline{1\,8} \\ 2\,0 \\ \underline{1\,8} \\ 2 \end{array}$$

Divide.
Change the decimal quotient to a percent.

Therefore, $\frac{2}{3} = 66\frac{2}{3}\%$.

■ **Talk About Math** Segment *RS* is 40 cm long. Explain how its length compares to that of a segment 80% as long as segment *AB* in Example A.

Check Understanding

For another example, see Set F, pages 404–405.

Express each ratio as a percent.

1. $\frac{89}{100}$ **2.** $\frac{1}{100}$ **3.** $\frac{3}{10} = \frac{}{100}$ **4.** $\frac{21}{28} = \frac{}{4} = \frac{}{100}$ **5.** $\frac{3}{25}$ **6.** $\frac{5}{8}$

Practice

For More Practice, see Set F, pages 406–407.

Write each percent as a ratio. **Remember** the meaning of *percent*.

7. 10% **8.** 26% **9.** 99% **10.** 65% **11.** 56% **12.** 3% **13.** 100%

14. 50% **15.** 21% **16.** 33% **17.** 42% **18.** 13% **19.** 78% **20.** 140%

Write each ratio as a percent.

21. $\frac{82}{100}$ **22.** $\frac{17}{100}$ **23.** $\frac{1}{10}$ **24.** $\frac{9}{10}$ **25.** $\frac{3}{5}$ **26.** $\frac{3}{4}$ **27.** $\frac{3}{20}$ **28.** $\frac{22}{55}$

29. $\frac{3}{10}$ **30.** $\frac{6}{10}$ **31.** $\frac{24}{48}$ **32.** $\frac{9}{12}$ **33.** $\frac{1}{5}$ **34.** $\frac{5}{20}$ **35.** $\frac{4}{40}$ **36.** $\frac{36}{72}$

37. $\frac{3}{8}$ **38.** $\frac{1}{6}$ **39.** $\frac{2}{7}$ **40.** $\frac{7}{12}$ **41.** $\frac{5}{9}$ **42.** $\frac{10}{11}$ **43.** $\frac{11}{15}$ **44.** $\frac{1}{200}$

Answer each problem with $>$, $<$, or $=$.

45. $\frac{1}{12}$ ▦ 10% **46.** $\frac{2}{5}$ ▦ 40% **47.** $\frac{4}{9}$ ▦ 50% **48.** $\frac{3}{11}$ ▦ 25% **49.** $\frac{3}{10}$ ▦ 30%

Problem Solving

Describe each with a percent.

50. 73 out of 100

51. Half up, half down

52. $\frac{1}{10}$ with coats, $\frac{9}{10}$ without

53. Ratio of boys to girls is 2:3

54. **Critical Thinking** Jon answered 7 out of 10 questions correctly on a math test and 19 out of 25 questions correctly on a science test. On which test did he get the greater percent of items correct?

Collecting Data

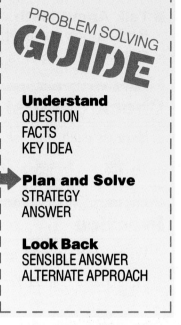

PROBLEM SOLVING
GUIDE

Understand
QUESTION
FACTS
KEY IDEA

▶**Plan and Solve**
STRATEGY
ANSWER

Look Back
SENSIBLE ANSWER
ALTERNATE APPROACH

Build Understanding

The students at Emerson School will select an animal mascot. When Brenda surveyed 40 students, she got the results shown below. What percent voted for the cougar?

School Mascot				
Lion 卌 l	Tiger 卌 ll	Cougar 卌 卌 ll	Eagle 卌 卌 l	Bulldog llll

Understand QUESTION   What percent selected the cougar?

FACTS   The tally table shows that 12 of 40 students selected the cougar.

KEY IDEA   The ratio 12:40 can be expressed as a percent.

**Plan and Solve**   To find the percent, find a ratio equal to 12:40 with a second term of 100.

$$\begin{array}{ccc} & \text{Survey} & \text{Percent} \\ \text{Cougar votes} \rightarrow \\ \overline{\text{Total votes}} \rightarrow & \dfrac{12}{40} = & \dfrac{b}{100} \end{array}$$

$$12 \times 100 = 40 \times b$$
$$1{,}200 = 40b$$
$$30 = b$$

Of the 40 students, 30% voted for the cougar.

Look Back   Since 12 is less than half of 40, the answer should be less than 50%.

■ **Talk About Math**   Did any animal get more than 30% of the votes? Explain how you could answer this question without calculating any more percents.

Check Understanding

1. How many students did not select the cougar? What percent is this?

2. What percent of the votes were for the bulldog?

Practice

You will need to gather data from outside sources to solve these problems.

3. Select any 5 animals and ask 10 classmates to choose their favorite of the five. Record the results on a tally sheet.

4. Find the percent of students who voted for each animal.

5. Select a sports team that is playing right now. Where might you find data about its won-lost record?

6. What percent of its last five games has your team won?

Choose a _____ **Strategy**

Be a Good Sport

7. Rita asked 21 classmates which of three sports they played. She found that eight students only swim, four only play basketball, and one only plays football. Some play one or two sports, but of these students 14 do not play football, six do not swim, and 11 do not play basketball. If all 21 students participate in at least one of these sports, how many classmates participate in all three?

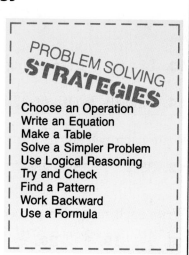

PROBLEM SOLVING STRATEGIES

Choose an Operation
Write an Equation
Make a Table
Solve a Simpler Problem
Use Logical Reasoning
Try and Check
Find a Pattern
Work Backward
Use a Formula

Skills Review

Use the picture to write a ratio for

1. black marbles to white marbles.

2. white marbles to all marbles.

Write three ratios that are equal to the given ratio.

3. $\frac{1}{3}$ **4.** $\frac{2}{5}$ **5.** $\frac{12}{18}$ **6.** $\frac{10}{10}$

Tell whether each pair of ratios forms a proportion.

7. $\frac{3}{4}, \frac{9}{12}$ **8.** $\frac{5}{7}, \frac{7}{5}$ **9.** $\frac{1}{2}, \frac{5}{10}$

10. Write a porportion for this situation. Three apples for $0.60 is the same as a dozen apples for $2.40.

Solve each proportion.

11. $\frac{a}{6} = \frac{5}{10}$ **12.** $\frac{0.8}{4} = \frac{3}{b}$

Use the similar figures for Exercises 13 and 14.

 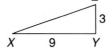

13. List the corresponding sides.

14. Find the length of $\overline{AB}$.

Write each percent as a ratio.

15. 35%   **16.** 4%   **17.** 80%

Write each ratio as a percent.

18. $\frac{1}{4}$ **19.** $\frac{2}{5}$ **20.** $\frac{3}{10}$ **21.** $\frac{5}{6}$

Problem-Solving Review

Solve each problem.

22. All freshmen students at Blake High School take a language course. This year, 72 students chose French, 41 chose Spanish, and 32 chose Latin. What is the ratio of the students who chose Latin to the total number of freshmen students?

23. A sum of the ages of two boys is 31. The difference in their ages is 7. How old is the younger of the two?

24. Suli wants to complete 15 hours of violin practice a week. She practices $2\frac{1}{2}$ hours each day, Monday through Friday. How many hours should she practice on the weekend to reach her goal?

25. Move 3 toothpicks to make 5 squares of the same size.

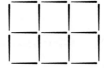

26. Data File Use the data on pages 410–411. Find the total length of the given African rivers.

27. Make a Data File Count the number of commercials during a commercial break on television and time the length of the break. What is the average length of the commercials in seconds?

Write each number in standard form.

1. Two hundred fifteen billion, six hundred million, fifty-two thousand, one hundred eight

2. Five and three hundred fourteen thousandths

Estimate. Then compute.

3. 83.56 + 4.259

4. 25 − 4.85

5. 34.7 × 6.41

6. 2.015 × 0.07

7. $65\overline{)520}$

8. $3.5\overline{)192.5}$

Use the figure for Exercises 9–11.

9. Name two rays with endpoint A.

10. Name an acute angle.

11. Name a line which intersects $\overleftrightarrow{AC}$.

For each number, write the prime factorization using exponents.

12. 216 **13.** 500 **14.** 81

Write the fractions in order from least to greatest.

15. $\frac{3}{4}, \frac{3}{5}, \frac{5}{8}$ **16.** $\frac{2}{5}, \frac{3}{10}, \frac{1}{4}$

Add or subtract.

17. $\frac{2}{3} + \frac{5}{8}$ **18.** $\frac{5}{6} - \frac{3}{4}$

19. $2\frac{1}{2} + 3\frac{3}{5}$ **20.** $4\frac{1}{4} - 1\frac{5}{8}$

Multiply. Use mental math.

21. $\frac{6}{5} \times \frac{5}{6} \times \frac{3}{4}$ **22.** $2\frac{1}{2} \times 10$

Multiply or divide.

23. $\frac{2}{3} \times \frac{6}{7}$ **24.** $6 \times \frac{3}{7}$ **25.** $\frac{1}{2} \div \frac{1}{8}$

Find each missing number.

26. 260 g = ▦ kg

27. 3 ft 6 in. = ▦ in.

28. 4 qt 1 pt = ▦ pt

Find the perimeter of each figure.

29.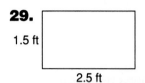

30.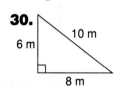

Find the area of the figure in

31. Exercise 29. **32.** Exercise 30.

Find the circumference and the area of each circle. Use 3.14 for π.

33. Radius: 5 in. **34.** Diameter: 20 cm

Use the prism for Exercises 35 and 36.

35. Find the volume.

36. Find the surface area.

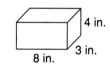

Write three ratios that are equal to the given ratio.

37. $\frac{3}{4}$ **38.** $\frac{3}{9}$ **39.** $\frac{15}{20}$ **40.** $\frac{7}{7}$

Write each percent as a ratio.

41. 63% **42.** 7% **43.** 40%

Reteaching

Set A pages 376–377

In the first basketball game, find the ratio of points scored by Ellen to the number of points scored by the team.

	Game 1	Game 2	Game 3
Ellen	12	16	15
Team	32	34	38

Ellen scored → $\frac{12}{32}$
Team scored →

Remember that a ratio gives a rate or makes a comparison.

Use the table at the left for Exercises 1–3.

1. The points scored by Ellen to the points scored by the team in game 2

2. The total number of points scored by Ellen to the total scored by the team

3. The team points scored in game 1 to the points scored in game 2

Set B pages 378–381

Equal ratios are obtained by multiplying or dividing both terms by the same nonzero number.

Write two ratios equal to $\frac{12}{15}$.

a. Using division:

$\frac{12 \div 3}{15 \div 3} = \frac{4}{5}$

b. Using multiplication:

$\frac{12 \times 2}{15 \times 2} = \frac{24}{30}$

Remember that a rate is a ratio that compares one quantity to a different quantity, such as miles per gallon.

Find three ratios that are equal to the given ratio. In Exercises 1–3, use multiplication. In Exercises 4–6, use division.

1. $\frac{1}{5}$ 2. $\frac{8}{3}$ 3. $\frac{5}{6}$

4. $\frac{30}{60}$ 5. $\frac{12}{12}$ 6. $\frac{45}{15}$

Set C pages 382–383

Mixing 2 tablespoons of cocoa with 8 ounces of milk is the same as mixing 6 tablespoons with 24 ounces. Set up a proportion that describes this.

Tablespoons → $\frac{2}{8} = \frac{6}{24}$
Ounces →

Remember to write corresponding terms in a proportion in the same order.

Set up a proportion that describes each situation.

1. Six bulbs for $1.80 is the same price as two bulbs for $0.60.

2. Getting 20 miles per gallon is the same as traveling 80 miles on 4 gallons.

Set D pages 384–387

Solve this proportion.

$\frac{3}{7} = \frac{27}{n}$

$\frac{3}{7} = \frac{27}{n}$ Use cross-products.

$3 \times n = 7 \times 27$ Divide both sides
$3 \times n = 189$ of the equation
$n = 63$ by 3.

Remember to check the answer by substituting the answer for n in the proportion.

Solve each proportion. Then check.

1. $\frac{3}{5} = \frac{n}{60}$ 2. $\frac{d}{16} = \frac{12}{48}$ 3. $\frac{a}{15} = \frac{2}{3}$

4. $\frac{n}{25} = \frac{300}{75}$ 5. $\frac{n}{40} = \frac{9}{10}$ 6. $\frac{b}{20} = \frac{25}{2}$

Set E pages 392–395

The triangles are similar. Find the length of $\overline{FD}$.

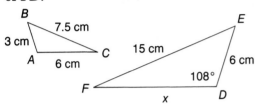

Corresponding sides:

$\frac{AB}{DE} = \frac{3}{6} = \frac{1}{2}, \frac{BC}{EF} = \frac{7.5}{15} = \frac{1}{2}, \frac{AC}{DF} = \frac{6}{x}$

Proportion: $\frac{1}{2} = \frac{6}{x}$

$x = 12$

The length of $\overline{FD}$ is 12 cm.

Remember that in similar figures the corresponding sides are proportional.

1. These triangles are similar. List the pairs of corresponding sides.

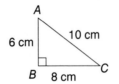

2. These rectangles are similar. Find the value of x.

Set F pages 398–399

Write the ratio $\frac{2}{25}$ as a percent.

Use proportions:
$4 \times 25 = 100$, so
$x = 4 \times 2$ or 8.

$\frac{2}{25} = \frac{x}{100}$

$\frac{2}{25} = \frac{8}{100} = 8\%$

Use division:
Divide 2 by 25.

$$\begin{array}{r} 0.08 = 8\% \\ 25\overline{)2.00} \\ \underline{2\ 00} \\ 0 \end{array}$$

Remember that percent means "hundredths."

Write each ratio as a percent.

1. $\frac{34}{100}$ 2. $\frac{7}{10}$ 3. $\frac{2}{5}$ 4. $\frac{3}{4}$

5. $\frac{1}{50}$ 6. $\frac{7}{25}$ 7. $\frac{15}{20}$ 8. $\frac{7}{40}$

9. $\frac{19}{20}$ 10. $\frac{39}{50}$ 11. $\frac{11}{25}$ 12. $\frac{43}{200}$

More Practice

Set A   pages 376–377

Use the picture. Write the ratio for

1. circles to squares.

2. squares to circles.

3. circles to all the figures shown.

4. squares to all the figures shown.

	1988	1989	1990
Won	12	11	20
Lost	10	11	2

The record for the Hawks baseball team is given at the right. What is the ratio of

5. wins to losses in 1988?

6. losses to wins in 1989?

7. wins to losses in 1990?

8. total wins to total losses?

Set B   pages 378–381

Make a diagram for each ratio.

1. 4 people per square mile

2. 3 banners for $6.00

Find three ratios that are equal to the given ratio. In Exercises 3–5, use multiplication. In Exercises 6–8, use division.

3. $\frac{1}{4}$

4. $\frac{6}{5}$

5. $\frac{5}{6}$

6. $\frac{24}{32}$

7. $\frac{12}{12}$

8. $\frac{80}{20}$

Copy and complete the table to show equal ratios.

9.

Miles	54	108	162	216		324
Gallons	2	4	6		10	

Set C   pages 382–383

Mental Math   Tell whether each pair of ratios forms a proportion.

1. $\frac{1}{3}, \frac{10}{30}$

2. $\frac{8}{4}, \frac{12}{8}$

3. $\frac{5}{13}, \frac{10}{26}$

4. $\frac{17}{34}, \frac{1}{3}$

5. $\frac{9}{10}, \frac{8}{9}$

6. $\frac{5}{6}, \frac{20}{24}$

7. $\frac{7}{12}, \frac{12}{17}$

Set up a proportion that describes the situation.

8. Eight apples for $2.00 is the same as two apples for $0.50.

9. Traveling 44 feet per second means going 352 feet in 8 seconds.

Set D   pages 384–387

Solve each proportion.

1. $\frac{7}{10} = \frac{a}{50}$ **2.** $\frac{d}{15} = \frac{30}{18}$ **3.** $\frac{17}{100} = \frac{n}{25}$ **4.** $\frac{n}{40} = \frac{3}{10}$ **5.** $\frac{4}{16} = \frac{6}{x}$

⊞ Calculator   Solve each proportion by using cross-products. Check your answers.

6. $\frac{5}{16} = \frac{h}{24}$ **7.** $\frac{15}{24} = \frac{3}{x}$ **8.** $\frac{7}{5} = \frac{56}{n}$ **9.** $\frac{16}{k} = \frac{40}{15}$ **10.** $\frac{a}{20} = \frac{16}{50}$

Mixed Practice   For Exercises 11–15, tell whether you would use paper and pencil, a calculator, or mental math to solve the proportion. Then solve.

11. $\frac{n}{42} = \frac{8}{21}$ **12.** $\frac{b}{49} = \frac{1}{14}$ **13.** $\frac{3}{10} = \frac{d}{14}$ **14.** $\frac{9}{28} = \frac{s}{42}$ **15.** $\frac{5}{7} = \frac{10}{c}$

Set E   pages 392–395

Are the pairs of figures similar? If so, list three equal ratios to show how the sides correspond.

1.   **2.**

For each pair of similar figures below, tell whether you would use paper and pencil, a calculator, or mental math to find x. Then solve for x.

3. 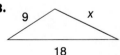   **4.**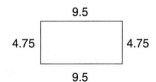

Set F   pages 398–399

Write each percent as a ratio.

1. 12%   **2.** 28%   **3.** 98%   **4.** 55%   **5.** 46%   **6.** 2%

Write each ratio as a percent.

7. $\frac{44}{100}$ **8.** $\frac{1}{25}$ **9.** $\frac{2}{10}$ **10.** $\frac{23}{50}$ **11.** $\frac{3}{5}$ **12.** $\frac{1}{4}$

Enrichment

Conversion Factors

The fractions $\frac{3}{3}$, $\frac{17}{17}$, and $\frac{100}{100}$ are all equal to 1 because the numerator and denominator are equal.
In a similar way, each ratio below is equal to 1.

$\frac{1 \text{ ft}}{12 \text{ in.}}$	$\frac{12 \text{ in.}}{1 \text{ ft}}$	$\frac{60 \text{ sec}}{1 \text{ min}}$	$\frac{1 \text{ min}}{60 \text{ sec}}$	$\frac{1 \text{ day}}{24 \text{ h}}$	$\frac{1 \text{ h}}{60 \text{ min}}$	$\frac{5{,}280 \text{ ft}}{1 \text{ mi}}$

Ratios such as these are called **conversion factors**. Conversion factors are used to convert one unit of measurement to a related unit of measurement.

An athlete runs 3 miles in 1 hour. How many feet does the athlete travel in an hour? You want to change miles per hour to feet per hour. Use a conversion factor with feet in the numerator.

Write the distance run in an hour as a ratio. ⟶ ⟵ Multiply by the conversion factor.

$$\frac{3 \text{ mi}}{1 \text{ hr}} \times \frac{5{,}280 \text{ ft}}{1 \text{ mi}} = \frac{3 \text{ mi} \times 5{,}280 \text{ ft}}{1 \text{ hr} \times 1 \text{ mi}}$$

Divide the units that are similar in both terms.

$$\frac{3 \text{ mi} \times 5{,}280 \text{ ft}}{1 \text{ hr} \times 1 \text{ mi}} = \frac{3 \times 5{,}280 \text{ ft}}{1 \text{ hr}} = \frac{15{,}840 \text{ ft}}{1 \text{ hr}}$$

Complete the following.

1. $\dfrac{480 \text{ mi}}{1 \text{ h}} \times \dfrac{1 \text{ h}}{\text{▦}} = \dfrac{\text{▦}}{1 \text{ min}}$
2. $\dfrac{72 \text{ ft}}{1 \text{ sec}} \times \dfrac{\text{▦}}{1 \text{ min}} = \dfrac{\text{▦}}{1 \text{ min}}$

Choose a conversion factor from the list at the top of the page and convert each rate as indicated.

3. $\dfrac{20 \text{ mi}}{1 \text{ h}} = \dfrac{\text{▦ ft}}{1 \text{ h}}$
4. $\dfrac{10{,}560 \text{ ft}}{1 \text{ h}} = \dfrac{\text{▦ ft}}{1 \text{ min}}$
5. $\dfrac{120 \text{ ft}}{1 \text{ sec}} = \dfrac{\text{▦ ft}}{1 \text{ min}}$

Solve the following problems by using the appropriate conversion factor.

6. A migrating bird flew at a rate of 10 miles per hour. How many feet per hour did it fly?

7. A horse and carriage traveled 528 feet in a minute. How many feet do they travel in an hour? How many miles in an hour?

Chapter 11 Review/Test

1. In 7 games, the Fliers won 3 games and lost 4 games. Write the ratio of wins to games played.

2. Complete the list of equal ratios.

   $\frac{7}{9} = \frac{14}{\text{▦}} = \frac{\text{▦}}{27} = \frac{28}{\text{▦}}$

3. Write a proportion for this situation. If one watch costs $35, it will cost $245 to buy 7 watches.

For each proportion, show that the cross-products are equal.

4. $\frac{5}{8} = \frac{25}{40}$ 5. $\frac{9}{12} = \frac{15}{20}$

Do the ratios form a proportion? Write *yes* or *no*.

6. $\frac{12}{18}$ $\frac{14}{20}$ 7. $\frac{9}{21}$ $\frac{12}{28}$

Use cross-products to find *n*.

8. $\frac{8}{12} = \frac{n}{15}$ 9. $\frac{36}{40} = \frac{18}{n}$

10. For these similar figures find *n*.

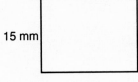

15 mm   20 mm   16 mm   *n*

Write an equation. Then solve it.

11. If a 3-pack of cassette tapes costs $5, how much will 12 tapes cost?

Write each ratio as a percent.

12. $\frac{3}{4}$ 13. $\frac{7}{25}$ 14. $\frac{2}{3}$

Read the problem below. Then answer the question.

In a survey 50 people were asked to name their favorite fruit juice. Pineapple juice was named by 16 people. What percent preferred pineapple juice?

15. What key idea can you use to solve the problem?

    a. The number of people who did not prefer pineapple juice is not stated.
    b. A ratio can be written as a percent.
    c. The number of people surveyed is not part of the ratio.

16. If 1 inch represents 30 miles on a scale drawing, then how many inches represents 150 miles?

Read the problem below. Then answer the question.

A sleeping bag is on sale for $40. The regular price was $50. What is the percent of discount?

17. Which number sentence would you use to solve the problem?

    a. $10 is 20% of $50.
    b. $50 + $40 = $90
    c. 40% of $50 is $20.
    d. $50 × 2 = $100

18. **Write About Math**   How can cross-products be used to find out if two ratios are equal?

1. Diagram

Tennis Court

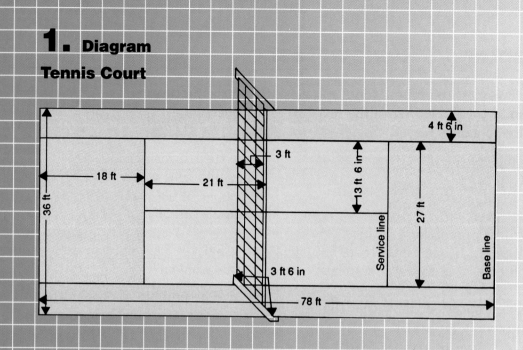

18 ft

21 ft

3 ft

4 ft 6 in

13 ft 6 in

Service line

27 ft

Base line

36 ft

3 ft 6 in

78 ft

2. Recipe

1. Diagram: Notice that the inner sidelines are used for singles play and the outer sidelines for doubles play.

2. Recipe: This Citrus Fruit Juice is all-natural.

3. Bar Graph: The bar graph shows that the Missouri-Mississippi River is the second longest river in the world.

4. Table: This conversion table is helpful when buying ingredients for recipes and for choosing pans of the appropriate size.

Citrus Fruit Juice

1 cup crushed ice

$\frac{1}{2}$ cup grapefruit juice

$\frac{5}{8}$ cup orange juice

$\frac{1}{4}$ cup lemon juice

Makes 4 servings.

3. Bar Graph

Seven Longest Rivers in the World

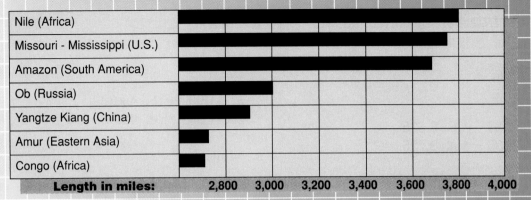

	Length in miles:	2,800	3,000	3,200	3,400	3,600	3,800	4,000
Nile (Africa)								
Missouri - Mississippi (U.S.)								
Amazon (South America)								
Ob (Russia)								
Yangtze Kiang (China)								
Amur (Eastern Asia)								
Congo (Africa)								

4. Table

Approximate Measurement Conversions for Cooking

Customary to Metric		Metric to Customary	
1 teaspoon	5 milliliters	1 milliliter	$\frac{1}{5}$ teaspoon
1 tablespoon	15 milliliters	1 liter	34 fluid ounces, or
1 fluid ounce	30 milliliters		4 cups + 3 tablespoons, or
1 cup	240 milliliters		2 pints + 3 tablespoons, or
1 pint	0.47 liter		1 quart + 3 tablespoons
1 quart	0.95 liter		

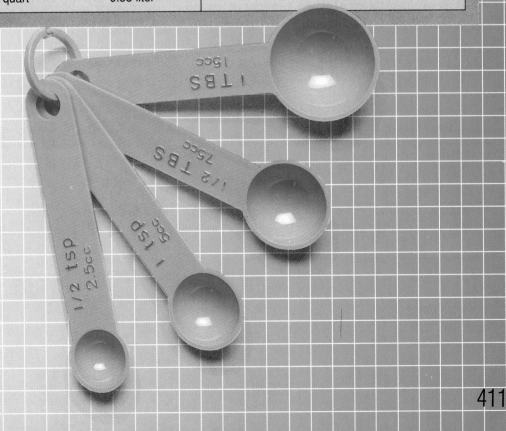

Cumulative Review/Test Chapters 1–11

Give the letter for the correct answer.

1. Add.

```
  7,486
+ 1,249
```

   a. 8,735   **b.** 8,625
   c. 8,635   **d.** 8,725

2. Multiply.

```
  4,962
×    45
```

   a. 222,280   **b.** 44,658
   c. 223,290   **d.** 189,310

3. Divide.

$72\overline{)37,945}$

   a. 527 R1   **b.** 624 R17
   c. 520 R55   **d.** 527 R11

4. What is six tenths written as a decimal?

   a. 10.6   **b.** 0.610
   c. 0.06   **d.** 0.6

5. Which numbers are written in order from least to greatest?

   a. 8.108   8.801   8.081
   b. 8.081   8.108   8.801
   c. 8.801   8.108   8.081
   d. 8.801   8.081   8.108

6. Add.

```
  3.16
+ 4.88
```

   a. 7.94   **b.** 8.04
   c. 7.04   **d.** 8.94

7. Subtract.

```
  42.17
−  1.29
```

   a. 41.98   **b.** 40.88
   c. 41.89   **d.** 40.98

8. Multiply.

```
  0.06
× 0.4
```

   a. 0.024   **b.** 0.24
   c. 0.0024   **d.** 2.4

9. Divide.

$0.21\overline{)6.3}$

   a. 3.0   **b.** 0.03
   c. 0.30   **d.** 30

10. Choose the equation that should be used to solve the problem. Then solve the problem.

A cap costs $8.50 plus 6% for sales tax. Find the amount of the tax.

   a. $8.50 − 0.06 = n;$ $7.90
   b. $8.50 + 0.06 = n;$ $8.56
   c. $8.50 − 0.06 = n;$ $8.54
   d. $8.50 × 0.06 = n;$ $0.51

11. What is $\frac{6}{18}$ in lowest terms?

   a. $\frac{1}{6}$ **b.** $\frac{2}{3}$
   c. $\frac{1}{3}$ **d.** $\frac{5}{6}$

12. What is the least common denominator of $\frac{1}{3}$ and $\frac{2}{5}$?

   a. 3   **b.** 15
   c. 5   **d.** 30

13. Which statement is true?

a. $\frac{3}{10} < \frac{3}{13}$ **b.** $\frac{3}{10} > \frac{7}{20}$

c. $\frac{3}{10} > \frac{2}{5}$ **d.** $\frac{3}{10} < \frac{3}{5}$

14. Add.

$$1\frac{3}{4}$$
$$+ \quad \frac{5}{8}$$

a. $2\frac{5}{8}$ **b.** $2\frac{3}{8}$

c. 2 **d.** $3\frac{3}{8}$

15. Subtract.

$$7\frac{1}{3}$$
$$- 2\frac{5}{9}$$

a. $5\frac{7}{9}$ **b.** $5\frac{2}{9}$

c. $4\frac{7}{9}$ **d.** $4\frac{2}{3}$

16. Multiply.

$$2\frac{1}{3} \times \frac{6}{7}$$

a. $2\frac{2}{7}$ **b.** $2\frac{7}{18}$

c. 2 **d.** $2\frac{7}{10}$

17. Divide.

$$2 \div \frac{3}{8}$$

a. $5\frac{1}{3}$ **b.** $1\frac{5}{8}$

c. $\frac{3}{4}$ **d.** 6

18. Choose the most sensible measure for the volume of a kitchen cabinet.

a. 6 sq ft **b.** 6 ft
c. 6 sq in. **d.** 6 cu ft

19. What is the circumference of this circle?

18 ft

a. About 28 ft
b. About 127 ft
c. About 254 ft
d. About 56 ft

20. What is the area of the circle?

a. About 127 sq ft
b. About 56 sq ft
c. About 28 sq ft
d. About 254 sq ft

21. Solve this proportion.

$$\frac{n}{40} = \frac{9}{10}$$

a. $n = 90$
b. $n = 36$
c. $n = 360$
d. $n = 400$

22. Which percent is the same as the ratio $\frac{9}{10}$?

a. 9% **b.** 45%
c. 90% **d.** 99%

Read the problem below. Then answer the question.

If you can hike 8 miles in 3 hours, how far could you hike in 7 hours?

23. Which proportion would you solve to find the answer?

a. $\frac{7}{3} = \frac{8}{n}$ **b.** $\frac{8}{3} = \frac{7}{n}$

c. $\frac{3}{8} = \frac{7}{n}$ **d.** $\frac{3}{8} = \frac{n}{7}$

Relating Percents, Fractions, and Decimals

Did You Know: The Recording Industry Association of America presents gold, platinum, and multi-platinum records to performers who sell 500,000, 1,000,000, and 2,000,000 records respectively. The first gold record awarded for an album went to the musical *Oklahoma* in 1958.

Number-Sense Project

Estimate
If you took a survey of popular songs, which song do you think would be the favorite?

Gather Data
List 5 songs that you think are the most popular. Survey 25 people and have them tell you which of the 5 songs is their favorite.

Analyze and Report
Determine what percent of the people surveyed picked each song. List the songs in order from most popular to least popular. Compare results among your classmates.

Percents and Decimals

Build Understanding

A. Look at the floor plan for the computer lab. The plan shows 100 identical squares. What percent of the total space does the office take up?

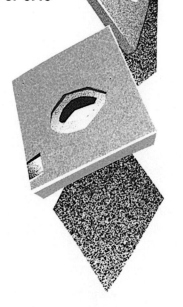

The office takes up 9 out of 100 squares.
9 out of 100 = 9 hundredths = 0.09

0.09 = 9%   Percent means "hundredths." 9 hundredths is 9 percent.

The office takes up 9% of the total space.

B. Write 0.5 as a percent.

0.5 = 5 tenths, or 50 hundredths
0.5 = 50%

C. Write 46% as a decimal.

46% = 46 hundredths, or 0.46
46% = 0.46

D. Write 5% as a decimal.

5% = 5 hundredths, or 0.05
5% = 0.05

■ **Talk About Math** Look at each percent and each group of decimals shown below. What patterns do you see? Do you see the same patterns in Examples A–D?

0%	10%	20%	30%	40%	50%	60%	70%	80%	90%	100%

0.00	0.10	0.20	0.30	0.40	0.50	0.60	0.70	0.80	0.90	1.00
0.0	0.1	0.2	0.3	0.4	0.5	0.6	0.7	0.8	0.9	1.0

Check Understanding

For another example, see Set A, pages 442–443.

1. Is 0.9 the same as 0.9%? as 9%? as 90%?

Write each decimal as a percent.

2. 0.38   **3.** 0.2   **4.** 0.03   **5.** 0.185

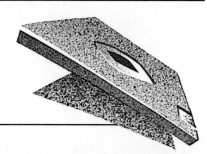

Practice

For More Practice, see Set A, pages 444–445.

Copy each percent bar. Write each decimal as a percent.
Then find the percent of the bar that is shaded.

6. 0% 20% 40% 60% 80% 100%

0.23   0.75

7. 0% 20% 40% 60% 80% 100%

0.09   0.66

What percent of $1 (100 cents) does each group of coins represent?

8. 2 quarters and 7 pennies

9. 4 dimes and 2 nickels

10. A nickel and 3 pennies

11. 3 quarters, a dime, and 4 pennies

Write each percent as a decimal. **Remember** that percent means "hundredths."

12. 2% **13.** 29% **14.** 46% **15.** 67% **16.** 80% **17.** 40%

18. 20% **19.** 9% **20.** 100% **21.** 7% **22.** 4.8% **23.** 0.9%

Write each decimal as a percent.

24. 0.37 **25.** 0.55 **26.** 0.67 **27.** 0.98 **28.** 0.08 **29.** 0.7

30. 0.34 **31.** 0.021 **32.** 0.57 **33.** 0.22 **34.** 0.92 **35.** 0.75

36. 0.06 **37.** 0.5 **38.** 0.09 **39.** 0.3 **40.** 0.375 **41.** 3.75

Problem Solving

The Computer Club has 100 members.

42. If 32% of the members are seventh graders, how many seventh graders is this?

43. If 45 of the members are eighth graders, what percent of the members are eighth graders?

Use the diagram in Example A. What percent of the total lab space is occupied by the

44. closet? **45.** kitchen? **46.** computers and office?

47. On a 100-square grid, draw a floor plan of a basement. Use heavy black lines to show the following sections: 15%–darkroom, 20%–laundry room, 24%–storage closet, the rest–a recreational area.

TIPS FOR PROBLEM SOLVERS

Compare problems to help you relate new problems to ones you've solved before.

Percents and Fractions

Build Understanding

A. Concept Cards
Materials: Graph paper, construction paper
Groups: Small groups of 3 or 4 students

a. Cut 14 ten × ten grids out of the graph paper. Shade an appropriate number of squares to show 1%, 5%, 10%, 20%, 25%, 30%, 40%, 50%, 60%, 70%, 75%, 80%, 90%, 100%. Paste each grid on construction paper. Write the percent below each grid.

b. Cut out 14 more ten × ten grids. Paste a grid on the back of each percent card. On each grid, show a fraction in lowest terms that is equal to the percent. Write the fraction.

c. Use the concept cards as flashcards. Take turns identifying equivalent percents and fractions.

B. One fourth of this grid is red. What percent of the grid is red?

C. Five percent of this grid is green. What fraction is that?

$\frac{1}{4} = \frac{25}{100}$ Since percent means "hundredths," write a fraction equal to $\frac{1}{4}$ with a denominator of 100.

$\frac{25}{100} = 25\%$ Write the numerator with a % sign.

25% of the grid is red.

$5\% = \frac{5}{100}$ Percent means "hundredths."

$\frac{5}{100} = \frac{1}{20}$ Write the fraction in lowest terms.

$\frac{1}{20}$ of the grid is green.

D. Sometimes it is easier to write a fraction as a decimal first and then to write the decimal as a percent. Remember that you can divide to write a fraction as a decimal.

Write $\frac{1}{3}$ as a percent.

$$0.33\frac{1}{3} = 33\frac{1}{3}\%$$

$$\begin{array}{r} 3\overline{)1.00} \\ \underline{9} \\ 10 \\ \underline{9} \\ 1 \end{array}$$

Divide through the hundredths place. Write the remainder as a fraction. Then write the percent.

■ **Talk About Math** Which of these fractions are greater than $33\frac{1}{3}\%$? $\frac{1}{2}, \frac{2}{3}, \frac{1}{4}, \frac{3}{4}$

Check Understanding

For another example, see Set B, pages 442–443.

Tell whether each fraction is the same as $33\frac{1}{3}\%$.

1. **2.** $\frac{5}{15}$ **3.** **4.** $\frac{2}{12}$ **5.** **6.** $\frac{3}{8}$

Practice

For More Practice, see Set B, pages 444–445.

Write each percent as a fraction in lowest terms.
Remember that a fraction is in lowest terms when the GCF of the numerator and the denominator is 1.

7. 13%   **8.** 32%   **9.** 1%   **10.** 85%   **11.** 30%   **12.** 70%   **13.** 52%

Write each fraction as a percent.

14. $\frac{60}{100}$ **15.** $\frac{73}{100}$ **16.** $\frac{3}{100}$ **17.** $\frac{11}{100}$ **18.** $\frac{15}{20}$ **19.** $\frac{7}{25}$ **20.** $\frac{1}{8}$ **21.** $\frac{1}{10}$

22. $\frac{1}{25}$ **23.** $\frac{13}{50}$ **24.** $\frac{2}{5}$ **25.** $\frac{4}{5}$ **26.** $\frac{11}{12}$ **27.** $\frac{5}{6}$ **28.** $\frac{4}{9}$ **29.** $\frac{2}{7}$

Number Sense What percent of the first 20 nonzero whole numbers (1, 2, 3, 4, . . .) are of the given type?

30. Odd   **31.** Prime   **32.** A multiple of 5   **33.** Not a multiple of 2 or 3

Problem Solving

Visual Thinking What percent of the area of the given figure is shaded?

34. **35.** **36.** **37.** **38.** **39.**

40. Critical Thinking Suppose you have 40% of a dollar in your pocket. You have no pennies. List the combinations of coins that could be in your pocket.

A
L
G
E
B
R
A

Percents, Decimals, and Fractions

Build Understanding

Every country has its own currency. Some names for currency, however, are used by more than one country. For example, Spain uses pesetas, while Mexico, the Dominican Republic, Argentina, Bolivia, Colombia, and Chile use pesos.

A. Pedro spent $\frac{3}{5}$ of his pesos to buy a book. What percent of his pesos did he spend?

Use the percent bar below. Indicated along the top edge of the bar are percents from 0% to 100%. Some of the decimal and fraction forms of the percents are indicated below the bar.

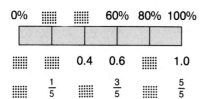

$\frac{3}{5}$ is 0.6,
which is 60%.

Pedro spent 60% of his pesos.

B. Write 80% as a decimal and as a fraction.

$$80\% = 0.80 = 0.8 \qquad 80\% = 0.8 = \frac{8}{10} = \frac{4}{5}$$

One country's pesos have a different value than another country's pesos.

■ **Talk About Math** Suppose a bus ride costs about 1,000 pesos. What is 20% $\left(\frac{1}{5}\right)$ of the cost? What is 60% $\left(\frac{3}{5}\right)$ of the cost?

Check Understanding

For another example, see Set C, pages 442–443.

1. Copy and complete the percent bar in Example A.

2. Write 10% as a fraction.

3. Write 0.15 as a fraction.

4. Write $\frac{3}{10}$ as a decimal and as a percent.

5. Write $\frac{7}{10}$ as a decimal and as a percent.

Practice

For More Practice, see Set C, pages 444–445.

Copy and complete the percent bars.

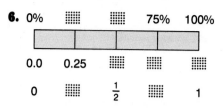

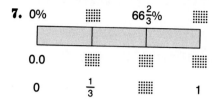

Write each percent as a decimal and as a fraction.
Remember to write fractions in lowest terms.

8. 44%   **9.** 90%   **10.** 8%   **11.** 62%   **12.** 28%   **13.** 77%

Write each fraction as a decimal and as a percent.

14. $\frac{1}{8}$ **15.** $\frac{5}{6}$ **16.** $\frac{3}{5}$ **17.** $\frac{1}{2}$ **18.** $\frac{1}{9}$ **19.** $\frac{7}{11}$

Complete the charts.

Fraction	Decimal	Percent
$\frac{11}{20}$	**20.**	**21.**
22.	0.2	**23.**
24.	**25.**	30%

Fraction	Decimal	Percent
26.	**27.**	99%
$\frac{2}{3}$	**28.**	**29.**
30.	**31.**	44%

Problem Solving

Solve each problem.

32. French currency is called francs. Michele spent $\frac{1}{8}$ of her francs on cards and 0.08 on stamps. Which item cost more?

This 1988 commemorative franc was issued to celebrate the anniversary of the election of Charles de Gaulle as President of France.

33. Rosa spent $\frac{1}{5}$ of her Peruvian soles on a trip, 0.07 on clothes, and 25% on food. Which item cost the most? What percent of her soles does she have left?

34. Tony had 35% of his currency in English pounds, $\frac{1}{3}$ in Italian lire and 0.30 in Indian rupees. Of which currency is the greatest percent of his money?

421

Using a Fraction or a Decimal to Find a Percent of a Number

Build Understanding

A. In 1989, about 66 million families lived in the United States. The circle graph shows the percent of families of different sizes. How many million families had only 2 people?

To answer the question, find 40% of 66.

You could solve a proportion.

$$\frac{40}{100} = \frac{n}{66}$$

You could also solve an equation.
Use a fraction or a decimal for the percent.

What is 40% of 66?

$$
\begin{array}{ccccc}
\downarrow & \downarrow & \downarrow & \downarrow & \downarrow \\
n & = & 0.40 & \times & 66 \\
n & = & 26.4 & &
\end{array}
$$

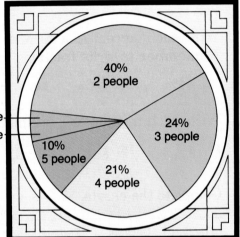

People who live alone (families of 1) were not included in the given statistics.

(Circle graph labels: 40% 2 people; 24% 3 people; 21% 4 people; 10% 5 people; 3% 6 people; 2% 7 or more people)

40% of 66 is 26.4. In 1989, 26.4 million U.S. families had only 2 people.

For some percents, it is easier to work with a fraction instead of a decimal. The information in this table may be helpful in solving percent problems.

Percent	10%	20%	25%	$33\frac{1}{3}\%$	50%	$66\frac{2}{3}\%$	75%
Fraction	$\frac{1}{10}$	$\frac{1}{5}$	$\frac{1}{4}$	$\frac{1}{3}$	$\frac{1}{2}$	$\frac{2}{3}$	$\frac{3}{4}$
Decimal	0.1	0.2	0.25	$0.33\frac{1}{3}$	0.5	$0.66\frac{2}{3}$	0.75

B. What is $33\frac{1}{3}\%$ of 51?

$$n = \frac{1}{3} \times 51$$

Remember that $\frac{1}{3} \times 51$ means $51 \div 3$.

$$n = 17$$

17 is $33\frac{1}{3}\%$ of 51.

c.  **Calculator** Find 15% of 60 with this key sequence:

60 ⌧× 15 ⌧% *9*.

Here is another possible key sequence:

⌧. 15 ⌧× 60 ⌧= *9*.

■ **Talk About Math** Explain why it is easier to use a fraction rather than a decimal in Example B.

Check Understanding

For another example, see Set D, pages 442–443.

1. In 1989, how many U.S. families had 3 people? Use the information from the circle graph in Example A.

Solve each exercise. In each case, first decide if it is easier to use a decimal or a fraction.

2. 25% of 600 = $\frac{1}{4} \times$ ▦ = ▦

3. 27% of 600 = 0.27 × ▦ = ▦

4. $33\frac{1}{3}\%$ of 600 = ▦ × ▦ = ▦

5. 75% of 600 = ▦ × ▦ = ▦

6. 50% of 600 = ▦

7. 40% of 600 = ▦

8. 45% of 600 = ▦

9. 66% of 600 = ▦

10. $66\frac{2}{3}\%$ of 600 = ▦

11. 85% of 600 = ▦

12. Find 50% of 826. First, use a decimal for the percent. Then use a fraction. Which way was easier for you?

Number Sense Pick three numbers to use for Exercises 13 and 14.

13. Find 100% of each number.

14. Find 0% of each number.

15. Write a statement for finding 100% of any number and a statement for finding 0% of any number.

Practice

For More Practice, see Set D, pages 444–445.

Find each answer.

16. 50% of 62   **17.** 25% of 84   **18.** 40% of 180   **19.** 60% of 120

20. $33\frac{1}{3}$% of 123   **21.** 75% of 4,800   **22.** 0% of 220   **23.** 8% of 3,500

24. 100% of 6   **25.** 20% of 4,000   **26.** 40% of 480   **27.** 9% of 1,200

28. 45% of 180   **29.** 85% of 1,600   **30.** 22% of 96   **31.** 4% of 1,860

32. 38% of 30   **33.** 19% of 50   **34.** 8% of 750   **35.** 3% of 625

36. 68% of 250 is what number?   **37.** 6% of 848 is what number?

38. 25% of 680 is what number?   **39.** 84.8% of 60 is what number?

Calculator   Find each answer.

40. 14.5% of 978   **41.** 87.5% of 2,052   **42.** 450% of 1,626

43. 67.9% of 371 is what number?   **44.** 93.45% of 3,343 is what number?

For Exercises 45–62, tell whether you would use paper
and pencil, mental math, or a calculator. Then solve.

45. 19% of 500 is what number   **46.** 6% of 340 is what number?

47. 5% of 1,900 is what number?   **48.** 3.4% of 600 is what number?

49. What is 50% of 84?   **50.** 27% of 285 is what number?

51. 17% of 321 is what number?   **52.** What is 20% of 75?

53. What is 70% of 45?   **54.** Find $12\frac{1}{2}$% of 48.

55. Find $66\frac{2}{3}$% of 15.   **56.** What is 55% of 60?

57. 10% of 450 is what number?   **58.** $33\frac{1}{3}$% of 9 is what number?

59. What is 53% of 263?   **60.** Find 100% of 117.

61. 37.5% of 104 is what number?   **62.** What is 3.5% of 650?

Problem Solving

Use the circle graph in Example A to find the
number of families with the given number of people.

63. 5   **64.** 4   **65.** 3   **66.** 2 or 3   **67.** fewer than 5

68. How many families had 3 or more people?

69. How many more families had 2 people than had
5 people?

70. What percent of families had fewer than
7 people?

Critical Thinking   Use paper and pencil or a calculator
to find each pair of answers.

71. 37% of 91   **72.** 28% of 25   **73.** 65% of 10   **74.** 78% of 50
    91% of 37   25% of 28   10% of 65   50% of 78

75. What pattern do you notice in
Exercises 71–74? Make up two sets
of similar problems. Does the
pattern work for each set?

76. How can following the pattern you
found in Exercise 75 help you solve
problems such as 36% of 25, 89%
of 10, and 16% of 50?

Midchapter ✓ Checkup

Write each percent as a decimal and as a fraction in
lowest terms.

1. 10%   **2.** 85%   **3.** 7%   **4.** 50%   **5.** 40%   **6.** 15%   **7.** 6%

At a day camp, 34.5% of the 400 campers were 6 years old
and $\frac{3}{8}$ of the campers were 7 years old. Solve each problem.

8. How many campers were
6 years old?

9. Were more campers age 6 or
age 7?

Find each answer.

10. 37% of 200   **11.** 25% of 360   **12.** $66\frac{2}{3}$% of 930   **13.** 100% of 60

Problem Solving WORKSHOP

Real-Life Decision Making

Suppose you are having a garage sale and want to advertise it in the Daily Chronicle and in the weekly Buyer's Flier.

Buyer's Weekly Flier
Published Each Wednesday
Advertising Rates:
30¢/Word
(10 Word Minimum)

DAILY CHRONICLE
ADVERTISING RATES:
(3 line minimum)

3 lines for 3 days - $8.50
Add $3.25 for each additional line
Add $2.00 for each additional day
Add $.80 extra for Sunday paper

Use this form to write your ad. There are 23 spaces per line. Each letter, number, punctuation mark, and space in your ad counts as one space.

	1	2	3	4	5	6	7	8	9	10	11	12	13	14	15	16	17	18	19	20	21	22	23
1 line																							
2 lines																							
3 lines																							
4 lines																							
5 lines																							
6 lines																							

GARAGE SALE

SATURDAY   8:00 AM TO   4:00 PM

CLOTHES, TOYS, RECORDS, 3-SPEED BICYCLE,
BOOKS, TOOLS, MISCELLANEOUS ITEMS

1263 EAST LINCOLN ROAD

Here is the ad you have written:

a. How many words are in the ad? What will it cost to run the ad in the Buyer's Flier?

b. How many lines are in the ad? What will it cost to run the ad in the newspaper for three days?

c. Decide where and for how long you would run the ad. Explain your decision.

d. How could you possibly reduce your costs of advertising?

Math-at-Home Activity

Play a game of "Fraction-Decimal-Percent Matchup" with someone in your family.

Use 30 index cards to make a set of cards like those shown here. Shuffle the cards and put them face down on a desk or table.

The first player turns over any 2 cards. If they match, the player keeps the cards and takes another turn. If they do not match, the cards are returned face down. Players take turns until all of the cards have been taken. The winner is the person with the most cards.

$\frac{6}{10}$	$\frac{2}{5}$	0.75	$\frac{4}{10}$	0.2
$\frac{1}{2}$	$\frac{1}{4}$	65%	$\frac{1}{3}$	$\frac{2}{3}$
50%	25%	$\frac{3}{4}$	$33\frac{1}{3}\%$	$66\frac{2}{3}\%$
$\frac{1}{5}$	$\frac{3}{3}$	$\frac{3}{5}$	$\frac{4}{5}$	1
20%	40%	0.6	1.0	100%
0.65	0.4	60%	80%	$\frac{2}{10}$

Number-Sense Project

Look back at pages 414-415.

1. About 2,000 tickets have been sold for a local performance of *Oklahoma*. If the play starts at 8:00 P.M, what percent of the people would you expect to have arrived by each of the following times?

a. 6:00 P.M.

b. 7:00 P.M.

c. 7:15 P.M.

d. 7:30 P.M.

e. 7:45 P.M.

f. 8:00 P.M.

2. Discuss your answers with other members of your class. As a group, decide on the percent of the people that would arrive at each time. Use these percents to estimate the number of people that would have arrived.

a. 6:00 P.M.   **b.** 7:00 P.M.

c. 7:15 P.M.   **d.** 7:30 P.M.

e. 7:45 P.M.   **f .** 8:00 P.M.

Mental Math: Percents

Build Understanding

A. About 40% of your body is muscle. If you weighed 120 pounds, how many pounds of muscle would you have?

10%   40%   100%

0 12   48   120

**Think: 10% of 120 = 12,
so 40% of 120 = 4 × 10% of 120.
4 × 12 = 48**

You would have 48 pounds of muscle.

B. What is 60% of 200?

**Think: 10% of 200 = 20,
so 60% of 200 = 6 × 20 = 120.
Or think: 60% of 100 = 60,
so 60% of 200 = 2 × 60 = 120.**

Many people exercise in order to increase the ratio of muscle to fat in their bodies.

■ **Talk About Math** Describe two ways in which you can mentally compute 20% of a number.

Check Understanding

For another example, see Set E, pages 442–443.

1. How do you know that 10% of 200 = 20?

Use mental math to find each percent of 400.

2. 50%   **3.** 25%   **4.** 10%   **5.** 5%   **6.** 1%   **7.** 20%   **8.** 75%

Describe how you can use your answers to Exercises 2–8 to solve each problem mentally. Then give each answer.

9. 6% of 400   **10.** 9% of 400   **11.** 26% of 400   **12.** 51% of 400

Practice

For More Practice, see Set E, pages 444–445.

Use mental math to find each answer.

13. 50% of 300   **14.** 75% of 800   **15.** $33\frac{1}{3}$% of 60   **16.** 10% of 570

17. 75% of 200   **18.** 25% of 200   **19.** 20% of 250   **20.** $66\frac{2}{3}$% of 300

21. 50% of 700   **22.** 10% of 900   **23.** $33\frac{1}{3}$% of 150   **24.** 25% of 840

Find each answer. Try to solve at least one exercise of each pair mentally.

25. 50% of 48; 48% of 48

26. 36% of 48; 25% of 48

27. $33\frac{1}{3}$% of 48; 42% of 48

28. 12% of 48; 10% of 48

29. 20% of 250; $33\frac{1}{3}$% of 250

30. 25% of 333; $66\frac{2}{3}$% of 333

31. 40% of 444; 25% of 444

32. $33\frac{1}{3}$% of 750; 75% of 750

33. 110% of 100; 150% of 100

34. 140% of 250; 125% of 250

Problem Solving

About 20% of a man's body weight is fat. Use this fact and the information in Example A to answer the following questions.

35. Ralph weighs 100 pounds. About how many pounds of muscle does he have?

36. Mr. Oliva weighs 150 pounds. About how many pounds of fat does he have?

37. About what percent of a man's body is either fat or muscle?

38. Mr. Saunders weighs 180 pounds. About how many more pounds of muscle does he have than fat?

Skills _____ Review   pages 276–281

Multiply.

1. $\frac{5}{6} \times \frac{1}{4}$ **2.** $8 \times 5\frac{5}{6}$ **3.** $7\frac{1}{2} \times 4\frac{2}{3}$ **4.** $2\frac{1}{12} \times 4\frac{4}{5}$

5. $5\frac{5}{9} \times 5\frac{1}{4}$ **6.** $6\frac{1}{4} \times 6\frac{4}{5}$ **7.** $7\frac{1}{3} \times \frac{7}{10} \times 2\frac{1}{2}$ **8.** $6 \times 8\frac{1}{3}$

Estimating with Percents

Build Understanding

A. In 1990, 52.8% of the 91,947,000 households in the United States had cable television. About how many households was this?

To estimate the number of households with cable TV, round the percent and the total number of households and compute mentally.

Think: 52.8% is close to 50%.
91,947,000 is about 90 million.
Find 50% of 90 million.

U.S. Households
Having Cable TV in 1990

52.8%

Method 1
50% of $90 = \frac{1}{2} \times 90$
$= 45$

Method 2
10% of $90 = 9$
50% of $90 = 5 \times 9 = 45$

About 45 million households had cable TV in 1990.

B. Estimate 27% of 600.

Use compatible numbers this time.

27% is close to 25%. $25\% = \frac{1}{4}$
$\frac{1}{4}$ **of 600 = 600 ÷ 4 = 150**
27% of 600 ≈ 150

Since 25% is less than 27%, the estimate is less than the exact answer.

■ **Talk About Math**   In Example A, can you tell if the estimate is greater than or less than the exact answer? Why or why not?

Check Understanding

For another example, see Set F, pages 442–443.

Number Sense   Choose the most sensible answer.

1. 47% of 250
   a. 118   **b.** 12   **c.** 200

2. 89% of 475
   a. 48   **b.** 423   **c.** 225

3. René paid 15% down on a $95 radio. About how much money was this?
   a. $50   **b.** $15   **c.** $1.50   **d.** $75

Practice

For More Practice, see Set F, pages 444–445.

Estimate. Tell if your estimate is greater or less than the exact answer.

4. 49% of 800   **5.** 34% of 900   **6.** 19% of 800   **7.** 74% of 800

8. 50% of 795   **9.** $66\frac{2}{3}$% of 907   **10.** 20% of 397   **11.** 60% of 2,008

12. 24% of 400   **13.** 40% of 703   **14.** 75% of 3,945   **15.** 59% of 60

16. 19% of 19   **17.** 80% of 211   **18.** 51% of 90   **19.** 5% of 20,188

20. 78% of 987   **21.** 41% of 1,500   **22.** 52% of 1,023   **23.** 28% of 49

Number Sense   Choose the most sensible answer.

24. 73% of 635
   a. 72   **b.** 464   **c.** 762

25. 56% of 224
   a. 125   **b.** 34   **c.** 207

26. 7% of 278
   a. 19   **b.** 52   **c.** 194

27. 29% of 1,532
   a. 64   **b.** 941   **c.** 444

28. 62% of 444
   a. 275   **b.** 24   **c.** 2,728

29. 8% of 5,677
   a. 48   **b.** 454   **c.** 4,500

Problem Solving

Critical Thinking   Suppose you know what 10% of a number is. Explain how you would find

30. 15% of the number.   **31.** 40% of the number.   **32.** 95% of the number.

Choose a _____ Strategy

Thumbs Down

33. A rule of thumb in the publishing business: "If you increase your subscription price by 10%, you lose 10% of your subscribers." Experiment with various values for the price and the number of subscribers. Determine if you gain or lose money in this situation.

431

Multiple-Step Problems

Build Understanding

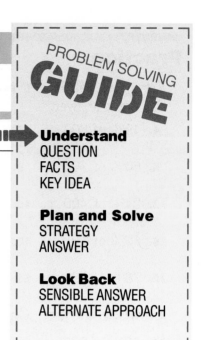

10-SPEED BICYCLES	**NOW**
Regular price $145.99	**15% off**

What is the sale price of the 10-speed bicycle?

▶ **Understand** QUESTION   What is the price after the discount?

FACTS   According to the ad, the regular price is $145.99 and the discount is 15% of that price.

KEY IDEA   The discount is 15% of $145.99. The sale price is the regular price minus the discount.

Plan and Solve Find the discount. Round to the nearest cent.

What is 15% of $145.99?
$$\downarrow \quad \downarrow \quad \downarrow \quad \downarrow \quad \quad \downarrow$$
$$n \ = 0.15 \ \times \ 145.99$$
$$n \ \approx 21.90$$

The discount is $21.90.

Subtract to find the sale price.
$145.99 - 21.90 = 124.09$

The sale price is $124.09.

Look Back ALTERNATE APPROACH   The bicycle will cost 85% of the regular price.

85% of $145.99 = $124.09

■ **Write About Math** Write a problem about the sale price of tennis shoes that usually cost $34.00.

Spring Sale at
SUPER SPORTS SHOPS

Tennis shoes regular $34.00   NOW 25% off

Baseball gloves: 20% off

Baseball bats: 20% off

Basketball backboard: 25% off

Skis and ski equipment: 50% off

All athletic shoes: 25% off

All sports bags: $33\frac{1}{3}$% off

10-speed bicycles: 15% off

Golf clubs: 15% off

Check Understanding

1. At a discount store, the sale price of the bicycle on page 432 is $114 plus 5% for assembling. Compare the prices, before sales tax, at the two stores.

2. What is the cost of the discounted bicycle on page 432 including 8% sales tax?

Practice

Use data from the ad on page 432. Find each sale price.

3. Baseball glove
   Regular: $47

4. Golf clubs
   Regular: $195

5. Backboard
   Regular: $105

6. Tennis bag
   Regular: $22.95

7. Running shoes
   Regular: $35.50

8. Baseball bat
   Regular: $14.88

Find the total price including the sales tax.

9. Baseball
   $14 plus 5% tax

10. Bicycle
    $129.95 plus 4% tax

11. Golf set
    $350.88 plus 7% tax

Answer each question.

12. **Calculator** Find 80% of $47. Compare this amount with the sale price of the baseball glove in Exercise 3.

13. If you know the regular price of an item and the percent of the discount, how can you find the sale price in one step?

Reading _____ Math

Vocabulary For each sentence, write *true* or *false* on your paper. If the statement is false, make it true.

1. To find the sale price, subtract the regular price from the discount.

2. A 5% sales tax adds five cents for every dollar to the cost of an item.

3. If you buy shoes at 25% off, you pay 25% of the regular price.

Finding What Percent One Number Is of Another

Build Understanding

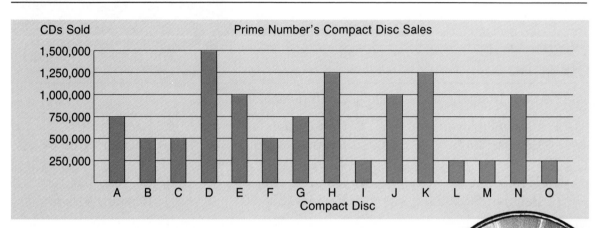

CDs Sold   Prime Number's Compact Disc Sales

Compact Disc

A. What percent of Prime Number's compact discs have sold at least a million copies?

From the graph you can see that 6 compact discs have sold at least 1 million copies. Since the total number of compact discs is 15, you need to find what percent 6 is of 15.

You have used proportions to solve problems like this one.

$$\frac{6}{15} = \frac{r}{100}$$

Another method is to write and solve an equation. Find the decimal value of r. Then write it as a percent.

What percent of 15 is 6?

$$\downarrow \quad \downarrow \quad \downarrow \quad \downarrow \quad \downarrow$$

$r \times 15 = 6$	Write the equation.
$\dfrac{r \times 15}{15} = \dfrac{6}{15}$	Divide both sides of the equation by 15.
$r = \dfrac{6}{15}$	Remember that $\frac{6}{15}$ is the same as $6 \div 15$.
$r = 0.4$	Write the decimal as a percent.
$r = 40\%$	

40% of 15 is 6.

40% of the compact discs have sold at least a million copies.

434

Estimation To see if your answer is reasonable, make a percent bar for 15. Choose a factor of 15, such as 5, and write the corresponding percents.

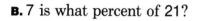

0%   33⅓%   66⅔%   100%

0   5   10   15

Since 6 is a little more than 5, the answer should be a little more than 33⅓%.

B. 7 is what percent of 21?

$$7 = s \times 21$$

$\dfrac{7}{21} = \dfrac{s \times 21}{21}$ Divide both sides by 21.

$\dfrac{7}{21} = s$ Remember that $\dfrac{7}{21}$ is the same as $7 \div 21$.

$\dfrac{1}{3} = s$ Write $\dfrac{7}{21}$ in lowest terms.

$\dfrac{1}{3} = 33\dfrac{1}{3}\%$ Write the fraction as a percent.

7 is 33⅓% of 21.

Estimation Check your answer. This percent bar shows that 7 is one third of 21. The computed answer should be 33⅓%.

0%   33⅓%   66⅔%   100%

0   7   14   21

■ **Talk About Math** Look at the graph in Example A. How many compact discs have sold 500,000 copies or more? Is this number greater or less than 40% of the compact discs? How can you tell without computing?

Check Understanding

For another example, See Set G, pages 442–443.

1. In Example A, $r = 0.4$. Why isn't the answer 0.4%?

2. Estimation Mark a percent bar to help you estimate what percent 8 is of 36.

3. 15 is what percent of 75?

4. What percent of 80 is 12?

5. Which of the Exercises 6–13 will have answers greater than 50%?

Practice

For More Practice, see Set G, pages 444–445.

Find each answer. **Remember** to express your answer as a percent.

6. What percent of 400 is 10?

7. What percent of 96 is 64?

8. 32 is what percent of 40?

9. Find what percent 12 is of 16.

10. Find what percent 21 is of 35.

11. 6 is what percent of 240?

12. What percent of 88 is 66?

13. What percent is 5 of 40?

14. 15 is what percent of 50?

15. Find what percent 4 is of 80.

16. What percent of 600 is 420?

17. What percent of 300 is 45?

18. 32 is what percent of 96?

19. Find what percent 120 is of 2,000.

20. Find what percent 44 is of 55.

21. 1.5 is what percent of 3?

Mental Math Copy and complete each pattern.

22. 8 is 20% of 40
8 is ▦ % of 80
8 is ▦ % of 160

23. 14 is 7% of 200
14 is ▦ % of 20
14 is ▦ % of 2

24. 30 is 5% of 600
60 is ▦ % of 600
90 is ▦ % of 600

25. 330 is 11% of 3,000
33 is ▦ % of 300
3.3 is ▦ % of 30

26. 9 is 30% of 30
9 is ▦ % of 60
9 is ▦ % of 120

27. 45 is 9% of 500
45 is ▦ % of 50
45 is ▦ % of 5

Mixed Practice Estimate. Then compute using paper and pencil or a calculator.

28. What is 12% of 9?

29. Find 4% of 150.

30. 9 is what percent of 40?

31. 72 is what percent of 800?

32. Find 45% of 20.

33. Find what percent 132 is of 200.

34. 120 is what percent of 300?

35. What is 15% of 60?

36. What is 99% of 50?

37. Find 200% of 77.

38. 88 is what percent of 80?

39. Find what percent 0.03 is of 0.15.

436

Problem Solving

In a survey of 40 students, Kerry found that Prime Number
was the favorite rock group of 12 of the students. One fourth of
the students surveyed preferred the Acute Angles, and 35%
favored the Square Roots. The rest were undecided.

40. What percent of the students preferred Prime Number?

41. Which rock group was the most popular among those surveyed?

42. Exactly how many of the students surveyed were undecided?

43. What percent of the students surveyed were undecided?

Calculator The latest release of Prime Number
has sold 250,000 compact discs and 75,000 cassettes.
The compact discs sell for $12.50 and the cassettes sell for $9.95.

44. How much money was received for the sale of the cassettes and the compact discs?

45. What percent of the money received was from compact discs? Round to the nearest percent.

46. What percent of the money received was from cassettes? Round to the nearest percent.

47. Use Data Use the ad for Super Sports Shops on page 432 and the total you found in Problem 44 of this page. If Prime Number had given the same discount as Super Sports Shops gave on baseball bats, how much money would Prime Number have received?

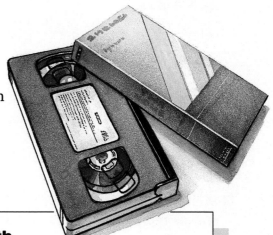

Explore ———— Math

You know that 40% of 100 is 40.

48. What percent of 200 is 40?

49. What percent of 400 is 40?

50. What percent of 800 is 40?

51. What pattern do you see? If the whole keeps doubling while the part does not change, what happens to the percent?

Use Data from a Graph

Build Understanding

Michelle has a job delivering newspapers. The graph shows what she plans to do with the money she earns. Last month Michelle earned $45. How much money will she save if she follows her budget?

Understand   QUESTION   How many dollars will Michelle save?

FACTS   Michelle earned $45.

DATA FROM THE GRAPH   Find the percent she plans to save.

KEY IDEA   Find a percent of a number.

Plan and Solve   What is $33\frac{1}{3}\%$ of $45?

$n = \frac{1}{3} \times \$45$ Remember that $33\frac{1}{3}\% = \frac{1}{3}$.

$n = 15$

Look Back   ALTERNATE APPROACH   Solve the proportion.

$$\frac{1}{3} = \frac{n}{45}$$

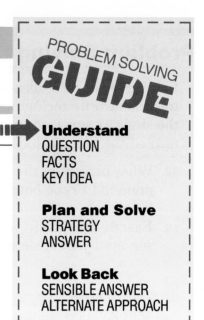

PROBLEM SOLVING GUIDE

Understand
QUESTION
FACTS
KEY IDEA

Plan and Solve
STRATEGY
ANSWER

Look Back
SENSIBLE ANSWER
ALTERNATE APPROACH

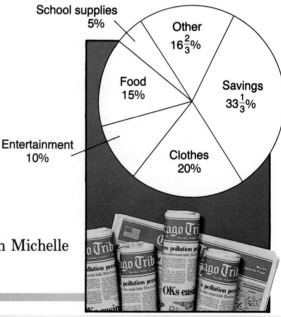

School supplies 5%

Other $16\frac{2}{3}\%$

Food 15%

Savings $33\frac{1}{3}\%$

Entertainment 10%

Clothes 20%

■ **Write About Math**   Write a problem in which Michelle spends more money on food than she budgets.

Check Understanding

1. In the circle graph, what percent does the entire circle represent?

2. What fraction of the circle would be used to show 50%?

3. In the pictograph on page 439, what does each newspaper represent? What does one fourth of a newspaper represent?

4. In the line graph on page 439, what does each number on the vertical scale represent?

Practice

Give each answer.

Michelle plans to earn $600 this year. According to her budget, how much does Michelle plan to spend on each of the following?

5. Clothes   **6.** Savings   **7.** School Supplies

8. Entertainment   **9.** Food   **10.** Other

11. The pictograph shows where Frank delivers newspapers. How many papers does he deliver in all?

What percent of the newspapers that Frank delivers are on each of these streets?

12. Elm Street   **13.** Maple Street

14. Vine Street   **15.** Pine Street

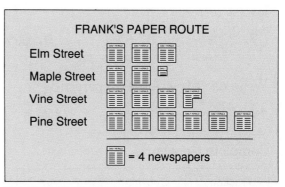

FRANK'S PAPER ROUTE

= 4 newspapers

16. In what year did both papers share the same percent of the market? What was this percent?

17. For what percent of the 10 years shown did *The Globe* have a greater circulation than *The Sun?*

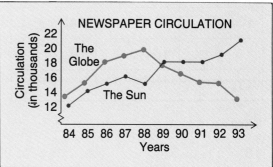

NEWSPAPER CIRCULATION

Choose a ———— Strategy

18. The circulation of the *Weekly Advertiser* increased 50% from 1988 to 1989 and 100% from 1987 to 1988. The circulation was 15,000 in 1989. What was the circulation at the beginning of 1987?

19. The 15,000 circulation of the *Weekly Advertiser* decreased $33\frac{1}{3}$% in 1990. It decreased in 1991 and in 1992 by the same percent. In 1992 the circulation was 6,400. By what percent did it decrease in 1991?

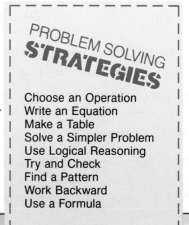

PROBLEM SOLVING
STRATEGIES

Choose an Operation
Write an Equation
Make a Table
Solve a Simpler Problem
Use Logical Reasoning
Try and Check
Find a Pattern
Work Backward
Use a Formula

Skills Review

Write each percent as a decimal.

1. 62%   **2.** 70%   **3.** 8%

Write each decimal as a percent.

4. 0.53   **5.** 0.02   **6.** 0.1

Write each percent as a fraction in lowest terms.

7. 23%   **8.** 5%   **9.** 60%

Write each fraction as a percent.

10. $\frac{47}{100}$ **11.** $\frac{3}{25}$ **12.** $\frac{3}{8}$

Complete the chart.

Fraction	Decimal	Percent
13.	0.9	**14.**
$\frac{3}{4}$	**15.**	**16.**
17.	**18.**	4%

Find each answer.

19. 75% of 320   **20.** $33\frac{1}{3}$% of 96

21. 5% of 200   **22.** 0% of 45

Use mental math to find each answer.

23. 25% of 800   **24.** $66\frac{2}{3}$% of 30

Estimate. Tell if your estimate is greater or less than the exact answer.

25. 23% of 880   **26.** $33\frac{1}{3}$% of 64

Find each answer.

27. What percent of 200 is 50?

28. 8 is what percent of 320?

Problem-Solving Review

Solve each problem.

29. Mrs. Acosta is grocery shopping and wants to buy frozen yogurt for her family. Which is the better buy, 1 pint for $0.79 or $\frac{1}{2}$ gallon for $2.59?

30. While on vacation, Bena bought 6 bracelets. Each bracelet cost $4.95. What was the total cost of the bracelets?

31. What is the volume of an aquarium that is 10 inches by 24 inches by 12 inches?

32. Mr. Borges has a garden that measures 20 feet by 50 feet. He planted 20% of his garden in corn. How many square feet of his garden were planted in corn?

33. Ms. Asano's salary is $15,500 per year. She budgets 12% of her salary for transportation. How much money can she spend on transportation during the year?

34. **Data File** Use the data on pages 542–543. Find the number of kids who chose pizza as their favorite food for dinner and the number who chose hamburger. Then compare. How many more chose pizza?

35. **Make a Data File** Take a survey of 25 people to find out what kind of pets they like best. Make a table listing the pets in order of their popularity.

Write each number in words.

1. 35,406,220,500   **2.** 19.30562

Use mental math to compute.

3. 300×70 **4.** 4.586×100

5. $3,600 \div 90$ **6.** $5.25 \div 100$

Name each polygon.

7.   **8.**   **9.**

Write three fractions equal to the given fraction.

10. $\frac{3}{4}$ **11.** $\frac{2}{5}$ **12.** $\frac{8}{16}$

Estimate by rounding each mixed number to the nearest whole number.

13. $6\frac{5}{12} + 2\frac{2}{15}$ **14.** $6\frac{2}{7} - 4\frac{1}{9}$

Compute.

15. $\frac{4}{9} + \frac{2}{3}$ **16.** $\frac{4}{5} - \frac{1}{6}$

17. $\frac{3}{5} \div \frac{2}{15}$ **18.** $\frac{5}{8} \div \frac{5}{12}$

Measure the straw to the nearest

19. half inch.   **20.** centimeter.

Solve.

21.   4 hr 55 min   **22.**   8 hr 15 min
        + 2 hr 20 min   − 2 hr 45 min

Find each missing number.

23. 5 yd = ▦ ft   **24.** 4 m = ▦ mm

Find the perimeter of each figure.

25. 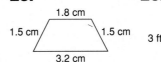   **26.**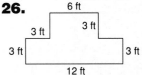

Find the surface area of each figure.

27.   **28.**

29. Find the volume of the figure in Exercise 27.

Tell whether each pair of ratios forms a proportion.

30. $\frac{2}{3}, \frac{8}{12}$ **31.** $\frac{8}{9}, \frac{9}{8}$ **32.** $\frac{3}{5}, \frac{10}{15}$

Write each ratio as a percent.

33. $\frac{8}{10}$ **34.** $\frac{2}{5}$ **35.** $\frac{1}{3}$ **36.** $\frac{11}{25}$

Use the similar figures for Exercises 37 and 38.

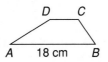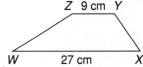

37. List the corresponding sides.

38. Find the length of $\overline{CD}$.

Write each percent as a decimal.

39. 65%   **40.** 3%   **41.** 100%

42. 55% of 120 is what number?

43. What percent of 50 is 35?

Reteaching

Set A   pages 416–417

What percent of the grid at the right is shaded?

12 out of 100 squares are shaded
12 out of 100 = 12 hundredths
12 hundredths = 0.12
Since percent means "hundredths,"
0.12 = 12%.

Remember that percent means hundredths.

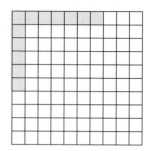

Write each decimal as a percent.

1. 0.45   **2.** 0.04   **3.** 0.8

4. 0.275   **5.** 0.71   **6.** 0.1

Set B   pages 418–419

Write $\frac{1}{4}$ as a percent.

Since percent means hundredths, write a fraction equal to $\frac{1}{4}$ with a denominator of 100.

$$\frac{1}{4} = \frac{25}{100}$$

To write this as a percent, write the numerator, 25, with a % sign.

$$\frac{25}{100} = 25\%$$

Remember that you can also divide the numerator by the denominator to write a decimal for a fraction. You then write a percent for the decimal.

Write each fraction as a percent.

1. $\frac{75}{100}$ **2.** $\frac{6}{100}$ **3.** $\frac{14}{100}$

4. $\frac{2}{4}$ **5.** $\frac{3}{5}$ **6.** $\frac{17}{20}$

7. $\frac{9}{50}$ **8.** $\frac{3}{25}$ **9.** $\frac{3}{10}$

Set C   pages 420–421

Write 40% as a decimal and as a fraction.

40% = 0.40   40% = 0.4
   = 0.4 $= \frac{4}{10} = \frac{2}{5}$

Remember to write fractions in lowest terms.

Copy and complete the percent bar.

0%	20%	40%	60%	80% 100%

0.0   0.2   **1.** ▦   0.6   0.8 **2.** ▦

0    $\frac{1}{5}$ **3.** ▦   **4.** ▦ $\frac{4}{5}$ $\frac{5}{5}$

Write each percent as a decimal and as a fraction.

5. 35%   **6.** 30%   **7.** 16%   **8.** 98%

Set D　pages 422–425

What is 24% of 62?

Write an equation.
What is 24% of 62?
$$\downarrow \quad \downarrow \quad \downarrow \quad \downarrow \quad \downarrow$$
$$n \quad = 0.24 \times 62$$
$$n = 14.88$$

Remember that you can also solve a proportion to find a percent of a number.

Find each answer.

1. 25% of 60　　**2.** 10% of 200

3. 60% of 320　　**4.** 30% of 80

Set E　pages 428–429

Forty students took an exam, and 75% of them got a C or better. How many of them got a C or better?

Think: 75% = 3 × 25%
　　　25% of 40 = 10
　　　3 × 10 = 30
Thirty students got a C or better.

Remember that sometimes you can compute the percent of a number mentally.

Use mental math to find each answer.

1. 10% of 480　　**2.** 75% of 120

3. 50% of 600　　**4.** 20% of 350

Set F　pages 430–431

Estimate 79% of 450.
Round the percent. 79% ≈ 80%

Find 80% of 450.
Think: 80% is 4 × 20%.

20% of 450 is $\frac{1}{5} \times 450 = 90$.
80% of 450 is 4 × 90 = 360.

80% of 450 = 360
79% of 450 ≈ 360

Remember that you may have to round both numbers to estimate the percent of a number.

Estimate.

1. 18% of 400　　**2.** 32% of 61

3. 52% of 84　　**4.** 76% of 195

5. 24% of 164　　**6.** 91% of 307

Set G　pages 434–437

9 is what percent of 24?

$$9 = n \times 24$$
$$\frac{9}{24} = \frac{n \times 24}{24}$$
$$\frac{9}{24} = n$$
$$\frac{3}{8} = n$$
$$\frac{3}{8} = 0.375 = 37.5\%$$

Remember that you can make a percent bar to see if your answer is reasonable.

Find each answer. Remember to express your answer as a percent.

1. 16 is what percent of 40?

2. What percent of 200 is 10?

3. Find what percent 9 is of 45.

4. 45 is what percent of 150?

More Practice

Set A   pages 416–417

Write each percent as a decimal.

1. 4%   **2.** 17%   **3.** 36%   **4.** 59%   **5.** 30%   **6.** 90%

7. 70%   **8.** 6%   **9.** 11%   **10.** 1%   **11.** 82%   **12.** 99%

Write each decimal as a percent.

13. 0.25   **14.** 0.53   **15.** 0.76   **16.** 0.82   **17.** 0.06   **18.** 0.6

19. 0.03   **20.** 0.9   **21.** 0.4   **22.** 0.01   **23.** 0.1   **24.** 0.22

Set B   pages 418–419

Write each percent as a fraction in lowest terms.

1. 11%   **2.** 36%   **3.** 2%   **4.** 65%   **5.** 40%   **6.** 90%

Write each fraction as a percent.

7. $\frac{62}{100}$ **8.** $\frac{8}{100}$ **9.** $\frac{3}{10}$ **10.** $\frac{8}{25}$ **11.** $\frac{4}{5}$ **12.** $\frac{3}{20}$

Set C   pages 420–421

Copy and complete the percent bar.

1.

0%	12.5%	25%	37.5%	50%	62.5%	75%	87.5%	100%

0.0	0.125	0.25	0.375	0.5	▦	0.75	▦	1
0	$\frac{1}{8}$	▦	▦	$\frac{1}{2}$	$\frac{5}{8}$	$\frac{3}{4}$	$\frac{7}{8}$	1

Mixed Practice

Complete the charts.

Fraction	Decimal	Percent
$\frac{7}{20}$	**2.**	**3.**
4.	0.4	**5.**
$\frac{3}{8}$	**6.**	**7.**

Fraction	Decimal	Percent
8.	**9.**	77%
$\frac{4}{5}$	**10.**	**11.**
12.	0.04	**13.**

Set D pages 422–425

Find each answer.

1. 30% of 90 **2.** 25% of 64 **3.** 50% of 88 **4.** 70% of 210

5. 75% of 800 **6.** $33\frac{1}{3}$% of 360 **7.** 1% of 200 **8.** 6% of 3,200

For Exercises 9–12, tell whether you would use paper and
pencil, mental math, or a calculator. Then solve.

9. What is 25% of 60? **10.** 42% of 386 is what number?

11. Find 20% of 3,800. **12.** What is 12.5% of 80?

Set E pages 428–429

Use mental math to find each answer.

1. 50% of 400 **2.** 25% of 320 **3.** 75% of 1,200 **4.** $33\frac{1}{3}$% of 450

5. 10% of 680 **6.** 20% of 500 **7.** 50% of 2,800 **8.** 25% of 480

Find each answer. Try to solve at least one of each pair mentally.

9. 10% of 52; 11% of 52 **10.** 25% of 88; 24% of 88

Set F pages 430–431

Estimation Estimate. Is your estimate *greater than* or
less than the exact answer?

1. 22% of 500 **2.** 47% of 900 **3.** 25% of 192 **4.** 50% of 391

Number Sense Choose the most sensible answer.

5. 9% of 378
   a. 4 **b.** 34 **c.** 420

6. 68% of 688
   a. 467 **b.** 68 **c.** 234

Set G pages 434–437

Find each answer.

1. 20 is what percent of 60? **2.** What percent of 88 is 22?

3. Find what percent 15 is of 24. **4.** 35 is what percent of 50?

Mixed Practice Estimate. Then compute.

5. What is 18% of 36? **6.** Find 12% of 400. **7.** 16 is what percent of 80?

445

Enrichment

Percents Greater Than 100% and Less Than 1%

The student council at Grant School is taking orders
for school sweatshirts. Their goal is to sell 400 sweatshirts.

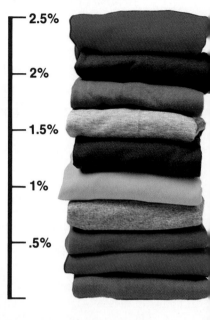

If they sell 4 shirts, they have
reached 1% of their goal.

1% = 0.01
0.01 × 400 = 4

If they sell fewer than 4 shirts, they have
reached less than 1% of their goal.

Selling 2 shirts is 0.5% of their goal.

0.5% = 0.005
0.005 × 400 = 2

If they sell 400 shirts, they have
reached 100% of their goal.

100% = 1
1 × 400 = 400

If they sell more than 400 shirts, they have
reached more than 100% of their goal.

Selling 440 shirts is 110% of their goal.

110% = 1.10
1.10 × 400 = 440

1. To reach 50% of the goal, how
many sweatshirts must be sold?

2. To reach 120% of the goal, how
many sweatshirts must be sold?

What percent of the goal would be reached by selling

3. 3 shirts?   **4.** 500 shirts?   **5.** 600 shirts?   **6.** 820 shirts?

Find each answer.

7. 140% of 1,000   **8.** 250% of 36   **9.** $166\frac{2}{3}$% of 45

10. 0.5% of 600   **11.** 0.1% of 2,000   **12.** 0.04% of 500

Does the statement make sense? Why or why not?

13. 160% of the shirts sold had long
sleeves.

14. Laura earned 125% of the price of
the skates she wanted.

15. In 1998 this savings bond will be
worth 150% of its value today.

16. Stan saved 115% of the amount
that he earned.

Chapter 12 Review/Test

Write each percent as a decimal.

1. 47%   **2.** 80%   **3.** 7%

Write each decimal as a percent.

4. 0.23   **5.** 0.09   **6.** 0.4

Write each percent as a fraction in lowest terms.

7. 25%   **8.** 49%   **9.** 55%

Write each fraction as a decimal and as a percent.

10. $\frac{3}{4}$ **11.** $\frac{7}{25}$ **12.** $\frac{2}{3}$

Find the following.

13. 75% of 36   **14.** 2% of 48

15. $33\frac{1}{3}$% of 27   **16.** 20% of 60

Write each answer, solving mentally when possible.

17. 20% of 50   **18.** 10% of 980

19. 75% of 24   **20.** $33\frac{1}{3}$% of 99

Choose the most sensible answer.

21. 12% of 265

   a. 6   **b.** 32   **c.** 113

22. 74% of 494

   a. 366   **b.** 420   **c.** 474

23. What percent of 20 is 15?

24. 18 is what percent of 45?

25. Juanita has $20.85. Does she have enough to buy a sweater that costs $18.50 plus 5% sales tax?

Use the graph to solve the problem.

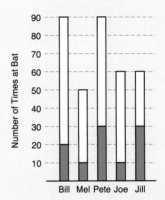

26. The graph shows the number of times at bat (entire bar) and the number of hits (shaded part) for 5 members of a softball team. All numbers are rounded to the nearest ten. Who has the highest batting average (number of hits divided by the number of times at bat)?

Read the problem below. Then answer the question.

A graph shows that 20% of Angie's monthly spending is for clothes. If she spends $115 per month, how much does she spend for clothes?

27. Which equation can you use to solve the problem?

   a. $0.20 \times 115 = n$
   b. $115 - 0.20 = n$
   c. $115 \div 0.20 = n$

28. **Write About Math** What are two ways that you can solve Problem 19?

Applying Statistics

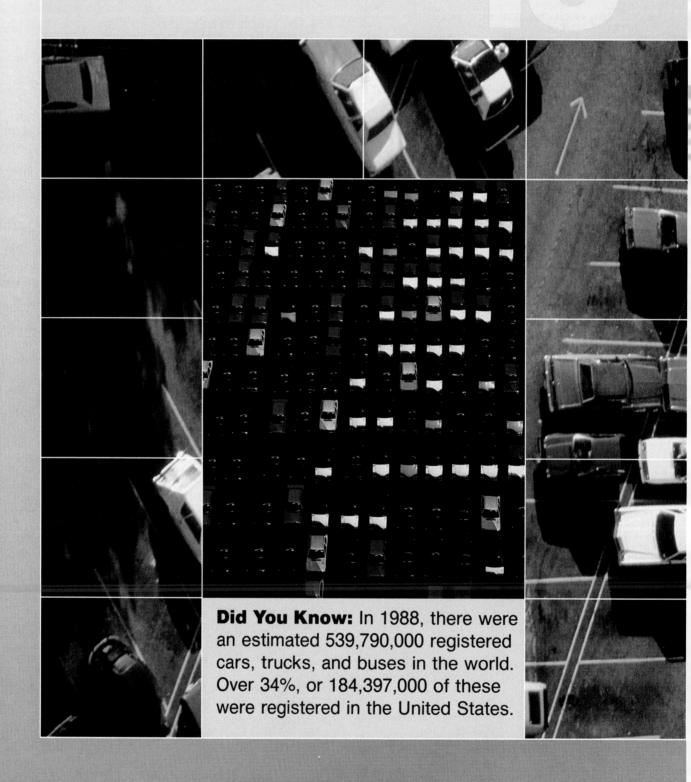

Did You Know: In 1988, there were an estimated 539,790,000 registered cars, trucks, and buses in the world. Over 34%, or 184,397,000 of these were registered in the United States.

Number-Sense Project

Estimate

What do you think is the most popular color car in your area?

Gather Data

Select a spot where you can observe 100 cars. Tally the color of the first 100 cars that pass this spot. Consider different shades of a color as the same.

Analyze and Report

Find the percent of each color car that passed your spot. Compare results. What color would you estimate is the favorite? How many cars out of 1,000 would you expect to be this color?

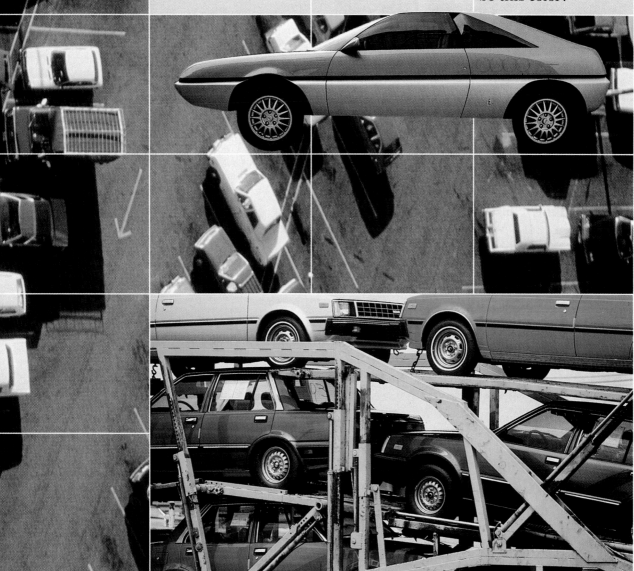

449

Range, Mean, Median, and Mode

Build Understanding

Favorite Number

Groups: An odd number of people per group

a. Write down the favorite number of each person in your group.

b. List all the numbers from least to greatest.

c. The *range* is the difference between the greatest and least numbers in a set of data. What is the range of the favorite numbers of your group?

d. Find the *mean*, or average, of your favorite numbers. First find the sum of the numbers. Then divide by the number of favorite numbers in your set of data. (If 5 people are in your group, you would divide by 5, for example.)

e. The *median* of a set of data is the number exactly in the middle of the set when the numbers are listed in order. What is the median of the favorite numbers of your group?

f. The number that occurs most often in a set of data is called the *mode*. Does any favorite number occur more often than any others? Does your set of data have a mode?

■ **Talk About Math** If an even number of people were in your group, how would you find the median?

Check Understanding

For another example, see Set A, pages 472–473.

Find the following for these favorite numbers: 3, 6, 48, 100, 3.

1. Range   **2.** Mean   **3.** Median   **4.** Mode

Practice

For More Practice, see Set A, pages 474–475.

For Exercises 5–20, tell whether you would use mental math, paper and pencil, or a calculator. Then find the range, mean, median, and mode for each set of numbers.

Set A: 16   30   17   18   22   24   27
5. Range   **6.** Mean   **7.** Median   **8.** Mode

Set B: 39   38   35   35   32   38   35   39   33   30
9. Range   **10.** Mean   **11.** Median   **12.** Mode

Set C: 7   15   9   28   22   13   15   20   17   15
13. Range   **14.** Mean   **15.** Median   **16.** Mode

Set D: 100   100   150   135   135   140   125   135
17. Range   **18.** Mean   **19.** Median   **20.** Mode

Find the missing numbers.

21. 95, 98, ▧, 120, ▧   Clues: Mean = 107, Mode = 120

22. 41, ▧, ▧, ▧, 58   Clues: Mean = 47, Mode = 41, Median = 43

23. ▧, 68, ▧, 75, ▧   Clues: Range = 29, Mode = 68, Mean = 76

24. 75, ▧, ▧, 135, ▧   Clues: Range = 65, Median = 125, Median = Mode

Problem Solving

Number Sense   Answer each question.

25. Could a set of numbers have more than one mode? Explain.

26. Give a set of 5 numbers whose mean, median, and mode are equal.

Critical Thinking   Give, if possible, an example of a set of 5 numbers having the following properties. If not possible, explain why.

27. The mean is greater than the median.

28. The mean is less than the median.

29. The mean is one of the numbers.

30. The median is not one of the numbers.

Give Sensible Answers

Build Understanding

PROBLEM SOLVING
GUIDE

▮▮▮▶ **Understand**
QUESTION
FACTS
KEY IDEA

Plan and Solve
STRATEGY
ANSWER

Look Back
SENSIBLE ANSWER
ALTERNATE APPROACH

One form of architecture developed by the American Indians was the adobe dwellings. Adobe houses are still built in our country, especially in the Southwest.

Suppose the Pueblo Company had the following weekly production of adobe bricks (in thousands).

Mon.	Tues.	Wed.	Thurs.	Fri.	Sat.
13	13	15	17	18	44

The manager wants to know the typical number of bricks produced per day. Should he use the mean, median, or mode?

▮▮▮▶ **Understand** QUESTION   Which of these "measures" best describes the data?

FACTS   The table shows the daily production of bricks.

KEY IDEA   Measures can be found in several ways.

Plan and Solve   To find the mean, add the number of bricks per day and divide the total by the number of days. The mean is 20,000.

To find the median, add the third and fourth numbers and divide by 2. The median is 16,000.

To find the mode, use the number that occurs most often. The mode is 13,000.

ANSWER   Use the median.

Look Back   SENSIBLE ANSWER   Five of the numbers are less than the mean. The mode represents the lowest numbers. The median shows the typical number.

■ **Talk About Math**   Is one very large or very small value likely to have the most effect on the mean, the median, or the mode?

People have used sun-dried bricks, or adobe, to build houses since ancient times.

452

Check Understanding

Suppose this table shows the number of bricks (in thousands) an *adobero*, a person who makes adobe bricks, made each year.

1987	1988	1989	1990	1991
31	20	26	31	32

1. Find the mean.

2. Find the median.

3. Find the mode.

Suppose the adobero made 30,000 bricks in 1992. What effect would this have on

4. the mean?

5. the median?

6. the mode?

Practice

Igloo is the Inuit word for "shelter."

The Inuit people, living in what is now called Canada, Alaska, and Greenland, build temporary shelters made of snow called igloos.

Which measure does each of the following describe about igloos—the mean, median, or mode? Give a reason for each answer.

7. Half of all snow igloos were less than 76 centimeters long.

8. The average width of the igloos was 3 meters.

9. The average height of an igloo in one town was 3.7 meters, but no igloos were that height.

10. To build an igloo, snow blocks with a height of 40 centimeters were used more than any other size.

Choose a _____ Strategy

Profit or Loss   This table shows the profit (indicated by +) and loss (indicated by −) of the Pueblo Company over a six-month period.

July	Aug.	Sept.	Oct.	Nov.	Dec.
−$1,000	+$1,500	+$2,000	−$500	−$1,500	+$2,500

11. How much money did the company lose in July, October, and November?

12. How much money did the Pueblo Company make in August, September, and December?

13. How much profit did the company make over the six-month period?

14. What was the mean monthly profit over the six months?

Statistical Graphs

Build Understanding

A. Which were the 3 best-selling car models in 1989?

Eight Best-Selling Car Models of 1989

Model	Number Sold
Arnel	334,876
Cavallo	307,028
Navarre	306,480
Elba	214,607
Brise	392,360
Sentinel	354,971
Vivace	219,296
Puma	263,610

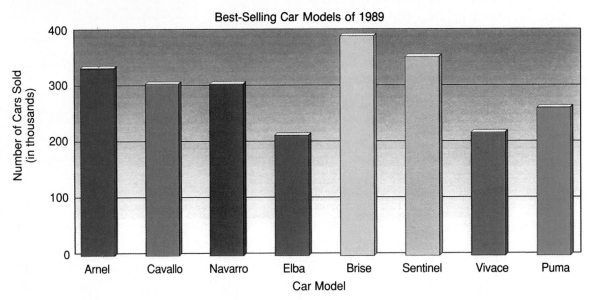

Best-Selling Car Models of 1989

Bar graphs show comparisons.

The 3 car models with the highest number of sales were the Brise, the Sentinel, and the Arnel.

Is the answer to the question easier to find from the bar graph or from the table?

The answer is easier to find from the bar graph because the heights of the bars show immediately which models had the most sales.

454

B. Other types of graphs are the **pictograph**, the **circle graph**, and the **broken-line graph**.

Pictographs show comparisons.

Value of Passenger Cars Imported to the U.S. (1987)

🍁	Canada	🚗🚗🚗🚗🚗🚗🚗🚗🚗🚗🚗
🇬🇧	United Kingdom	🚗
🇩🇪	West Germany	🚗🚗🚗🚗🚗🚗🚗🚗🚗
🇯🇵	Japan	🚗🚗🚗🚗🚗🚗🚗🚗🚗🚗🚗🚗🚗🚗🚗🚗🚗🚗🚗🚗🚗🚗🚗🚗

Key: Each 🚗 represents $1 billion in car sales.

Circle graphs show parts of a whole.

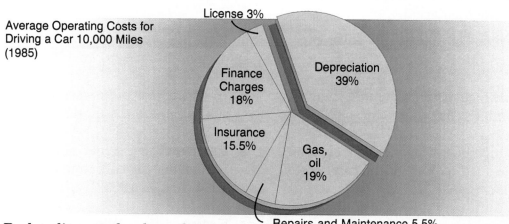

Average Operating Costs for Driving a Car 10,000 Miles (1985)

License 3%
Depreciation 39%
Finance Charges 18%
Insurance 15.5%
Gas, oil 19%
Repairs and Maintenance 5.5%

Broken-line graphs show change over time.

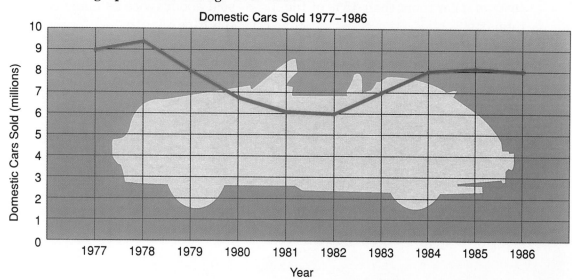

Domestic Cars Sold 1977–1986

Domestic Cars Sold (millions)

Year

■ **Talk About Math**   Would the bar graph or the table be more useful in finding out how many Vivaces were sold in 1989? Why?

Check Understanding

For another example, see Set B, pages 472–473.

Use the graphs in Example B to answer Exercises 1 and 2.

1. What units of measure are used in the scales of each graph?

2. What percent of operating costs is due to depreciation?

Practice

For More Practice, see Set B, pages 474–475.

Use the appropriate graph on page 454 or 455 to answer each question.

3. Which car models sold fewer cars than the Navarre?

4. Did U.S. car sales increase or decrease from 1981 to 1982?

5. In which years were more than 7 million domestic cars sold?

6. In which year did domestic car sales decrease the most?

7. Which operating cost of a car was the smallest part of the total cost?

8. **Estimation**   About how many more domestic cars were sold in 1984 than in 1983?

9. For which items were the operating costs of a car more than 15% of the total cost?

10. **Estimation**   Which model car sold about twice as many cars as the Elba?

11. From which country was the second highest dollar value of cars imported?

12. What was the total value of cars imported from Japan and Germany?

13. **Estimation**   By approximately how many cars did sales decrease from 1979 to 1980?

14. In 1985 one driver's expenses totaled $3,175 after 10,000 miles. How much more would you expect the driver to have spent on insurance, repairs, and maintenance than on gas and oil?

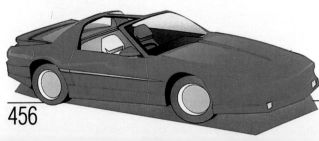

Problem Solving

Indicate which of the four types of graphs you would use to describe the given situation. Give a reason for your answer.

15. The number of imported cars sold in the U.S. from 1977 to 1986

16. The percent of time per day the average person spends driving a car for business, for family necessities, for pleasure, or to help other people

17. The monthly average amount of fuel used by cars during 1989

18. The average number of miles driven between mechanical checkups for passenger cars, buses, small trucks, and large truck rigs

Use Data Look at the graph for monthly temperatures in Honolulu on page 458. Calculate the following.

19. Median

20. Mean

```
┌─────────────────────────┐
│ TIPS FOR                │
│ PROBLEM SOLVERS         │
│                         │
│ Brainstorm to get       │
│ started—one idea will   │
│ lead to another.        │
└─────────────────────────┘
```

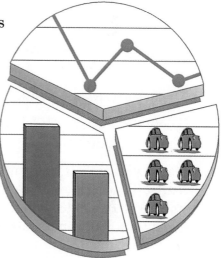

Reading 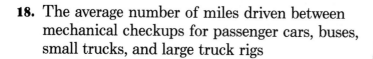 **Math**

Use the four graphs on pages 454 and 455 to answer these questions.

1. Does each title describe the data shown? Explain.

2. In the circle graph, what does the whole circle represent?

3. What unit of time is used in the line graph?

4. What quantity is changing over time?

5. What other type of graph could be used to compare the data shown in the pictograph?

Interpreting Graphs

Build Understanding

A. The graph at the right shows the normal monthly temperatures in Honolulu, Hawaii. The scale on this graph is a *broken scale*. The zig-zag mark at the bottom shows that the scale from 0 to 73 has been omitted. The range of temperatures is only 8°F.

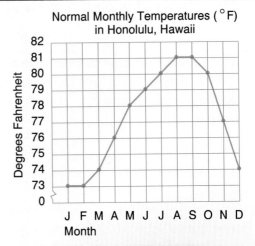

Normal Monthly Temperatures (°F) in Honolulu, Hawaii

B. The island Hawaii has an area of 4,038 square miles. The table at the right shows the areas of some of the other islands of the state of Hawaii. If you used this information to draw a bar graph, how could you label the scale to show the areas?

Try dividing your scale into eight parts. The range of areas is from 140 to 729 square miles. Draw the scale from 0 to 800 in intervals of 100.

Area of Some Hawaiian Islands (in square miles)

Island	Area
Kauai	553
Lanai	140
Maui	729
Molokai	261
Oahu	608

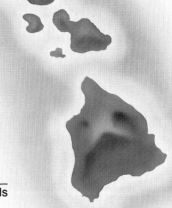

■ **Write About Math** Draw the vertical scale for the temperatures in Honolulu in 10° intervals from 0° to 80° and redraw the graph. Explain any differences in your impressions of the two graphs of the same data.

The state of Hawaii includes 132 islands spanning a distance of 1,523 miles.

Check Understanding

For another example, see Set C, pages 472–473.

The graphs on page 459 show monthly sales of scuba gear in a sporting goods store in Hawaii. Explain which graph you would use if you were

1. a salesman trying to get the store to order extra gear in the spring and fall.

2. the manager trying to show the owner that sales have been good all year.

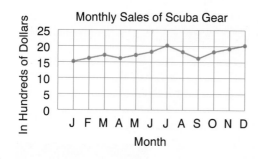

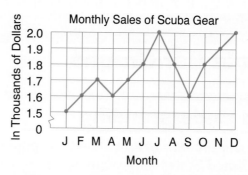

Practice

For More Practice, see Set C, pages 474–475.

Tell whether you would use a broken-line graph or a bar graph to show the following data. Then draw and label the numerical scale for each graph.

3. The population of Hawaii from 1900 to 1980 rose from 154,001 to 964,691 people.

4. The rainfall in Hawaii varies from 10 inches in the lowlands to 300 inches in the mountains.

5. The population density of Hawaii from 1920 to 1980 increased from 39.9 people per square mile to 150.1 people per square mile.

6. Complete the bar graph begun in Example B.

Problem Solving

7. Explain which graph at the top of this page you would use to convince the store manager to keep the same number of employees all year long.

Suppose you were illustrating a newspaper article about the fact that the Hawaiian state government payroll varied from $18,000,000 last year to $20,000,000 this year. Draw a bar graph of this data for each headline.

8. STATE GOVERNMENT PAYROLL UP!   **9. STATE PAYROLL STABLE**

Skills _____ Review   pages 292–295

Divide.

1. $6\frac{1}{3} \div 1\frac{1}{3}$ **2.** $6 \div 4\frac{1}{2}$ **3.** $1\frac{1}{2} \div 1\frac{1}{4}$ **4.** $3\frac{1}{3} \div 1\frac{1}{5}$ **5.** $5\frac{2}{3} \div 2$

Double Bar Graphs

Build Understanding

This ***double bar graph*** shows the population in the United States for certain age groups in 1980 and 1989.

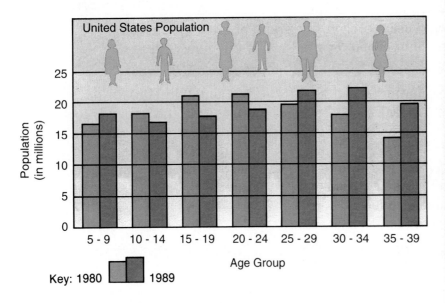

A double bar graph is used to compare related information. What information is given in the key?

■ **Talk About Math**   In 1980, about 12 million people were in the 40–44 age group. In 1989, about 17 million people were in this age group. Explain how you would graph this data.

Check Understanding

For another example, see Set D, pages 472–473.

1. Which age group had the least population in 1980?

2. Which age group had the least population in 1989?

3. Which age groups had the least amount of change in population between 1980 and 1989?

Practice

For More Practice, see Set D, pages 474–475.

Use the bar graph on page 460 for Exercises 4–11.

4. Which two age groups were the largest in 1989?

5. For which age groups was the population over 20 million in 1980?

6. For which age groups was the population more than 20 million in 1989?

7. For which age groups was there a decrease in population between 1980 and 1989?

8. For which age groups was the population in 1989 between 16 and 20 million?

9. For which age groups was the population in 1989 between 20 and 24 million?

10. For which age groups was the population in 1980 between 15 and 20 million?

11. For which age group was the population less than 15 million in 1980?

Problem Solving

Solve each problem.

12. In 1988, the population in Langston was about 20,000. Three tenths of the people are 20 years old or younger, and 0.1 are 60 years old or older. Write a decimal that represents the 21–59 age group.

13. **Mental Math** The population of Langston increased by 10% from 1988 to 1989 (see Exercise 12) and by 10% from 1989 to 1990. What was the population in 1990?

14. What would be Langston's population in 1992, if it continued to grow by 10% every year?

15. **Calculator** By what percent did Langston's population increase from 1988 to 1992?

Midchapter ✓ Checkup

Find the following for these numbers: 95, 82, 80, 95, 90, 42, 90.

1. Median   **2.** Mode   **3.** Mean   **4.** Range

Would a circle, bar, or line graph be best for the data?

5. Breakdown of yearly operating costs for a shoe store

6. Comparison of U.S. population by age groups in 1960 and 1990

Explore as a Team

As a team you will be making a set of questions and surveying 100 people for their answers. The results will be used as the basis for a game of *Classroom Conflict* to be played by two other teams in your class.

Decide on ten questions your team will ask. Each question should require a one or two-word answer. Then decide how many people each team member will survey so that a total of 100 people are questioned.

Each team member should prepare a survey sheet for recording answers and a signature sheet for people to sign after they have answered the questions. Do not survey other students in your class.

After your team has completed their survey, combine your results and assign a percent to each answer. Have two other teams in your class play Classroom Conflict using your results.

Read one question and have each team decide on three answers. Each team receives points equal to the percent of people who answered the same way. The game is over when all questions have been asked. The winner is the team with the most points.

1. What is your favorite sport?
2. What is your favorite school subject?
3. What is your favorite movie?

5.

6.

7.

8.

9.

10.

TIPS FOR WORKING TOGETHER

To make sure your group understands the task or solution have each group member say it in his/her own words, summarize the steps, or give an example.

Explore with a Computer

Use the *Graphing and Probability Workshop Project* for this activity.

1. Substances can be an acid, neutral, or a base. The pH values of substances range from 0-6 (acids), 7 (neutral), and 8-14 (bases). At the computer, record the following information in the table:

Substance	pH Value
Tomato	4.2
Water	7.2
Egg	8.0
Ammonia	11.0

2. View the data as a **Bar Graph**. What do the bars show?

3. Predict the pH value for the following substances: apple juice, blood, baking soda, milk, soft drink, and bread. Use a science book or encyclopedia to check your predictions. Add the data to the table. Make or print a graph of the data.

Number-Sense Project

Look back at pages 448-449.

Suppose an automobile dealership kept this record of cars sold by color.

Color	Number Sold
White	60
Black	40
Gray	32
Red	20
Other	48

The dealer plans to order 50 new cars. Based on this data, he should order how many

a. white cars?   **b.** black cars?   **c.** gray cars?   **d.** red cars?

463

Circle Graphs

Build Understanding

A. A *circle graph* is used to compare parts of a whole. This graph shows the percent of the U.S. population in each age group in 1960. How many were in the 14–24 age group?

The whole is 180,000,000, and 15% of these people were in the 14–24 age group.

15% of 180,000,000 =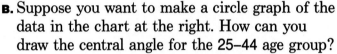

0.15 × 180,000,000 = 27,000,000

There were 27,000,000 people in the 14–24 age group.

B. Suppose you want to make a circle graph of the data in the chart at the right. How can you draw the central angle for the 25–44 age group?

Use a ratio to compare the population of the 25–44 age group to the total population.

$\dfrac{74.4}{240}$ ⟶ 74.4 ÷ 240 = 0.31 = 31%

The whole circle represents 360°.
Find 31% of 360°.

31% × 360° = 111.6°, or 112° to the nearest degree.

■ **Talk About Math**   What age group in Example B will have the smallest central angle? How do you know? What will the measure of that angle be?

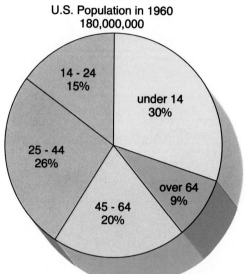

U.S. Population in 1960
180,000,000

under 14
30%

14 - 24
15%

25 - 44
26%

45 - 64
20%

over 64
9%

U.S. Population in 1985
240,000,000 People

Age	Number of People (in Millions)
Under 14	43.2
14–24	48
25–44	74.4
45–64	44.4
over 64	30

The first census to determine the population of the United States was conducted in 1790.

Check Understanding

For another example, see Set E, pages 472–473.

Use the graph in Example A for Exercises 1 and 2.

1. What percent of the population is over 64? under 25?

2. What percent of the population is under 65?

Practice

For More Practice, see Set E, pages 474–475.

The graphs at the right show the percent of the U.S. population living in each region of the country in 1950 and in 1985.

3. How many people lived in the Northeast in 1950? in 1985?

4. Which regions had a greater percent of the U.S. population in 1985 than in 1950?

5. How many more people lived in the South in 1985 than in 1950?

6. **Critical Thinking** The Midwest had a smaller percent of the U.S. population in 1985 than in 1950. Were fewer people living there in 1985 than in 1950? Explain.

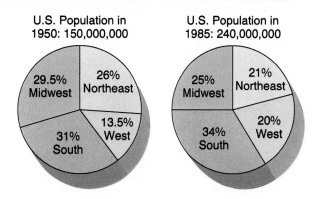

U.S. Population in 1950: 150,000,000

29.5% Midwest
26% Northeast
31% South
13.5% West

U.S. Population in 1985: 240,000,000

25% Midwest
21% Northeast
34% South
20% West

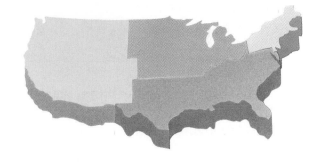

Problem Solving

Explore _____ Math

Calculator Plan a circle graph for the data in the table.

7. Find the percent of the population in each age group to the nearest whole percent.

8. Find the central angles to the nearest degree for the graph.

Population Age Groups in Greenville	
Under 14	15,985
14–24	19,479
25–44	25,932
45–64	14,250
Over 64	11,704
Total	87,350

9. What is the sum of the central angle measures you obtained in Exercise 8?

10. What angles would you actually use to draw your circle graph? Why?

Make a Graph

Build Understanding

As part of "How's Your Heart Week" Michi and Roberto took the pulse rate of 50 people. This frequency table shows the data.

Pulse rate	Tally	Frequency
68	||||	4
72	卌 卌 卌 |	16
76	卌 卌 卌 卌	20
80	卌 |||	8
84	||	2

What type of graph will best show their data?

Understand   What type of graph will show the results of the pulse rates best? Michi and Roberto want to make a graph to compare the frequencies.

 **Plan and Solve**   STRATEGY   Bar graphs are best for comparing this kind of data. Make a bar graph. Draw and label the two scales. Draw bars to show each frequency. Title the graph.

ANSWER

Look Back   SENSIBLE ANSWER   A circle graph would not be as visual and a line graph usually shows changes over time. A bar graph is the best choice.

■ **Talk About Math**   When might it be sensible to make a circle graph for the pulse-rate data?

Check Understanding

Explain why the following graphs are the best choice to show:

1. Your family's budget; circle graph

2. The population of your state from 1900 to 1990; line graph

3. The mileage from your home to five cities; bar graph

Practice

Decide what type of graph will best show each set of data.
Draw the graph. **Remember** to use a title and label the scales.

4. Patient's Temperature Over a 16-Hour Period

Time	8 A.M.	NOON	4 P.M.	8 P.M.	MIDNIGHT
Temperature	98.8	99	98.2	100	99

5. Pulse Rate for Fifty People

Rate	68	72	76	80	84
Percent	10%	26%	40%	20%	4%

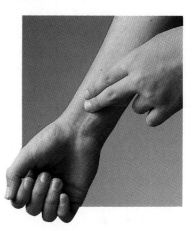

Mixed Practice   Use the data in Problems 4
and 5 to answer each question.

6. What was the range of the
patient's temperature over the
16-hour period?

7. What was the patient's average
temperature over the 16-hour
period?

8. **Critical Thinking**   Suppose that five more people's pulse rates
are taken. If each person's pulse rate falls into one of each of
the five rate categories, which percent will remain the same?

Choose a ——— Strategy

Big Spenders   Jane, Sandy, Amos, and Clyde each left a tip of
20% for the food server. Sandy left $1 more than Amos did.
Amos's lunch cost more than Jane's and $2 less than Clyde's.

9. Who left the smallest tip?

10. Based on the size of the tip, write
the names in decreasing order.

Stem-and-Leaf Plots

Build Understanding

As part of a science project, Julio tested
20 size-AA batteries to see how long each
would last. He followed these steps to make a
stem-and-leaf plot of the data in his table.

**Lifetime of Batteries
To the Nearest Hour**

56	67	63	70
46	57	71	67
58	60	72	67
57	60	90	63
88	78	49	65

a. Find the least and greatest values
in the table. The least value,
46, has a 4 in the tens place, and
the greatest value, 90, has a 9 in
the tens place. The stems are the
tens digits 4 through 9.

b. Write the stems in a column. Draw a
vertical line to the right.

```
4 |
5 |
6 |
7 |
8 |
9 |
```

c. The leaves are the ones digits. Write
each leaf to the right of its stem.

```
4 | 6     Battery Age: 46
5 |       Stem = 4, leaf = 6
6 |
7 |
8 |
9 | 0     Battery Age: 90
          Stem = 9, leaf = 0
```

d. Enter each battery lifetime from
the chart.

```
4 | 6, 9
5 | 6, 7, 8, 7
6 | 7, 3, 7, 0, 7, 0, 3, 5
7 | 0, 1, 2, 8
8 | 8
9 | 0
```

e. Rewrite each leaf in increasing
order.

```
4 | 6, 9
5 | 6, 7, 7, 8
6 | 0, 0, 3, 3, 5, 7, 7, 7
7 | 0, 1, 2, 8
8 | 8
9 | 0
```

■ **Write About Math**   Using the information from
the stem-and-leaf plot, write a paragraph describing
the results of Julio's test.

Check Understanding

For another example, see Set F, pages 472–473.

1. Explain how you would find the range and mode using Julio's stem-and-leaf plot.

2. Why is performing step **e** useful in making a stem-and-leaf plot?

3. What is the median of the data in Julio's stem-and-leaf plot?

4. 🖩 **Calculator**   Find the mean of Julio's data.

Practice

For More Practice, see Set F, pages 474–475.

Make a stem-and-leaf plot for each set of data.

5. Lifetime of D Batteries to the Nearest Hour

27	40	31	33	32
31	25	35	40	28
32	36	37	28	40

6. Lifetime of Lithium Batteries to the Nearest Week

72	76	66	63	57	80
64	59	84	70	77	74
66	74	52	76	83	66

For Exercises 7–12 tell whether you would use paper and pencil, mental math, or a calculator. Then find each answer.

7. The range for Exercise 5

8. The mode for Exercise 5

9. The median for Exercise 5

10. The range for Exercise 6

11. The mode for Exercise 6

12. The median for Exercise 6

Problem Solving

13. Number Sense   Julio tested 20 alkaline batteries. The median was 68 hours, and the tenth leaf was 66 hours. What was the eleventh leaf?

14. Mental Math   The range for the alkaline-battery test was 37 hours. The poorest battery lasted 44 hours. How long did the best one last?

Critical Thinking   The manufacturer of the size-AA batteries made the following claim:

BATTERIES LAST UP TO 90 HOURS!

15. On the basis of Julio's data, is this a true statement?

16. Is it a fair or misleading statement? Why?

Skills Review

For the data listed below, find the

1. median.   **2.** mode.   **3.** mean.

| 19 | 39 | 44 | 17 | 19 | 33 | 25 |

Would you use a bar graph, a broken-line graph, or a circle graph to describe each situation?

4. The average yearly precipitation where you live between the years 1970 and 1993

5. The percent of your day spent in activities such as sleeping, eating, and studying

Use the graph for Exercises 6 and 7.

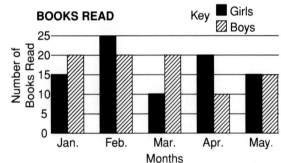

BOOKS READ Key ■ Girls ▨ Boys

6. In which two months did the boys read more books than the girls?

7. In which two months did the girls read more than 15 books?

Use the circle graph for Problem 8.

8. How many cups of orange juice are needed to make 30 cups of punch?

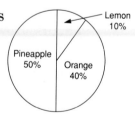

Lemon 10%
Pineapple 50%
Orange 40%

9. Make a stem-and-leaf plot for these test scores: 85, 88, 96, 90, 95, 86, 87, 75, 65, 79, 83, 95, 78, 93, 95, 88.

Problem-Solving Review

Solve each problem.

10. Last week Tao sold 150 roses and 50 bunches of carnations. There were 6 carnations in each bunch. Write the ratio of roses to carnations that Tao sold last week.

11. For his family, Mr. Schuman bought 4 dinners at $5.95 each, 2 dinners at $3.95 each, and 2 cups of coffee that cost $1 in all. Was the total he spent more or less than $30?

12. A survey showed that 475 out of 1,250 students have jobs. What percent of the students have jobs?

13. Which is the warmer temperature, 25°C or 25°F?

14. Mr. Bryant earns $31,500 a year. Mrs. Bryant earns $34,500 a year, and their daughter Mari earns $12,000 a year. What is the mean of the three salaries?

15. **Data File** Use the data on pages 542–543. Make a line graph showing the winners' scores in the U.S. Open for the years 1895–1904. Then make another line graph for the years 1979–1988. Compare the graphs. Describe any trends you see.

16. **Make a Data File** Use a reference book to find the sales-tax rate for 10 different states. List the states in order from the least sales tax to the greatest sales tax.

Write the numbers in order from least to greatest.

1. 12.54   1.254   15.24   0.154

2. 23.1   3.21   2.31   32.1   231

Estimate each answer by using compatible numbers.

3. 4 × 26

4. 12 × 472

5. 703 ÷ 9

6. 302.6 ÷ 24

Use triangle *DEF* for Exercises 7 and 8.

7. Is triangle *DEF* acute, right, or obtuse?

8. Is triangle *DEF* scalene, isosceles, or equilateral?

Find the GCF for each set of numbers.

9. 12, 16

10. 18, 54

Compute.

11. $2\frac{3}{8} + 5\frac{5}{6}$

12. $10\frac{2}{5} - 3\frac{1}{2}$

13. $3\frac{2}{3} \times 1\frac{1}{2}$

14. $1\frac{1}{4} \div 2\frac{1}{2}$

15. The temperature goes from −5°C to −11°C. Tell whether it has fallen or risen and by how much.

Find the area of each figure. Use 3.14 for π.

16. 5 yd / 5 yd   **17.** 4 m / 4 m / 6 m / 4 m   **18.** 2 ft

19. Find the circumference of the circle in Exercise 18.

Write a ratio for

20. Xs to Ts.

X	X	X	
Y	Y	Y	Y
T	T	T	T	T

21. Ys to all letters.

Solve each proportion.

22. $\frac{n}{8} = \frac{6}{20}$

23. $\frac{1.5}{p} = \frac{5}{11}$

Complete the chart.

Fraction	Decimal	Percent
$\frac{1}{3}$	**24.**	**25.**
26.	0.04	**27.**
28.	**29.**	20%

For the data listed below, find the

30. median.   **31.** mode.   **32.** mean.

7	9	7	8	8	2	2	2	9

Solve.

33. What number is $66\frac{2}{3}\%$ of 24?

34. 12 is what percent of 60?

35. Would you use a bar graph or a broken-line graph to compare the populations of 5 cities?

Use the graph for Exercises 36 and 37. Elena earned $400.

ELENA'S BUDGET

36. How much did she budget for food?

37. How much more did she budget for food than for savings?

Reteaching

Set A pages 450–451

Find the mean for this set of numbers.
4, 5, 12, 6, 4, 4, 7

To find the mean, add the numbers. Then divide the sum by the number of numbers.
4 + 5 + 12 + 6 + 4 + 4 + 7 = 42
42 ÷ 7 = 6
The mean is 6.

Remember that the mean need not be one of the numbers in the set of data.

Find the mean for each set of numbers.

1. 36 37 41 43 43

2. 4 15 16 17 18 25 17

Set B pages 454–457

The bar graph at the right shows the sales of video games at Video Plus. The most popular game is the Chase Race. The least popular game is Max is Magic.

Remember that bar graphs are used to show comparisons.

Use the bar graph to find the answer.

1. Which video games had sales greater than 20? less than 20?

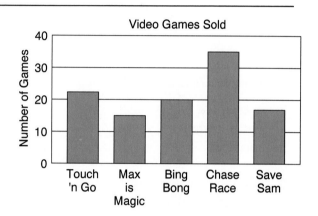

Set C pages 458–459

These two graphs show the same data but use different intervals on the vertical scale.

Remember to consider the intervals on the numerical scale when looking at a graph.

1. Which graph would you use to give the impression that sales grew at a rapid rate?

2. Who might use Graph A to show monthly sales, the sales manager or a competing company?

Set D   pages 460–461

This double bar graph shows the number of miles from San Francisco by road and by air.

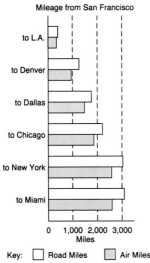

Mileage from San Francisco

to L.A.

to Denver

to Dallas

to Chicago

to New York

to Miami

0   1,000 2,000 3,000
Miles

Key: ☐ Road Miles   ▨ Air Miles

Remember that a double bar graph is used to compare related information.

Use the bar graph shown.

1. Which cities are less than 1,500 miles from San Francisco by road?

2. About how much farther is San Francisco from Chicago than from Dallas by air?

3. Which is greater in each case, the number of road miles or the number of air miles?

Set E   pages 464–465

A garage serviced 400 vehicles. The circle graph shows the percent of each type of vehicle serviced.

How many trucks were serviced?

Find 27% of 400.

$$0.27 \times 400 = 108$$

108 trucks were serviced.

Remember that a circle graph is used to compare parts of a whole.

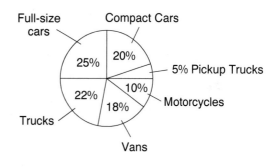

Full-size cars   Compact Cars

25%   20%

5% Pickup Trucks

22%   10%

18%   Motorcycles

Trucks

Vans

Use the circle graph. Find the number of each vehicle serviced.

1. Vans   **2.** Full-sized cars

Set F   pages 468–469

The results of 15 games are shown in the chart. In the stem-and-leaf plot, the stems are the tens digits of each number. The leaves are the ones digits.

41	28	36	42	46
27	26	31	32	44
32	33	35	27	31

```
2 | 6 7 7 8
3 | 1 1 2 2 3 5 6
4 | 1 2 4 6
```

Remember that the range, mode, and median can often be read easily from a stem-and-leaf plot.

1. Make a stem-and-leaf plot for these test grades: 68, 75, 81, 72, 84, 90, 83, 76, 67, 92, 86, 73, 75, 93, 69

2. Find the median grade.

More Practice

Set A   pages 450–451

For Exercises 1–8, tell whether you would use mental math, paper and pencil, or a calculator.

Set A: 23   33   19   23   27   24   19
For Set A, find

1. the range.   **2.** the mean.   **3.** the median.   **4.** the mode.

Set B: 24   39   26   25   28   29   32
For Set B, find

5. the range.   **6.** the mean.   **7.** the median.   **8.** the mode.

Set B   pages 454–457

Use the bar graph for Exercises 1–2. Use the circle graph for Exercises 3–4.

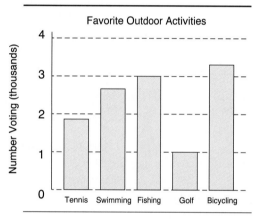

Favorite Outdoor Activities

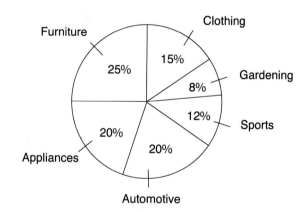

Sales By Department

1. What was the most popular outdoor activity?

2. Estimation Bicycling received about 3 times as many votes as which activity?

3. Which department had the most sales?

4. Estimation Which department had sales that were about twice that of the sports department?

Set C   pages 458–459

Tell whether you would use a line graph or a bar graph to show the following data. Then draw and label the numerical scale for each graph.

1. The areas of the five Great Lakes vary from about 22,000 to about 81,000 square miles.

2. The number of cars sold by a dealer over an eight-month period had a monthly low of 50 cars to a high of 250 cars.

Set D   pages 460–461

Use the bar graph at the right for the following exercises.

1. Which item cost the least in 1980?

2. Which items sold for $1 or more in 1980?

3. Which items sold for $1 or more in 1990?

4. Which item had the largest increase in price from 1980 to 1990?

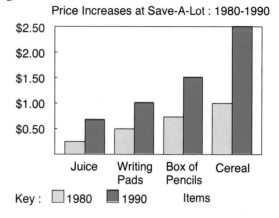

Price Increases at Save-A-Lot : 1980-1990

Key : ☐ 1980   ■ 1990   Items

Set E   pages 464–465

Use the circle graph at the left for Exercises 1–2. Use the circle graph at the right for Exercises 3–4.

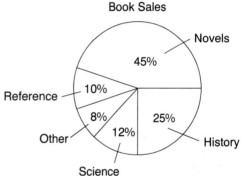

Food Sales

Book Sales

The PTA raised $3,000 from food sales.

1. Which food item brought in the most money? How much money?

2. How much more money was raised selling desserts than beverages?

The PTA raised $4,000 from book sales.

3. How much was raised by the PTA from the sales of history books?

4. How much money was raised selling science and "other" books?

Set F   pages 468–469

Make a stem-and-leaf plot for the data.

1. Number of Customers Each Hour at the Fifteen-Hour Sale

40	61	42	70	54
62	53	63	59	41
63	51	53	61	63

Tell whether you would use paper and pencil, mental math, or a calculator. Then find Exercise 1's

2. range.   3. median.   4. mode.   5. mean.

Enrichment

Random Samples

Many companies use market research to determine the need for new products or to find out what people like about a certain product. Researchers cannot question every single person, so they choose a smaller group, called a **sample**. The sample should reflect the opinions of the entire population.

In a **random sample**, each person has as much chance as any other person to be included. For example, suppose you wanted to find out which breakfast cereal children like. Asking only sixth-graders in a school would tell you nothing about what cereals children of other ages liked.

Explain why each method might not give a random sample.

1. A market researcher questions 25 people at a shopping mall to find out if they like a certain brand of frozen yogurt. The poll is taken on Wednesday morning when school is in session.

2. A survey is being conducted to determine the average amount of gasoline per week used by drivers in a certain state. Fifty drivers passing through a toll booth on an interstate highway are questioned.

3. A car dealer wants to determine how many people plan to buy a new car in the next year. A survey is sent to 1,000 people who bought a car last year.

Answer this question.

4. Suppose you want to conduct a survey to determine how many people at your school plan to attend an upcoming ballgame. How might you conduct the survey to get a random sample?

Chapter 13 Review/Test

Find the range, mean, median, and mode for the set of numbers.

Set A: 12 27 12 20 30 28

1. Range   **2.** Mean

3. Median   **4.** Mode

Study the graph. Then answer the question.

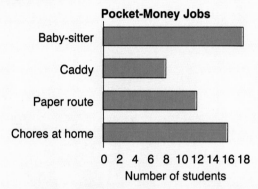

Pocket-Money Jobs

5. What is the most popular job?

6. Draw a line graph based on the data in the table below.

	Number of games won by Team A
1974	10
1975	15
1976	5
1977	20
1978	10

7. How many kilograms of sand are needed to make 90 kg of concrete mix?

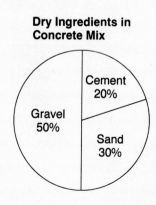

Dry Ingredients in Concrete Mix

Cement 20%
Gravel 50%
Sand 30%

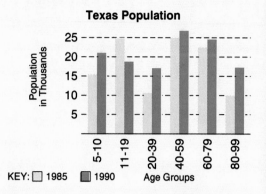

Texas Population

KEY: ☐ 1985 ■ 1990   Age Groups

8. Which two age groups were the largest in 1985?

9. For which age group was there a decrease in population between 1985 and 1990?

10. What is the median of the data in this stem-and-leaf plot?

4	5, 2, 6, 3
5	2, 4, 0
6	1, 0

Read the information below. Then answer the question.

Monthly apartment rents listed in the newspaper were $900, $800, $495, $400, $350, and $350.

11. If you wanted to compare these rents with average rents in other cities, which statistical fact would be the most useful to find?

a. Mean   **b.** Mode   **c.** Median

12. **Write About Math** Which would you use to show a steady increase in population in your city over 10 years—a bar graph or a broken-line graph? Explain.

Investigating Probability

Did You Know: There are four girls and no boys in the Lee family. Assuming that it is equally likely that any given child is a boy or a girl, this is not uncommon.

Number-Sense Project

Estimate
If there are 50 families with 4 children each at a picnic, in how many of the families do you think all 4 children are girls?

Gather Data
You can simulate a family of four children by tossing a coin four times for each family. Do this simulation of four tosses for each of the 50 families. Consider heads a girl and tails a boy. Record the results.

Analyze and Report
How many times out of 50 did you get a family of four girls (4 heads)? Compare your results with those of your classmates.

479

Introducing Probability

Build Understanding

Pick a Color
Materials: A bag; 6 cards or chips (3 green, 2 blue, 1 red)
Groups: 4 students

The **probability** of an event is a number from 0 to 1.

What is the probability of the event "draw a blue chip from the bag" [written P(blue)]? One way to answer is to perform an experiment.

a. Put the cards or chips in the bag. Without looking, draw one chip from the bag and record the color in a chart like this one.

Color	Tally	Number
Green		
Blue		
Red		

b. Put the chip back in the bag. Do 19 more **trials.** Replace the chip each time after recording the color.

c. How many times out of 20 did you draw a blue chip?

d. If you drew a blue chip 7 times, then your approximation of the probability of drawing a blue chip is $\frac{7}{20}$. The probability can be approximated by the fraction

$$P(\text{event}) = \frac{\text{Number of successes}}{\text{Number of trials}}$$

Such a fraction is called the **experimental probability** of an event. Give your experimental probability for each event:

$$P(\text{red}) = \frac{}{20} \qquad P(\text{green}) = \frac{}{20} \qquad P(\text{blue}) = \frac{}{20}$$

e. The greater the probability of an event, the **more likely** it is to occur. The smaller the probability of an event, the **less likely** it is to occur. According to your experimental probabilities, list the events ("draw green," "draw blue," "draw red") from least likely to most likely.

■ **Talk About Math** Give an example of an event in your life that you consider (1) certain; (2) impossible; (3) likely but not certain; (4) unlikely but not impossible.

Check Understanding

For another example, see Set A, pages 500–501.

Lian's tallies for her experiment are shown. Write her approximation for the probability of each event.

Color	Tally
Green	IIII
Blue	IIII II
Red	IIII IIII

1. P(green)   **2.** P(blue)   **3.** P(red)

4. Do you think there is anything unusual about Lian's results? Explain your answer.

Practice

For More Practice, see Set A, pages 502–503.

Make eight cards like the ones shown. Put the cards in a bag and draw one without looking. Record your results. Replace the card. Perform 20 trials of the experiment. Approximate each probability using your results.

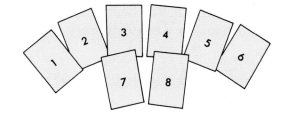

5. $P(2)$ **6.** P(less than 4)   **7.** P(odd number)

8. P(prime number)   **9.** P(1 or 8)   **10.** P(even and prime)

Perform the above activity again, drawing out 2 cards. Approximate each probability using your results.

11. P(2 odd numbers)   **12.** P(2 prime numbers)

13. P(2 numbers less than 8)   **14.** P(odd and even number)

Problem Solving

Suppose you performed 12,000 trials of the experiment for the activity on page 480. What would you expect the approximate value of each probability below to be? Give a reason for your answer.

15. P(green)   **16.** P(blue)   **17.** P(red)   **18.** P(green or red)

Critical Thinking   How would you expect the experimental probabilities in the example on page 480 to change if you put these cards in the bag?

19. 1 green, 2 blue, 3 red   **20.** 6 green, 4 blue, 3 red   **21.** 3 green, 2 blue, 0 red

481

Probability from Tables and Graphs

Build Understanding

A. Real estate agent, Gail Cardona, made this table showing the number of each style of home she sold. She can use the table to approximate the probability of a buyer's preference.

Out of 100 homes sold, 36 were traditional and 29 were contemporary. To approximate the probability that a client will want either a traditional or a contemporary home, Gail added:

P(traditional or contemporary) = $\frac{36 + 29}{100} = \frac{65}{100} = \frac{13}{20} = 0.65 = 65\%$.

The probability that a client will want a traditional or a contemporary home is 65%.

B. The circle graph shows the areas in which Gail's clients prefer to live. Give the probability that a client will want to live in the city as a fraction.

$5\% = 0.05 = \frac{5}{100} = \frac{1}{20}$.

The probability that a client will want to live in the city is $\frac{1}{20}$.

Urban areas cover less than 2 percent of the land in the United States but account for the housing of about three fourths of the people.

Style	Number of Buyers
Traditional	36
Contemporary	29
Colonial	17
Victorian	3
Spanish	7
Tudor	2
Other	6

Areas in Which Clients Want to Live

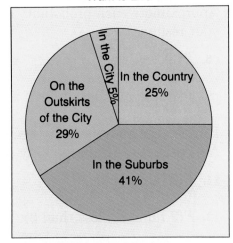

■ **Talk About Math** If Gail makes a table of the styles of the next 100 homes she sells, would you expect it to be exactly like the table in Example A? Explain your answer.

Check Understanding

For another example, see Set B, pages 500–501.

Use Example A to approximate the probability that Gail's next client will

1. want a Victorian or a Tudor home.

2. not want to live in the country or in the city.

Practice

For More Practice, see Set B, 502–503.

Approximate the probability that the next person to buy a house from Gail Cardona will

3. not buy a home in the city.

4. not buy a traditional home.

5. buy a contemporary or a colonial home.

6. buy neither a Spanish home nor a Tudor home.

Kelly Washington runs a rental agency. Based on the most recent 100 renters, the first chart shows the number of rooms in each house that was rented. The second chart shows the number of bathrooms in each house rented.

Approximate the probability that the next person to rent a house through Mr. Washington's agency will

Number of Rooms	Number of Renters
1	2
2	3
3	24
4	34
5	20
6	10
7	4
8 or more	3

7. rent a 5-room house.

8. rent a 3-room house.

9. rent a 4- or 6-room house.

10. rent a house with $1\frac{1}{2}$ bathrooms.

11. rent a house with 1 or more bathrooms.

Number of Bathrooms	Number of Renters
1	75
$1\frac{1}{2}$	12
2 or more	13

12. A national survey shows that for every 42,000 owners of homes with a garage or carport, there are only about 9,000 renters that have one. What is the probability that a renter would rent a home with a garage or carport?

Problem Solving

Estimation   If Gail sells 1,000 homes, how many would you expect to be

13. traditional?   **14.** in the suburbs?   **15.** not Victorian?

16.  **Calculator**   Last year Gail received 539 phone calls about homes for sale. There were 91 calls about homes in the city, 207 calls about homes in the country, 174 about homes on the outskirts of the city, and the rest about homes in the suburbs. Approximate the probability that a caller will ask about a home in the suburbs.

Theoretical Probability

Build Understanding

Theory vs. Experiment
Materials: 50 slips of paper, a box
Groups: 3 or 4 students per group

a. The map shows the postal abbreviations for each of the 50 states. Write the postal abbreviations on slips of paper. Put the slips of paper in a box.

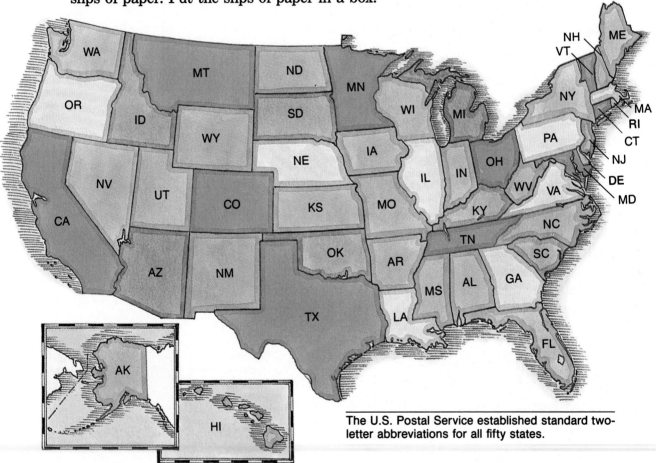

The U.S. Postal Service established standard two-letter abbreviations for all fifty states.

b. Suppose you perform this experiment: Close your eyes. Draw one of the slips of paper from the box. What is the probability that the postal abbreviation will begin with the letter M?

There are 50 abbreviations. They are all equally likely to be drawn. For equally likely outcomes, the probability of an event is

$$P(\text{event}) = \frac{\text{Number of favorable outcomes}}{\text{Number of possible outcomes}}$$

For the event "draw an abbreviation beginning with the letter M," there are 8 *favorable outcomes* (MA, MD, ME, MI, MN, MO, MS, MT) and 50 *possible outcomes.*

$P(\text{abbreviation beginning with M}) =$
$\frac{8}{50} = \frac{4}{25} = 0.16$, which is equal to 16%.

This is the *theoretical probability* that the postal abbreviation will begin with the letter M.

If an experiment with equally likely outcomes is performed a large number of times, we expect the experimental probability and the theoretical probability to be almost equal.

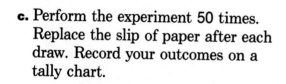

c. Perform the experiment 50 times. Replace the slip of paper after each draw. Record your outcomes on a tally chart.

d. What was your experimental probability for drawing an abbreviation that begins with the letter M?

■ **Talk About Math** For the event "draw an abbreviation beginning with the letter M," were the theoretical probability and your experimental probability the same? If not, what could you do so your next approximation is closer to the theoretical probability?

Check Understanding

For another example, see Set C, pages 500–501.

For each experiment, find the theoretical probability if you can. Write E if you would have to do the experiment. Perform several trials and find an experimental probability.

1. *Experiment:* Close your eyes. Spin a globe. When it stops, point to a spot.
Find: P(landing on Africa)

2. *Experiment:* Open an 85-page atlas at random.
Find: P(the ones digit of the page number is 5)

3 *Experiment:* Each of the 50 cards in a box has a drawing of one of the United States on the front. Take one card.
Find: P(choosing Iowa)

Practice

For More Practice, see Set C, pages 502–503.

Find each theoretical probability for the experiment in the activity on page 484. **Remember** to count all the favorable outcomes.

4. *P*(the first letter of the abbreviation is an I)

5. *P*(the first letter of the abbreviation is a D)

6. *P*(the first letter of the abbreviation is a B)

7. *P*(the first letter of the abbreviation is a vowel)

8. *P*(the abbreviation stands for two words)

9. *P*(the first letter of the abbreviation is an A)

10. *P*(the letters in the abbreviation can be reversed to make another abbreviation)

11. *P*(the state shares part of its border with Mexico)

12. *P*(the state is surrounded on all sides by other states)

13. *P*(the state is east of the Mississippi River)

14. *P*(the state touches an ocean or a gulf)

15. *P*(the state does not border a coast or another country)

16. *P*(the state is west of the Mississippi River and begins with a vowel)

A 17. A world atlas has 60 pages showing 1 or more of the United States. If this is 25% of all the pages, write an equation to find the total number of pages in the atlas. Then tell the probability of opening the atlas to one of these pages.

18. Number Sense The full name of each state is put in a box. If the theoretical probability of selecting the name of a state with more than 10 letters is 22%, is it correct to say that the theoretical probability of drawing the name of a state with less than 10 letters is 78%? Explain your reasoning.

Problem Solving

Number Sense Suppose you print the whole numbers from 1 through 100 on slips of paper and put them in a box. You close your eyes, reach into the box, and pull out one of the slips of paper. What is each probability?

19. P(the number is a multiple of 5)

20. P(the number is a multiple of 3)

21. P(the number is prime)

22. P(the number is odd and composite)

TIPS FOR PROBLEM SOLVERS

Share your thinking with others. Explaining your ideas helps you think better.

Use Data For the experiment on page 480, find each theoretical probability.

23. P(red)   **24.** P(green)   **25.** P(red or blue)

26. P(neither red nor green)   **27.** P(blue or yellow)

Midchapter Checkup

Fernando tossed a number cube with the numbers 1 through 6 on the faces. He recorded the outcomes in this table. Give the experimental and theoretical probability of each event.

Outcome	Tally
1	||||
2	|||| ||
3	|||| |
4	|||
5	|||| |||
6	|||| ||

1. $P(1)$ **2.** $P(4)$

3. $P(5)$ **4.** $P(6)$

5. $P(3 \text{ or } 4)$ **6.** $P(8)$

7. P(a number greater than 4)

8. P(an even number)

Problem-Solving Workshop

Explore as a Team

1. Have one member of your team toss two number cubes numbered 1–6. Record the sum of the two numbers. Predict how many times your team would toss the same sum if they tossed the cubes 100 times.

2. Make a list of all the possible sums your team could toss.

3. Toss the number cubes 100 times. Record the sum of each toss.

4. Compare your team's results with that of the other teams in your class. Are the results the same?

5. If your team tossed the cubes another 100 times, do you think you would get the same results? Why or why not?

TIPS FOR **WORKING TOGETHER**

Help keep your group on task.

Math-at-Home Activity

1. Have each person in your family make a bar graph to chart the number of minutes he or she watches television each week.

2. After a week has gone by, discuss the charts. Who watched the most television? The least television? On what day did each person watch the most television?

3. Have each person find the average number of minutes he or she watches television each day.

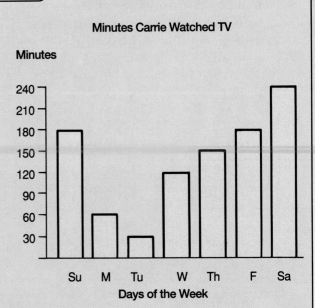

Minutes Carrie Watched TV

Minutes

Days of the Week

Explore with a Computer

Use the *Graphing and Probability Workshop Project* for this activity.

Terry and Chris are playing a coin tossing game. They toss four coins at a time. Terry gets a point if the result is 3 heads and 1 tail. Chris gets a point if the result is 4 tails.

1. Think about the possible combinations of heads and tails. Predict the theoretical probability that Chris will get a point.

2. At the computer, toss four coins 100 times. **Transform** the data into fractions. What is the experimental probability of 3 heads and 1 tail?

3. Explain the difference in your prediction and the actual result.

Number-Sense Project

Look back at pages 478–479.

1. Show all of the possibilities for families of four children, including the order in which the children are born.

2. How many different possibilities are there?

3. What is the probability of a family of 2 girls and 2 boys in any order?

4. Which is more likely, a family of 4 boys or a family in which the oldest is a boy, the middle two children are girls, and the youngest is a boy?

5. Out of 50 families of 4 children, about how many would expect to have 4 girls?

489

Draw a Diagram

Build Understanding

Mrs. Thundercloud's sixth-grade class is electing officers. The candidates are listed below. What possible teams of president and secretary could be elected?

President	Secretary
Tom, Beth, Roberto	Sue, Lynn, Carmen, Art

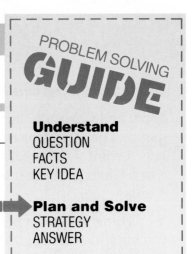

PROBLEM SOLVING
GUIDE

Understand
QUESTION
FACTS
KEY IDEA

▶ **Plan and Solve**
STRATEGY
ANSWER

Look Back
SENSIBLE ANSWER
ALTERNATE APPROACH

Understand   Each candidate for president can be teamed with each of the candidates for secretary.

Plan and Solve   STRATEGY   One way to find the possible teams is to draw a *tree diagram* like the one below.

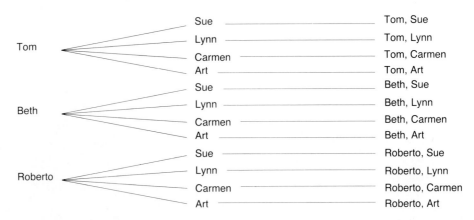

ANSWER   You can see by the tree diagram that 12 teams are possible.

Look Back   SENSIBLE ANSWER   Each presidential candidate can be paired with 4 secretarial candidates. Since there are three presidential candidates, the number of choices is 4 + 4 + 4, or 12.

■ **Talk About Math**   Can you assume that all of the president-secretary teams are equally likely to be elected? Give reasons for your answer.

Check Understanding

Use the data in the chart on page 490 for Exercises 1 and 2.

1. Draw another tree diagram for the possible teams. This time, put the secretarial candidates in the first column. Is the number of possible teams the same?

2. Suppose Brian and Alicia are running for treasurer. Complete the tree diagram begun at the right to show all of the choices for class officers.

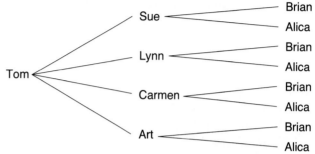

Practice

Draw a tree diagram to find the total number of choices for each election.

3.

Student Council Representative	Homeroom Representative
Wayne, Pam, Tai, Mark	Yoko, Colin, Alan, Arnelle

4.

Basketball Captain	Winter Dance Queen	Dance Chairperson
Manuela, Leonard, Frank	Sally, Claire, Janis, Han	Myrna, Paolo, Jeremy

---

Choose a Strategy

In or Out?   Solve each problem.

5. Eight teams entered a volleyball tournament. If a team loses, it is out of the tournament. How many games are needed to determine the winner?

6. If 32 teams play in the tournament, how many games will have to be played?

PROBLEM SOLVING STRATEGIES

Choose an Operation
Write an Equation
Make a Table
Solve a Simple Problem
Use Logical Reasoning
Try and Check
Find a Pattern
Work Backward
Use a Formula
Make a Graph
Draw a Diagram

Methods of Counting Choices

Build Understanding

Basketmaking is one of the oldest African art forms. This art form was brought to the United States over 300 years ago.

Mary Lee Jackson continues this craft at her home near Charleston, South Carolina. For a plain basket, her customers can choose from the following options:

Shape	Round (R), oval (V)
Handles	0, 1, or 2
Size	Medium (M) or large (L)

How many possible choices are there? To solve the problem, you could make a tree diagram or an *organized list:*

R, 0, M	R, 2, M	V, 1, M
R, 0, L	R, 2, L	V, 1, L
R, 1, M	V, 0, M	V, 2, M
R, 1, L	V, 0, L	V, 2, L

This African American basket was made using the coiling method, one of four methods of basketmaking. The others are weaving, plaiting, and twining.

You can also find the total number of choices by multiplying:

$$2 \times 3 \times 2 = 12$$

2	×	3	×	2	=	12
Choices for shape		Choices for handles		Choices for size		Total number of choices

■ **Talk About Math**   Explain when multiplication works for finding the total number of choices. Give an example of a case where it would be easier to make an organized list.

Check Understanding

For another example, see Set D, pages 500–501.

Find the number of possible choices if

1. only 1 or 2 handles are offered.

2. there were only round baskets.

3. each basket could be dyed light or dark.

4. the baskets could be made from reeds, pine needles, or sweetgrass.

Practice

For More Practice, see Set D, pages 502–503.

Christy Wolf will use one of each type of material shown for her new basket.

Grasses	sweetgrass, reeds
Trees	leaves, bark, wood, twigs
Fibers	cotton, jute

5. Multiply to find the total number of choices.

6. Make an organized list to show all the choices.

Mixed Practice   In selecting a fruit basket, a customer needs to choose one of each of the options listed.

Material	reeds, fabric
Color	red, brown
Method	coiled, woven, twined
Handles	0, 1

7. Multiply to find the total number of choices.

8. Make a tree diagram to show all the possible choices.

Problem Solving

In choosing a Southwest Indian shallow basket, a customer has to make a selection based on these choices.

Group	Tohono O'Odham, Hopi, Apache
Size	small, medium, large
Color	light, dark

People of many Indian nations in the Southwest use shallow baskets to winnow corn before grinding it.

9. How many choices does a customer have if a large basket is wanted?

10. How many choices does a customer have if the dark color is wanted?

11. What is the total number of choices for a small Hopi basket?

12. How many choices are there for a tray made by Apache Indians in a light color?

Skills _____ **Review**   pages 428–429

Mental Math   Find each percent mentally.

1. 25% of 40   **2.** 40% of 200   **3.** 30% of 90   **4.** 70% of 400

Making Predictions

Build Understanding

Which Shape?
Materials: Forty 3 × 5 cards
Groups: 4 students

a. Draw a square on ten cards, a circle on ten cards, a triangle on ten cards, and a star on ten cards.

b. Mix the 40 cards well. Then count out 25 cards without looking at them.

c. Make a table like the following:

Square	Triangle	Circle	Star	Total
				25

d. Mix your 25 cards well. Draw one card. Record the shape in your table. Put the card back in your 25-card deck.

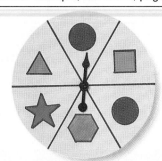

e. Repeat Step **d** until you have recorded 25 draws.

f. Use the data from your table. Find your experimental probability of drawing each shape.

g. Count the number of cards of each shape in your 25-card deck.

h. Suppose you draw a card. Find the theoretical probability of drawing each shape.

■ **Talk About Math** Compare your theoretical and experimental probabilities. Give reasons for any differences.

Check Understanding

For another example, see Set E, pages 500–501.

Use the spinner at the right for Exercises 1–4. What is the probability of landing on

1. a circle?

2. a polygon?

3. a figure with more than 4 sides?

4. a triangle?

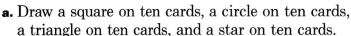

494

For More Practice, see Set E, pages 502–503.

Practice

For each Mind Bender problem a student solves, Mrs. Forsythe writes the student's name on a slip of paper and places the slip in a box. Then she draws one slip to select the winner of the Mind Bender Prize. Use the chart to solve each problem. **Remember** to count the possible outcomes.

Mind Benders	
John	♀♀♀♀♀♀♀♀♀
Heather	♀♀♀♀♀♀
Kimiko	♀♀♀♀
Bobby	♀
Alonzo	♀♀♀
Ramon	♀♀♀♀
Irene	♀♀♀♀♀♀
Taro	♀♀♀♀

Each ♀ = 1 problem solved

5. Which student has the best chance to win the prize?

6. What is the probability that Alonzo will win the prize?

7. What is the probability that Bobby will not win the prize?

8. Compute each student's probability of winning.

9. If each ♀ stood for 5 problems solved, explain how the probability would change.

10. Miriam's 6 problems were not on the chart. Explain how including them would change each student's probability of winning.

Problem Solving

Solve the problem.

11. Critical Thinking In the activity on page 494, do you think the experimental probabilities would be closer to the theoretical probabilities with 25 draws or 2,500 draws?

Explore ———— Math

Jacob spun several spinners 100 times each. Each spinner had regions of equal size and each region was colored one of the indicated colors. On the basis of the data given, draw and color each spinner Jacob might have used. How many regions will you draw? What colors will those regions be?

12.		**13.**		**14.**		**15.**	
Green	47	Green	39	Green	9	Green	21
Blue	53	Blue	19	Blue	54	Blue	41
		Red	42	Red	37	Red	32
						Brown	6

Collecting Data

PROBLEM SOLVING
GUIDE

Build Understanding

 **Understand**
QUESTION
FACTS
KEY IDEA

Plan and Solve
STRATEGY
ANSWER

Look Back
SENSIBLE ANSWER
ALTERNATE APPROACH

The Parents' Club is donating $4,000 to King Middle School clubs. They will give each club a percent of the $4,000 equal to the percent of students choosing that club as their favorite. They surveyed the students in Mr. Stewart's math class to determine students' favorite clubs. If the Parents' Club uses only these results, how much of their donation will go to the Science Club?

Understand   QUESTION   How much of the $4,000 should go to the Science Club?

FACTS   The table shows the survey results. Of the 20 students surveyed, 6 chose the Science Club.

KEY IDEA   The percent of the $4,000 that goes to the Science Club should be equal to the percent of the students whose favorite club is the Science Club.

Results of Club Survey	
Stamp Club	2
Music Club	5
Science Club	6
Art Club	4
Pep Club	2
Chess Club	1

Plan and Solve   The Science Club was the favorite of $\frac{6}{20}$, or $\frac{3}{10}$, or 30%, of the students. Find 30% of $4,000.

$0.3 \times 4,000 = 1,200$

If the survey results alone are used, the Science club should get $1,200.

Look Back   A little more than $\frac{1}{4}$ of the students chose the Science Club as their favorite. Since $\frac{1}{4}$ of $4,000 is $1,000, the answer is reasonable.

■ **Talk About Math**   Do you think the survey data from Mr. Stewart's math class are representative of all of King Middle School? Why or why not?

Check Understanding

On the basis of the survey of Mr. Stewart's class,
how much of $4,000 should the Parents' Club give to

1. the Stamp Club?　　**2.** the Chess Club?　　**3.** the Music Club?

4. the Art Club?　　**5.** the Pep Club?

Practice

Take a survey to find the favorite clubs of students in your
class. Make a table to show your data.

6. Using your data, decide how much of the $4,000
the Parents' Club should give to each club.

Extend your survey. Have each student in your class
survey 3 other students. Make a table to show your data.

7. Using the results of the extended
survey, decide how much of the
$4,000 should be given to each club.
List the amount for each club.

8. Critical Thinking If you were
president of the Parents' Club, which
of the two surveys would you
recommend using to decide how
much to give to each club?

Choose a_____ Strategy

Did You See It? Barbara asked each of the 20 students in her
class if they had seen the movies *Icy Planet* and *Superperson*. The
table shows the results of her survey.

	Saw *Icy Planet*	Did not see *Icy Planet*
Saw *Superperson*	10	5
Did not see *Superperson*	4	1

Among a group of 100 students in Barbara's school, how
many would you predict saw

9. *Superperson?*　　**10.** *Icy Planet?*　　**11.** one movie but not both?

Skills Review

A bag contains green, blue, and red blocks. Jon drew 20 blocks one at a time, returning each to the bag. The tallies show his results. Give each experimental probability.

Color	Tally
Green	卌 III
Blue	III
Red	卌 IIII

1. P(green)   **2.** P(blue)   **3.** P(red)

4. If a bag contains 4 green, 3 blue, and 2 red blocks, what is the theoretical probability of picking a red block?

Use the chart. Write a percent for the probability that a student's favorite pet is

Favorite Pets

Pet	Number of Students
Bird	25
Cat	28
Dog	35
Fish	12

5. a dog.

6. a cat or a fish.

7. A sandwich can be made with white, wheat, or rye bread. The filling can be ham or chicken. The bread can be toasted or untoasted. How many choices are there?

The chart shows the number of books read by 5 students. For each book read, a slip of paper with the student's name is put in a box. One name is drawn to receive a prize.

Student	Books Read
Mel	2
Anna	6
Chen	1
Josh	8
Bryan	3

8. Which student has the best chance to win?

9. What is the probability that Josh will win the prize?

Problem-Solving Review

Solve each problem.

10. One cup of milk powder has 879 milligrams of calcium. It takes $1\frac{1}{3}$ cups of milk powder to make 1 quart of milk. How much calcium is in 1 quart of milk?

11. Ada bought a used piano for $495 plus 6% sales tax. What was the total cost?

12. Fred has four different colors of shirts he wears to work with two different colors of pants. How many different outfits can Fred wear to work?

13. Shannon and Robin shared the cost of a new television equally. The television cost $145.98 plus 6% sales tax. How much money did each girl spend?

14. Martin bought a pair of shoes and a belt. The shoes cost 4 times as much as the belt. The shoes cost $27.80. Write and solve an equation to find the cost of the belt.

15. Data File Use the data on pages 542–543. Suppose you want to see two movies for the price of one, but you must leave the theater before 6:00. How many choices do you have for pairs of movies to see? List all possible choices.

16. Make a Data File Use a reference book to find the calorie content of one serving of six different foods. Present your findings in a bar graph.

498

Round 24,367.28349 to the nearest

1. thousand   **2.** ten-thousandth.

Estimate each product or quotient using compatible numbers.

3. 31 × 48   **4.** 55 × 364

5. 325 ÷ 4   **6.** 428 ÷ 68

Describe how to move from Figure I to Figure II. Write *slide*, *flip*, or *turn*.

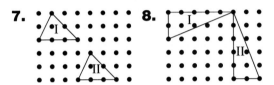

7.   **8.**

Compare. Use <, >, or =.

9. $\frac{5}{6}$ ⬚ $\frac{7}{8}$ **10.** $\frac{20}{4}$ ⬚ $5\frac{1}{4}$

Compute.

11. $5\frac{1}{2} + 3\frac{1}{6}$ **12.** $2\frac{5}{6} \div 2\frac{1}{2}$

Choose the most sensible measure.

13. Height of a door
    2 cm   2 m   2 km

Use the prism for Exercise 14.

14. Find the volume and the surface area of the prism.

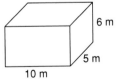

Write each percent as a ratio.

15. 95%   **16.** 3%   **17.** 50%

Use the similar figures for Exercise 18.

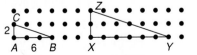

18. Find the length of $\overline{XY}$.

Find each answer.

19. 25% of 80   **20.** $66\frac{2}{3}$% of 96

21. What percent of 50 is 30?

22. 28 is what percent of 56?

23. Make a stem-and-leaf plot for the data below.

Number of Video Rentals Per Hour						
56	54	38	45	48	54	41
63	32	54	48	38	66	

For the data above, find the

24. range.   **25.** mode.

26. median.   **27.** mean.

Would you use a bar graph, a broken-line graph, or a circle graph to describe each situation?

28. The number of new homes sold each year between 1980 and 1993

29. The percent of library books checked out by category such as novels, history, or science

Cards with the letters for the word MISSISSIPPI are put in a bag. One card is drawn. Find each probability.

30. P(S)   **31.** P(M)   **32.** P(M or P)

33. P(a vowel)   **34.** P(M, S, I, or P)

Solve each problem.

35. How many choices for outfits do you have if your shirt can be red, blue, or green and your pants can be black or white?

Reteaching

Lou performed 25 trials of drawing a colored chip from a bag and replacing it. The chart at the right shows the results. She then computed each probability using this fraction.

$P(\text{event}) = \frac{\text{Number of successes}}{\text{Number of trials}}$

Remember that the probability of an event is a number from 0 to 1.

Color	Tally	Number
Green	IIII IIII	9
Blue	IIII III	8
Yellow	IIII	5
Red	III	3

Find an approximation for the probability of each event.

1. $P(\text{green})$ **2.** $P(\text{blue})$

3. $P(\text{yellow})$ **4.** $P(\text{red})$

The table below shows the results of a survey of 100 people.

Entertainment	Number
Television	21
Sports	23
Movies	27
Games	13
Concerts	16

To approximate the probability that the next person asked will prefer movies or sports, you add.

$P(\text{movies or sports}) = \frac{27 + 23}{100} = \frac{50}{100}, \text{ or } \frac{1}{2}$

Remember that a probability of 0 means than an event will never occur. A probability of 1 means an event is certain to happen.

Use the table at the left to approximate the probability that the next person asked will

1. prefer games or concerts.

2. prefer television or movies.

3. prefer sports, movies, or concerts.

The letters of the word WASHINGTON are written on separate cards and placed in a box. After mixing up the cards, one is drawn without looking. Since there are 10 cards, the theoretical probability of drawing the letter N is

$P(\text{event}) = \frac{\text{Number of Favorable Outcomes}}{\text{Number of Possible Outcomes}}$

$P(N) = \frac{2}{10}$ There are 2 Ns.
        There are 10 cards.

$\quad\quad = \frac{1}{5}$

Remember that the probability ratio is used when all the events are equally likely to be drawn.

Find each theoretical probability for the activity described in the left column.

1. $P(W)$ **2.** $P(A \text{ or } N)$

3. $P(E)$ **4.** $P(\text{a vowel})$

5. $P(\text{a consonant})$ **6.** $P(A \text{ or } I)$

Set D   pages 492–493

This is today's menu at Quick Stop Burgers. How many possible choices are there for lunch? To solve the problem, make an organized list. Use R for regular burger, C for Cheeseburger, P for Pizzaburger, M for milk, H for hot chocolate, F for fruit cup, and Y for frozen yogurt.

HAMBURGERS
Regular burger
Cheeseburger
Pizzaburger
BEVERAGES
Milk
Hot Chocolate
DESSERTS
Fruit Cup
Frozen Yogurt

R, M, F   C, M, F   P, M, F
R, M, Y   C, M, Y   P, M, Y
R, H, F   C, H, F   P, H, F
R, H, Y   C, H, Y   P, H, Y

Remember that you can find the total number of choices by multiplying.

The following sign shows the types of bread, loaf sizes, and the types of slices available at a bakery.

BREAD	LOAF	SLICE
Pumpernickel Whole Wheat	12-ounce 16-ounce 24-ounce	Regular Thin

1. Make an organized list to show all the choices.

2. A customer wants to buy whole wheat bread. How many choices are there?

Set E   pages 494–495

Jack kept this record of each of his 25 spins. Each of the 5 regions on the spinner is the same size.

Spinner Number	1	2	3	4	5	Total
Number of Times	4	5	6	7	3	25

The number 4 came up 7 times out of 25.

The experimental probability is:

$P(4) = \frac{7}{25}$

He compared this with the theoretical probability.

$P(4) = \frac{1}{5}$

Remember that the more trials you make, the closer the experimental probability will be to the theoretical probability.

Refer to this spinner for Exercises 1–5.

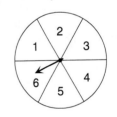

1. What is the probability of landing on the number 2?

2. What is the probability of landing on an even number?

3. How many numbers on the spinner are greater than 2?

4. What is the probability of landing on a number greater than 2?

5. What is the probability of landing on a number less than 3?

More Practice

Set A   pages 480–481

Make six cards like these. Put the cards in a bag and draw one without looking. Replace the card. Perform 20 trials of the experiment. Be sure to record the results.

| 1 | 2 | 3 |

| 4 | 5 | 6 |

Approximate each probability using your results.

1. $P(1)$

2. $P(\text{odd number})$

3. $P(\text{less than 3})$

4. $P(\text{prime number})$

5. $P(2 \text{ or } 5)$

6. $P(1, \text{ or } 2, \text{ or } 3)$

Add these four cards to the six you made for Exercises 1–6. Put all ten cards in a bag and draw one without looking. Replace the card. Perform 25 trials of the experiment. Be sure to record your results.

| 7 | 8 | 9 | 10 |

Approximate each probability using your results.

7. $P(1)$

8. $P(\text{even number})$

9. $P(\text{less than 7})$

10. $P(\text{prime number})$

11. $P(2 \text{ or } 5)$

12. $P(\text{more than 6})$

Set B   pages 482–483

This table shows the results of a survey of 100 people. These people were asked to name their favorite local attraction.

Attraction	Number of People
Public beach	40
Municipal zoo	14
Amusement park	35
Wildlife sanctuary	11

This table shows the results of a survey of 100 people. These people were asked to name their favorite food from a list of four foods.

Food	Number of People
Hamburger	40
Hot dog	19
Pizza	31
Taco	10

1. Approximate the probability that a person would not name the public beach as their favorite attraction.

2. Approximate the probability that a person would not name the public beach or the amusement park as their favorite attraction.

3. Approximate the probability that a person would not name a hot dog as their favorite food.

4. Approximate the probability that a person would not name pizza or hamburger as their favorite food.

Set C pages 484–487

The letters of the word CALIFORNIA are written on separate cards and placed in a box. After mixing up the cards, one is drawn without looking.

Find each theoretical probability.

1. $P(A)$

2. $P(C)$

3. $P(F \text{ or } I)$

4. $P(N, R, \text{ or } A)$

5. $P(\text{a vowel})$

6. $P(\text{a consonant})$

The letters of the word MATHEMATICAL are written on separate cards and placed in a box. After mixing up the cards, one is drawn without looking.

Find each theoretical probability.

7. $P(A)$

8. $P(M)$

9. $P(I)$

10. $P(C, T, \text{ or } H)$

11. $P(\text{a vowel})$

12. $P(\text{a consonant})$

Set D pages 492–493

A car that you want to buy has these options available.

1. Multiply to find the total number of choices.

2. Make an organized list to show all the options.

Exterior Colors	Red, blue, black, white
Interior Colors	Red, black, white
Seat Fabric	Vinyl, leather

Mixed Practice A Jasper car has these options available.

3. Multiply to find the total number of choices.

4. Make a tree diagram to show all the possible choices.

Style	Two door, four door
Seat Fabric	Vinyl, leather, cloth
Windows	Power, regular
Transmission	Automatic, manual

Set E pages 494–495

Each time a student collects 10 aluminum cans, the teacher writes the student's name on a slip of paper and places the slip in a box. At the end of the drive, a winner of the grand prize will be chosen by drawing one slip from the box.

1. Which student has the best chance of winning the prize?

2. Compute each student's probability of winning.

ALUMINUM CAN DRIVE

Rene ⊟ ⊟ ⊟ ⊟ ⊟

Willis ⊟ ⊟ ⊟ ⊟

Jake ⊟ ⊟ ⊟ ⊟ ⊟ ⊟ ⊟ ⊟ ⊟

Rita ⊟ ⊟ ⊟ ⊟ ⊟ ⊟ ⊟

Art ⊟ ⊟ ⊟ ⊟ ⊟ ⊟

Nancy ⊟ ⊟ ⊟ ⊟ ⊟

Key: ⊟ = 10 aluminum cans

Enrichment

Arrangements and Combinations

In a classroom, Todd, Chris, and Lee Ann sit behind each other in single file. In how many ways can they be seated?

One possible way to solve this problem is to list all possible *arrangements*. Each possible arrangement involves the order of seating.

1. Todd	**1.** Todd	**1.** Chris	**1.** Chris	**1.** Lee Ann	**1.** Lee Ann
2. Chris	**2.** Lee Ann	**2.** Todd	**2.** Lee Ann	**2.** Chris	**2.** Todd
3. Lee Ann	**3.** Chris	**3.** Lee Ann	**3.** Todd	**3.** Todd	**3.** Chris

There are six possible arrangements.

In some problems, order is not important. For example, suppose five pizza toppings are available: cheese, sausage, onion, mushroom, and pepperoni. If Iola picks two toppings, how many *combinations* are possible?

In this case, if Iola picks cheese and sausage, that is the same as picking sausage and cheese. The order of the topping is not important. If you list all the possible combinations, you have ten different possibilities:

cheese	cheese	cheese	cheese	sausage
sausage	onion	mushroom	pepperoni	onion
sausage	sausage	onion	onion	mushroom
mushroom	pepperoni	mushroom	pepperoni	pepperoni

Solve the following problems by listing all the possible arrangements or combinations.

1. Ti, Carlotta, Ricky, and Kathy board an airplane in single file. In how many ways can they board?

2. If Iola picks three pizza toppings instead of two, how many combinations are possible?

3. Ossie must pick three different activities out of six possible choices: swimming, basketball, soccer, tennis, archery, and softball. In how many ways can he pick three activities?

Chapter 14 Review/Test

A bag contains 3 red marbles, 4 blue marbles, 1 white marble, and 1 green marble. A marble is picked without looking and the color is recorded.

1. In 45 draws, a blue marble was picked 22 times. Use these results to approximate P(blue).

2. What is the theoretical probability of picking a blue marble from the bag?

Candidate	Number of Votes
Ramirez	174
Schwartz	90
Zepeda	210
Wentworth	126

The chart shows the result of a survey of 600 registered voters. Write each probability as a percent.

3. The probability that a voter will vote for Schwartz

4. The probability that a voter will vote for Zepeda or Wentworth

Suppose you wrote the letters of the alphabet on 26 slips of paper and drew one of the slips from the bag. Write each probability as a fraction.

5. P(the slip shows a vowel)

6. P(the slip shows the first letter of your first name)

Draw a tree diagram for Exercise 7.

7. Vicente has 3 ski badges from Vail, 2 from Aspen, and 4 from Squaw Valley. In how many ways can he choose one badge from each place?

8. Mrs. Marple must travel from Boston to New York to Pittsburgh to Dallas. She can choose to fly or drive to New York; to fly or take the train to Pittsburgh; and then fly, take the train, or take the bus to Dallas. Make an organized list to find the number of different ways she can plan her trip.

9. A telephone book has 744 pages. What is the probability that you will open it on the first try to a given page number?

Read the problem below. Then answer the question.

Sixteen teams entered a soccer tournament. If a team loses, it is out of the tournament. How many games are needed to determine the winner?

10. Which strategy could you use to solve the problem?

   a. Use a formula
   b. Draw a diagram.
   c. Write an equation.

11. **Write About Math** Suppose that only science students were asked to name their favorite subject. Would this survey represent the views of all of the students? Explain.

Understanding Integers

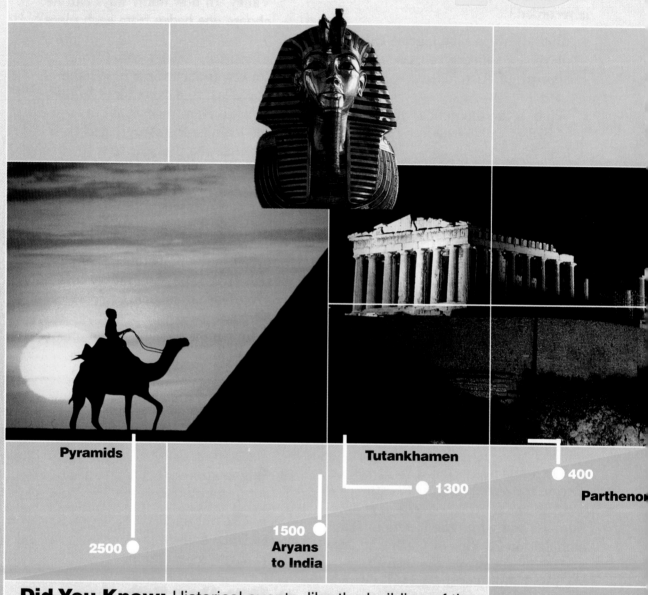

Pyramids

Tutankhamen

● 400

Parthenon

● 1300

2500 ●

1500 ●
**Aryans
to India**

Did You Know: Historical events, like the building of the pyramids in Egypt are often recorded on a time line. A time line is like a number line without the 0 point. The year 1 A.D. and points to the right represent dates A.D. The year 1 B.C. and points to the left represent dates B.C.

Number-Sense Project

Estimate
When do you think the pyramids were constructed? Where would this data be on the time line?

Gather Data
Determine dates for three events that occurred in times B.C. and three events that occurred in times A.D. Include the building of the pyramids in Egypt as one of the events.

Analyze and Report
Put your events on a time line. As a class you might make a time line to show all the dates reported.

Wright Brothers

Colosseum

2000

1500 ● **1900**

Modern Cities

Tiberius Caesar

800 ●

● **100**

Vikings

Columbus

Meaning of Integers

Build Understanding

On February 16, the low temperature in Chicago was ⁻15°F. On the same day, the low temperature in San Diego was 58°F and in New York it was 0°F.

Integers include whole numbers and their opposites. Zero, ⁻15, and ⁺58 are integers. The integer ⁻15 is *negative* and ⁺58 (or 58) is *positive.* Zero is neither positive nor negative.

■ **Talk About Math**   Name other examples of the uses of positive and negative integers.

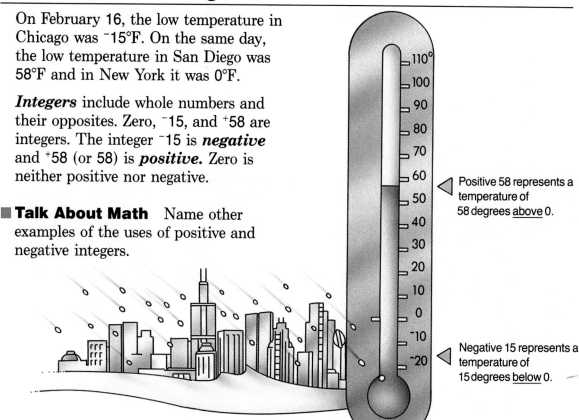

Positive 58 represents a temperature of 58 degrees <u>above</u> 0.

Negative 15 represents a temperature of 15 degrees <u>below</u> 0.

Check Understanding

For another example, see Set A, pages 536–537.

Number Sense   For Exercises 1 and 2, refer to the example above. **Remember** to use the symbol for Fahrenheit, F, when writing the temperatures.

1. On February 16, the low temperature in Minot, North Dakota, was 10 degrees colder than the low temperature in Chicago. Find the low temperature in Minot.

2. Copy and complete. ___?___ integers show temperatures greater than zero. ___?___ integers show temperatures less than zero.

3. Describe a situation requiring the use of positive integers.

4. Describe a situation requiring the use of negative integers.

Write an integer to represent each situation.
Remember to write the sign for each integer
and to label each answer.

5. A temperature of 98 degrees above
zero

6. A temperature of 10 degrees below
zero

7. A profit of $125

8. A loss of $456

9. A weight loss of 21 pounds

10. Backward by 27 steps

11. Down 4 flights of stairs

12. A bank withdrawal of $47

13. 683 feet above sea level

14. A $15 increase in pay

15. A bank deposit of $45

16. Up 2 flights of stairs

17. A $25 decrease in pay

18. A 4-point drop in the stock market

19. A 12 point rise in the stock market

20. 368 feet below sea level

21. A temperature of 0°

22. Altitude at sea level

Problem Solving

Write an integer for each situation.

23. The level of water in the river
dropped five inches during the
drought.

24. On the hottest day of the summer,
the temperature reached
112° Fahrenheit.

25. The first stage of the rocket
separated 126 seconds after liftoff.

26. Marty spent $13 on a birthday gift
for his father.

27. The jeweler sold a watch for $250
more than she paid for it.

28. The top of the hill was 1,500 feet
above sea level.

Solve the problem.

29. Critical Thinking Suppose the only temperatures
labeled on a thermometer are 0°F and 10°F. How
would you find the location of ⁻10°F? of 45°F?

Integers on the Number Line

Build Understanding

Let the Integers Roll
Materials: Four number cubes numbered 1–6,
two red ones and two green ones
Groups: 4 students

a. Toss the four number cubes.

b. Copy the number line below, leaving more space
between the integers. Place the red number cubes
on the negative integers corresponding to the
numbers tossed.

Place the green number cubes on the positive
integers corresponding to the numbers tossed.

If you have two number cubes on the same integer,
move one onto the 0.

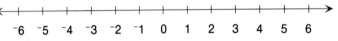

$$\overset{\longleftarrow \quad |\quad|\quad|\quad|\quad|\quad|\quad|\quad|\quad|\quad|\quad|\quad|\quad|\quad \longrightarrow}{\quad ^-6 \;\; ^-5 \;\; ^-4 \;\; ^-3 \;\; ^-2 \;\; ^-1 \;\; 0 \;\; 1 \;\; 2 \;\; 3 \;\; 4 \;\; 5 \;\; 6}$$

c. On a horizontal number line, the integer on the
right is greater. Write your integers in order from
least to greatest.

d. Use $<$, $>$, or $=$ to compare each integer to 0.

e. Pairs of integers that are the same distance from
0, such as $^-6$ and 6, are called *opposites.* Name
any opposites you tossed.

■ **Write About Math**   Write a statement for comparing
a positive integer to a negative integer.

Check Understanding

For another example, see Set B, pages 536–537.

Fill in the blanks.

1. The opposite of $^-63$ is ___?___

2. 0 is less than any ___?___ integer.

3. As you move from left to right on
the number line, the integers become
___?___.

4. On the number line, the integer
between $^-6$ and $^-4$ is ___?___.

Practice

For More Practice, see Set B, pages 538–539.

Use the number line below. Write the integer for each point. **Remember** to write a negative sign for negative integers.

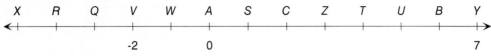

5. *Q*   **6.** *W*   **7.** *R*   **8.** *B*   **9.** *S*   **10.** *Z*   **11.** *X*   **12.** *T*

Compare these integers. Use >, < or =.

13. 40 ⬚ 2   **14.** 30 ⬚ 8   **15.** 54 ⬚ ⁻3   **16.** ⁻17 ⬚ ⁻5   **17.** ⁻3 ⬚ ⁻7

18. 90 ⬚ ⁻9   **19.** ⁻18 ⬚ ⁻3   **20.** ⁻85 ⬚ 62   **21.** 18 ⬚ ⁻18   **22.** ⁻12 ⬚ 16

Arrange the integers from least to greatest.

23. 2 4 1 7   **24.** 10 ⁻3 0 ⁻6   **25.** 0 ⁻2 ⁻7 5

26. ⁻5 3 ⁻2 1   **27.** ⁻7 8 ⁻6 1   **28.** 2 ⁻3 7 ⁻5

Problem Solving

Use Data   Use the thermometer at the top of page 508. Which temperature is warmer?

29. 32° or 80°   **30.** ⁻15° or 0°   **31.** ⁻15° or ⁻7°   **32.** 4° or ⁻12°

Explore _____ Math

Number Sense   Do this experiment.

a. Pick any two integers *a* and *b*. Compare them. Use < or >.
b. Find the opposites of *a* and *b*. Compare them. Use < or >.
c. Repeat step a and step b for 5 other pairs of integers.
Use the results of your experiment. Complete each
sentence. Write < or >.

33. If $a > b$, then the opposite of *a*   **34.** If $a < b$, then the opposite of *a*
⬚ the opposite of *b*.   ⬚ the opposite of *b*.

Adding Integers

Build Understanding

A. Nathan deposited $9 into his bank account on Tuesday and $8 on Friday. What is the total of the two deposits? Putting money into an account is a ***deposit***.

Find 9 + 8.

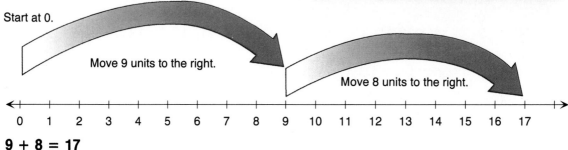

Start at 0.

Move 9 units to the right.

Move 8 units to the right.

9 + 8 = 17

Nathan deposited $17.

B. Last week, Katherine made a withdrawal of $12 from her bank account. This week she made a withdrawal of $6. What is the total of the two withdrawals? Taking money out of an account is a ***withdrawal.***

Find ⁻12 + ⁻6.

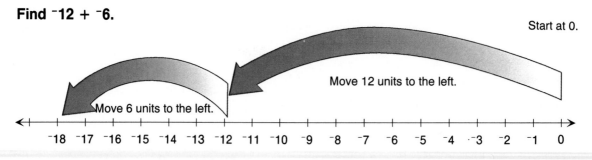

Start at 0.

Move 12 units to the left.

Move 6 units to the left.

⁻12 + ⁻6 = ⁻18

Katherine withdrew a total of $18.

To add two integers with the same sign, add the integers. Then place the sign of the integers in the answer.

c. Leon opened a checking account with $12. He wrote a check for $18. A bank account is ***overdrawn*** if more money is taken out than is in the account. By how much is his account overdrawn?

Find 12 + ⁻18.

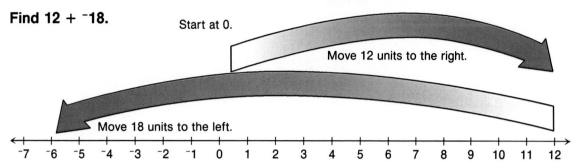

Start at 0.

Move 12 units to the right.

Move 18 units to the left.

$$-7 \quad -6 \quad -5 \quad -4 \quad -3 \quad -2 \quad -1 \quad 0 \quad 1 \quad 2 \quad 3 \quad 4 \quad 5 \quad 6 \quad 7 \quad 8 \quad 9 \quad 10 \quad 11 \quad 12$$

12 + ⁻18 = ⁻6

Leon's account is overdrawn by $6.

To add two integers with different signs, consider the distance each integer is from zero. Subtract the shorter distance from the longer distance. Then use the sign of the number farther from zero in your answer.

D. ▦ **Calculator**   You can use the [+/–] key on a calculator to add integers. The [+/–] key changes the number in the display to its opposite.

Add: ⁻42 + 26	Add: 83 + ⁻37
Press: 42 [+/–]	**Press:** 83 [+] 37 [+/–] [=]
Display: ⁻42.	**Display:** 46.
Press: [+] 26 [=]	83 + ⁻37 = 46
Display: ⁻16.	
⁻42 + 26 = ⁻16	

■ **Talk About Math**   When is the sum of one positive number and one negative number positive? When is the sum negative? When is it zero?

Check Understanding

For another example, see Set C, pages 536–537.

Draw a number line for each exercise. Begin at zero. Move right to show deposits and left to show withdrawals. Write an integer to show the sum.

1. Deposit $10; withdraw $6

2. Withdraw $6; withdraw $8

3. Withdraw $7; deposit $5

4. Deposit $10; withdraw $10

5. What is the sum of an integer and its opposite?

Practice

For More Practice, see Set C, pages 538–539.

Find each sum. **Remember** to watch the signs.

6. $-4 + 1$ **7.** $-7 + 3$ **8.** $3 + -7$ **9.** $5 + -5$ **10.** $-9 + 6$

11. $-3 + -5$ **12.** $-5 + -3$ **13.** $-3 + 8$ **14.** $-1 + -10$ **15.** $7 + -5$

16. $8 + -12$ **17.** $-4 + -3$ **18.** $6 + -11$ **19.** $-4 + 13$ **20.** $-8 + -6$

21. $10 + -3$ **22.** $-9 + -9$ **23.** $-8 + 0$ **24.** $8 + -6$ **25.** $-11 + 9$

26. $-6 + -4$ **27.** $-4 + 12$ **28.** $9 + -8$ **29.** $5 + -2$ **30.** $-4 + 4$

Mental Math   Use what you know about opposites to find each sum mentally.

31. $-3 + 12 + 3$ **32.** $5 + -5 + -6$ **33.** $-14 + 11 + -11 + 14$

34. $9 + -9 + 5$ **35.** $8 + 7 + -7$ **36.** $-23 + -16 + 16$

37. $-10 + -10 + 10$ **38.** $13 + -3 + 3$ **39.** $12 + 0 + -12 + 0$

For Exercises 40–59, tell whether you would use mental math, paper and pencil, or a calculator. Then find each sum.

40. $12 + -7$ **41.** $-3 + 3$ **42.** $10 + -20$ **43.** $(-15 + 28) + 3$

44. $9 + -18$ **45.** $24 + 0$ **46.** $-15 + 0$ **47.** $-18 + 27$

48. $612 + -115 + 115$ **49.** $34 + (12 + -18)$ **50.** $(234 + 412) + -318$

51. $-4 + 12 + 4$ **52.** $-415 + (128 + 93)$ **53.** $8 + -8 + -8$

54. $26 + -12 + -14$ **55.** $-85 + 66 + -48$ **56.** $107 + -82 + 56$

57. $126 + (-318 + -203)$ **58.** $-25 + -25 + -25$ **59.** $237 + -138 + -237$

Number Sense   Complete.

60. The sum of two or more positive integers is always ___?___.

61. The sum of two or more negative integers is always ___?___.

62. The sum of a positive integer and a negative integer is sometimes ___?___ and sometimes ___?___.

63. The sum of a number and its opposite is always ___?___.

Problem Solving

Use integers to solve. **Remember** to label answers with a dollar sign ($) when writing about money.

64. Leslie deposited $22 into her checking account. She then made a withdrawal of $5. How much of her $22 is left?

65. Jan had $19 in her bank account. She wrote a check for $25. By how much is her account overdrawn?

66. Helen Marie had no money in her checking account. She deposited $30. She wrote a check for $30 and deposited $17. What is the amount in her account?

67. Vince's account was $8 overdrawn. The bank charged $5 for being overdrawn. Then he made a $40 deposit. How much is in his account?

Critical Thinking Solve each problem.

68. Write a rule for finding the sum of any integer and 0.

69. Does the commutative property of addition apply to integers? Explain. Then give an example.

70. Write an equation for the grouping of addends when you add three integers.

Skills _____ **Review**   Pages 378–381, 384–387

Write three other ratios equal to each ratio.

1. $\frac{3}{3}$ **2.** $\frac{2}{8}$ **3.** $\frac{1}{5}$ **4.** $\frac{2}{12}$ **5.** $\frac{8}{4}$ **6.** $\frac{7}{3}$

Solve each proportion.

7. $\frac{9}{n} = \frac{6}{2}$ **8.** $\frac{h}{3} = \frac{2}{1}$ **9.** $\frac{10}{16} = \frac{30}{s}$ **10.** $\frac{5}{9} = \frac{t}{45}$ **11.** $\frac{7}{10} = \frac{8}{d}$

Subtracting Integers

Build Understanding

Positive and negative integers may be used to show distances above and below sea level.

A. How thick is the iceberg from top to bottom? You can find the answer by subtracting.

$$4 - {}^-8 = 4 + 8 = 12$$

Notice that the scale of the graph is in hundreds of feet.

The distance is 1,200 feet.

To subtract an integer, add its opposite.

B. Find ${}^-6 - ({}^-12)$.

$${}^-6 - ({}^-12) = {}^-6 + (12) = 6$$

C. Subtract: ${}^-17 - 10$.

$${}^-17 - (10) = {}^-17 + ({}^-10) = {}^-27$$

■ **Write About Math** Write three examples to find out whether $a - b$ always equals $b - a$. Is subtraction of integers commutative?

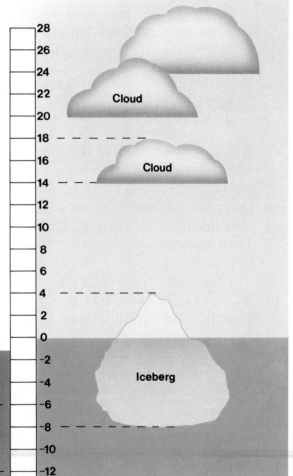

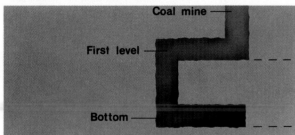

Check Understanding

For another example, see Set D, pages 536–537.

Find each difference.

1. $14 - {}^-5 = 14 + \text{▦} = \text{▦}$

2. ${}^-8 - 3 = {}^-8 + \text{▦} = \text{▦}$

3. ${}^-4 - {}^-9 = {}^-4 + \text{▦} = \text{▦}$

4. $7 - {}^-5 = 7 + \text{▦} = \text{▦}$

Practice

For more Practice, see Set D, pages 538–539.

Find each difference.

5. 5 − 12　　**6.** 7 − ⁻6　　**7.** 9 − 4　　**8.** ⁻20 − 30

9. 14 − ⁻15　　**10.** 35 − 36　　**11.** 10 − ⁻10　　**12.** 8 − ⁻5

13. ⁻12 − 12　　**14.** ⁻14 − ⁻14　　**15.** 0 − 5　　**16.** 0 − ⁻11

17. 6 − ⁻4　　**18.** 9 − ⁻6　　**19.** 25 − ⁻25　　**20.** ⁻8 − ⁻3

21. ⁻37 − 18　　**22.** ⁻34 − 78　　**23.** ⁻15 − 7　　**24.** ⁻18 − ⁻7

⊞ Calculator　Find each difference.

25. ⁻78 − 46　　**26.** 88 − ⁻17　　**27.** ⁻67 − ⁻33　　**28.** 45 − 78

29. 67 − ⁻29　　**30.** 39 − 72　　**31.** ⁻42 − ⁻51　　**32.** 49 − ⁻31

33. ⁻83 − ⁻56　　**34.** ⁻64 − 38　　**35.** 16 − 43　　**36.** ⁻52 − 25

Mixed Practice　Add or subtract. **Remember** to watch the signs.

37. 7 + ⁻13　　**38.** ⁻9 − 7　　**39.** 15 + ⁻5　　**40.** ⁻9 − ⁻9

41. ⁻13 − ⁻6　　**42.** ⁻20 + 5　　**43.** ⁻8 − 4　　**44.** 7 + ⁻10

45. ⁻9 + 15 + ⁻4　　**46.** 11 − 15 + ⁻3　　**47.** ⁻4 + ⁻6 − ⁻10

48. ⁻4 − ⁻6 − ⁻3　　**49.** ⁻7 + 13 + ⁻1　　**50.** ⁻12 + 6 − ⁻9

51. 19 − 6 + ⁻12　　**52.** ⁻5 + ⁻14 − ⁻11　　**53.** 10 − 8 + ⁻16

Problem Solving

Solve each problem.

54. Compute 25 − (12 − 8) and (25 − 12) − 8. Does the way in which you group numbers for subtraction affect the answer?

55. Number Sense　Explain how you can tell if the difference of two integers will be positive or negative.

56. Use the diagram on page 516. How far is it from the bottom of the cloud to the bottom of the coal mine?

A
L
G
E
B
R
A

Multiplying and Dividing Integers

Build Understanding

Myths and folk tales are stories that express ideas, explain how things occur, and tell the adventures of heros.

A Hawaiian folk tale explains that the Hawaiian Islands were created when Maui, a Polynesian god, fished them up out of the ocean. In Greek mythology, King Sisyphus was condemned to roll a huge stone to the top of a steep hill forever. Each time he neared the top of the hill, the stone rolled back down and he had to start over again.

A. On a good day, Sisyphus can roll the stone 6 feet in an hour. How far can he roll it in 5 hours?

5 × 6 = 30

He can roll the stone 30 feet in 5 hours.

B. Despite the king's efforts, the stone has been rolling backward for the last 4 hours at the rate of 3 feet an hour. How far back has it rolled? Think of a backward roll of 3 feet as ⁻3. Use repeated addition.

⁻3 + ⁻3 + ⁻3 + ⁻3 = ⁻12
4 × ⁻3 = ⁻12

The product of a positive integer and a negative integer is always a negative integer.

Greek myths were written as early as 775 B.C.

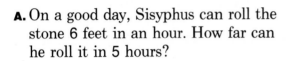

c. In the past 5 days, the stone has rolled backward 6 feet each day. How much farther ahead was Sisyphus 5 days ago?

Think of 5 days ago as ⁻5. A loss of 6 feet is ⁻6.

Just as with whole numbers, parentheses can be used to show multiplication of integers.

(⁻5)(⁻6) = 30

The product of two negative integers is always a positive integer.

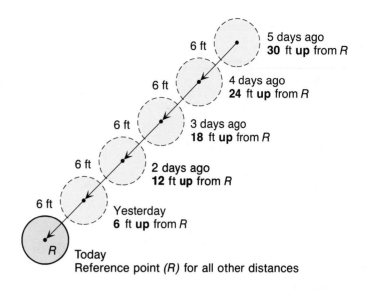

5 days ago **30 ft up** from R

6 ft

4 days ago **24 ft up** from R

6 ft

3 days ago **18 ft up** from R

6 ft

2 days ago **12 ft up** from R

6 ft

Yesterday **6 ft up** from R

6 ft

R

Today Reference point (R) for all other distances

D. To divide integers, think of a related multiplication problem.

⁻36 ÷ ⁻4 = 9 because 9 × ⁻4 = ⁻36.

If two integers are negative, their quotient is always a positive integer.

E. 56 ÷ ⁻8 = ⁻7 because ⁻7 × ⁻8 = 56.

If two integers have different signs, their quotient is always negative.

■ **Talk About Math** What is the quotient of 0 ÷ 25? What is the quotient of 0 ÷ ⁻25? Explain.

In a Korean folk tale, eclipses of the sun are said to happen when a monster dog takes bites out of the sun.

Check Understanding

For another example, see Set E, pages 536–537.

Number Sense Fill in each blank.

1. The product 4 × 3 is a __?__ integer.

2. The product ⁻4 × ⁻3 is a __?__ integer.

Multiply or divide.

3. ⁻4 × 5 **4.** 6 × ⁻8 **5.** ⁻56 ÷ 8 **6.** ⁻64 ÷ ⁻8 **7.** 100 ÷ ⁻20

Practice

For More Practice, see Set E, pages 538–539.

Multiply.

8. 30 × ⁻3   **9.** 11 × ⁻7   **10.** ⁻10 × 15   **11.** ⁻20 × 20   **12.** ⁻9 × ⁻10

13. 25 × ⁻4   **14.** ⁻12 × ⁻10   **15.** 25 × 10   **16.** ⁻30 × 20   **17.** 15 × ⁻8

18. 12 × ⁻8   **19.** ⁻20 × ⁻6   **20.** ⁻16 × 5   **21.** ⁻25 × 6   **22.** 10 × ⁻40

Compute each of these products.

23. ⁻8(⁻50)   **24.** (⁻50)2   **25.** 15(⁻5)   **26.** ⁻4(⁻13)   **27.** (⁻9)(12)

28. ⁻12(10)   **29.** (⁻5)(⁻5)   **30.** ⁻10(10)   **31.** (15)(⁻2)

32. 10(⁻6)(⁻3)   **33.** (⁻9)(⁻1)(⁻1)   **34.** 25(⁻4)(6)   **35.** (2)(25)(⁻3)

Divide.

36. 48 ÷ ⁻8   **37.** ⁻64 ÷ 8   **38.** ⁻99 ÷ ⁻9   **39.** ⁻84 ÷ ⁻7   **40.** 39 ÷ 13

41. 45 ÷ ⁻5   **42.** ⁻72 ÷ 36   **43.** 140 ÷ ⁻14   **44.** 0 ÷ ⁻7   **45.** ⁻52 ÷ ⁻1

46. ⁻60 ÷ ⁻4   **47.** 48 ÷ ⁻12   **48.** ⁻200 ÷ 20   **49.** 54 ÷ ⁻6   **50.** ⁻72 ÷ ⁻3

51. ⁻88 ÷ 11   **52.** 42 ÷ ⁻7   **53.** 13 ÷ ⁻1   **54.** ⁻80 ÷ ⁻4   **55.** 0 ÷ ⁻15

Mixed Practice   Solve.

56. ⁻90 ÷ 15   **57.** ⁻16 × ⁻3   **58.** ⁻80 − 55   **59.** 75 + ⁻50

60. 35 − ⁻30   **61.** 96 ÷ ⁻8   **62.** ⁻40 × ⁻4   **63.** ⁻30 + ⁻60

64. 52 ÷ ⁻4   **65.** ⁻30 × ⁻3   **66.** ⁻6 − ⁻6   **67.** ⁻120 ÷ ⁻30

68. ⁻12 + 18   **69.** 25 + ⁻25   **70.** 27 − ⁻12   **71.** ⁻9 × 0

Problem Solving

Use integers to solve each problem.

72. How far has Sisyphus's stone rolled backward in 6 hours if it has rolled back 7 feet per hour?

73. Sisyphus rolled his stone forward 48 feet in 8 hours. How many feet per hour did he roll the stone?

74. In Greek mythology, Penelope wove a cloth during the day and removed rows of weaving at night. Suppose she removed 2 more rows than she wove each day for one week. How much farther ahead was she the week before?

75. According to a folk tale, the gods of the Norsemen of ancient Scandinavia lived on a mountaintop in the city of Asgard. Suppose Asgard was 7,500 feet above sea level and the underworld was 7,500 feet below sea level. Find the difference in height between Asgard and the underworld.

Thor was the Norse god of thunder and work.

Midchapter Checkup

Write an integer to represent each situation.

1. 40 feet below sea level

2. A bank deposit of $50

3. A profit of $22

4. A temperature of 9°F below 0

5. The altitude at sea level

6. A weight loss of 6 pounds

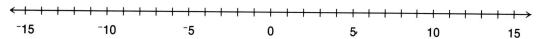

Compare these integers. Use > or <.
The number line above may be helpful.

7. 0 ▦ 4   **8.** ⁻5 ▦ 5   **9.** 12 ▦ 4   **10.** ⁻9 ▦ 0   **11.** ⁻6 ▦ ⁻7

Arrange the integers in order from least to greatest.

12. 0 ⁻6 5 6   **13.** 4 ⁻1 7 ⁻3   **14.** 9 0 ⁻9 5

Add or subtract.

15. ⁻5 + ⁻2   **16.** 7 − ⁻6   **17.** 0 + ⁻15   **18.** ⁻7 − 3   **19.** ⁻9 − ⁻3

Multiply and divide.

20. 0 × ⁻6   **21.** ⁻45 ÷ ⁻5   **22.** ⁻7 × ⁻8   **23.** ⁻72 ÷ 6   **24.** ⁻12 × 12

Number-Sense Project

Look back on pages 506–507.

1. Six historic events are listed below.

3000 BC—First writing system, Cuneiform, appeared

1440 AD—Printing press invented

1500 BC—Olmec Indians settled in Mexico

1620 AD—Pilgrims settled in New England

776 AD—First Olympic games held

1896 AD—First modern Olympic games held

List the events in order beginning with the most recent.

2. Tell if the time elapsed between the following events is between (A) 4,000 and 5,000 years, (B) 3,000 and 4,000 years, (C) 2,000 and 3,000 years, (D) 1,000 and 2,000 years, or (E) less than 1,000 years.

a. Cuneiform writing appearing and the invention of the printing press

b. Olmec Indians settling in Mexico and the Pilgrims landing in New England

c. First ancient Olympic games and the first modern games

d. Today and the first modern Olympic games

e. Today and the Olmec Indians settling in Mexico

Visual Thinking Activity

This is the outside view of part of a woven basket. Which of the four pictures shows the inside center?

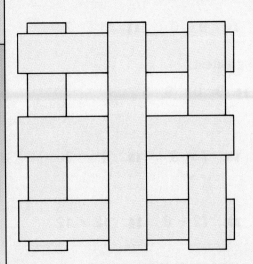

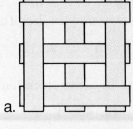
a.

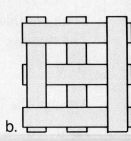
b.

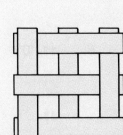
c.

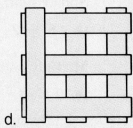
d.

Explore with a Computer

Use the *Spreadsheet Workshop Project* for this activity.

During a football game, the 6th-grade Panthers kept statistics for each play to record gains and losses on the field. Use the **Addition worksheet** to find the gains and losses for each play.

File   Edit   Forms   Change   Extras   Help
Addition worksheet

	A	B	C	D	E
1	14	+	-8	=	6
2		+		=	
3		+		=	
4		+		=	
5		+		=	
6		+		=	
7		+		=	
8		+		=	
9		+		=	

A2

Use arrows to move the highlight.
Press Esc for menus.

1. On the first play, they moved forward 14 yards. What was the penalty if the gain was 4 yards?

2. On the second play, they were pushed back 11 yards, and received a penalty of 10 yards. What was the loss?

3. On the third play, a pass was thrown from the 50-yard line and received at the 35-yard line. The receiver ran for another 5 yards. What was the total gain?

Real-Life Decision Making

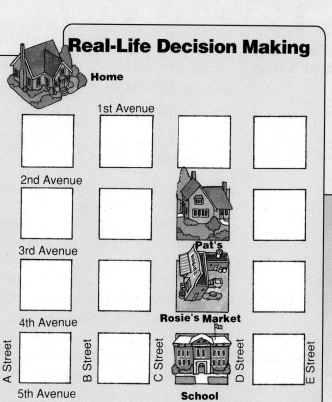

Suppose you walk to school each day.

1. How many paths can you take from home to your friend Pat's house at C Street and 2nd Avenue?

2. How many different paths can you take from home to Rosie's Market at C Street and 3rd Avenue?

3. How many different paths can you take from home to school at C Street and 5th Avenue? What could influence which path you will take?

523

A
L
G
E
B
R
A

Choose an Operation

PROBLEM SOLVING
GUIDE

Understand
QUESTION
FACTS
KEY IDEA

Plan and Solve
STRATEGY
ANSWER

Look Back
SENSIBLE ANSWER
ALTERNATE APPROACH

Build Understanding

Mrs. Marklund's sixth-grade class kept track of changes in the Dow Jones average on the New York Stock Exchange. Use the table below to find the average daily change in the Dow Jones this week.

Changes in the Dow Jones Average

Day	Monday	Tuesday	Wednesday	Thursday	Friday
Change	⁻6	⁻10	⁻3	5	9

Understand   QUESTION   If the stocks had changed by the same amount each day, what would the amount be?

FACTS   The daily changes were ⁻6, ⁻10, ⁻3, 5, 9.

KEY IDEA   You need to *choose the operations* you will use to find the average.

Plan and Solve   STRATEGY   Use the procedure for finding an average. First find the sum of the changes.

$$^-6 + {}^-10 + {}^-3 + 5 + 9 = {}^-5$$

Then divide the sum by 5, the number of days. $^-5 \div 5 = {}^-1$

ANSWER   The Dow Jones changed an average of ⁻1 point each day. In other words, it went down an average of 1 point per day.

The New York Stock Exchange was first organized in 1792.

Look Back   ALTERNATE APPROACH   Add all the positive integers: $5 + 9 = 14$. Add all the negative integers: $^-6 + {}^-10 + {}^-3 = {}^-19$. Add 14 and ⁻19. Divide the sum, ⁻5, by 5.

■ **Talk About Math**   If the Dow Jones average was 1,954 at the beginning of the week, what was the average at the end of the week?

Check Understanding

During the 5 business days last week, each share of stock in A & B Food Company lost an average of 2 points per day.

1. What integer would you use to describe the average daily change in price per share?

2. What was the total amount of change in the price of each share during the week?

3. If the price of stock was $35 per share at the beginning of the week, what was the price at the end of the week?

4. How much less was the stock worth at the end of the week than at the beginning of the week?

Practice

Use integers to solve these problems.
Remember to watch the signs.

5. What was the average change in the price of the stock for the seven days shown?

Day	1	2	3	4	5	6	7
Change	⁻8	4	9	0	⁻2	⁻9	⁻8

6. Last Wednesday, the price of a share of Amalgamated Gold Company stock was $24. By Friday, it had dropped to $16. What was the change in the price of a share of stock?

Choose a ——— Strategy

Moving On   At the end of the school year, 33 students were in the sixth grade class. Over the past four years some students have left the class and others have arrived.

7. How many students were in the class at the beginning of sixth grade?

8. How many students were in the class at the beginning of fifth grade?

9. How many students were in the class at the beginning of the third grade?

Grade	Left	Arrived
3	6	5
4	5	7
5	2	5
6	3	7

Locating Points in Four Quadrants

ALGEBRA

Build Understanding

A police dispatcher locates the positions of police cars using a grid. The *x*-axis and the *y*-axis, perpendicular reference lines, divide the grid into four regions called **quadrants.** The quadrants are labeled I, II, III, and IV as shown.

A point in the plane can be located with an ordered pair of integers called **coordinates.** The point with coordinates (0, 0) is called the **origin.**

The first coordinate tells you how far to move to the right (+) or to the left (−) from the origin along the *x*-axis.

Then the second coordinate tells you how far to move up (+) or down (−).

A. The dispatcher is at (0, 0). Locate Police Car *A* by naming its coordinates.

Police Car *A* is 8 units to the left of the origin and 4 units down from the origin. The coordinates of Police Car *A* are (⁻8, ⁻4).

B. Give the letter of the police car located at (6, ⁻4).

To find the vehicle located at (6, ⁻4), move 6 units to the right of the origin and 4 units down. Police Car *V* is located at (6, ⁻4).

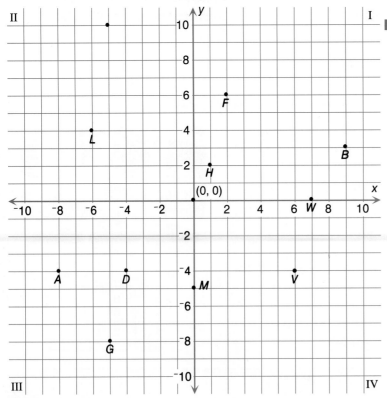

■ **Talk About Math**
Pick any point on the *x*-axis. What is the second coordinate of that point? Explain. Pick any point on the *y*-axis. What is the first coordinate of that point? Explain.

Check Understanding

For another example, see Set F, pages 536–537.

For Exercises 1–8, use the graph on page 526. Name
the coordinates of the vehicle.

1. Point F **2.** Point G **3.** Point H **4.** Point M

Name the police car located at each point.

5. (9, 3)   **6.** (7, 0)   **7.** ($^-$6, 4)   **8.** ($^-$4, $^-$4)

Practice

For More Practice, see Set F, pages 538–539.

Use graph paper. Plot the following points. Name the
quadrant or the axis that contains each point.

9. (6, 7)   **10.** (5, $^-$1)   **11.** ($^-$7, 4)   **12.** (0, 2)   **13.** ($^-$6, 0)

Use graph paper. Plot and sketch each shape.

14. The four vertices of a square have
these coordinates: ($^-$3, 3); ($^-$3, 7);
($^-$7, 7); ($^-$7, 3).

15. The five vertices of a pentagon
have these coordinates: (0, 8);
(7, 6); (9, 0); (7, $^-$6); (0, $^-$8).

16. The six vertices of a hexagon
have these coordinates: (4, $^-$4);
(7, $^-$4); (10, 0); (7, 4); (4, 4); (0, 0).

17. The four vertices of a trapezoid
have these coordinates: (9, $^-$2);
(6, 1); ($^-$2, 1); ($^-$5, $^-$2).

Problem Solving

Critical Thinking   Give the new location for each
vehicle by naming the coordinates.

18. Police Car U was at point
($^-$3, $^-$5). It traveled 4 blocks east
and 8 blocks south to a
warehouse fire.

19. While Police Car U was at the
warehouse fire, the dispatcher
called it to an emergency 2 blocks
west and 3 blocks north.

Skills _____ **Review**   pages 430–431, 434–437

1. Estimate 32% of 9,033.

2. Estimate 91% of 10,322.

3. What percent of 84 is 42?

4. 130 is what percent of 1,040?

Use Data from a Graph

Build Understanding

The skipper of a fishing fleet has anchored his twelve boats as shown on the radar screen. Where are the four boats in Quadrant II located?

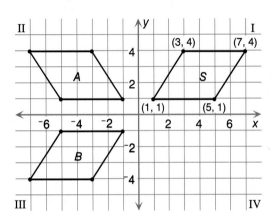

PROBLEM SOLVING
GUIDE

Understand
QUESTION
FACTS
KEY IDEA

Plan and Solve
STRATEGY
ANSWER

Look Back
SENSIBLE ANSWER
ALTERNATE APPROACH

Understand QUESTION What are the coordinates of the boats in Quadrant II?

FACTS The coordinates of the boats in Quadrant I are labeled on the diagram.

KEY IDEA Parallelogram A is a flip over the y-axis of parallelogram S. If you folded the graph over the y-axis, polygons A and S would be on top of one another.

Plan and Solve STRATEGY Read the coordinates of the vertices of parallelogram S. Change each x-coordinate to its opposite.

ANSWER The boats in Quadrant I are at:
      (1, 1)   (5, 1)   (7, 4)   (3, 4)

Therefore, the boats in Quadrant II are at:
      (⁻1, 1)   (⁻5, 1)   (⁻7, 4)   (⁻3, 4)

Look Back SENSIBLE ANSWER Check the answer. Count the number of units along the x-axis and then locate each vertex of parallelogram A.

■ **Talk About Math** Explain how you can use the signs of the coordinates to decide in which quadrant a point is located.

528

Check Understanding

Use the graph on page 528.

1. What are the coordinates of the four points in parallelogram *B*?

2. Describe the relationship between the coordinates in parallelogram *S* and those in parallelogram *B*.

3. Is parallelogram *B* a flip of parallelogram *A*? Explain.

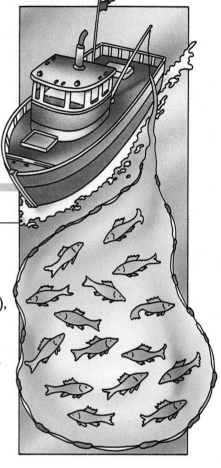

Practice

Use grid paper. Draw each figure by connecting the points in order. Then flip the figure over the *y*-axis. Do each exercise on a separate grid.

4. (1, 1), (7, 1), (7, 7), (1, 1)

5. (⁻1, 2), (⁻7, 2), (⁻7, 5), (⁻1, 5), (⁻1, 2)

6. (⁻4, ⁻1), (⁻7, ⁻4), (⁻4, ⁻7), (⁻1, ⁻4), (⁻4, ⁻1)

7. (0, 6), (⁻3, 2), (⁻8, 2), (0, 6)

Draw the flip over the *x*-axis for the figure in

8. Exercise 6.

9. Exercise 7.

Solve.

10. One ship is located at point (5, ⁻5). Another ship is located at point (⁻7, ⁻5). How far apart are the two ships?

Choose a _____ Strategy

At 9:00, Dan left camp on his bicycle riding 12 miles per hour. Sharon left at 10:00 riding 18 miles per hour.

How far had Dan ridden
11. in 2 hours?   **12.** in 3 hours?

13. Did Sharon catch up with Dan? If so, at what time?

Graphing in Four Quadrants

Build Understanding

A. Graph the rule $y = x + 5$. First replace x in $y = x + 5$ with some numbers. Then add 5 to each number to get a corresponding y.

Then plot the points for (6, 11); (0, 5); and (⁻9, ⁻4). A line can be drawn through the points. The line is the graph of $y = x + 5$.

B. Is the point for (4, ⁻1) on the graph of $y = x + 5$?

Plot the point for (4, −1). You can see that it is *not* on the line. It is not part of the graph of $y = x + 5$.

■ **Talk About Math** How could you decide whether the point (4, ⁻1) is on the graph of $y = x + 5$ without plotting points?

$y = x + 5$

x	6	0	⁻9
y	11	5	⁻4

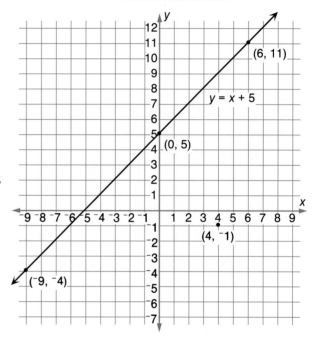

Check Understanding

For another example, see Set G, pages 536–537.

Solve.

1. Choose the ordered pair for the point that is on the graph of $y = x - 4$.

   a. (3, 7)   **b.** (8, 4)   **c.** (⁻10, ⁻6)

2. Choose the ordered pair for the point that is on the graph of $y = x + ⁻2$.

   a. (0, ⁻2)   **b.** (4, ⁻4)   **c.** (7, 9)

3. Complete the table and graph the rule.

$y = x + ⁻3$

x	7	3	0	⁻2
y	4			

Practice

For More Practice, see Set G, pages 538–539.

Complete each table and graph the rule.
Draw each graph on a separate set of axes.

4. $y = x + {}^-3$

x	6	1	0	$^-2$	$^-8$	$^-12$
y	3	$^-2$				

5. $y = x - {}^-1$

x	4	0	$^-4$	$^-6$	$^-10$	$^-20$
y	5					

6. $y = x - 2$

x	5	1	0	$^-3$	$^-7$	$^-9$
y	3					

7. $y = x + 4$

x	4	0	$^-4$	$^-8$	$^-11$	$^-16$
y	8					

8. $y = x + {}^-6$

x	7	6	3	0	$^-1$	$^-3$
y						

9. $y = x - {}^-2$

x	3	1	0	$^-2$	$^-5$	$^-8$
y						

Problem Solving

Solve each problem.

10. Is the point (12, $^-3$) on the graph of
$y = x - 12$?

11. Is the point ($^-5$, $^-10$) on the graph of
$y = x - 5$?

12. Is the point (0, 0) on the graph of both
$y = x$ and $y = x + {}^-2$?

Take risks. Try your
hunches. They often work.

Explore ———— Math

Use grid paper. Draw coordinate axes.

13. Draw any line parallel to the x-axis.

14. Name three points on the line.

15. What do you notice about the
coordinates of the three points?

16. Repeat Exercises 13–15 for
another line.

17. Write a generalization about the coordinates of lines that
are parallel to the x-axis.

Make a Graph

Build Understanding

Hari wrote from Saskatoon, Saskatchewan, that the temperature was ⁻20° Celsius. Kitti wants to know what ⁻20°C equals on the Fahrenheit scale. On a local bank's sign, Kitti has seen temperature comparisons like the ones in this table:

°C	10°	0°	⁻5°
°F	50°	32°	23°

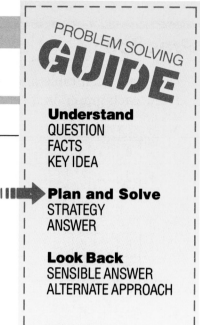

PROBLEM SOLVING GUIDE

Understand
QUESTION
FACTS
KEY IDEA

▶ **Plan and Solve**
STRATEGY
ANSWER

Look Back
SENSIBLE ANSWER
ALTERNATE APPROACH

Understand   QUESTION   What does ⁻20°C mean in degrees Fahrenheit?

FACTS   Kitty knows three pairs of equivalent temperatures.

KEY IDEA   The three pairs of temperatures can be plotted on a graph.

▶ **Plan and Solve**   STRATEGY   Draw a graph with degrees Celsius on the x-axis and degrees Fahrenheit on the y-axis. Plot the three points and connect them with a line. Extend the line through ⁻20° on the Celsius scale and read the Fahrenheit temperature from the y-axis.

ANSWER   A temperature of ⁻20°C is about ⁻4°F.

Look Back   SENSIBLE ANSWER   Look at the table. A temperature of ⁻20°C is colder than ⁻5°C, so the Fahrenheit reading for ⁻20°C has to be colder than 23°F.

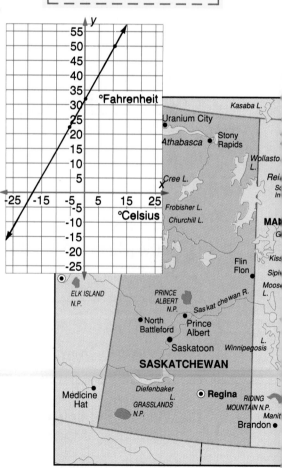

Saskatchewan is a Canadian province that borders Montana and North Dakota. Saskatoon is its largest city.

■ **Talk About Math**   Notice that (0, 0) is not on the graph of Fahrenheit and Celsius temperatures. What does that tell you about 0°F and 0°C?

Check Understanding

Estimation   Use the thermometer on page 328 to decide if each statement is *true* or *false*.

1. 75°F is about 25°C.

2. ⁻30°C is about ⁻20°F.

3. ⁻4°C is about ⁻20°F.

4. 55°F is about 13°C.

Practice

Copy the temperature grid on a sheet of graph paper. Plot these three points: (21, 70); (⁻10, 14); (⁻23, ⁻10). Draw a line through the points and extend it in both directions.

5. What Fahrenheit temperature corresponds to 10°C?

6. What Celsius temperature corresponds to 5°F?

7. What Celsius temperature corresponds to ⁻4°F?

8. What Farenheit temperature corresponds to 15°C?

9. The point (20, 68) lies on the graph. 68°F is equal to ▦°C.

10. The point (5, 41) lies on the graph. 5°C is equal to ▦°F.

11. Do the points (10, 50); (0, 32); and (⁻5, 23) lie on the graph?

12. Do the points (50, 10); (32, 0); and (23, ⁻5) lie on the graph?

Choose a ———— Strategy

Making Music   Solve each problem.

Ben, Bonnie, and Bud are in the school orchestra. One person plays the piano, one plays the cello, and the other plays the tuba.

13. Ben's instrument is too large to carry. What instrument does he play?

14. Bonnie doesn't play a wind instrument. Which of the two remaining instruments does she play?

15. What instrument does Bud play?

Skills Review

Write an integer for each situation.

1. Going down 3 floors

2. Losing 5 pounds

3. Earning $10

Write the opposite of each integer.

4. 4   **5.** ⁻12   **6.** ⁻5   **7.** 16

List the integers from least to greatest.

8. 5, ⁻5, 2, 0   **9.** ⁻2, 4, ⁻3, ⁻5

Compute. Watch the signs.

10. 4 + ⁻2   **11.** ⁻6 + ⁻6

12. ⁻4 + 3   **13.** ⁻2 − 6

14. ⁻5 − ⁻2   **15.** 7 − ⁻1

16. ⁻3 × ⁻2   **17.** 15 ÷ ⁻5

Give the ordered pair for each point.

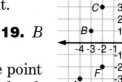

18. A   **19.** B

Name the point at each ordered pair.

20. (⁻2, 3)   **21.** (⁻2, ⁻2)

22. Complete the table.

$y = x + ^-2$

x	5	2	1	⁻3	⁻4	⁻9
y	3	0				

23. Graph the rule in Exercise 22.

Problem-Solving Review

Solve each problem.

24. Brad's math quiz scores were 75, 72, 88, 83, 82, 88, and 95. What is the median and the mode of his scores?

25. Sonja has 4 sweaters, each a different color. They are red, yellow, brown, and white. What is the probability that the sweater she chooses to wear today will be the red one?

26. Western Samoa has an area of 1,133 square miles. In 1985, the population density was 146 per square mile. What was the total population to the nearest thousand?

27. Louisiana's lowest elevation is 5 ft below sea level. How much lower is this than the highest point in Louisiana, which is 535 ft above sea level?

28. For dinner, Matthew ate food totaling 715 calories. If his total intake of calories for the day was 2,400 calories, about what percent of the total was his dinner?

29. **Data File** Use the data on pages 542–543. What is the difference between the mountain's highest and lowest elevations shown? between points B and C?

30. **Make a Data File** Use a newspaper to research the costs of real estate. Prepare a table listing the costs of 10 homes advertised for sale.

Compare. Use <, >, or =.

1. 0.61 ▒ 0.165   **2.** 3.75 ▒ 3.51

3. $\frac{1}{6}$ ▒ $\frac{3}{18}$ **4.** $\frac{17}{12}$ ▒ $1\frac{7}{12}$

Estimate each answer by rounding to the nearest tenth. Then compute.

5. 35.86
    + 4.3785

6. 300.2
    − 25.75

7. 2.06
    × 0.05

Estimate each quotient by using compatible numbers.

8. $95\overline{)380}$ **9.** $7.4\overline{)222}$

Name each figure.

10.   **11.**

Compute.

12. $6 \times 5\frac{3}{4}$ **13.** $6\frac{1}{4} - 2\frac{3}{5}$

Choose the best estimate for the length of the segment.

———————

14. $\frac{1}{2}$ in.   2 in.   12 in.

15. Find the perimeter of a hexagon when each side is 5 inches long.

16. Set up a proportion for this situation. If it costs $12 to buy 2 shirts, it will cost $42 to buy 7 shirts.

Write each number as a percent.

17. 0.72   **18.** 0.6   **19.** $\frac{2}{5}$

20. What is 15% of 80?

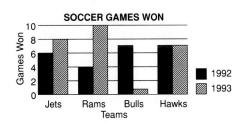

SOCCER GAMES WON

Use the graph above. Which team won

21. the most games in 1993?

22. more games in 1992 than 1993?

23. fewer than 5 games in 1992?

24. the fewest games in 1993?

Cards with the numbers 1–9 are put in a box. One card is drawn. Find each probability.

25. P (an odd number) **26.** P (2 or 4)

27. P (neither 7 nor 9) **28.** P (11)

The chart shows options for a bicycle.

Color	red, blue, green
Speed	10-speed, 12-speed
Seat	banana, regular

How many choices are there for

29. a bike with a banana seat?

30. a red bike?   **31.** any bike?

Compare the integers. Use < or >.

32. ⁻4 ▒ ⁻6   **33.** ⁻8 ▒ 2

Compute.

34. ⁻6 + ⁻3   **35.** 4 + ⁻3

36. ⁻2 × ⁻7   **37.** ⁻12 ÷ 2

Reteaching

Set A pages 508–509

In the following situations, the key words that mean positive or negative are underlined.

Situation	Integer
A bank <u>deposit</u> of $6	$^+6$
A <u>drop</u> of 60 feet	$^-60$
The water <u>rose</u> 3 feet	$^+3$
A <u>loss</u> of 18 pounds	$^-18$

Remember to watch for key words that mean negative or positive.

Write an integer to represent each situation.

1. A growth of 4 inches

2. 12 feet below sea level

Set B pages 510–511

Use a number line to help you compare these integers.

$^-6$ and $^-2$

Think: $^-6$ is to the left of $^-2$ on a number line. Therefore, $^-6 <^- 2$.

Remember that the inequality symbol always points to the smaller number.

Compare these integers. Use $>$, $<$, or $=$.

1. $^-5 ⦂⦂⦂ ^-1$ **2.** $6 ⦂⦂⦂ 8$

3. $4 ⦂⦂⦂ ^-2$ **4.** $^-18 ⦂⦂⦂ ^-20$

5. $6 ⦂⦂⦂ ^-6$ **6.** $^-3 ⦂⦂⦂ 0$

Set C pages 512–515

Use a number line to find $7 + ^-10$.

Start at 0.
Move 7 units to the right.
Move 10 units left.

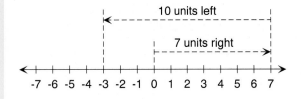

Read the answer: $7 + ^-10 = ^-3$

Remember to use the sign of the integer farther from zero when you add two integers with different signs.

Find each sum.

1. $6 + ^-4$ **2.** $^-1 + 7$

3. $12 + ^-20$ **4.** $6 + ^-9$

5. $^-4 + 15$ **6.** $^-2 + 6$

7. $^-9 + ^-6$ **8.** $^-8 + 3$

Set D pages 516–517

To subtract an integer, add its opposite.

Use the rule to find $8 - ^-9$.
The opposite of $^-9$ is 9.
$8 - ^-9 = ⦂⦂⦂ → 8 + 9 = 17$

Remember that integers which are the same distance from 0 are called opposites.

Find each difference.

1. $7 - 8$ **2.** $7 - ^-8$ **3.** $^-7 - ^-8$

4. $^-5 - 4$ **5.** $^-6 - ^-8$ **6.** $9 - ^-8$

Set E pages 518–521

Find ⁻6 × 3.

The product of a negative integer and a positive integer is always a negative integer.
⁻6 × 3 = ⁻18

Remember to look at the signs when multiplying integers.

Multiply.

1. ⁻2 × 2 **2.** 2 × 44

3. 12 × ⁻4 **4.** ⁻5 × ⁻20

5. ⁻7 × 13 **6.** ⁻10 × ⁻30

Set F pages 526–527

Plot (3, ⁻4).

Start at the origin. Move three units to the right, because 3 is positive.
Move down 4 units, because 4 is negative.

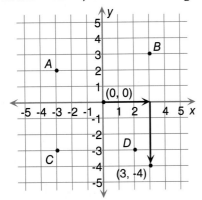

Remember that a point in the plane can be located by an ordered pair of integers.

Use the graph at the left for Exercises 1–4. Name the coordinates of

1. Point *A*. **2.** Point *B*.

3. Point *C*. **4.** Point *D*.

5. Use graph paper. Plot and sketch a rectangle whose vertices have these coordinates:
(⁻2, 2), (4, 2), (4, ⁻3), (⁻2, ⁻3)

Set G pages 530–531

Complete this table for the given rule.

$y = x - 2$

x	2	0	⁻2
y			

The rule states:
"Subtract 2 from each *x* value."
For $x = 2$: $y = 2 - 2 = 0$
For $x = 0$: $y = 0 - 2 = ⁻2$
For $x = ⁻2$: $y = ⁻2 - 2 = ⁻2 + ⁻2 = ⁻4$

Remember that the line you draw for an equation is the graph of the equation.

Complete each table.

1. $y = x + 3$

x	3	0	⁻3
y			

2. $y = x - 1$

x	1	0	⁻1
y			

3. $y = x - ⁻2$

x	2	0	⁻2
y			

More Practice

Set A   pages 508–509

Write an integer to represent each situation.

1. Up 3 flights of stairs

2. A drop of 22 feet

3. 6 fathoms below sea level

4. A profit of $100

5. A $20 raise in pay

6. A deduction of 3 points

7. A bank deposit of $50

8. A loss of 2 yards

Set B   pages 510–511

Use the number line below. Write the integer for
each point.

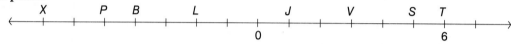

1. J 2. P 3. V 4. B 5. X 6. S

Compare these integers. Use >, <, or =.

7. 21 ▦ 5   8. 16 ▦ 18   9. 36 ▦ ⁻5   10. ⁻15 ▦ ⁻1

11. 70 ▦ ⁻6   12. ⁻50 ▦ 2   13. ⁻30 ▦ 30   14. 1 ▦ 0

Arrange these integers from least to greatest.

15. 5   9   1   6   16. 8   ⁻7   0   ⁻2   17. ⁻9   4   3   ⁻4

Set C   pages 512–515

Find each sum.

1. 6 + ⁻3   2. ⁻6 + 3   3. ⁻5 + 0   4. 8 + ⁻8

5. ⁻1 + ⁻4   6. ⁻7 + ⁻9   7. ⁻6 + 4   8. ⁻2 + ⁻9

9. 7 + ⁻14   10. ⁻6 + 10   11. 8 + ⁻17   12. ⁻5 + 19

For Exercises 13–20, tell whether you would use mental
math, paper and pencil, or a calculator. Then find
each sum.

13. 18 + ⁻6   14. (⁻8 + 30) + 6   15. ⁻18 + 18   16. ⁻28 + 39

17. 10 + ⁻3 + 3   18. ⁻45 + 0   19. ⁻6 + 9 + 6   20. (36 + 18) + ⁻3

Set D   pages 516–517

Find each difference.

1. 6 − 13

2. 8 − ⁻3

3. 12 − 8

4. ⁻40 − 10

5. 18 − 19

6. 18 − ⁻19

7. 0 − ⁻4

8. 13 − ⁻13

Mixed Practice   Add or subtract.

9. 16 + ⁻13

10. ⁻9 + 20

11. ⁻6 − ⁻9

12. ⁻13 − 6

Set E   pages 518–521

Multiply.

1. 20 × ⁻4

2. ⁻12 × ⁻7

3. ⁻10 × 20

4. 18 × ⁻5

Compute each of these products.

5. ⁻6(⁻40)

6. (⁻20)4

7. ⁻5(⁻11)

8. (⁻9)8

Divide.

9. 42 ÷ ⁻7

10. ⁻63 ÷ 9

11. ⁻66 ÷ ⁻11

12. 96 ÷ ⁻32

13. ⁻125 ÷ 25

14. 48 ÷ 12

15. 0 ÷ ⁻5

16. ⁻16 ÷ ⁻1

Mixed Practice   Solve.

17. 32 + ⁻16

18. ⁻7 × ⁻8

19. 54 ÷ ⁻9

20. ⁻20 + ⁻20

Set F   pages 526–527

Use graph paper. Plot and sketch each shape.

1. The vertices of a parallelogram have these coordinates: (⁻3, ⁻1), (⁻2, 3), (4, 3), (3, ⁻1).

2. The five vertices of a pentagon have these coordinates: (⁻2, 3), (2, 3), (3, 0), (0, ⁻3), (⁻3, 0).

Set G   pages 530–531

Complete each table and graph the rule. Draw each graph on a separate set of axes.

1. $y = x + {}^-5$

x	3	4	0	⁻2
y	⁻2	⁻1		

2. $y = x - {}^-2$

x	2	0	⁻2	4
y	4			

3. $y = x + 5$

x	⁻11	⁻8	⁻10	⁻5
y	⁻6			

4. $y = x - 6$

x	6	0	⁻6	4
y	0			

Rotations of Figures on a Grid

Maureen drew a triangle by joining these three points on a grid: (1, 1), (4, 3), (5, 2). She labeled the points *A*, *B*, and *C*.

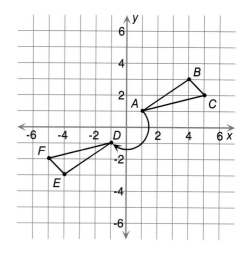

Then Maureen changed the signs of both numbers in each ordered pair. The new points were: (−1, −1), (−4, −3), (−5, −2). She joined these points to draw another triangle and labeled the points *D*, *E*, and *F*.

If you turn, or **rotate**, triangle *ABC* about the origin as shown by the arrow, triangle *ABC* will cover triangle *DEF*. Triangle *DEF* is a 180° **rotation** of triangle *ABC* about the origin.

For each ordered pair in Exercises 1 and 2, draw the triangle that results when each set of points is joined. Then change the signs of both numbers in each pair. On the same grid, draw the triangle that results from connecting these sets of points.

1. (0, 0), (−2, 4), (−5, 3)

2. (−3, −1), (−6, −5), (−4, −4)

3. Complete the following:

a. Graph the points (0, 0), (5, 1), (1, 5). Connect the points.

b. Change the sign of the second number in each ordered pair. Plot and connect the points. The second figure is a **reflection** of the first figure over the *x*-axis.

c. Change the sign of the first number in each ordered pair from step b. Plot and connect these points. The resulting figure is a reflection over the *y*-axis.

d. How does reflecting a figure over the *x*-axis and then over the *y*-axis compare to rotating the figure through an angle of 180°?

Chapter 15 Review/Test

Write an integer to represent each situation.

1. Earning $23 babysitting

2. Cutting 1 inch off your hair

3. Riding down 3 floors in an elevator

4. Flying at 20,000 feet

Arrange the integers from least to greatest.

5. 0 ⁻7 3   6. 5 ⁻6 4 ⁻8

Give the opposite of each integer.

7. ⁻3   8. ⁺2   9. ⁻7

Compare the integers. Use < or >.

10. 1 ▦ ⁻4   11. ⁻3 ▦ ⁻1

Add or subtract.

12. ⁻3 + ⁻5   13. 2 + ⁻7

14. ⁻6 + 6   15. ⁻2 − 5

16. ⁻4 − ⁻8   17. ⁻3 − ⁻1

Multiply or divide.

18. ⁻4 × 15   19. 49 ÷ ⁻7

20. ⁻33 ÷ ⁻1   21. ⁻6 × ⁻12

Give the ordered pair that locates each point.

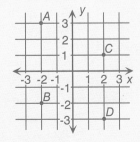

22. A

23. D

24. Complete the table and graph the rule.

$y = x - 2$

x	0	3		
y			⁻3	0

25. On a grid, draw the figure by joining the given points in order. Change the sign of the first number in each ordered pair. Then draw the new figure.

(2, 1), (4, 1), (4, 3), (2, 1)

Read the problem. Then answer the problem.

During five business days a share of Health Products, priced at $37 a share, lost an average of 2 points a day. What was the total amount of change in the price per share during the week?

26. Which strategy would you use to solve the problem?

    a. Add or multiply integers.
    b. Multiply or subtract integers.
    c. Divide or multiply integers.
    d. Subtract or add integers.

27. **Write About Math** What sign does the product of three negative integers have? Explain.

28. Graph the information below. Find the number of miles approximately equal to 86 km.

km	100	80	32
mi	62	50	20

1. Favorite Choice of Food for Dinner (Survey of 12,000 Kids)

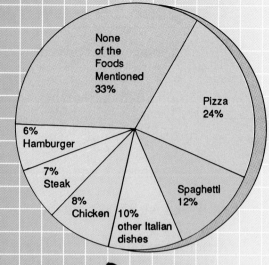

None of the Foods Mentioned 33%

Pizza 24%

6% Hamburger

7% Steak

8% Chicken

10% other Italian dishes

Spaghetti 12%

2.

1. Circle Graph:
The ages of the kids surveyed ranged from 6 years to 14 years.

2. Winners Chart:
The U.S. Open is a 72-hole golf championship that began in 1895. The list shows the winners and their scores for the first ten years and for the ten years from 1979 through 1988.

3. Diagram:
This elevation diagram shows the height above sea level or the depth below sea level of certain land areas.

4. Movie Schedule:
Beginning times for six movies are given.

5. Population Table:
These are 1980 statistics.

List of Winners
U.S. Open

The winners	Score
1895 Horace Rawlins	173
1896 James Foulis	152
1897 Joe Lloyd	162
1898 Fred Herd	328
1899 Willie Smith	315
1900 Harry Vardon (GB)	313
1901 Willie Anderson	331
1902 Laurie Auchterlonie	307
1903 Willie Anderson	307
1904 Willie Anderson	303
1979 Hale Irwin	284
1980 Jack Nicklaus	272
1981 David Graham (Aust)	273
1982 Tom Watson	282
1983 Larry Nelson	280
1984 Fuzzy Zoeller	276
1985 Andy North	279
1986 Ray Floyd	279
1987 Scott Simpson	277
1988 Curtis Strange	278

3. Elevation Diagram

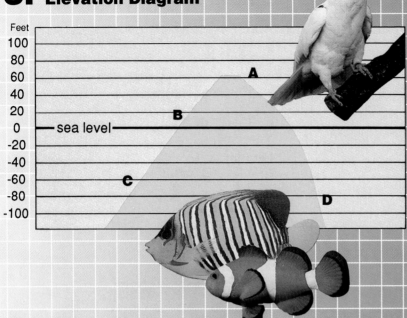

Feet	
100	
80	
60	A
40	
20	B
0	— sea level
-20	
-40	
-60	c
-80	D
-100	

4. Movie Schedule

Laugh Club	Might and Right	Westridge USA
2:15 3:45 5:15	2:05 4:20	1:30 3:30 5:30
7:45 9:15 10:45	6:35 8:50	7:30 9:30
City vs Country	**Revenge of the Giant Salamander**	**Haunts and Horrors**
1:45 3:30	2:00 4:00	1:50 3:50 5:50
5:30 7:15 9:00	6:00 8:00	7:50 9:50

All Movies
Before 7:00

2 for the
price of 1!

(15 minutes
between
showings)

5. Population Table

Country	% of Population 15 and Under	Country	% of Population 15 and Under
Australia	26	India	41
Bolivia	41	Kenya	50
Canada	24	Mexico	44
China	52	U.S.S.R	24
Honduras	49	U.S.	27

Give the letter for the correct answer.

1. Round 47,639 to the nearest thousand.

   a. 47,000   **b.** 50,000
   c. 48,000   **d.** 40,000

2. Multiply.

$$\begin{array}{r} 426 \\ \times\ 34 \\ \hline \end{array}$$

   a. 18,318   **b.** 14,484
   c. 14,364   **d.** 18,108

3. Subtract.

$$\begin{array}{r} 6.41 \\ -\ 1.63 \\ \hline \end{array}$$

   a. 5.88   **b.** 4.78
   c. 5.78   **d.** 4.88

4. Divide.

$$10\overline{)6.12}$$

   a. 612   **b.** 61.2
   c. 0.0612   **d.** 0.612

5. Choose the equation that should be used to solve this problem. Then solve the problem.

A merchant's store earned $54,000 in 6 months. What was the mean amount of money taken in per month?

   a. $54,000 − 6 = x; $53,994
   b. $54,000 × 6 = x; $324,000
   c. $54,000 ÷ 6 = x; $9,000
   d. $54,000 + 6 = x; $54,006

6. Add.

$$\frac{3}{4} + \frac{2}{3} + \frac{5}{12}$$

   a. $\frac{5}{6}$ **b.** $1\frac{11}{12}$
   c. $1\frac{5}{6}$ **d.** $1\frac{3}{4}$

7. Divide.

$$\frac{3}{10} \div \frac{6}{5}$$

   a. $\frac{1}{2}$ **b.** $\frac{1}{4}$
   c. $\frac{8}{60}$ **d.** $\frac{15}{16}$

8. The Eiffel Tower is 300 meters tall. Which measure is closest to this height?

   a. 500 ft   **b.** 750 ft
   c. 1,000 ft   **d.** 2,000 ft

9. What is the perimeter of the polygon shown below?

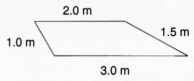

   a. 7.5 m   **b.** 4.5 m
   c. 9.0 m   **d.** 6.0 m

10. What is the area of a rectangle 7 mm long and 3 mm wide?

   a. 10 mm²   **b.** 21 mm²
   c. 20 mm²   **d.** 18 mm²

Cumulative Review/Test

11. Which ratio comes next in the series below?

$\frac{2}{7} = \frac{4}{14} = \frac{6}{21} = $ ▦

a. $\frac{8}{35}$ **b.** $\frac{12}{48}$
c. $\frac{12}{35}$ **d.** $\frac{8}{28}$

12. Which of these pairs of ratios form a proportion?

a. $\frac{1}{3}$ $\frac{6}{9}$ **b.** $\frac{2}{3}$ $\frac{3}{8}$
c. $\frac{3}{8}$ $\frac{6}{16}$ **d.** $\frac{3}{4}$ $\frac{8}{12}$

13. What is 42% written as a decimal?

a. 4.2   **b.** 42.0
c. 0.042   **d.** 0.42

14. What is $\frac{7}{20}$ written as a percent?

a. 7%   **b.** 14%
c. 35%   **d.** 27%

15. What is 4% of 32?

a. 12.8   **b.** 2.56
c. 25.6   **d.** 1.28

16. Suppose you print each letter of the alphabet on 26 cards and put them in a box. If you pull out one card, what is the probability the card shows a consonant?

a. $\frac{26}{26}$ **b.** $\frac{21}{26}$
c. $\frac{13}{26}$ **d.** $\frac{5}{26}$

17. How many choices does Meaghan have for her new bike that can be blue, red, or green and 10-speed or 12-speed?

a. 5   **b.** 6
c. 10   **d.** 12

18. Add.

$14 + {}^-6$

a. $^-8$ **b.** 20
c. 8   **d.** $^-20$

19. Multiply.

$^-3 \times 6$

a. 3   **b.** 18
c. $^-18$ **d.** $^-2$

20. Divide.

$^-64 \div {}^-4$

a. 16   **b.** $^-16$
c. $^-8$ **d.** 256

Read the problem below. Then answer the question.

Ben's account was $9 overdrawn. The bank charged $5 for being overdrawn. Then Ben made a $30 deposit. What is his new balance?

21. Which of the following operations would be the first step in solving the problem?

a. $^-9 + {}^-5$
b. $9 + {}^-5$
c. $^-9 + 5$
d. $9 + 5$

545

Reading and Writing Whole Numbers

Review

Grand Teton National Park in Wyoming covers over 309,990 acres.

The number 309,990 has three 9s. Remember that a digit's place in a number determines its meaning.

9 thousands 9 hundreds 9 tens

3 0 9,9 9 0

hundred-thousands	ten-thousands	thousands	hundreds	tens	ones
3	0	9	9	9	0

three hundred nine thousand, nine hundred ninety

Standard form
309,990

Expanded form
300,000 + 9,000 + 900 + 90

Practice

Write the standard form of each number.

1. 40,000 + 7,000 + 100 + 50 + 9

2. 60,000 + 4,000 + 300 + 10 + 3

3. 500,000 + 20,000 + 300 + 7

4. 700,000 + 5,000 + 30 + 9

5. Two thousand, six hundred fifteen

6. Six thousand, one hundred twenty

7. Fifteen thousand, two hundred six

8. Nine hundred thousand, twelve

9. Ten thousand, five hundred eleven

10. Forty-two thousand, one hundred

Write each number in words.

11. 5,304   **12.** 8,729   **13.** 44,792   **14.** 61,078   **15.** 605,419   **16.** 832,764

Write the expanded form of each number.

17. 2,186   **18.** 7,042   **19.** 58,025   **20.** 18,327   **21.** 426,285   **22.** 800,906

Tell what the 7 means in each number.

23. 70,852   **24.** 9,627   **25.** 148,729   **26.** 17,253   **27.** 879   **28.** 715,630

Meaning of Decimals

Review

Each square below represents 1 one.
Divide 1 one into 10 equal parts. Each part is 1 tenth.
Then divide each tenth into 10 equal parts. Each part is 1 hundredth.

 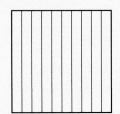 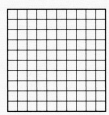

If you divide each hundredth into 10 equal parts, each part is 1 thousandth.

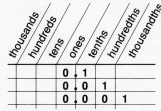

The decimal for one tenth is 0.1.
The decimal for one hundredth is 0.01.
The decimal for one thousandth is 0.001.

Practice

Write each decimal.

1. Seven tenths   **2.** Sixteen hundredths   **3.** Forty-five hundredths

4. Four hundred fifteen thousandths   **5.** One hundred five thousandths

6. Seventy hundredths   **7.** Nine hundredths   **8.** Nineteen thousandths

9. Two thousandths   **10.** Twenty thousandths   **11.** Six thousandths

Write each decimal in words.

12. 0.16   **13.** 0.3   **14.** 0.516   **15.** 0.08   **16.** 0.004   **17.** 0.075

Tell what the 8 means in each number.

18. 3.845   **19.** 5.368   **20.** 0.98   **21.** 8.36   **22.** 0.008   **23.** 5.082

Rounding Whole Numbers

Review

The driving distance from Boston to San Francisco is 3,174 miles.

A. Round 3,174 to the nearest thousand.

3,174

3,000   4,000

The number 3,174 is between 3,000 and 4,000, but it is closer to 3,000. To the nearest thousand, 3,174 rounds to 3,000.

B. Each of these numbers is between 310,000 and 320,000. Round each number to the nearest ten thousand. In each case, the ten-thousands digit is 1.

310,243	**318,243**	**315,243**
The next digit, 0, is less than 5, so the ten-thousands digit, 1, remains the same.	The next digit, 8, is greater than 5, so the ten-thousands digit, 1, increases by one.	The next digit is 5, so the ten-thousands digit, 1, increases by one.
310,000	**320,000**	**320,000**

Practice

Round to the nearest hundred.

1. 529   **2.** 261   **3.** 9,850   **4.** 4,316   **5.** 8,209   **6.** 14,783

7. 308   **8.** 593   **9.** 908   **10.** 2,086   **11.** 86   **12.** 1,964

Round to the nearest thousand.

13. 3,867   **14.** 6,459   **15.** 90,722   **16.** 13,500   **17.** 51,156   **18.** 92,562

19. 4,767   **20.** 8,942   **21.** 50,887   **22.** 79,369   **23.** 26,451   **24.** 29,843

Round to the nearest ten-thousand.

25. 41,375   **26.** 58,655   **27.** 109,592   **28.** 605,500   **29.** 96,387

30. 28,865   **31.** 45,800   **32.** 437,159   **33.** 293,426   **34.** 109,592

Adding Whole Numbers

Review

Find 589 + 742 + 96.

```
  1
  5 8 9   Add the ones.
  7 4 2
+   9 6   17 ones =
      7   1 ten 7 ones
```

```
  2 1
  5 8 9   Add the tens.
  7 4 2
+   9 6   22 tens =
    2 7   2 hundreds 2 tens
```

```
  2 1
  5 8 9   Add the hundreds.
  7 4 2
+   9 6   14 hundreds =
1,4 2 7   1 thousand 4 hundreds
```

Practice

Add.

1. 472 + 356	**2.** 651 + 294	**3.** 226 + 548	**4.** 537 + 235	**5.** 242 + 264	**6.** 384 + 471
7. 3,476 + 5,865	**8.** 9,597 + 4,828	**9.** 7,783 + 2,865	**10.** 3,647 + 5,456	**11.** 6,585 + 4,188	**12.** 8,483 + 8,967
13. 193 621 + 127	**14.** 333 777 + 888	**15.** 4,237 3,528 + 1,967	**16.** 3,946 65,278 + 937	**17.** 57,193 4,621 + 3,127	**18.** 12,401 1,858 + 56,823

19. 2,546 + 7,365

20. 8,948 + 3,589 + 847

21. 3,946 + 27,556 + 721

22. 396,522 + 84,256

23. 27,329 + 5,999 + 624

24. 48,321 + 689 + 724

25. 498 + 56,302

26. 51,287 + 243 + 8,927

27. 16,291 + 5,287 + 2,189

28. 725 + 683 + 927 + 823

29. 5,648 + 9,278 + 2,156 + 9,834

30. 1,528 + 7,562 + 7,856 + 283

31. 78,527 + 3,621 + 8,222 + 785

32. 863,452 + 198,529 + 382,563

33. 5,863,227 + 98,324 + 150,089

34. 76,500 + 7,560 + 756

35. 18,000 + 82,000 + 9,576

36. 24,000,000 + 36,000,000 + 50,000

37. 75,075,075 + 25,025,025 + 50

38. 1,111,111 + 999,999 + 111,112

39. 8,899,999 + 1,000,001 + 100,000

Adding Decimals

Review

A. Find 3.6 + 7.48 + 9.005.
Since 9.005 has three decimal places, write the other decimals with three decimal places.

3.6 = 3.600   Remember that 6 tenths = 600 thousandths and
7.48 = 7.480   48 hundredths = 480 thousandths.

Then line up the decimal points and add as you would with whole numbers.

```
 1
 3.600
 7.480
 9.005
20.085
```
Write the decimal point in the answer.

B. Find 417 + 213.6.

```
    1
  417.0
+ 213.6
  630.6
```
Write the decimal point and one zero to show tenths.
Then line up the decimal points and add.
Write the decimal point in the answer.

Practice

Add.

1. 5.3 + 7.8
2. 8.9 + 6.5
3. 64.72 + 8.35
4. 35.64 + 2.73
5. 7.493 + 3.485
6. 7.832 + 8.171

7. 27.63 + 82.97
8. 43.21 + 8.37
9. 14.53 + 6.38
10. 5.68 + 37.43

11. 4.35 + 76.8
12. 53.02 + 9.8
13. 9.25 + 83.007
14. 476.3 + 4.986

15. 7.864 + 42.68
16. 63.92 + 5.608
17. 2.6 + 3.57
18. 0.346 + 1.29

19. 75.2 + 98
20. 7.005 + 8 + 16
21. 9 + 7.35 + 17
22. 15 + 1.5 + 0.15

23. 16 + 32.59 + 8.2
24. 16.378 + 23.9 + 8.74
25. 11.011 + 110.11 + 1.011

26. 18.003 + 19 + 6.5
27. 0.04 + 0.26 + 0.7
28. 19.63 + 78.56 + 8.745

Subtracting Whole Numbers

Review

A. Find 576 − 398.

```
  6 16
  5 7 6        You need more ones.
− 3 9 8        Rename to get 10 more ones.
─────          7 tens 6 ones = 6 tens 16 ones
      8        Subtract the ones.
```

```
      16
  4 6 16
  5 7 6        You need more tens.
− 3 9 8        Rename to get 10 more tens.
─────          5 hundreds 6 tens = 4 hundreds 16 tens
  1 7 8        Subtract the tens. Subtract the hundreds.
```

B. Find 7,008 − 456.

```
  7,0 0 8      Subtract the ones.
−   4 5 6
────────
        2
```

```
        9
    6 10 10
  7,0 0 8      To get more tens, first rename to get more
−   4 5 6      hundreds. Then rename to get more tens.
────────       Subtract the tens. Subtract the hundreds.
  6,5 5 2      Subtract the thousands.
```

Practice

Subtract.

1. 673 − 419	**2.** 608 − 324	**3.** 592 − 437	**4.** 4,708 − 136	**5.** 7,352 − 236	**6.** 6,037 − 5,136
7. 517 − 249	**8.** 723 − 365	**9.** 308 − 149	**10.** 635 − 567	**11.** 5,348 − 3,662	**12.** 5,013 − 4,678
13. 62,804 − 5,371	**14.** 80,503 − 4,285	**15.** 50,709 − 28,925	**16.** 75,600 − 49,324	**17.** 46,000 − 38,291	**18.** 83,327 − 45,849

19. 600 − 257   **20.** 900 − 194   **21.** 6,235 − 4,657   **22.** 8,243 − 2,987

23. 3,107 − 498   **24.** 5,076 − 894   **25.** 5,600 − 2,443   **26.** 3,700 − 1,467

27. 81,498 − 12,476   **28.** 73,298 − 19,489   **29.** 100,500 − 93,500

30. 529,881 − 2,749   **31.** 90,000 − 57,080   **32.** 1,000,001 − 9,009

33. 80,406 − 12,658   **34.** 42,300 − 9,892   **35.** 705,807 − 47,999

36. 305,049 − 79,680   **37.** 5,070,080 − 692,485   **38.** 120,907 − 86,049

Subtracting Decimals

Review

A. Find $97.8 - 64.53$.

Since 64.53 has two decimal places, write 97.8 with two decimal places.

$97.8 = 97.80$

Then line up the decimal points and subtract as you would with whole numbers.

$$
\begin{array}{r}
^{7\,10}\\
9\,7.8\,\cancel{0}\\
-\,6\,4.5\,3\\
\hline
3\,3.2\,7
\end{array}
$$

Rename to get more hundredths.
8 tenths 0 hundredths = 7 tenths 10 hundredths.
Subtract.
Write the decimal point in the answer.

B. Find $3 - 1.687$.

$$
\begin{array}{r}
^{9\ 9}\\
2\,\cancel{10}\cancel{10}\cancel{10}\\
3.\cancel{0}\,\cancel{0}\,\cancel{0}\\
-\,1.6\,8\,7\\
\hline
1.3\,1\,3
\end{array}
$$

Write the decimal point and three zeros to show thousandths.
Rename and subtract.
Write the decimal point in the answer.

Practice

Subtract.

1. $\begin{array}{r}4.6\\-\,1.9\\\hline\end{array}$	**2.** $\begin{array}{r}7.3\\-\,4.8\\\hline\end{array}$	**3.** $\begin{array}{r}16.592\\-\ \ 8.729\\\hline\end{array}$	**4.** $\begin{array}{r}23.296\\-\ \ 6.897\\\hline\end{array}$	**5.** $\begin{array}{r}6.410\\-\,3.358\\\hline\end{array}$	**6.** $\begin{array}{r}72.910\\-\,46.257\\\hline\end{array}$

7. $0.24 - 0.17$ **8.** $3.4 - 0.8$ **9.** $7.653 - 4.984$ **10.** $0.802 - 0.513$

11. $3.015 - 2.84$ **12.** $12.68 - 9.3$ **13.** $7.3 - 6.914$ **14.** $0.2 - 0.184$

15. $0.67 - 0.379$ **16.** $78 - 24.321$ **17.** $63.78 - 45.928$ **18.** $14.5 - 9.63$

19. $26.7 - 12.42$ **20.** $0.5 - 0.29$ **21.** $141.3 - 37.604$ **22.** $17.62 - 8.957$

23. $0.146 - 0.009$ **24.** $8.09 - 3.963$ **25.** $43.01 - 18.962$ **26.** $17.42 - 9.7$

27. $6 - 0.379$ **28.** $23 - 20.027$ **29.** $217 - 146.914$ **30.** $2 - 0.184$

31. $63 - 49.53$ **32.** $75 - 24.321$ **33.** $354 - 245.92$ **34.** $145 - 98.63$

Meaning of Multiplication

Review

Remember, an array can be used to represent a multiplication fact.

A. This array has 5 rows of dots with 7 dots in each row.

· · · · · · ·
· · · · · · ·
· · · · · · ·
· · · · · · ·
· · · · · · ·

This array represents the multiplication fact $5 \times 7 = 35$.

B. This array has 7 rows with 5 dots in each row.

· · · · ·
· · · · ·
· · · · ·
· · · · ·
· · · · ·
· · · · ·
· · · · ·

This array represents the multiplication fact $7 \times 5 = 35$.

Practice

Use the array in Example A and write a multiplication fact represented by the given number of rows.

1. 4 rows   **2.** 3 rows   **3.** 2 rows   **4.** 1 row

Multiply.

5. 8×3 **6.** 2×6 **7.** 5×3 **8.** 9×2 **9.** 8×6 **10.** 5×5

11. 7×9 **12.** 8×4 **13.** 6×6 **14.** 4×4 **15.** 3×7 **16.** 8×5

17. 4×9 **18.** 6×5 **19.** 3×6 **20.** 7×5 **21.** 9×8 **22.** 7×7

23. 9×3 **24.** 4×5 **25.** 8×7 **26.** 9×9 **27.** 8×8 **28.** 9×5

Write two multiplication facts for each set of numbers. Then make an array to represent each fact.

29. 3   7   21   **30.** 24   6   4   **31.** 9   36   4   **32.** 63   7   9

33. 7   4   28   **34.** 6   8   48   **35.** 72   8   9   **36.** 2   18   9

Meaning of Division

Review

These arrays represent two multiplication facts and two division facts.

5 × 8 = 40   5 rows of 8

40 ÷ 5 = 8   40 dots in 5 rows

8 × 5 = 40   8 rows of 5

40 ÷ 8 = 5   40 dots in 8 rows

Practice

Divide.

1. 56 ÷ 8   **2.** 24 ÷ 3   **3.** 20 ÷ 4   **4.** 30 ÷ 5   **5.** 32 ÷ 4   **6.** 12 ÷ 3

7. 16 ÷ 2   **8.** 42 ÷ 6   **9.** 14 ÷ 2   **10.** 0 ÷ 7   **11.** 54 ÷ 6   **12.** 28 ÷ 7

13. 20 ÷ 5   **14.** 12 ÷ 2   **15.** 16 ÷ 4   **16.** 14 ÷ 7   **17.** 0 ÷ 3   **18.** 48 ÷ 8

19. 63 ÷ 7   **20.** 54 ÷ 9   **21.** 24 ÷ 6   **22.** 63 ÷ 9   **23.** 36 ÷ 4   **24.** 64 ÷ 8

25. 56 ÷ 7   **26.** 45 ÷ 5   **27.** 72 ÷ 8   **28.** 36 ÷ 6   **29.** 81 ÷ 9   **30.** 48 ÷ 6

Write two division facts and two multiplication facts using the given numbers.

31. 1, 8, 8   **32.** 2, 4, 8   **33.** 2, 8, 16   **34.** 5, 7, 35   **35.** 3, 9, 27   **36.** 6, 5, 30

37. 3, 8, 24   **38.** 9, 5, 45   **39.** 8, 7, 56   **40.** 3, 7, 21   **41.** 18, 2, 9   **42.** 6, 54, 9

43. 7, 9, 63   **44.** 4, 28, 7   **45.** 9, 8, 72   **46.** 4, 9, 36   **47.** 6, 42, 7   **48.** 9, 9, 1

Write a multiplication fact and a division fact using each set of numbers. Then make an array that represents both facts.

49. 3   3   9   **50.** 6   6   36   **51.** 49   7   7   **52.** 5   25   5

Meaning of Fractions

Review

A. The rectangle at the right is separated into 8 equal parts. Three of the parts are blue. Three eighths of the rectangle is blue.

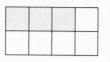

numerator → **3** ← number of blue parts
denominator → **8** ← number of equal parts

| 2 | 3 | 5 | 1 | 4 |

B. What fraction of the cards show even numbers? There are 5 cards in all. Two of the cards show even numbers.

The fraction of the cards that shows even numbers is $\frac{2}{5}$ (two fifths).

Practice

Write each fraction.

1. Two thirds   **2.** Nine tenths   **3.** Five sixths   **4.** Four fifths

In Example A, what fraction of the rectangle is

5. yellow?   **6.** red?   **7.** not red?   **8.** blue or yellow?

In Example B, what fraction of the cards shows

9. odd numbers?   **10.** letters of the alphabet?   **11.** whole numbers?

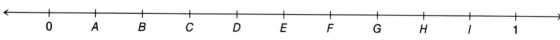

On this number line, the distance from zero to one is divided into 10 equal parts. Write a fraction for the distance from zero to each point named.

12. A **13.** B **14.** C **15.** D **16.** E **17.** F **18.** G **19.** H **20.** I

21. What fraction with denominator 10 is another name for zero?

22. What fraction with denominator 10 is another name for one?

Adding Fractions

Review

Find $\frac{3}{4} + \frac{3}{4}$.

The denominators are the same, so add the numerators.

$$\frac{3}{4} + \frac{3}{4} = \frac{3+3}{4} = \frac{6}{4}$$

$$= 1\frac{2}{4} = 1\frac{1}{2}$$ Rename the sum as a mixed number and write the fraction in lowest terms.

You can also show the work vertically.

$$\frac{3}{4}$$
$$+ \frac{3}{4}$$
$$\frac{6}{4} = 1\frac{2}{4} = 1\frac{1}{2}$$

Practice

Add.

1. $\frac{1}{4} + \frac{2}{4}$　　**2.** $\frac{2}{6} + \frac{3}{6}$　　**3.** $\frac{1}{5} + \frac{3}{5}$　　**4.** $\frac{2}{8} + \frac{3}{8}$　　**5.** $\frac{5}{10} + \frac{4}{10}$　　**6.** $\frac{5}{12} + \frac{2}{12}$

7. $\frac{3}{8} + \frac{4}{8}$　　**8.** $\frac{6}{10} + \frac{2}{10}$　　**9.** $\frac{1}{6} + \frac{3}{6}$　　**10.** $\frac{3}{10} + \frac{2}{10}$　　**11.** $\frac{2}{5} + \frac{1}{5}$　　**12.** $\frac{2}{10} + \frac{5}{10}$

13. $\begin{array}{r} \frac{3}{16} \\ + \frac{9}{16} \\ \hline \end{array}$　　**14.** $\begin{array}{r} \frac{5}{10} \\ + \frac{7}{10} \\ \hline \end{array}$　　**15.** $\begin{array}{r} \frac{5}{6} \\ + \frac{3}{6} \\ \hline \end{array}$　　**16.** $\begin{array}{r} \frac{2}{3} \\ + \frac{2}{3} \\ \hline \end{array}$　　**17.** $\begin{array}{r} \frac{7}{8} \\ + \frac{3}{8} \\ \hline \end{array}$　　**18.** $\begin{array}{r} \frac{3}{5} \\ + \frac{4}{5} \\ \hline \end{array}$

19. $\begin{array}{r} \frac{3}{4} \\ + \frac{3}{4} \\ \hline \end{array}$　　**20.** $\begin{array}{r} \frac{7}{8} \\ + \frac{7}{8} \\ \hline \end{array}$　　**21.** $\begin{array}{r} \frac{9}{10} \\ + \frac{7}{10} \\ \hline \end{array}$　　**22.** $\begin{array}{r} \frac{3}{8} \\ + \frac{5}{8} \\ \hline \end{array}$　　**23.** $\begin{array}{r} \frac{9}{16} \\ + \frac{11}{16} \\ \hline \end{array}$　　**24.** $\begin{array}{r} \frac{7}{10} \\ + \frac{5}{10} \\ \hline \end{array}$

25. $\frac{5}{12} + \frac{5}{12} + \frac{5}{12}$　　**26.** $\frac{5}{16} + \frac{9}{16} + \frac{3}{16}$　　**27.** $\frac{3}{8} + \frac{1}{8} + \frac{5}{8}$　　**28.** $\frac{1}{3} + \frac{2}{3} + \frac{2}{3}$

29. $\frac{7}{10} + \frac{9}{10} + \frac{3}{10}$　　**30.** $\frac{7}{15} + \frac{1}{15} + \frac{13}{15}$　　**31.** $\frac{7}{16} + \frac{11}{16} + \frac{3}{16}$　　**32.** $\frac{9}{20} + \frac{19}{20} + \frac{3}{20}$

Subtracting Fractions

Review

Find $\frac{9}{16} - \frac{5}{16}$.

The denominators are the same, so subtract the numerators.

$\frac{9}{16} - \frac{5}{16} = \frac{9-5}{16} = \frac{4}{16} = \frac{1}{4}$ Write the difference in lowest terms.

You can also show the work vertically.

$$\begin{array}{r} \frac{9}{16} \\ -\frac{5}{16} \\ \hline \frac{4}{16} = \frac{1}{4} \end{array}$$

Practice

Subtract.

1. $\frac{5}{6} - \frac{4}{6}$ 2. $\frac{7}{8} - \frac{3}{8}$ 3. $\frac{2}{3} - \frac{1}{3}$ 4. $\frac{9}{10} - \frac{7}{10}$ 5. $\frac{4}{5} - \frac{3}{5}$ 6. $\frac{2}{3} - \frac{2}{3}$

7. $\frac{7}{8} - \frac{5}{8}$ 8. $\frac{9}{10} - \frac{6}{10}$ 9. $\frac{3}{4} - \frac{1}{4}$ 10. $\frac{5}{12} - \frac{1}{12}$ 11. $\frac{5}{5} - \frac{1}{5}$ 12. $\frac{5}{6} - \frac{2}{6}$

13. $\frac{7}{16} - \frac{5}{16}$ 14. $\frac{7}{12} - \frac{5}{12}$ 15. $\frac{13}{16} - \frac{5}{16}$ 16. $\frac{5}{8} - \frac{1}{8}$ 17. $\frac{7}{5} - \frac{3}{5}$ 18. $\frac{11}{16} - \frac{3}{16}$

19. $\begin{array}{r} \frac{9}{16} \\ -\frac{7}{16} \\ \hline \end{array}$ 20. $\begin{array}{r} \frac{7}{10} \\ -\frac{3}{10} \\ \hline \end{array}$ 21. $\begin{array}{r} \frac{11}{12} \\ -\frac{4}{12} \\ \hline \end{array}$ 22. $\begin{array}{r} \frac{5}{10} \\ -\frac{3}{10} \\ \hline \end{array}$ 23. $\begin{array}{r} \frac{15}{16} \\ -\frac{3}{16} \\ \hline \end{array}$ 24. $\begin{array}{r} \frac{37}{100} \\ -\frac{17}{100} \\ \hline \end{array}$

25. $\begin{array}{r} \frac{11}{24} \\ -\frac{5}{24} \\ \hline \end{array}$ 26. $\begin{array}{r} \frac{15}{16} \\ -\frac{7}{16} \\ \hline \end{array}$ 27. $\begin{array}{r} \frac{9}{8} \\ -\frac{3}{8} \\ \hline \end{array}$ 28. $\begin{array}{r} \frac{7}{4} \\ -\frac{3}{4} \\ \hline \end{array}$ 29. $\begin{array}{r} \frac{8}{5} \\ -\frac{4}{5} \\ \hline \end{array}$ 30. $\begin{array}{r} \frac{7}{6} \\ -\frac{5}{6} \\ \hline \end{array}$

31. $\begin{array}{r} \frac{19}{20} \\ -\frac{7}{20} \\ \hline \end{array}$ 32. $\begin{array}{r} \frac{47}{50} \\ -\frac{9}{50} \\ \hline \end{array}$ 33. $\begin{array}{r} \frac{24}{25} \\ -\frac{19}{25} \\ \hline \end{array}$ 34. $\begin{array}{r} \frac{41}{48} \\ -\frac{27}{48} \\ \hline \end{array}$ 35. $\begin{array}{r} \frac{31}{36} \\ -\frac{9}{36} \\ \hline \end{array}$ 36. $\begin{array}{r} \frac{51}{60} \\ -\frac{23}{60} \\ \hline \end{array}$

Length, Area, Volume

Review

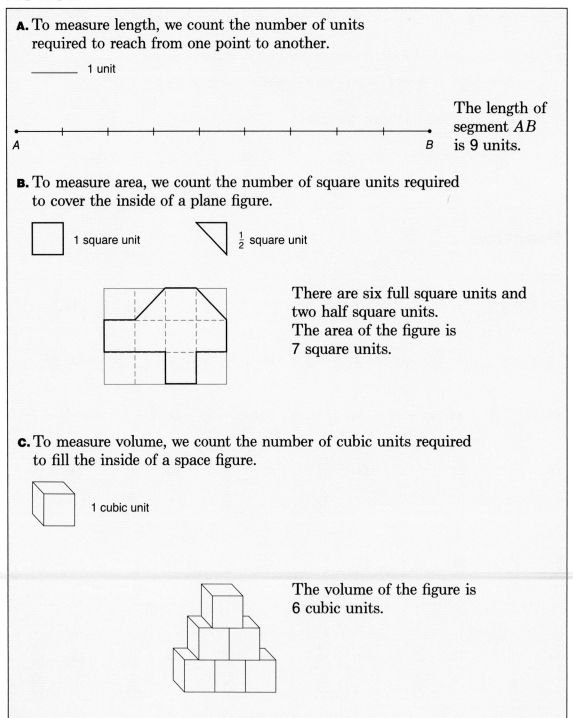

A. To measure length, we count the number of units required to reach from one point to another.

_____ 1 unit

The length of segment AB is **9** units.

A   B

B. To measure area, we count the number of square units required to cover the inside of a plane figure.

☐ 1 square unit   ◺ $\frac{1}{2}$ square unit

There are six full square units and two half square units.
The area of the figure is 7 square units.

C. To measure volume, we count the number of cubic units required to fill the inside of a space figure.

1 cubic unit

The volume of the figure is 6 cubic units.

Practice

Give the length from A to B using the unit of length shown in Example A.

1.

2.

3.

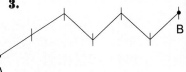

Give the area of each plane figure using the square unit shown in Example B.

4.

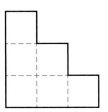

5.

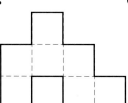

6.

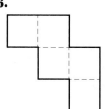

7.

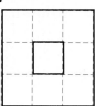

8.

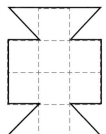

9.

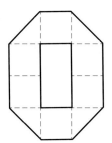

10.

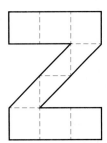

11.

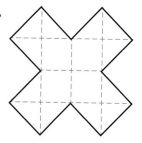

Give the volume of each space figure, using the cubic unit shown in Example C.

12.

13.

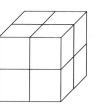

14.

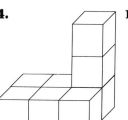

15.

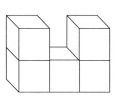

16.

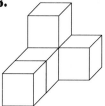

17.

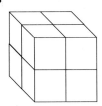

18.

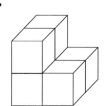

19.

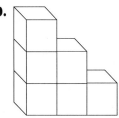

Independent Study Handbook

Contents

How to Use a Calculator

Calculators are used in everyday life at home and at work. They are useful tools when computing with large numbers or when computations involve many numbers. *Remember*:

▶ **Do** estimate to check whether you pushed the correct buttons.

▶ **Don't** use a calculator when paper and pencil or mental math is faster.

Calculator displays

▶ **Number of digits** How many digits will your calculator display? If you press 99,999 × 99,999 to generate a number with more digits than the display can show, most calculators will show some kind of "error" message.

▶ **Unnecessary zeros** If you add 2.10 and 3.20, does your display show 5.3 or 5.30? Calculators usually drop unnecessary zeros.

▶ **Rounding** If you divide 2 by 3, do you see 0.6666666 or 0.6666667? Many calculators drop any digits after 8 digits, rather than round.

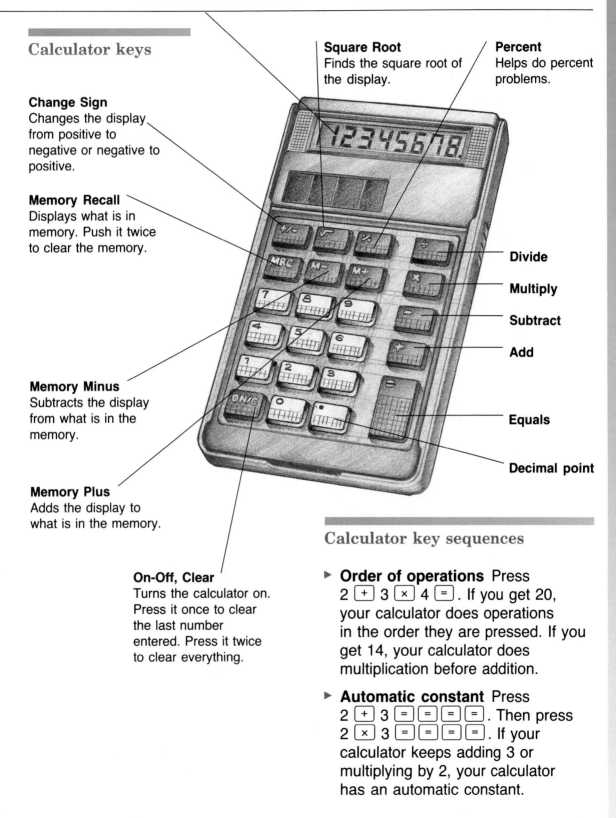

Display
Shows the number that is being used in a calculation or the solution to a calculation.

Calculator keys

Square Root
Finds the square root of the display.

Percent
Helps do percent problems.

Change Sign
Changes the display from positive to negative or negative to positive.

Memory Recall
Displays what is in memory. Push it twice to clear the memory.

Memory Minus
Subtracts the display from what is in the memory.

Memory Plus
Adds the display to what is in the memory.

On-Off, Clear
Turns the calculator on. Press it once to clear the last number entered. Press it twice to clear everything.

Divide

Multiply

Subtract

Add

Equals

Decimal point

Calculator key sequences

▶ **Order of operations** Press 2 ⊞ 3 ⊠ 4 ⊜. If you get 20, your calculator does operations in the order they are pressed. If you get 14, your calculator does multiplication before addition.

▶ **Automatic constant** Press 2 ⊞ 3 ⊜ ⊜ ⊜ ⊜. Then press 2 ⊠ 3 ⊜ ⊜ ⊜ ⊜. If your calculator keeps adding 3 or multiplying by 2, your calculator has an automatic constant.

Problem-Solving Help File

Use these pages to help you solve problems more effectively.

Problem-Solving Guide

There is no recipe or magic formula for solving problems. But keeping a problem-solving guide in mind can help you become a better problem solver.

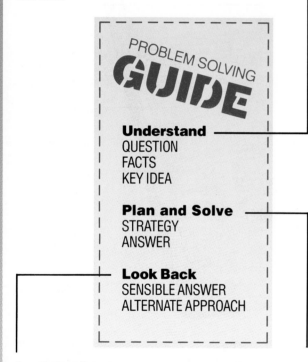

PROBLEM SOLVING **GUIDE**

Understand
QUESTION
FACTS
KEY IDEA

Plan and Solve
STRATEGY
ANSWER

Look Back
SENSIBLE ANSWER
ALTERNATE APPROACH

Understand
QUESTION
▶ What are you asked to find?
▶ Try to state the question in your own words.
▶ Is an exact answer needed?

FACTS
▶ What facts are given?
▶ Is there too much or too little information?
▶ Is data needed from a picture, table, graph?
▶ Do you need to collect some data?

KEY IDEA
▶ How are the facts and the question related?
▶ Are there groups that are part of a whole?
▶ Are two groups being compared?
▶ Are there groups that are joining or separating?
▶ Are there groups of the same size?

Plan and Solve
STRATEGY
▶ What can you do to solve the problem?
▶ Can the problem be solved by computing?
▶ Estimate the answer.
▶ Choose a strategy. Try another, if needed.

ANSWER
▶ Give the answer in a sentence.
▶ Do you need to interpret a remainder?
▶ Is rounding needed?

Look Back
SENSIBLE ANSWER
▶ Did you check your work?
▶ Did you use all the needed data?
▶ Does your answer have the correct units?
▶ Is your answer close to the estimate?
▶ Is your answer reasonable for the situation?

ALTERNATE APPROACH
▶ Is there another way to get the same answer?
▶ Could you use the same strategy differently?
▶ Would another strategy be faster or simpler?

Problem-Solving Strategies

You might think of problem-solving strategies as problem-solving tools that you own and use when needed. One or more strategies might be used for a problem. And if one strategy doesn't work, try another one.

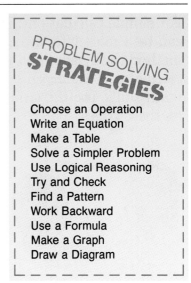

PROBLEM SOLVING STRATEGIES

Choose an Operation
Write an Equation
Make a Table
Solve a Simpler Problem
Use Logical Reasoning
Try and Check
Find a Pattern
Work Backward
Use a Formula
Make a Graph
Draw a Diagram

Problem-Solving Behaviors and Attitudes

When you solve problems, do you give up quickly or lack confidence? Behaviors and attitudes can affect your work. So, remember these tips. They can help you become a better problem solver.

TIPS FOR PROBLEM SOLVERS

Don't give up. Some problems take longer than others.

Tips for Problem Solvers

▶ **Don't give up.** Some problems take longer than others.

▶ **Be flexible.** If you get stuck, try another idea.

▶ **Be confident** so you can do your best.

▶ **Take risks.** Try your hunches. They often work.

▶ **Brainstorm to get started**—one idea will lead to another.

▶ **Visualize the problem** in your mind to help you understand it better.

▶ **Compare problems** to help you relate new problems to ones you've solved before.

▶ **Think about your thinking.** Pause to ask, "How is this going to help me solve the problem?"

▶ **Share your thinking with others.** Explaining your ideas helps you think better.

▶ **Organize your work** to help you think clearly.

Mental Math Strategies

For simple calculations, mental math can be a more effective computation method than paper and pencil or a calculator. To sharpen your mental math skills, use the strategies shown on these pages.

Breaking Apart Numbers

Break apart one or more numbers to get numbers that are easier to use.

54 + 23	
54 + 20 + 3	Break apart 23.
74 + 3	
77	

87 × 2	
(80 + 7) × 2	Break apart 87.
(80 × 2) + (7 × 2)	Use the distributive property.
160 + 14	
174	

35 + 48	
(30 + 5) + (40 + 8)	Break apart 35 and 48.
(30 + 40) + (5 + 8)	Regroup the numbers.
70 + 13	
83	

60% of 900	
6 × 0.10 × 900	Break apart 60%.
6 × 90	Find 10% of 900.
540	Then multiply by 6.

Compatible Numbers

Compatible numbers are pairs of numbers that are easy to use. Look for numbers like 1, 10, 100 or 3, 30, 300 that are easy to use.

40 + 30	**28 × 10**
70	280

180 ÷ 60
3

When there are 3 or more numbers, look for pairs of numbers that are compatible.

3 + 48 + 7

3 + 7 + 48
10 + 48
58

$\frac{1}{3}$ × 7 × 12

$\frac{1}{3}$ × 12 × 7

4 × 7
28

Using Equivalent Forms

Divide to find "fraction of."

$$\frac{1}{3} \times 180$$
$$180 \div 3$$
$$60$$

Change decimals or percents to fractions to get a number that is easier to use.

25% of 32

$$\frac{1}{4} \text{ of } 32$$
$$32 \div 4$$
$$8$$

Compensation

Change one number to make it easy to use. Then change the answer to compensate.

57 + 29

$57 + 30 = 87$	Add 1 to 29 to get 30.
$87 - 1 = 86$	Subtract 1 from the answer.

165 − 97

$165 - 100 = 65$	Add 3 to 97 to get 100.
$65 + 3 = 68$	Add 3 to the answer.

Change one number to make it easy to use. Then change the other number to compensate.

66 + 19

$$65 + 20$$
$$85$$

Add 1 to 19 and subtract 1 from 66.

157 − 98

$$159 - 100$$
$$59$$

Add 2 to 98 and to 157.

Estimation Strategies

In everyday life, an exact answer is often unnecessary. For example, you can estimate while shopping to see if you have enough money.

When you do need an exact answer, estimation helps you find possible errors. Estimation is especially important for checking whether you pushed a wrong button on a calculator.

To help you make good estimates, use the estimation strategies shown on these pages.

Front-End Digits

Use just the first digit in each number to help you make an estimate.

$$
\begin{array}{r}
173 \\
421 \\
+348 \\
\end{array}
\qquad
\begin{array}{r}
100 \\
400 \\
+300 \\
\hline
800 \\
\end{array}
$$

You can also adjust the estimate by adding 100 to get 900.

$$4\tfrac{1}{2} + 6\tfrac{5}{8} + 2\tfrac{1}{3}$$

$$4 + 6 + 2$$

$$12$$

Rounding

Round to one nonzero digit.

$$
\begin{array}{r}
425 \\
\times\ 28 \\
\end{array}
\qquad
\begin{array}{r}
400 \\
\times 30 \\
\hline
12{,}000 \\
\end{array}
$$

Round to the same place.

$$
\begin{array}{r}
28.45 \\
-\ 3.79 \\
\end{array}
\qquad
\begin{array}{r}
28 \\
-\ 4 \\
\hline
24 \\
\end{array}
$$

$$13\tfrac{1}{4} + 8\tfrac{7}{8}$$

$$13 + 9$$

$$22$$

Round to the nearest half.

$$\tfrac{3}{8} + 2\tfrac{5}{8} + \tfrac{1}{4}$$

$$\tfrac{1}{2} + 2\tfrac{1}{2} + \tfrac{1}{2}$$

$$3\tfrac{1}{2}$$

Round both numbers up and both numbers down to get a range.

$$57 \times 84 \qquad \begin{array}{l} 60 \times 90 = 5{,}400 \\ 50 \times 80 = 4{,}000 \end{array}$$

57×84 is between 4,000 and 5,400.

Substituting Compatible Numbers

Use numbers that are close to the original numbers.

$23\overline{)476}$
$24\overline{)480}$ or $23\overline{)460}$ or $25\overline{)500}$
$23\overline{)476}$ is about 20.

24 × 78 × 4
25 × 78 × 4
100 × 78
24 × 78 × 4 is about 7,800.

$\frac{1}{3} \times 187$
$\frac{1}{3} \times 180$
$\frac{1}{3} \times 187$ is about 60.

26% of 32
25% of 32
$\frac{1}{4} \times 32$
26% of 32 is about 8.

Clustering

Look for groups of numbers that are close to the same number.

6,278	Each number
6,589	is about 6,000,
5,893	so the sum is
+6,134	about
	4 × 6,000 or
	24,000.

$$4\frac{7}{8} + 5\frac{1}{5} + 4\frac{2}{3}$$

Each number is about 5, so the sum is about 3 × 5 or 15.

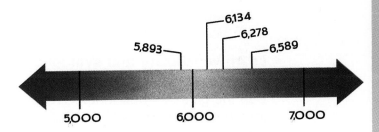

Comparing to a Reference Point

Compare the numbers to numbers you can work with easily.

346	Both numbers are less than 500, so the
+438	sum is less than 1,000.

$\frac{5}{8} + \frac{3}{5}$	Both numbers are greater than $\frac{1}{2}$, so the sum is greater than 1.

Math Study Skills

Try these math study skills to help
you do your best.

Before a Lesson

▶ **Preview the lesson.** Look over the
lesson to see what it's about.

▶ **Set a purpose.** Are you about to
learn a new topic or revisit a familiar
one?

▶ **Recall what you know.** What have
you learned about this topic
previously?

Build Understanding

Reading the lesson

▶ **Read slowly.** Don't try to read a
math book as fast as a story book.

▶ **Learn vocabulary and symbols.**
Note new math terms and symbols.
Use the glossary and index. Watch
for words like "product" that have
other meanings outside of math.

▶ **Read diagrams, tables, graphs.**
Use a ruler to help you read rows
and columns.

▶ **Do the examples.** Work the
examples yourself as you go through
them.

Doing Activities

▶ **Use materials.** Keep the materials
organized. Use them to explore new
ideas.

▶ **Work with others.** When you work
with others, use the tips for working
together given on page 570.

Build Understandin

A. A market gets boxes of l
24 heads in each box. H
heads of lettuce are in 4

Since each box contai
same number of he

Check Understanding

Trying on your own

▸ **Note what you don't understand.** When you try some exercises, be aware of what you don't understand.

▸ **Reread the lesson.** When you don't understand, reread the "Build Understanding" section.

Preventing errors

▸ **Find another example.** When you need another example, turn to the "Reteaching" set at the back of the chapter.

▸ **Try again.** Keep trying until you feel you understand.

Practice and Problem Solving

Reading the exercises

▸ **Read directions.** Read carefully.

▸ **Read word problems.** Read slowly and reread, if needed.

Doing written work

▸ **Show your work.** Record what you did. Make your paper easy to follow and the answer easy to find.

▸ **Check your work.** Read what you write.

▸ **Find more practice.** Use the "More Practice" at the back of the chapter when needed.

After a Lesson

▸ **Look back.** Summarize the lesson. Can you explain what you learned to another student?

▸ **Connect to other lessons.** Think about how this lesson is related to other lessons.

Working in Groups

Working in groups during math class will help you learn and enjoy mathematics. You will also learn to work as a member of a team.

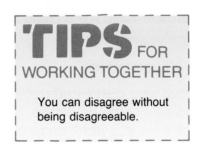

TIPS FOR
WORKING TOGETHER

You can disagree without being disagreeable.

Roles for Group Members

When you work in a group, it can be helpful for each person to have a role. Some roles are:

▶ **Reporter**—This person summarizes the group's thinking.

▶ **Encourager**—This person encourages group members to take part and to work together well.

▶ **Recorder**—This person records the group's work.

▶ **Checker**—This person asks group members to explain their thinking or may ask others if they agree.

▶ **Materials Manager**—This person gets any materials that are needed and returns them at the end of class.

Tips for Working Together

Here are some tips for working well with others in a group.

▶ Involve your whole group. Help everyone to participate.

▶ Help keep your group on task.

▶ To make sure your group understands the task or solution, have each group member say it in his or her own words, summarize the steps, or give an example.

▶ Work as a group. If you understand, help another group member. Don't work ahead of the others.

▶ Be a good tutor. Make up similar problems or easier ones to help someone understand.

▶ When you are unsure, ask someone in your group for help or say you don't understand.

▶ Tell someone when he or she does or says something that helps you.

▶ Don't decide by voting. Try to understand which might be the best solution and why.

▶ Remember, you can disagree without being disagreeable.

Tables

Metric System

Length

$$10 \text{ millimeters (mm)} = 1 \text{ centimeter (cm)}$$
$$\left.\begin{array}{r}10 \text{ centimeters} \\ 100 \text{ millimeters}\end{array}\right\} = 1 \text{ decimeter (dm)}$$
$$\left.\begin{array}{r}10 \text{ decimeters} \\ 100 \text{ centimeters}\end{array}\right\} = 1 \text{ meter (m)}$$
$$1{,}000 \text{ meters} = 1 \text{ kilometer (km)}$$

Area

$$100 \text{ square millimeters (mm}^2) = 1 \text{ square centimeter (cm}^2)$$
$$10{,}000 \text{ square centimeters} = 1 \text{ square meter (m}^2)$$
$$100 \text{ square meters} = 1 \text{ are (a)}$$
$$10{,}000 \text{ square meters} = 1 \text{ hectare (ha)}$$

Volume

$$1{,}000 \text{ cubic millimeters (mm}^3) = 1 \text{ cubic centimeter (cm}^3)$$
$$1{,}000 \text{ cubic centimeters} = 1 \text{ cubic decimeter (dm}^3)$$
$$1{,}000{,}000 \text{ cubic centimeters} = 1 \text{ cubic meter (m}^3)$$

Mass (weight)

$$1{,}000 \text{ milligrams (mg)} = 1 \text{ gram (g)}$$
$$1{,}000 \text{ grams} = 1 \text{ kilogram (kg)}$$
$$1{,}000 \text{ kilograms} = 1 \text{ metric ton (t)}$$

Capacity

$$1{,}000 \text{ milliliters (mL)} = 1 \text{ liter (L)}$$

Time

$$60 \text{ seconds} = 1 \text{ minute}$$
$$60 \text{ minutes} = 1 \text{ hour}$$
$$24 \text{ hours} = 1 \text{ day}$$
$$7 \text{ days} = 1 \text{ week}$$
$$\left.\begin{array}{l}365 \text{ days} \\ 52 \text{ weeks} \\ 12 \text{ months}\end{array}\right\} = 1 \text{ year}$$
$$366 \text{ days} = 1 \text{ leap year}$$

Addition-Subtraction Table

+	0	1	2	3	4	5	6	7	8	9
0	0	1	2	3	4	5	6	7	8	9
1	1	2	3	4	5	6	7	8	9	10
2	2	3	4	5	6	7	8	9	10	11
3	3	4	5	6	7	8	9	10	11	12
4	4	5	6	7	8	9	10	11	12	13
5	5	6	7	8	9	10	11	12	13	14
6	6	7	8	9	10	11	12	13	14	15
7	7	8	9	10	11	12	13	14	15	16
8	8	9	10	11	12	13	14	15	16	17
9	9	10	11	12	13	14	15	16	17	18

Multiplication-Division Table

×	1	2	3	4	5	6	7	8	9
1	1	2	3	4	5	6	7	8	9
2	2	4	6	8	10	12	14	16	18
3	3	6	9	12	15	18	21	24	27
4	4	8	12	16	20	24	28	32	36
5	5	10	15	20	25	30	35	40	45
6	6	12	18	24	30	36	42	48	54
7	7	14	21	28	35	42	49	56	63
8	8	16	24	32	40	48	56	64	72
9	9	18	27	36	45	54	63	72	81

Customary System

Length

$$12 \text{ inches (in.)} = 1 \text{ foot (ft)}$$
$$\left.\begin{array}{r}3 \text{ feet} \\ 36 \text{ inches}\end{array}\right\} = 1 \text{ yard (yd)}$$
$$\left.\begin{array}{r}1{,}760 \text{ yards} \\ 5{,}280 \text{ feet}\end{array}\right\} = 1 \text{ mile (mi)}$$
$$6{,}076 \text{ feet} = 1 \text{ nautical mile}$$

Area

$$144 \text{ square inches (sq in.)} = 1 \text{ square foot (sq ft)}$$
$$9 \text{ square feet} = 1 \text{ square yard (sq yd)}$$
$$4{,}840 \text{ square yards} = 1 \text{ acre (A)}$$

Volume

$$1{,}728 \text{ cubic inches (cu in.)} = 1 \text{ cubic foot (cu ft)}$$
$$27 \text{ cubic feet} = 1 \text{ cubic yard (cu yd)}$$

Weight

$$16 \text{ ounces (oz)} = 1 \text{ pound (lb)}$$
$$2{,}000 \text{ pounds} = 1 \text{ ton (T)}$$

Capacity

$$8 \text{ fluid ounces (fl oz)} = 1 \text{ cup (c)}$$
$$2 \text{ cups} = 1 \text{ pint (pt)}$$
$$2 \text{ pints} = 1 \text{ quart (qt)}$$
$$4 \text{ quarts} = 1 \text{ gallon (gal)}$$

Glossary

Abundant number A number for which the sum of its proper factors is greater than the number itself.

Acute angle An angle with a measure less than 90°.

Acute triangle Triangle with three acute angles.

Addition property of zero The sum of zero and a number is that number.

Adjacent angles Angles that have a common vertex and a common side between them.

Angle (∠) The figure formed by two rays with the same endpoint.

Area A number given in square units that indicates the size of the inside of a plane figure.

Arrangement A selection of objects with regard to order.

Associative property (Grouping property) The way in which addends (or factors) are grouped does not affect the sum (or product).
$(7 + 2) + 5 = 7 + (2 + 5)$
$(7 \times 2) \times 5 = 7 \times (2 \times 5)$

Average A number obtained by dividing the sum of two or more addends by the number of addends.

Base (of an exponent) The number to be raised to a power. In 4^3, 4 is the base.

Base (in geometry) A name used for a side of a polygon or surface of a space figure.

Betweenness property For any two numbers, there is another number between them.

Bisect To divide into two congruent parts.

Central angle An angle with its vertex at the center of a circle.

Chord A segment with both endpoints on a circle. A diameter is a special chord.

Circle A plane figure with all points the same distance from a given point called the *center*.

Circle graph A drawing that compares the parts of a quantity with the whole quantity.

Circumference The distance around a circle.

Clustering An estimation method used when all the numbers are close to the same number.

Combination A selection of objects without regard to order.

Common denominator A common multiple of two or more denominators. A common denominator for $\frac{1}{6}$ and $\frac{3}{8}$ is 48.

Common factor A number that is a factor of two or more numbers. A common factor of 6 and 12 is 3.

Commutative property (Order property) The order in which numbers are added (or multiplied) does not affect the sum (or product).
$4 + 6 = 6 + 4$
$4 \times 6 = 6 \times 4$

Compass An instrument used for drawing circles and for doing geometric constructions.

Compatible number A number close to the number in the problem being solved that is used for mental computation.

Complementary angles Two angles whose measures add up to 90°.

Composite number A whole number, greater than 0, that has more than two factors.

Cone A space figure formed by connecting a circle to a point not in the plane of the circle.

Congruent figures Two figures with the same size and shape.

Construction The drawing of a figure using only a compass and a straightedge.

Conversion factor A ratio used to convert one unit of measure to a related unit of measure.

Coordinates Integers in an ordered pair giving the location of a point in a coordinate plane.

Cross-products The cross-products of the ratios $\frac{3}{4}$ and $\frac{9}{12}$ are 3×12 and 4×9.

Cube A prism with all square faces.

Cylinder A space figure with two circular bases that are parallel and congruent.

Data A collection of gathered information that has not been organized.

Decimal A number used to name a whole quantity and/or a fractional part. It is written in standard form with a point to separate the whole number and fraction parts.

Deficient number A number for which the sum of its proper factors is less than the number itself.

Degree (of an angle) A unit for measuring angles.

Deposit Money given to a bank to open or add to a checking or a savings account.

Diagonal A segment with two nonadjacent vertices of a polygon as its endpoints.

Diameter In a circle, a segment that passes through the center and that has both endpoints on the circle.

Distributive property
When a factor is a sum, multiplying each addend before adding does not change the product.

Dividend A number that is divided by another number.

Divisible One number is divisible by another if the remainder is zero after dividing.

Divisor The number by which another number is divided.

Double bar graph A drawing that uses two bars to compare related information.

Edge Segment where two faces of a polyhedron meet.

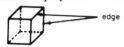

Equation A mathematical sentence with the = symbol.

Equilateral triangle
Triangle with three congruent sides.

Estimate A number that is close to another number. A name used for a calculation not requiring an exact answer.

Experimental probability
Ratio of number of successes to number of trials.

Exponent A number that tells how many times the base is to be used as a factor.
$4^3 = 4 \times 4 \times 4$

Expression A mathematical phrase that uses numbers, variables, and operation symbols to represent a value.

Face Flat surface that is part of a polyhedron.

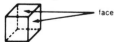

Factor (1) A number to be multiplied. (2) A number that divides evenly into a given second number is a factor of that number.

Favorable outcome A result in a probability

experiment that meets a specific condition.

Flip A transformation that creates a mirror image (reflection) of a figure.

Formula An equation that states a general fact or rule by using variables.

Fraction A number that names a part of a whole or of a set. It is written in the form $\frac{a}{b}$.

Frequency The number of times a certain item occurs in a set of data.

Googol 10 to the one hundredth power. 10^{100}

Graph A drawing used to show information in an organized way.

Greatest common factor
1) The greatest number that is a factor of two or more numbers.
2) The greatest number that divides two or more numbers with no remainder.

Height The segment from a vertex perpendicular to the line containing the opposite side.

Hexagon A six-sided polygon.

Improper fraction A fraction whose numerator is greater than or equal to its denominator.

Inequality A mathematical sentence with one of the following symbols: $\neq$, $<$, $>$, $\leq$, $\geq$.

Integers The whole numbers and their opposites. Some integers are $+3$, -3, 0, $+16$, -16.

Intersecting lines Lines that meet at a point.

Inverse operations Two operations that have the opposite effect on a number. Addition and subtraction are inverse operations. Multiplication and division are inverse operations.

Isosceles triangle Triangle with two congruent sides.

Least common denominator (LCD) The least common multiple of the denominators of two or more fractions. The least common denominator of $\frac{1}{2}$ and $\frac{2}{3}$ is 6.

Least common multiple (LCM) The smallest number that is a common multiple of two given numbers. The least common multiple for 6 and 8 is 24.

Line A set of points continuing without end in both directions.

Line of symmetry A line on which a figure can be folded into two congruent parts.

Line segment Two points and the straight path between them.

Lowest terms A fraction for which 1 is the greatest common factor of both the numerator and the denominator.

Mean Average of a group of numbers. The mean of 2, 4, 5, 6, 6 is 23 ÷ 5, or 4.6.

Median The middle number in a group of numbers when the numbers are listed in order. The median of 2, 4, 5, 6, 6 is 5.

Metric system The system of measures that uses meter, liter, gram, and degrees Celsius.

Midpoint A point that divides a segment into two congruent segments.

Mixed number A number that has a whole number part and a fraction part.

Mode Number that occurs most often in a set of data.

Multiple A multiple of a number is the product of that number and a whole number.

Multiplication property of one The product of one and a number is that number.

Multiplication property of zero The product of zero and a number is zero.

Negative integer An integer less than 0, such as −5 or −10.

Obtuse angle An angle with a measure greater than 90° and less than 180°.

Obtuse triangle Triangle with one obtuse angle.

Octagon An eight-sided polygon.

Opposites Two numbers whose sum is 0. +5 and −5 are opposites because +5 + (−5) = 0.

Ordered pair A pair of numbers arranged so there is a first number and a second number, used to locate a point on a grid.

Order of operations Rules for finding the value of an expression.

Organized list All the possibilities for a situation written in a certain order.

Origin On a coordinate grid, the point, (0, 0), where the two number lines, or axes, intersect.

Outcome A possible result in a probability experiment.

Parallel lines Lines in a plane that never meet.

Parallelogram A quadrilateral with opposite sides parallel and congruent.

Pentagon A five-sided polygon.

Percent (%) A word meaning "hundredths" or "out of 100." 45 percent (45%) equals 0.45 or $\frac{45}{100}$.

Perfect number A number for which the sum of its proper factors is equal to the number itself.

Perimeter The sum of the lengths of the sides of a polygon.

Perpendicular bisector (of a segment) A line which divides the segment into two congruent parts and is perpendicular to it.

Perpendicular lines Lines that intersect to form right angles.

Pi (π) The number obtained by dividing the circumference of any circle by its diameter. A common approximation for π is 3.14.

Place value The number each digit represents is determined by the position the digit occupies.

Plane A flat surface that extends without end in all directions.

Point An exact location in space.

Polygon A closed plane figure made by line segments.

Polyhedron A space figure made up of flat surfaces called *faces*. Each face is a polygon.

Positive integer An integer greater than 0, such as +1 or +35.

Power 4^2 is read "4 to the second power" or "4 squared." $4^2 = 16$. The second power of 4 is 16. *See* Exponent.

Prime factorization A number written as the product of prime numbers. $30 = 2 \times 3 \times 5$

Prime number A whole number, greater than 1, that has exactly two factors: itself and 1.

Prism A polyhedron with two parallel, congruent faces, called *bases*. All other faces are parallelograms.

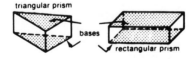

triangular prism / bases / rectangular prism

Probability A number from 0 to 1 that tells how likely it is that a given event will occur. The closer to 1, the *more likely* the event is to occur. The closer to 0, the *less likely* it is to occur.

Proper factors All the factors of a number except the number itself.

Proportion A statement that two ratios are equal. $\frac{2}{5} = \frac{12}{30}$

Protractor An instrument used to measure angles.

Pyramid The space figure formed by connecting points of a polygon to a point not in the plane of the polygon. The polygon and its interior is the *base*.

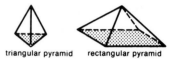

triangular pyramid   rectangular pyramid

Quadrant One of the four parts into which a plane is divided by two perpendicular lines.

Quadrilateral A four-sided polygon.

Quotient The answer after dividing one number by another.

Radius (1) In a circle, a segment that connects the center of the circle with a point on the circle. (2) In a circle, the distance from the center to a point on the circle.

Range The difference between the greatest and the least numbers in a set of data.

Rate A ratio that compares one quantity to a different kind of quantity.

Ratio A pair of numbers that expresses a rate or a comparison.

Ray A set of points that has one endpoint and that extends without end in one direction.

Reciprocals Two numbers whose product is 1. $\frac{3}{4}$ and $\frac{4}{3}$ are reciprocals because $\frac{3}{4} \times \frac{4}{3} = 1$.

Rectangle A parallelogram with four right angles.

Reflection A change in location of a figure by flipping it over a line.

Regular polygon A polygon with all sides congruent and all angles congruent.

Repeating decimal A decimal in which one or more digits keep repeating, such as 0.518181818...

Rhombus A parallelogram with four congruent sides.

Right angle An angle with a measure of 90°.

Right triangle Triangle with one right angle.

Rotation A change in location of a figure by turning it about a point.

Sample Part of a group upon which an experiment or survey is conducted.

Scale drawing A drawing made so that distances in the drawing are proportional to actual distances.

Scalene triangle Triangle with no congruent sides.

Sequence A set of numbers formed by a pattern.

Similar figures Figures with the same shape but not necessarily the same size.

Skew lines Lines that are in two different planes.

Slide A transformation that moves a figure without turning it.

Sphere A space figure with all points the same distance from a given point called the *center*.

Square (in geometry) A rectangle with four congruent sides.

Square (in numeration) To multiply a number by itself.

Square root A number a is the square root of a number b if $a \times a = b$. 3 is the square root of 9.

Standard form The notation for writing numbers using the digits 0-9 and each place represents a power of ten.

Statistics Numerical facts that are collected, organized and analyzed.

Stem-and-leaf plot A method for representing numerical data in which tens digits (stems) appear in a vertical line and ones digits (leaves) appear in horizontal lines.

Straight angle An angle with a measure of 180°.

Straightedge An instrument, such as an unmarked ruler, used in geometric constructions.

Supplementary angles Two angles whose measures add up to 180°.

Surface area The sum of the areas of all the surfaces of a space figure.

Symmetric figure A plane figure that can be folded in half so the two halves match.

Terminating decimal A decimal with an exact number of nonzero digits, such as 0.375.

Terms In a ratio $a{:}b$, a is the first term and b is the second term.

Theoretical probability Ratio of the favorable outcomes to the possible outcomes for an event.

Time zone A geographical region within which the same standard time is used.

Transformation A flip, slide, or turn that changes the location of a figure on a plane without changing its size or shape.

Transversal A line that intersects two or more lines.

Trapezoid A quadrilateral with one pair of parallel sides.

Tree diagram An organized way to list all possible outcomes of an experiment.

Trial An attempt to carry out an event.

Triangle A three-sided polygon.

Triangular numbers A sequence of numbers that can be shown by dots arranged in the shape of a triangle.

Turn A transformation that turns a figure around a given point.

Twenty-four hour clock An instrument for showing time in relationship to midnight.

Unit fraction A fraction with a numerator of one.

Vertex (1) The common endpoint of two rays that form an angle. (2) The point of intersection of two sides of a polygon. (3) The point of intersection of the edges of a polyhedron.

Volume A number given in cubic units that indicates the size of the inside of a space figure.

Whole number One of the numbers 0, 1, 2, 3, and so on.

Withdrawal Money taken out of a savings account.

Index

ACKNOWLEDGMENTS

Design
Covers and Special Features:
SHELDON COTLER + ASSOCIATES

Identity Center, Lipman Hearne, Rosa + Wesley Design Associates, Jack Weiss Associates

Photographs
Abbreviations for page positions are as follow: T for top; C for center; B for bottom; L for left; and R for right.

Cover: Richard Chesnut, Fred Schenk. ScottForesman photographs by: Richard Chesnut 65, 117, 125, 140, 179, 246, 266B, 267T, 285, 388; Arie deZanger 153, 267C, 278–279, 484, 489; unless otherwise acknowledged, all photographs are the property of ScottForesman. AlaskaStock: Chris Arend 286; Brandon 453; Crandall 387. Allstock: Art Wolfe xiiiTR. Robert Amft 14. Peter Arnold, Inc.: 233TR, Steve Kaufman 198TL; Stephen J. Krasemann 266C; K. Schafer 160BL. Lee Boltin: 286. Trustees of the British Museum: 248. Cameramann International: 24, 160 (Egypt, Teotihuacan), 165, 186, 386. Woodfin Camp & Associates, Inc.: Jeff Lowenthal 87B; Bill Ross 270–271. Click/Chicago/Tony Stone: Chris Baker 460; Oliver Benn 331; Suzanne Murphy 384; Ed Pritchard 94–95; L. T. Rhodes 255; Tony Stone 330; Bob Thomason 95. Bruce Coleman: Bruce Coleman 160 (Bolivia stone statue; M. Sherman 160 (Bolivia stone face). Comstock: John Batchelor 507R. Culver Pictures: 3CR. Tim Davis; 128BL. Duomo: Rick Rickman 128–129. Ellis Wildlife Collection: Ken Deitcher 233BR; Gerry Ellis 198TF, 232–233, 240–241, 354. Focus on Sports: 428. David R. Frazier Photolibrary: David R. Frazier 513, 524; Aaron Haupt 476. Grant Heilman: Lefever/Grushow 277; Larry Lefever 32, 100T. Museum of the American Indian, The Heye Foundation: 187, 286 LR. From *The*

Firedogs, copyright © 1990 by Hollym Corp. Illustration by Pak Mi-son 519. The Image Bank: Ira Block 506R; Cliff Feulner 506L, 521; Gary Gay 340C; William Rivelli 340BL; Al Satterwhite 21. The Image Works: David Wells xixBL. ImpactPhoto: Christopher Cormack 149. Bruce Iverson: 304–305. Courtesy International Business Machines Corp.: xv. Courtesy International Pumpkin Association: 33. Jerry Jacka: 493. Kelly/Mooney Photography: xiv. Landslides: 527. From THE ART OF THE PUPPET by Bil Baird, The Ridge Press Inc., published by the Macmillan Company, NY, 1965. All rights reserved. Photo: Arie de Zanger 257. David Madison: 8, 129C, 141. Magnum Photos: Eve Arnold 448–449; Ara Guler 506T; Richard Kalvar 449BR; Erich Lessing 507CL. Courtesy Mexican Fine Arts Center Museum: 343. Michael K. Nichols 448C. NASA: 17, 44–45. Courtesy National Park Service: xiiiBL. Odyssey Productions: Robert Frerck 250. Courtesy Oriental Institute, University of Chicago: 264. Panoramic Stock Images: David Larence 235. PhotoEdit: Tony Freeman xviiiB, xivBR, 403; Dennis MacDonald 203; Alan Oddie xvi; Mark Richards xvi–xvii. Photo Researchers, Inc.: H. Dosal 160 (Chichen Itza w/people); Eric Grave/Science Source 318; G. Holton 160 (Chichen Itza w/posts). Ernest H. Robl: 30. The Museum of African Art, Smithsonian Institution. James Smithson Society, 89-8-19: 25. Stock Boston: Jose Carillo xvi; Bob Daemmrich xii–xiii; Charles Gupton 100B; Peter Menzel xivT; Jeffry W. Myers 74; Ilene Perlman xiiiBR. Frank Siteman xvii. The Stock Market: David Ball 86–87, 375R; David Barbes 507TL; Berenhottz 198–199; Robert Frerck 178; Stan Osolinski 198B; Kunio Owaki 199BL, 375L; John Reis 86; Christopher Springman 104; Peter Steiner 335; Joe Towers 191. Superstock: Kobal Collection 414–415, 426–427,

462, 463, 488, 542–543. The Time Museum: 2B, 31R. The Tokyo Museum: 287. Union Pacific Railroad Museum Collection: 34. Stamp design © 1986 U.S. Postal Service, reproduced by permission: 342. Van Cleve: Fred Myers 452.

Illustrations
JoAnna Adamska, Jaques Auger, John Batchelor, Marty Braun, Nan Brooks, David Cain, Ron Criswell, Tony Crnkovich, Paul Dolan, Fred and Jill Duanno, Cameron Eagle, David Frampton, Janice Fried, Byron Gin, Dale Glasgow, Glen Gustafson, Brad Hamann, Clint Hansen, Steve Henry, Monica Incisa, Mike Jones, Robert Korta, Andy Levine, Tom Lochray, Susan Mills, Leonard Morgan, Mike Muir, Eileen Mueller Neill, R. Kenton Nelson, Melanie Parks, Brenda Pepper, Rodica Prato, Mike Quon, Joe Rogers, Ellen Rixford, Donna Ruff, Scott Sawyer, Judy Seckler, Dan Siculan, Margo Stahl, Maria Stroster, Suzanne Snider, John Trotta, Justin Wager & John Walter, John Walter, Jr., Leslie Wolf

Data
pp. 86–87, 104 on The American Eagle® Ride reprinted by permission of Six Flags Great America, Gurnee, IL; p. 102 from *Statistical Abstract of the United States 1982–83 National Data Book;* p. 124 courtesy of NASA; p. 125 Uptown Sales, Inc. advertisement reprinted by permission of Uptown Sales, Inc., Chambersburg, PA; pp. 128, 141 from *World Almanac, 1989,* p. 860; p. 214 from *World Almanac, 1989,* pp. 412–413; p. 247 courtesy of Columbus Zoo, Columbus, Ohio; table on p. 411 from *Pocket Pathfinder* by Ann Kay. Copyright © 1987 by *Kingfisher Books Ltd.* Reprinted by permission of *Random House, Inc;* p. 542 from *3-2-1 Contact and Kid City,* a survey of 12,000 youth ages 6–14; p. 543 from *UNICEF,* 1980 statistics

ScottForesman Staff

ScottForesman gratefully acknowledges the contributions
of the following individuals.

Editorial
Karen Usiskin, Janice Ziebka, Therese Smith, Clare Froemel,
Nancy Baty, Rosi Marshall, Mary Jane Wolfe, Mary Schaefer,
Iromie Fernando

Design
Barbara Schneider, Virginia Pierce, George Roth, David Dumo,
Tom Gorman

Production
Mary Lou Beals, Joy Kelly, Barbara Albright, Kathy Oberfranc,
Lois Nelson, Fran Simon, Sally Buehne, JoAnn Ballwanz

Marketing
Cathie Dillender, Nan Simpson, Muffet Fox

Business
Elizabeth A. Dietz, Elizabeth R. Semro

Picture Research/Photo Studio
Nina Page, Rosemary Hunter, John Moore, Phoebe Novak

Photo Lab/Keyline
Marilyn Sullivan, Mark Spears, Madeline Oton-Tarpey, Gwen
Plogman